OCM: Oracle Database 10g Administrator Certified Master Exam Guide

About Prudent Solutions

Prudent Solutions specializes in developing & implementing solutions based on Oracle's best practices for Information Technology. Using our decade of hands-on experience, we provide solutions that suit every client's requirements and budget. We remain equipped with 'Skilled Oracle Resources' that help our prized clients to implement Oracle environments at optimum level. All the Prudent Solutions' consultants are masters in their respective fields and deliver specialized solutions for every Oracle practice. Be it requirement for comprehensive solutions; customized setup, on-call support; or anything in between, we render proficient solutions to the optimal approval of every client. We nurture the objective not just of using technology for our convenience, but also to solve every business issue with comprehensive intent and plan.

At Prudent Solutions, we believe in edifying lucrative productivity within reasonable operation costs.

Prudent Solutions LLC.
172 Point Comfort Ln.
Cary NC USA 27519

www.prusolutions.com
Prudent Provides Proficiency

OCM: Oracle Database 10g Administrator Certified Master Exam Guide

(Oracle Database 10g DBA Practical Handbook)

Nilesh Kakkad
Oracle Certified Master

Prudent Solutions LLC. USA

OCM: Oracle Database 10g Administrator Certified Master Exam Guide
(Oracle Database 10g DBA Practical Handbook)

ISBN: 978-0-615-48193-7

Published by
Prudent Solutions LLC.
172 Point Comfort Ln.
Cary NC USA 27519

Printed in India for Prudent Solutions LLC USA

Editorial Supervisor
Pinki Gadhia

Technical Review
Prudent's Team

Project Editor
Pinki Gadhia

Copy Editor
Sunil Shukla

Typesetter
Sudhir Vats

Cover Designer
Rohit Kathuria

Preface

Oracle's OCM Certification is the elite credential in the database world. This certification will help the readers to get acknowledgement as proven performers who have demonstrated their skills and have a scalable understanding of their job-role. Thorough study of this practical guide will help in pertinent use of Oracle products.

Since the scope of Oracle's providence is very extensive, there is a lot to go through and implore. This practical guide offers thorough exam preparation and a great on-the-job reference for the Oracle Database.

All those who want to award themselves with the acclaim of elite DBA... must acquire this guide for its thorough study.

About the Author

Nilesh Kakkad is an Oracle 10g Certified Master with more than a decade of experience, having complete understanding of OLTP/Data Warehouse Architecture and Design. Present book grew out of the author's involvement with major Oracle Databases in association of various clients. Currently, he is working as an independent consultant.

Contents at a Glance

Contents

Hardware and Software Requirements

Hardware Requirements

- Laptop or Desktop 64 bit with 8GB Memory and 500GB Hard Disk

Software Requirements

- Download VMware Server 2.0x trial version
  http://downloads.vmware.com/d/info/datacenter_downloads/vmware_server/2_0
- Download following trial software for Linux 32 bit from Oracle
  http://edelivery.oracle.com/EPD/GetUserInfo/get_form?caller=LinuxWelcome
  - V10142-01
  - V10143-01
  - V10145-01
- Download Oracle Clusterware and Oracle 10g Database software for Linux 32 bit
  http://www.oracle.com/technetwork/database/10201linuxsoft-097986.html
  - 10201_database_linux32.zip (668,734,007 bytes) (cksum - 2737423041)
  - 10201_companion_linux32.zip (705,274,421 bytes) (cksum - 1240689190)
  - 10201_clusterware_linux32.zip (228,239,016 bytes) (cksum - 2639036338)
- Download Oracle Enterprise Manager Software
  http://www.oracle.com/technetwork/oem/grid-control/downloads/linuxsoft-099441.html
  - gc_102011_linux
  - Linux_Grid_Control_agent_download_10_2_0_2_0
  - gc_10205_part1of2
  - gc_10205_part2of2
  - Download jdk and oracleasmlib software

    http://www.oracle.com
  - jdk-6u21-linux-i586-rpm.bin
  - oracleasmlib-2.0.2-1.i386.rpm
- Download Oracle Documentation for 10g Database
  http://www.oracle.com/technetwork/database/database10g/overview/index.html

How to prepare for the OCM Exam and use this Exam Guide

Oracle Database 10g Administrator Certification Master combines training, experience, and testing to ensure that you have a strong foundation and expertise in the industry's most advanced database management system.

- For OCM Certifications following conditions should be met
  - You should be Oracle Database 10g Administrator Certified Professional (OCP) to appear for the OCM exam.
  - OCM candidates must take two courses from the Advanced/Specialty list or from the Oracle Database 10g Administrator Certified Master – Additional Approved Courses list.

    http://education.oracle.com/pls/web_prod-plq-dad/db_pages.getpage?page_id=244#3

- You can appear for the OCM exam without taking two Advance Courses, but Oracle will not tell your OCM exam results unless you have taken two Advance Courses, so it is better to attend the training before appearing for the OCM Exam.

  Suggested courses are mentioned below. Please do not jump on 11g courses, do training in Oracle 10g as you are preparing for the OCM 10g.

  Attend training for subject where you have less experience or feel you may need more attention.

  Oracle Database 10g: RAC for Administrator Release 2

  Oracle Database 10g: Performance Tuning

  Oracle Enterprise Manager 10g Grid Control Release 2

  Oracle Database 10g: Data Guard Administration

  Oracle Database 10g: OCM Exam Preparation Workshop Ed 1

- Do not wait for OCM exam dates to appear for the OCM exam, instead, call Oracle University and request them to conduct OCM exam at location of your choice and preferred date. Once Oracle gets at least 6 candidates for that location Oracle will conduct the OCM exam immediately.

- Make sure you have appropriate hardware and software before using this book.

- Each section of this book is important for OCM exam, so do not miss any section, at many places it is suggested to navigate through Oracle Document. Please visit those pages and read them thoroughly.

- Before starting exercise for any chapter, read that chapter in entirety along with suggested Oracle Documentation Read in that chapter then start the exercises.

  Wherever in the book backup is suggested, please take Backup for future exercises.

- All UNIX commands in this book are in bold and all sql commands starts with **SQL>**

- In OCM exam, if you face any difficult situation do not lose confidence find alternative solutions. For example, if you are NOT able to install Oracle's OEM Grid Control then install dbcontrol to do rest of the exercises using dbcontrol. In this way, you will lose marks only for Oracle's OEM Grid Control, but you will be able to perform other exercises using dbcontrol. Learn to switch between dbcontrol and Grid Control by stopping and starting agent and dbcontrol.

Acknowledgements

This book is a reflection of over a decade of my experience with Oracle Databases. This book reflects my expertise and proficiency that I have earned while working at various clients and using the product in multitude situations.

I feel honored and blessed to be able to write this book with a passionate zeal and offer my true thanks to God for enabling me to accomplish this.

I always had passion for Oracle and I am inspired to write this book by my Guruji Shri Acharya Batuk Prasad Sharma Shastri.

I would also like to thank my wife Pinki and my two sons Yash and Neel for allowing me the time to work on this book and for bearing my busy writing sessions.

Finally, I recognize the efforts of all for culminating my earnest efforts into this book.

1

Configure Linux Machines on VMware

1.1 Install VMware Server

- Double Click on VMware Software "VMware-server-2.0.2-203138" then Click Next

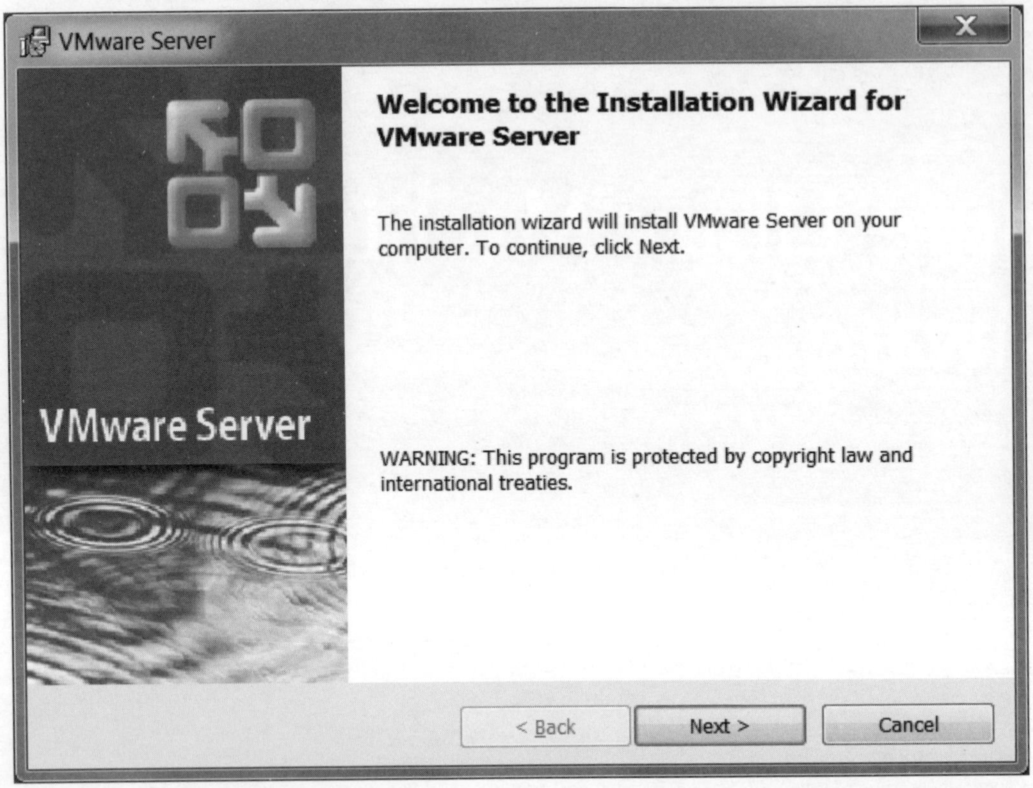

- Accept License Agreement

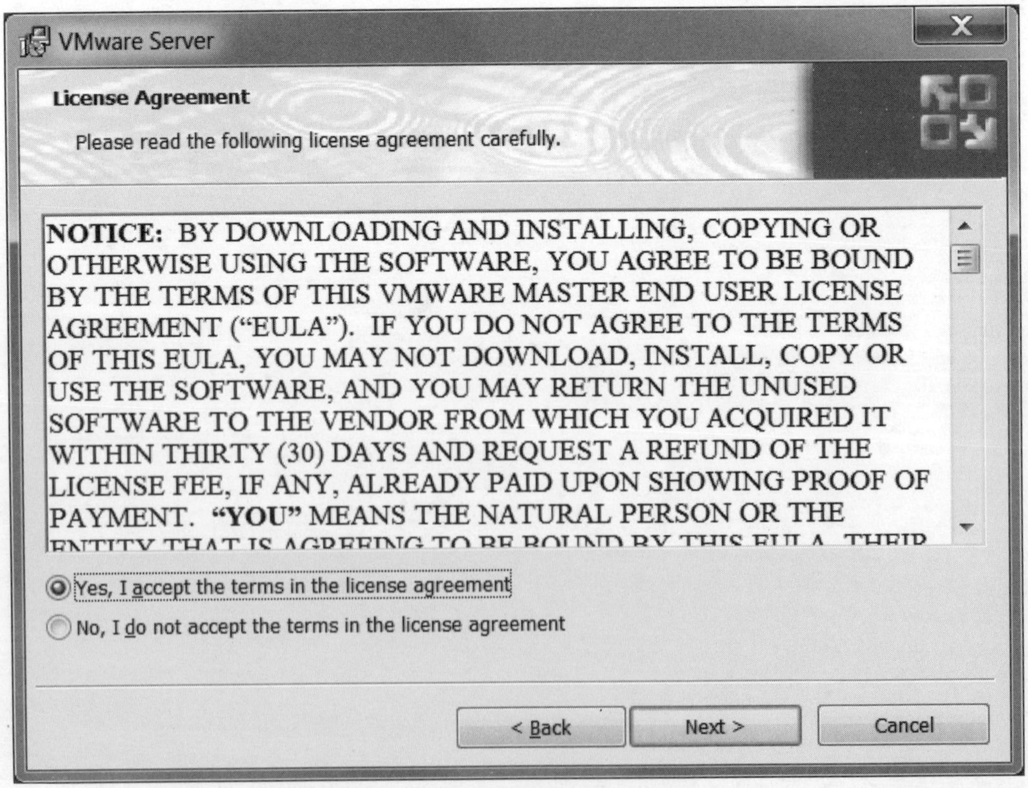

- Click Install

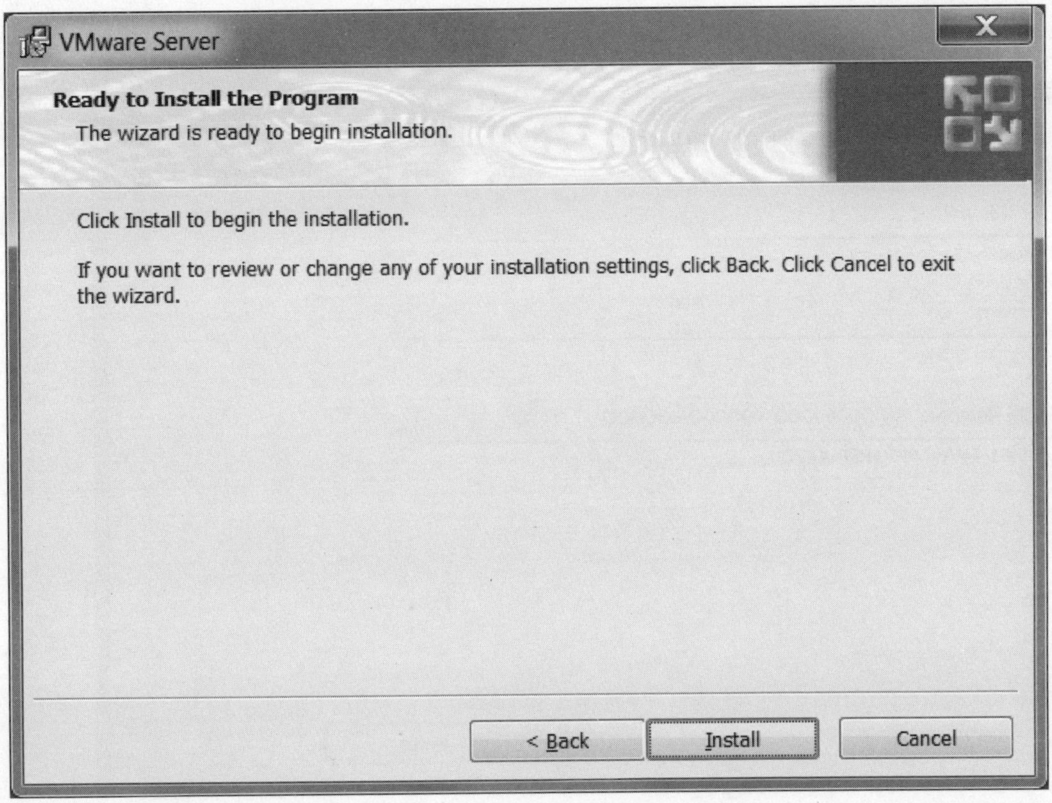

- Enter Host Name

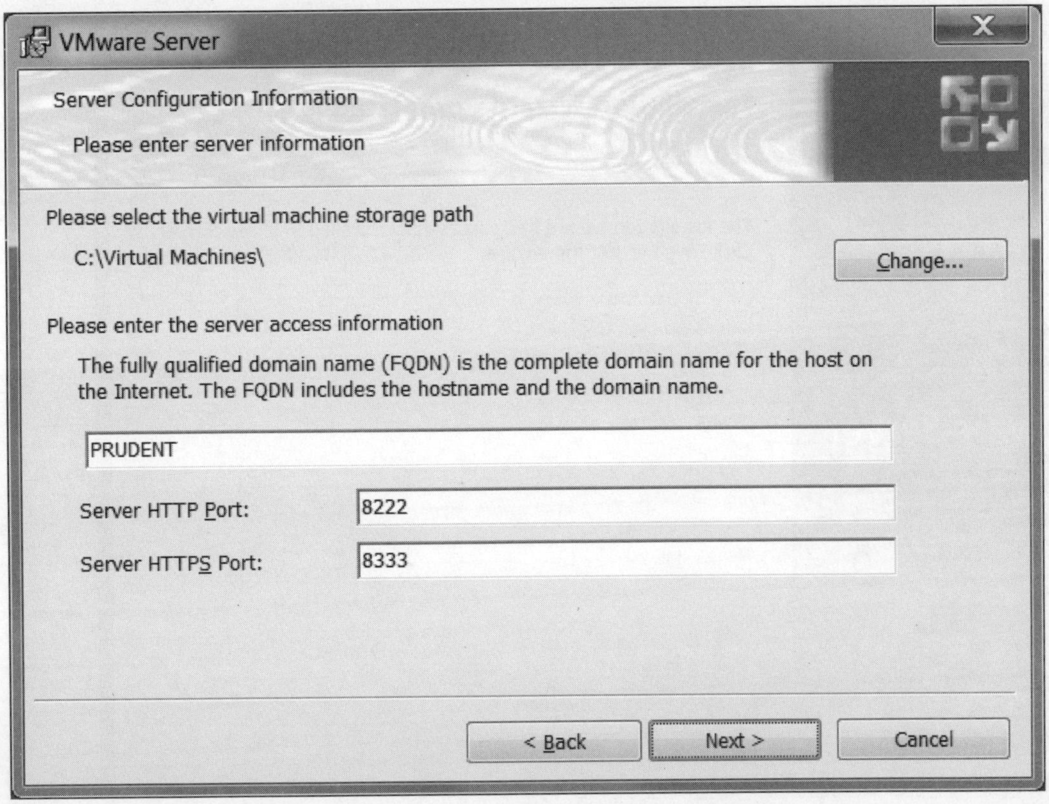

- Enter Host Username and Software Serial Number

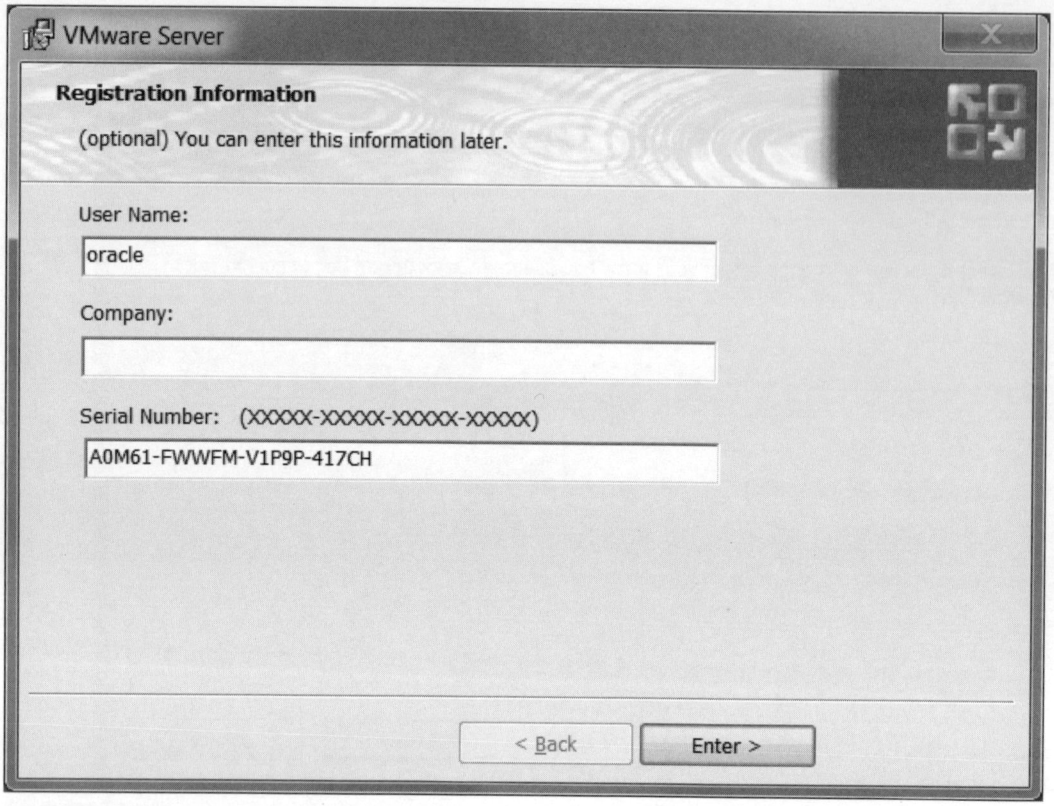

- Finish Install

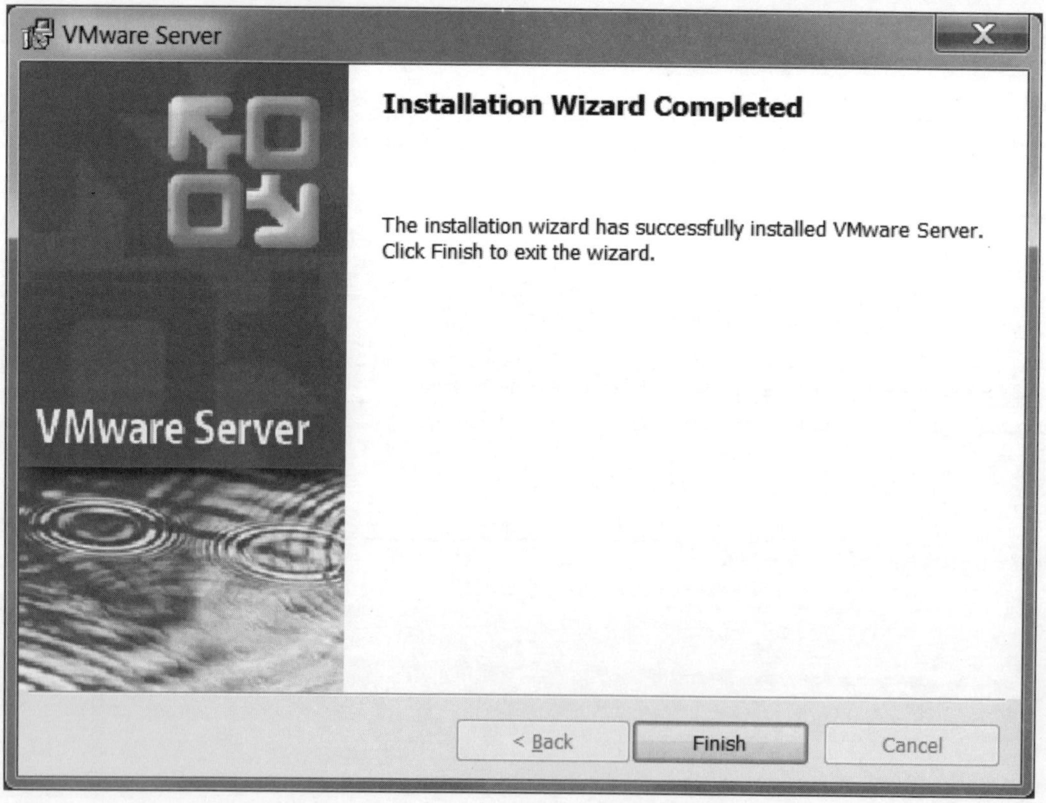

1.2 Install and Configure Oracle Linux Software

- Create folder c:\vm\rac\ which will be used for Datastores for VMware
- Copy the Linux iso files mentioned below into c:\vm\rac, that were downloaded from Oracle
  - Enterprise-R4-U4-i386-disc1
  - Enterprise-R4-U4-i386-disc2
  - Enterprise-R4-U4-i386-disc3
- Start VMware Server

- Click Continue to this Website [not recommended]

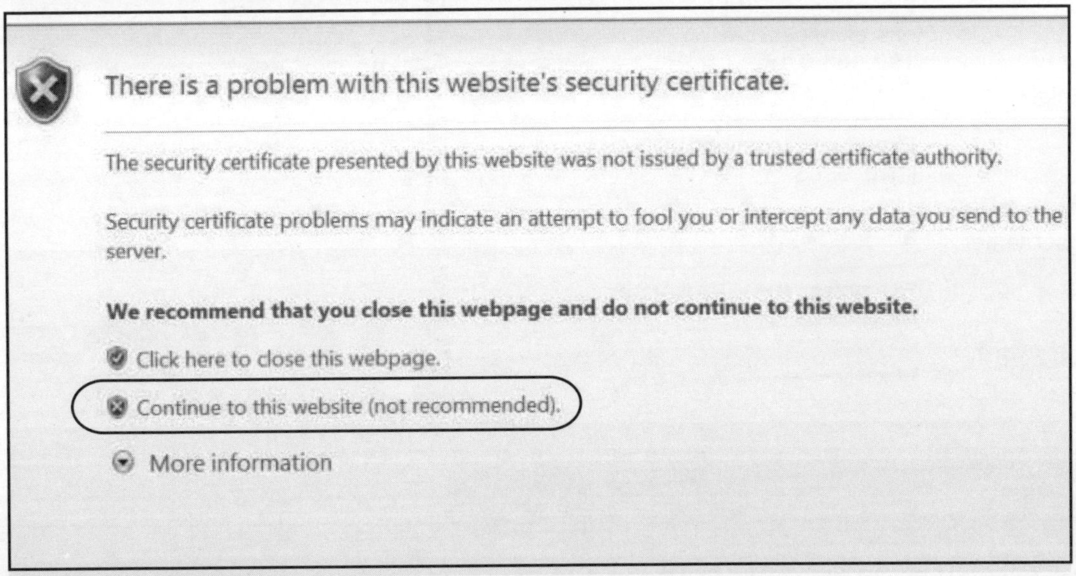

- Windows Username/Password having Administrator Rights

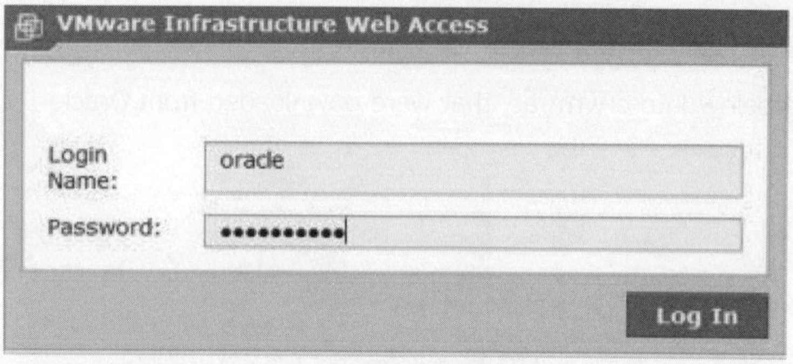

- Add Local Datastore "rac" in VMware c:\vm\rac

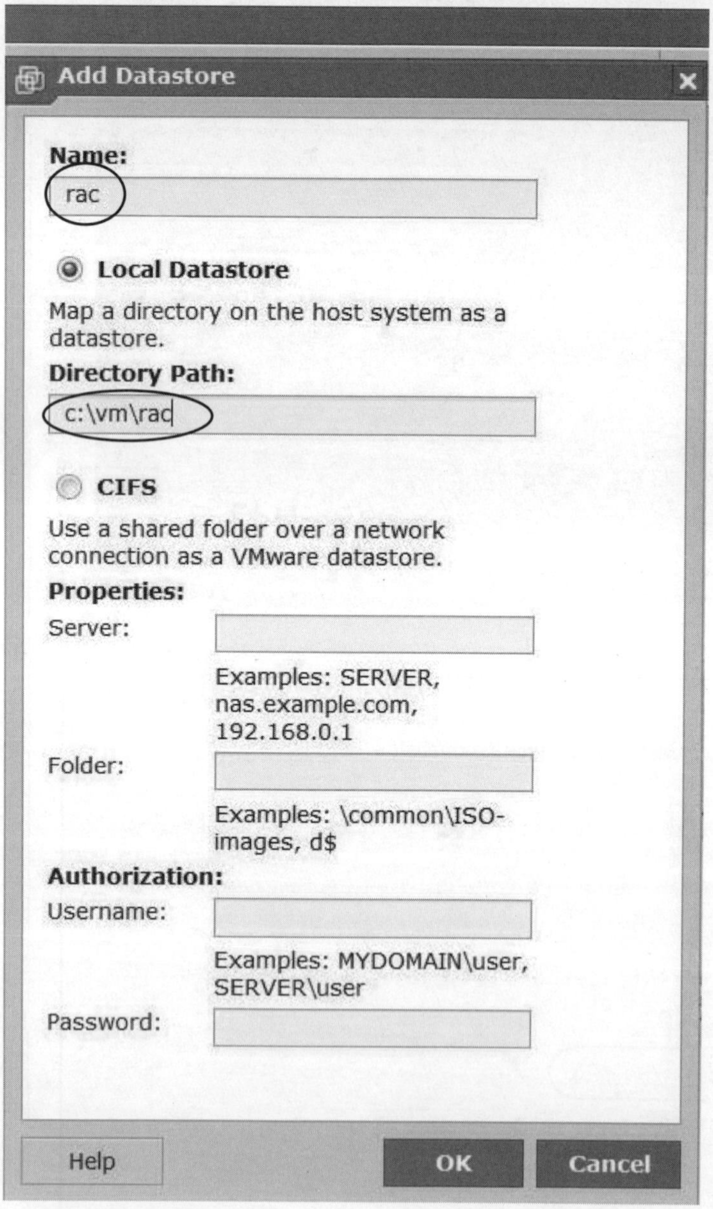

- Create a New Virtual Machine "ocm" Linux Operating System Red Hat Enterprise Linux (32 bit) Memory 1024 MB

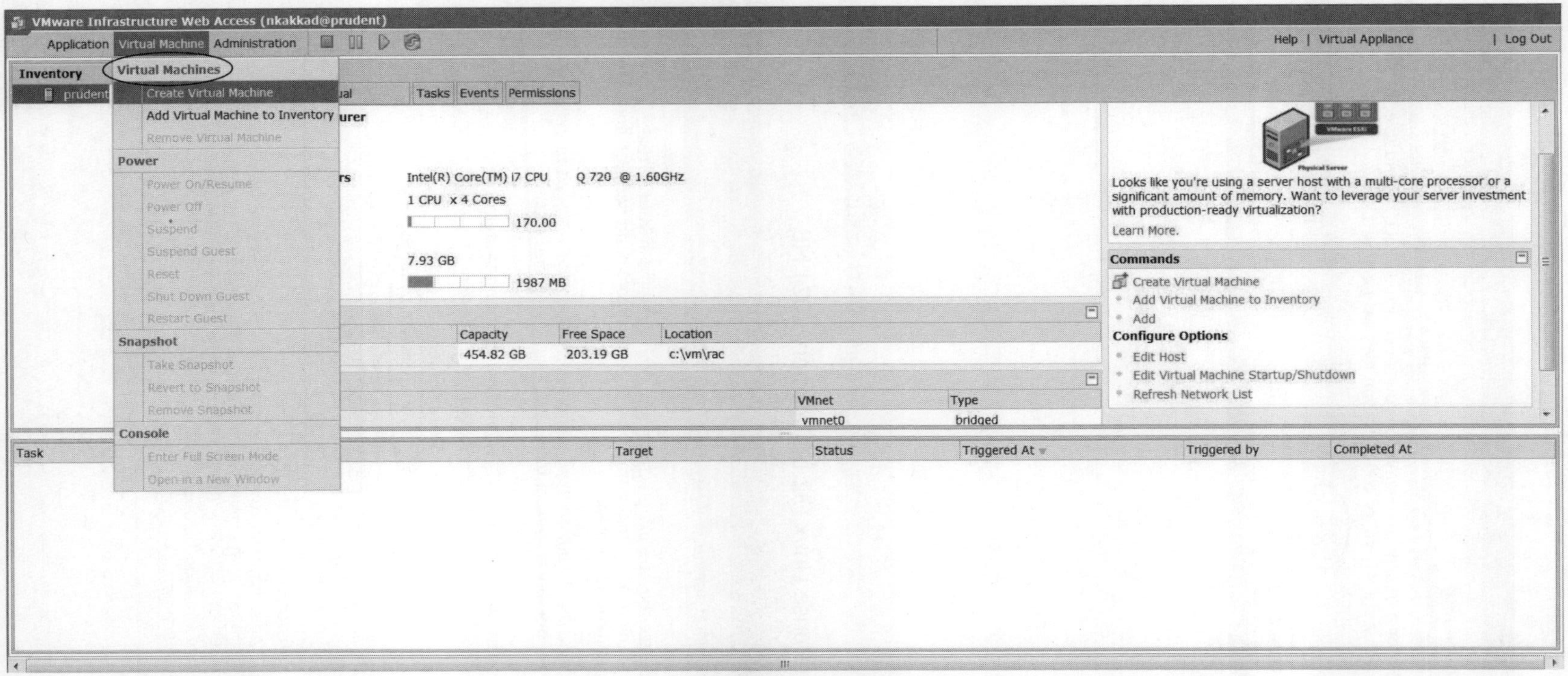

- Virtual Machine "ocm"

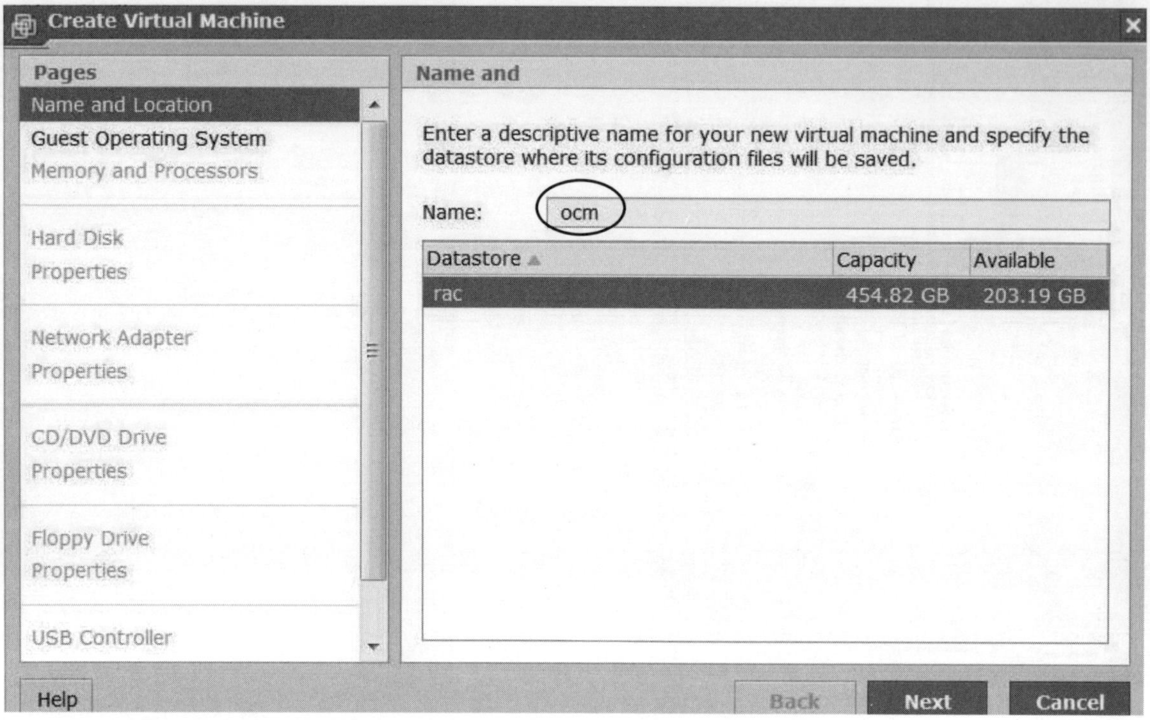

- Linux Operating System Red Hat Enterprise Linux (32 bit) Memory 1024 MB

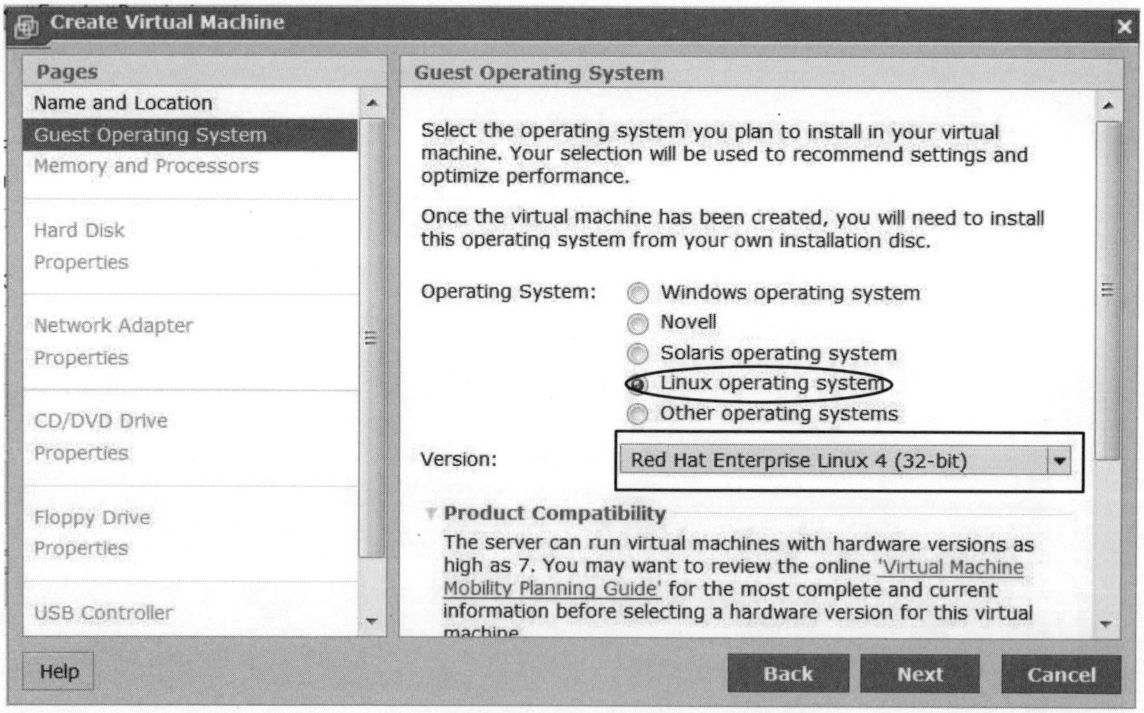

- Add the following Hardware to virtual machine "ocm" from Commands section of VMware

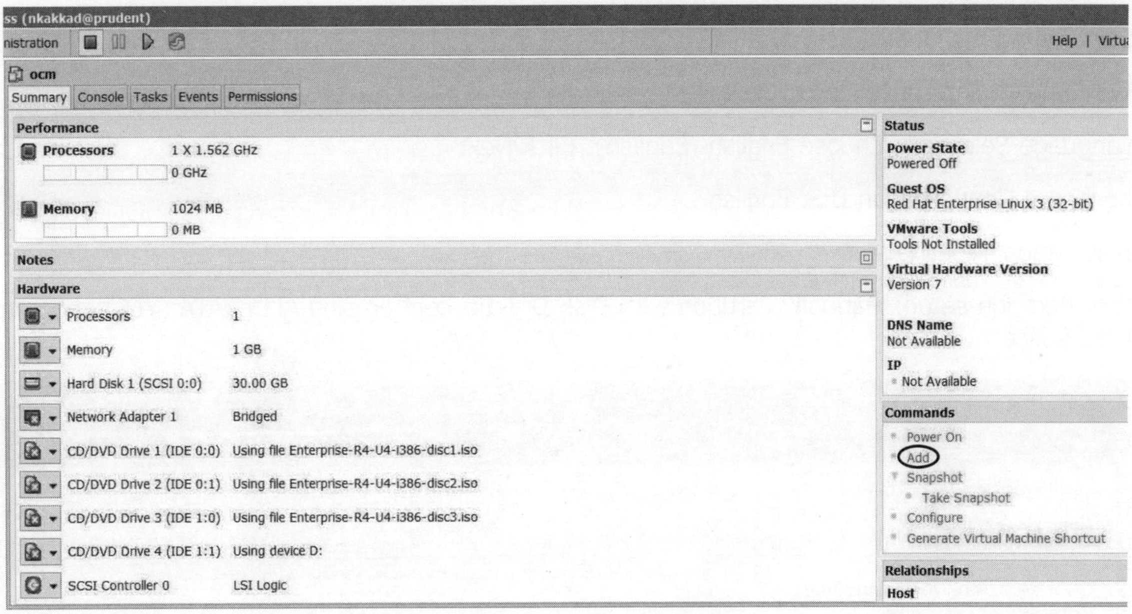

- Create new virtual disk localdisk size 30GB path [rac] ocm/localdisk.vmdk
  - File Options: Deselect "Allocate all disk space now"
  - Disk Mode: Independent Persistent
  - Virtual Device Mode: Adapter SCSI 0 Device 0
  - Policies: optimize for Safety
  - Add a network: Bridge Network, connect at power on
- Add CD/DVD Drive Use an ISO image mentioned below
  - c:\vm\rac\Enterprise-R4-U4-i386-disc1 (Adaptor IDE 0 Device 0)
- Do not "Add a Floppy" and "USB drive" and Finish the operations
- Add more Hardware
  - c:\vm\rac\Enterprise-R4-U4-i386-disc2 (Adaptor IDE 0 Device 1)
  - c:\vm\rac\Enterprise-R4-U4-i386-disc3 (Adaptor IDE 1 Device 0)
  - Use a Physical Host Drive D: (Adaptor IDE 1 Device 1)
- Modify the virtual machine configuration file c:\vm\rac\ocm\ocm.vmxf and add the following lines
  - disk.locking = "FALSE"
  - diskLib.dataCacheMaxSize = "0"
- Power on Virtual Machine, go to console tab and click Install plugin, and follow the instructions
- After VMware plugin is installed again logon to virtual machine

1.3 Installation of Linux Operating System continued

- Skip testing CD Media
- Welcome to Enterprise Linux: Click Next
- Language Selection: Choose English (English): Click Next
- Keyboard Configuration U.S. English
- Installation Type: Custom
- Disk partition setup: Manually Partition with Disk Druid accept erasing ALL_DATA (YES) and edit Free Space

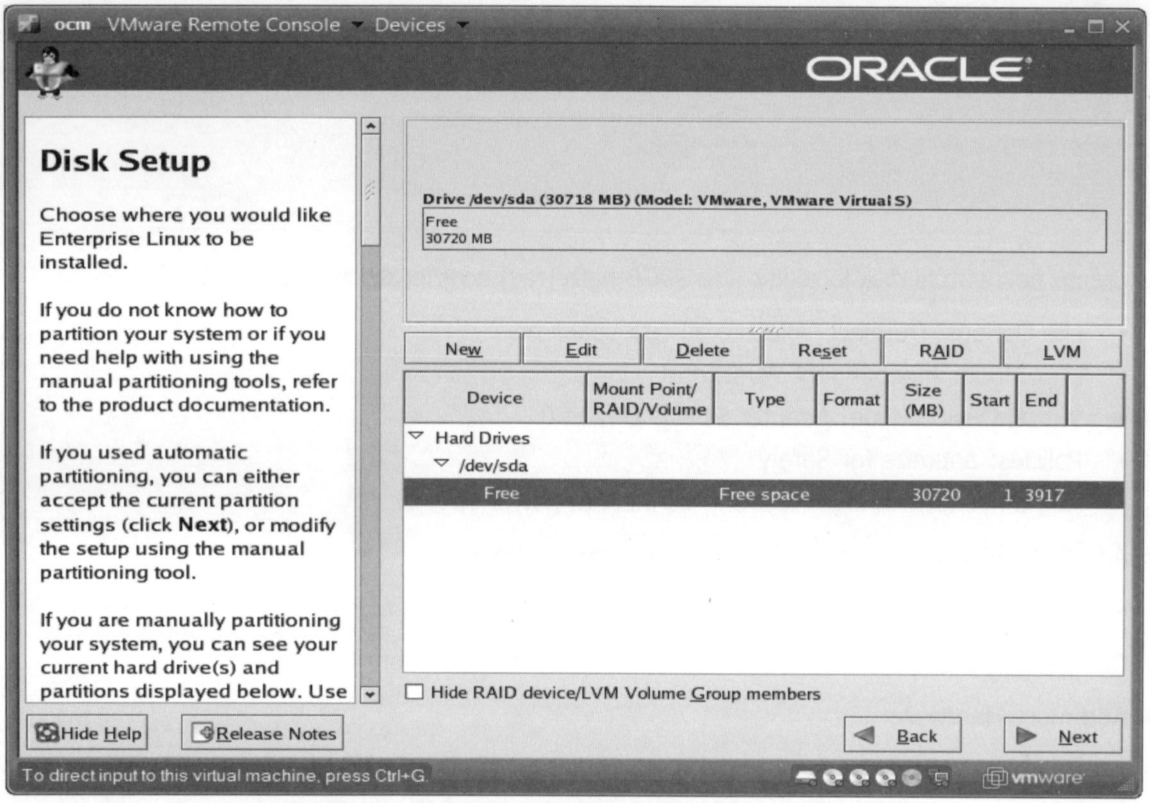

- Add partitions in Free space 30G as show in picture above
  - Mount Point: /, File System Type: ext3, Start Cylinder: 1, End Cylinder: 1020 check force primary partition.
  - File System Type: SWAP, Start Cylinder: 1021, End Cylinder:1410
  - Mount Point: /u01, File System Type: ext3, Start Cylinder: 1411, End Cylinder: 3916
  - Boot Loader Configuration: Select Default Enterprise /dev/sda1
- Network Configuration: Edit Network Device eth0
  - Deselect Configure Using DHCP
  - Select Activate on Boot
  - IP address: 192.168.2.121/192.168.1.121 (this depends on what is your default gateway for your router to access internet)

- If your default gateway is 192.168.2.1 then choose 192.168.2.121 or if default gateway is 192.168.1.1 then choose 192.168.1.121 and all other machines ip addresses should be assigned accordingly.
- Netmask address: 255.255.255.0
- Hostname: select manually "ocm.prusolutions.com" (One can choose any domain, In this book, prusolutions.com is used)
- This Book assumes the Subnet is 192.168.2.1 and all the ip addresses will be assigned accordingly
- Miscellaneous Settings Gateway: 192.168.2.1

- Firewall Configuration: No Firewall, SELinux: Disable
    - Warning No Firewall Click on Proceed
- Additional Language: English (USA)
- Time Zone Selection America/New_York Eastern Time
- Set Root Password: "oracle"
- Package Group Selection: Select the following packages to be installed
    - X Windows System
    - GNOME Desktop Environment
    - Editors
    - Graphical Internet
    - Text Based Internet
    - Office Productivity
    - Sound and Video
    - Graphics
    - Server Configuration Tools
    - FTP Server
    - Legacy Network Server (extra packages apart from default selected)
    - rsh-server
    - telnet-server
    - Development Tools
    - Legacy Software Development
    - Administration Tools
    - System Tools (extra packages apart from default selected)
        i. ocfs2-2.6.9-42.0.0.0.1.ELsmp
        ii. ocfs2-tools
        iii. ocfs2console
        iv. oracleasm-2.6.9-42.0.0.0.1.ELsmp
        v. sysstat
        vi. vnc
- Printing Support
- About to Install: Click Next and then Continue
- Some extra packages are installed that are not required on single instance, as same machine will be copied to create Real Application Clusters.

- Reboot

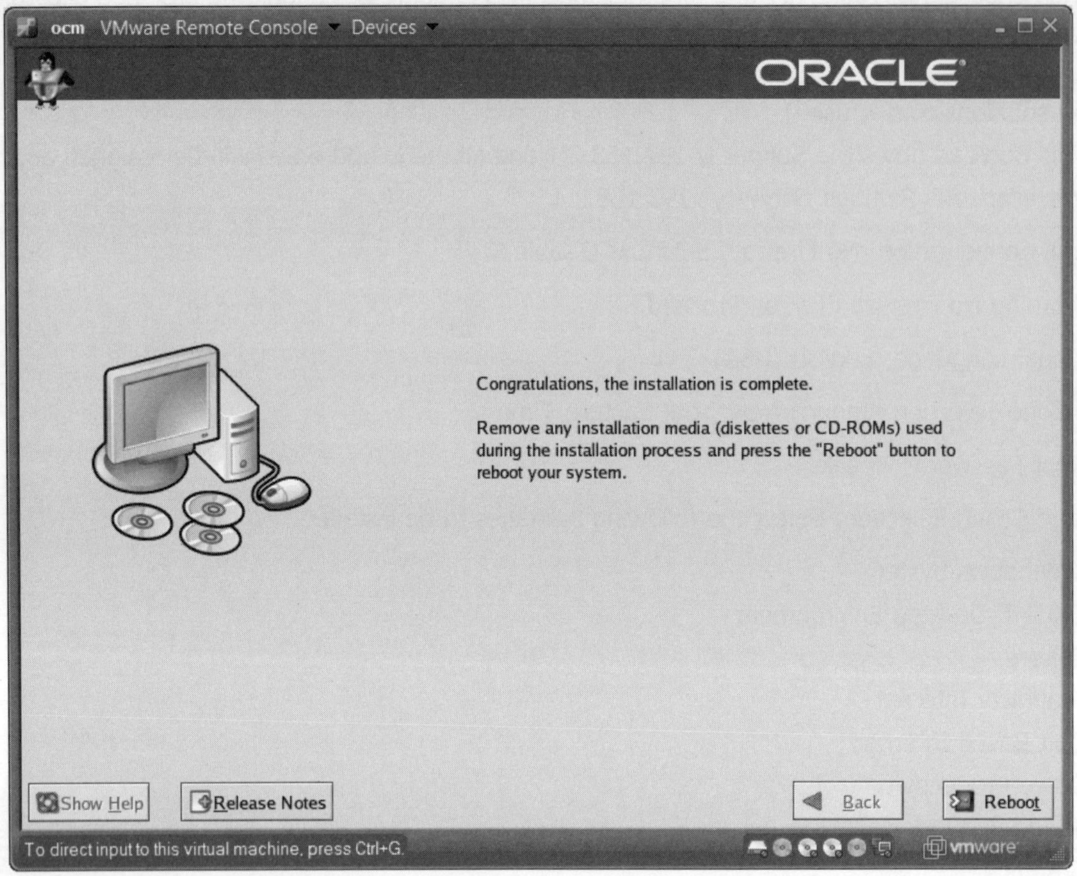

- Welcome Screen: Click Next
- License Agreement: Yes, I agree to the License Agreement
- Set Date and Time
- Display: Click Next
- System User: Leave it Blank and continue
- Additional CDs: Click Next
- Finish Setup: Click Next
- On Summary, page of VMware Click Install VMware Tools

- Double Click VMware Tool and VMwareTools-7.7.6-203138.i386.rpm

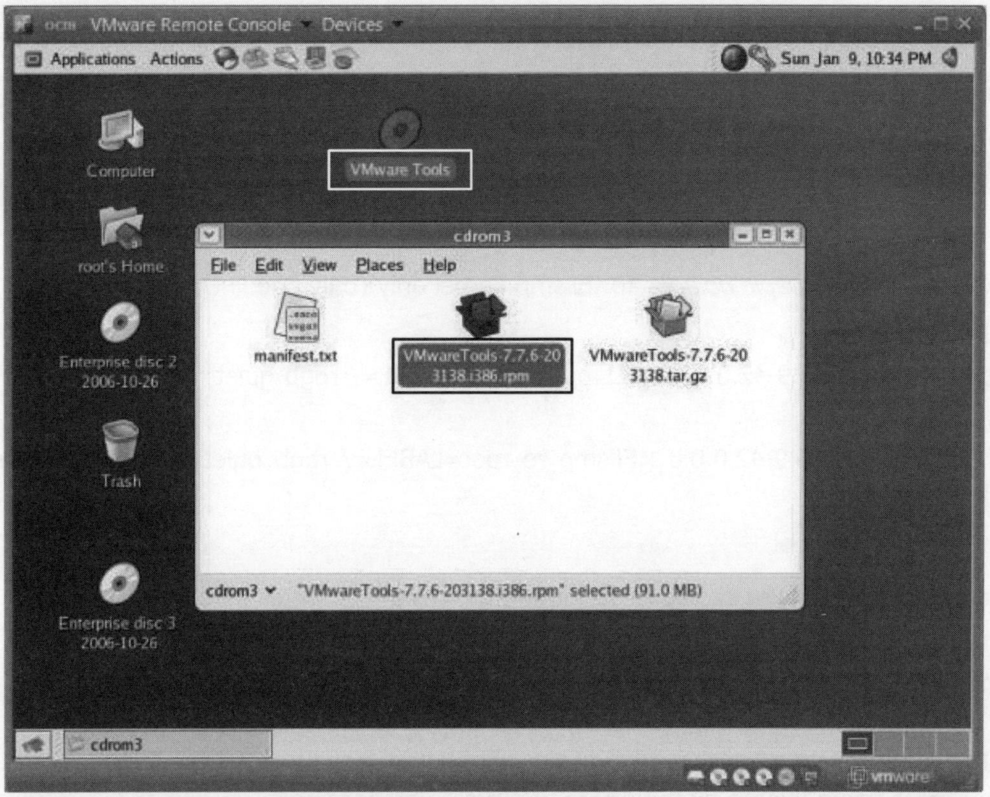

- Shutdown machine and in Commands section of VMware Click Configure VM and on "power" tab Advance section select "Synchronize guest time with host" and restart

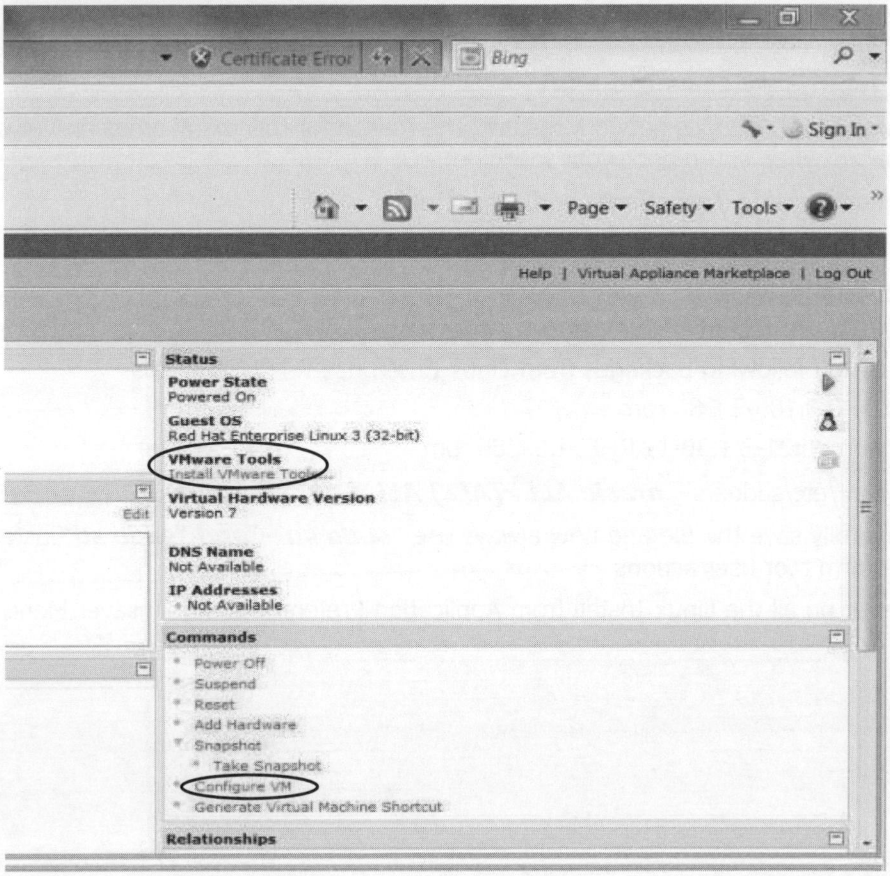

1.4 Configuration of OCM Machine

- Open a terminal in Linux and execute the following

  [root@ocm ~]# vmware-config-tools.pl

  For VMware File sync driver select default **[no]**

  For Display, select option **[12]** or that suits your machine for proper display.

- As a root user edit **/boot/grub/grub.conf** (Please be careful when you modify this file)

  - Add "*clock=pit nosmp noapic nolapic*" to .ELsmp kernel only (only one line is modified)

    Before Modification

    kernel /boot/vmlinuz-2.6.9-42.0.0.0.1.ELsmp ro root=LABEL=/ rhgb quiet

    After Modification

    kernel /boot/vmlinuz-2.6.9-42.0.0.0.1.ELsmp ro root=LABEL=/ rhgb quiet **clock=pit nosmp noapic nolapic**

- Reboot "ocm" machine: reboot

  Only the errors mentioned below should occur during the restart of "ocm" machine.

  Mounting HGFS shares [FAILED]

  Mounting other filesystems: Error: cannot mount filesystems: Protocol error [FAILED]

  Starting smartd [FAILED]

  If you get any other errors, please fix the errors first before proceeding.

- In OCM machine make the following changes

  - Set default gateway of host in resolv.conf, In book example **nameserver 192.168.2.1**
  - Start ftp process **/sbin/service vsftpd start**
  - Restart network again /sbin/service network restart (The reason for this many times on VMware server network hangs when you reboot your machine)
  - Add name of windows host in **/etc/hosts** with ip address
  - Add following lines to **/etc/rc.d/rc.local**

    i. /sbin/service vsftpd start

    ii. /sbin/service network restart

    iii. As root user install following packages from Linux Enterprise-R4-U4-i386 cds

    iv. rpm -Uvh libaio-0.3.105-2.i386.rpm

    v. rpm -Uvh openmotif21-2.1.30-11.RHEL4.6.i386.rpm

  - Add following line in /etc/sudoers ***oracle ALL=(ALL) ALL***

    — use wq! to forcefully save the file and now always use "***sudo su –"and "sudo su"*** instead to use root to perform root user actions.

  - Disable screen saver on all the Linux Install from Application Preferences Screensaver Menu

1.5 Kernel Parameters to Install Oracle Software

- Check hosts names, files option should be the first

  # cat /etc/nsswitch.conf | grep hosts

  make sure it has **file** option first then dns

- Modify Kernel Parameters mentioned below

  - **/etc/sysctl.conf**

```
kernel.shmall = 2097152                    # (2mb)
kernel.shmmax = 2147483648                 # (2g)
kernel.shmmni = 4096                       # (4k)
kernel.sem = 250 32000 100 128
fs.file-max = 65536                        # (64k)
net.ipv4.ip_local_port_range = 1024 65000
net.core.rmem_default = 1048576            # (1mb)
net.core.rmem_max = 1048576                # (1mb)
net.core.wmem_default = 262144             # (256k)
net.core.wmem_max = 262144                 # (256k)
```

  - **/etc/security/limits.conf**

```
oracle    soft    nproc 2047
oracle    hard    nproc 16384
oracle    soft    nofile 1024
oracle    hard    nofile 65536
```

  - **/etc/pam.d/login**

```
session   required   /lib/security/pam_limits.so
session   required   pam_limits.so
```

  - **/etc/profile**

```
if [ $USER = "oracle" ]; then
        if [ $SHELL = "/bin/ksh" ]; then
            ulimit -p 16384
            ulimit -n 65536
        else
            ulimit -u 16384 -n 65536
        fi
fi
```

- Add following to **/etc/hosts** (Extra hosts are added and they will be created in later exercises)

```
127.0.0.1           localhost
# Oracle Database ip addresses
192.168.2.121       ocm.prusolutions.com           ocm
# Oracle Enterprise Manager ip addresses
192.168.2.161       oem.prusolutions.com           oem
192.168.2.162       oms.prusolutions.com           oms
# Oracle RAC ip addresses
192.168.2.131       crs1.prusolutions.com          crs1
192.168.2.31        crs1-vip.prusolutions.com      crs1-vip
10.10.10.31         crs1-priv.prusolutions.com     crs1-priv
192.162.2.132       crs2.prusolutions.com          crs2
```

```
192.168.2.32     crs2-vip.prusolutions.com      crs2-vip
10.10.10.32      crs2-priv.prusolutions.com     crs2-priv
# Oracle RAC Data Guard ip addresses
192.168.2.141    crsdg1.prusolutions.com        crsdg1
192.168.2.41     crsdg1-vip.prusolutions.com    crsdg1-vip
10.10.10.41      crsdg1-priv.prusolutions.com   crsdg1-priv
192.162.2.142    crsdg2.prusolutions.com        crsdg2
192.168.2.42     crsdg2-vip.prusolutions.com    crsdg2-vip
10.10.10.42      crsdg2-priv.prusolutions.com   crsdg2-priv
```

- Create User Oracle for Software Install (Password for oracle user is **oracle**)

```
# groupadd -g 500 oinstall
# groupadd -g 501 dba
# useradd -u 500 -d /home/oracle -g "oinstall" \
  –G "dba" -m -s /bin/bash oracle
# grep nobody /etc/passwd
  nobody:x:99:99:Nobody:/:/sbin/nologin
# chown oracle:dba /home/oracle /u01
# passwd oracle
```

- Check following parameters swap should be 3G and memory 1G and temp space at least 512M

```
# grep MemTotal /proc/meminfo
# grep SwapTotal /proc/meminfo
# df -k /tmp
```

- Make sure Linux required packages are installed and if not, install the missing packages.

```
binutils-2.15.92.0.2-21
compat-db-4.1.25-9
compat-libstdc++-33-3.2.3-47.3
gcc-3.4.6-3.1
gcc-c++-3.4.6-3.1
glibc-2.3.4-2.25
glibc-common-2.3.4-2.25
gnome-libs-1.4.1.2.90-44.2
libstdc++-3.4.6-3.1
libstdc++-devel-3.4.6-3.1
make-3.80-6.EL4
pdksh-5.2.14-30.3
sysstat-5.0.5-11.rhel4
xscreensaver-4.18-5.rhel4.12
setarch-1.6-1
libaio-0.3.105-2.i386.rpm
openmotif21-2.1.30-11.RHEL4.6.i386.rpm
```

- If different version of Linux is installed then packages may be as mentioned below or combination of both.

```
binutils-2.15.92.0.2-13.EL4
compat-db-4.1.25-9
compat-libstdc++-296-2.96-132.7.2
control-center-2.8.0-12
gcc-3.4.3-22.1.EL4
```

gcc-c++-3.4.3-22.1.EL44
glibc-2.3.4-2.9
glibc-common-2.3.4-2.9
gnome-libs-1.4.1.2.90-44.1
libstdc++-3.4.3-22.1
libstdc++-devel-3.4.3-22.1
make-3.80-5
pdksh-5.2.14-30
sysstat-5.0.5-1
xscreensaver-4.18-5.rhel4.2
setarch-1.6-1
libaio-0.3.105-2.i386.rpm
openmotif21-2.1.30-11.RHEL4.6.i386.rpm

- FTP downloaded jdk-6u21-linux-i586-rpm.bin to ocm in folder /u01/software/jdk

  [root@ocm ~]# /u01/software/jdk/jdk-6u21-linux-i586-rpm.bin

  [root@ocm ~]# which java
  /usr/bin/java

- Check "iptables" is unchecked

  [root@ocm ~]# system-config-services

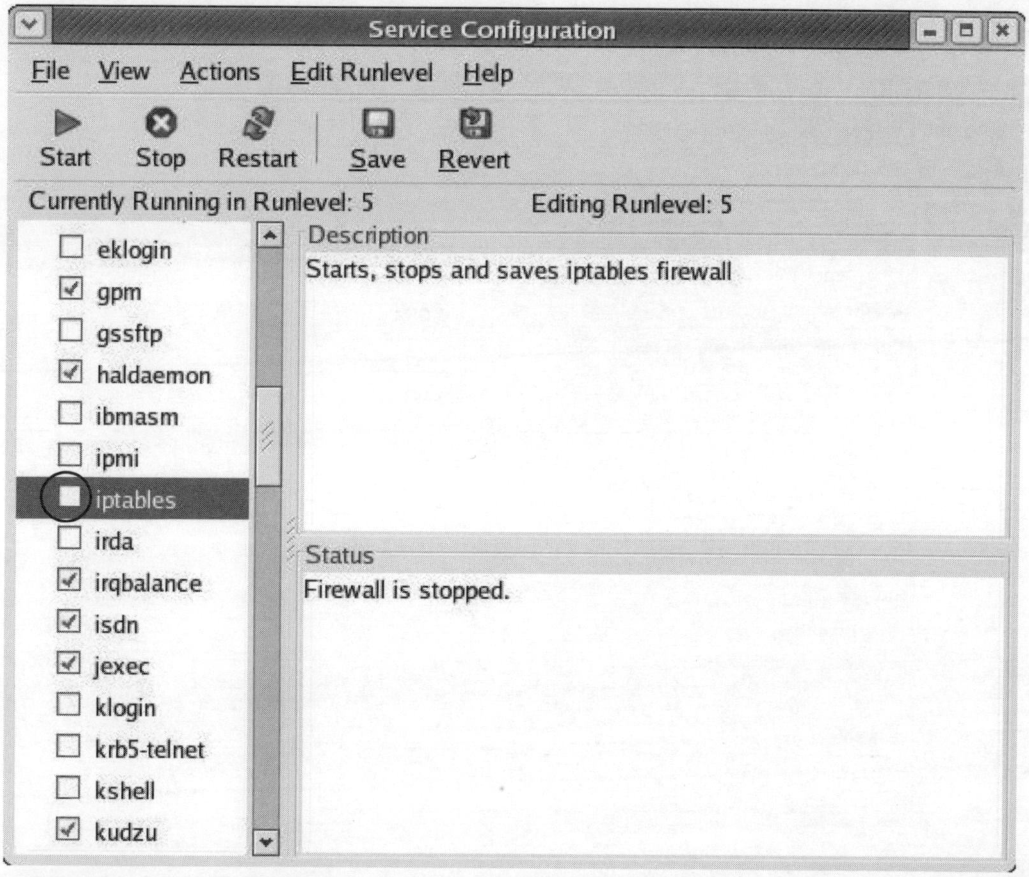

- **[root@ocm ~]# ifconfig**
- **Make sure all above configurations are set properly as this is the key to rest of the exercises.**
- Reboot the machine, recheck all above configurations and test you can ping oracle.com from Linux machine.

1.6 Create the other machines from OCM machine

- Shutdown "ocm" machine again
- COPY and PASTE c:/vm/rac/ocm folders 4 times and name them as follows

  i. c:/vm/rac/**oem**
  ii. c:/vm/rac/**oms**
  iii. c:/vm/rac/**crs1**
  iv. c:/vm/rac/**crsdg1**

- Modify the parameter displayName = "<new machine name>" in VMware configuration file c:/vm/rac/<new machine name>/*ocm.vmx*

FILE	PARAMETER CHANGE
i. c:/vm/rac/oem/ocm.vmx	displayName = "oem"
ii. c:/vm/rac/oms/ocm.vmx	displayName = "oms"
iii. c:/vm/rac/crs1/ocm.vmx	displayName = "crs1"
iv. c:/vm/rac/crsdg1/ocm.vmx	displayName = "crsdg1"

- Configuration of OEM machine [rac] oem/ocm.vmx
  - Start VMware console and "Add Virtual Machine to Inventory"

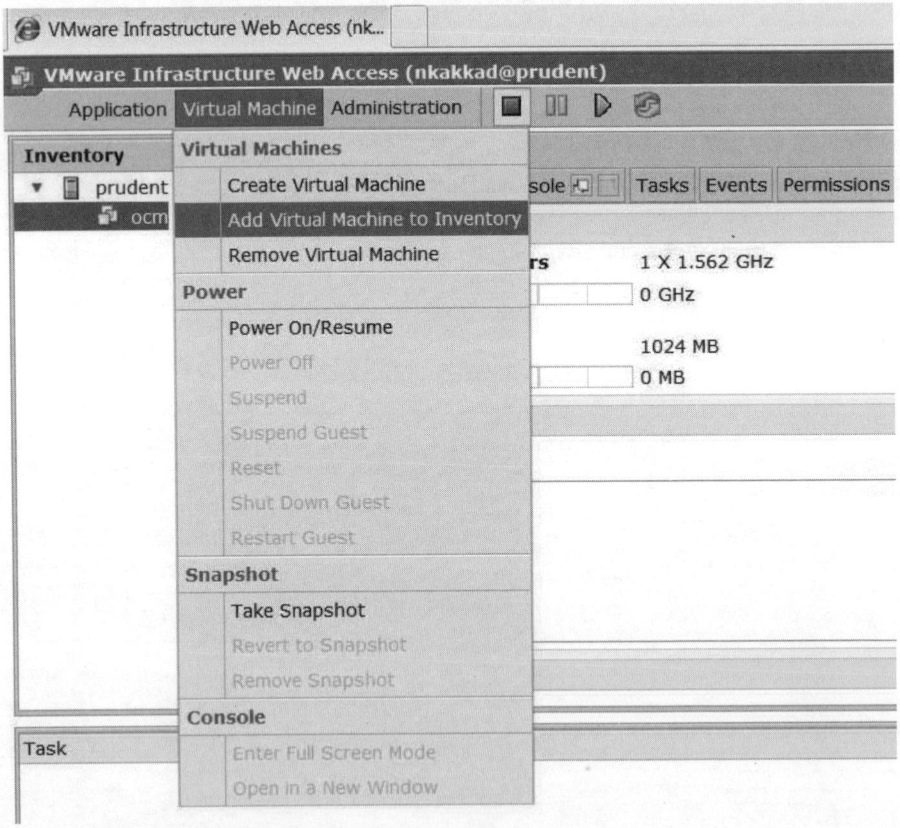

- Select **[rac] oem/ocm.vmx** for "oem" machine. There is no need to change the name of configuration file ocm.vmx. just the parent folder should be oem.

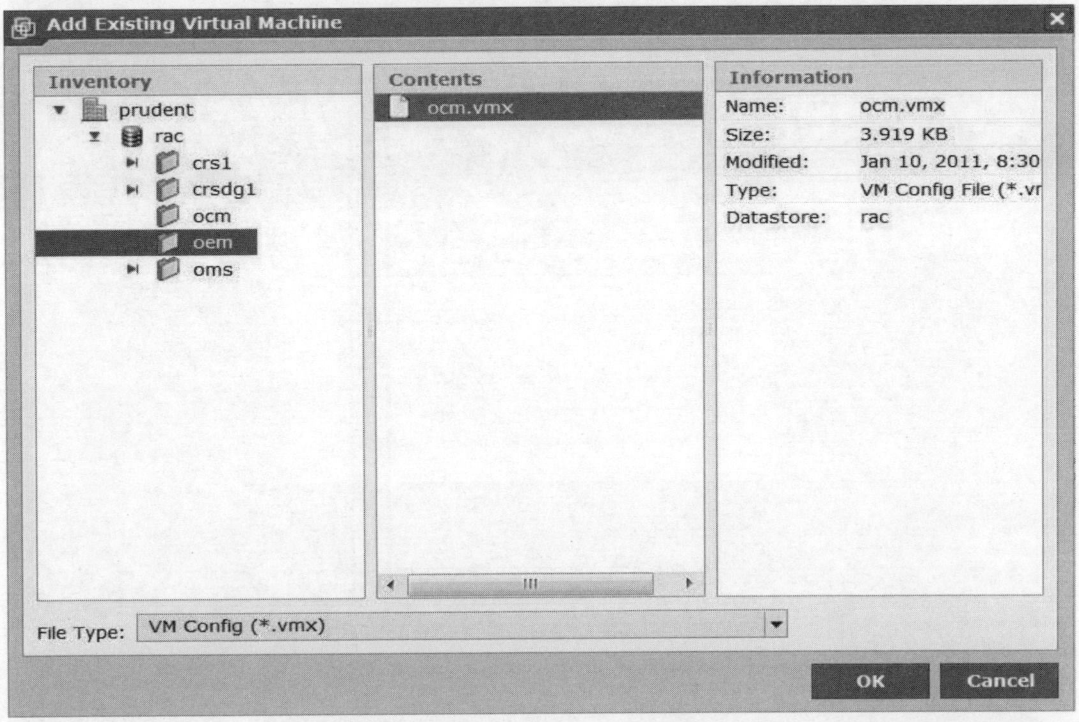

- Start the new OEM machine and choose the option "I_copied", once machine starts, double click on "Console" tab to see the virtual machine.

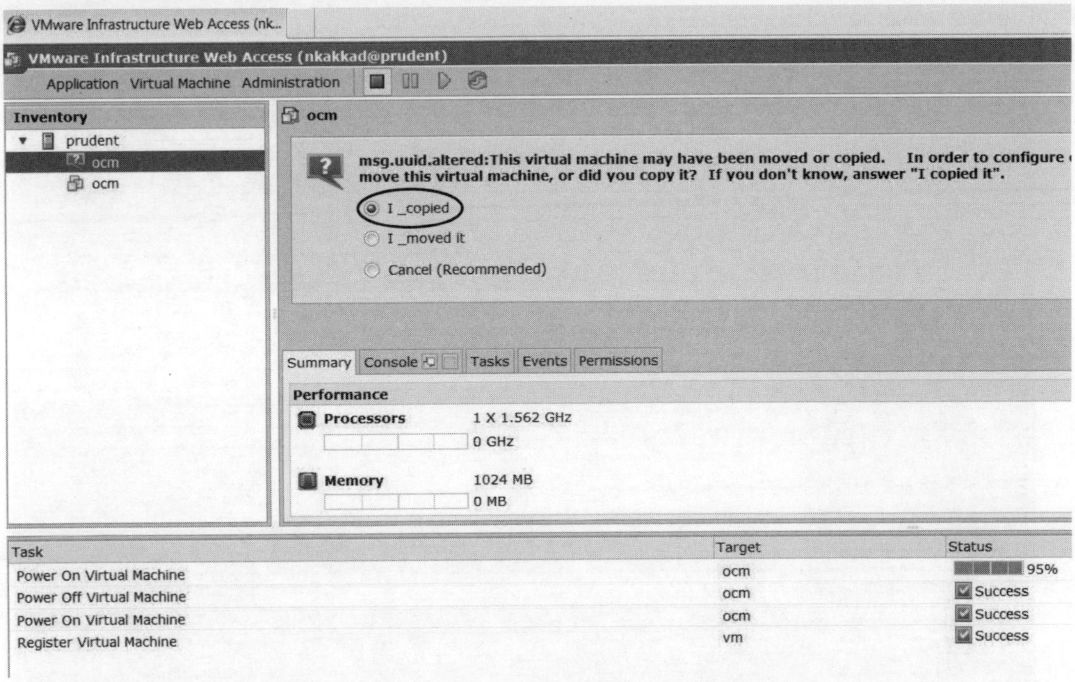

- Hardware Changes Screen: Double Click to make network changes

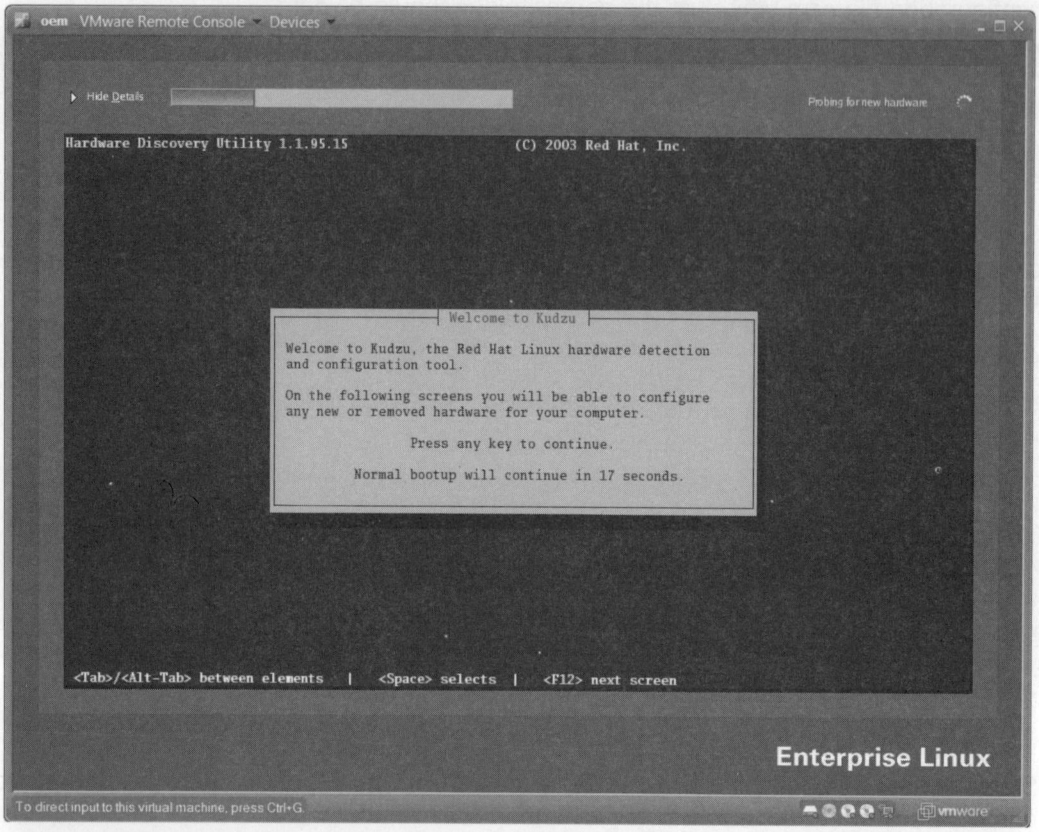

- Hardware Removed Screen: Click "Remove Configuration"

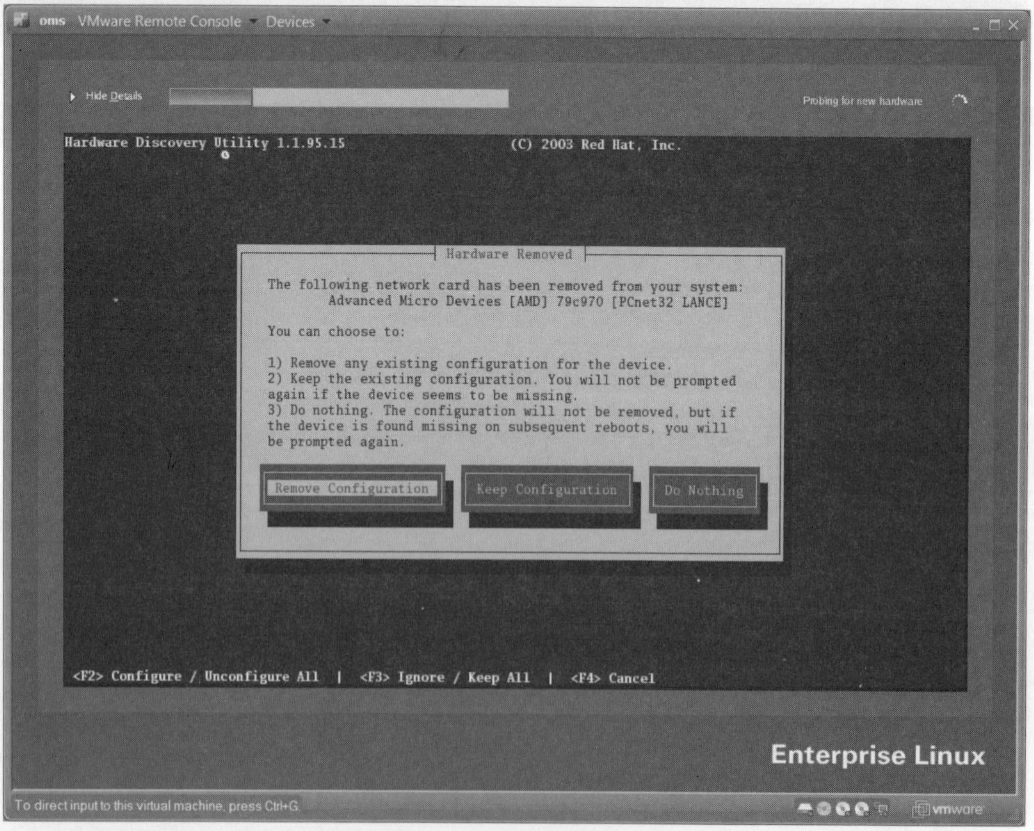

- Hardware Added Screen: Click "Configure"

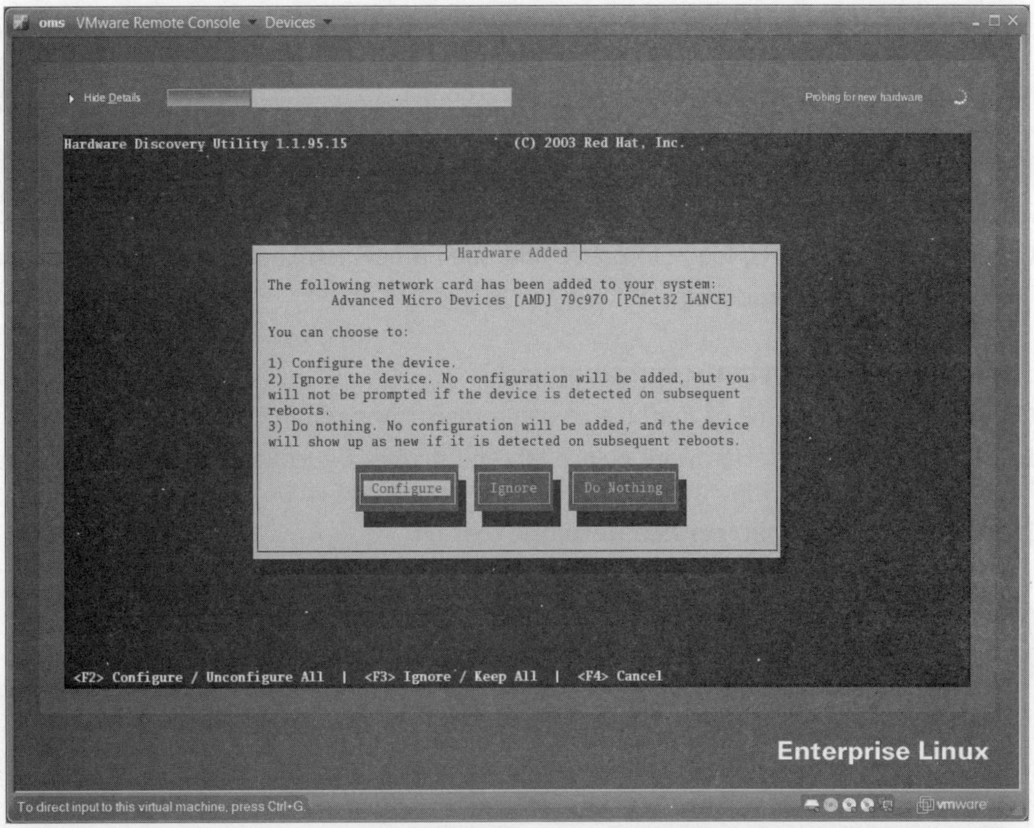

- On Configure TCP/IP Screen: Deselect **[ ]** Use dynamic IP configuration (BOOT/DHCP)

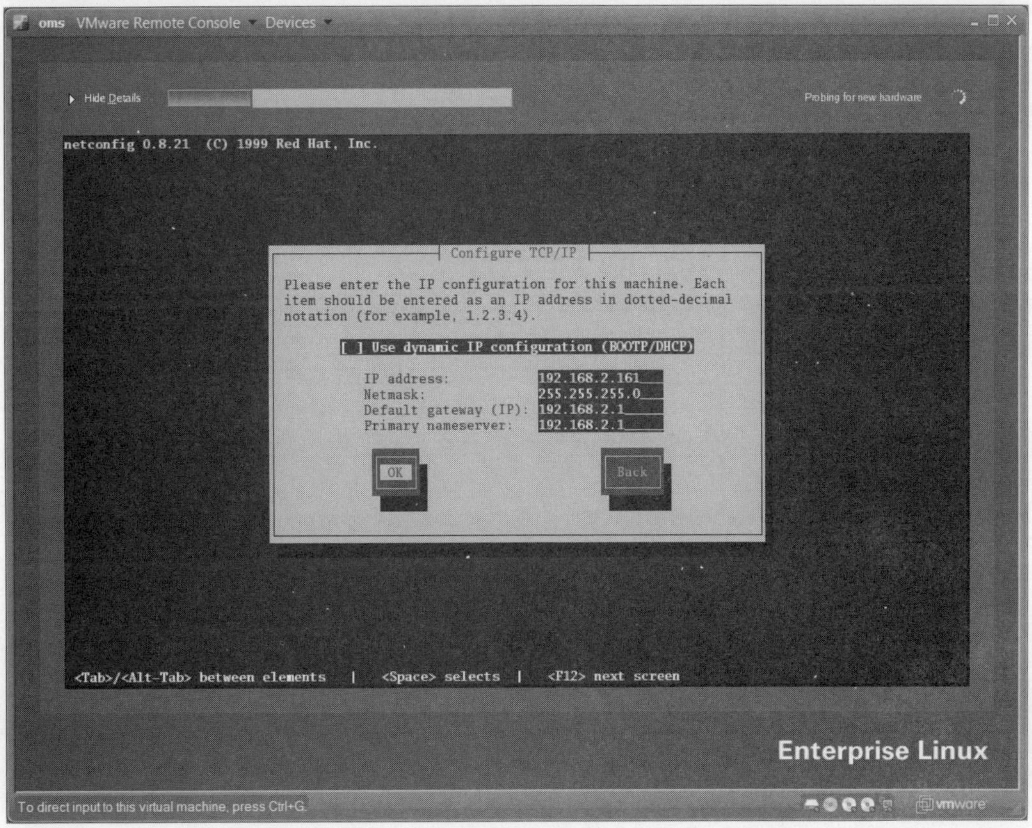

Add the following

i.	IP address:	192.168.2.161
ii.	Netmask:	255.255.255.0
iii.	Default gateway (IP)	192.168.2.1
iv.	Primary nameserver	192.168.2.1
v.	All eth0 network cards should have ip addresses starting 192.168.2. ..	
vi.	All eth1 network cards should have ip addresses starting 10.10.10. ..	

- Once the machine starts, logon to oracle and open a new terminal and execute command

  [oracle@ocm ~]$ sudo su -
  Password: **oracle**

  [root@ocm ~]# system-config-network

- On dns tab change name of machine to oem.prusolutions.com

  Edit Ethernet card Click Hardware device tab and **probe.** Deactivate and Activate the eth0 Do the above step for the entire network device configured later.

  [root@oem ~]# /sbin/service network restart

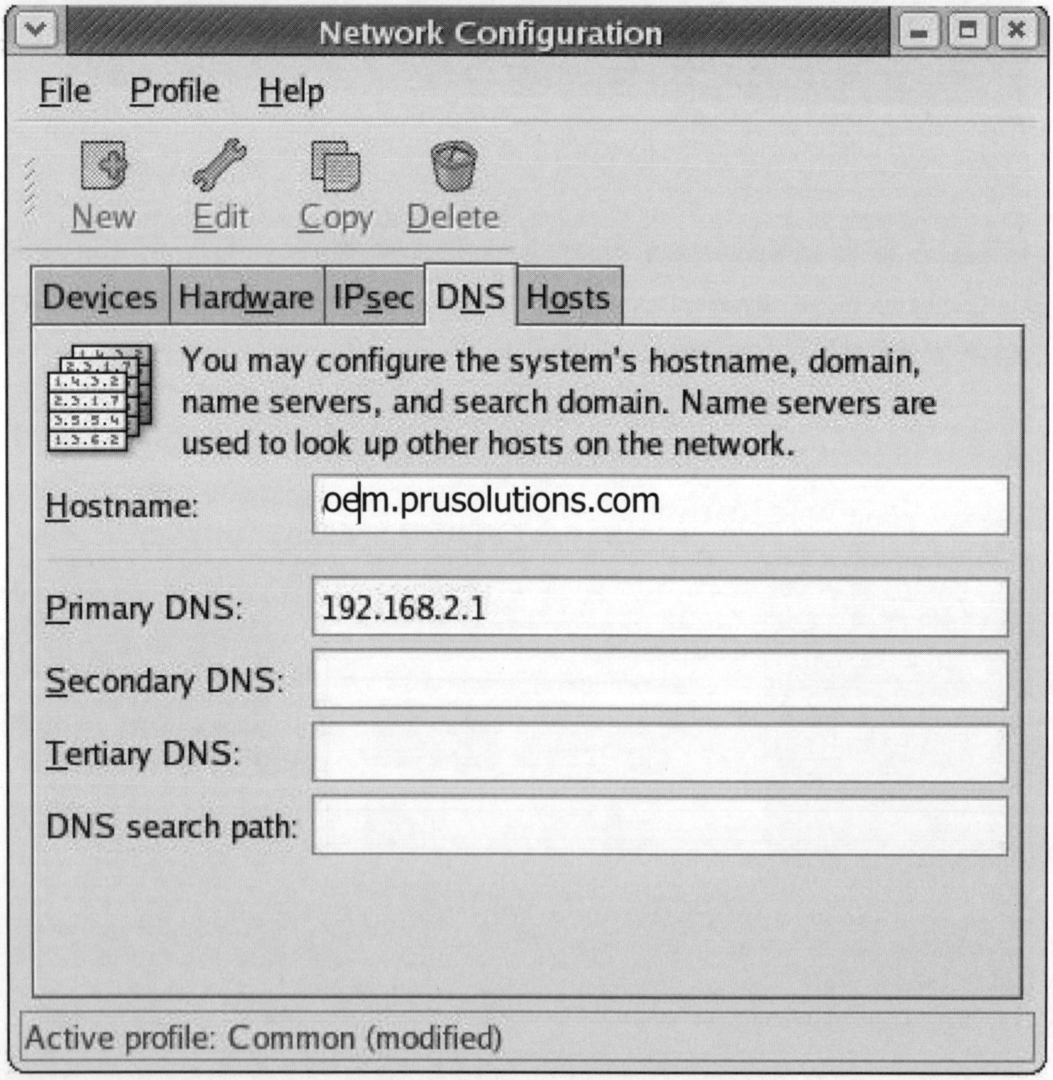

- Make sure following lines are there in **/etc/hosts** (same ip addresses as added in ocm machine)

```
127.0.0.1          localhost
# Oracle Database ip addresses
192.168.2.121      ocm.prusolutions.com            ocm
# Oracle Enterprise Manager ip addresses
192.168.2.161      oem.prusolutions.com            oem
192.168.2.162      oms.prusolutions.com            oms
# Oracle RAC ip addresses
192.168.2.131      crs1.prusolutions.com           crs1
192.168.2.31       crs1-vip.prusolutions.com       crs1-vip
10.10.10.31        crs1-priv.prusolutions.com      crs1-priv
192.162.2.132      crs2.prusolutions.com           crs2
192.168.2.32       crs2-vip.prusolutions.com       crs2-vip
10.10.10.32        crs2-priv.prusolutions.com      crs2-priv
# Oracle RAC Data Guard ip addresses
192.168.2.141      crsdg1.prusolutions.com         crsdg1
192.168.2.41       crsdg1-vip.prusolutions.com     crsdg1-vip
10.10.10.41        crsdg1-priv.prusolutions.com    crsdg1-priv
192.162.2.142      crsdg2.prusolutions.com         crsdg2
192.168.2.42       crsdg2-vip.prusolutions.com     crsdg2-vip
10.10.10.42        crsdg2-priv.prusolutions.com    crsdg2-priv
```

- Make sure following lines are in **/etc/rc.d/rc.local**
  i. /sbin/service vsftpd start
  ii. /sbin/service network restart
- Make sure jdk is installed

  [root@oem ~]# which java
  /usr/bin/java

■ Configure other machines oms, crs1, crsdg1 in the same way as "oem" is configured

i. [rac] oms/ocm.vmx
ii. [rac] crs1/ocm.vmx
iii. [rac] crsdg1/ocm.vmx

	FILE	**PARAMETER CHANGE**
i.	c:/vm/rac/oms/ocm.vmx	displayName = "oms"
ii.	c:/vm/rac/crs1/ocm.vmx	displayName = "crs1"
iii.	c:/vm/rac/crsdg1/ocm.vmx	displayName = "crsdg1"

■ Make sure you have correct ip addresses for all machine as mentioned in **/etc/hosts** file.

 # system-config-network

i. "oms" ip address: 192.168.2.162 Netmask: 255.255.255.0 Default Gateway: 192.168.2.1
ii. "crs1" ip address: 192.168.2.131 Netmask: 255.255.255.0 Default Gateway: 192.168.2.1
iii. "crsdg1" ip address: 192.168.2.141 Netmask: 255.255.255.0 Default Gateway: 192.168.2.1

1.7 Extra configuration for Real Application Cluster machines

Create crs2 machine from crs1.

- Additional Configuration of "crs1" machine [rac] crs1/ocm.vmx
  - Create a folder c:/vm/rac/shared
  - Shutdown crs1 machine and go to summary tab of crs1 on VMware
  - Double Click "Add Hardware"

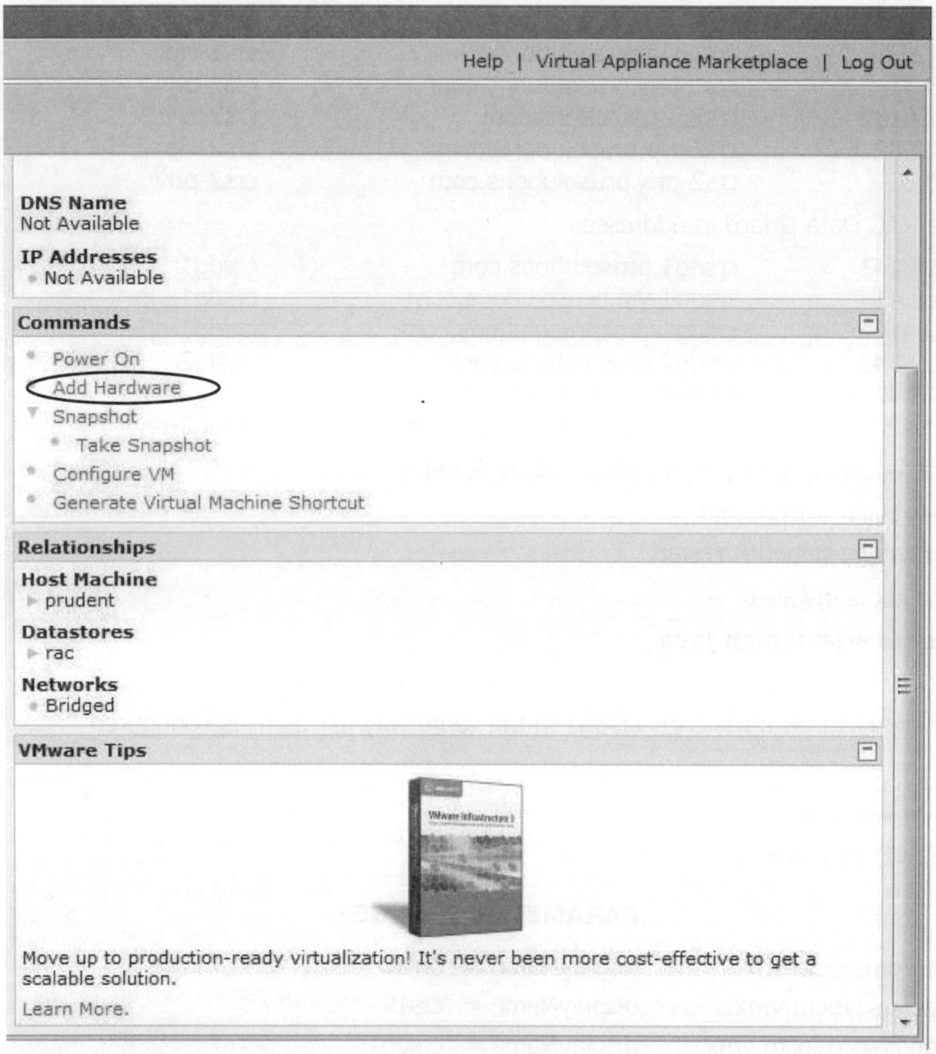

  - Network Adapter: Bridge
  - Hard Disk:

Create a New Virtual Disk

Capacity : 0.5 GB

Location : [rac] shared/ocrdisk1.vmdk

File Options : Select Allocate all the disk space Now

Disk Mode : Indepented, Persistent

Virtual Device : Adapter : **SCSI 1**, Device :0

Policies : Optimize for Safety

Finish the operations

- Repeat the above operations for more virtual disks
- Add Hardware

Create a New Virtual Disk
Capacity : 0.5 GB
Location : [rac] shared/ocrdisk2.vmdk
File Options : Select Allocate all the disk space Now
Disk Mode : Independent, Persistent
Virtual Device : Adapter : SCSI 1, Device : 1
Policies : Optimize for Safety
Finish the operations

Create a New Virtual Disk
Capacity : 0.5 GB
Location : [rac] shared/votdisk1.vmdk
File Options : Select Allocate all the disk space Now
Disk Mode : Independent, Persistent
Virtual Device : Adapter : SCSI 1, Device : 2
Policies : Optimize for Safety
Finish the operations

Create a New Virtual Disk
Capacity : 0.5 GB
Location : [rac] shared/votdisk2.vmdk
File Options : Select Allocate all the disk space Now
Disk Mode : Independent, Persistent
Virtual Device : Adapter : SCSI 1, Device : 3
Policies : Optimize for Safety
Finish the operations

Create a New Virtual Disk
Capacity : 0.5 GB
Location : [rac] shared/votdisk3.vmdk
File Options : Select Allocate all the disk space Now
Disk Mode : Independent, Persistent
Virtual Device : Adapter : SCSI 1, Device : 4
Policies : Optimize for Safety
Finish the operations

Create a New Virtual Disk
Capacity : 4 GB
Location : [rac] shared/asmdisk1.vmdk
File Options : Select Allocate all the disk space Now
Disk Mode : Independent, Persistent
Virtual Device : Adapter : SCSI 1, Device :5
Policies : Optimize for Safety
Finish the operations

Create a New Virtual Disk
Capacity : 4 GB
Location : [rac] shared/asmdisk2.vmdk
File Options : Select Allocate all the disk space Now
Disk Mode : Independent, Persistent
Virtual Device : Adapter : SCSI 1, Device : 6
Policies : Optimize for Safety
Finish the operations

Create a New Virtual Disk
Capacity : 0.5 GB
Location : [rac] shared/asmdisk3.vmdk
File Options : Select Allocate all the disk space Now
Disk Mode : Independent, Persistent
Virtual Device : Adapter : SCSI 1, Device :8
Policies : Optimize for Safety
Finish the operations

Create a New Virtual Disk
Capacity : 0.5 GB
Location : [rac] shared/asmdisk4.vmdk
File Options : Select Allocate all the disk space Now
Disk Mode : Independent, Persistent
Virtual Device : Adapter : SCSI 1, Device :9
Policies : Optimize for Safety
Finish the operations

Create a New Virtual Disk
Capacity : 0.5 GB
Location : [rac] shared/asmdisk5.vmdk
File Options : Select Allocate all the disk space Now
Disk Mode : Independent, Persistent
Virtual Device : Adapter : SCSI 1, Device :10
Policies : Optimize for Safety
Finish the operations

Create a New Virtual Disk
Capacity : 0.5 GB
Location : [rac] shared/asmdisk6.vmdk
File Options : Select Allocate all the disk space Now
Disk Mode : Independent, Persistent
Virtual Device : Adapter : SCSI 1, Device :11
Policies : Optimize for Safety
Finish the operations

Create a New Virtual Disk
Capacity : 0.5 GB
Location : [rac] shared/asmdisk7.vmdk
File Options : Select Allocate all the disk space Now
Disk Mode : Independent, Persistent
Virtual Device : Adapter : SCSI 1, Device :12
Policies : Optimize for Safety
Finish the operations

Create a New Virtual Disk
Capacity : 0.5 GB
Location : [rac] shared/asmdisk8.vmdk
File Options : Select Allocate all the disk space Now
Disk Mode : Independent, Persistent
Virtual Device : Adapter : SCSI 1, Device :13
Policies : Optimize for Safety
Finish the operations

Create a New Virtual Disk
Capacity : 0.5 GB
Location : [rac] shared/asmdisk9.vmdk

File Options : Select Allocate all the disk space Now
Disk Mode : Independent, Persistent
Virtual Device : Adapter : SCSI 1, Device :14
Policies : Optimize for Safety
Finish the operations

- Start machine crs1

i. Configure the **2nd network** device in same way as network was configured for oem machine.

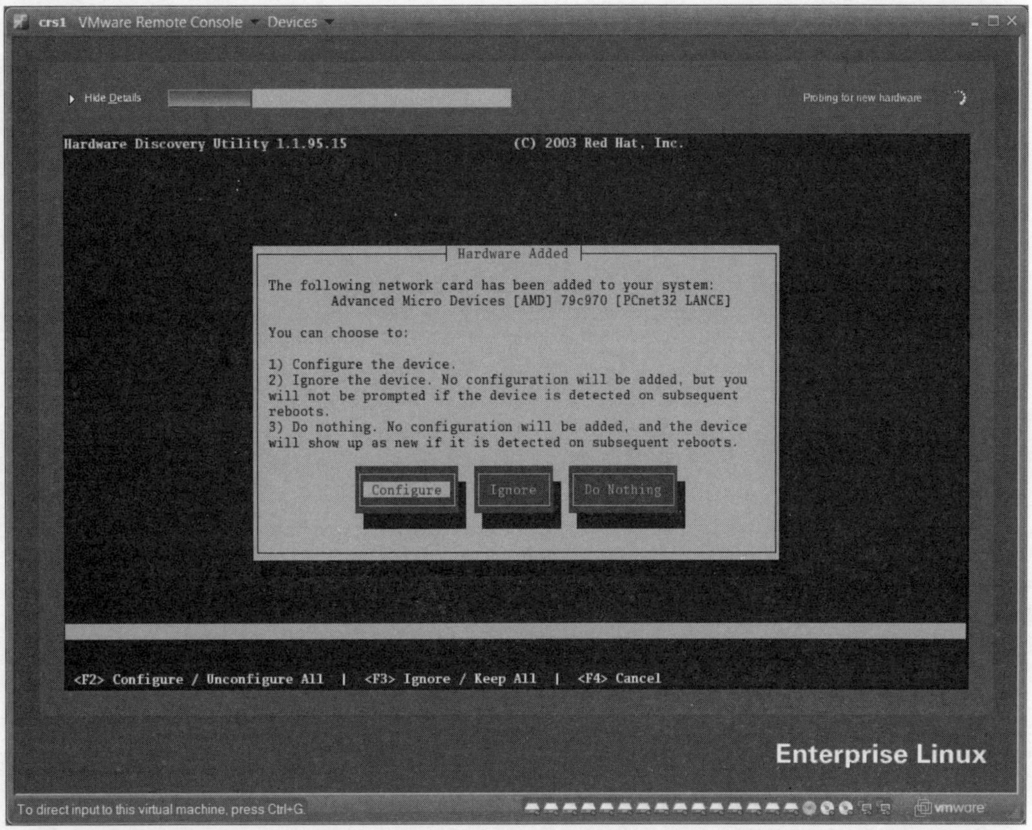

ii. On Configure TCP/IP Screen: Deselect **[ ]** Use dynamic IP configuration (BOOT/DHCP)

IP address:	10.10.10.31
Netmask:	255.255.255.0
Default gateway (IP)	
Primary nameserver	

iii. All eth0 network cards will have ip addresses starting 192.168.2. ..

iv. All eth1 network cards will have ip addresses starting 10.10.10. ..

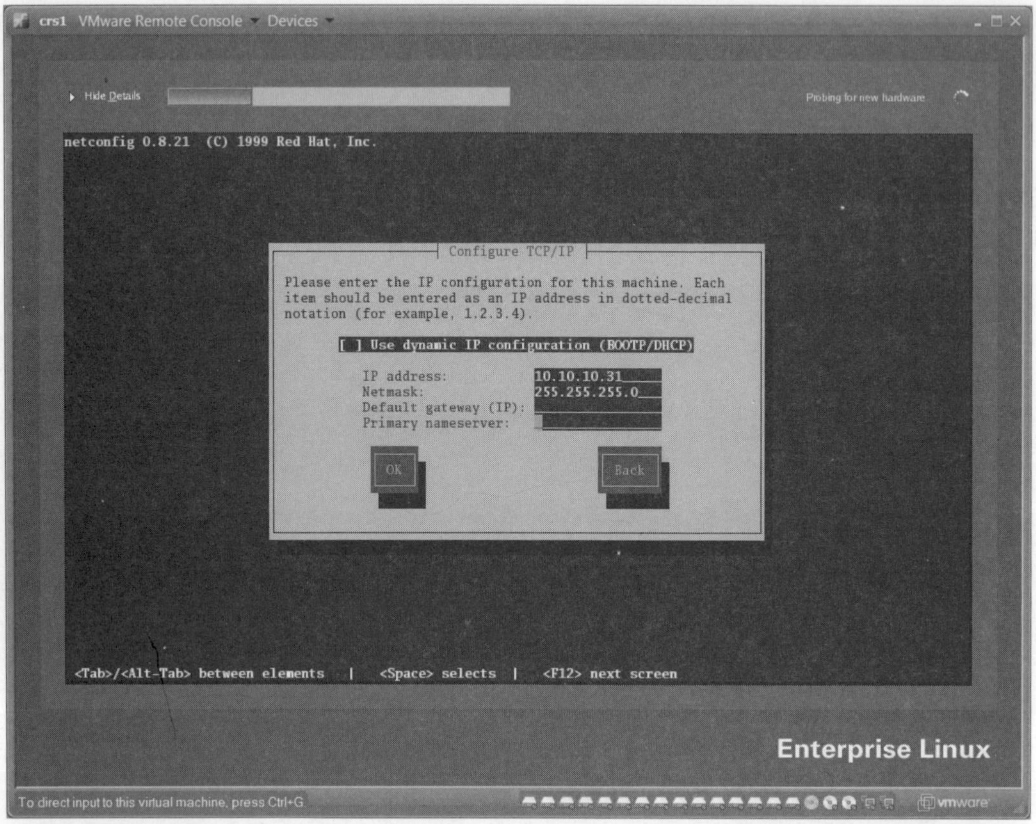

- Configure LSI Logic for SCSI 1 Disks

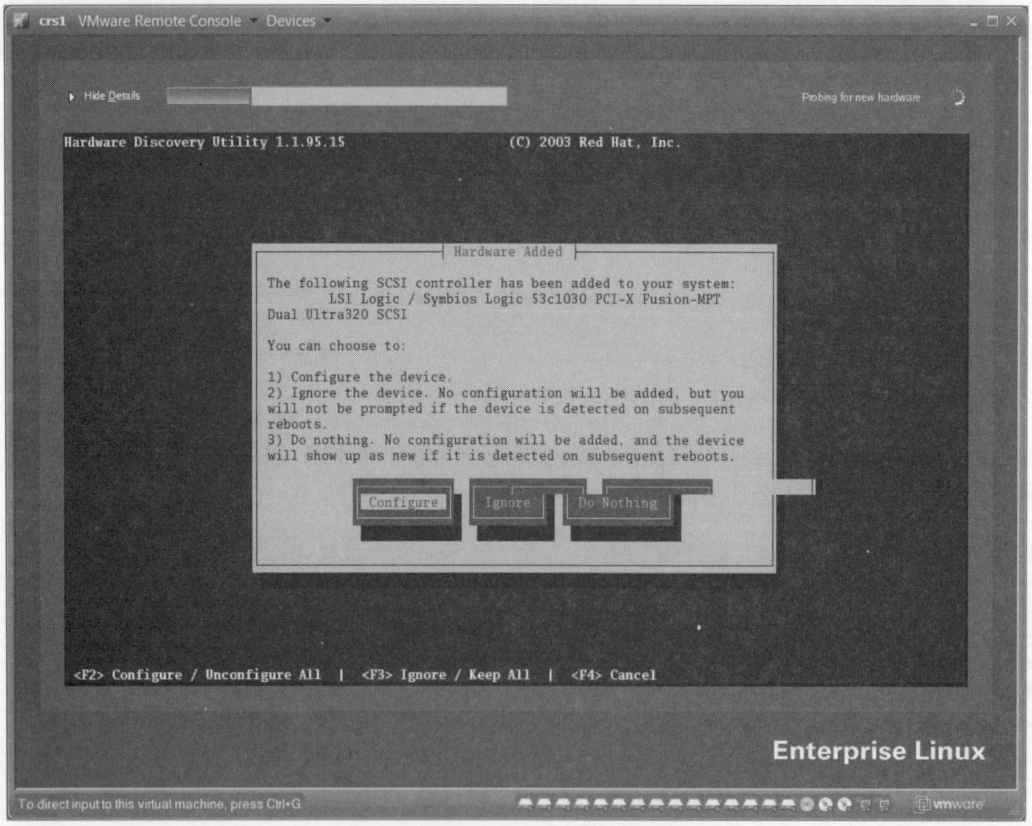

- After crs1 is started logon as oracle users and **sudo su -**

  [root@crs1 ~]# system-config-network

- On dns tab change name of machine to crs1.prusolutions.com

  Edit Ethernet card click Hardware device tab and **probe.** Deactivate and Activate the eth0, eth1

- Make sure following ip addresses are in **/etc/hosts** (same ip addresses as added in ocm machine)

```
127.0.0.1         localhost
# Oracle Database ip addresses
192.168.2.121     ocm.prusolutions.com          ocm
# Oracle Enterprise Manager ip addresses
192.168.2.161     oem.prusolutions.com          oem
192.168.2.162     oms.prusolutions.com          oms
# Oracle RAC ip addresses
192.168.2.131     crs1.prusolutions.com         crs1
192.168.2.31      crs1-vip.prusolutions.com     crs1-vip
10.10.10.31       crs1-priv.prusolutions.com    crs1-priv
192.162.2.132     crs2.prusolutions.com         crs2
192.168.2.32      crs2-vip.prusolutions.com     crs2-vip
10.10.10.32       crs2-priv.prusolutions.com    crs2-priv
# Oracle RAC Data Guard ip addresses
192.168.2.141     crsdg1.prusolutions.com       crsdg1
192.168.2.41      crsdg1-vip.prusolutions.com   crsdg1-vip
10.10.10.41       crsdg1-priv.prusolutions.com  crsdg1-priv
192.162.2.142     crsdg2.prusolutions.com       crsdg2
192.168.2.42      crsdg2-vip.prusolutions.com   crsdg2-vip
10.10.2.42        crsdg2-priv.prusolutions.com  crsdg2-priv
```

- Make sure following lines are in **/etc/rc.d/rc.local**

  i. /sbin/service vsftpd start

  ii. /sbin/service network restart

- Shutdown crs1 and modify the VMware configuration file c:/vm/rac/crs1/ocm.vmx for crs1

  i. Modify scsi1.sharedBus = "none" to scsi1.sharedBus = "virtual"

  ii. Add a line for all scsi1 virtual disks as shown in bold letters below.

```
scsi1:0.deviceType = "disk"
:
scsi1:14.deviceType = "disk"
```

- Typical virtual machine configuration file

```
.encoding = "windows-1252"
config.version = "8"
virtualHW.version = "7"
floppy0.present = "FALSE"
mks.enable3d = "TRUE"
pciBridge0.present = "TRUE"
pciBridge4.present = "TRUE"
pciBridge4.virtualDev = "pcieRootPort"
pciBridge4.functions = "8"
pciBridge5.present = "TRUE"
```

```
pciBridge5.virtualDev = "pcieRootPort"
pciBridge5.functions = "8"
pciBridge6.present = "TRUE"
pciBridge6.virtualDev = "pcieRootPort"
pciBridge6.functions = "8"
pciBridge7.present = "TRUE"
pciBridge7.virtualDev = "pcieRootPort"
pciBridge7.functions = "8"
vmci0.present = "TRUE"
nvram = "ocm.nvram"
virtualHW.productCompatibility = "hosted"
ft.secondary0.enabled = "TRUE"
tools.upgrade.policy = "useGlobal"
powerType.powerOff = "soft"
powerType.powerOn = "hard"
powerType.suspend = "hard"
powerType.reset = "soft"
displayName = "crs1"
extendedConfigFile = "ocm.vmxf"
disk.locking = "FALSE"
diskLib.dataCacheMaxSize = "0"
scsi0.present = "TRUE"
scsi0.sharedBus = "none"
scsi0.virtualDev = "lsilogic"
memsize = "1024"
scsi0:0.present = "TRUE"
scsi0:0.fileName = "localdisk.vmdk"
scsi0:0.writeThrough = "TRUE"
scsi0:0.mode = "independent-persistent"
ide0:0.present = "TRUE"
ide0:0.fileName = "c:\vm\rac\Enterprise-R4-U4-i386-disc1.iso"
ide0:0.deviceType = "cdrom-image"
ide0:0.allowGuestConnectionControl = "FALSE"
ide1:0.present = "TRUE"
ide1:0.fileName = "c:\vm\rac\Enterprise-R4-U4-i386-disc3.iso"
ide1:0.deviceType = "cdrom-image"
ide1:0.allowGuestConnectionControl = "FALSE"
ide1:1.present = "FALSE"
ide1:1.fileName = "c:\vm\rac\Enterprise-R4-U4-i386-disc2.iso"
ide1:1.deviceType = "cdrom-image"
ide1:1.allowGuestConnectionControl = "FALSE"
ethernet0.present = "TRUE"
ethernet0.allowGuestConnectionControl = "FALSE"
ethernet0.features = "1"
ethernet0.wakeOnPcktRcv = "FALSE"
ethernet0.networkName = "Bridged"
ethernet0.addressType = "generated"
guestOS = "rhel4"
uuid.location = "56 4d 8c 47 6e 77 a1 ab-39 3b 9f 4c a1 15 2a f1"
uuid.bios = "56 4d 8c 47 6e 77 a1 ab-39 3b 9f 4c a1 15 2a f1"
vc.uuid = "52 5d a8 ce 77 d4 51 3b-49 fb 7d a6 6d 28 7c 79"

ide0:1.present = "TRUE"
ide0:1.fileName = "c:\vm\rac\Enterprise-R4-U4-i386-disc2.iso"
ide0:1.deviceType = "cdrom-image"
ide0:1.allowGuestConnectionControl = "FALSE"
```

ide0:0.startConnected = "FALSE"
ethernet0.generatedAddress = "00:0c:29:15:2a:f1"
tools.syncTime = "TRUE"
scsi0:0.redo = ""
vmotion.checkpointFBSize = "134217728"
pciBridge0.pciSlotNumber = "17"
pciBridge4.pciSlotNumber = "21"
pciBridge5.pciSlotNumber = "22"
pciBridge6.pciSlotNumber = "23"
pciBridge7.pciSlotNumber = "24"
scsi0.pciSlotNumber = "16"
ethernet0.pciSlotNumber = "32"
vmci0.pciSlotNumber = "33"
ethernet0.generatedAddressOffset = "0"
vmci0.id = "-1913533590"

ethernet1.present = "TRUE"
ethernet1.allowGuestConnectionControl = "FALSE"
ethernet1.features = "1"
ethernet1.wakeOnPcktRcv = "FALSE"
ethernet1.networkName = "Bridged"
ethernet1.addressType = "generated"

scsi1.present = "TRUE"
scsi1.sharedBus = "virtual"
scsi1.virtualDev = "lsilogic"
scsi1:0.present = "TRUE"
scsi1:0.fileName = "c:\vm\rac\shared\ocrdisk1.vmdk"
scsi1:0.writeThrough = "TRUE"
scsi1:0.mode = "independent-persistent"
scsi1:0.deviceType = "disk"

scsi1:1.present = "TRUE"
scsi1:1.fileName = "c:\vm\rac\shared\ocrdisk2.vmdk"
scsi1:1.writeThrough = "TRUE"
scsi1:1.mode = "independent-persistent"
scsi1:1.deviceType = "disk"

scsi1:2.present = "TRUE"
scsi1:2.fileName = "c:\vm\rac\shared\votdisk1.vmdk"
scsi1:2.writeThrough = "TRUE"
scsi1:2.mode = "independent-persistent"
scsi1:2.deviceType = "disk"

scsi1:3.present = "TRUE"
scsi1:3.fileName = "c:\vm\rac\shared\votdisk2.vmdk"
scsi1:3.writeThrough = "TRUE"
scsi1:3.mode = "independent-persistent"
scsi1:3.deviceType = "disk"

ethernet1.generatedAddress = "00:0c:29:15:2a:fb"
scsi1:0.redo = ""
scsi1:1.redo = ""
scsi1:2.redo = ""
scsi1:3.redo = ""

```
scsi1.pciSlotNumber = "34"
ethernet1.pciSlotNumber = "35"
ethernet1.generatedAddressOffset = "10"

scsi1:4.present = "TRUE"
scsi1:4.fileName = "c:\vm\rac\shared\votdisk3.vmdk"
scsi1:4.writeThrough = "TRUE"
scsi1:4.mode = "independent-persistent"
scsi1:4.deviceType = "disk"

scsi1:5.present = "TRUE"
scsi1:5.fileName = "c:\vm\rac\shared\asmdisk1.vmdk"
scsi1:5.writeThrough = "TRUE"
scsi1:5.mode = "independent-persistent"
scsi1:5.deviceType = "disk"

scsi1:6.present = "TRUE"
scsi1:6.fileName = "c:\vm\rac\shared\asmdisk2.vmdk"
scsi1:6.writeThrough = "TRUE"
scsi1:6.mode = "independent-persistent"
scsi1:6.deviceType = "disk"

scsi1:8.present = "TRUE"
scsi1:8.fileName = "c:\vm\rac\shared\asmdisk3.vmdk"
scsi1:8.writeThrough = "TRUE"
scsi1:8.mode = "independent-persistent"
scsi1:8.deviceType = "disk"

scsi1:9.present = "TRUE"
scsi1:9.fileName = "c:\vm\rac\shared\asmdisk4.vmdk"
scsi1:9.writeThrough = "TRUE"
scsi1:9.mode = "independent-persistent"
scsi1:9.deviceType = "disk"

scsi1:4.redo = ""
scsi1:5.redo = ""
scsi1:6.redo = ""
scsi1:8.redo = ""
scsi1:9.redo = ""

scsi1:10.present = "TRUE"
scsi1:10.fileName = "c:\vm\rac\shared\asmdisk5.vmdk"
scsi1:10.writeThrough = "TRUE"
scsi1:10.mode = "independent-persistent"
scsi1:10.deviceType = "disk"

scsi1:11.present = "TRUE"
scsi1:11.fileName = "c:\vm\rac\shared\asmdisk6.vmdk"
scsi1:11.writeThrough = "TRUE"
scsi1:11.mode = "independent-persistent"
scsi1:11.deviceType = "disk"

scsi1:12.present = "TRUE"
scsi1:12.fileName = "c:\vm\rac\shared\asmdisk7.vmdk"
scsi1:12.writeThrough = "TRUE"
```

```
scsi1:12.mode = "independent-persistent"
scsi1:12.deviceType = "disk"

scsi1:13.present = "TRUE"
scsi1:13.fileName = "c:\vm\rac\shared\asmdisk8.vmdk"
scsi1:13.writeThrough = "TRUE"
scsi1:13.mode = "independent-persistent"
scsi1:13.deviceType = "disk"

scsi1:14.present = "TRUE"
scsi1:14.fileName = "c:\vm\rac\shared\asmdisk9.vmdk"
scsi1:14.writeThrough = "TRUE"
scsi1:14.mode = "independent-persistent"
scsi1:14.deviceType = "disk"

scsi1:10.redo = ""
scsi1:11.redo = ""
scsi1:12.redo = ""
scsi1:13.redo = ""
scsi1:14.redo = ""
```

- Restart crs1 machine, login as oracle then sudo su –
- Run following command to make sure you can see all the disks

  [root@crs1 ~]# fdisk -l | grep -i disk

■ Create CRS2 machi'ne from CRS1 machine [rac] crs2/ocm.vmx

- "crs1" is ready. Shutdown crs1 and make a copy as "crs2"

  i. **Copy** c:/vm/rac/crs1 to c:/vm/rac/crs2
  ii. Modify the file c:/vm/rac/crs2/ocm.vmx

FILE	PARAMETER CHANGE
c:/vm/rac/crs2*/ocm.vmx*	*displayName = "crs2"*

- "Add Virtual Machine to Inventory" and select *[rac] crs2/ocm.vmx for* crs2 machine. There is no need to change the name of configuration file ocm.vmx

- Add **crs2** machine to VMware, Start the machine crs2 and choose the option "I_copied", once machine starts, double click on console window to see the virtual machine.

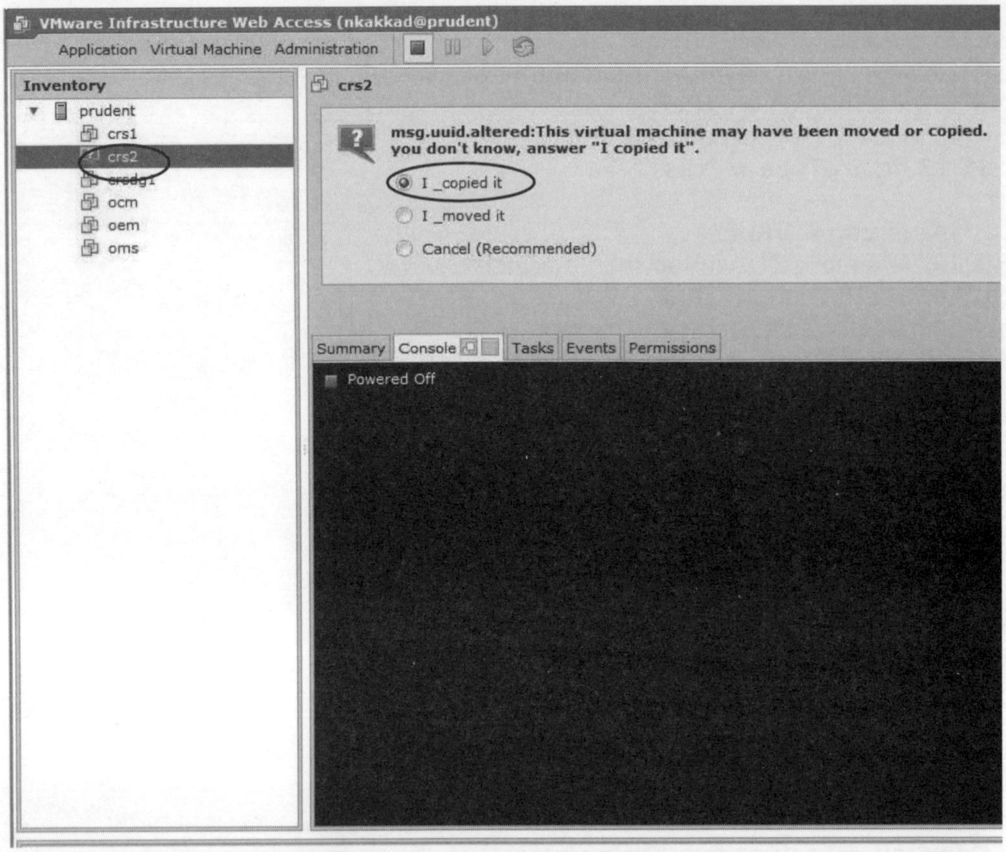

- Hardware Changes Screen: Double Click to make network changes

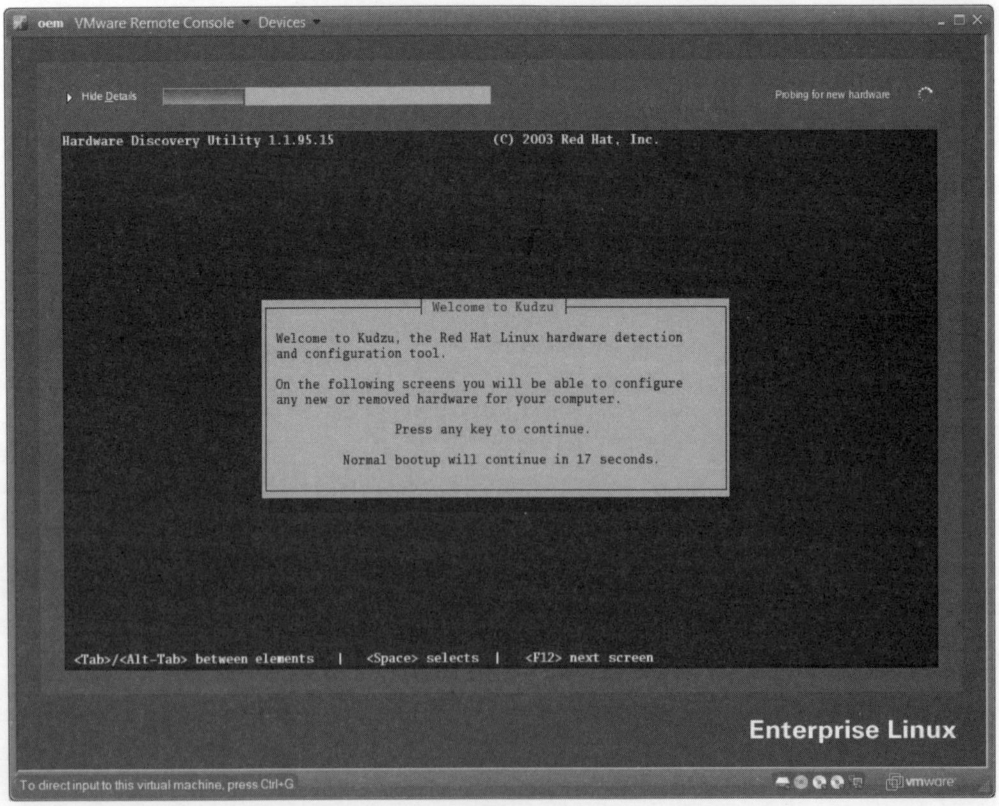

- Hardware Removed Screen : Click "Remove Configuration" twice

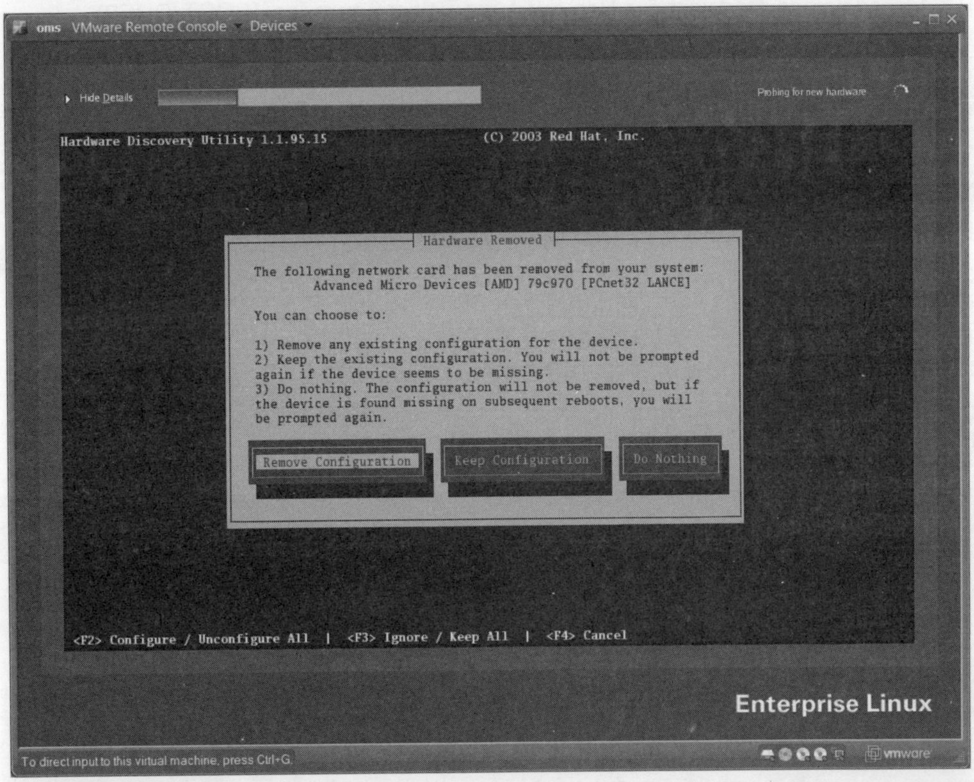

- Make sure you have correct ip addresses 2nd network card (eth1) which you will "Configure" first. If you have to do two-network configuration then the first network will always be eth1.

  The 2nd network device (eth1) on crs2 will be configured in same way as crs1 and the ip address will 10.10.10.32.

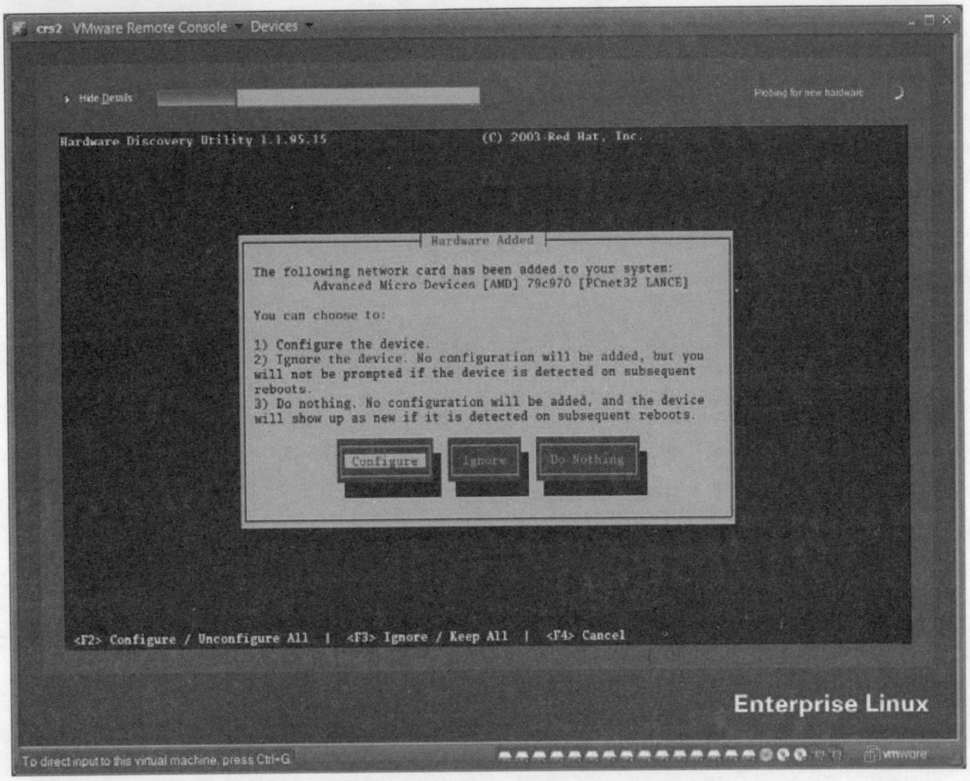

Configure **2nd** network card eth0

On IP address screen Deselect **[ ]** Use dynamic IP configuration (BOOT/DHCP)

IP address:	10.10.10.32
Netmask:	255.255.255.0
Default gateway (IP)	
Primary nameserver	

- Configure **1st** network card eth0

  On IP address screen Deselect **[ ]** Use dynamic IP configuration (BOOT/DHCP)

IP address:	192.168.2.132
Netmask:	255.255.255.0
Default gateway (IP)	192.168.2.1
Primary nameserver	192.168.2.1

All eth0 network cards will have ip addresses starting 192.168.2. ..
All eth1 network cards will have ip addresses starting 10.10.10. ..

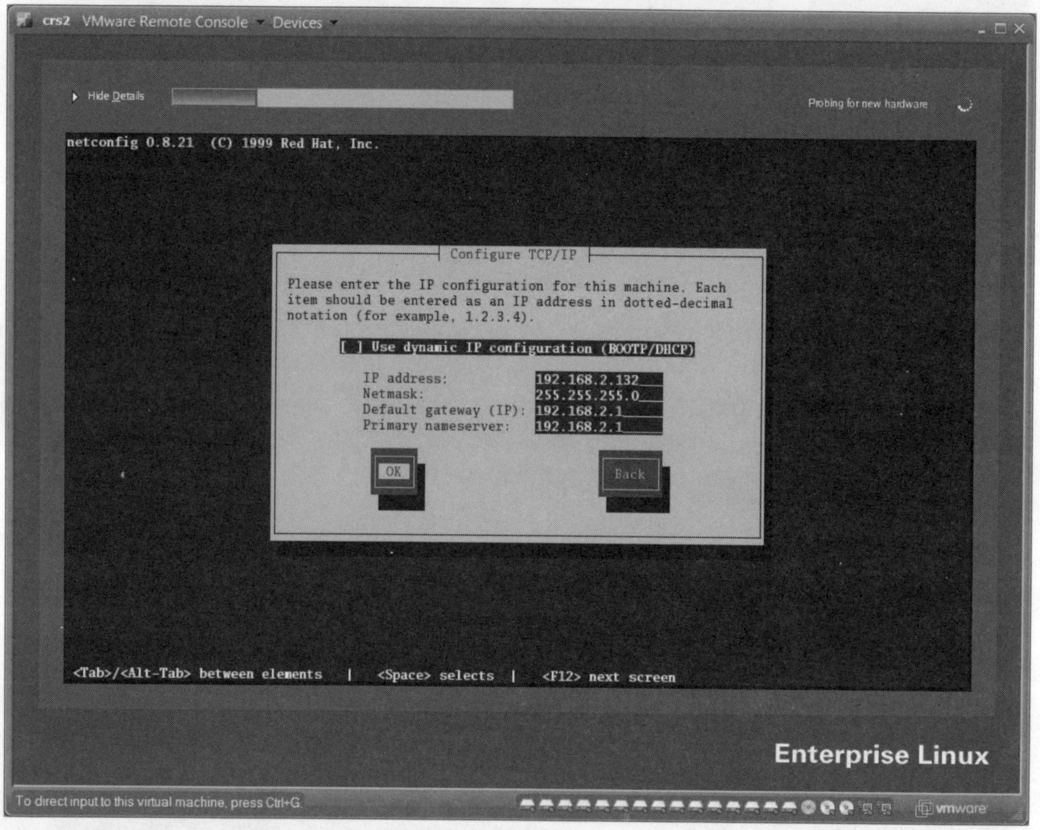

- After crs2 is started login are oracle then "sudo su –"

  Run following command to make sure you can see all the disks

  [root@crs2 ~]# fdisk -l | grep -i disk

  [root@crs2 ~]# system-config-network

- Edit Ethernet card click Hardware device tab and ***probe.*** On dns tab change name of machine to **crs2.prusolutions.com** Deactivate and Activate the eth0, eth1

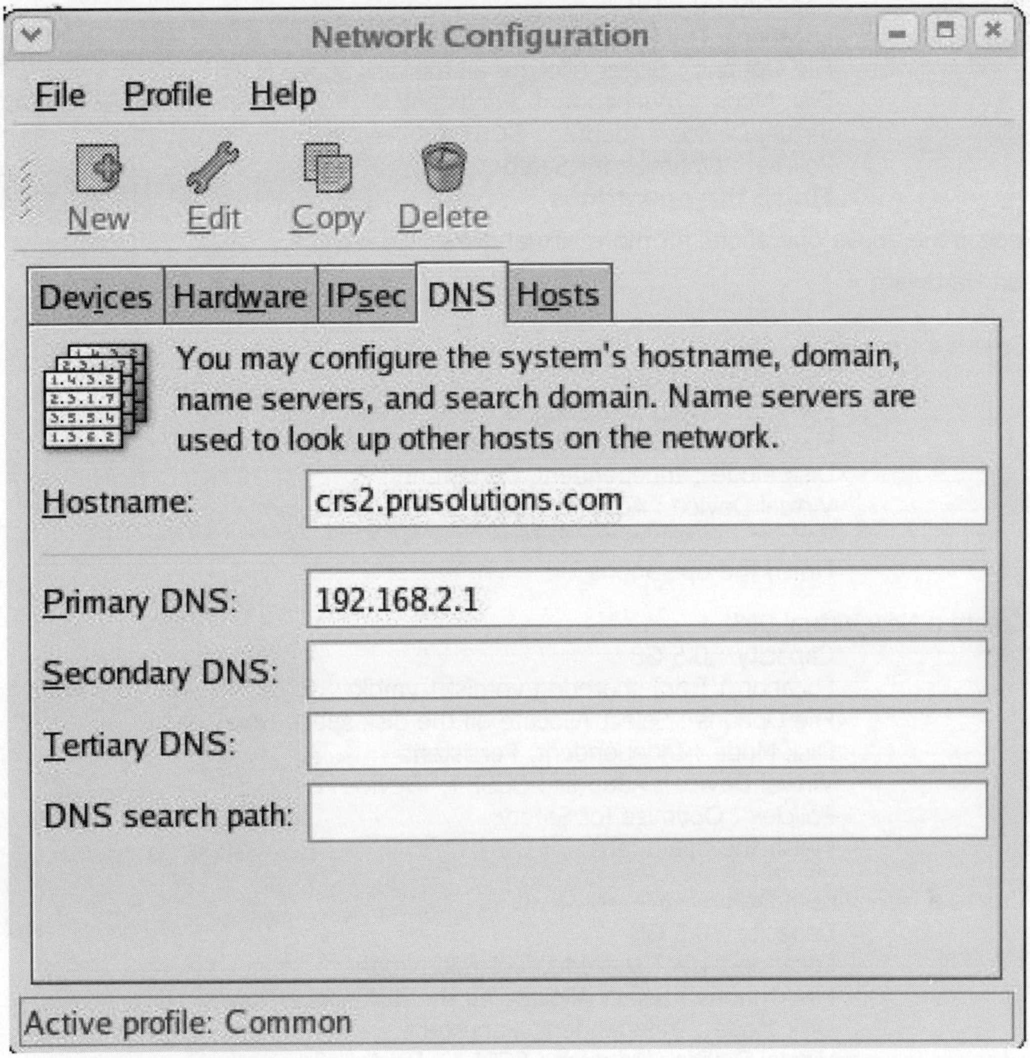

1.8 Extra configuration for Data Guard Real Application Cluster

Create crsdg2 machine from crsdg1.

- Additional Configuration of crsdg1 machine [rac] crsdg1/ocm.vmx
  - We have to follow same steps that we did in additional configuration of "crs1". The only difference is this time this shared folder will be "shareddg" and ip address for 2nd network eth1 is 10.10.10.41
  - Create a folder shareddg
  - Shutdown crsdg1 machine and go to summary tab of crsdg1 on VMware
  - Add Hardware
  - Network Adapter: Bridge

- Hard Disk:

  Create a New Virtual Disk

  Capacity : 0.5 GB
  Location : [rac] shareddg/ocrdisk1.vmdk
  File Options : Select Allocate all the disk space Now
  Disk Mode : Independent, Persistent
  Virtual Device : Adapter : **SCSI 1,** Device :0
  Policies : Optimize for Safety
  Finish the operations

- Repeat the above operations for more virtual disks
- Add Hardware

  Create a New Virtual Disk

  Capacity : 0.5 GB
  Location : [rac] shareddg/ocrdisk2.vmdk
  File Options : Select Allocate all the disk space Now
  Disk Mode : Independent, Persistent
  Virtual Device : Adapter : SCSI 1, Device :1
  Policies : Optimize for Safety
  Finish the operations

  Create a New Virtual Disk

  Capacity : 0.5 GB
  Location : [rac] shareddg/votdisk1.vmdk
  File Options : Select Allocate all the disk space Now
  Disk Mode : Independent, Persistent
  Virtual Device : Adapter : SCSI 1, Device :2
  Policies : Optimize for Safety
  Finish the operations

  Create a New Virtual Disk

  Capacity : 0.5 GB
  Location : [rac] shareddg/votdisk2.vmdk
  File Options : Select Allocate all the disk space Now
  Disk Mode : Independent, Persistent
  Virtual Device : Adapter : SCSI 1, Device :3
  Policies : Optimize for Safety
  Finish the operations

  Create a New Virtual Disk

  Capacity : 0.5 GB
  Location : [rac] shareddg/votdisk3.vmdk
  File Options : Select Allocate all the disk space Now
  Disk Mode : Independent, Persistent
  Virtual Device : Adapter : SCSI 1, Device :4
  Policies : Optimize for Safety
  Finish the operations

  Create a New Virtual Disk

  Capacity : 4 GB
  Location : [rac] shareddg/asmdisk1.vmdk
  File Options : Select Allocate all the disk space Now
  Disk Mode : Independent, Persistent
  Virtual Device : Adapter : SCSI 1, Device :5
  Policies : Optimize for Safety
  Finish the operations

Create a New Virtual Disk

Capacity : 4 GB
Location : [rac] shareddg/asmdisk2.vmdk
File Options : Select Allocate all the disk space Now
Disk Mode : Independent, Persistent
Virtual Device : Adapter : SCSI 1, Device :6
Policies : Optimize for Safety
Finish the operations

Create a New Virtual Disk

Capacity : 0.5 GB
Location : [rac] shareddg/asmdisk3.vmdk
File Options : Select Allocate all the disk space Now
Disk Mode : Independent, Persistent
Virtual Device : Adapter : SCSI 1, Device :8
Policies : Optimize for Safety
Finish the operations

Create a New Virtual Disk

Capacity : 0.5 GB
Location : [rac] shareddg/asmdisk4.vmdk
File Options : Select Allocate all the disk space Now
Disk Mode : Independent, Persistent
Virtual Device : Adapter : SCSI 1, Device :9
Policies : Optimize for Safety
Finish the operations

Create a New Virtual Disk

Capacity : 0.5 GB
Location : [rac] shareddg/asmdisk5.vmdk
File Options : Select Allocate all the disk space Now
Disk Mode : Independent, Persistent
Virtual Device : Adapter : SCSI 1, Device :10
Policies : Optimize for Safety
Finish the operations

Create a New Virtual Disk

Capacity : 0.5 GB
Location : [rac] shareddg/asmdisk6.vmdk
File Options : Select Allocate all the disk space Now
Disk Mode : Independent, Persistent
Virtual Device : Adapter : SCSI 1, Device :11
Policies : Optimize for Safety
Finish the operations

Create a New Virtual Disk

Capacity : 0.5 GB
Location : [rac] shareddg/asmdisk7.vmdk
File Options : Select Allocate all the disk space Now
Disk Mode : Independent, Persistent
Virtual Device : Adapter : SCSI 1, Device :12
Policies : Optimize for Safety
Finish the operations

Create a New Virtual Disk
Capacity : 0.5 GB
Location : [rac] shareddg/asmdisk8.vmdk
File Options : Select Allocate all the disk space Now
Disk Mode : Independent, Persistent
Virtual Device : Adapter : SCSI 1, Device :13
Policies : Optimize for Safety
Finish the operations

Create a New Virtual Disk
Capacity : 0.5 GB
Location : [rac] shareddg/asmdisk9.vmdk
File Options : Select Allocate all the disk space Now
Disk Mode : Independent, Persistent
Virtual Device : Adapter : SCSI 1, Device :14
Policies : Optimize for Safety
Finish the operations

- Start machine crsdg1
- Configure the **2nd** network device in same way as network was configured for crs1 machine.
  On IP address screen Deselect **[ ]** Use dynamic IP configuration (BOOT/DHCP)

IP address:	10.10.10.41
Netmask:	255.255.255.0
Default gateway (IP)	
Primary nameserver	

All eth0 network cards will have ip addresses starting 192.168.2. ..
All eth1 network cards will have ip addresses starting 10.10.10. ..

- Rest of Configuration is same as for crs1 machine
  After crsdg1 is started logon as oracle users and **sudo su -**
  [root@crsdg1 ~]# system-config-network
- On dns tab change name of machine to **crsdg1.prusolutions.com**
  Edit Ethernet card click Hardware device tab and **probe.** Deactivate and Activate the eth0, eth1
- Add following to /etc/hosts (same ip addresses as added in crs1 machine)

```
127.0.0.1         localhost
# Oracle Database ip addresses
192.168.2.121     ocm.prusolutions.com          ocm
# Oracle Enterprise Manager ip addresses
192.168.2.161     oem.prusolutions.com          oem
192.168.2.162     oms.prusolutions.com          oms
# Oracle RAC ip addresses
192.168.2.131     crs1.prusolutions.com         crs1
192.168.2.31      crs1-vip.prusolutions.com     crs1-vip
10.10.10.31       crs1-priv.prusolutions.com    crs1-priv
192.162.2.132     crs2.prusolutions.com         crs2
192.168.2.32      crs2-vip.prusolutions.com     crs2-vip
10.10.10.32       crs2-priv.prusolutions.com    crs2-priv
# Oracle RAC Dataguard ip addresses
192.168.2.141     crsdg1.prusolutions.com       crsdg1
```

192.168.2.41	crsdg1-vip.prusolutions.com	crsdg1-vip
10.10.10.41	crsdg1-priv.prusolutions.com	crsdg1-priv
192.162.2.142	crsdg2.prusolutions.com	crsdg2
192.168.2.42	crsdg2-vip.prusolutions.com	crsdg2-vip
10.10.10.42	crsdg2-priv.prusolutions.com	crsdg2-priv

- Make sure following lines are in /etc/rc.d/rc.local
  i. /sbin/service vsftpd start
  ii. /sbin/service network restart
- Shutdown crsdg1 and modify the VMware configuration file c:/vm/rac/crsdg1/ocm.vmx for crsdg1
  i. Modify scsi1.sharedBus = "none" to scsi1.sharedBus = "virtual"
  ii. Add a line for all scsi1 virtual disks as shown below
  scsi1:0.deviceType = "disk"
  :
  scsi1:14.deviceType = "disk"

■ Create CRSDG2 machine from CRSDG1 machine [rac] crs2/ocm.vmx

- Configure CRSDG2 same way as CRS2 above
- "crsdg1" is ready. Shutdown crsdg1 and make a copy as "crsdg2"
  i. **Copy** c:/vm/rac/crsdg1 to c:/vm/rac/crsdg2
  ii. Modify the file c:/vm/rac/crsdg2/ocm.vmx

FILE	PARAMETER CHANGE
c:/vm/rac/crsdg2/ocm.vmx	displayName = "crsdg2"

  iii. "Add Virtual Machine to Inventory" and select **[rac] crsdg2/ocm.vmx** for crs2 machine. There is no need to change the name of configuration file ocm.vmx
  iv. Add crsdg2 machine to VMware start the machine crsdg2 and choose the option I_copied, once machine started double click on console window to see the virtual machine
- Configure Hardware Changes: Click Enter to configure Hardware changes. It will take you to network configuration screen.
- Remove configuration twice and configure the network.
- You have to do two network configuration then the first network will be always eth1
- Make sure you have correct ip addresses 2nd network card (eth1) which the first you will configure.

  The 2nd network device (eth1) on crsdg2 will be configured same way as crsdg1 and the ip address will 10.10.10.42

  Network: eth1 ip address: 10.10.10.42 Netmask: 255.255.255.0 Default gateway:

  On IP address screen Deselect **[ ]** Use dynamic IP configuration (BOOT/DHCP)

IP address:	10.10.10.42
Netmask:	255.255.255.0
Default gateway (IP)	
Primary nameserver	

  On IP address screen Deselect **[ ]** Use dynamic IP configuration (BOOT/DHCP)

IP address:	192.168.2.142
Netmask:	255.255.255.0
Default gateway (IP)	192.168.2.1
Primary nameserver	192.168.2.1

  All eth0 network cards will have ip addresses starting 192.168.2. ..
  All eth1 network cards will have ip addresses starting 10.10.10. ..

- After crsdg2 is started login are oracle then **"sudo su –"**
  Run following command to make sure you can see all the disks
  [root@crsdg2 ~]# fdisk -l | grep -i disk
  [root@crsdg2 ~]# system-config-network
  Edit Ethernet card click Hardware device tab and **probe.** Deactivate and activate the eth0, eth1

1.9 Start all the machines, ping each other

Make sure you are able to ping all the machines from each other.

```
# ping crs1
# ping crs2
# ping crsdg1
# ping crsdg2
# ping ocm
# ping oem
# ping oms
```

And also ping the following from RAC and Dataguard machines, crs1, crs2, crsdg1, crsdg2

```
# ping crs1-priv
# ping crs2-priv
# ping crsdg1-priv
# ping crsdg2-priv
```

If there is any problem fix and then proceed further. If you are able to ping any machine by its ip address and not by name then **/etc/hosts** file may not be defined properly or the machine name may not be set correct. Use the commands below to detect problems.

```
# system-config-network
# /sbin/ifconfig -a
# /sbin/route -n
# /sbin/iptables -L
# chkconfig —list | grep iptables
#system-config-securitylevel
```

1.10 Shutdown all the machines and backup the parent folder

- **Copy c: /vm/rac to c: /vm/rac_bck.**

  The backup folder will be used to do all "ocm" exercises multiple times.

1.11 Machine Configuration

Whenever you need new machine, remove the old machine from VMware and add new machine in VMware. Do not select "Delete this virtual machine's file", instead delete the folder manually from c: /vm/rac/ and copy new folder in v: /vm/rac from c:/vm/rac_bck

2

Server Configuration

- Create the database
- Determine and set sizing parameters for database structures
- Create and manage temporary, permanent, and undo tablespaces
- Stripe data files across multiple physical devices and locations
- Configure the database environment to support optimal data access performance
- Create and manage database configuration files
- Create and manage bigfile tablespaces
- Create and manage multiple network configuration files
- Create and configure a listener
- Configure the database instance to support shared server connections
- Set up network tracing
- Manage Oracle network processes (the Listener Control utility)
- Configure the network environment to allow connections to multiple databases
- Use configurationless connections

2.1 Install Oracle Database Software

- Ftp and unzip Oracle 10g Database software and JDK

  Start "ocm" machine on VMware, logon to oracle user then create folder /u01/software ftp Oracle 10g Database software and JDK mentioned below to ocm Linux guest machine from Windows host. Unzip the oracle database 10g software files

  10201_database_linux32.zip
  10201_companion_linux32
  jdk-6u21-linux-i586-rpm.bin

  Sometimes while creating zip file some of the oracle install files becomes read only. Using user oracle on Linux change the permission to read, write, execute (chmod 755 <filename>) on those files if you get any error during install of any Oracle software on VMware.

- Check hosts names, files option should be the first

  # cat /etc/nsswitch.conf | grep hosts

  make sure it has **file** option first then dns

- Check Kernel Parameters are set properly (Converted into kb, mb, gb to remember easily)

  - **/etc/sysctl.conf**

```
kernel.shmall = 2097152                        # (2mb)
kernel.shmmax = 2147483648                     # (2g)
kernel.shmmni = 4096                           # (4k)
kernel.sem = 250 32000 100 128
fs.file-max = 65536                            # (64k)
net.ipv4.ip_local_port_range = 1024 65000
net.core.rmem_default = 1048576                # (1mb)
net.core.rmem_max = 1048576                    # (1mb)
net.core.wmem_default = 262144                 # (256k)
net.core.wmem_max = 262144                     # (256k)
```

  - **/etc/security/limits.conf**

```
oracle    soft   nproc 2047
oracle    hard   nproc 16384
oracle    soft   nofile 1024
oracle    hard   nofile 65536
```

  - **/etc/pam.d/login**

```
session   required   /lib/security/pam_limits.so
session   required   pam_limits.so
```

  - **/etc/profile**

```
if [ $USER = "oracle" ]; then
      if [ $SHELL = "/bin/ksh" ]; then
            ulimit -p 16384
            ulimit -n 65536
      else
            ulimit -u 16384 -n 65536
      fi
fi
```

- Check /etc/hosts for following values are set

```
127.0.0.1                 localhost
```

```
# Oracle Database ip addresses
192.168.2.121        ocm.prusolutions.com               ocm
# Oracle Enterprise Manager ip addresses
192.168.2.161        oem.prusolutions.com               oem
192.168.2.162        oms.prusolutions.com               oms
# Oracle RAC ip addresses
192.168.2.131        crs1.prusolutions.com              crs1
192.168.2.31         crs1-vip.prusolutions.com          crs1-vip
10.10.10.31          crs1-priv.prusolutions.com         crs1-priv
192.162.2.132        crs2.prusolutions.com              crs2
192.168.2.32         crs2-vip.prusolutions.com          crs2-vip
10.10.10.32          crs2-priv.prusolutions.com         crs2-priv
# Oracle RAC Dataguard ip addresses
192.168.2.141        crsdg1.prusolutions.com            crsdg1
192.168.2.41         crsdg1-vip.prusolutions.com        crsdg1-vip
10.10.10.41          crsdg1-priv.prusolutions.com       crsdg1-priv
192.162.2.142        crsdg2.prusolutions.com            crsdg2
192.168.2.42         crsdg2-vip.prusolutions.com        crsdg2-vip
10.10.10.42          crsdg2-priv.prusolutions.com       crsdg2-priv
```

- Check user oracle and nobody for software Install

```
# cat /etc/passwd
```

- Check following parameters swap should be 3G, memory 1G and temp space at least 512M

```
# grep MemTotal /proc/meminfo
# grep SwapTotal /proc/meminfo
# df -k /tmp
```

- Set up profile for user oracle

/home/oracle/.bash_profile

```
# Get the aliases and functions
if [ -f ~/.bashrc ]; then
        . ~/.bashrc
fi

# User specific environment and startup programs

export EDITOR=vi
export ORACLE_SID=ocmdb
export ORACLE_BASE=/u01/app/oracle
export ORACLE_HOME=$ORACLE_BASE/product/10.2.0/db_1
export PATH=$ORACLE_HOME/bin:/bin:/sbin :/usr/bin:/usr/sbin:/usr/local/bin:/usr/X11R6/bin
umask 022
```

- Set up agent_profile

/home/oracle/agent_profile

```
# agent_profile

# Get the aliases and functions
if [ -f ~/.bashrc ]; then
        . ~/.bashrc
fi
```

```
# User specific environment and startup programs
export EDITOR=vi
export ORACLE_BASE=/u01/app/oracle
export ORACLE_HOME=$ORACLE_BASE/product/10.2.0
export PATH=$ORACLE_HOME/bin:/bin:/sbin :/usr/bin:/usr/sbin:/usr/local/bin:/usr/X11R6/bin
umask 022
```

- To change environment variable use following

```
$. /home/oracle/.bash_profile
$. /home/oracle/agent10_profile
$ echo $ORACLE_HOME
```

- Check Linux required packages are installed

```
binutils-2.15.92.0.2-21
compat-db-4.1.25-9
compat-libstdc++-33-3.2.3-47.3
gcc-3.4.6-3.1
gcc-c++-3.4.6-3.1
glibc-2.3.4-2.25
glibc-common-2.3.4-2.25
gnome-libs-1.4.1.2.90-44.2
libstdc++-3.4.6-3.1
libstdc++-devel-3.4.6-3.1
make-3.80-6.EL4
pdksh-5.2.14-30.3
sysstat-5.0.5-11.rhel4
xscreensaver-4.18-5.rhel4.12
setarch-1.6-1
libaio-0.3.105-2.i386.rpm
openmotif21-2.1.30-11.RHEL4.6.i386.rpm
```

If the different version of Linux is installed then packages may be as mentioned below or combination of both

```
binutils-2.15.92.0.2-13.EL4
compat-db-4.1.25-9
compat-libstdc++-296-2.96-132.7.2
control-center-2.8.0-12
gcc-3.4.3-22.1.EL4
gcc-c++-3.4.3-22.1.EL44
glibc-2.3.4-2.9
glibc-common-2.3.4-2.9
gnome-libs-1.4.1.2.90-44.1
libstdc++-3.4.3-22.1
libstdc++-devel-3.4.3-22.1
make-3.80-5
pdksh-5.2.14-30
sysstat-5.0.5-1
xscreensaver-4.18-5.rhel4.2
setarch-1.6-1
libaio-0.3.105-2.i386.rpm
openmotif21-2.1.30-11.RHEL4.6.i386.rpm
```

- Make the following directories for Oracle Install

```
mkdir –p $ORACLE_HOME
mkdir –p $ORACLE_BASE/admin
mkdir –p $ORACLE_BASE/oradata/disk1/ocmdb
mkdir –p $ORACLE_BASE/oradata/disk2/ocmdb
mkdir –p $ORACLE_BASE/oradata/disk3/ocmdb
mkdir –p $ORACLE_BASE/oradata/disk4/ocmdb
mkdir –p $ORACLE_BASE/oradata/disk5/ocmdb
mkdir –p $ORACLE_BASE/admin/ocmdb/control
mkdir –p $ORACLE_BASE/admin/ocmdb/cdump
mkdir –p $ORACLE_BASE/admin/ocmdb/bdump
mkdir –p $ORACLE_BASE/admin/ocmdb/udump
mkdir –p $ORACLE_BASE/admin/ocmdb/adump
mkdir –p $ORACLE_BASE/admin/ocmdb/scripts
mkdir -p $ORACLE_BASE/flash_recovery_area
```

- Install Database Software only on ocm server

```
[oracle@ocm software]$ pwd
/u01/software
[oracle@ocm software]$ ls -ltr
total 738380
-rw-r—r— 1 oracle oinstall 675848454 Nov 26 18:40 database.zip
drwxr-xr-x 7 oracle oinstall      4096 Nov 26 18:44 database
-rw-r—r— 1 oracle oinstall  79491215 Jan 15 12:12 jdk-6u21-linux-i586-rpm.bin
```

[oracle@ocm software]$ cd database

[oracle@ocm database]$. /runInstaller

  - Select Installation Method : Advance Installation

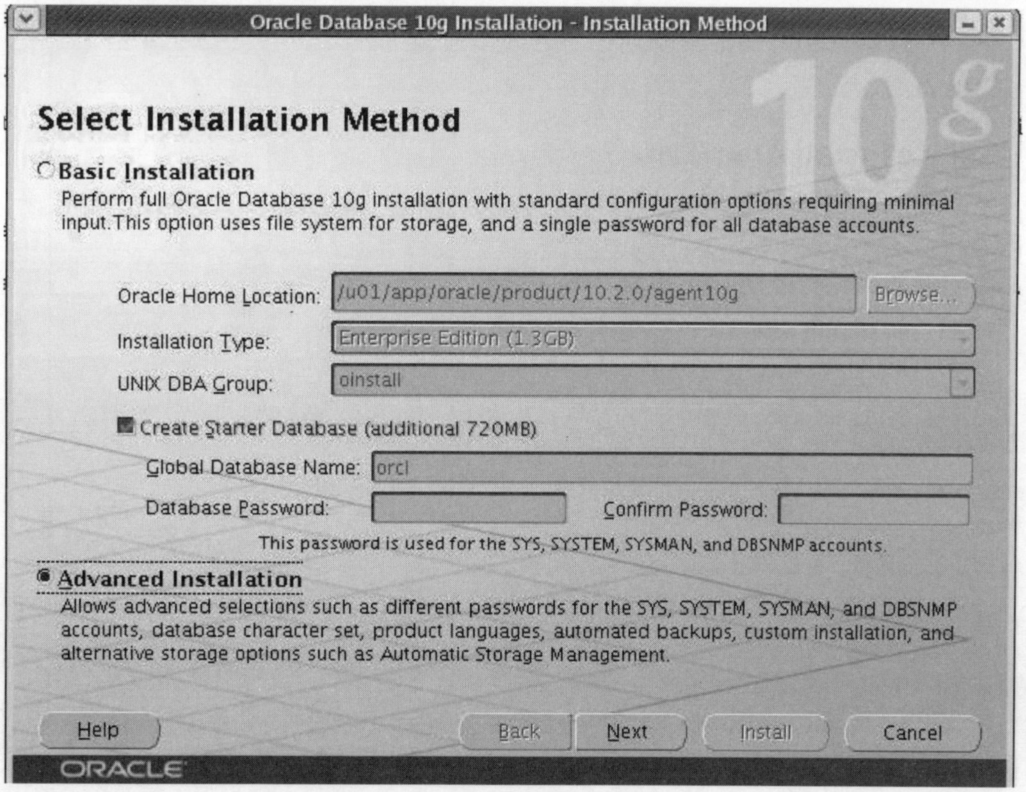

- Specify Inventory directory and credential
  i. Enter full path of the inventory directory: **/u01/app/oracle/oraInventory**
  ii. Specify operating system group name: **oinstall**

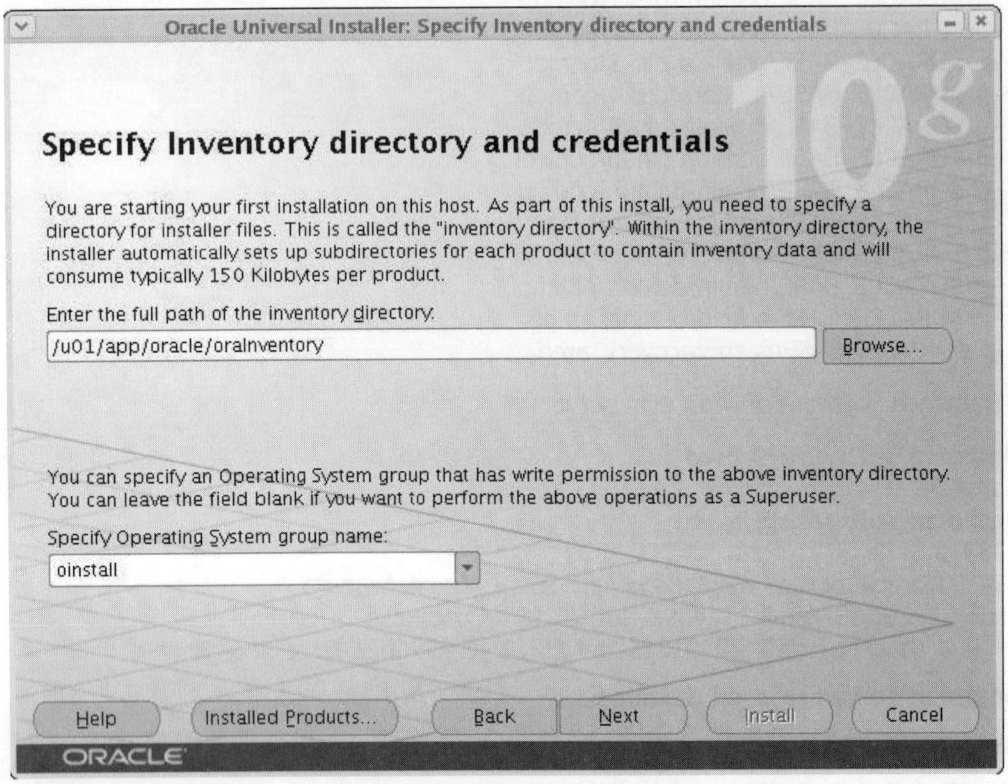

- Select Installation Type: **Enterprise Edition (1.24 GB)**

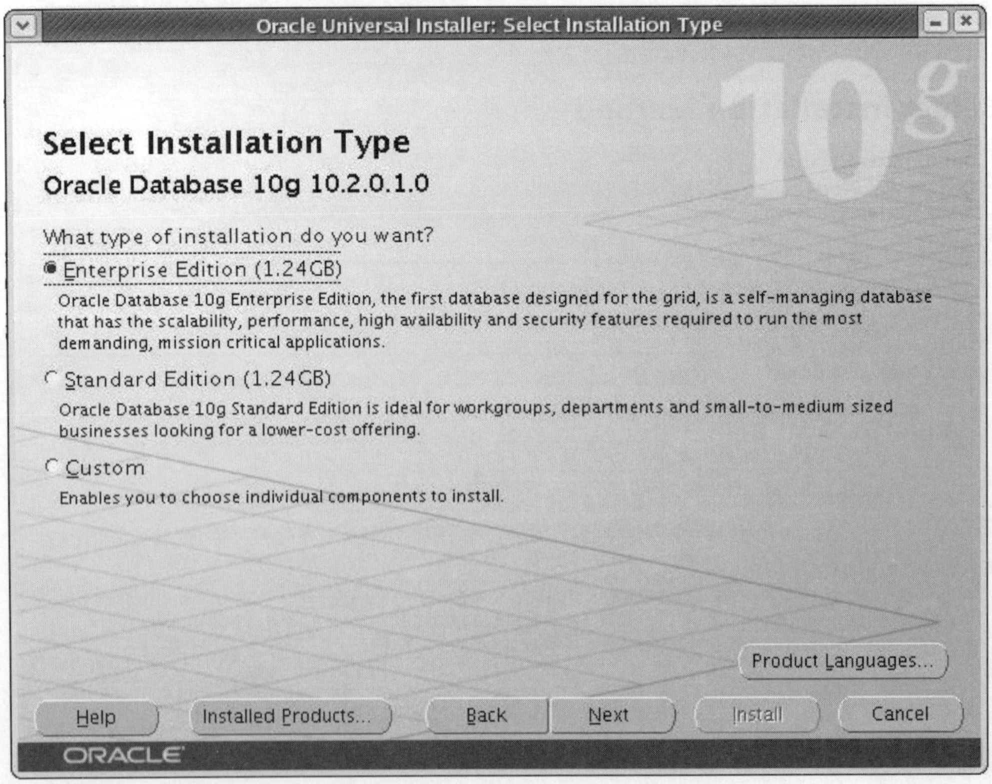

- Specify Home Details
  i. Name: **OraDb10g_home1**
  ii. Path: **/u01/app/oracle/product/10.2.0/db_1**

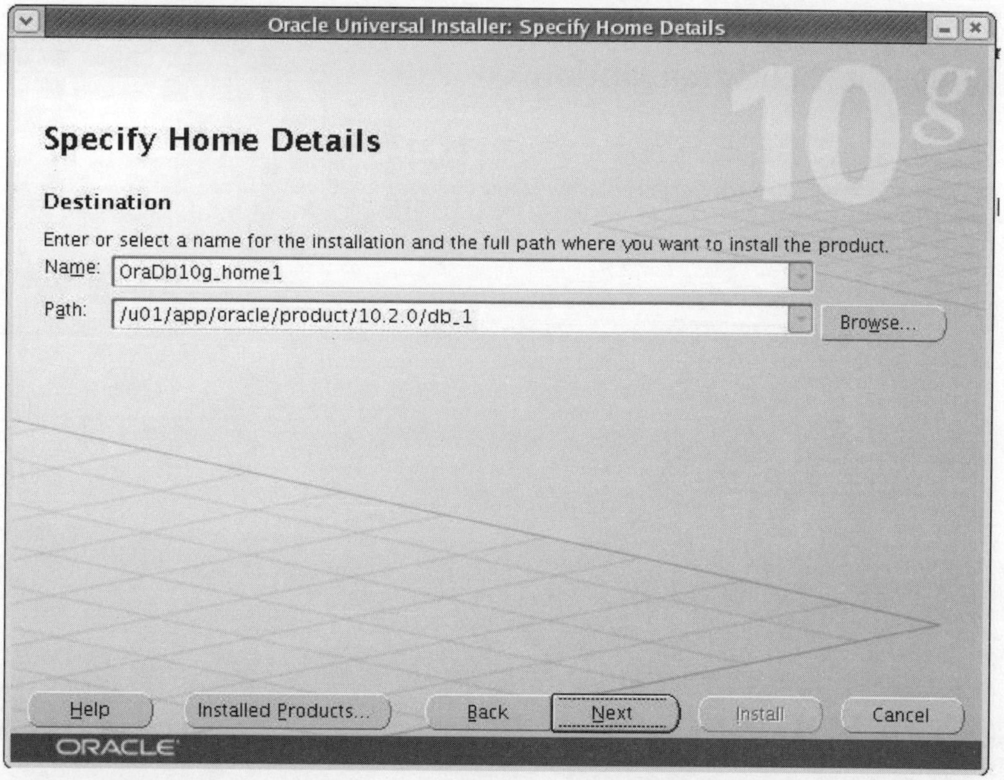

- Product-Specific Prerequisite Checks: **Check complete .The overall result of this check is passed**. Click Next

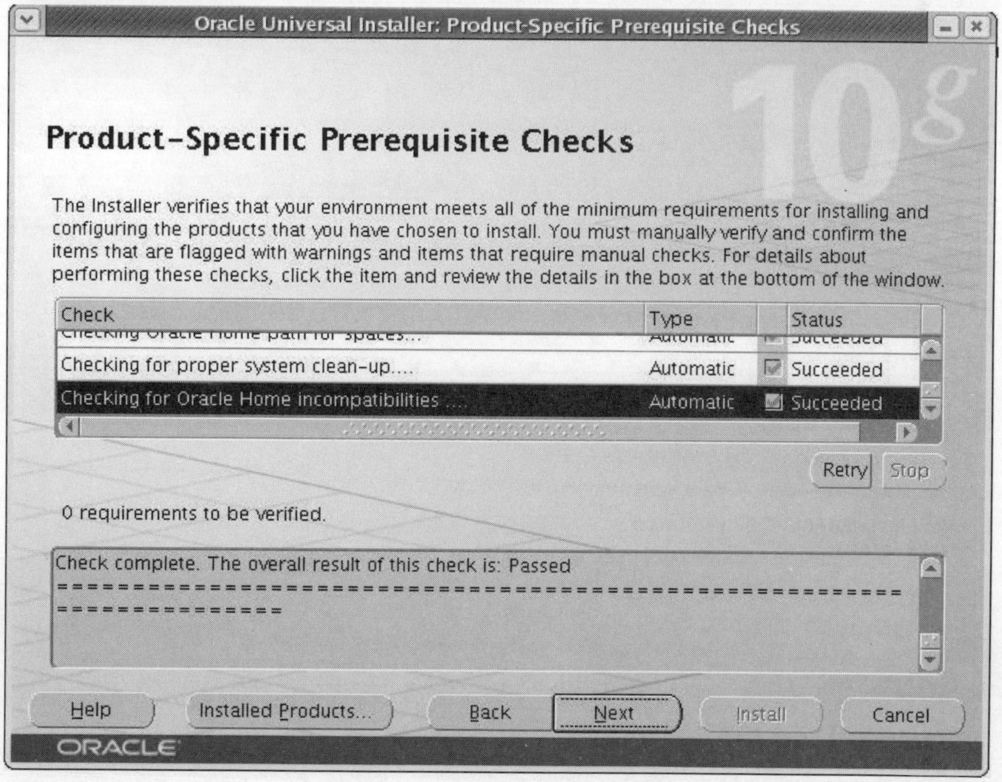

- Select Configuration Option: **Install database Software only**

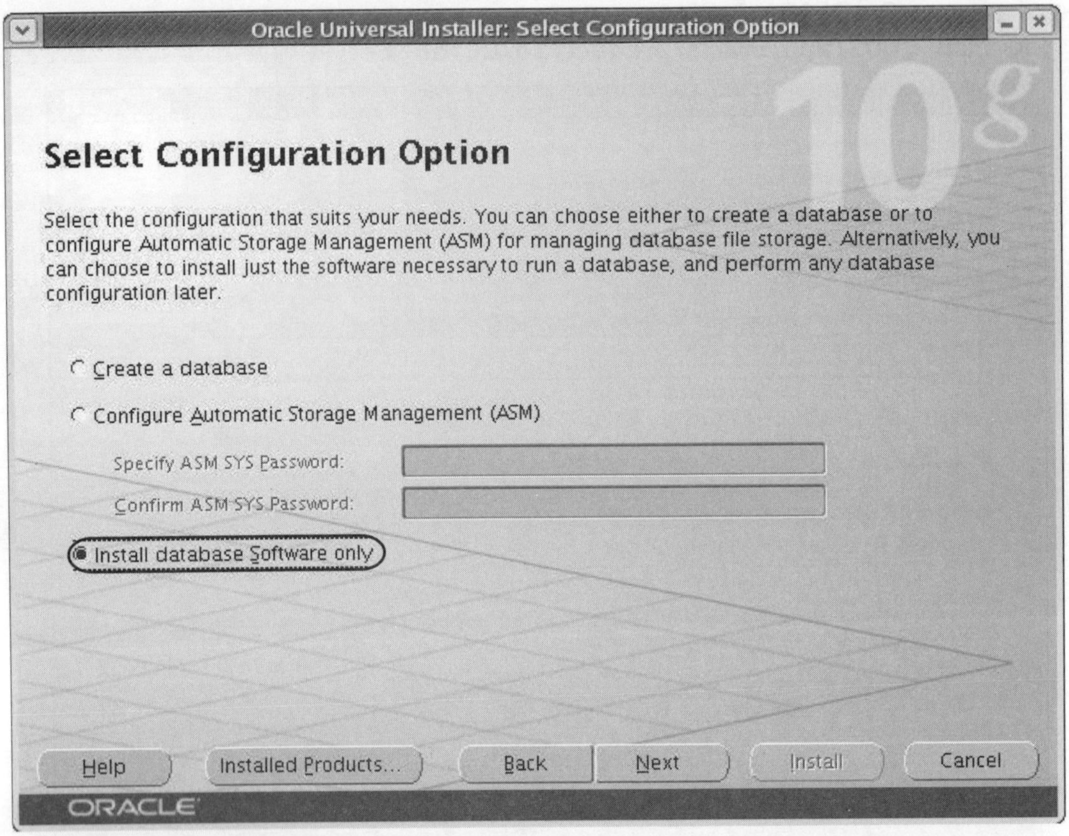

- Summary: **Click Install**

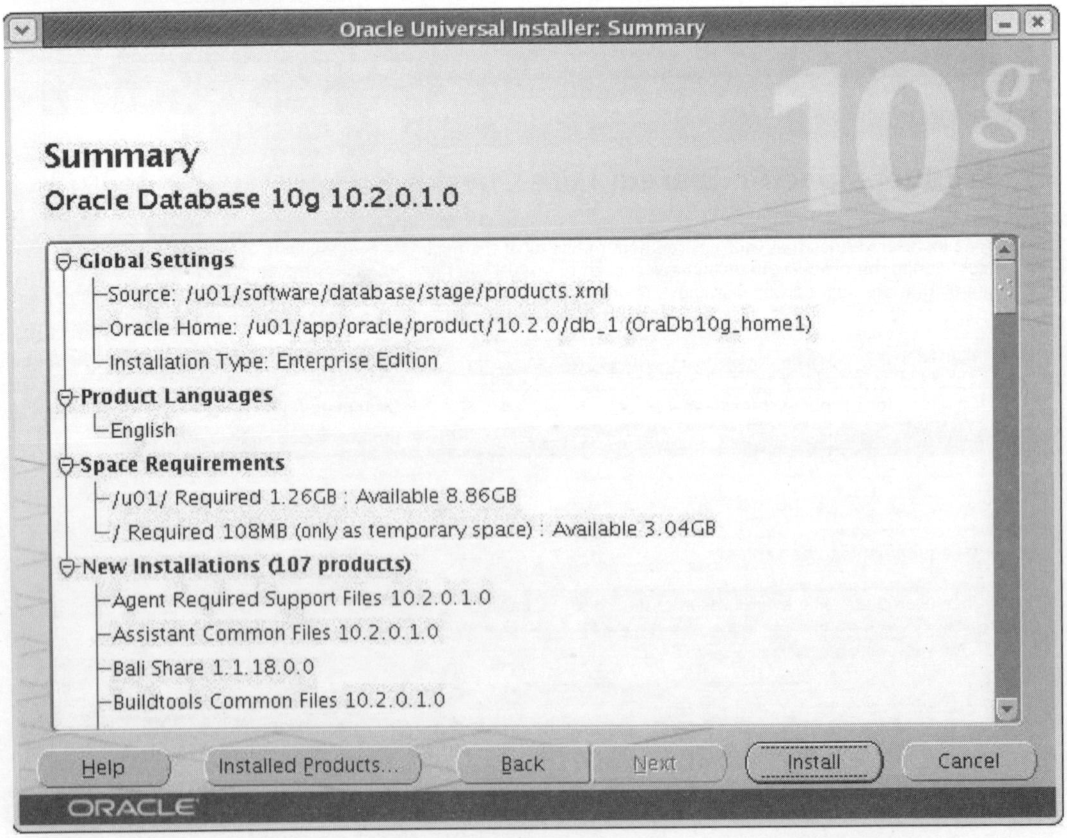

- Install

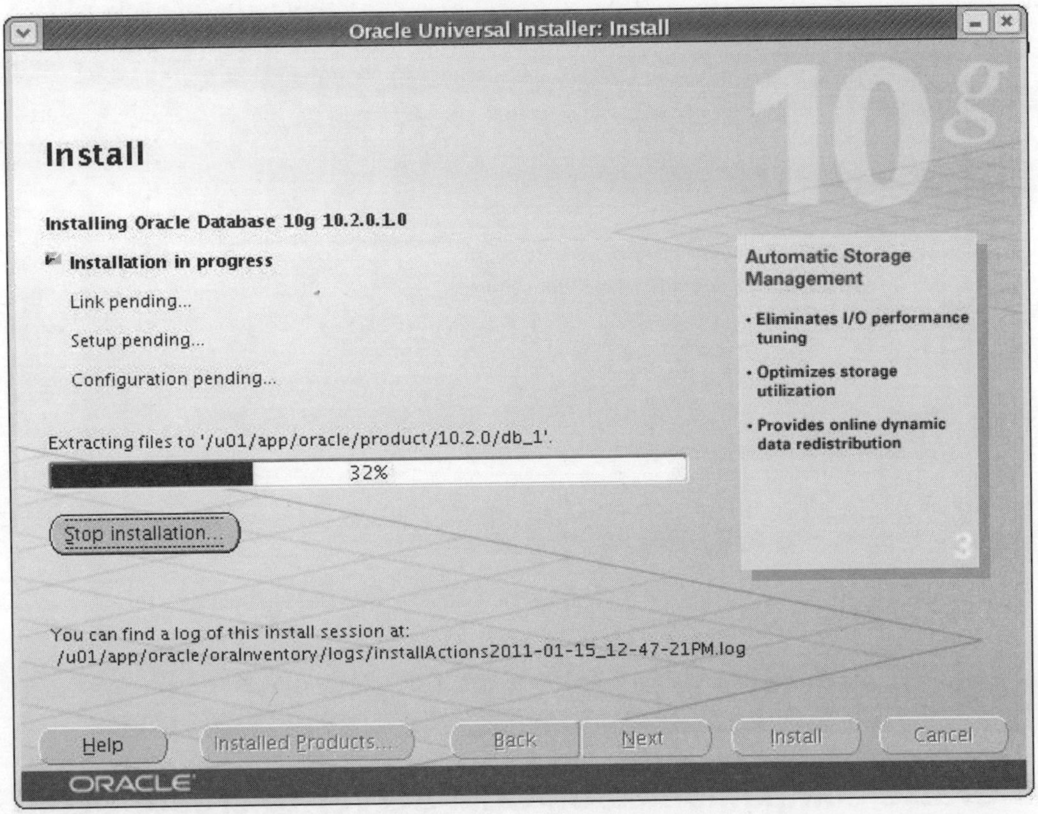

- Execute Configuration Scripts: Open a new terminal and sudo su and execute configuration script

[oracle@ocm ~]$ sudo su
Password:

[root@ocm oraInventory]#/u01/app/oracle/oraInventory/orainstRoot.sh
Changing permissions of /u01/app/oracle/oraInventory to 770.
Changing groupname of /u01/app/oracle/oraInventory to oinstall.
The execution of the script is complete

[root@ocm db_1]# $ORACLE_HOME/root.sh
Running Oracle10 root.sh script...
The following environment variables are set as:
ORACLE_OWNER= oracle
ORACLE_HOME= /u01/app/oracle/product/10.2.0/db_1

Enter the full pathname of the local bin directory: [/usr/local/bin]: <press Enter>
Copying dbhome to /usr/local/bin ...
Copying oraenv to /usr/local/bin ...
Copying coraenv to /usr/local/bin ...

Creating /etc/oratab file...
Entries will be added to the /etc/oratab file as needed by
Database Configuration Assistant when a database is created
Finished running generic part of root.sh script.
Now product-specific root actions will be performed.

- Go back to Execute Configuration Scripts: Click OK and EXIT from install

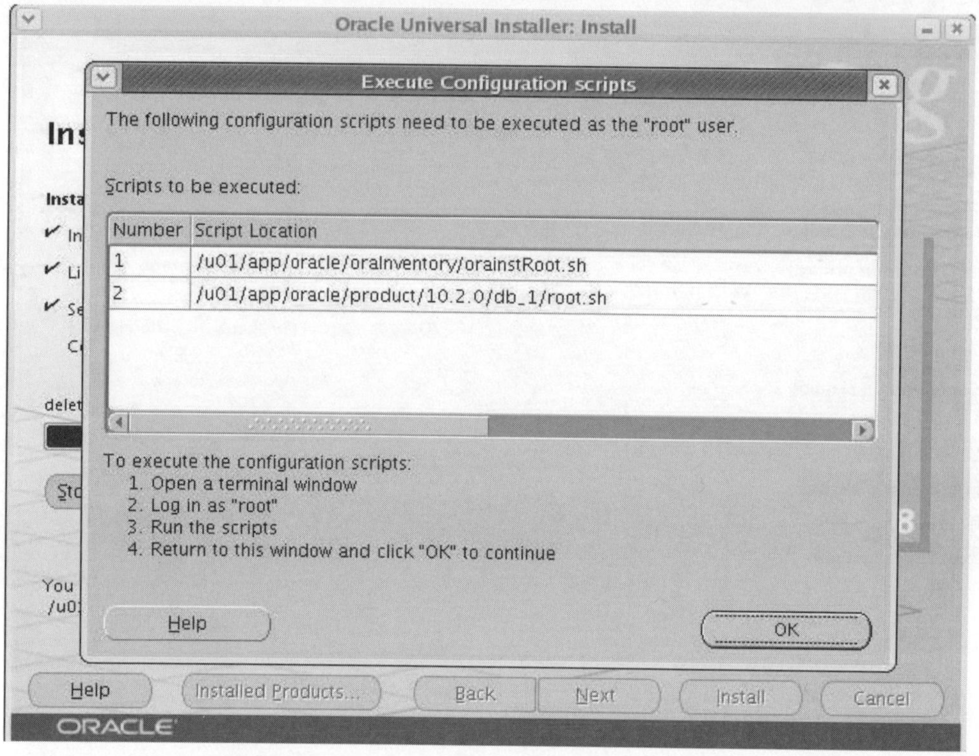

2.2 Install Oracle Companion cd on OCM Server to create DEMO Schemas

- Install Oracle Companion cd

  [oracle@ocm database]$. /runInstaller

- Specify a Product to Install: **Oracle Database 10g Products 10.2.0.1.0**

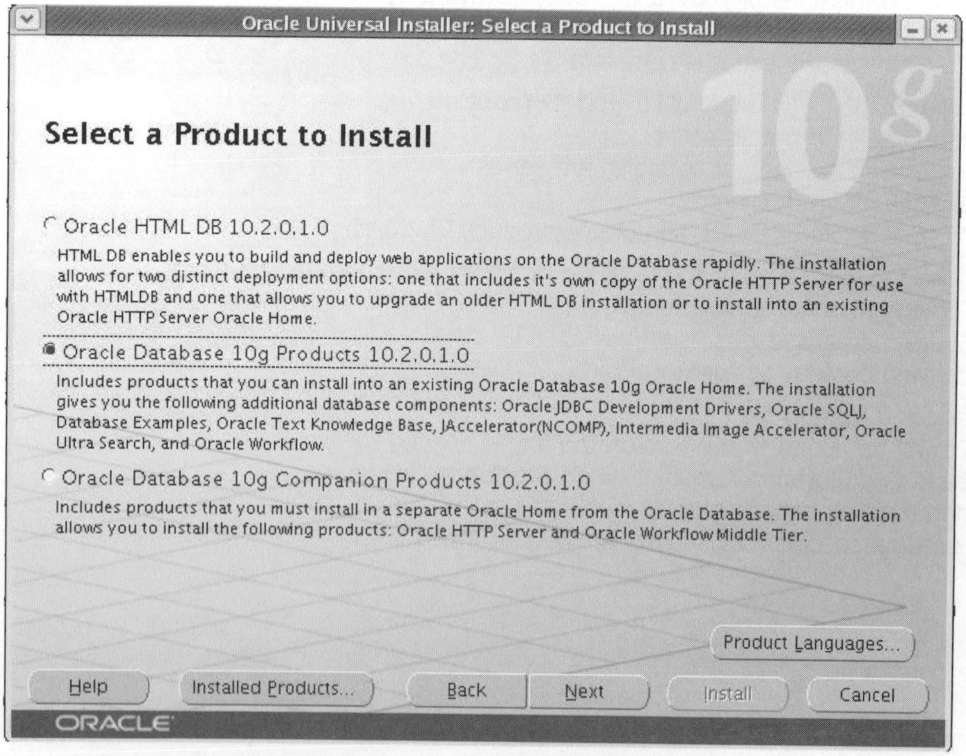

- Specify Home Details and Click Install

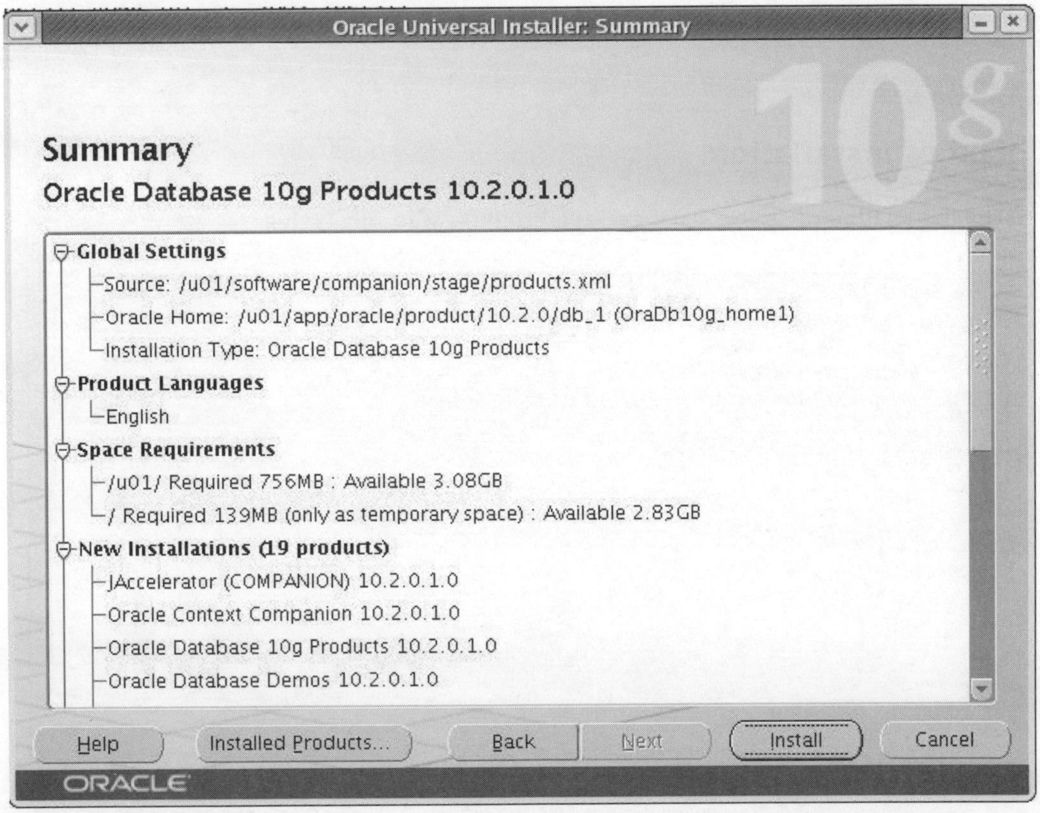

- Install Screen

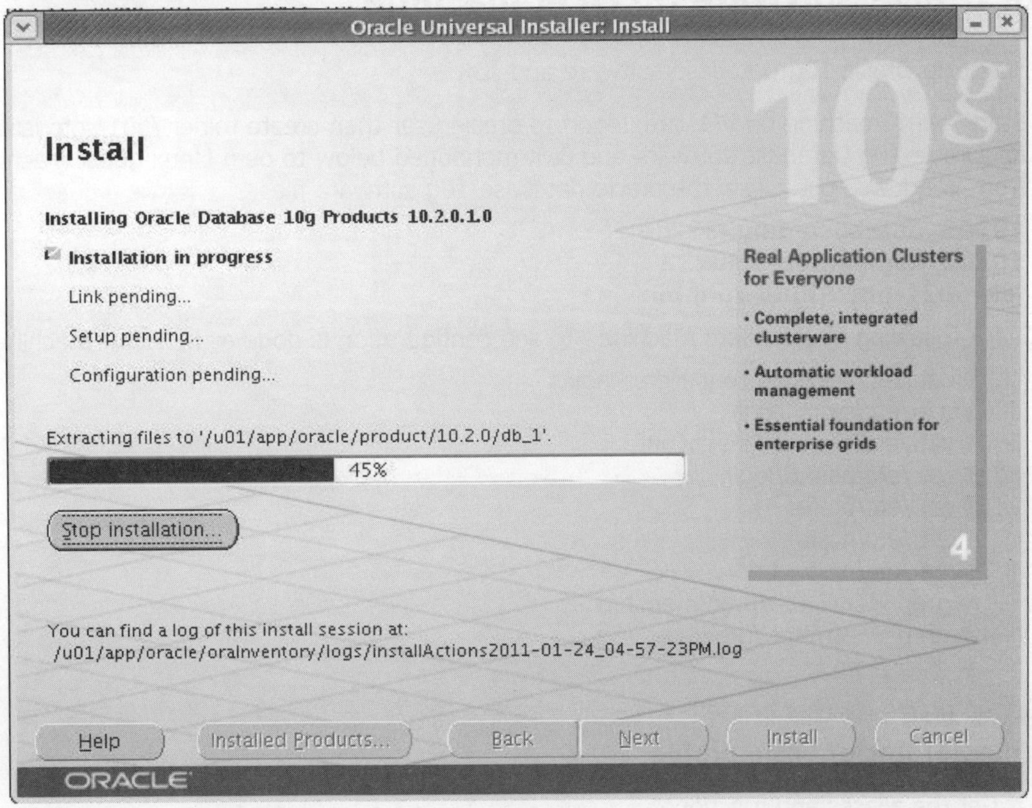

- End of Installations

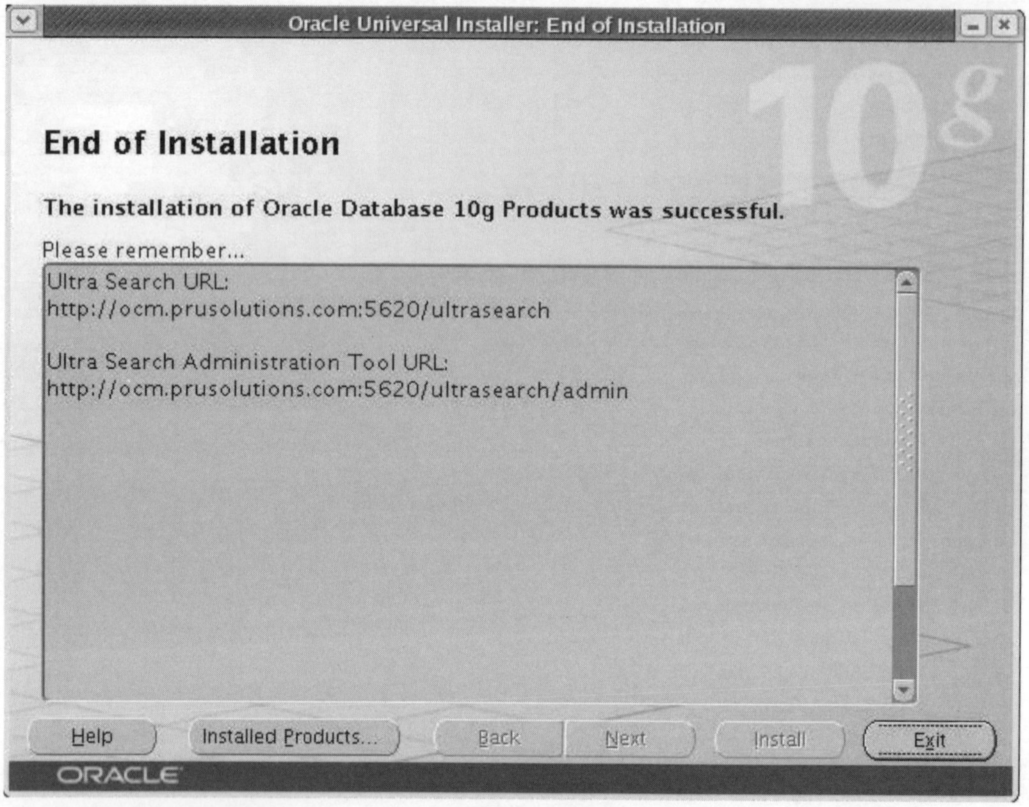

2.3 Install Oracle Software on OEM machine

- Ftp and unzip Oracle 10g Database software and JDK

  Start "oem" machine on VMware, logon to oracle user then create folder /u01/software ftp Oracle 10g Database software and JDK mentioned below to oem Linux guest machine from Windows host. Unzip the oracle database 10g software files

  10201_database_linux32.zip
  10201_companion_linux32
  jdk-6u21-linux-i586-rpm.bin

- Check following files on oem machine , to see configuration is done as in "ocm" machine

  i. $ cat /etc/nsswitch.conf | grep hosts
  ii. $ cat /etc/sysctl.conf
  iii. $ cat /etc/security/limits.conf
  iv. $ cat /etc/pam.d/login
  v. $ cat /etc/profile
  vi. $ cat /etc/hosts
  vii. $ cat /etc/passwd
  viii. # grep MemTotal /proc/meminfo
  ix. # grep SwapTotal /proc/meminfo
  x. # df -k /tmp

- Set up profile for user oracle

  /home/oracle/.bash_profile

```
# Get the aliases and functions
if [ -f ~/.bashrc ]; then
```

```
        . ~/.bashrc
fi
# User specific environment and startup programs
export EDITOR=vi
export ORACLE_SID=oemdb
export ORACLE_BASE=/u01/app/oracle
export ORACLE_HOME=$ORACLE_BASE/product/10.2.0/db_1
export PATH=$ORACLE_HOME/bin:/bin:/sbin :/usr/bin:/usr/sbin:/usr/local/bin:/usr/X11R6/
bin
umask 022
```

/home/oracle/agent_profile

```
# agent_profile
# Get the aliases and functions
if [ -f ~/.bashrc ]; then
        . ~/.bashrc
fi
# User specific environment and startup programs
export EDITOR=vi
export ORACLE_BASE=/u01/app/oracle
export ORACLE_HOME=$ORACLE_BASE/product/10.2.0
export PATH=$ORACLE_HOME/bin:/bin:/sbin:/usr/bin:/usr/sbin:/usr/local/bin:/usr/X11R6/bin
umask 022
```

- To change environment variable use the following

```
$. /home/oracle/.bash_profile
$. /home/oracle/agent10_profile
$ echo $ORACLE_HOME
```

- Create ORACLE_BASE and ORACLE_HOME directory

```
mkdir –p $ORACLE_HOME
mkdir –p $ORACLE_BASE/admin
mkdir –p $ORACLE_BASE/oradata
mkdir -p $ORACLE_BASE/flash_recovery_area
```

- Install Database Software only on oem Server

```
[oracle@ocm software]$ pwd
/u01/software
[oracle@ocm software]$ ls -ltr
total 738380
-rw-r—r—  1 oracle oinstall 675848454 Nov 26 18:40 database.zip
drwxr-xr-x  7 oracle oinstall      4096 Nov 26 18:44 database
-rw-r—r—  1 oracle oinstall  79491215 Jan 15 12:12 jdk-6u21-linux-i586-rpm.bin
```

The steps to install Oracle Software on oem will be different from that used for ocm. The database will be created for Oracle's OEM Grid, which needs **Oracle Label Security** only.

[oracle@ocm database]$. /runInstaller

- Select Installation Method: **Advanced Installation**

- Select Installation Type: **Custom**

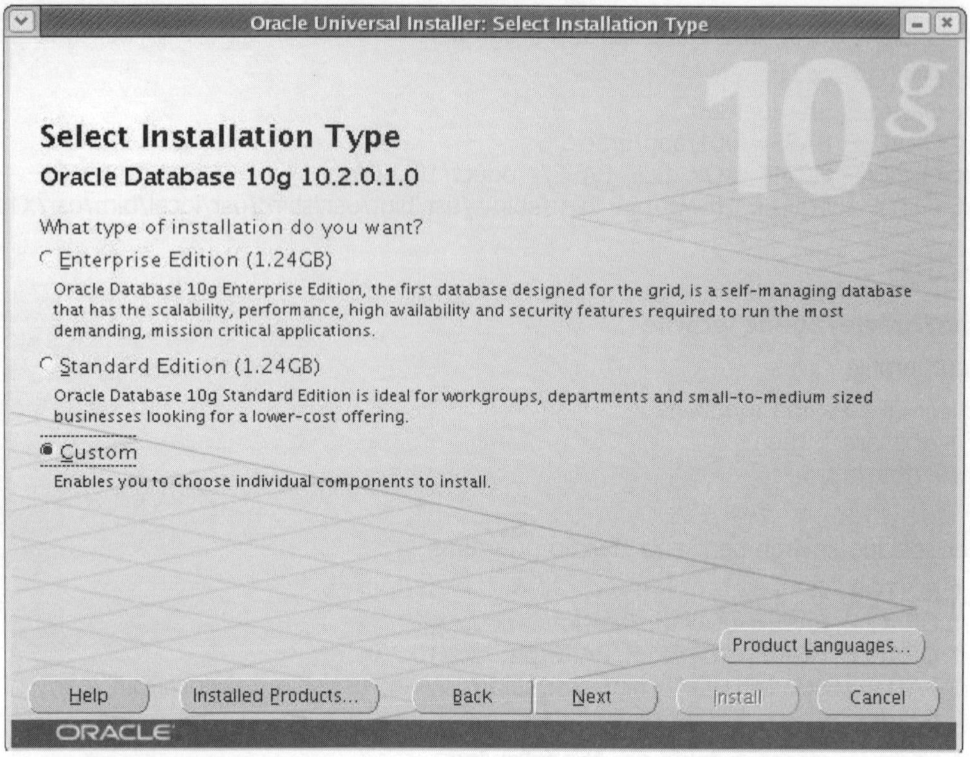

- Specify Home Details
  i. Name: **OraDb10g_home1**
  ii. Path: **/u01/app/oracle/product/10.2.0/db_1**
- Available Product Components Oracle Database 10g: **Oracle Label Security**

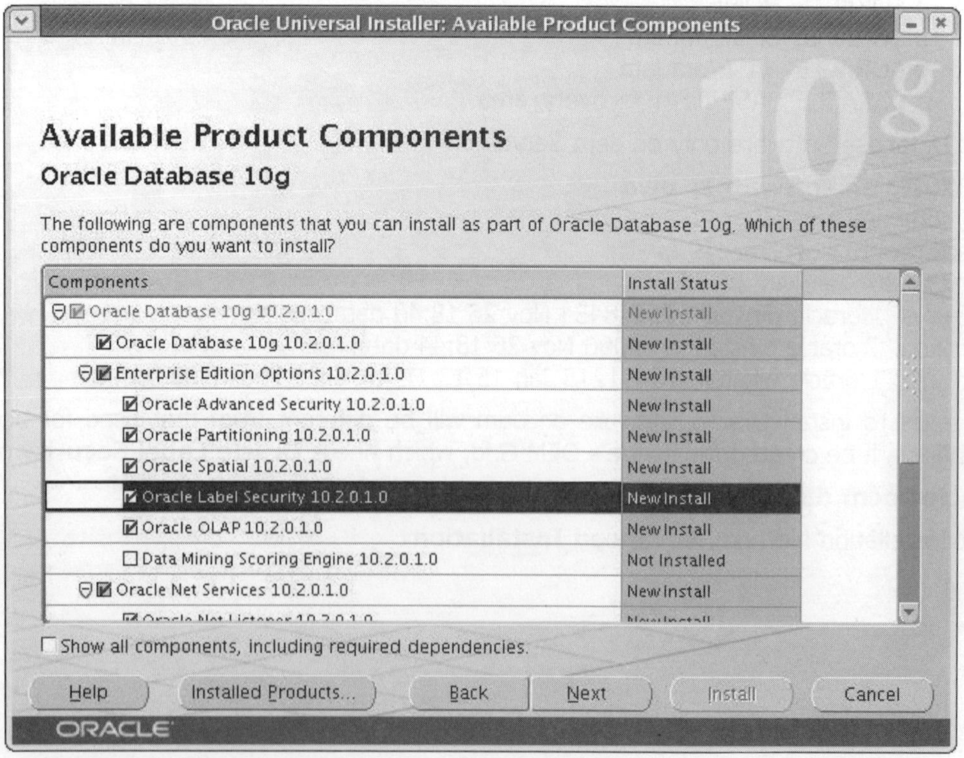

- Product- Specific Prerequisite Checks

  Check complete. The overall result of this check is: passed

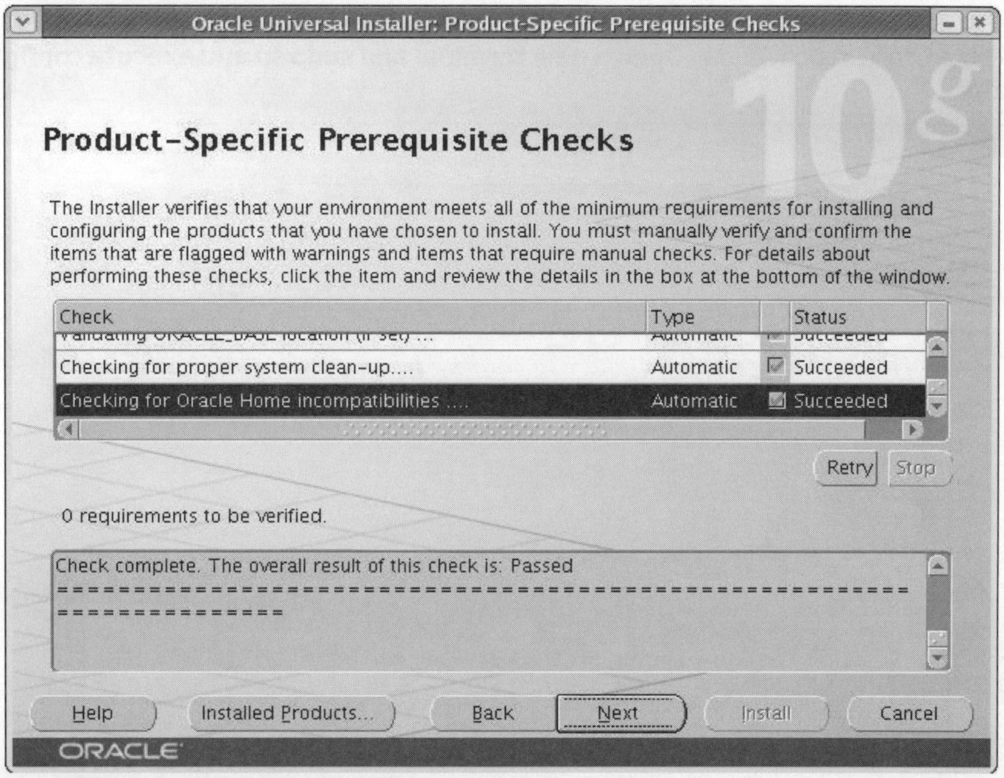

- Privilege Operating System Group
  i. Database Administrator (OSDBA) Group: **dba**
  ii. Database Operator(OSOPER) Group: **dba**

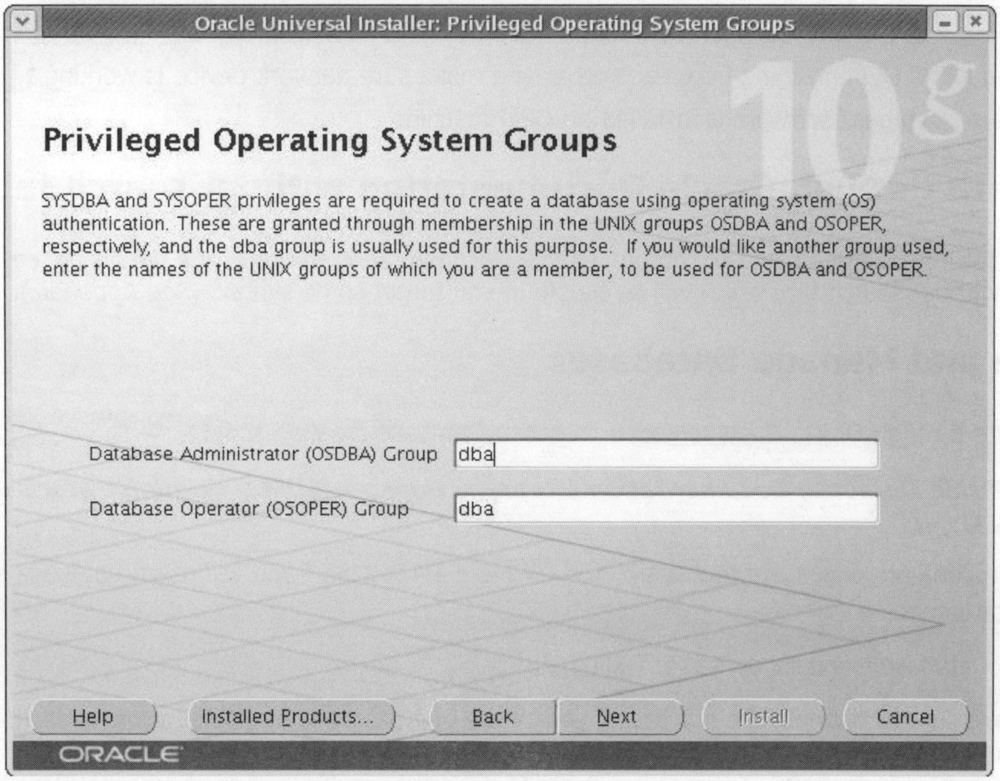

- Create Database: **Install Database Software only.** Click Next
- Summary : Click Install
- Install Screen: **Shows Installation in Progress**
- Execute Configuration Scripts: **Open a new terminal and sudo su and execute configuration script**

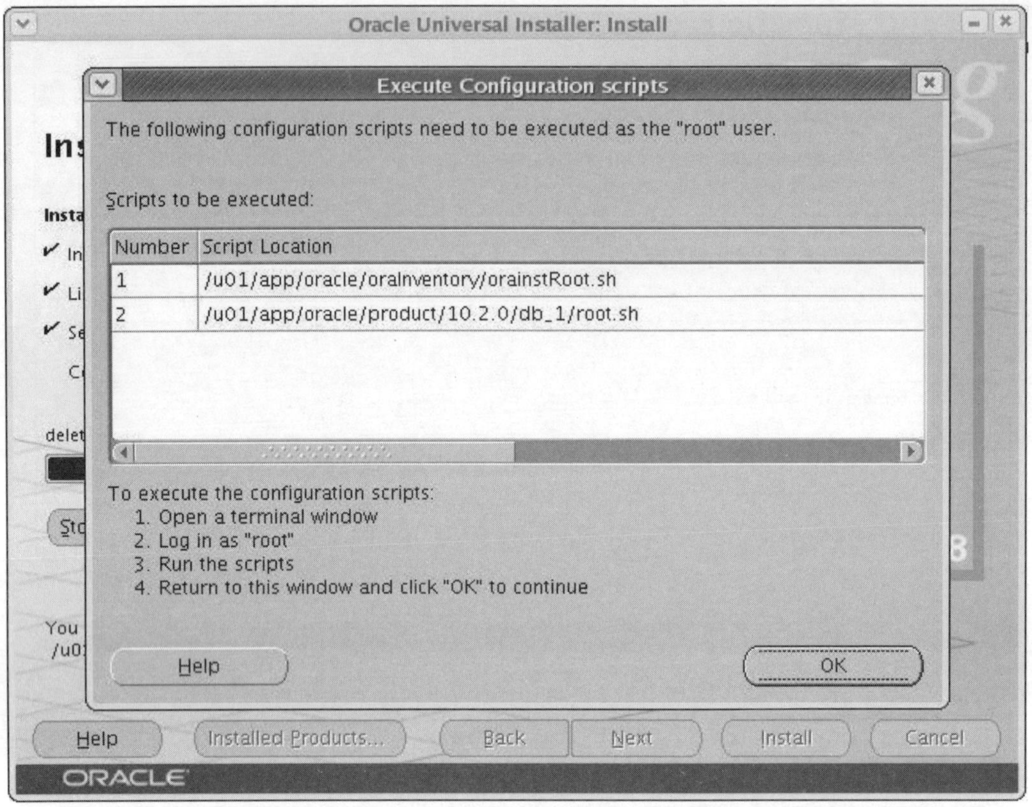

- Go back to Execute Configuration Scripts: Click OK and EXIT from install
- Ping OEM, OCM machine from each other and make sure network device is working
- Oracle Database software is installed on OEM machine

2.4 Navigate through Oracle Documentation without search tab

For all future exercises navigate through Oracle Documentation to get to the details for each exam topics without search tab, which will be helpful if you forget some syntax. (See Appendix).

2.5 Create and Manage Databases

- Navigate through Oracle Documentation to get to Database creation script

  Oracle Database Documentation Library > Books > ADM > Administrator's Guide > HTML

  On contents page Ctrl f and search for *"CREATE DATABASE"* you will reach database creation statement.

- Create Database Manually on server OEM
  - Make sure throughout the practice, if you create any database manually or using dbca, it should be of same character set and same compatible parameter.

- In this book it is character set **WE8ISO8859P1 and** compatible=**'10.2.0.1.0'**

Small file database

- Use sample initdw.ora file in $ORACLE_HOME/dbs directory and modify. Make a copy of initdw.ora file for precaution and modify then sample file
- **$cat initdw.ora | grep -v ^# | grep -v ^$ > initocmdb.ora**
- Modify the initocmdb.ora. Make a copy of initocmdb.ora file after every modification for precaution.
- Add/Modify following parameter to initocmdb.ora file (The values are set for faster modification)
  - i. db_name =ocmdb
  - ii. db_unique_name = ocmdb
  - iii. sga_max_size =512m
  - iv. sga_target =512m
  - v. shared_poool_size =120m
  - vi. db_cache_size = 130M
  - vii. pga_aggregate_target =130m
  - viii. undo_management=auto
  - ix. undo_tablespace=undotbs1
  - x. control_files=('/u01/app/oracle/oradata/disk1/ocmdb/control01.ctl','/u01/app/oracle/admin/ocmdb/control/control02.ctl')
- Remove obsolete parameter from initocmdb.ora
  - i. parallel_automatic_tuning = true
- Start database ocm in nomount state to check the parameter file is good

  $ sqlplus / as sysdba

  SQL> STARTUP NOMOUNT; (to make sure initocmdb.ora file is good)

  SQL> SHUTDOWN ABORT;

  SQL> exit;
- Create spfile from pfile

  $ sqlplus / as sysdba

  SQL> CREATE SPFILE='/u01/app/oracle/product/10.2.0/db_1/dbs/spfileocmdb.ora' FROM PFILE='/u01/app/oracle/product/10.2.0/db_1/dbs/initocmdb.ora';

  OR

  SQL> CREATE SPFILE FROM PFILE;

  SQL> STARTUP NOMOUNT;
- Modify following parameter using **alter system scope=spfile** (Use show parameter)
  - i. ALTER SYSTEM SET compatible='10.2.0.1.0' scope=spfile;
  - ii. ALTER SYSTEM SET sessions=200 SCOPE=SPFILE;
  - iii. ALTER SYSTEM SET processes=250 SCOPE=SPFILE;
  - iv. ALTER SYSTEM SET job_queue_processes=10 SCOPE=SPFILE;
  - v. ALTER SYSTEM SET db_recovery_file_dest_size =10G scope=spfile;
  - vi. ALTER SYSTEM SET db_recovery_file_dest= '/u01/app/oracle/flash_recovery_area' SCOPE=SPFILE;
- Create pfile from spfile and take backup of pfile

  SQL> CREATE PFILE='/u01/app/oracle/product/10.2.0/db_1/dbs/initocmdb.ora' FROM SPFILE='/u01/app/oracle/product/10.2.0/db_1/dbs/spfileocmdb.ora';

  SQL> SHUTDOWN IMMEDIATE;

  SQL> exit;

- Backup the initocmdb.ora
- Create password file using orapwd

  $ cd $ORACLE_HOME/dbs

  [oracle@ocm dbs]$ orapwd password=oracle entries=5 file=orapwocmdb

- Create small file database, use script as mentioned below
- Make sure the name of undo tablespace is same as in initocmdb.ora file, strip redo log members on separate disks, control_files and datafiles on separate disks.

  createocmdb1.sql

```
create database ocmdb
user sys identified by oracle
user system identified by oracle
maxinstances 8
maxlogmembers 4
maxlogfiles 32
maxloghistory 100
character set WE8ISO8859P1
national character set al16utf16
logfile
group 1 ('/u01/app/oracle/oradata/disk2/ocmdb/redo01a.log','/u01/app/oracle/oradata/
disk4/ocmdb/redo01b.log') size 50m reuse,
group 2 ('/u01/app/oracle/oradata/disk2/ocmdb/redo02a.log','/u01/app/oracle/oradata/
disk4/ocmdb/redo02b.log') size 50m reuse,
group 3 ('/u01/app/oracle/oradata/disk2/ocmdb/redo03a.log','/u01/app/oracle/oradata/
disk4/ocmdb/redo03b.log') size 50m reuse
datafile '/u01/app/oracle/oradata/disk3/ocmdb/system01.dbf' size 256m reuse autoextend
on next 1m maxsize unlimited extent management local
sysaux datafile '/u01/app/oracle/oradata/disk3/ocmdb/sysaux01.dbf' size 256m reuse
autoextend on next 1m maxsize 1024m
default tablespace users  datafile '/u01/app/oracle/oradata/disk3/ocmdb/users01.dbf'
size 256m reuse autoextend on next 1m maxsize 1024m
default temporary tablespace temp tempfile '/u01/app/oracle/oradata/disk3/ocmdb/
temp01.dbf' size 256m reuse autoextend on next 1m maxsize 1024m
undo tablespace undotbs1 datafile '/u01/app/oracle/oradata/disk3/ocmdb/
undotbs01.dbf' size 256m reuse autoextend on next 1m maxsize 1024m;
```

- Startup instance in nomount state and execute create database script

  $ sqlplus / as sysdba

  SQL> STARTUP NOMOUNT;

  SQL> @createocmdb1.sql

  If script gives some syntax error, fix the script and again execute, If script fails check any files are created in /u01/app/oracle/oradata/ocmdb and /u02/app/oracle/oradata/ocmdb Delete them and re-execute the script to create the database.

- Add the following line to /etc/oratab

  ocmdb:/u01/app/oracle/product/10.2.0/db_1:N
  to use ". oraenv" for above database

- After database is created execute following scripts as sys

  $ORACLE_HOME/rdbms/admin/catalog.sql

  $ORACLE_HOME/rdbms/admin/catproc.sql

  $ORACLE_HOME/rdbms/admin/dbmspool.sql

- Execute following scripts as user system
  $ORACLE_HOME/sqlplus/admin/plustrce.sql
  $ORACLE_HOME/sqlplus/admin/pupbld.sql
- To Install Label Security manually for Oracle's OEM Grid
  Connect sys as sysdba
  $ORACLE_HOME/rdbms/admin/catols.sql
  User LBACSYS/LBACSYS is created by above script and all packages are installed in that user
- To Install dbcontrol manually
  $ emca -config dbcontrol db -repos create
  $ emctl start dbconsole
- Create user Scott for testing in later exercises
  SQL> GRANT CREATE SESSION TO scott IDENTIFIED BY tiger;
- Make database in ARCHIVELOG mode and turn FLASHBACK database on;
  SQL> SHUTDOWN IMMEDIATE;
  SQL> STARTUP MOUNT;
  SQL> ALTER DATABASE ARCHIVELOG;
  SQL> ALTER DATABASE FLASHBACK ON;
- Switch logfile at least 3 times

- Backup your Database using RMAN immediately (Details provided in Managing Database Availability)

- To create Data Warehouse database using multiple block size and bigfile tablespace. There are few changes in parameter and database creation script mentioned below.
  - **initocmdb.ora** parameter changes mentioned below rest of parameters will be same
    i. db_block_size=16384
  - Create big file database creation script as mentioned below

createocmdb2.sql

```
create database ocmdb
user sys identified by oracle
user system identified by oracle
SET DEFAULT BIGFILE TABLESPACE
maxinstances 8
maxlogmembers 4
maxlogfiles 32
maxloghistory 100
character set WE8ISO8859P1
national character set al16utf16
logfile
group 1 ('/u01/app/oracle/oradata/disk2/ocmdb/redo01a.log','/u01/app/oracle/oradata/disk4/
ocmdb/redo01b.log') size 50m reuse,
group 2 ('/u01/app/oracle/oradata/disk2/ocmdb/redo02a.log','/u01/app/oracle/oradata/disk4/
ocmdb/redo02b.log') size 50m reuse,
group 3 ('/u01/app/oracle/oradata/disk2/ocmdb/redo03a.log','/u01/app/oracle/oradata/disk4/
ocmdb/redo03b.log') size 50m reuse
datafile '/u01/app/oracle/oradata/disk3/ocmdb/system01.dbf' size 256m reuse autoextend on
next 1m maxsize unlimited extent management local
sysaux datafile '/u01/app/oracle/oradata/disk3/ocmdb/sysaux01.dbf' size 256m reuse
autoextend on next 1m maxsize 1024m
```

smallfile default tablespace users datafile '/u01/app/oracle/oradata/disk3/ocmdb/users01.dbf' size 256m reuse autoextend on next 1m maxsize 1024m
smallfile default temporary tablespace temp tempfile '/u01/app/oracle/oradata/disk3/ocmdb/temp01.dbf' size 256m reuse autoextend on next 1m maxsize 1024m
smallfile undo tablespace undotbs1 datafile '/u01/app/oracle/oradata/disk3/ocmdb/undotbs01.dbf' size 256m reuse autoextend on next 1m maxsize 1024m
;

- Rest of the steps are same as mentioned above for smallfile database.
- The default block size is 16k, Now for some smaller dimension tables in Data Warehouse we have to create tablespace on 8k block sizes and for big fact tables of 32k block sizes. 8k and 32k block sizes can be created from Oracle' OEM Grid Control also.
- Steps to create 8k block size tablespace

SQL> ALTER SYSTEM SET db_8k_cache_size=100M SCOPE=BOTH;

SQL> CREATE TABLESPACE test_dim_8k DATAFILE '/u01/app/oracle/oradata/disk5/ocmdb/test_dim_8k_01.dbf' SIZE 100M BLOCKSIZE 8K SEGMENT SPACE MANAGEMENT AUTO EXTENT MANAGEMENT LOCAL UNIFORM SIZE 1M;

- As above database is for Data Warehouse and we have created redo logfiles, which are very small for Data Warehouse, database, so we will drop them and recreate them with larger size.

i. Make sure the logfile group which is being dropped and recreated is in **INACTIVE** status
Use sql below to find status of the logfile

```
SQL> SELECT l.group#,
            l.status,
            l.archived,
            BYTES / (1024 * 1024) size_mb,
            lf.MEMBER
     FROM v$log l, v$logfile lf
     WHERE l.group# = lf.group#;
```

ii. Drop the inactive logfile group and then add larger size

SQL> ALTER DATABASE DROP LOGFILE GROUP 1;

SQL> ALTER DATABASE ADD LOGFILE GROUP 1 ('/u01/app/oracle/oradata/disk2/ocmdb/redo01a.log','/u01/app/oracle/oradata/disk4/ocmdb/redo01b.log') SIZE 200M REUSE;

Use one of the commands to make current log group inactive status before dropping the log group

SQL> ALTER SYSTEM SWITCH LOGFILE;

SQL> ALTER SYSTEM ARCHIVE LOG CURRENT;

- Creating Database Using DBCA that will be used for Oracle Enterprise Manager (Oracle's OEM Grid Control)

[oracle@oem ~]$ echo $ORACLE_SID
[oracle@oem ~]$ echo $ORACLE_HOME
[oracle@oem ~]$ dbca

- Database Configuration Assistant: Welcome Screen: **Click Next**
- Select the operations that you want to perform: **Create Database**

- Select a template from the following list to create database: **Custom Database**

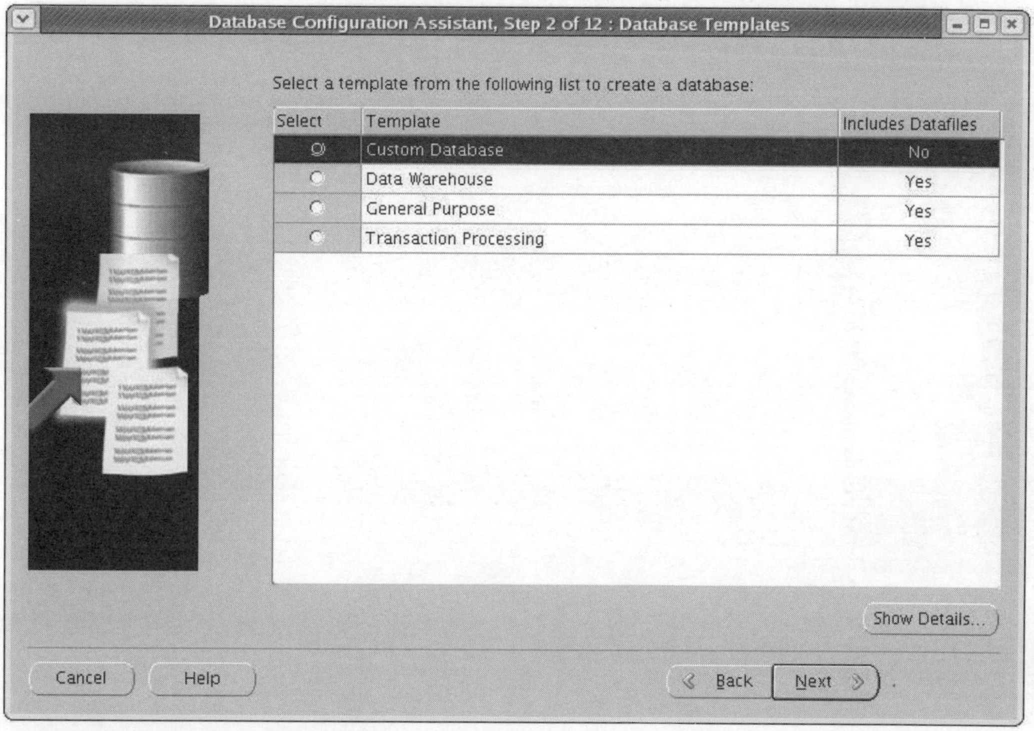

- Global Database Name: **oemdb**

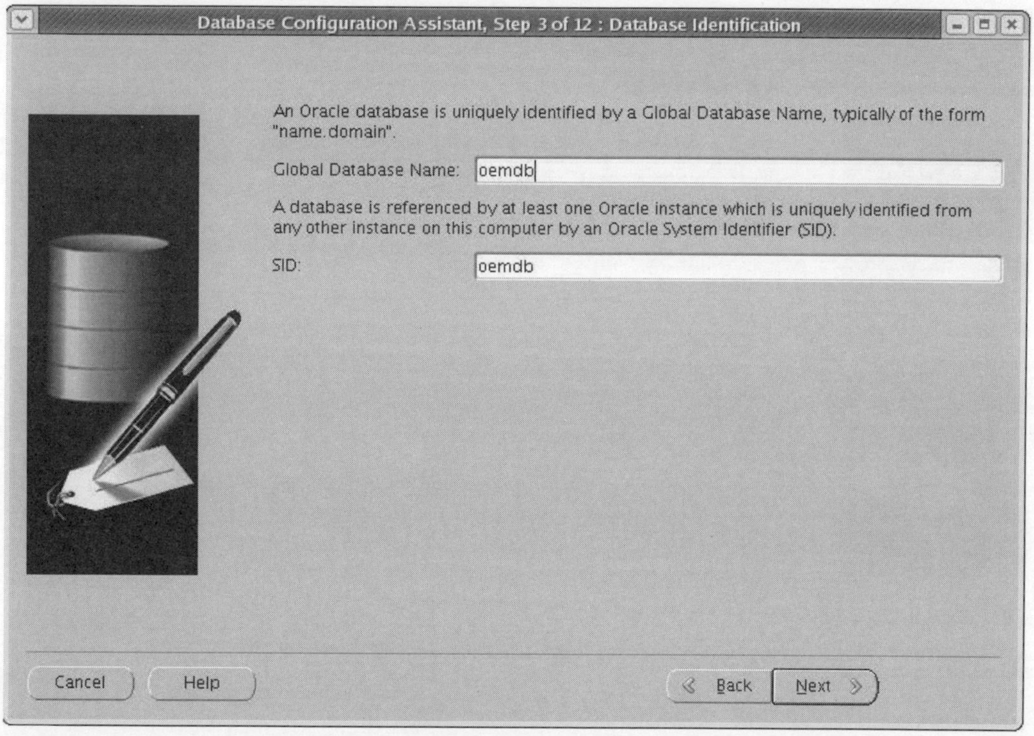

- Configure the Database with Enterprise Manager: **Deselect**

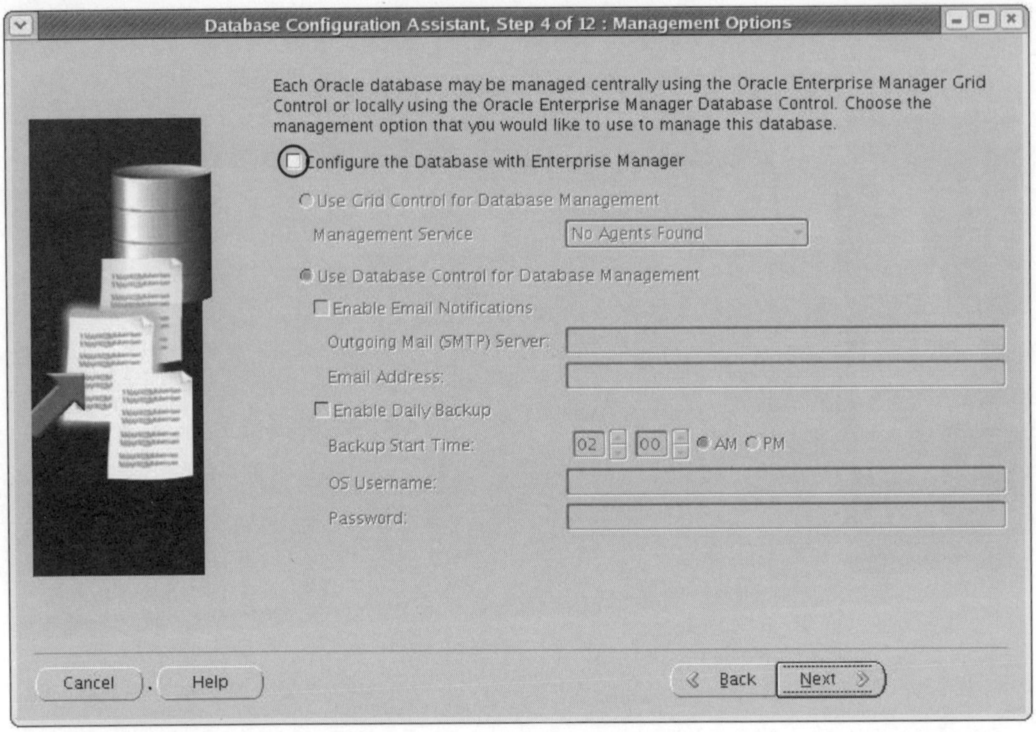

- Use Same Password for All Accounts: Password: **oracle**

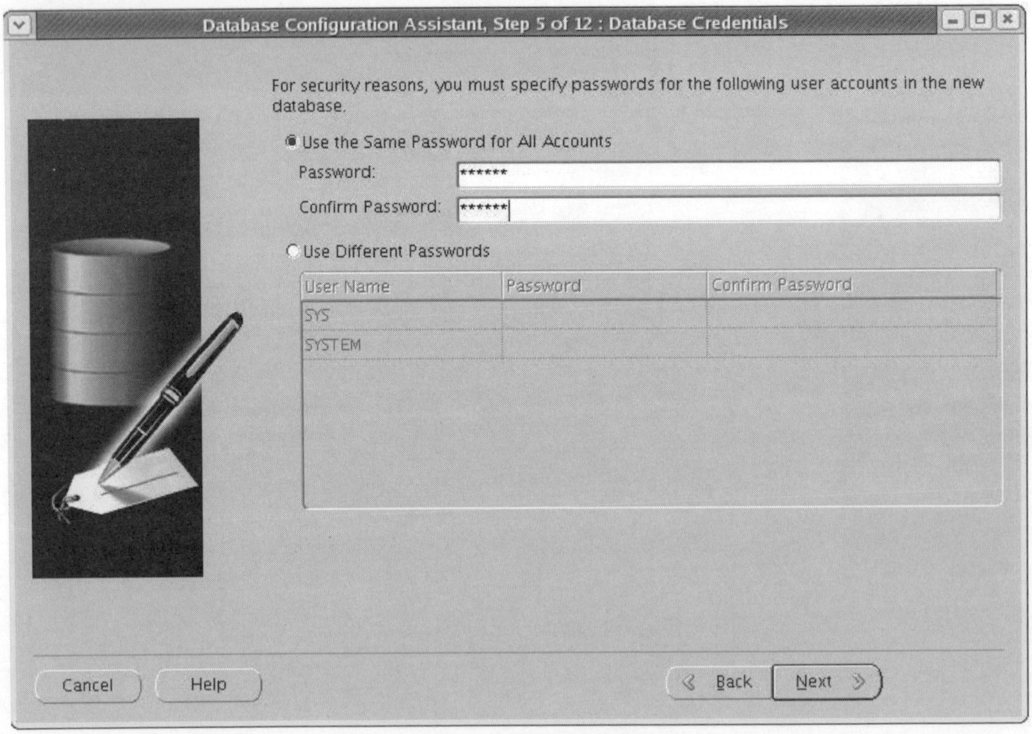

- Storage Mechanism: **File System**

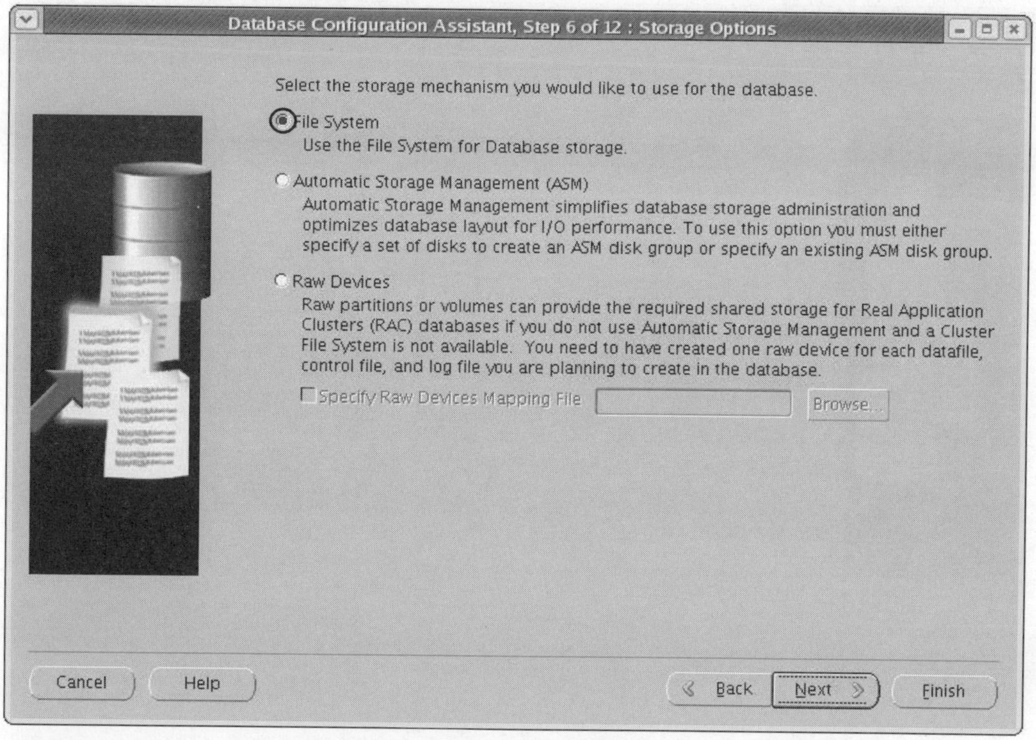

- Specify location for Datafiles: **Use Common Location for All Datafiles**

  Database Files Location: **/u01/app/oracle/oradata**

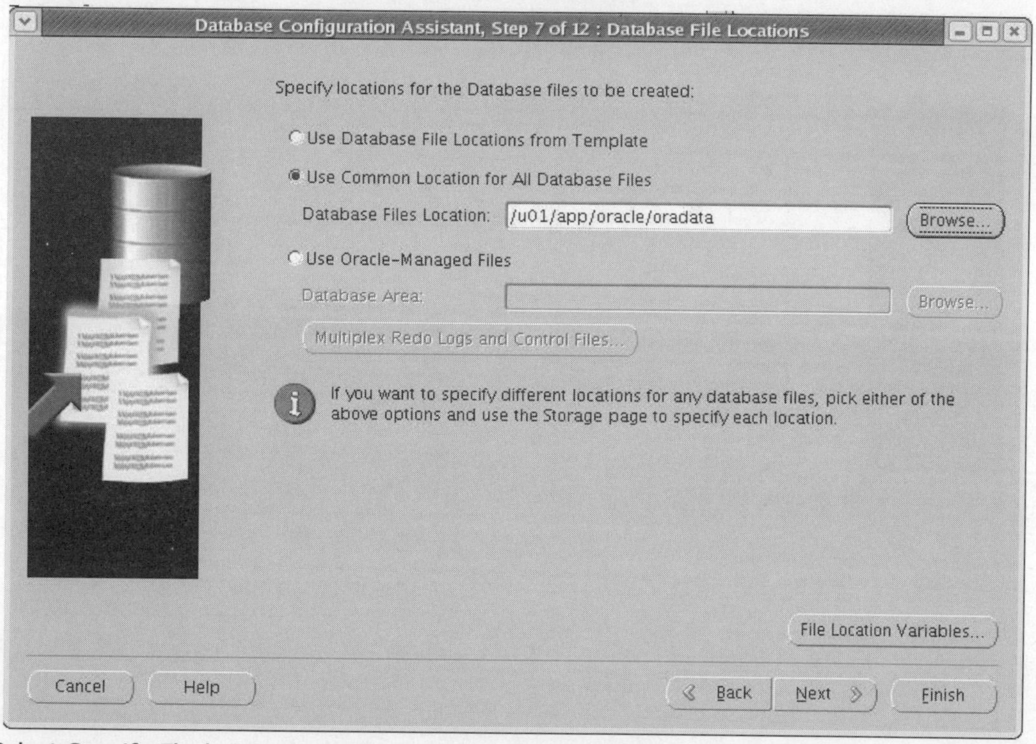

- Select Specify Flash Recovery Area and Enable Archiving
  i. Flash Recovery Area:**(ORACLE_BASE)/flash_recovery_area**
  ii. Flash Recovery area Size : **10240 M**

- Select Specify Flash Recovery Area and Enable Archiving

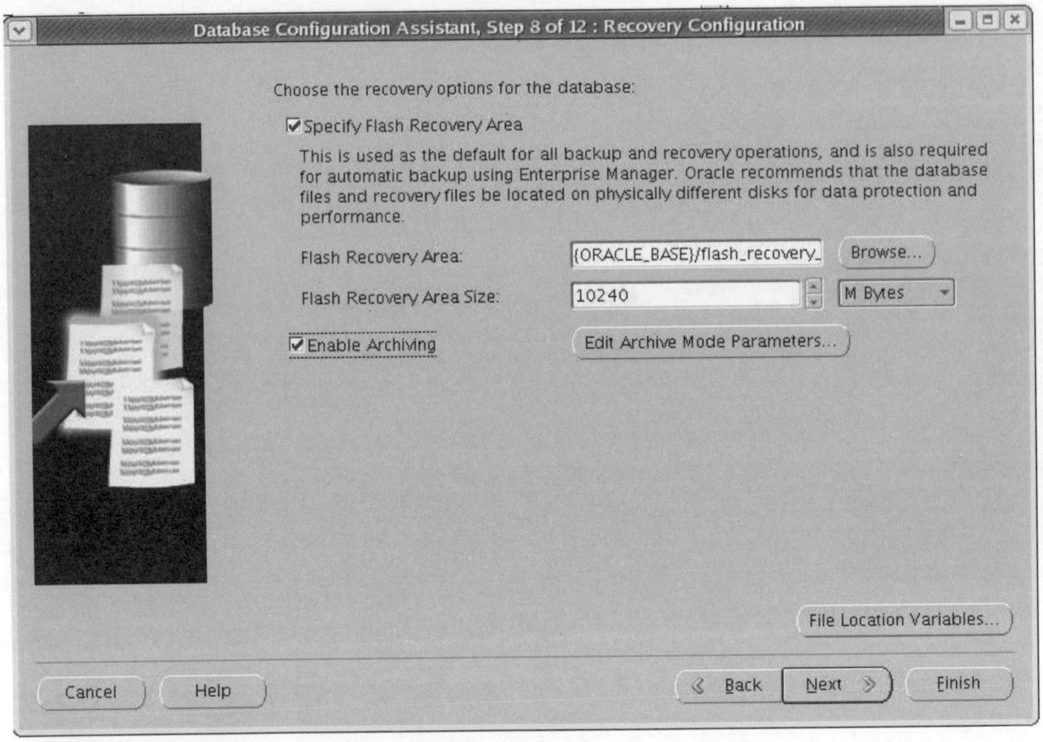

- Database Components: **Oracle Label Security**

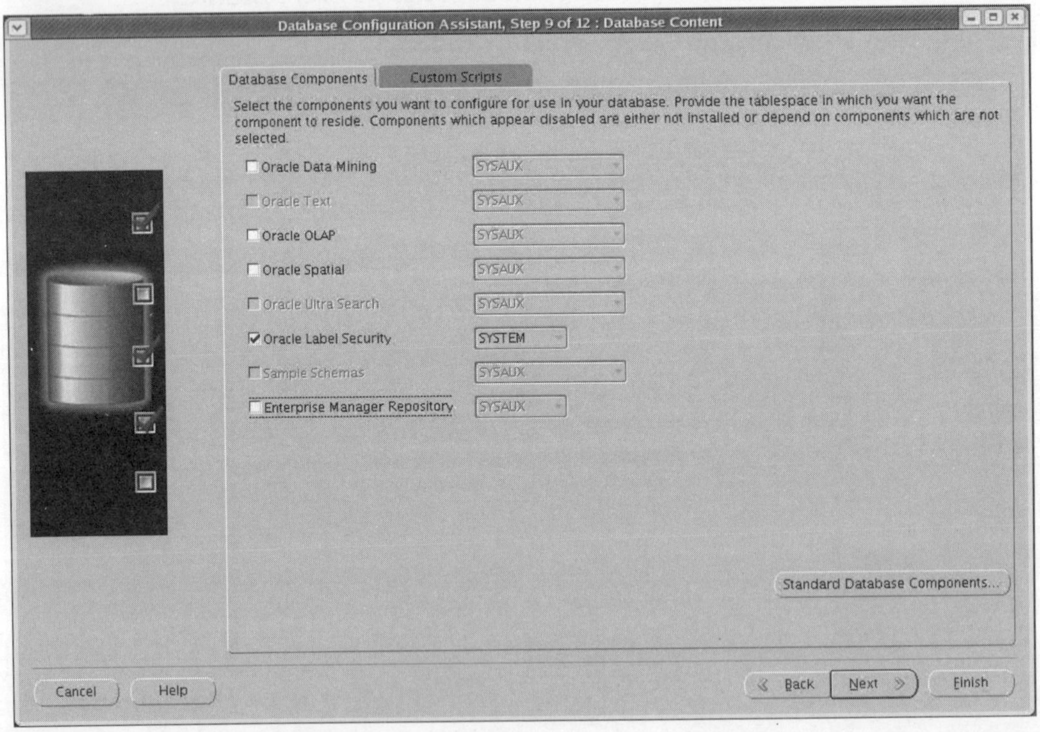

- Memory Parameters
  i. SGA Size: **512M**
  ii. PGA Size: **128M**

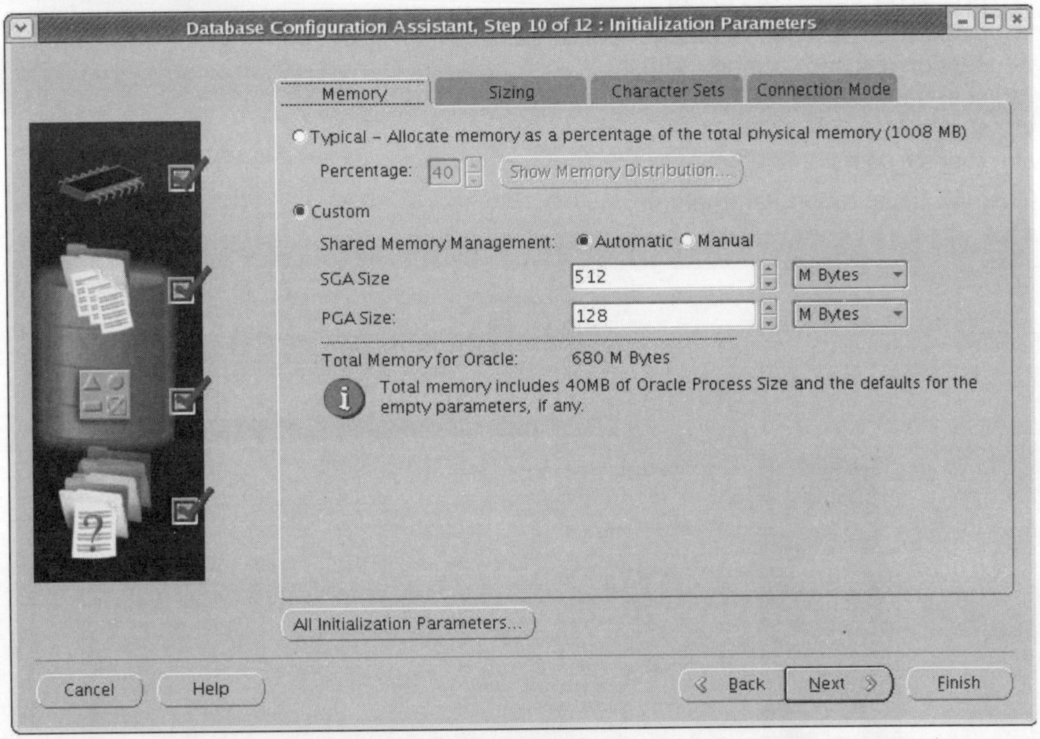

- Character Set: **Use the default WE8ISO8859P1**

  Throughout the practice, the database character set and compatible parameter should be same for all databases.

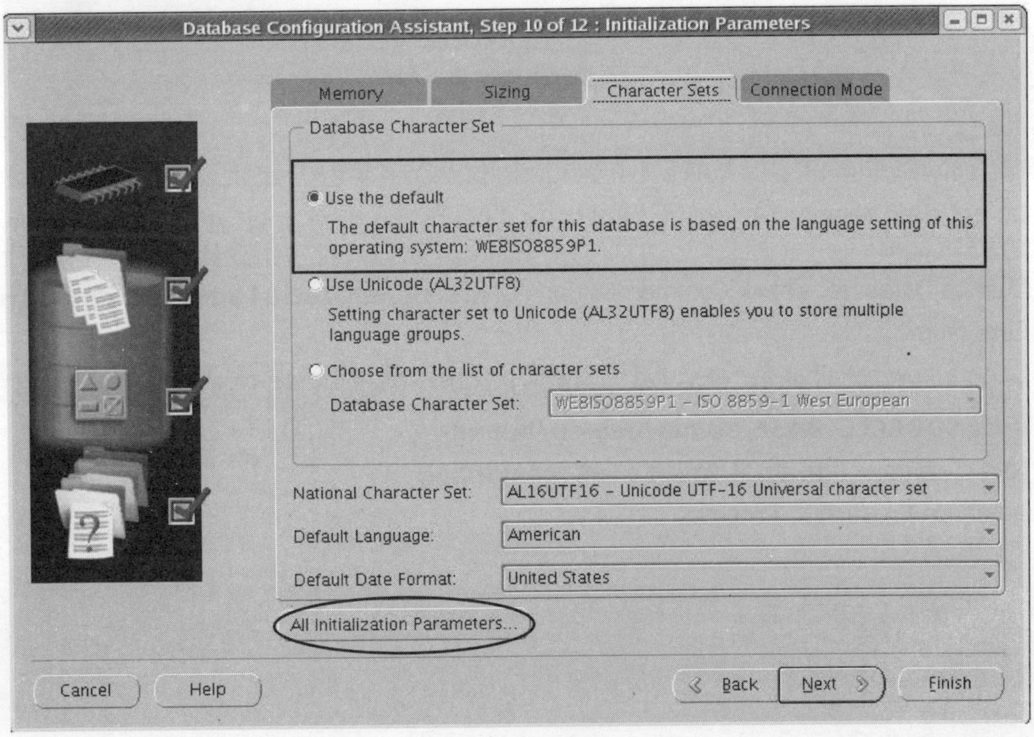

- Change the following parameter for Oracle's OEM Grid Database oemdb using All Initialization Parameters tab shown above.
  i. aq_tm_processes=10
  ii. db_cache_size=134217728
  iii. dispatcher (remove dispatcher parameter)
  iv. session_cached_cursors=200
  v. sga_max_size=536870912
  vi. sga_target=536870912
  vii. shared_pool =268435456
- Close All Initialization Parameters.

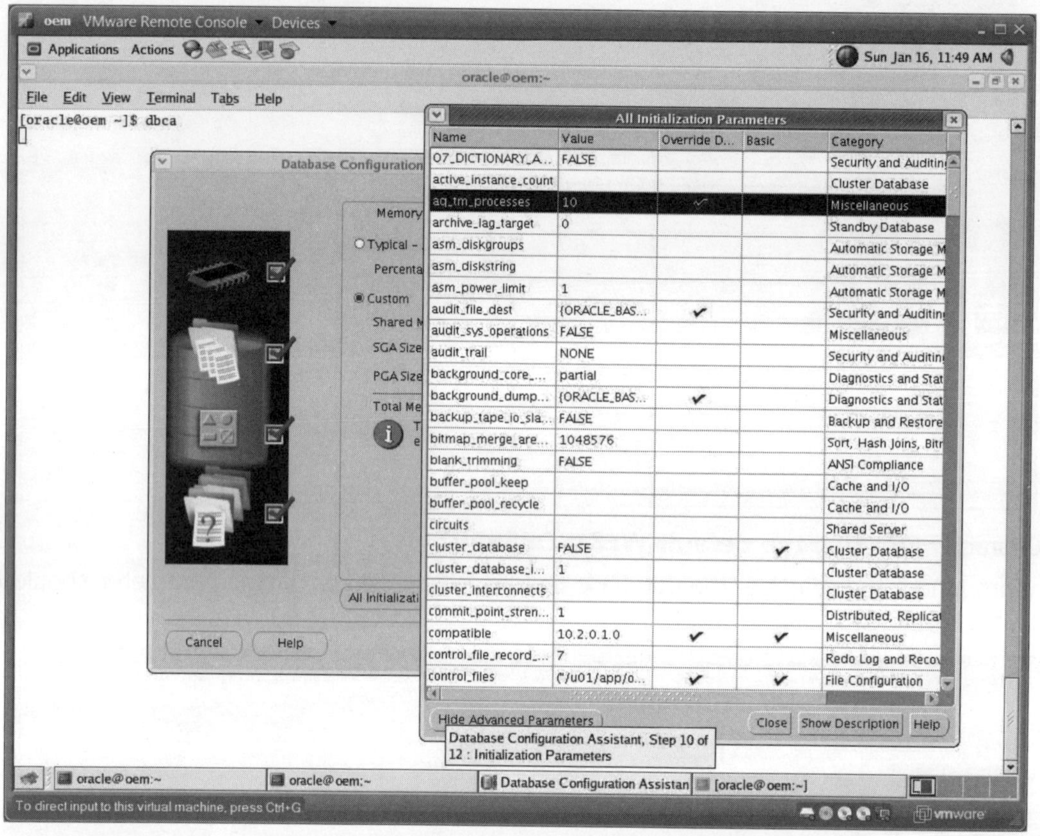

- Do not click Memory TAB again, sometimes it hangs the dbca, then you have to start whole dbca process again.
- Custom Database: Check Common Options to make sure **Oracle Label Security is true**
- Click Finish
- Open a new terminal see alert log to check progress of database creation.

  $ cd $ORACLE_BASE/admin/oemdb/bdump

  [oracle@oem bdump]$ tail -f alert_oemdb.log
- Database Creation in Progress

- Database Creation Complete: Click Exit

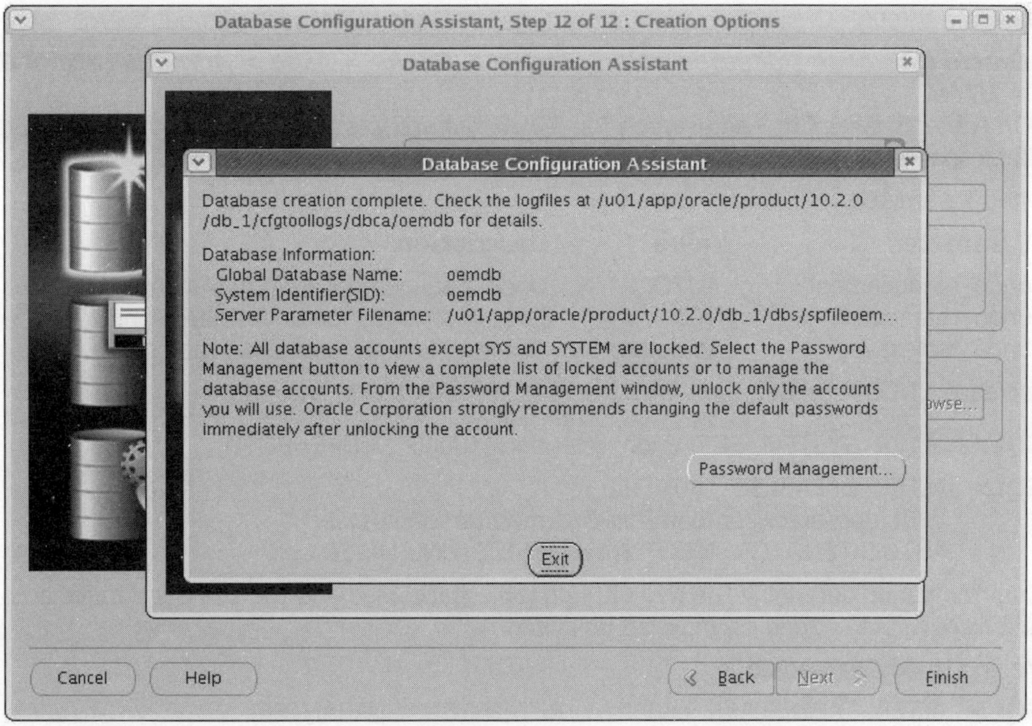

- Install the following packages required by grid control installations
  i. $ORACLE_HOME/rdbms/admin/dbmspool.sql
  ii. $ORACLE_HOME/rdbms/admin/prvtpool.plb
- Database for Oracle Enterprise manager is created.

■ Managing temporary tablespace

- Navigate through Oracle Documentation to get to Temporary Tablespace details

  Oracle Database Documentation Library > Books > ADM > Administrator's Guide > HTML

  On contents page Ctrl f and search for *"Temporary Tablespaces"* you will reach Temporary Tablespaces.

- Adding tablespace to tablespace group

  SQL> ALTER TABLESPACE temp TABLESPACE GROUP group1;

- Create tablespace with default group

  SQL> CREATE TEMPORARY TABLESPACE temp1 TEMPFILE '/u01/app/oracle/oradata/disk3/ocmdb/temp01.dbf ' SIZE 100M REUSE EXTENT MANAGEMENT LOCAL UNIFORM SIZE 8M TABLESPACE GROUP group1;

- Making group1 as default temporary tablespace

  SQL> ALTER DATABASE DEFAULT TEMPORARY TABLESPACE group1;

- Dictionary Views to get information of Temporary Tablespaces
  i. DBA_TEMP_FILES
  ii. DBA_TABLESPACES

- Managing Undo tablespace
  - Navigate through Oracle Documentation to get to Undo tablespace without search tab

    Oracle Database Documentation Library > Books > ADM > Administrator's Guide > HTML

    On contents page Ctrl f and search for *"Undo Tablespaces"* you will reach Managing Undo Tablespaces.
  - Undo Parameters

Parameter	Value	Description
undo_management	AUTO	Undo Management AUTO/MANUAL
undo_retention	900	Time in seconds for Undo Retention
undo_tablespace	undotbs1	Name to use multiple undo tablespace

  - Increase UNDO retention time for 5 hours (5*60*60) 18000 seconds

```
SQL> ALTER SYSTEM SET undo_retention=18000 SCOPE=BOTH;
SQL> ALTER DATABASE DATAFILE
     '/u01/app/oracle/oradata/disk3/ocmdb/undotbs01.dbf'
     AUTOEXTEND ON NEXT 1M MAXSIZE UNLIMITED;
```

Over the period determine the size of undo tablespace used and the size the datafile accordingly and remove autoextend on maxsize unlimited.

  - Making Undo Guaranteed

```
SQL> ALTER TABLESPACE undotbs1 RETENTION GUARANTEE;
```

Oracle will make sure the undo blocks are their till undo_retention time even if other transactions fail due to lack of undo tablespace.

  - To remove undo Guarantee use following Sql.

```
SQL> ALTER TABLESPACE undotbs1 RETENTION NOGUARANTEE;
```

  - Migrating from Manual Undo to Automatic Undo Management use function below to find the sizing of undo tablespace

```
SQL> variable undo_MB number;
SQL> DECLARE
              undo_MB    NUMBER;
     BEGIN
              : undo_MB:= DBMS_UNDO_ADV.RBU_MIGRATION;
     END;
     /
SQL> print undo_MB
```

OR

Use Undo Advisory from Oracle's OEM Grid/dbcontrol to estimate size of undo tablespace datafile.

  - Setting undo_retention=0, Oracle automatically manages undo retention.
  - Create another Undo tablespace in database.

```
SQL> CREATE UNDO TABLESPACE undotbs02 DATAFILE
     '/u01/app/oracle/oradata/disk5/undotbs201.dbf'
     SIZE 100M REUSE AUTOEXTEND ON NEXT 1M MAXSIZE UNLIMITED;
```

  - Making undo tablespace undotbs02 default tablespace

```
SQL> ALTER SYSTEM SET undo_tablespace=undotbs02 SCOPE=BOTH;
```

  - Adding/Dropping undo tablespace file

```
SQL> ALTER TABLESPACE undotbs1 ADD DATAFILE
     '/u01/app/oracle/oradata/disk5/ocmdb/undotbs02.dbf'
     SIZE 100M AUTOEXTEND ON NEXT 1M MAXSIZE UNLIMITED;
```

SQL> ALTER TABLESPACE undotbs1 DROP DATAFILE '/u01/app/oracle/oradata/disk5/ocmdb/undotbs02.dbf';

- Making datafile of undo tablespace unlimited

  SQL> ALTER DATABASE DATAFILE '/u01/app/oracle/oradata/disk3/ocmdb/undotbs01.dbf' AUTOEXTEND ON NEXT 1 MAXSIZE UNLIMITED;

- Dropping Undo Tablespace (Cannot drop current undo tablespace)

  SQL> DROP TABLESPACE undotbs1;

- ORA-01555 snapshot too old error message.

This happens when a long query needs to get data from undo segments which is already been over written. If this is happening on regular basis then to prevent it
Increase undo_retention, Increase the size of undo tablespace and at last set tablespace undo retention guaranteed mode.

- Data Dictionary Views for Undo Management

  i. V$UNDOSTAT
  ii. V$ROLLSTAT
  iii. V$TRANSACTION
  iv. DBA_UNDO_EXTENTS
  v. DBA_HIST_UNDOSTAT
  vi. DBA_TABLESPACES

- Creating Permanent Tablespaces

  i. Uniform extent size, segment management auto and extent management local

  SQL> CREATE TABLESPACE test1 DATAFILE '/u01/app/oracle/oradata/disk5/ocmdb/test101.dbf' SIZE 100M SEGMENT SPACE MANAGEMENT AUTO EXTENT MANAGEMENT LOCAL UNIFORM SIZE 1M;

  ii. Auto allocate extent, segment management auto and extent management local

  SQL> CREATE TABLESPACE example DATAFILE '/u01/app/oracle/oradata/disk5/ocmdb/example01.dbf' SIZE 100M AUTOEXTEND ON NEXT 1M MAXSIZE 2048M EXTENT MANAGEMENT LOCAL AUTOALLOCATE;

  iii. Auto allocate extent, segment management manual and extent management local

  SQL> CREATE TABLESPACE test3 DATAFILE '/u01/app/oracle/oradata/disk5/ocmdb/test301.dbf' SIZE 100M EXTENT MANAGEMENT LOCAL SEGMENT SPACE MANAGEMENT MANUAL AUTOALLOCATE;

  iv. Oracle Managed Files (OMF).

  For Oracle managed files set following parameters for datafiles db_create_file_dest and logfile db_create_on line_log_dest_1.

  SQL> ALTER SYSTEM SET db_create_file_dest='/u01/app/oracle/oradata/disk5' SCOPE=BOTH;

  SQL> CREATE TABLESPACE test4;

  SQL> CREATE TABLESPACE test5 DATAFILE SIZE 256M AUTOEXTEND ON NEXT 1M MAXSIZE 1024M EXTENT MANAGEMENT LOCAL UNIFORM SIZE 1M;

  v. Create tablespace on non-default block size

  SQL> ALTER SYSTEM SET db_16k_cache_size=100M SCOPE=BOTH;

  SQL> CREATE TABLESPACE test6 DATAFILE '/u01/app/oracle/oradata/disk5/ocmdb/test601.dbf' SIZE 100M BLOCKSIZE 16K SEGMENT SPACE MANAGEMENT AUTO EXTENT MANAGEMENT LOCAL UNIFORM SIZE 1M;

vi. Create big file tablespace

```
SQL> CREATE BIGFILE TABLESPACE test7 DATAFILE
'/u01/app/oracle/oradata/disk5/ocmdb/test701'
SIZE 100M AUTOEXTEND ON NEXT 1024M MAXSIZE 10240G;

SQL> CREATE BIGFILE TABLESPACE test8 DATAFILE
'/u01/app/oracle/oradata/disk5/ocmdb/test801' SIZE 100M
AUTOEXTEND ON NEXT 1024M MAXSIZE 10240G BLOCKSIZE 16K;
```

vii. Details of Tablespaces created above

```
SQL> SELECT tablespace_name,
     block_size,
     bigfile,
     segment_space_management,
     extent_management,
     allocation_type
     FROM dba_tablespaces;
```

viii. Dropping tablespace with manual segment management and recreating with segment management auto

```
SQL> DROP TABLESPACE test3 INCLUDING CONTENTS AND DATAFILES;

SQL> CREATE TABLESPACE test3 DATAFILE
     '/u01/app/oracle/oradata/disk5/ocmdb/test301.dbf' SIZE 100M EXTENT
     MANAGEMENT LOCAL SEGMENT SPACE MANAGEMENT AUTO AUTOALLOCATE;
```

2.6 Create Sample Schema for Future Exercises

Oracle 10g companion cd already installed above and example tablespace created.

- Execute the following script and ignore some errors generated as those objects not needed for our practise.

  $ORACLE_HOME/demo/schema/mksample.sql

  Provide password for system, sys and for other users, log file directory for log files.

2.7 Network Configuration

- Typical listener.ora file with default port 1521.

The **extproc, ipc** (in bold) is configured only on one listener in this example listener "LISTENER"

listener.ora

```
# listener.ora Network Configuration File:
# /u01/app/oracle/product/10.2.0/db_1/network/admin/listener.ora
# Generated by Oracle configuration tools.

LISTENER=
  (DESCRIPTION=
    (ADDRESS_LIST=
      (ADDRESS=(PROTOCOL=tcp)(HOST=ocm.prusolutions.com)(PORT=1521))
      (ADDRESS=(PROTOCOL=ipc)(KEY=extproc))
      ))
SID_LIST_LISTENER=
  (SID_LIST=
    (SID_DESC=
      (GLOBAL_DBNAME=ocmdb)
      (ORACLE_HOME=/u01/app/oracle/product/10.2.0/db_1)
```

```
  (SID_NAME=ocmdb))
(SID_DESC=
  (SID_NAME=plsextproc)
  (ORACLE_HOME=/u01/app/oracle/product/10.2.0/db_1)
  (PROGRAM=extproc))
   )
```

- Navigate through Oracle Documentation to get to listener.ora file without search tab

  Oracle Database Documentation Library > Books > NET > Net Services Reference > HTML

  On contents page Ctrl f and search for *"listener.ora"* you will reach sample listener.ora file.

- Notes on Listener

  i. One listener can listen multiple databases and thousands of connections.
  ii. You cannot duplicate IPC Key values in single or multiple listeners.
  iii. You cannot duplicate TCP Port values in single or multiple listener running on **single** ip address/ network card.
  iv. To configure non-default listener port (default is 1521) requires to setup LOCAL_LISTENER parameter in initocmdb.ora parameter file.
  v. **Make sure that any parenthesis is not in far left margin in listener.ora file.**
  vi. Make sure there is not any blank line in end of listener.ora or tnsnames.ora file

- Add **LOCAL_LISTENER** to listener.ora file.

  Always backup network files like listener.ora before making any modifications manually.

  Apart from having default port 1521 LISTENER as shown above we can add non-default port 2010. To make LOCAL_LISTENER work LISTENER_OCM parameters should be added in tnsnames.ora file also.

```
LISTENER_OCM =
 (DESCRIPTION_LIST =
  (DESCRIPTION =
   (ADDRESS = (PROTOCOL = TCP)(HOST = ocm.prusolutions.com)(PORT = 2010))
      )
 )
SID_LIST_LISTENER_OCM =
 (SID_LIST =
  (SID_DESC =
   (GLOBAL_DBNAME = ocmdb)
   (ORACLE_HOME = /u01/app/oracle/product/10.2.0/db_1)
   (SID_NAME = ocmdb)
      )
 )
```

- Other listener.ora parameters

Parameter	Description
STARTUP_WAIT_TIME	Listener wait time to respond to lsnrctl status command.
SAVE_CONFIG_ON_STOP	Used to save modifications made by lsnrctl session on exit.
INBOUND_CONNECT_TIMEOUT	It defines listener wait time for valid response from client
PASSWORDS	Specifies password required to use lsnrctl command line utility
TRACE_LEVEL	Sets trace level for listener values (OFF, USER, SUPPORT, ADMIN)
TRACE_FILE	Defines location of listener trace files Default $ORACLE_HOME\network\trace\listener.trc

LOG_FILE	Define location of listener logfile file Default $ORACLE_HOME\network\log\ listener.log.

- For other listener parameters for Transparent Application Failover, Load Balancing
  - Navigate through Oracle Documentation to get to Transparent Application Failover without search tab

    Oracle Database Documentation Library > Books > NET > **Net Services Administrator's Guide** ***> HTML***

    On contents page Ctrl f and search for 'Configuring Transparent Application Failover "you will reach sample Configuring Transparent Application Failover

- Listener commands basic syntax: lsnrctl command <LISTENER_NAME>

Command	**Description**
$ lsnrctl start listener	Start Default listener.
$ lsnrctl start listener_ocm	Start listener "listener_ocm".
$ lsnrctl stop listener	Stop Default listener.
$ lsnrctl stop listener_ocm	Stop listener "listener_ocm".
$ lsnrctl reload listener	Reload new listener parameters without stopping listener.
$ lsnrctl reload listener_ocm	Reload new listener_ocm parameters without stopping listener.
$ lsnrctl service listener	Shows details of all databases and services supported by listener.
$ lsnrctl service listener_ocm	Shows details of all databases and services supported by listener_ocm.
$ lsnrctl status listener	Shows status of listener.
$ lsnrctl status listener_ocm	Shows status of listener_ocm.

- Learn all the listener commands from Oracle Documentation. Read about Dynamically Register Services in Oracle 10g
  - Navigate through Oracle Documentation to get to Dynamically Register Services without search tab

    Oracle Database Documentation Library > Books > NET > **Net Services Administrator's Guide** ***> HTML***

    On contents page Ctrl f and search for 'Listener Architecture "you will reach Dynamically Register Services.

  - Get listener parameter help

    [oracle@ocm ~]$ lsnrctl help

    LSNRCTL for Linux: Version 10.2.0.1.0 - Production on 17-JAN-2011 10:53:32

    Copyright (c) 1991, 2005, Oracle. All rights reserved.

    The following operations are available

    An asterisk (*) denotes a modifier or extended command:

```
start           stop        status
services        version     reload
save_config     trace       spawn
change_password quit        exit
set*            show*
```

- Listener Configuration using netca
  - Backup current listener.ora file before doing changes through **netca** and **netngr** mentioned below and see the difference between old and new listener.ora file
  - Adding new listener using netca

    [oracle@ocm ~]$ netca
  - Welcome Screen: **Select Listener Configuration**

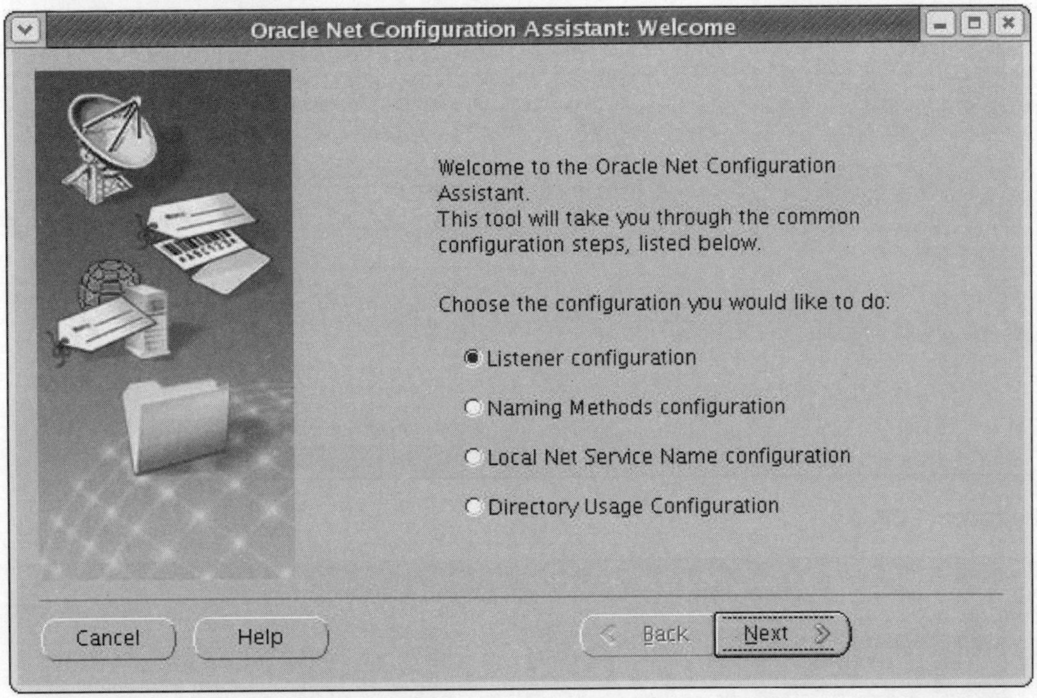

  - Listener Configuration Screen: **Add**

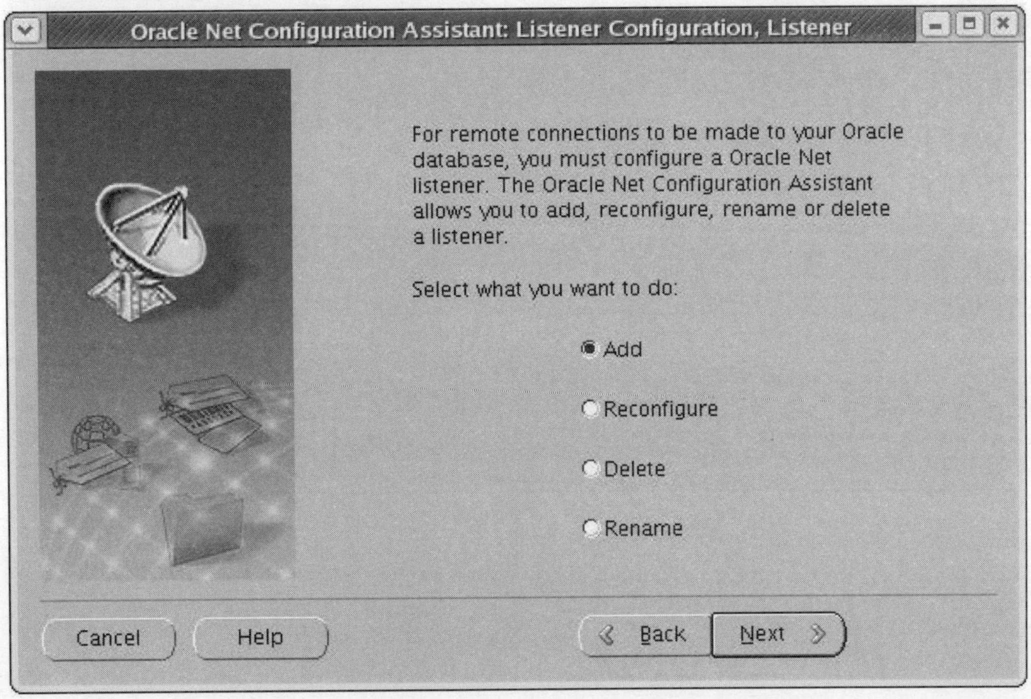

- Listener Name: **LISTENER_TEST**

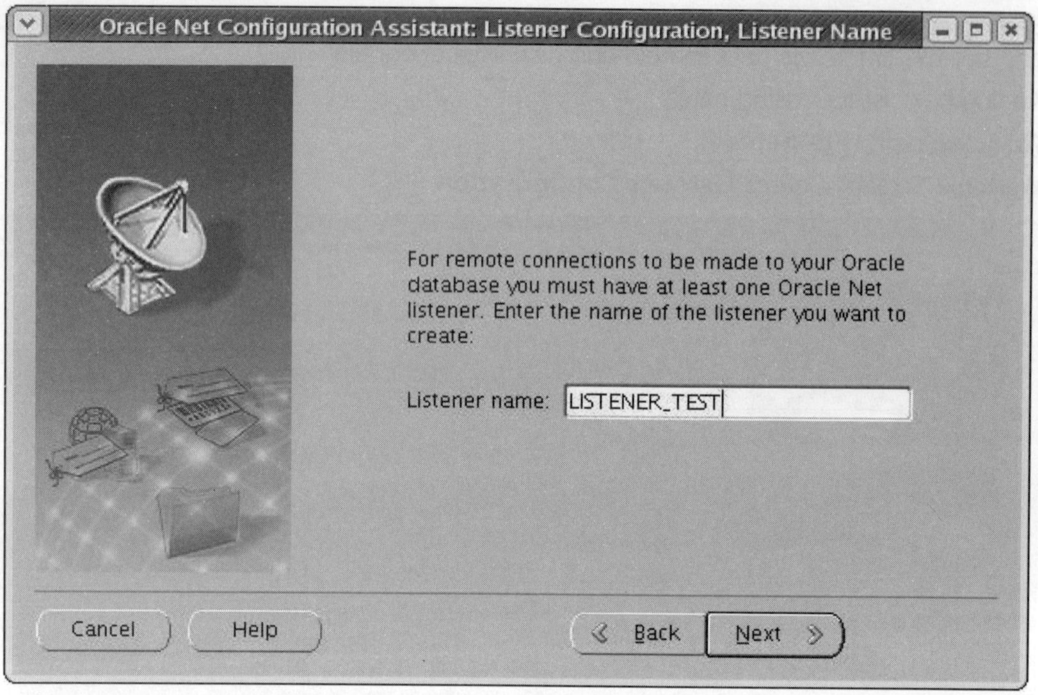

- Protocol: **TCP**

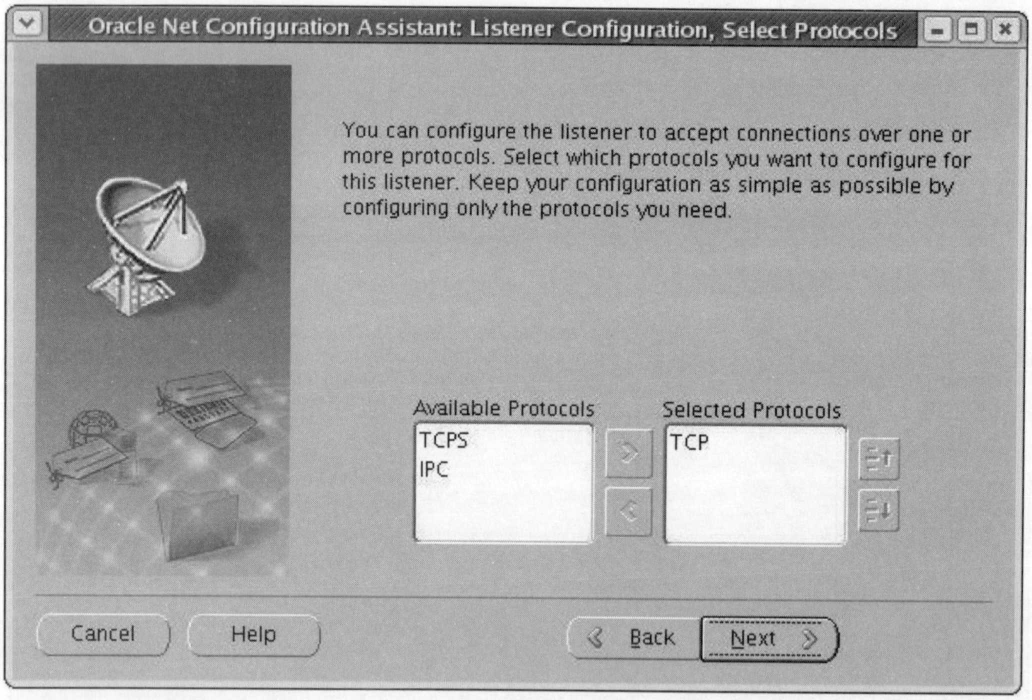

- Port: **2012**

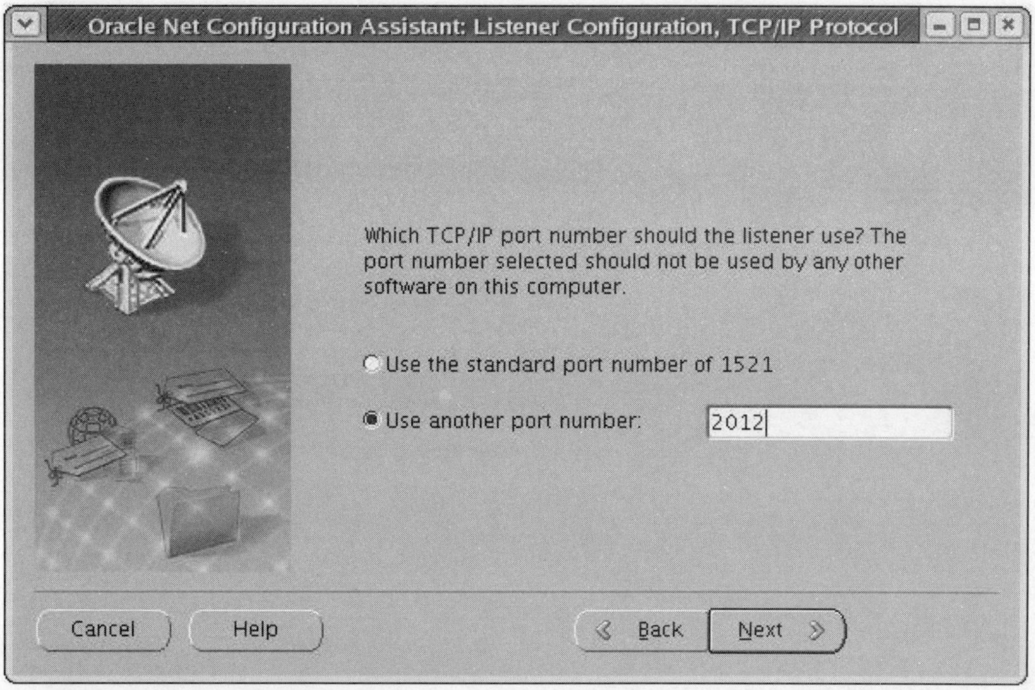

- Configure Another Listener: **NO**

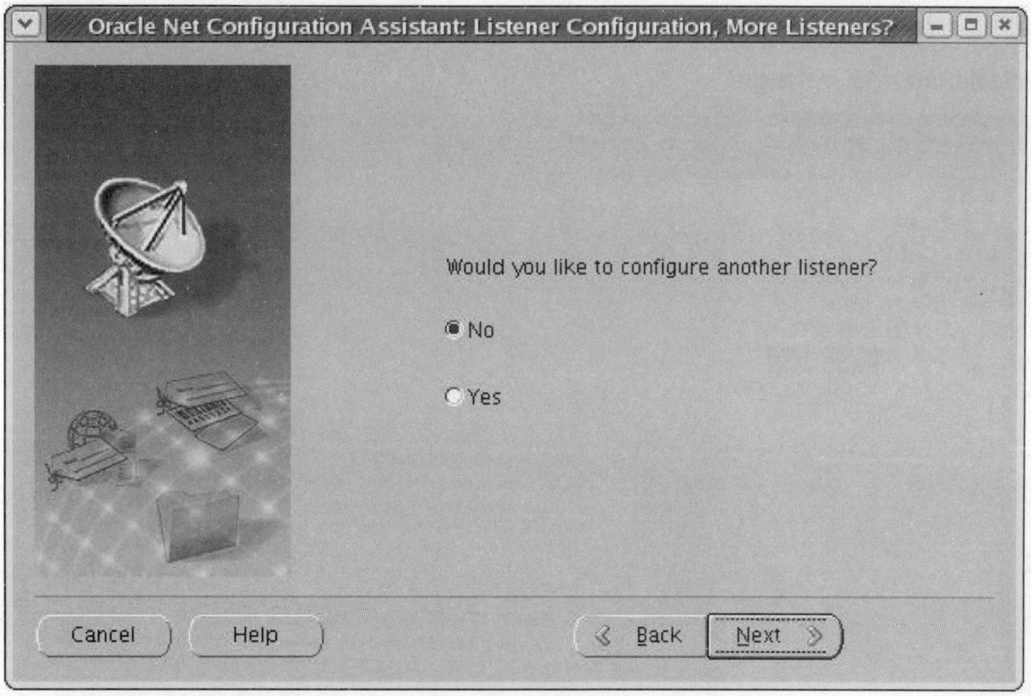

- Welcome Screen: **Click Finish**

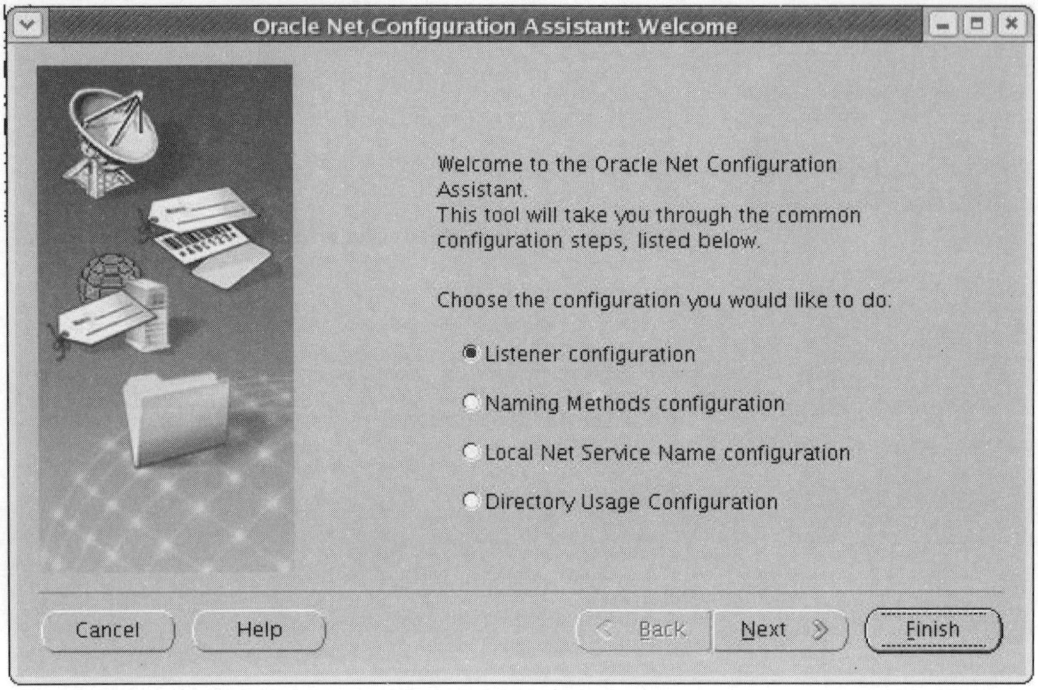

- In same way you can Reconfigure, Delete, Rename listener

■ Managing listener.ora using netmgr

[oracle@ocm ~]$ netmgr

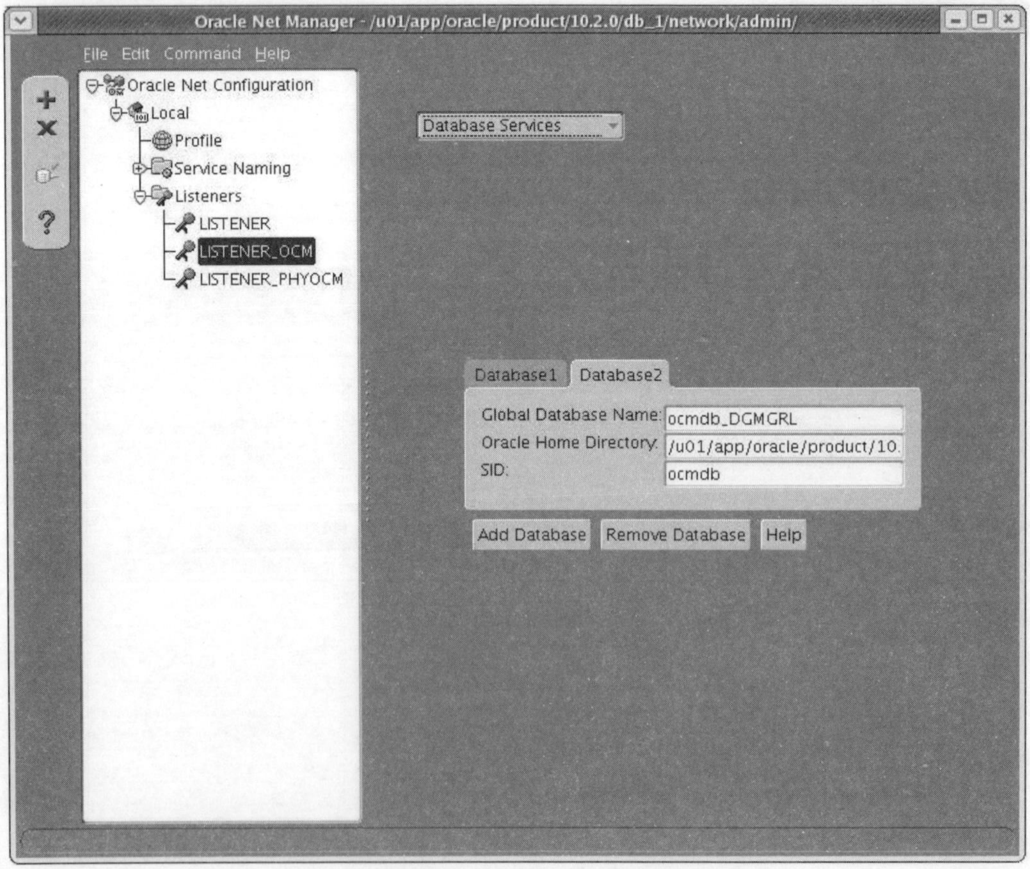

- Configuring tnsnames.ora file manually

  - Navigate through Oracle Documentation to get to tnsnames.ora file without search tab
    Oracle Database Documentation Library > Books > NET > Net Services Reference > HTML

    On contents page Ctrl f and search for *"Perform Functional Upgrade"* you will reach sample tnsnames.ora file.

  - Typical tnsnames.ora for default port 1521

```
ocmdb=
(DESCRIPTION=
  (ADDRESS=(PROTOCOL=tcp)(HOST=ocm.prusolutions.com)(PORT=1521))
 (CONNECT_DATA=
   (SERVICE_NAME=ocmdb)
   (SERVER=DEDICATED)
     )
 )
```

  - TNSPING ocmdb and connect through sqlplus to make sure listener.ora and tnsnames.ora and orapwocmdb are configured properly

```
[oracle@ocm admin]$ tnsping ocmdb
[oracle@ocm admin]$ sqlplus /nolog
SQL> connect scott/tiger@ocmdb
         Connected.
```

    If you are not able to connect, check the errors and fix the problems before proceeding further

  - Add entry to tnsnames.ora files for non-Default port 2010 for local listener

```
ocmdb_test=
(DESCRIPTION=
  (ADDRESS=(PROTOCOL=tcp)(HOST=ocm.prusolutions.com)(PORT=2010))
 (CONNECT_DATA=
   (SERVICE_NAME=ocmdb)
   (SERVER=DEDICATED)
    )
     )
LISTENER_OCM =
 (DESCRIPTION_LIST =
  (DESCRIPTION =
   (ADDRESS = (PROTOCOL = TCP)(HOST = ocm.prusolutions.com)(PORT = 2010))
  )
 )
SQL> ALTER SYSTEM SET local_listener='LISTENER_OCM' SCOPE=BOTH;
SQL> SHUTDOWN immediate;
SQL> STARTUP;
```

  - Make sure there are no blank lines at the end of tnsnames.ora file
  - Tnsping ocmdb_test and connect through sqlplus to make sure local_listener parameter is set properly and **restart database**.

```
[oracle@ocm admin]$ tnsping ocmdb_test
[oracle@ocm admin]$ sqlplus /nolog
```

SQL> connect scott/tiger@ocmdb_test
Connected.

If you are not able to connect, check the errors and fix the problems before proceeding further.

- Adding new tnsname entry in tnsnames.ora using netca

  [oracle@ocm admin]$ netca

  - Welcome Screen: **Local Net Service Name Configuration**

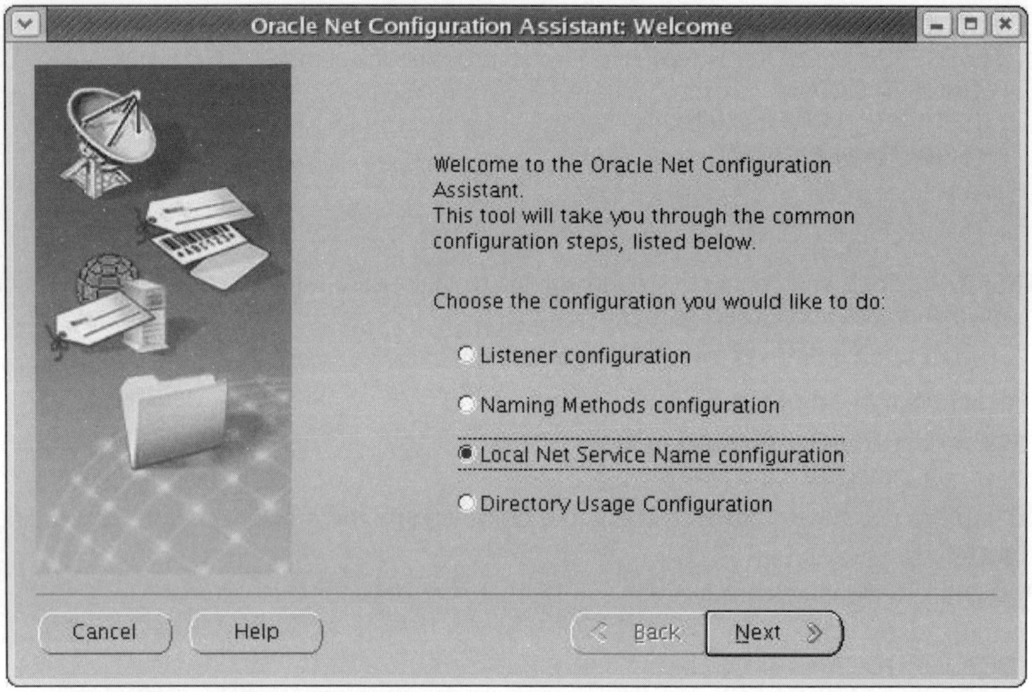

  - Net Service Name Configuration: **Add**

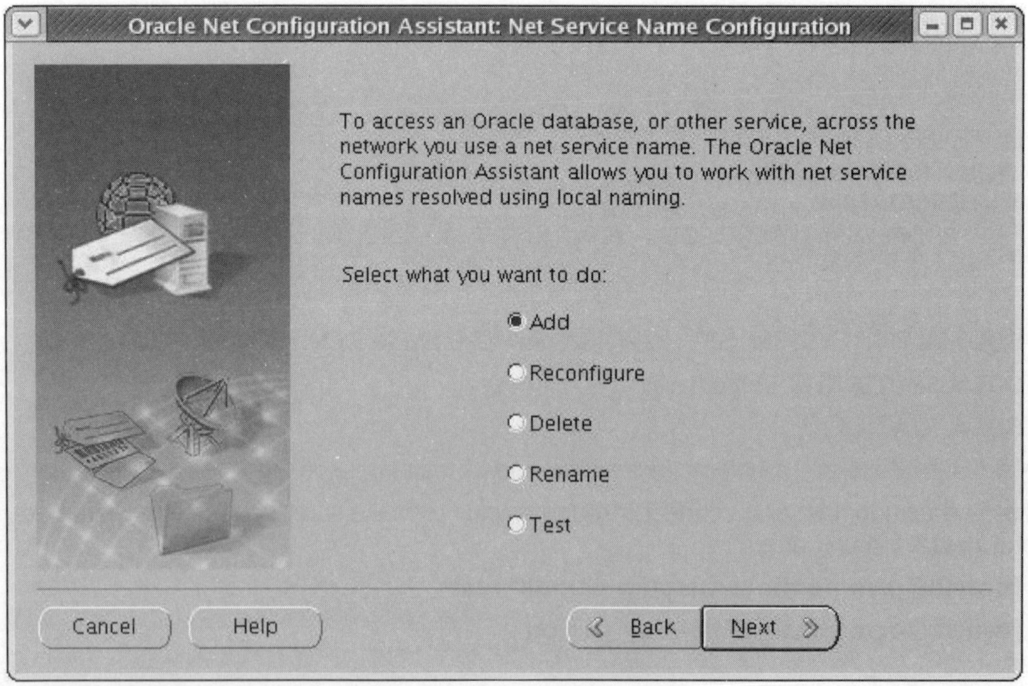

- Service Name:**ocmdb**

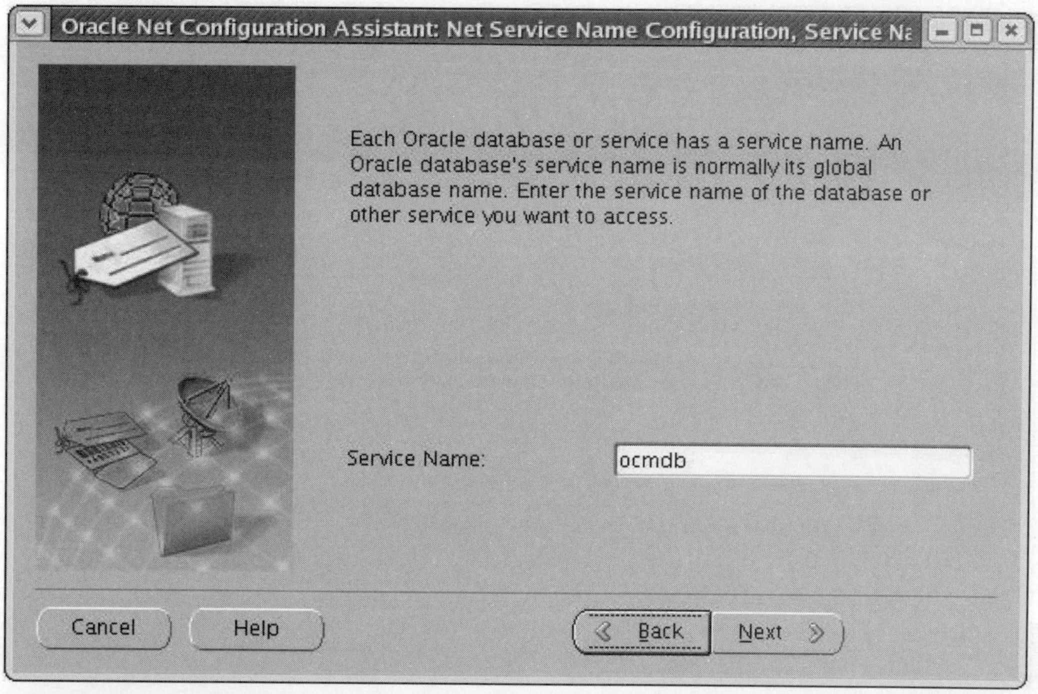

- Network Protocol:**TCP**

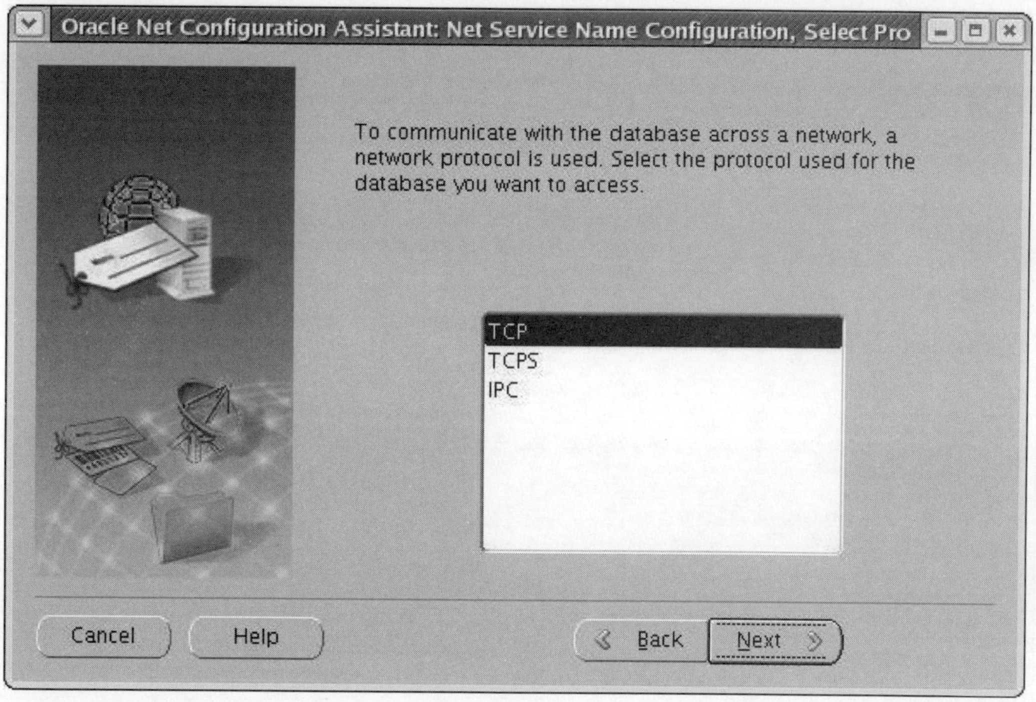

- Hostname: ocm.prusolutions.com Port Number: **2010**

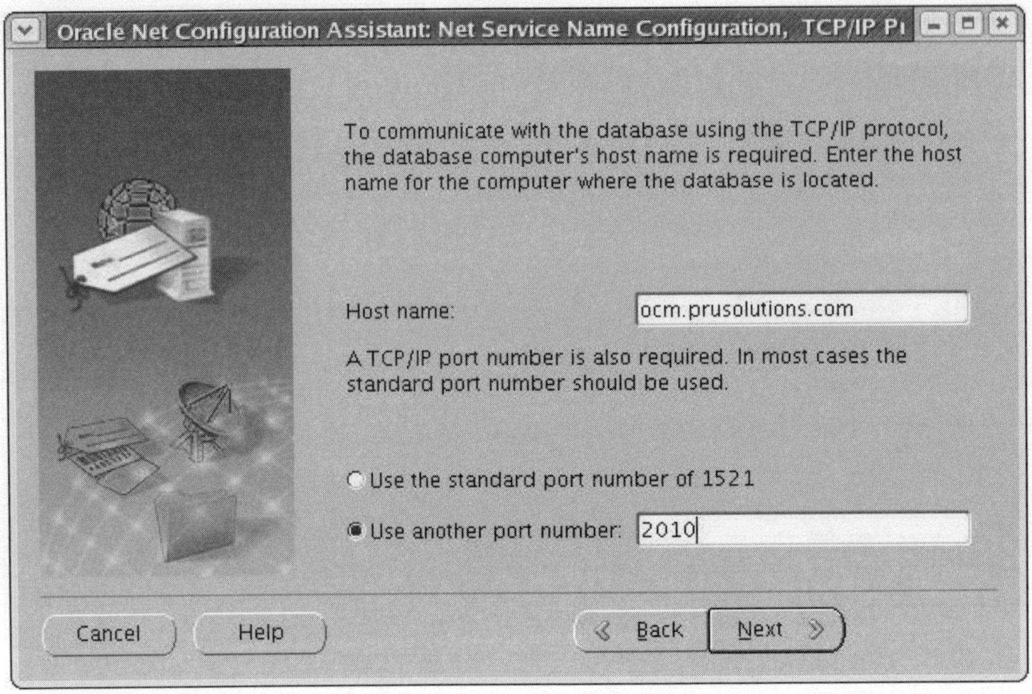

- Perform Test: **Yes**

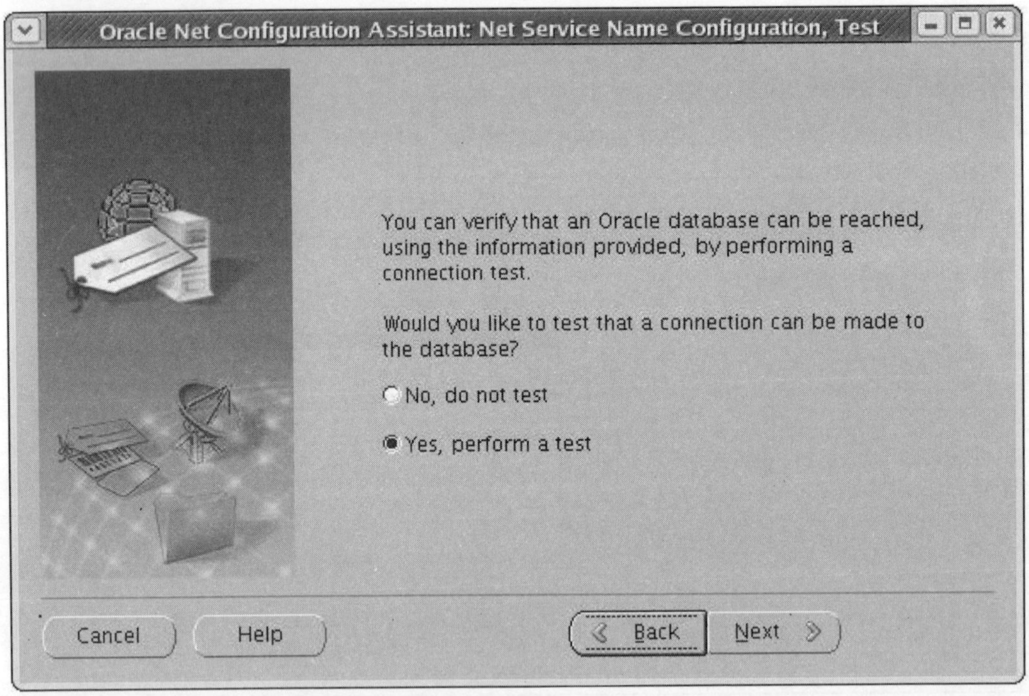

- Change Login: Username: **system** Password: **oracle**

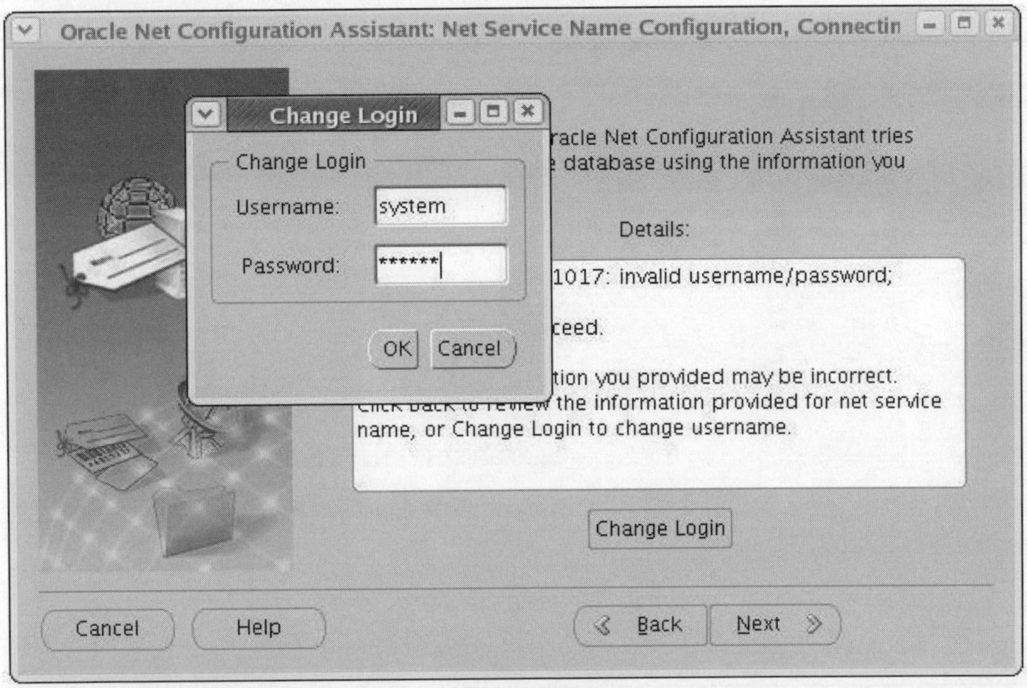

Enter a name for this Service name : **ocmdb_new**

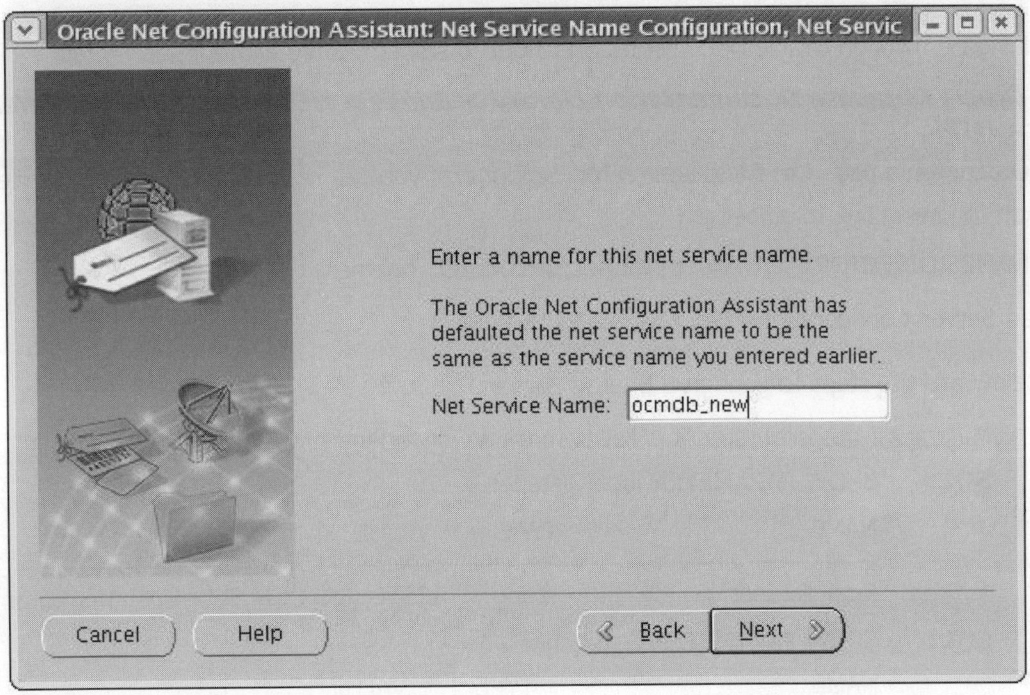

- Welcome Screen: **Click Finish**

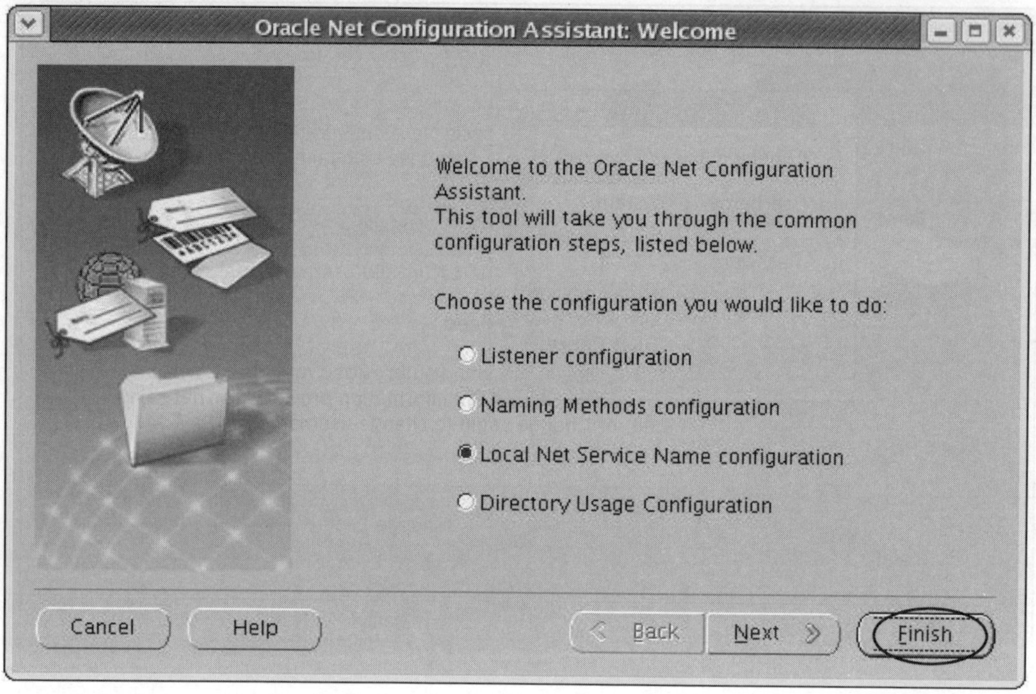

- Configuring sqlnet.ora file manually
  - Navigate through Oracle Documentation to get to sqlnet.ora file without search tab

    Oracle Database Documentation Library > Books > NET > Net Services Reference > HTML

    On contents page Ctrl f and search for *"sqlnet.ora"* you will reach sample sqlnet.ora file.
  - Add following line to sqlnet.ora

    NAMES.DIRECTORY_PATH= (tnsnames, ezconnect, onames)
- Shared Server Configurations
  - Below are the steps to configure Shared Server

    i. Make sure the local listener is set before and is working properly.

SQL> SHOW PARAMETER local_listener

NAME	TYPE	VALUE
local_listener	string	LISTENER_OCM Set dispatcher parameters

SQL> SHOW PARAMETER dispatcher

NAME	TYPE	VALUE
dispatchers	string	
max_dispatchers	integer	

SQL> ALTER SYSTEM SET dispatchers '(protocol=tcp)(dispatchers=2)(protocol=ipc)(dispatchers=2)' SCOPE=BOTH;

ii. The listener is only required in dispatchers parameters when local_listener is not defined.

SQL> ALTER SYSTEM SET dispatchers= '(protocol=tcp)(LISTENER=LISTENER_OCM)(dispatchers=2)' SCOPE=BOTH;

SQL> ALTER SYSTEM SET max_dispatchers=10 SCOPE=BOTH;

iii. Shared Server Configuration

SQL> SHOW PARAMETER shared_server

```
NAME                          TYPE        VALUE
----------------------------- ----------- ------------------------------
max_shared_servers            integer
shared_server_sessions        integer
shared_servers                integer     0
```

SQL> ALTER SYSTEM SET shared_servers=4 SCOPE=BOTH;

SQL> ALTER SYSTEM SET max_shared_servers=10 SCOPE=BOTH;

iv. Configure Virtual Circuits

SQL> SHOW PARAMETER circuits

```
NAME                          TYPE        VALUE
----------------------------- ----------- ------------------------------
circuits                      integer
```

Virtual circuits are user connections to the database through dispatchers and servers. This parameter specifies the total number of virtual circuits that are available for inbound and outbound network sessions. Set this parameter only if you want to limit the total number of connections users can make via the shared server architecture. This parameter is of interest because it is one of several parameters that contribute to the total SGA requirements of an instance. If Oracle Shared Server is configured, then the value of CIRCUITS will match that of SESSIONS. Otherwise, the value is 0.

SQL> ALTER SYSTEM SET circuits = 100 SCOPE=BOTH;

v. Configure Large Pool

SQL> SHOW PARAMETER large_pool

```
NAME                          TYPE        VALUE
----------------------------- ----------- ------------------------------
large_pool_size               big integer 0
```

SQL> ALTER SYSTEM SET large_pool_size=64M SCOPE=BOTH;

Add following tnsname entry to tnsnames.ora file

```
OCMDB_MTS=
(DESCRIPTION=
  (ADDRESS=(PROTOCOL=tcp)(HOST=ocm.prusolutions.com)(PORT=2010))
  (CONNECT_DATA=
    (SERVICE_NAME=ocmdb)
    (SERVER=SHARED)
     )
 )
```

- Easy Connect

  In Easy Connect, we have to supply all information required for the Oracle Net connection as part of the connect string.

  <username>/<password>@<hostname>:<listener port>/<servicename>

  [oracle@ocm admin]$ sqlplus system/oracle@ocm.prusolutions.com:2010/ocmdb

  - Make sure on ocm.prusolutions.com both listeners LISTENER, LISTENER_OCM and ocmdb database has started for further exercises.
  - Make sure on oem.prusolutions.com default LISTENER and oemdb database has started for further exercises

3

Enterprise Manager Grid Control

- Install the Enterprise Manager Grid Control software
- Configure the Enterprise Manager repository
- Create Enterprise Manager Grid Control users
- Use Enterprise Manager to modify a database configuration
- Configure Enterprise Manager to modify a database availability
- Create and manage jobs
- Create and monitor alerts
- Create notifications
- Implement Grid Control and Database Control
- Choose the appropriate tablespace type for the intended use
- Create Scheduler jobs
- Create schedules
- Assign jobs to windows
- Create programs
- Create job classes
- Install the Enterprise Manager Grid Control infrastructure
- Deploy Enterprise Manager Grid Control agents
- Configure Grid Control for business requirements

3.1 Install Oracle Enterprise Manager using existing Database

- Start the machine "oem" where custom oemdb database having Oracle Label Security Installed.
- Start the database oemdb listener and test connection-using sqlplus.
- Start the machine "oms" where Oracle Enterprise Manger will be installed.
- Ftp Oracle Enterprise Manager software previously downloaded gc_102011_linux to oms machine directory /u01/software.
- unzip gc_102011_linux in /u01/software
- As we have, already set kernel parameters to Install Oracle software make sure all the configuration is done properly.
- Check hosts names, files option should be the first.

  # cat /etc/nsswitch.conf | grep hosts
  make sure it has file option first then dns
- Check Kernel Parameters are set properly

  /etc/sysctl.conf

```
kernel.shmall = 2097152
kernel.shmmax = 2147483648
kernel.shmmni = 4096
kernel.sem = 250 32000 100 128
fs.file-max = 65536
net.ipv4.ip_local_port_range = 1024 65000
net.core.rmem_default = 1048576
net.core.rmem_max = 1048576
net.core.wmem_default = 262144
net.core.wmem_max = 262144
```

  /etc/security/limits.conf

```
oracle    soft    nproc 2047
oracle    hard    nproc 16384
oracle    soft    nofile 1024
oracle    hard    nofile 65536
```

  /etc/pam.d/login

```
session   required   /lib/security/pam_limits.so
session   required   pam_limits.so
```

  /etc/profile

```
if [ $USER = "oracle" ]; then
      if [ $SHELL = "/bin/ksh" ]; then
            ulimit -p 16384
            ulimit -n 65536
      else
            ulimit -u 16384 -n 65536
      fi
fi
```

- Check /etc/hosts for following values are set

```
127.1.0.0            localhost
# Oracle Database ip addresses
192.168.2.121        ocm.prusolutions.com        ocm
```

```
# Oracle Enterprise Manager ip addresses
192.168.2.161      oem.prusolutions.com          oem
192.168.2.162      oms.prusolutions.com          oms
# Oracle RAC ip addresses
192.168.2.131      crs1.prusolutions.com         crs1
192.168.2.31       crs1-vip.prusolutions.com     crs1-vip
10.10.10.31        crs1-priv.prusolutions.com    crs1-priv
192.162.2.132      crs2.prusolutions.com         crs2
192.168.2.32       crs2-vip.prusolutions.com     crs2-vip
10.10.10.32        crs2-priv.prusolutions.com    crs2-priv
# Oracle RAC Dataguard ip addresses
192.168.2.141      crsdg1.prusolutions.com       crsdg1
192.168.2.41       crsdg1-vip.prusolutions.com   crsdg1-vip
10.10.10.41        crsdg1-priv.prusolutions.com  crsdg1-priv
192.162.2.142      crsdg2.prusolutions.com       crsdg2
192.168.2.42       crsdg2-vip.prusolutions.com   crsdg2-vip
10.10.10.42        crsdg2-priv.prusolutions.com  crsdg2-priv
```

- Check user oracle and nobody for software Install

```
# cat /etc/passwd
```

- Check following parameters swap should be 3G ,memory 1G and temp at least 512M

```
# grep MemTotal /proc/meminfo
# grep SwapTotal /proc/meminfo
# df -k /tmp
```

- Set up profile for user oracle

/home/oracle/.bash_profile

```
# Get the aliases and functions
if [ -f ~/.bashrc ]; then
        . ~/.bashrc
fi
# User specific environment and startup programs
export EDITOR=vi
export ORACLE_BASE=/u01/app/oracle
export ORACLE_HOME=$ORACLE_BASE/OracleHomes/oms10g
export PATH=$ORACLE_HOME/bin:/bin:/sbin:/usr/bin:/usr/sbin:/usr/local/bin:/usr/X11R6/bin
umask 022
```

- Execute .bash_profile to set Oracle Environment.

```
$. /home/oracle/.bash_profile
$ echo $ORACLE_HOME
$ mkdir –p $ORACLE_HOME
$ mkdir –p $ORACLE_BASE/admin
$ ping oem.prusolutions.com
```

- Install to Oracle Enterprise Manager parent directory of in $ORACLE_HOME

$ORACLE_BASE/OracleHomes (/u01/app/oracle/OracleHomes)
Installer creates oms10g directory and installs in it.

- Make sure following parameters are set in oemdb database

i. aq_tm_processes=10
ii. db_cache_size=134217728

iii. dispatcher (remove dispatcher parameter)
iv. session_cached_cursors=200
v. sga_max_size=536870912
vi. sga_target=536870912
vii. shared_pool =268435456

- Make sure following scripts are executed in oemdb database
  i. $ORACLE_HOME/rdbms/admin/dbmspool.sql
  ii. $ORACLE_HOME/rdbms/admin/prvtpool.plb
- **If database was already created having dbcontrol, then drop dbcontrol repository from oemdb database.**
  i. For single instance

     $ORACLE_HOME/bin/emca -deconfig dbcontrol db -repos drop
  ii. For cluster database

     $ORACLE_HOME/bin/emca -deconfig dbcontrol db -repos drop –cluster

- Install Oracle's OEM Grid software on "OMS" machine.
  - Run Installer

    [oracle@oms Disk1]$ pwd
    /u01/software/Disk1
    [oracle@oms Disk1]$. /runInstaller
  - Specify Installation Type : **Enterprise Manager 10g Using Existing Database**

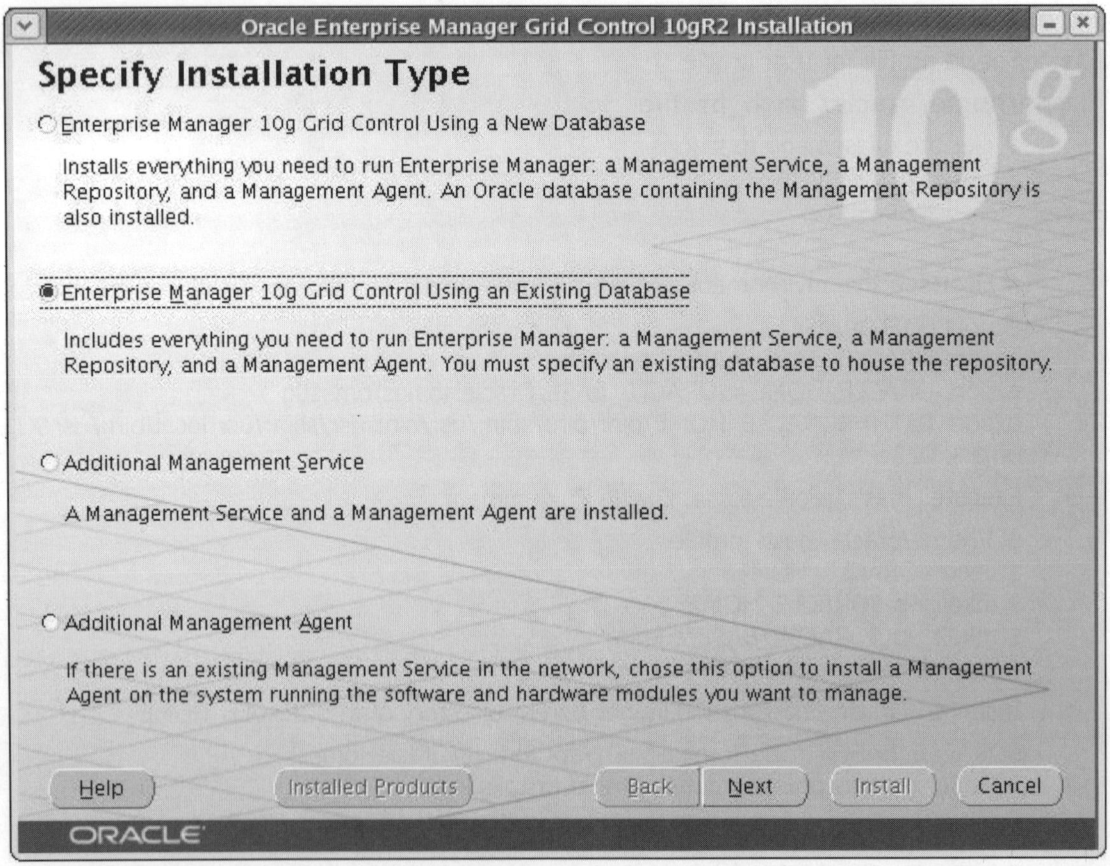

- Specify Installation Location: **/u01/app/oracle/OracleHomes**

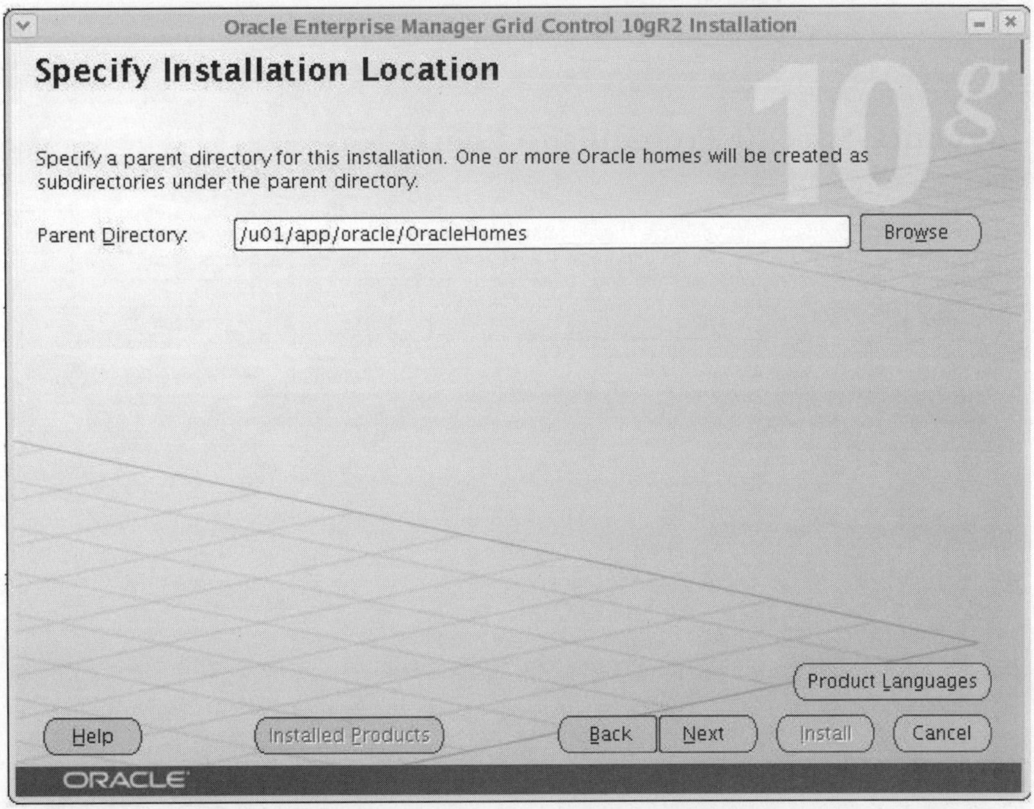

- Specify Inventory Diretcory and Credentials: **/u01/app/oraInventory**, OS Group: **oinstall**

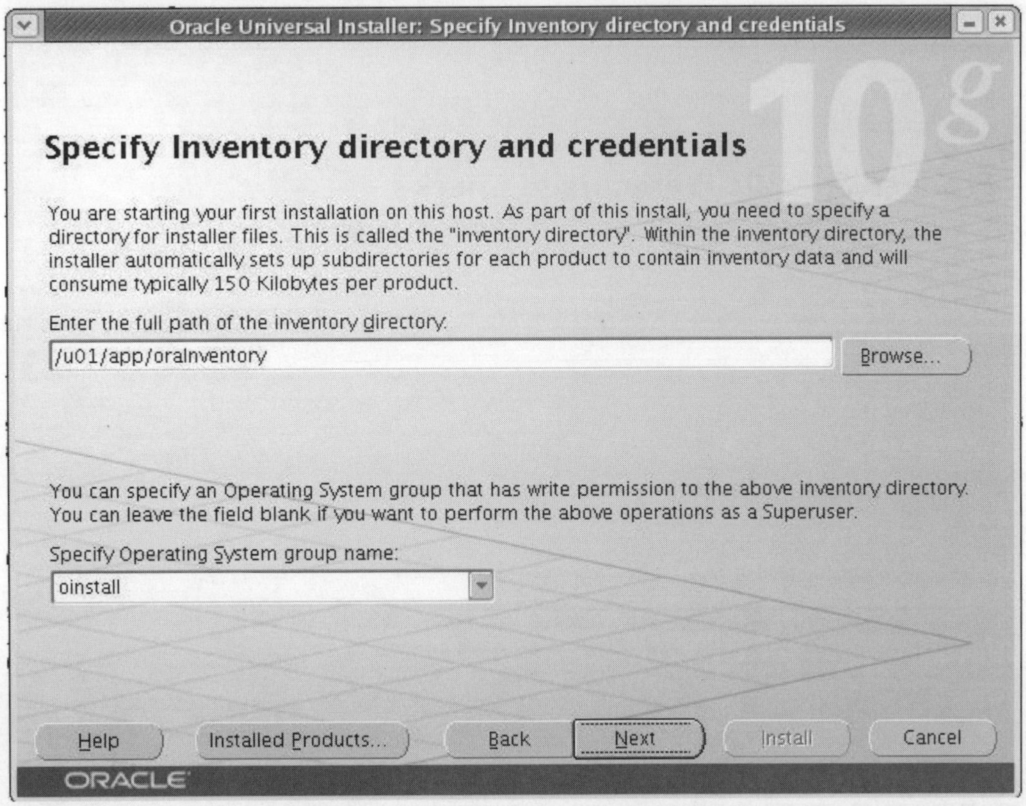

- Product-Specific Prerequisite Checks

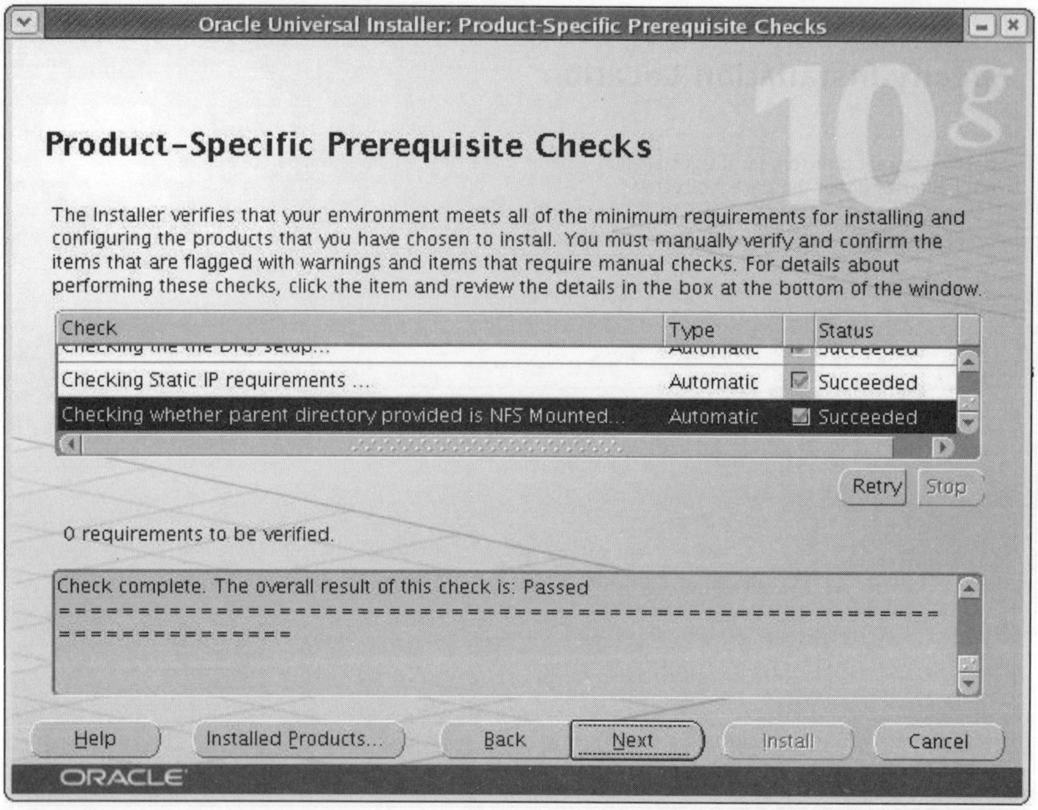

- Extra screen shots below: Sometime, if you get warnings as mentioned below, you could ignore and proceed. **Click YES**

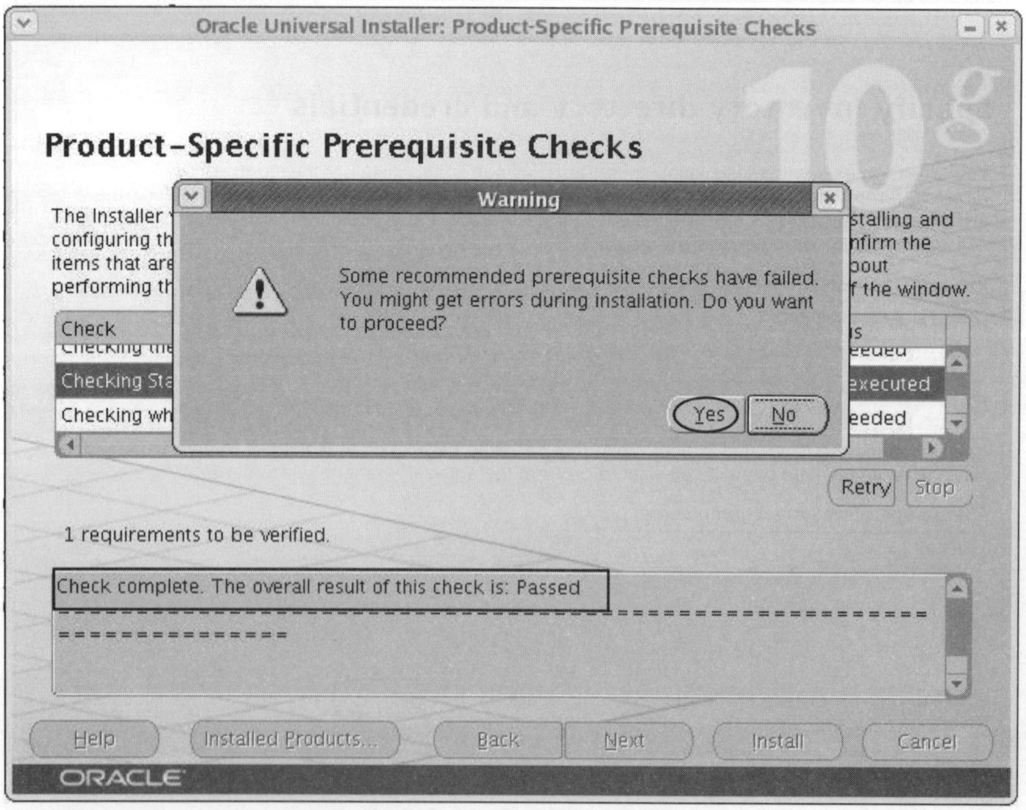

- Specify Repository Database Configuration.
  i. Database Hostname: **oem.prusolutions.com**
  ii. Port : **1521**
  iii. Service/SID: **oemdb**
  iv. SYS Password: **oracle**
  v. Management Tablespace Location: (Location of datafile on oemdb database) **/u01/app/oracle/oradata/oemdb/mgmt.dbf**
  vi. Configuration Data Tablespace Location: (Location of datafile on oemdb) **/u01/app/oracle/oradata/oemdb/mgmt_ecm_depot1.dbf**

  The above file location is common datafile file directory of **oemdb** database in oem machine

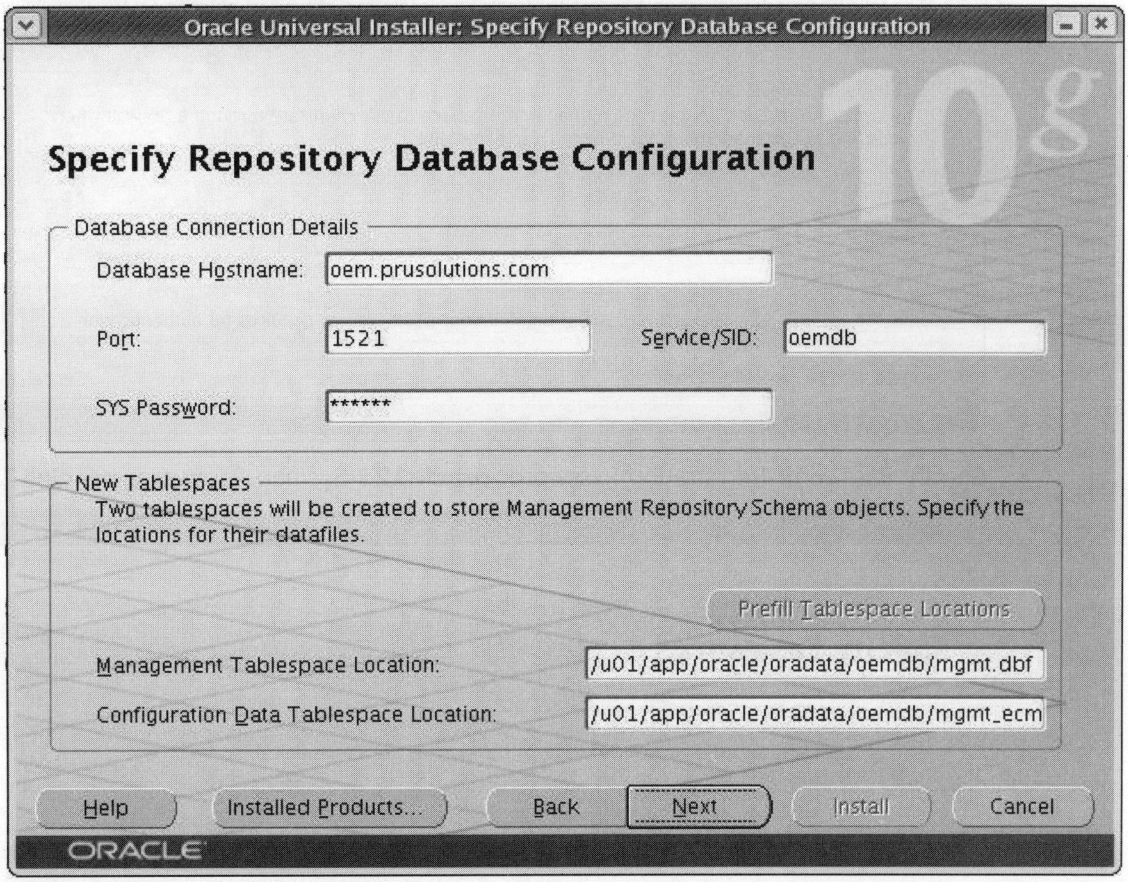

- Specify Optional Configuration : **Unselect** if not to configure oem through **METALINK**

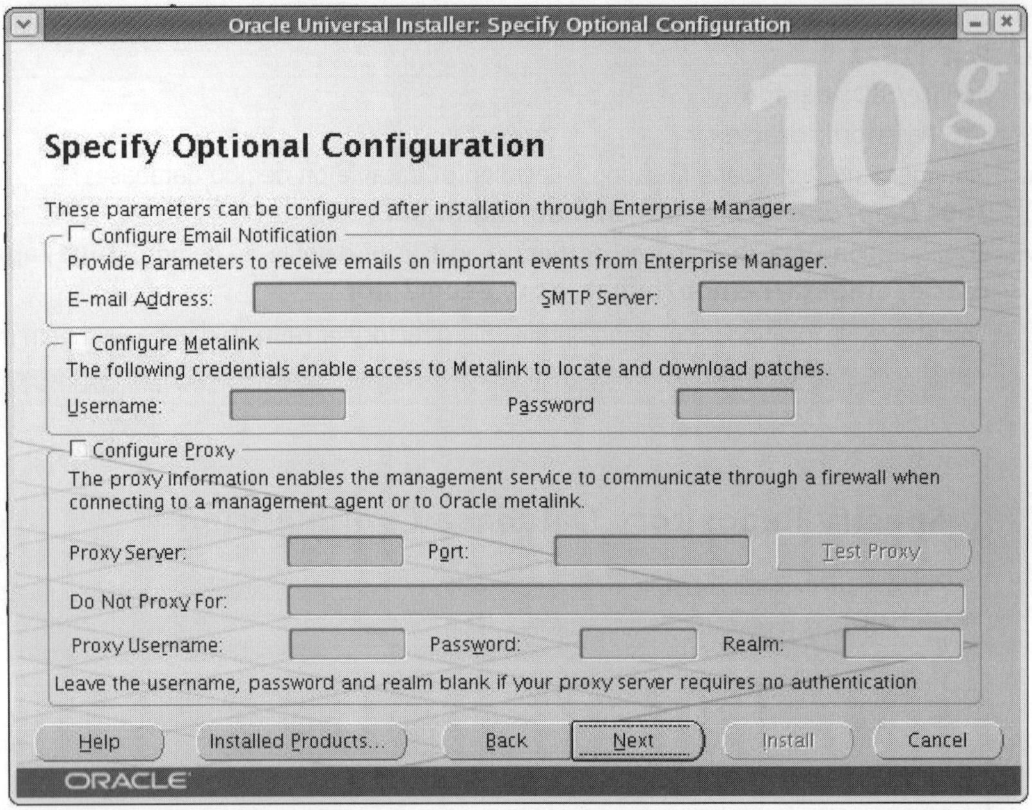

- Specify Password: Registration Password: **oracle123** Sysman Password: **oracle123**

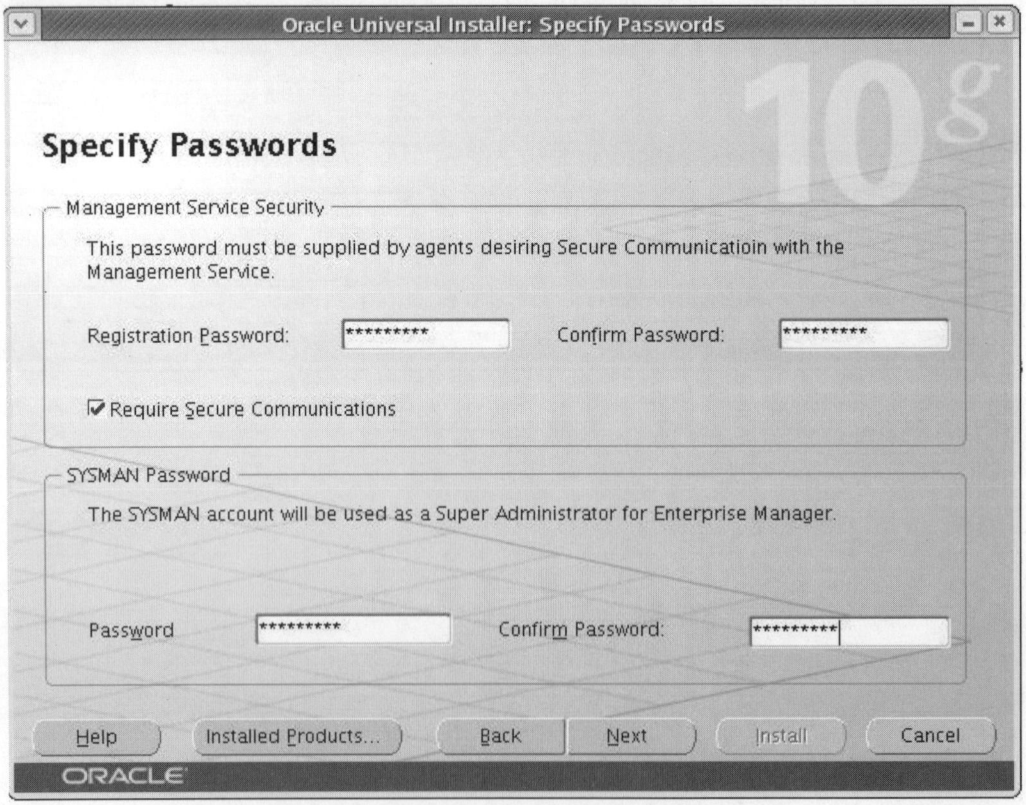

- Summary Screen : **Click Install**
- Install Screen : **Installation in Progress**
- On "oem" machine change directory to $ORACLE_BASE/admin/oemdb/bdump

[oracle@oem bdump]$ tail -f alert_oemdb.log

- Open a new Terminal window and sudo su and execute the scripts mentioned below in screen shot.

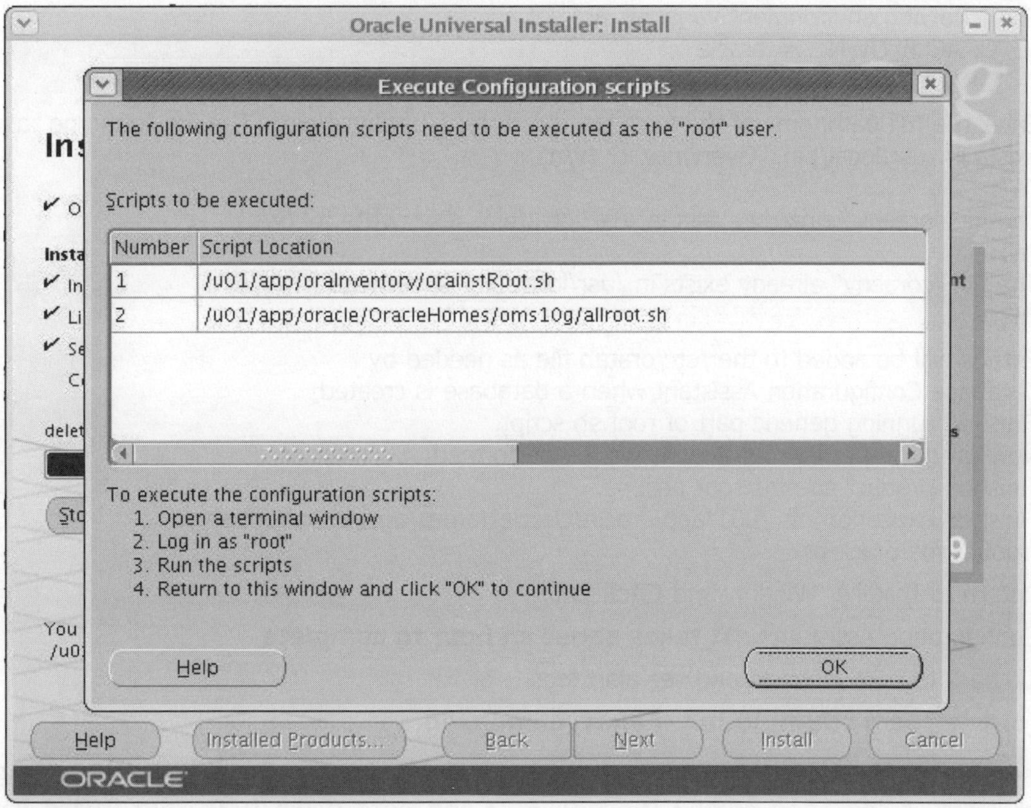

[oracle@oms ~]$ sudo su
Password:

[root@oms oracle]# /u01/app/oraInventory/orainstRoot.sh

Changing permissions of /u01/app/oraInventory to 770.
Changing groupname of /u01/app/oraInventory to oinstall.
The execution of the script is complete

[root@oms oracle]# /u01/app/oracle/OracleHomes/oms10g/allroot.sh

Starting to execute allroot.sh ...
Starting to execute /u01/app/oracle/OracleHomes/oms10g/root.sh ......
Running Oracle10 root.sh script...

The following environment variables are set as:
ORACLE_OWNER= oracle
ORACLE_HOME= /u01/app/oracle/OracleHomes/oms10g

Enter the full pathname of the local bin directory: [/usr/local/bin]:
Copying dbhome to /usr/local/bin ...
Copying oraenv to /usr/local/bin ...
Copying coraenv to /usr/local/bin ...

Creating /etc/oratab file...
Adding entry to /etc/oratab file...

```
    Entries will be added to the /etc/oratab file as needed by
Database Configuration Assistant when a database is created
Finished running generic part of root.sh script.
Now product-specific root actions will be performed.
Finished execution of  /u01/app/oracle/OracleHomes/oms10g/root.sh ......
Starting to execute /u01/app/oracle/OracleHomes/agent10g/root.sh ......
Running Oracle10 root.sh script...
The following environment variables are set as:
    ORACLE_OWNER= oracle
    ORACLE_HOME=  /u01/app/oracle/OracleHomes/agent10g
Enter the full pathname of the local bin directory: [/usr/local/bin]: The file "dbhome" already
exists in /usr/local/bin.  Overwrite it? (y/n)
[n]:
The file "oraenv" already exists in /usr/local/bin.  Overwrite it? (y/n)
[n]:
The file "coraenv" already exists in /usr/local/bin.  Overwrite it? (y/n)
[n]:
Entries will be added to the /etc/oratab file as needed by
Database Configuration Assistant when a database is created
Finished running generic part of root.sh script.
Now product-specific root actions will be performed.
Finished product-specific root actions.
Finished execution of  /u01/app/oracle/OracleHomes/agent10g/root.sh ......
[root@oms oracle]#
```

- Return to Installer Window and **Click OK**
- Configuration Assistants : **It takes about an hour to complete**
- Go back to oem machine and see alert logs

  [oracle@oem bdump]$ tail -f alert_oemdb.log

- The configuration will take an hour meanwhile you can create oracle user profile files for crs1,crs2,crsdg1 and crsdg2 (Section 8.3) and note down RAC Data Guard Parameters changes(Section 9.14) in notepad, that will be used when installing RAC and setting Data Guard.

- Configuration Assistants

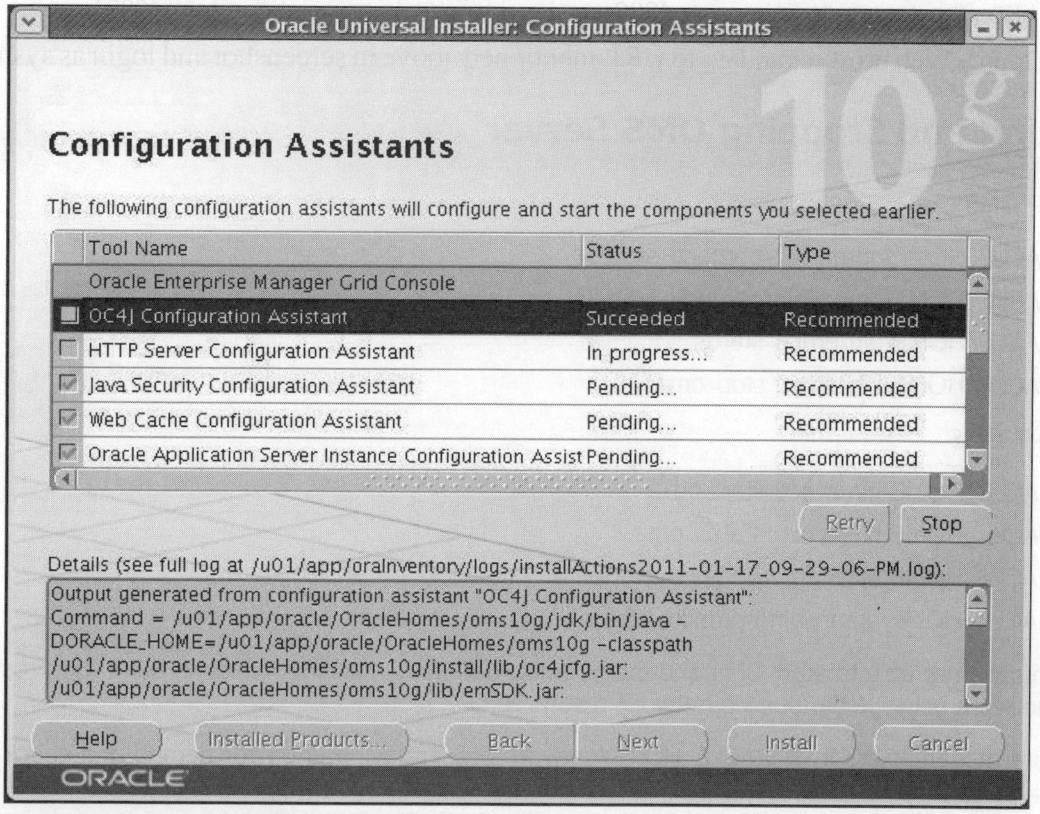

- End of Installation : **Exit**

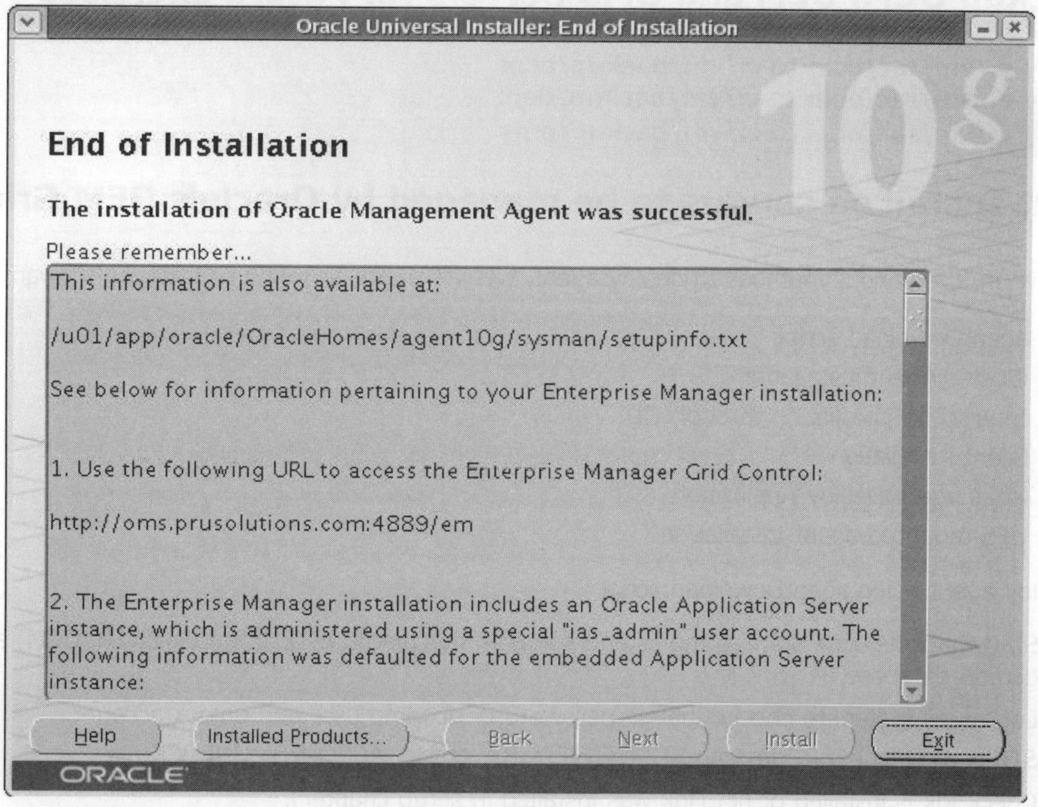

- Note the URL to access the Enterprise Manager Grid Control at End of Installation page http://hostname.domain.com: 4889/em i.e. http://oms.prusolutions.com:4889/em
- Open a Web browser and go to URL mentioned above in screenshot and login as sysman/oracle123

3.2 Starting and Stopping OMS Server

- STOP OMS

  $ORACLE_HOME/opmn/bin/opmnctl status
  $ORACLE_HOME/opmn/bin/opmnctl stopall
  $ORACLE_HOME/bin/emctl status
  $ORACLE_HOME/bin/emctl stop oms

- START OMS

  $ORACLE_HOME/bin/emctl start oms
  $ORACLE_HOME/bin/emctl status oms
  $ORACLE_HOME/opmn/bin/opmnctl startall
  $ORACLE_HOME/opmn/bin/opmnctl status

- If you are not able to start OMS and ping oemdb database machine, which is oem, then restart all network using /sbin/service network restart .
- Create tnsnames.ora in $ORACLE_HOME/network/admin having entry for oemdb and check if you are able to tnsping oemdb.

3.3 Backup OCM, OEM and OMS Servers for Future Exercises

Copy c:/vm/rac/ocm to c:/vm/backup/ocm
Copy c:/vm/rac/oem to c:/vm/backup/oem
Copy c:/vm/rac/oms to c:/vm/backup/oms

3.4 Agent Install on servers to be managed by Oracle's OEM Grid Control

- Below are the various methods to deploy agent, we will create as many possible on VMware server.

  i. agentDownload script
  ii. Cluster Agent installation
  iii. Interactive installation through OUI
  iv. Silent installation
  v. Mass agent Deploy Application
  vi. NFS-mounted agent installation

- Deploy agent using agentDownload script
  - Start machine ocm, start all the listeners in ocm machine (LISTENER, LISTENER_OCM) and startup ocmdb database.
  - Log on as system to check. Change password of dbsnmp user and unlock account.

    SQL> ALTER USER dbsnmp IDENTIFIED BY oracle ACCOUNT UNLOCK;
  - Check jdk is installed or not (jdk was installed in setup chapter).

    [oracle@ocm ~]$ which java

If not installed ftp the downloaded software **jdk-6u21-linux-i586-rpm.bin**
As a root user install **jdk-6u21-linux-i586-rpm.bin** on target server where agent has to install.
After install check, java is configured.

[root@ocm software]#/u01/software/jdk/jdk-6u21-linux-i586-rpm.bin

[root@ocm software]# which java
/usr/bin/java

- Logon to oms machine where Oracle's OEM Grid software is installed and secure copy **agentDownload.linux** to target machine <AGENT_HOME> parent directory where agent has to be deployed

  <OMS_HOME>/oms10g/sysman/agent_download/10.2.0.1.0/linux

  [oracle@oms ~]$ cd /u01/app/oracle/OracleHomes/oms10g/sysman/ agent_download/ 10.2.0.1.0/linux

  [oracle@oms linux]$ scp agentDownload.linux ocm:/u01/app/oracle/product/ 10.2.0

  The authenticity of host 'ocm (192.168.2.121)' can't be established.
  RSA key fingerprint is f4:ac:d2:7e:05:e8:4e:47:a9:6f:80:99:46:f9:f7:58.
  Are you sure you want to continue connecting (yes/no)? yes
  Warning: Permanently added 'ocm,192.168.2.121' (RSA) to the list of known hosts.
  oracle@ocm's password:
  agentDownload.linux 100% 22KB 22.3KB/s 00:00

- On ocm machine execute agent_profile

  . /home/oracle/agent_profile
  to change directory to parent directory of <AGENT_HOME>

  [oracle@ocm ~]$ cd /u01/app/oracle/product/10.2.0

  [oracle@ocm 10.2.0]$ ls –ltr

- Change agentDownload.linux file permission

  [oracle@ocm 10.2.0]$ chmod 755 agentDownload.linux

- Install Agent using agentDownload script

  [oracle@ocm 10.2.0]$ ./agentDownload.linux -b /u01/app/oracle/product/10.2.0 -m oms.prusolutions.com -r 4889

  The following configuration scripts need to be executed as the "root" user.
  #!/bin/sh
  #Root script to run
  /u01/app/oracle/product/10.2.0/agent10g/root.sh

- Open a new terminal, sudo su and execute root.sh script

  [oracle@ocm ~]$ sudo su
  Password:

  [root@ocm oracle]# /u01/app/oracle/product/10.2.0/agent10g/root.sh

- Once agent is installed, secure agent and upload agent to Oracle's OEM Grid.

  Here $ORACLE_HOME is <AGENT_HOME> **. /home/oracle/agent_profile**

  $ORACLE_HOME/bin/emctl stop agent
  $ORACLE_HOME/bin/emctl secure agent
  $ORACLE_HOME/bin/emctl clearstate agent
  $ORACLE_HOME/bin/emctl start agent
  $ORACLE_HOME/bin/emctl upload

- How to reset agent Time zone.

  Execute following command on OMS database oemdb as sysman user.

SQL> EXEC mgmt_target.set_agent_tzrgn('oem.prusolutions.com:3872','US/Eastern');

- If you get TIME ZONE errors, then apply Oracle's OEM Patch mentioned below and redo agent configuration again.

  i. gc_10205_part1of2
  ii. gc_10205_part2of2

- Configure Database in Oracle's OEM GRID Control

  On Oracle's OEM Grid page, Database tab, if Database is not configured then, configure database ocmdb manually.

  - Add Database Instance Target: Specify Host **ocm.prusolutions.com,** Click **Continue**

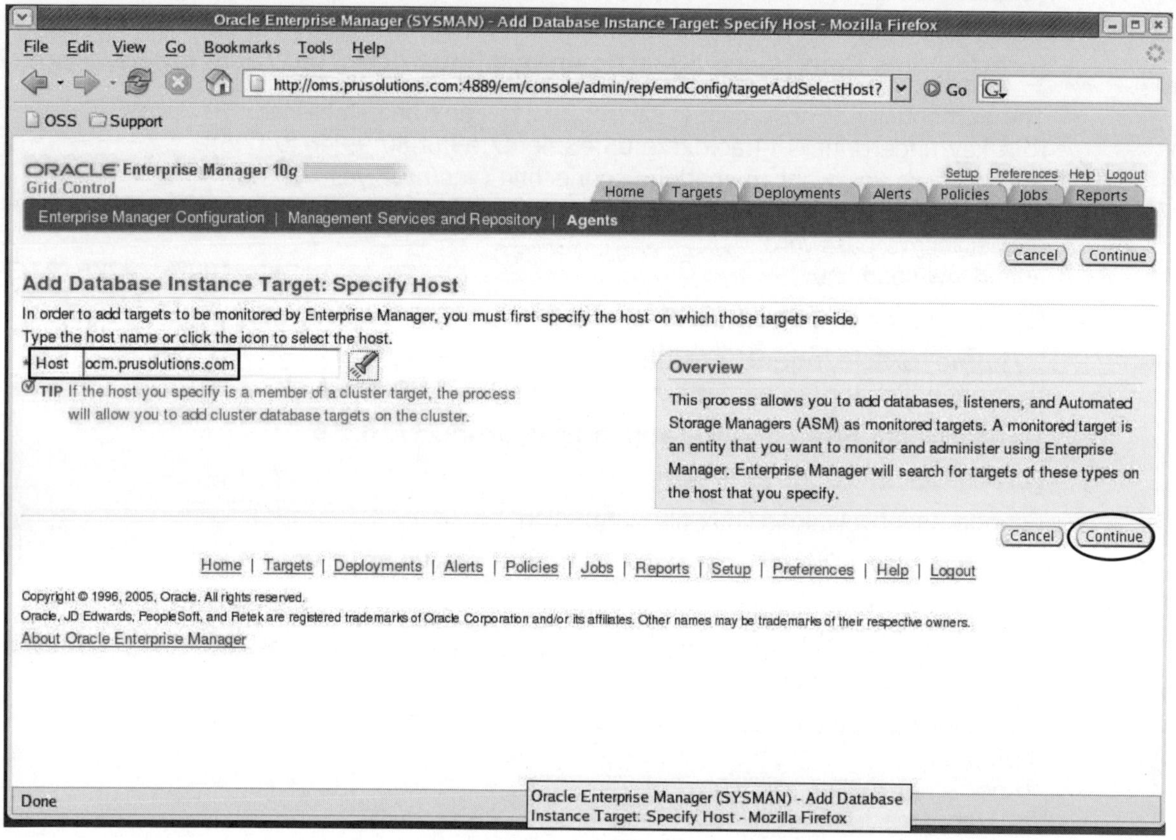

- On Targets page **Click Add**

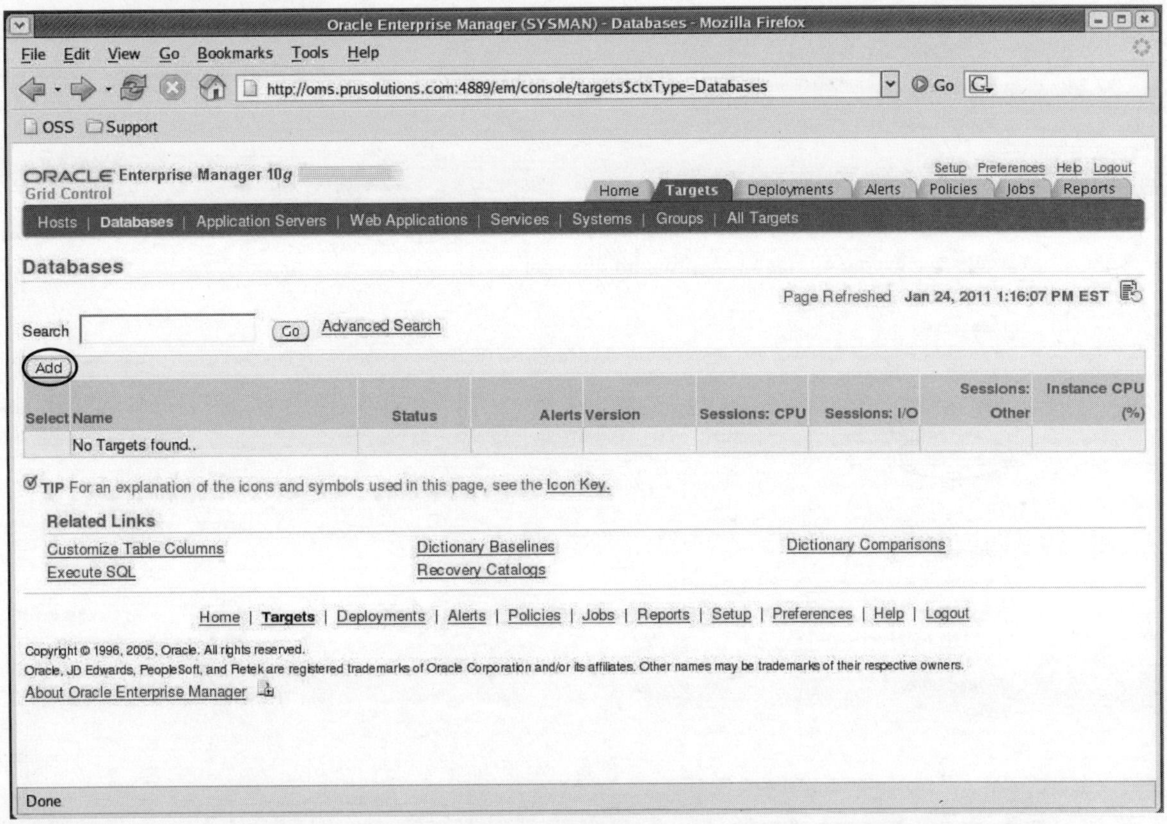

- Select host ocm.prusolutions.com and Click **Continue**

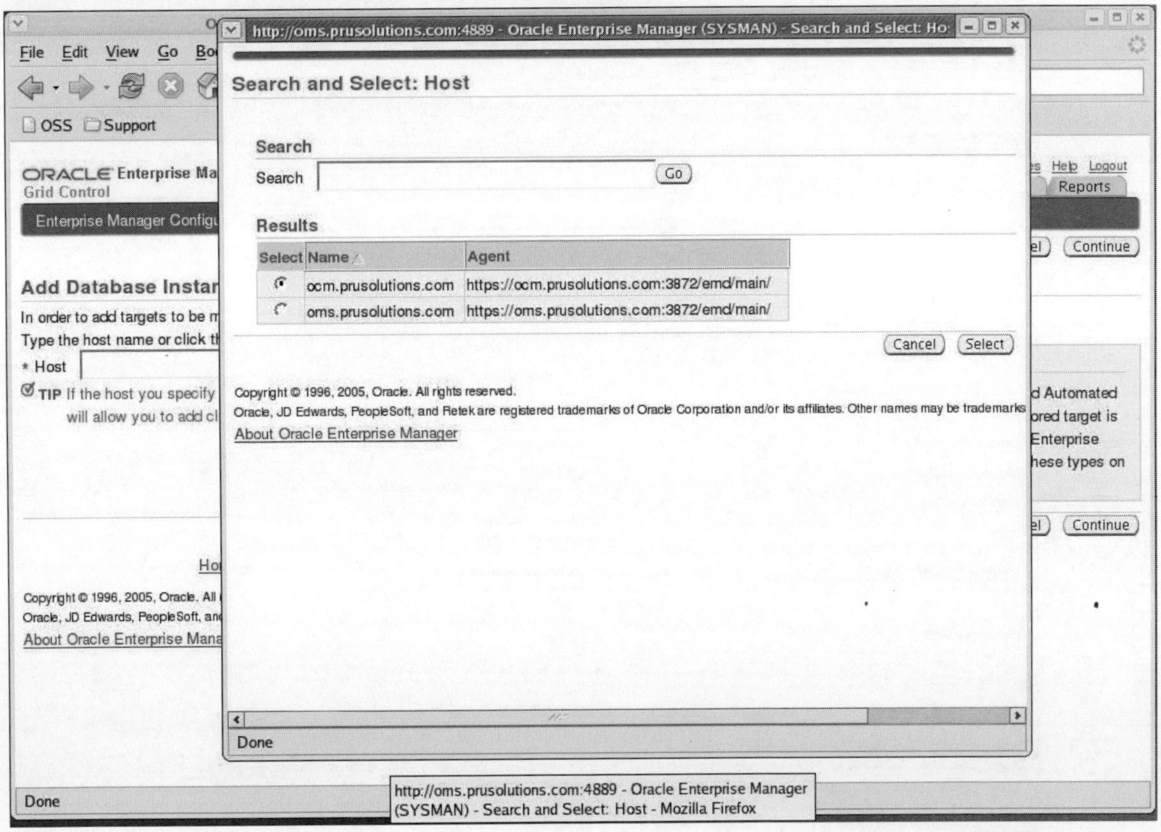

- On Targets Discovered on Host : **Manually Add Database**

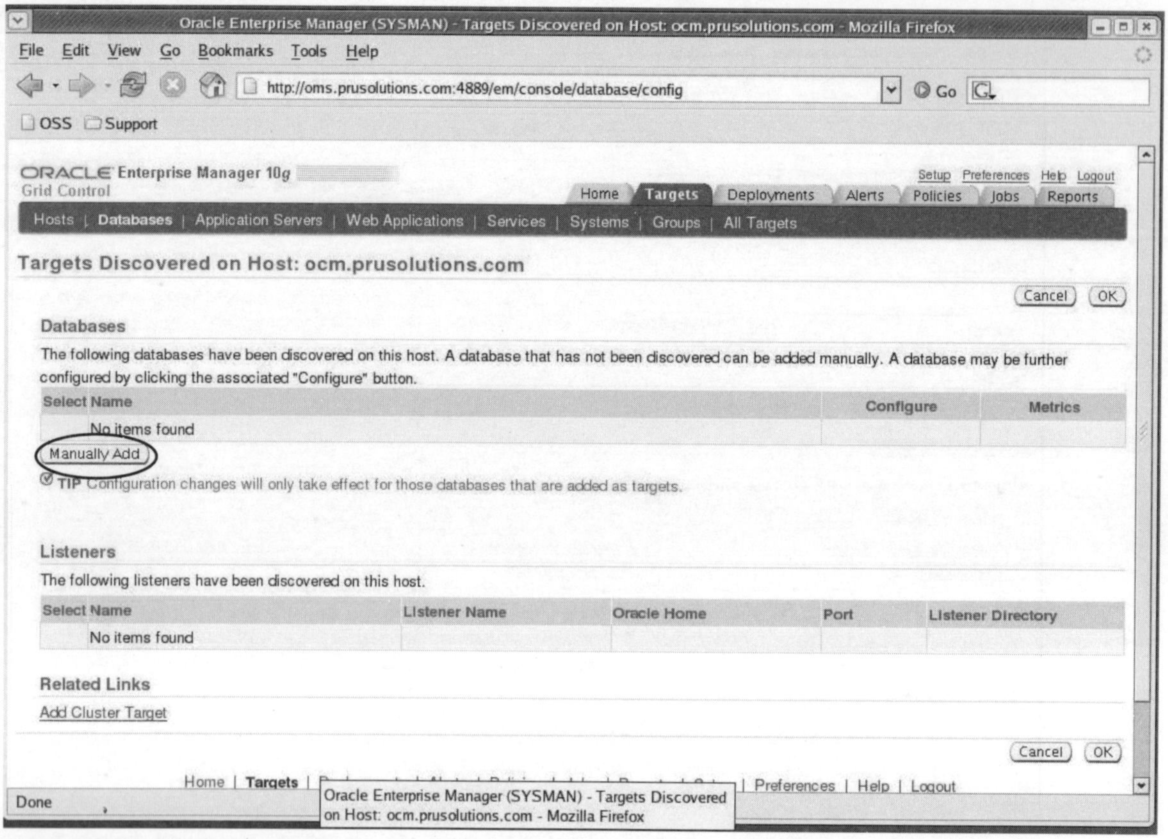

- Test Connection

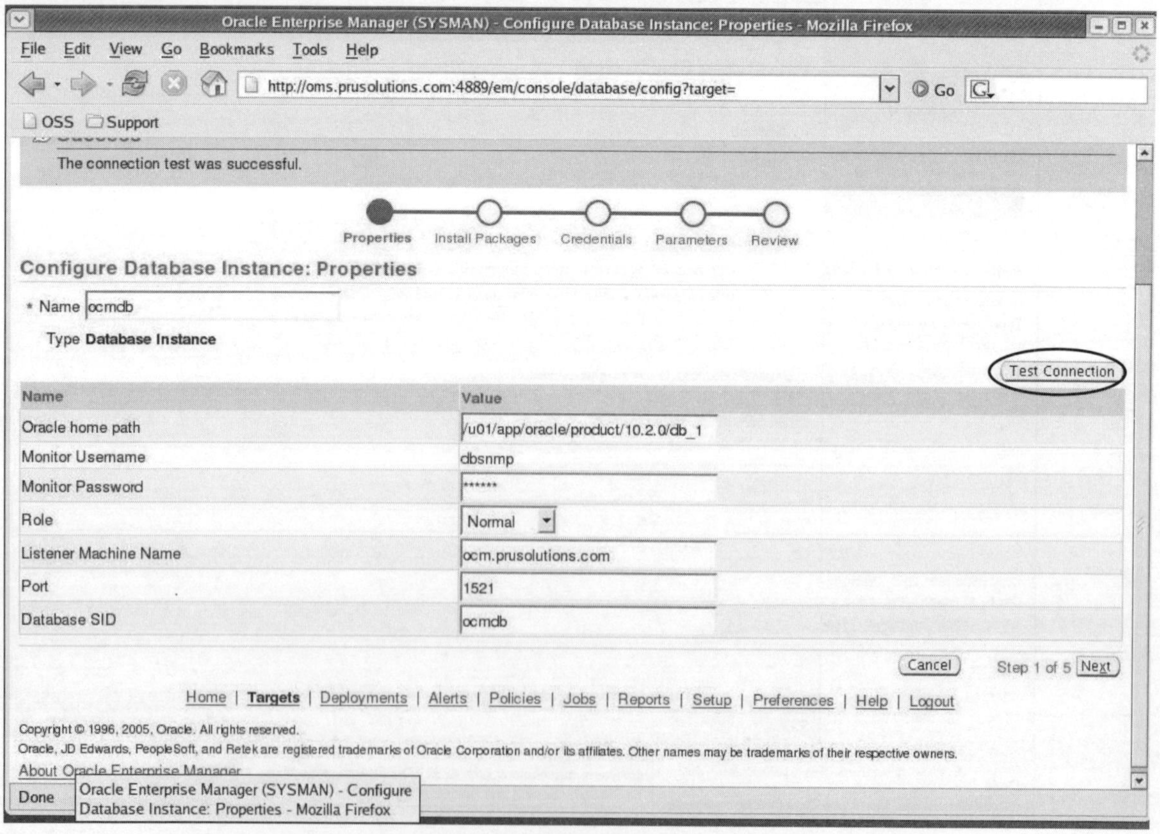

- Review the changes and Click OK

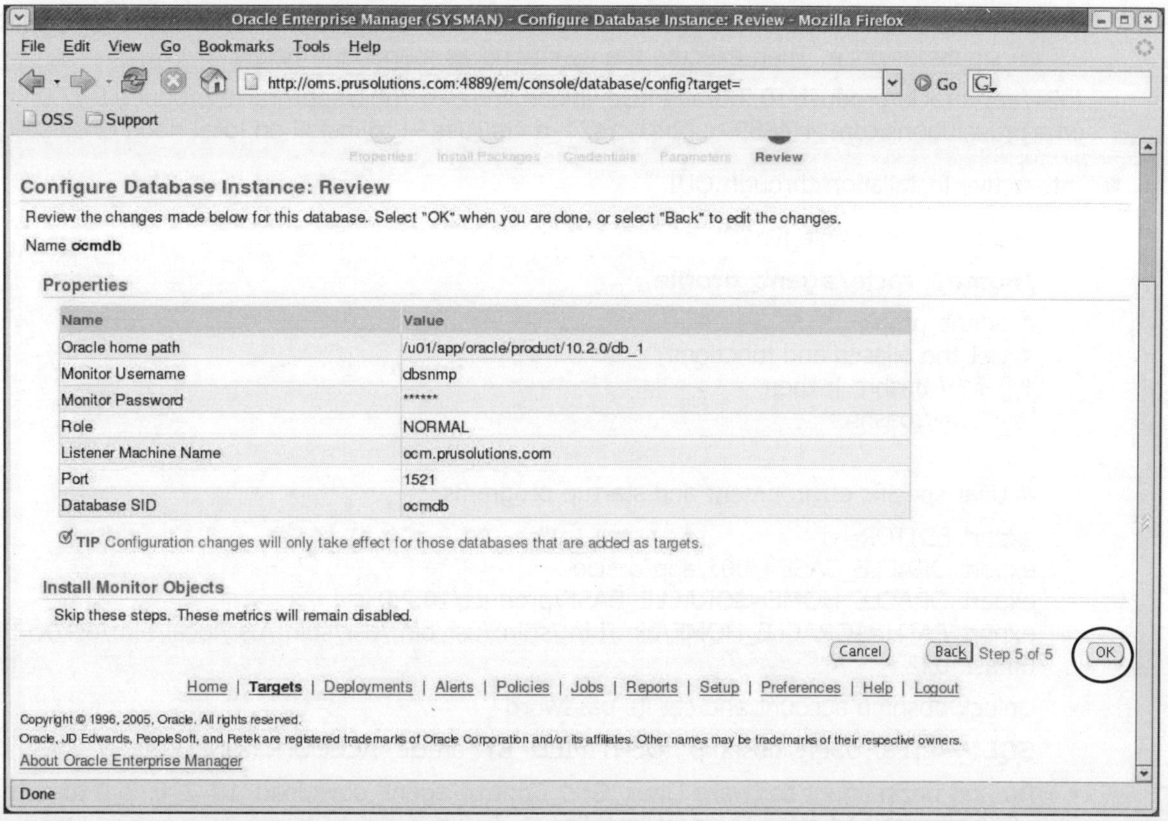

- Targets Tab Database Page: Target saving in Progress

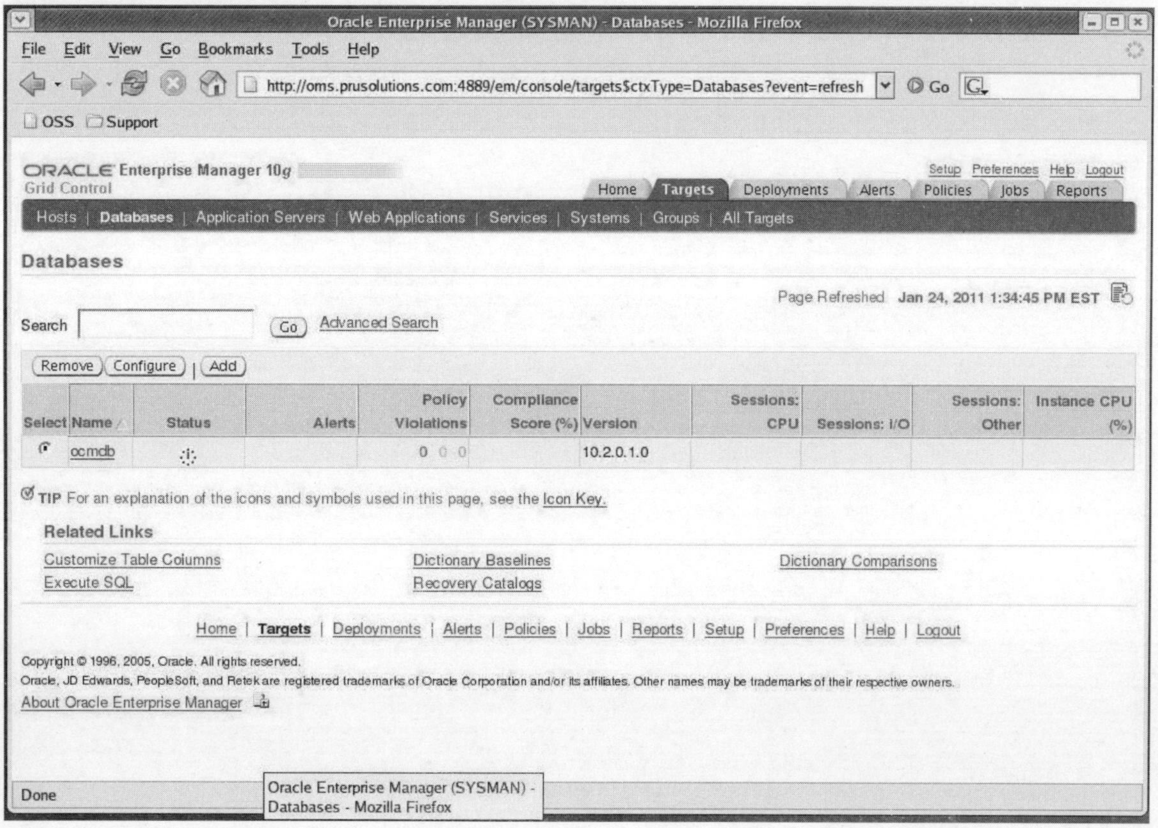

- Cluster Agent installation
  - Do setup on all nodes where agent has to be installed as setup was done above for agentDownload script on single instance. Then execute the command as mentioned below.

  /u01/app/oracle/product/10.2.0/agentDownload.linux -b /u01/app/oracle/product/10.2.0 -m oms.prusolutions.com -r 4889 -c "crs1,crs2" -n crs (use –l to install on local node of cluster)

- Interactive installation through OUI
  - Create agent_profile file

    /home/oracle/agent_profile

```
# agent_profile
# Get the aliases and functions
if [ -f ~/.bashrc ]; then
        . ~/.bashrc
fi

# User specific environment and startup programs

export EDITOR=vi
export ORACLE_BASE=/u01/app/oracle
export ORACLE_HOME=$ORACLE_BASE/product/10.2.0
export PATH=$ORACLE_HOME/bin:/bin:/sbin:/usr/bin:/usr/sbin:/usr/local/bin:/usr/X11R6/bin
umask 022
```

  - Unlock dbsnmp account and set its password

    SQL> ALTER USER dbsnmp IDENTIFIED BY oracle ACCOUNT UNLOCK;

  - ftp and unzip agent software Linux_Grid_Control_agent_download_10_2_0_2_0 to oem machine in /u01/software and execute agent installer
  - Run Installer

    [oracle@oem agent]$ /u01/software/linux/agent/runInstaller

- Specify Installation Type: **Additional Management Agent**

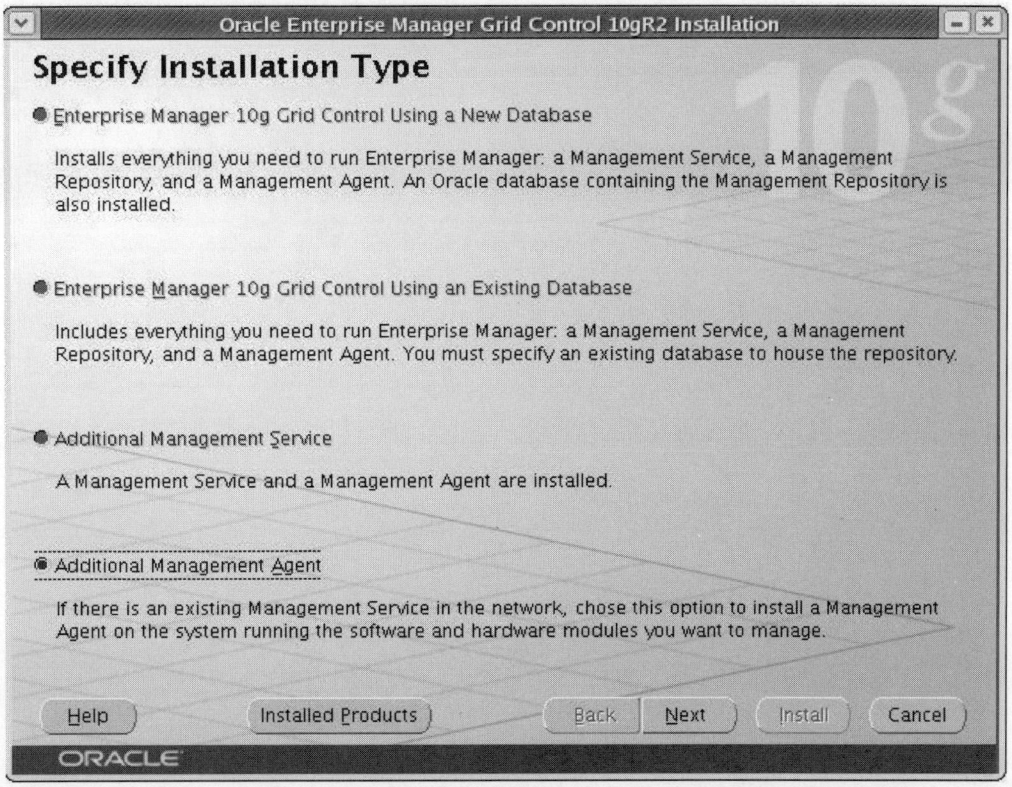

- Specify Installation Location :**Select parent directory of <AGENT_HOME>**

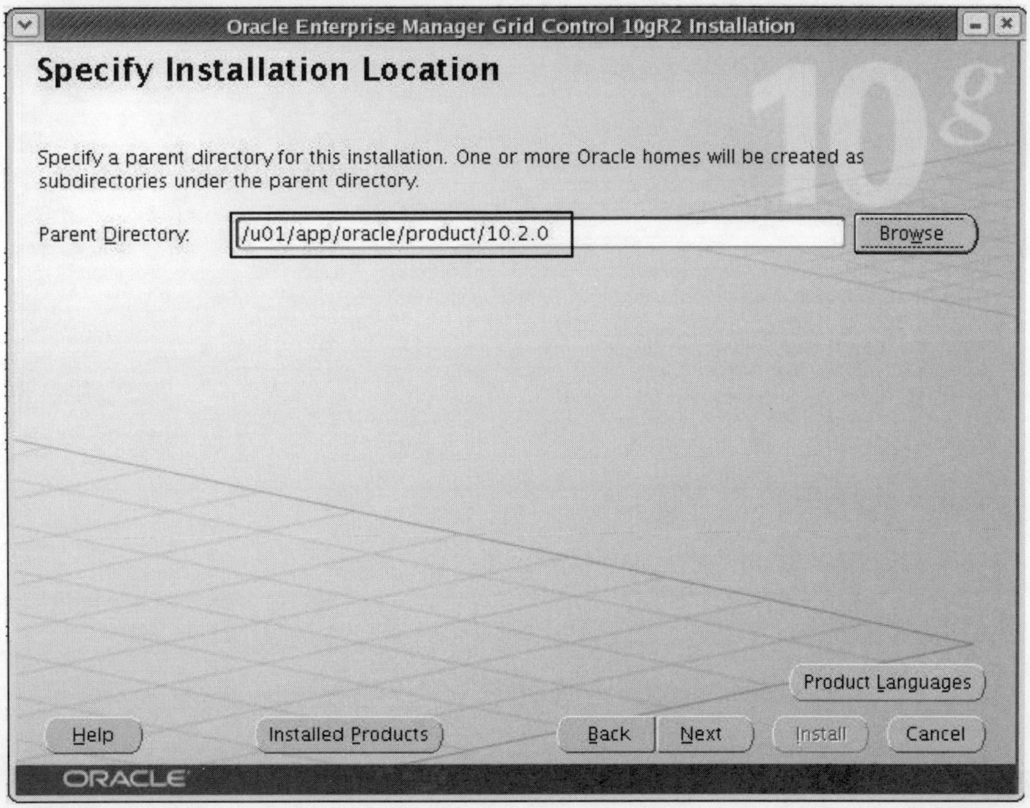

- Specify Oracle management Service Location: Management Service Host Name:**oms.prusolutions.com**, Management Service Port: **4889**

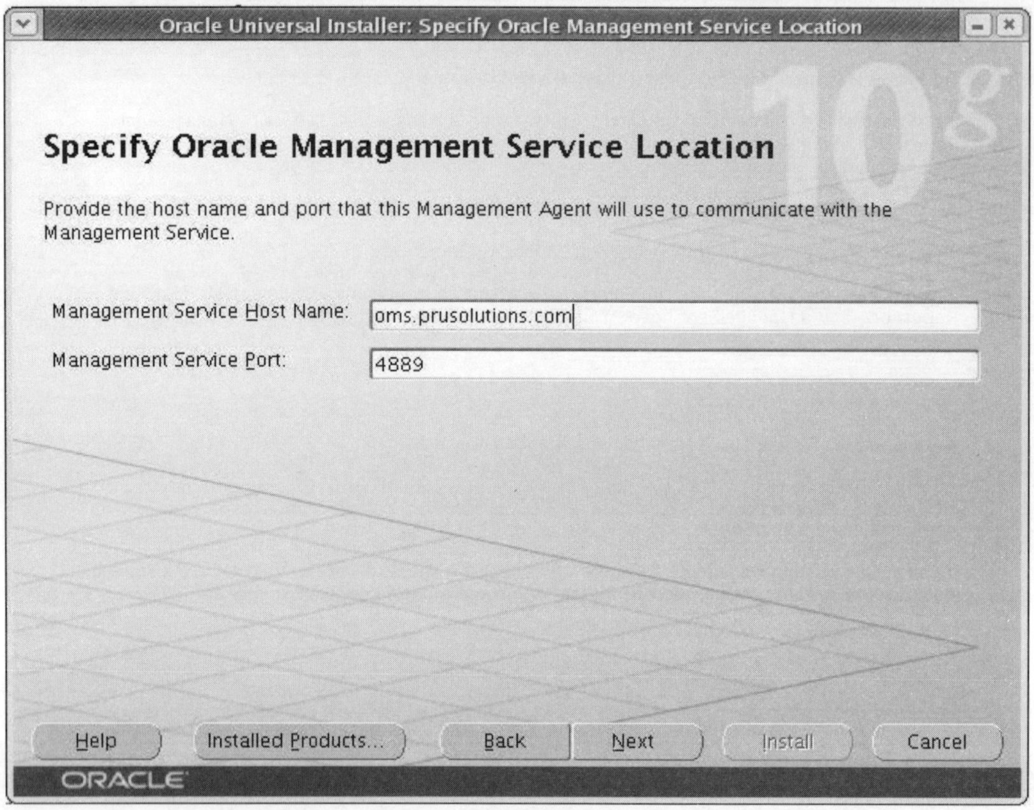

- Specify Agent Registration Password: **oracle123**

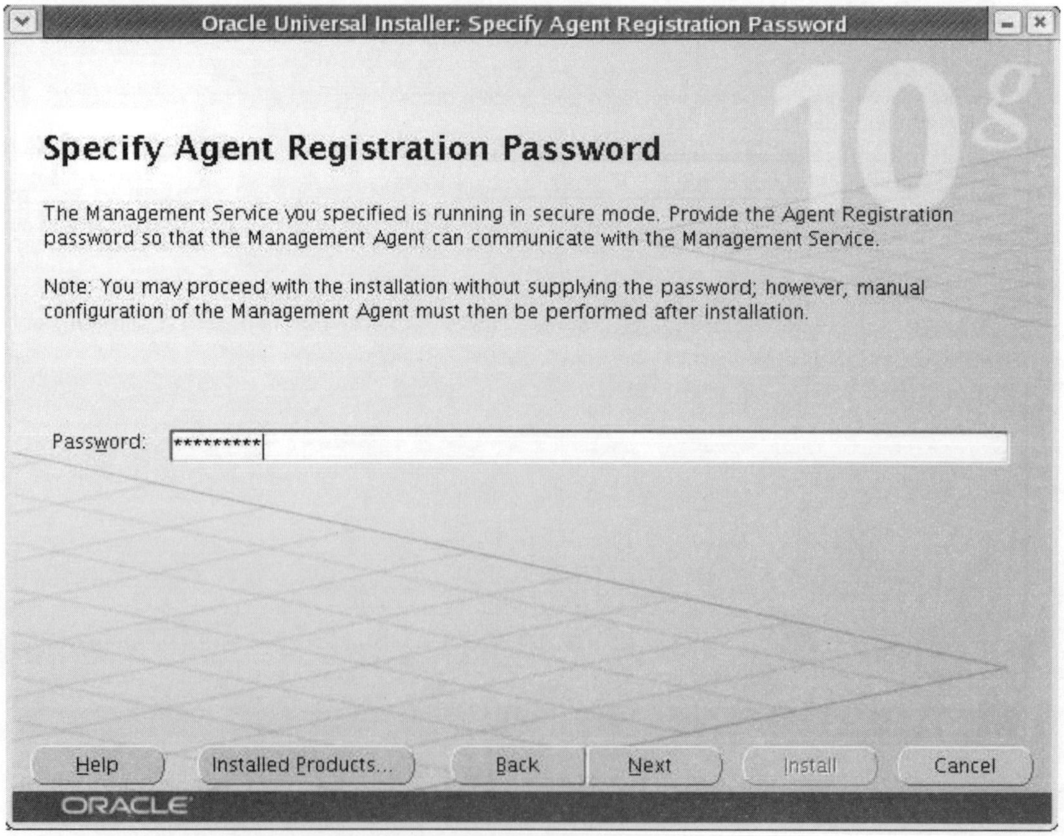

- Oracle Configuration Manager Agreement: **Decline License Agreement**

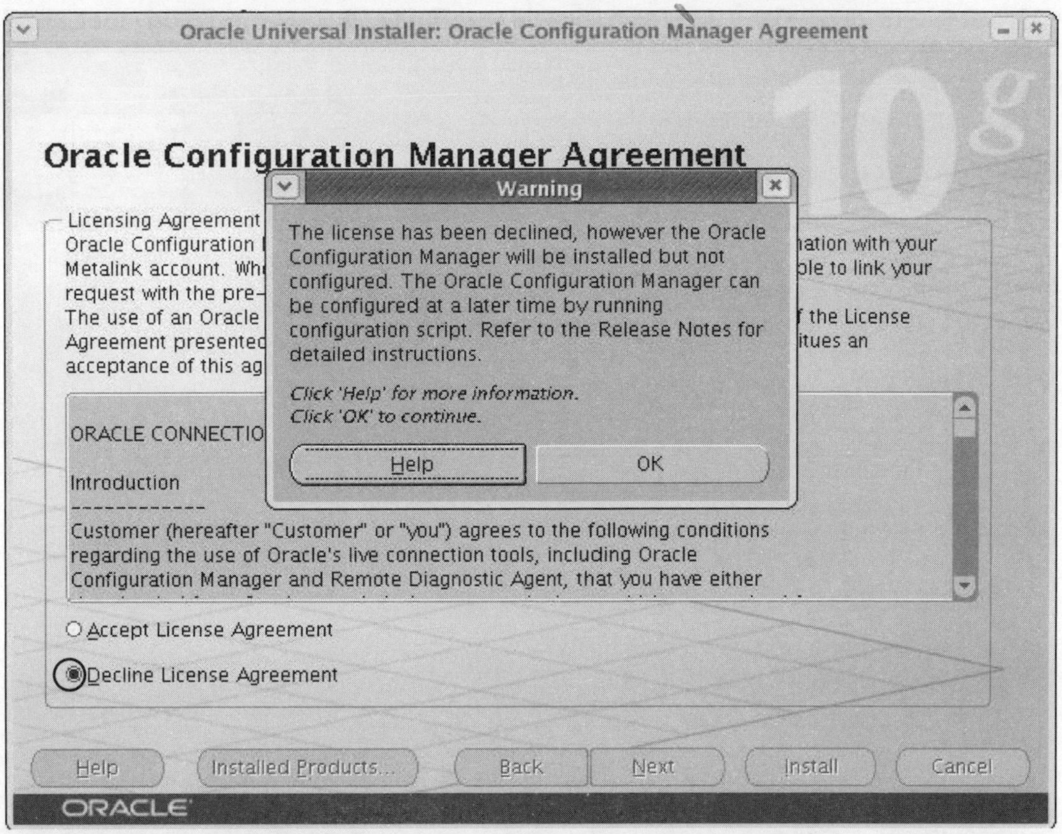

- Summary Page: **Click Install**

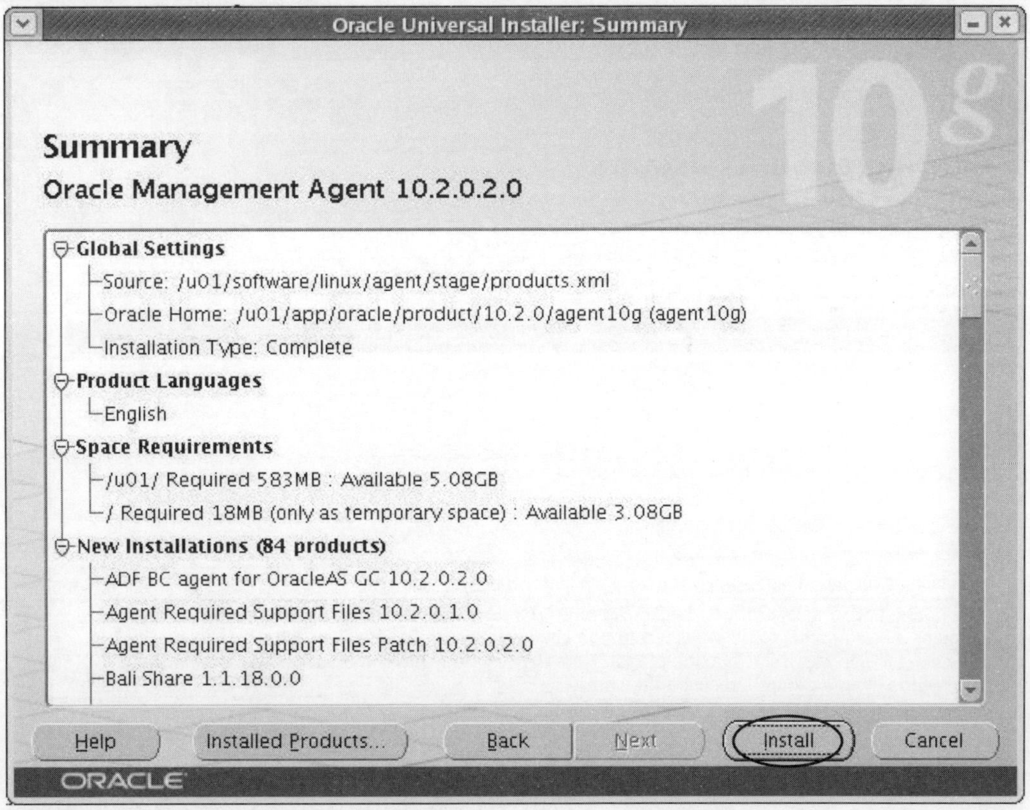

- Execute Configuration Scripts as root user

[root@oem oracle]# /u01/app/oracle/product/10.2.0/agent10g/root.sh

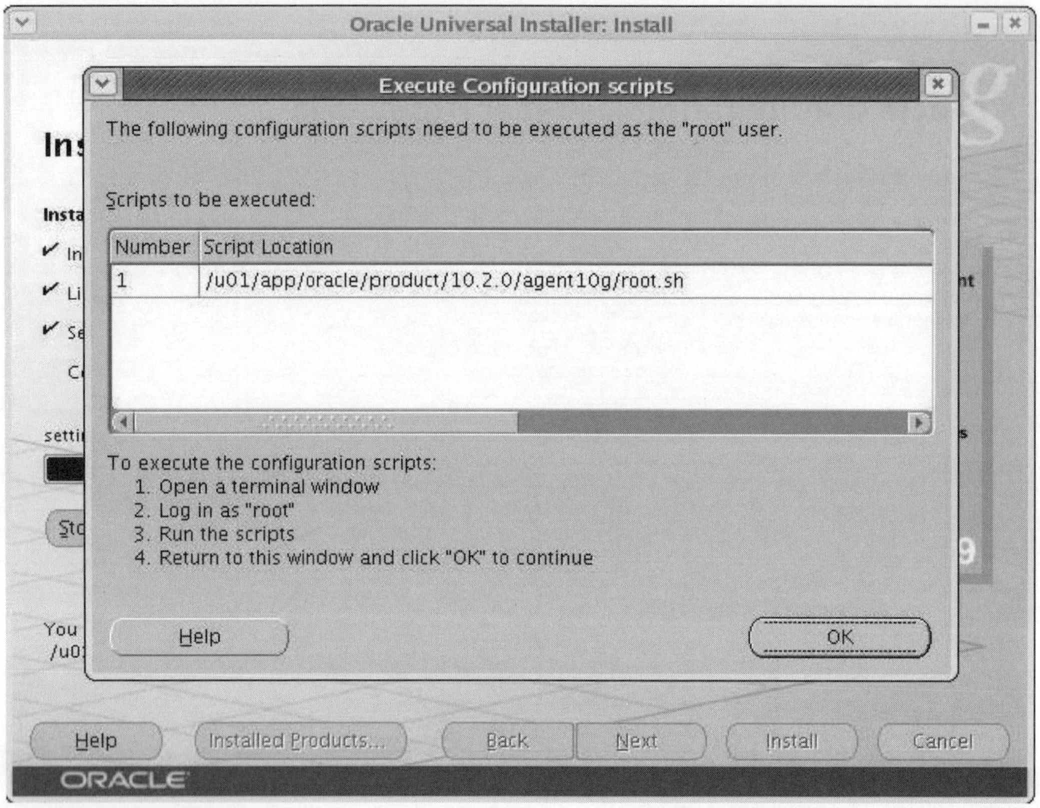

- Configuration Assistants

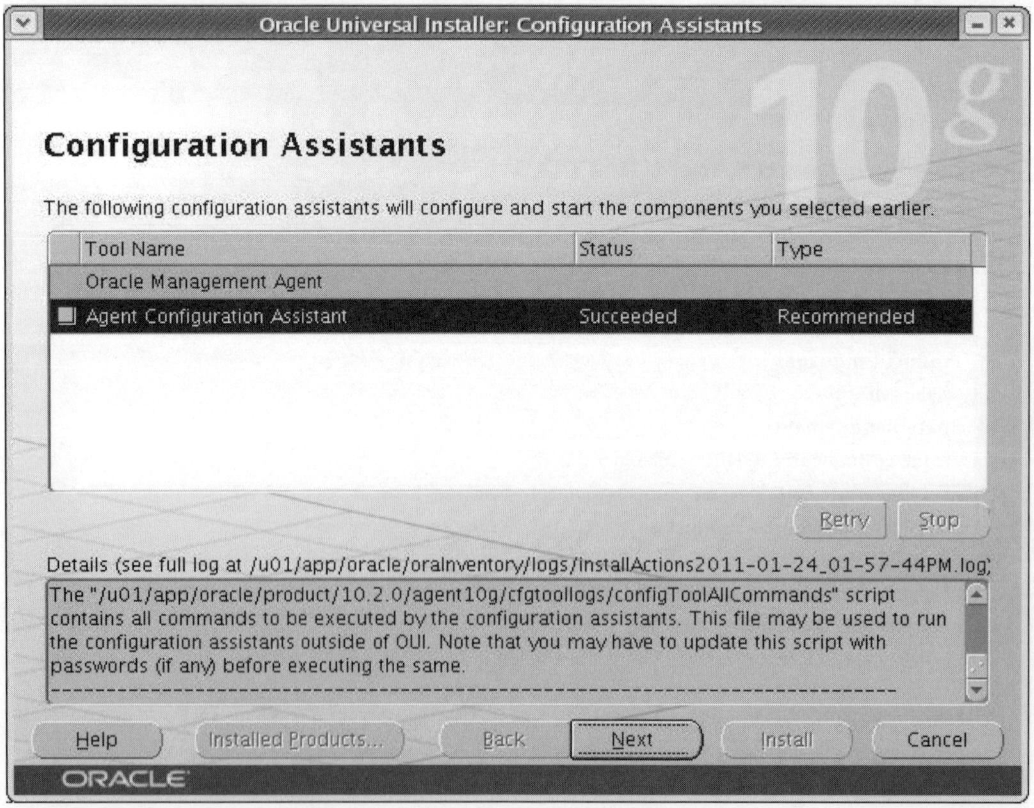

- End of Installation

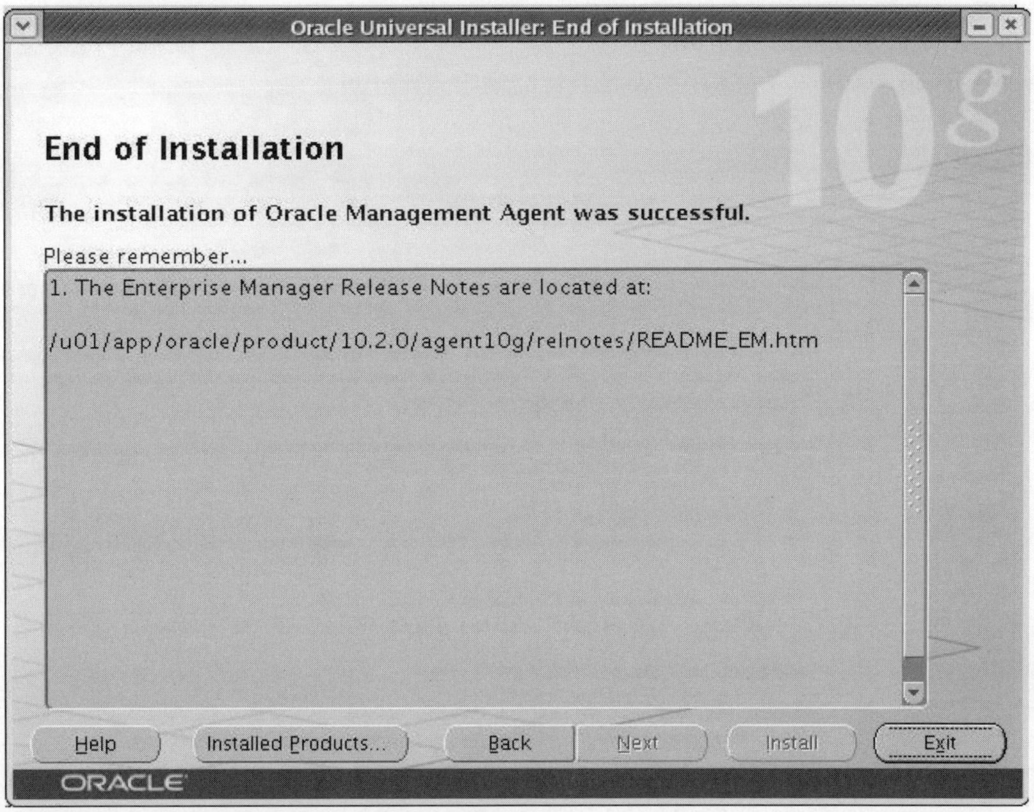

- Create Enterprise Manager Grid Control Users
  - Click Setup on upper right side corner

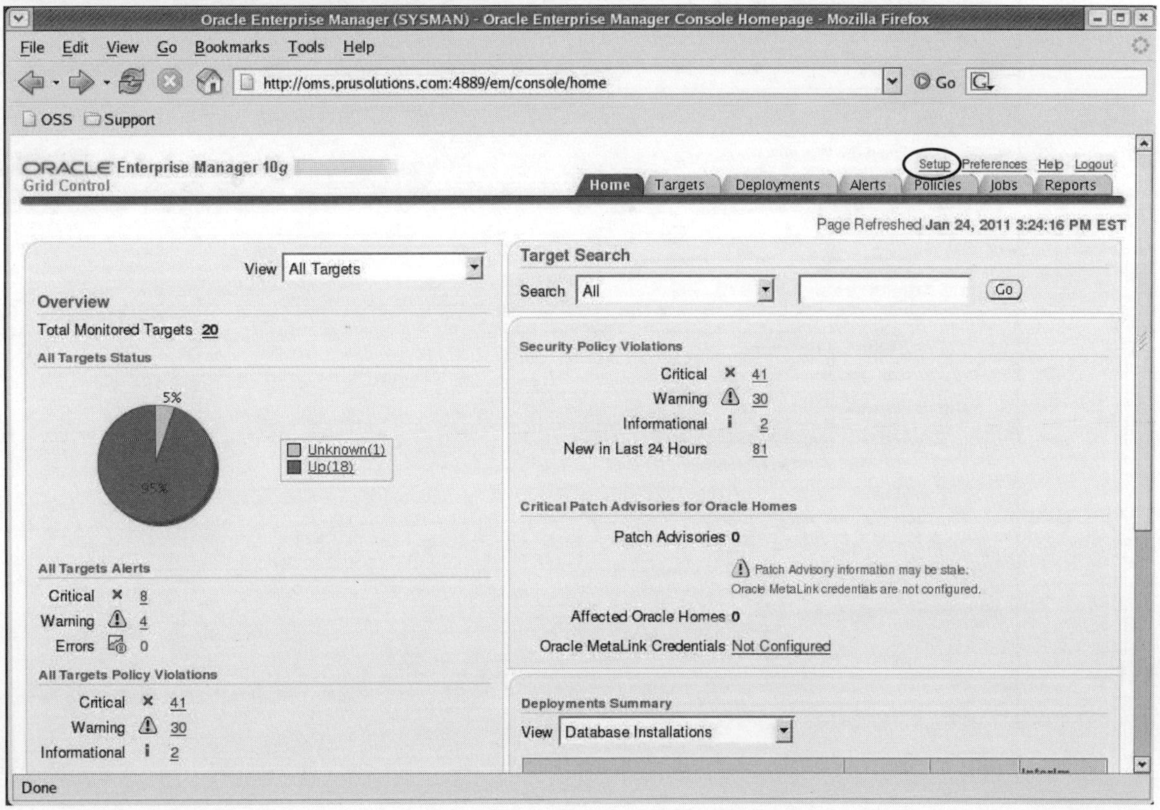

- Add Administrators

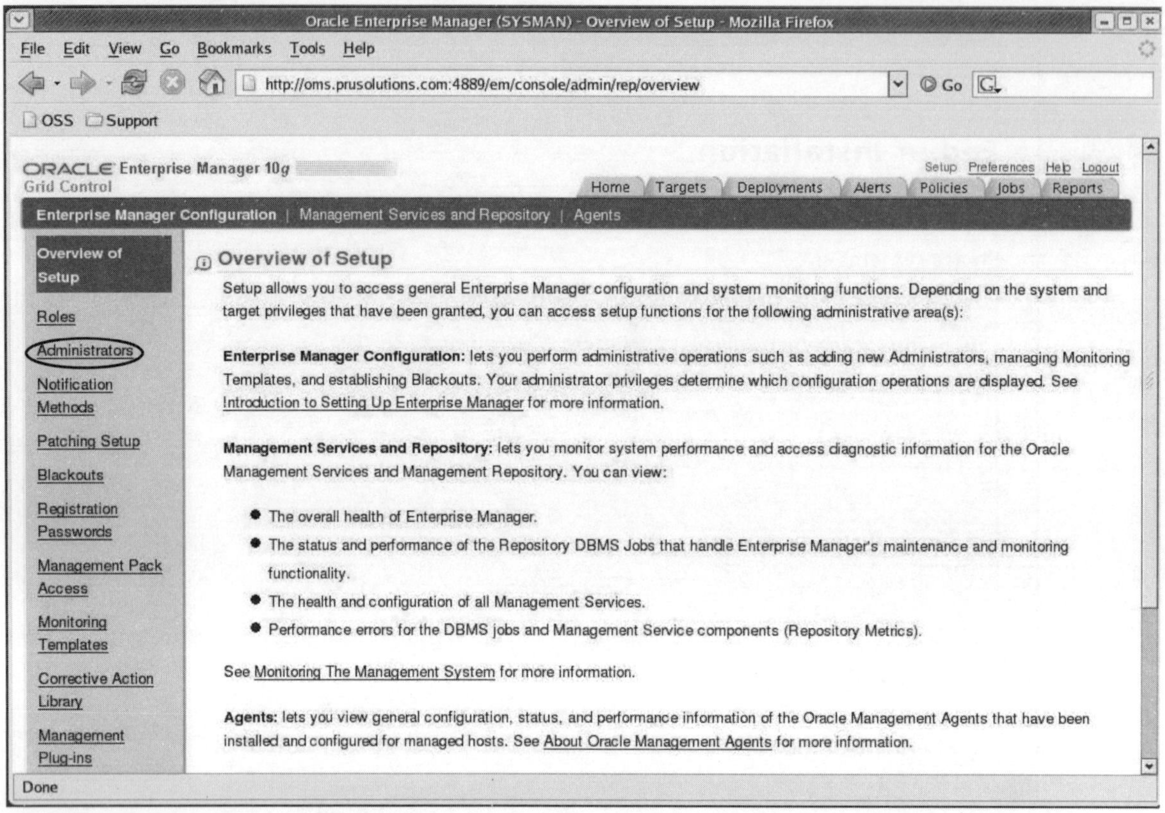

- Select SYSTEM and click **create like** and provide Username Password and Email Address Click Next and Finish Setup.

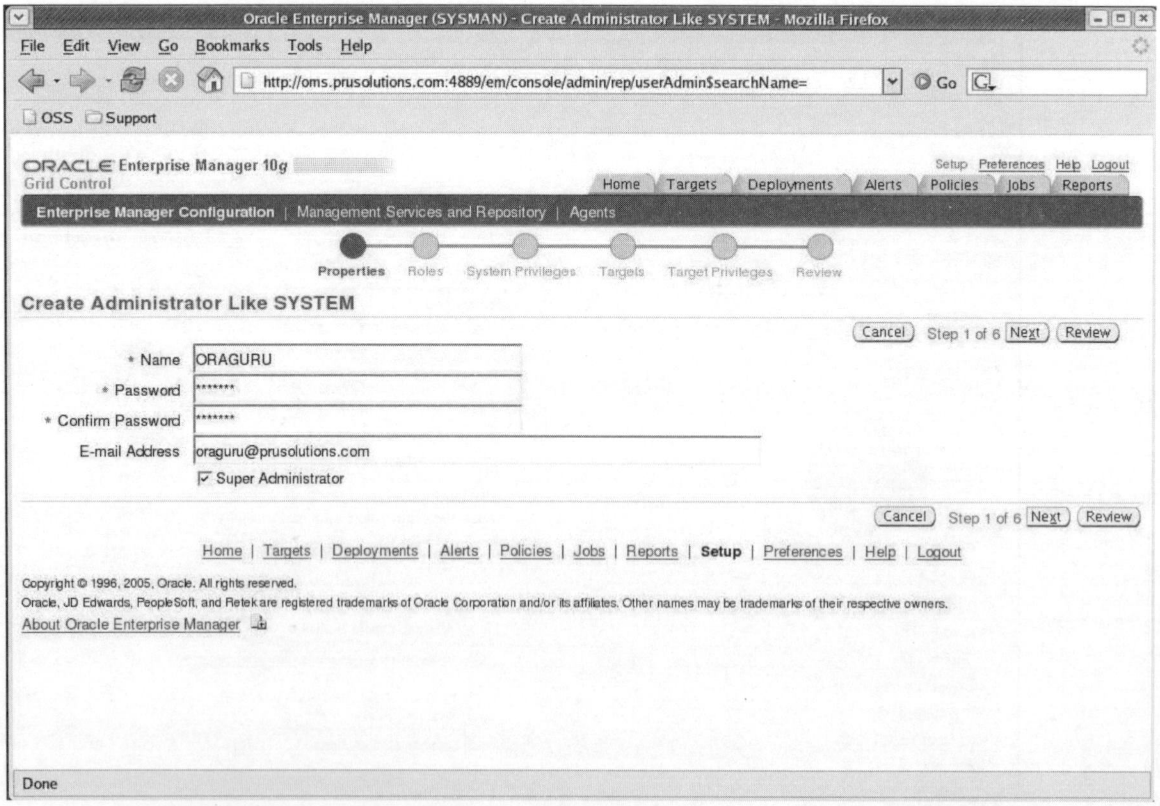

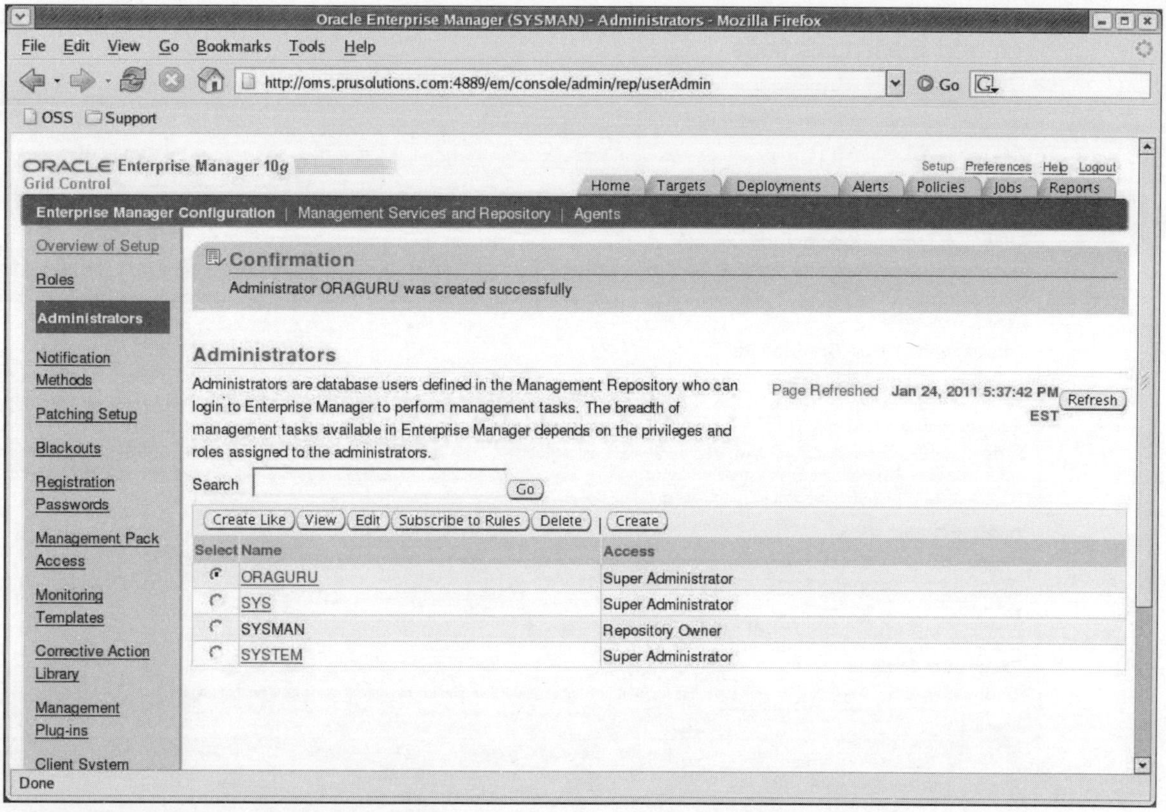

- Now we will perform all Oracle's OEM Grid exercises using **ORAGURU** user. Logout of Oracle's OEM Grid and then login as ORAGURU user
- Change **oms** Registration Password

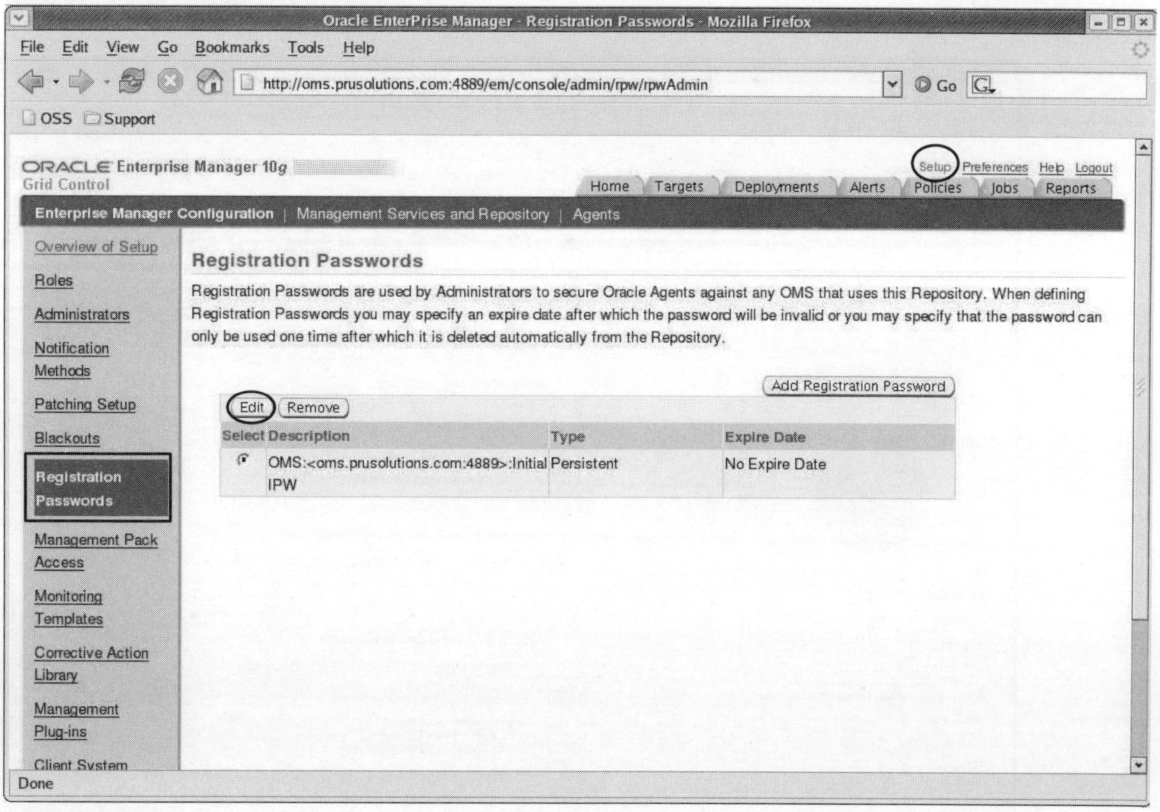

- Setting Preferred Credentials : Click Preferences on upper right side corner and go to Database Preferred Credentials page

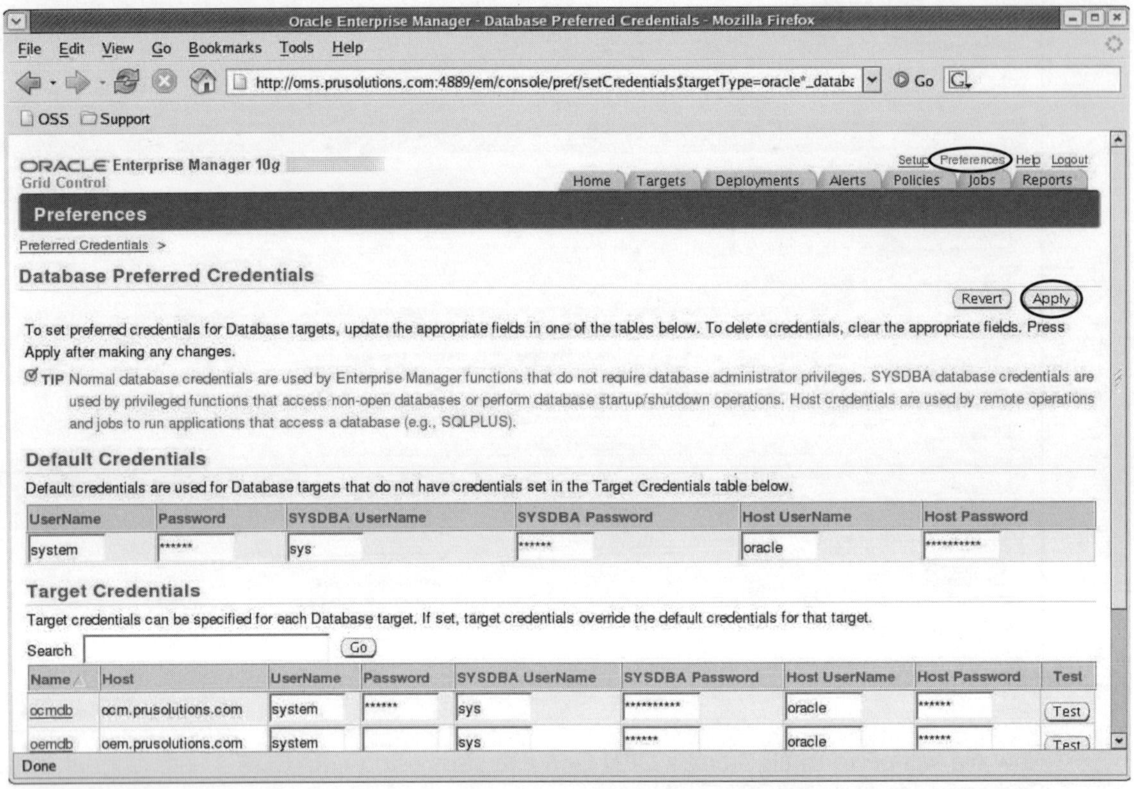

- Navigating through Oracle's OEM Grid pages, we will be using ocmdb database for all Oracle's OEM Grid exercises
- Enterprise Home Page

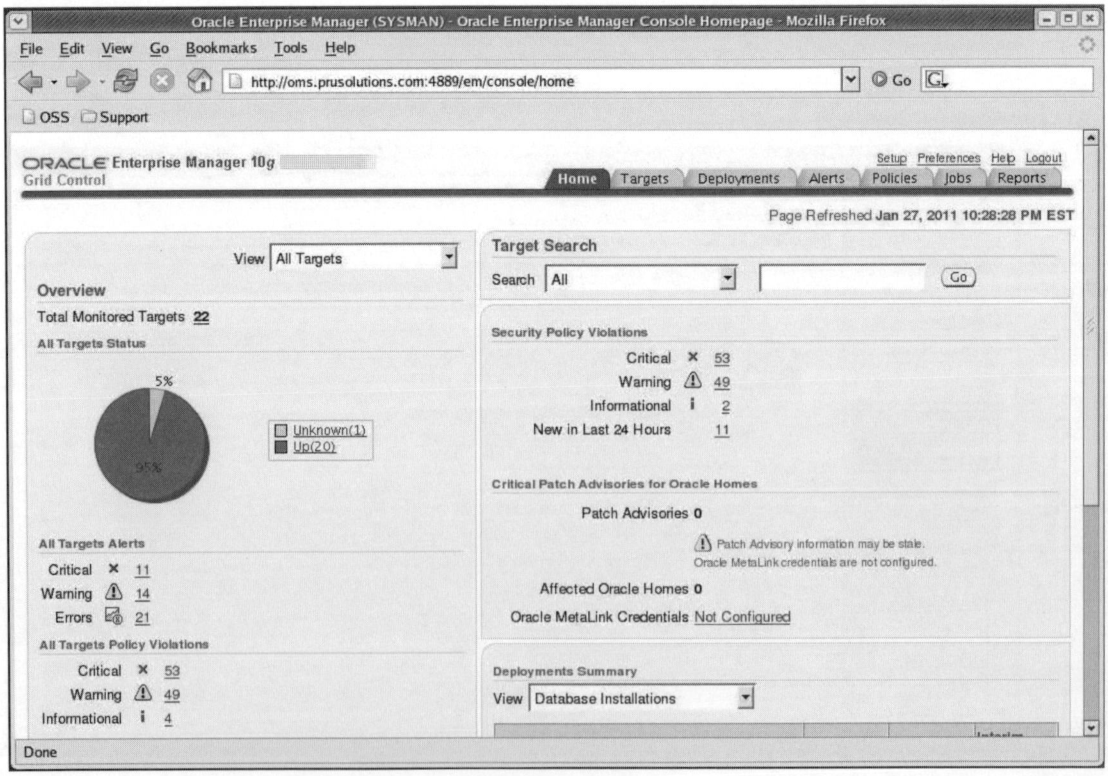

- Oracle 10gR2 Grid Control Details

  The Oracle's OEM Grid Control provides a single interface to monitor, entire Oracle technology stack and operating systems. It includes real time monitoring, health status, target availability, generating alerts job automation and enterprise reporting.

- Manually Configuring Targets
  - Go to Oracle's OEM Grid Targets tab and configure oemdb Database

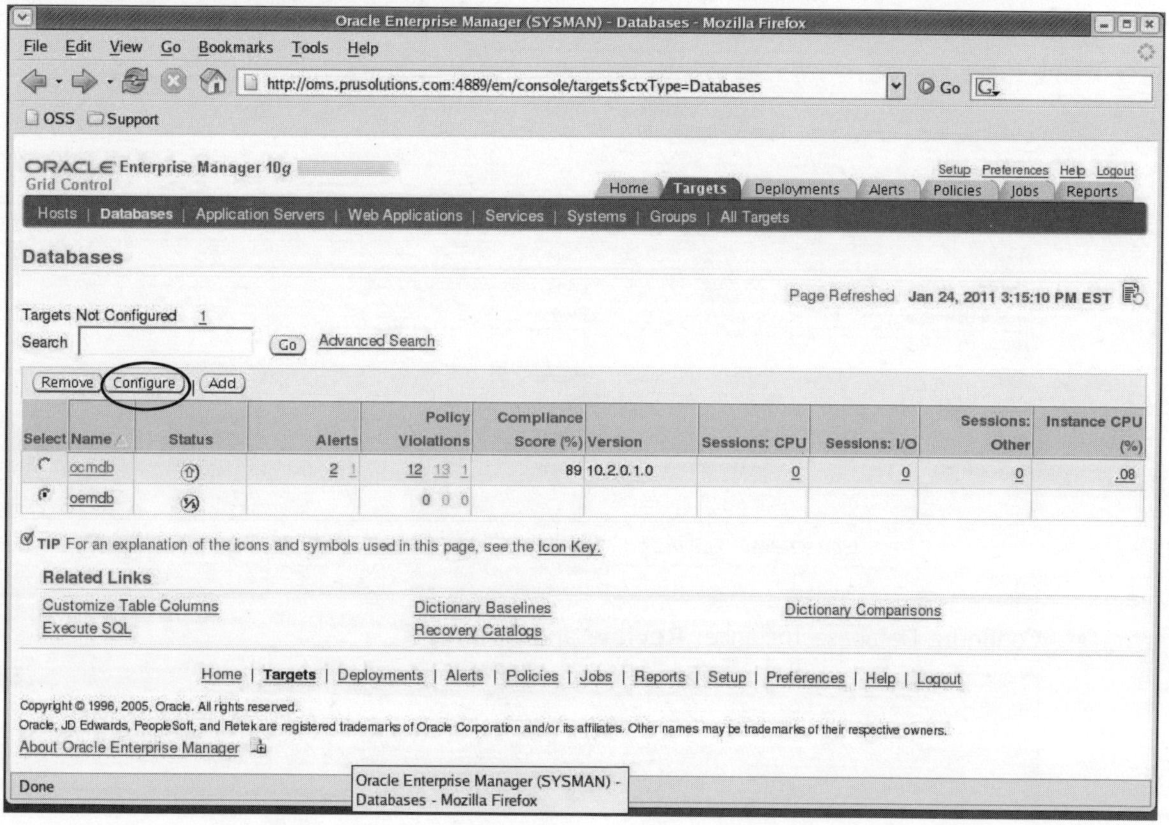

- Test Connections

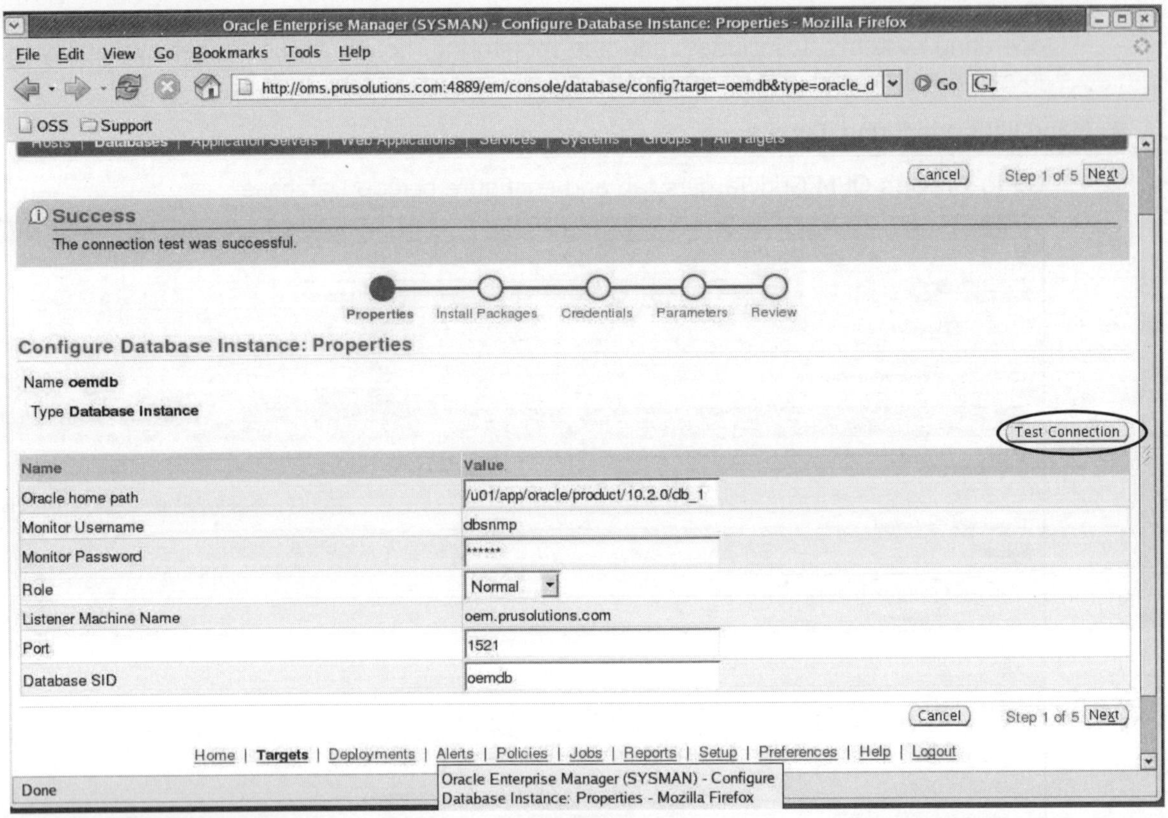

- Configure Database Instance: **Review** and **Submit**

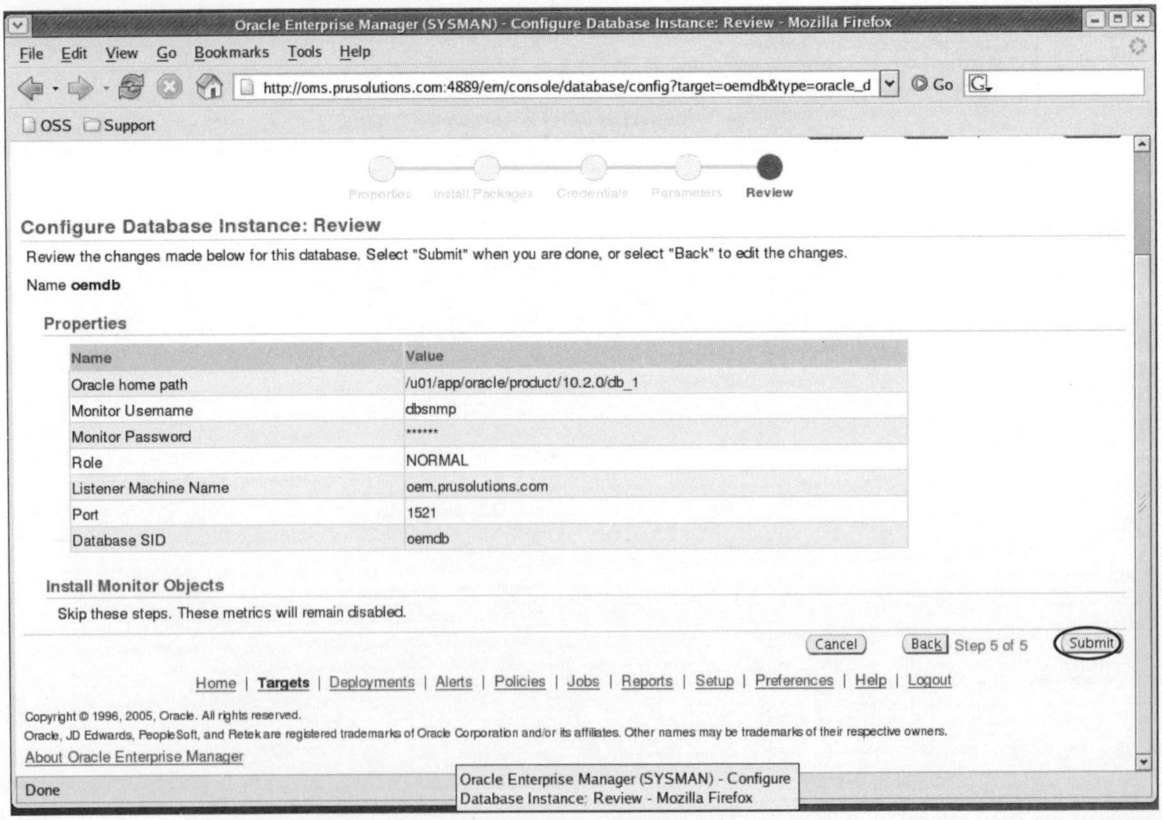

- Database Instance Configuration **Result**

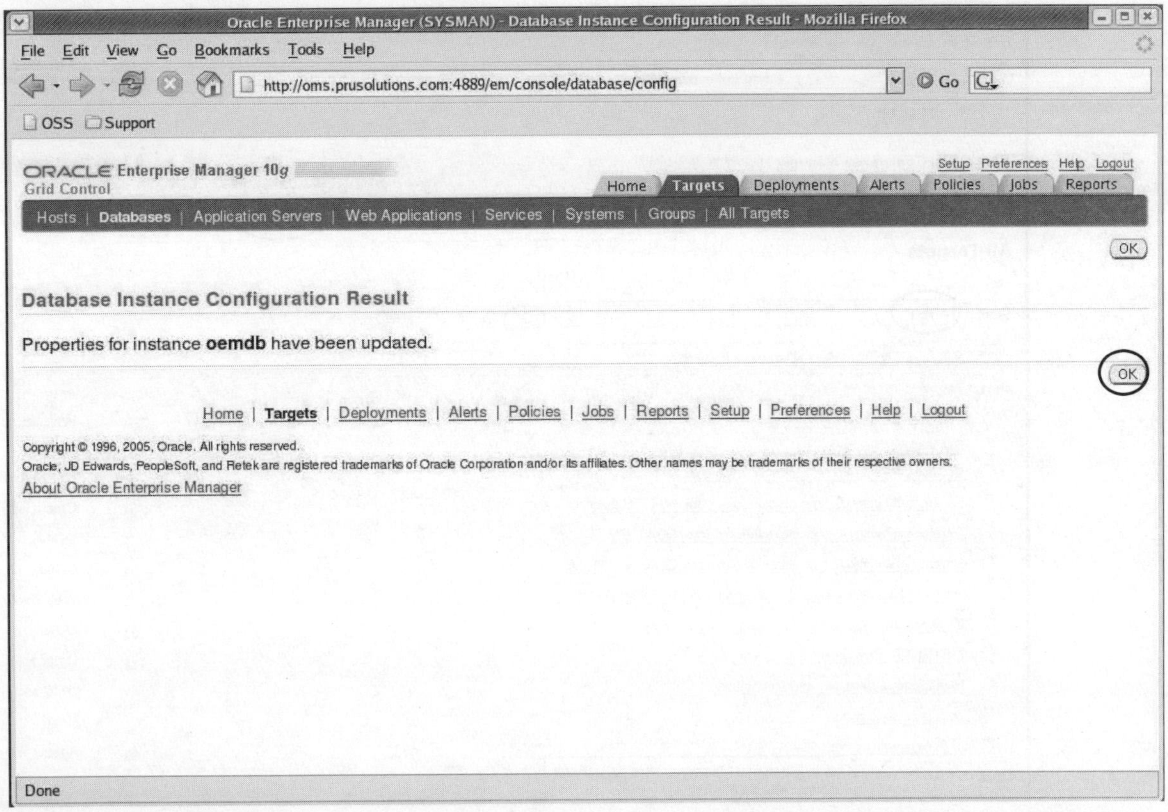

- Configure Listener Manually.

Click on the Targets tab and then on Databases Sub tab and go to ocmdb home page as shown below, you will notice that due to some error listener is not configured automatically.

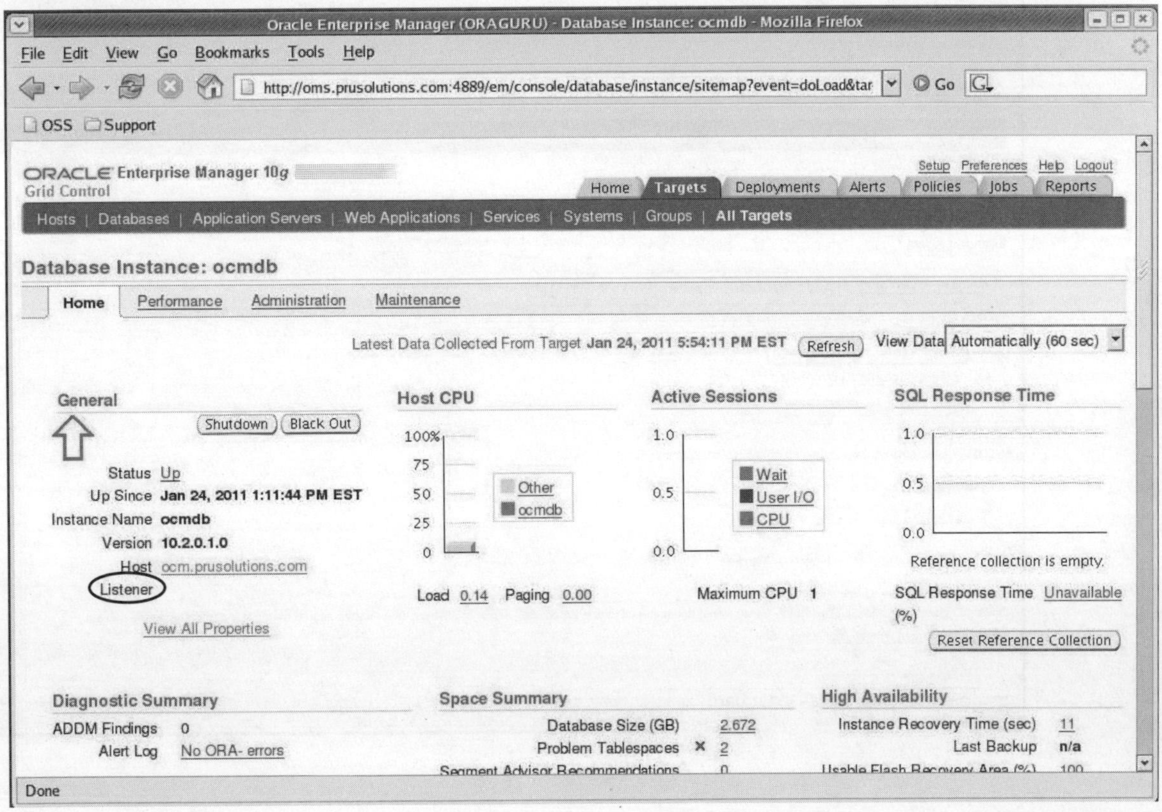

- Go to All Targets Sub tab and search for Agent and Click Go

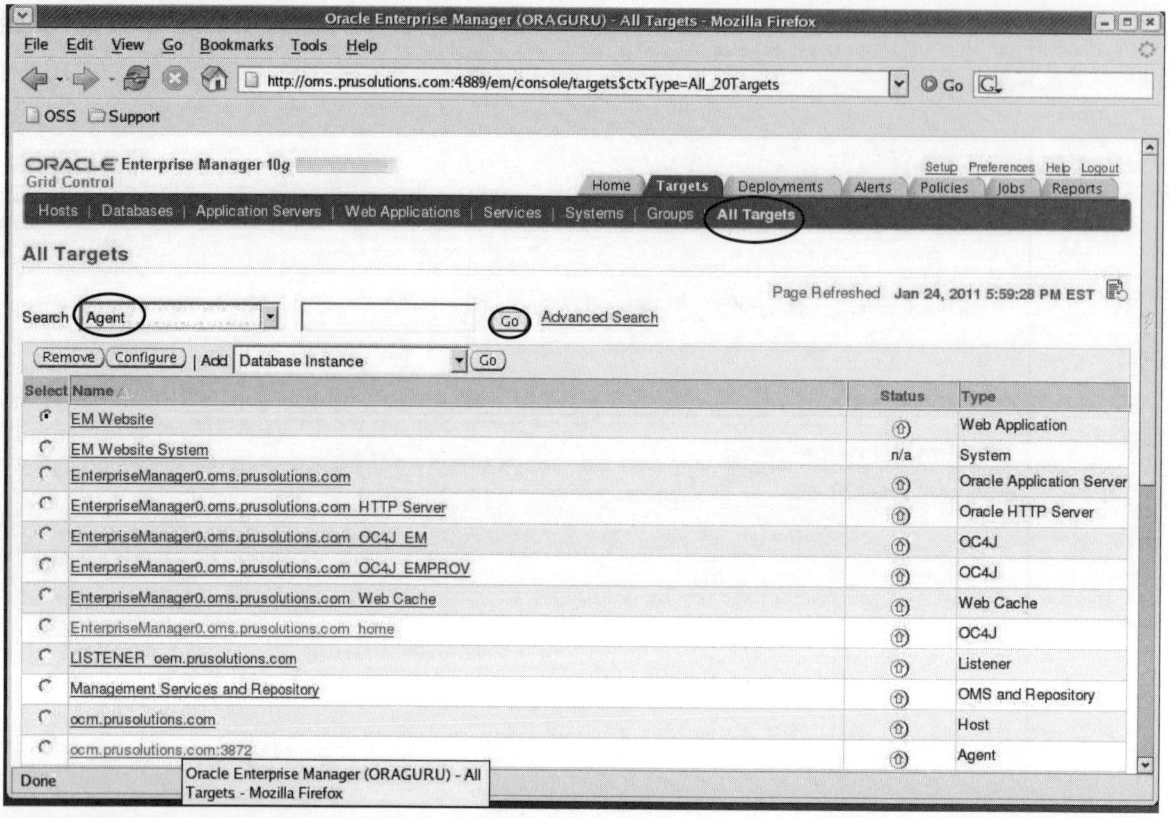

- Click link ocm.prusolutions.com.

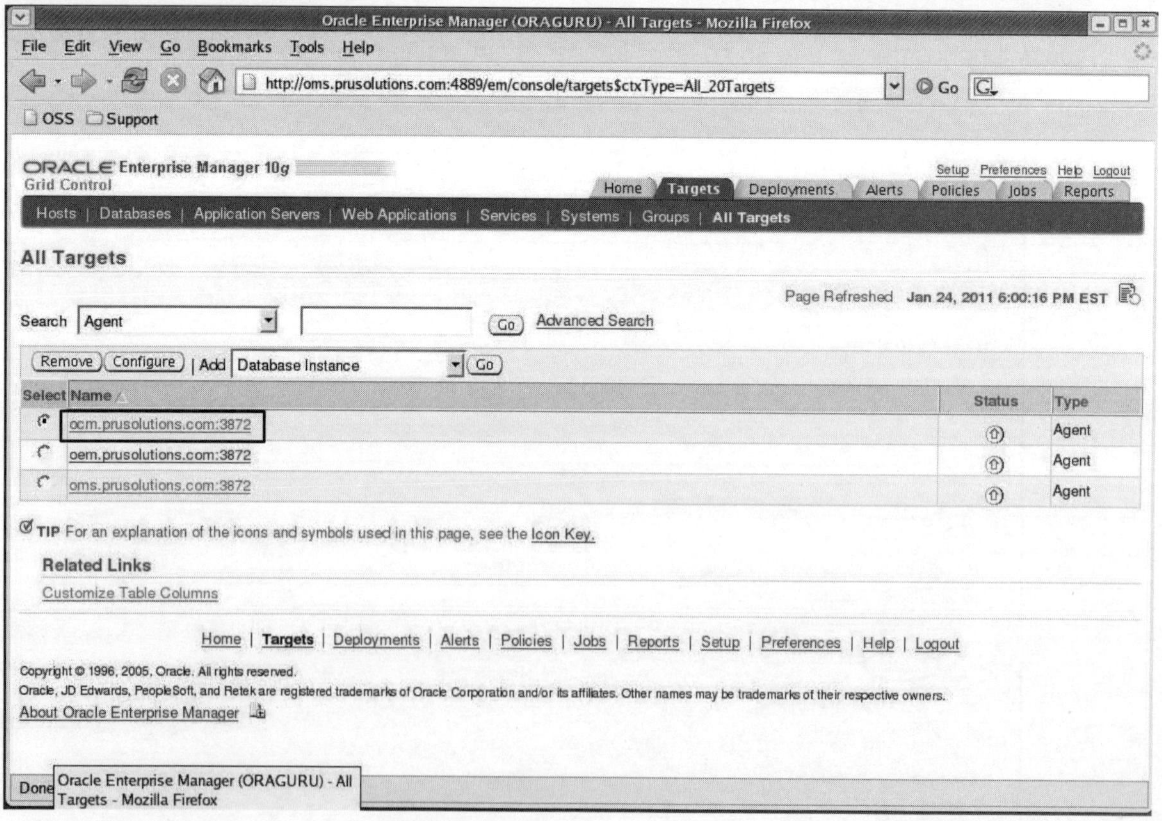

- On Agent Page in Add Drop Down select listener and Click Go

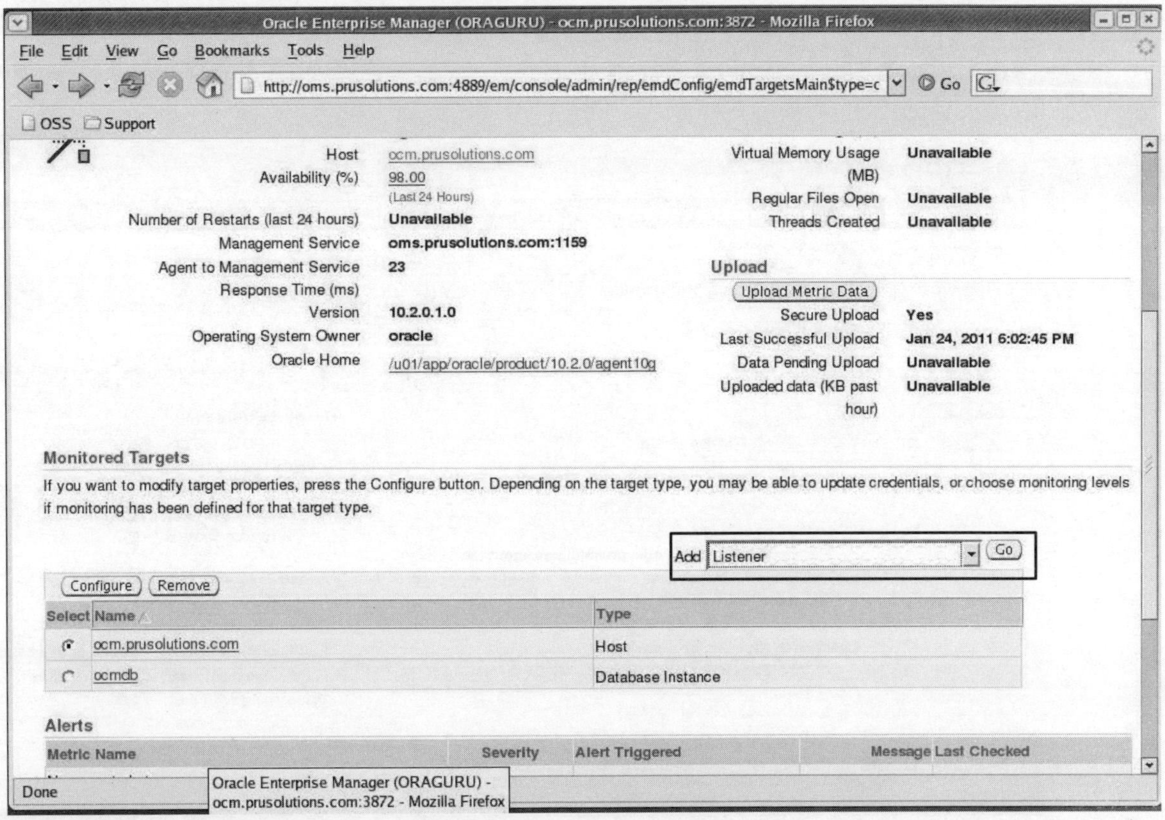

- Fill in all the required entry and recheck them. Click OK

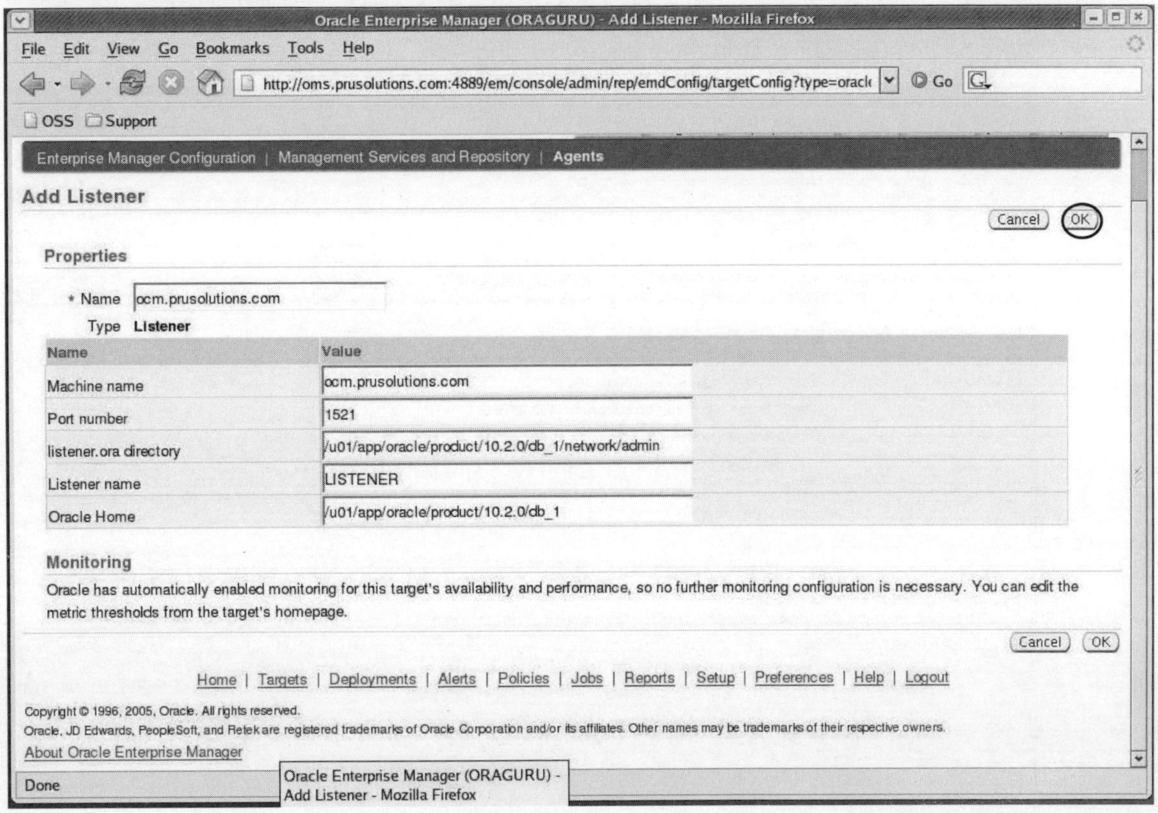

- Confirmation Page

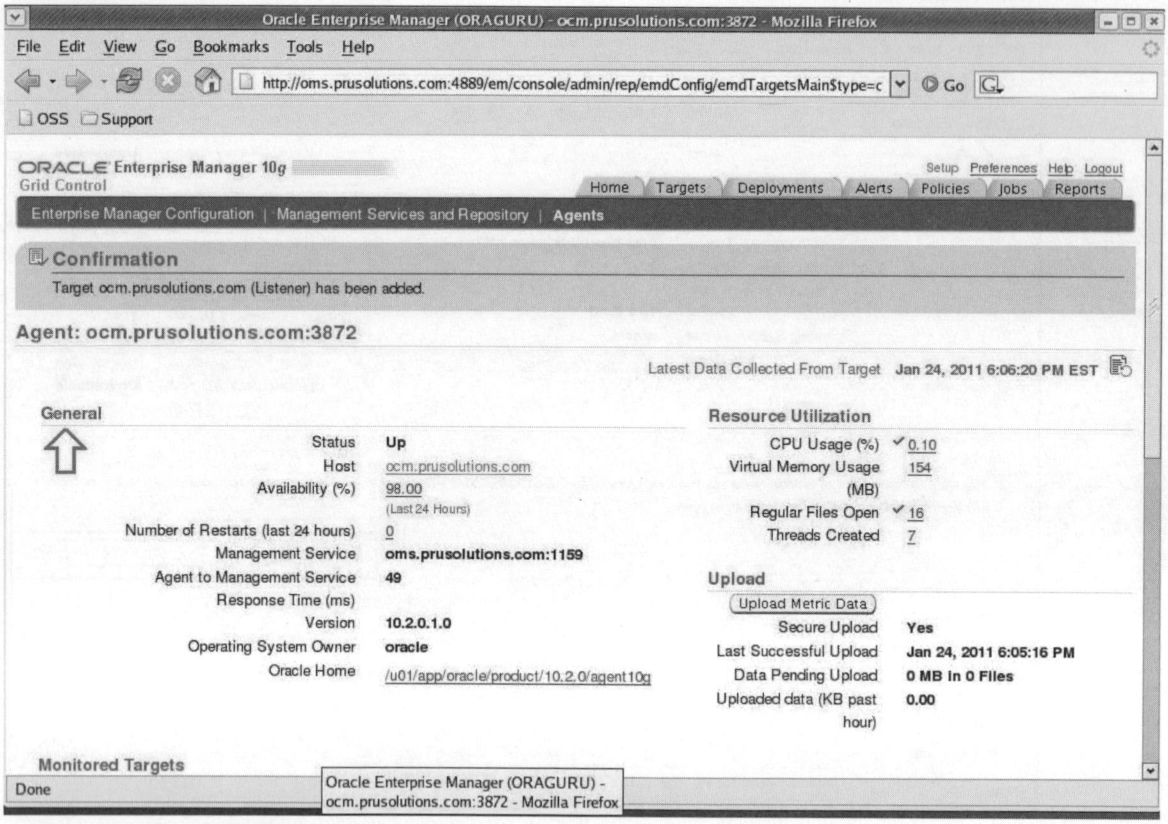

- Listener name LISTENER is added to Oracle's OEM Grid. In the same way you can add LISTENER_OCM and other objects that are not added automatically.
- Manage listener (start, stop reconfigure, tracing, etc. also from Oracle's OEM Grid Control).

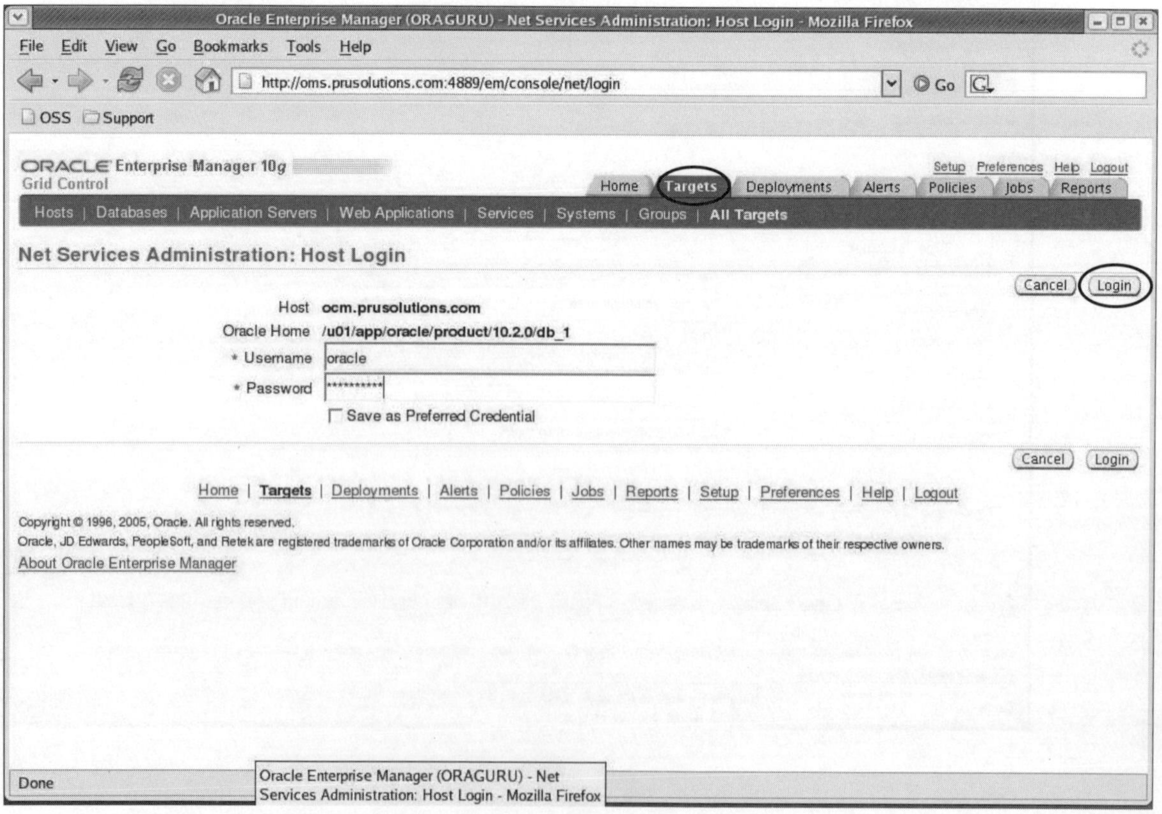

- Add Listener

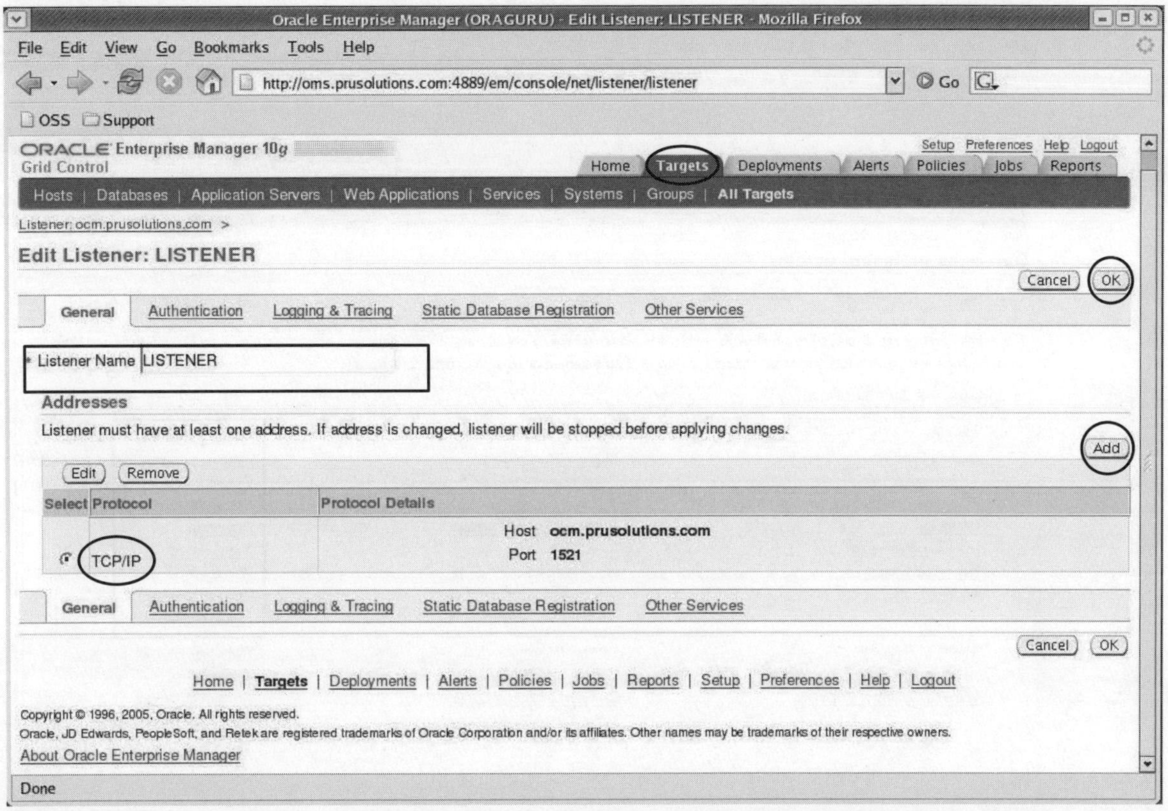

3.5 Navigate through all the Pages of Oracle Enterprise Manager

- Navigate through Oracle Documentation to get an Overview of Enterprise Manager without search tab

  Oracle Database Documentation Library > Books > ENT > Enterprise Manager Concepts > HTML

  On contents page Ctrl f and search for "Overview of Enterprise Manager" you will reach Overview of Enterprise Manager.

- Navigate through all the sections of Oracle's OEM Grid Control to get familiarize with Oracle's OEM Grid Control.

- Use Oracle Scheduler, Create Jobs, Modify Database Configuration, Set Alerts Thresholds and View Reports

- Oracle Scheduler

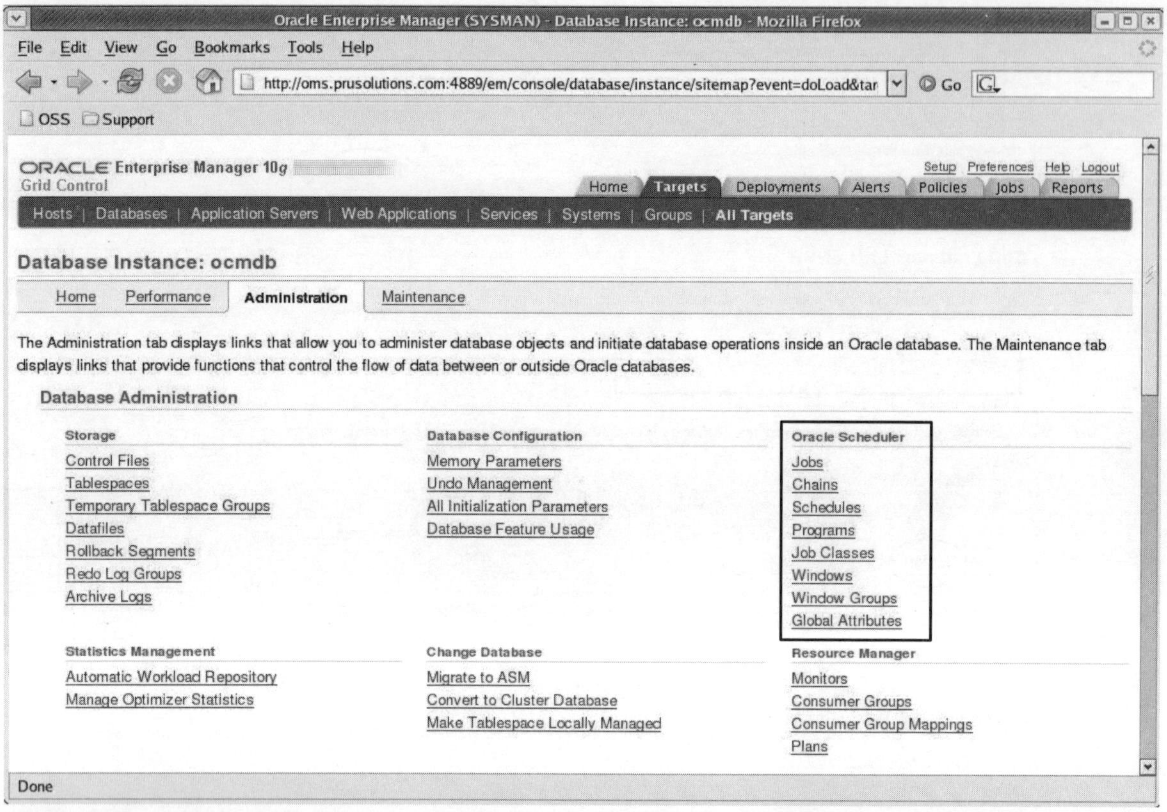

- Create Jobs: Learn to create jobs with all the Command Types mentioned in Slide below

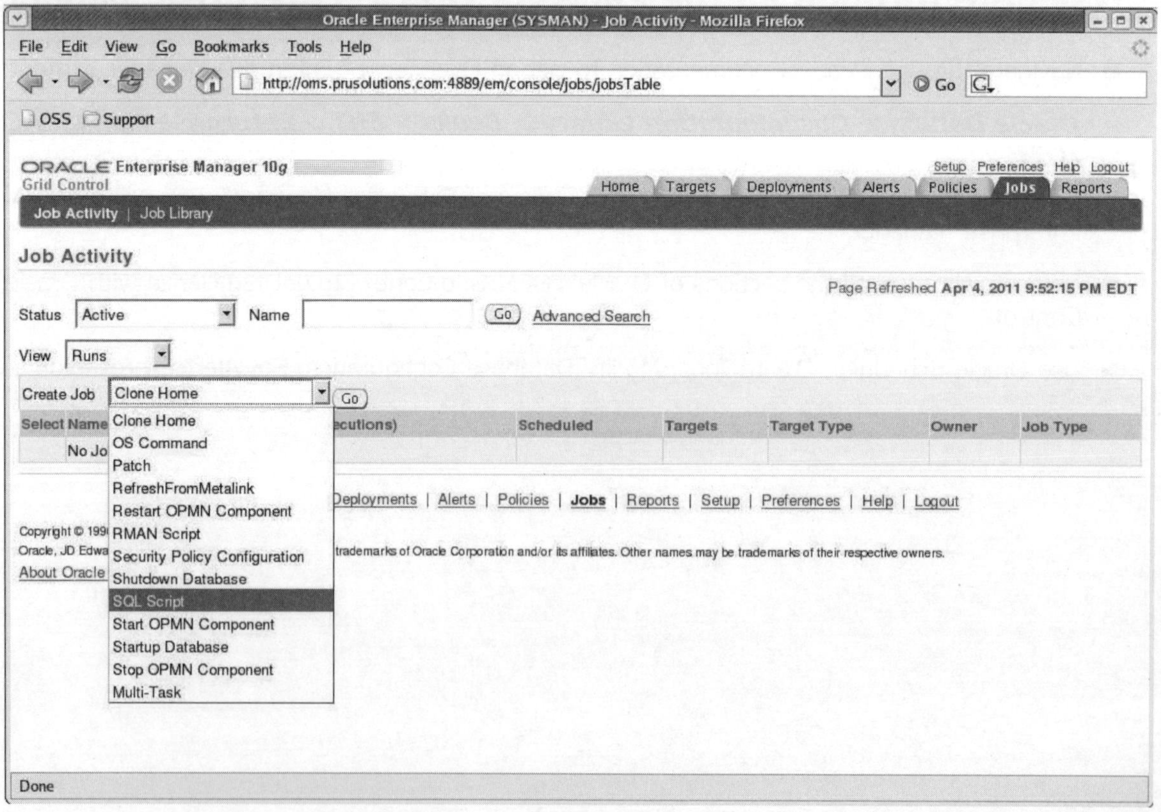

- Set Alerts Thresholds Using Metrics and Policy Settings

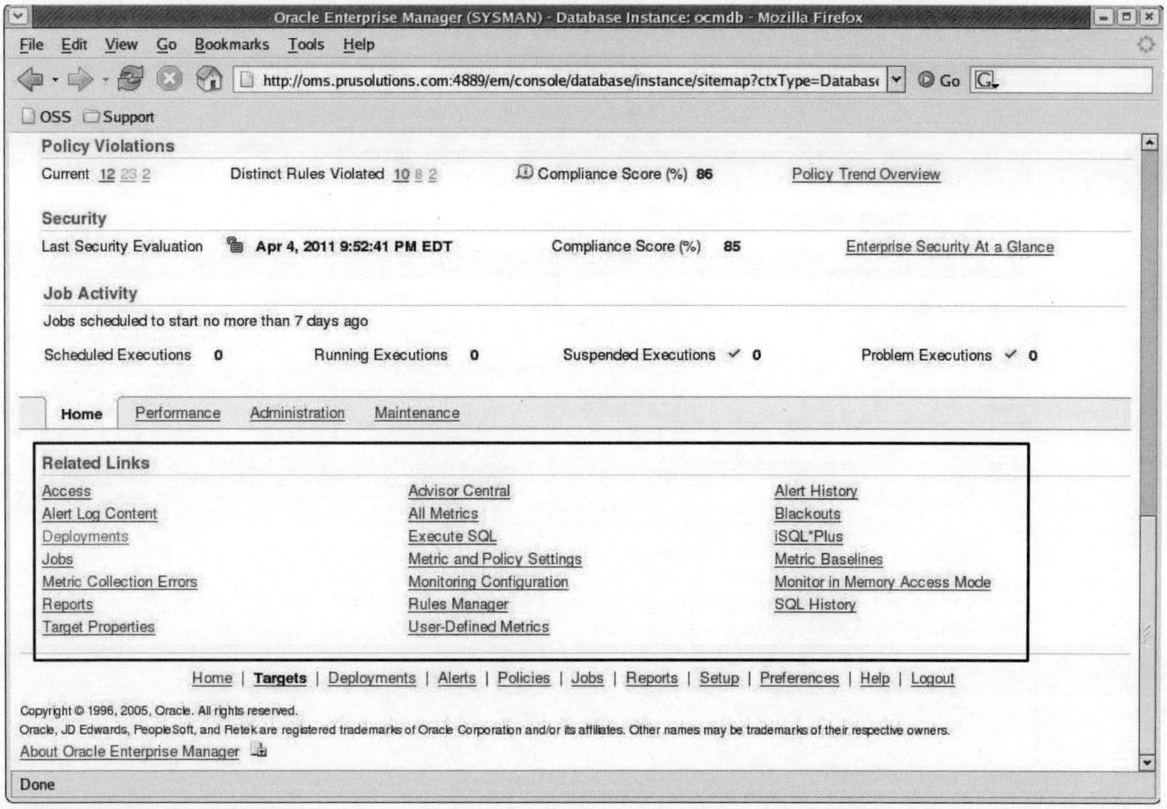

- View Reports

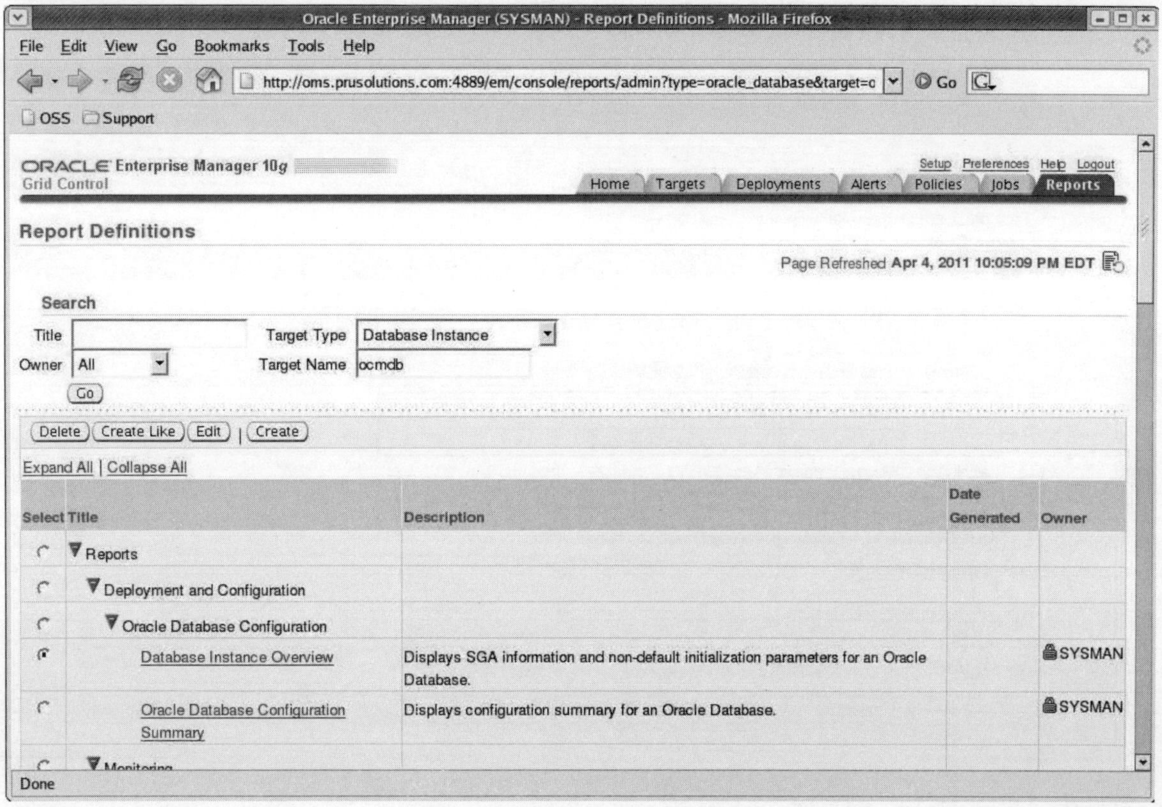

- Example : Create Job to collect schema statistics using SQL Scripts
  - On jobs tab, Job Activity page, Select SQL Scripts in Create Job Drop Down and Click Go

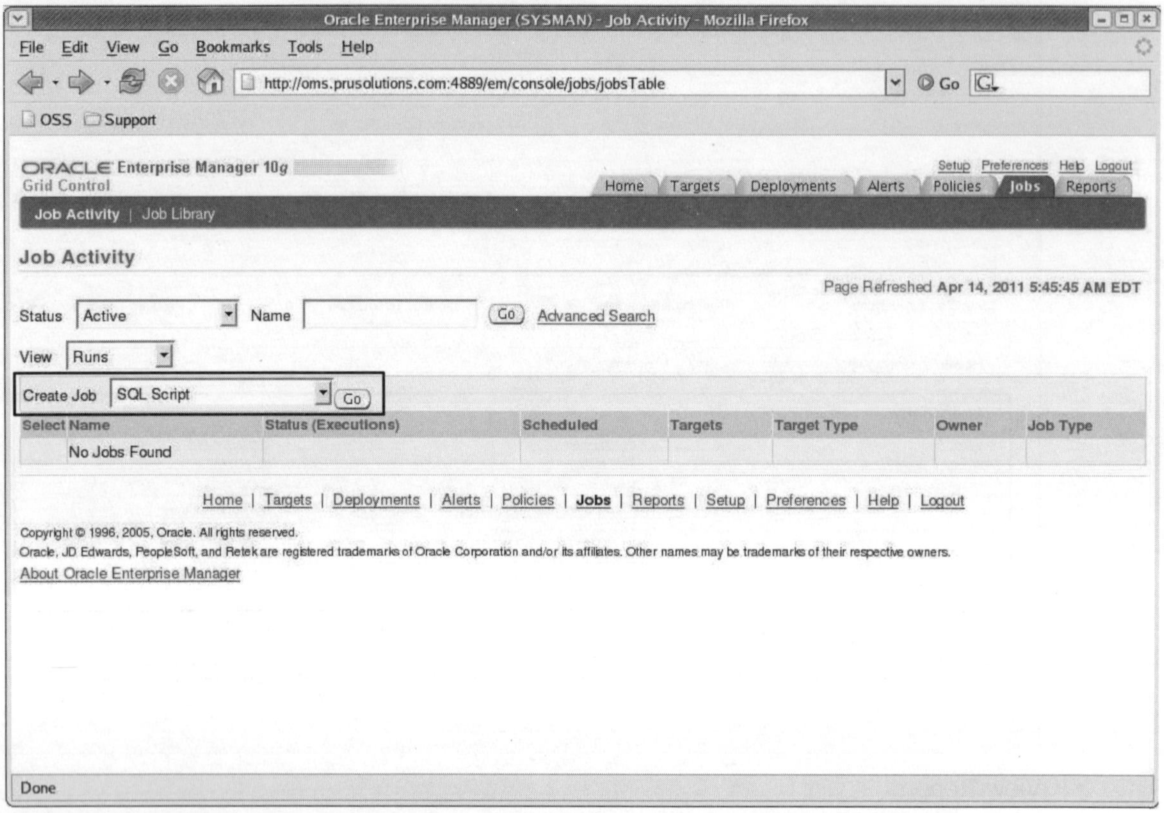

  - On General tab enter, Name : **OCMDB_SCHEMA_STATS**, Targets: Add **ocmdb**

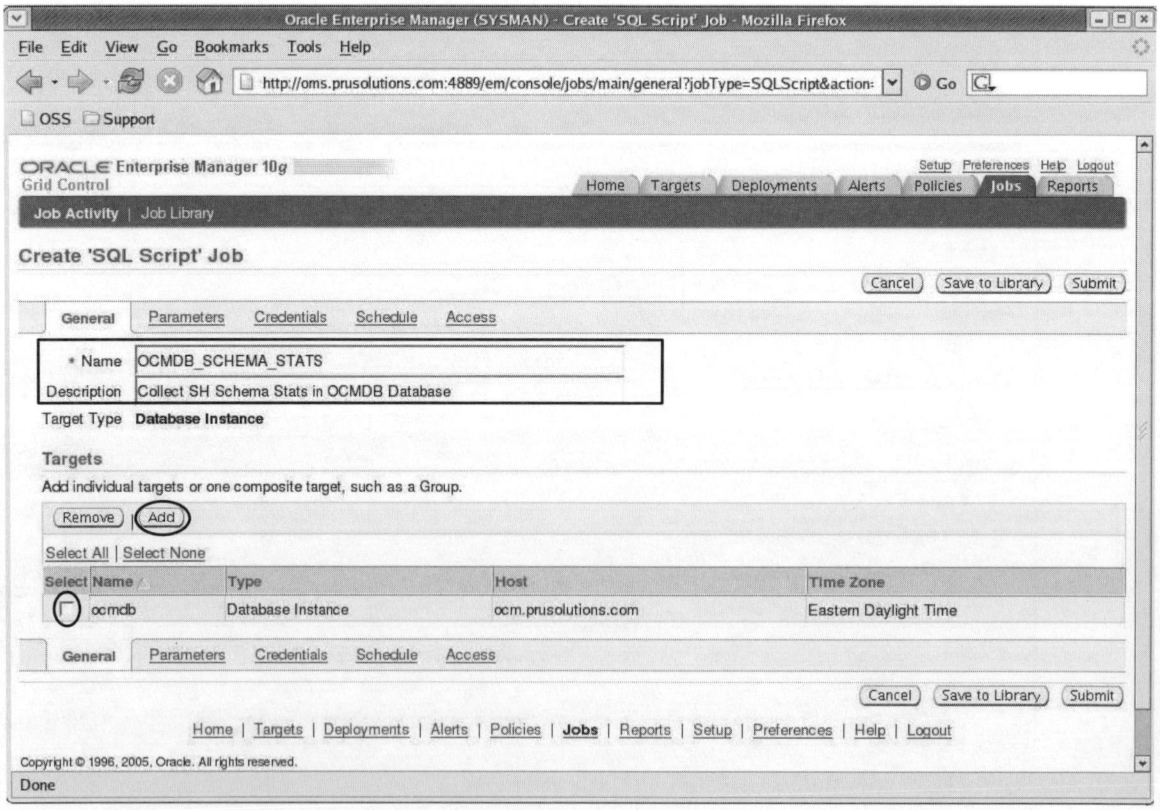

- Job Parameters

```
BEGIN
  SYS.DBMS_STATS.GATHER_SCHEMA_STATS (
        OwnName         => 'SH',
        Granularity     => 'DEFAULT',
        Options         => 'GATHER STALE',
        Gather_Temp     => FALSE,
        Method_Opt      => 'FOR ALL INDEXED COLUMNS SIZE AUTO ',
        Degree          => 4,
        Cascade         => TRUE,
        No_Invalidate   => FALSE);
END;
/
```

- Job Parameters Details

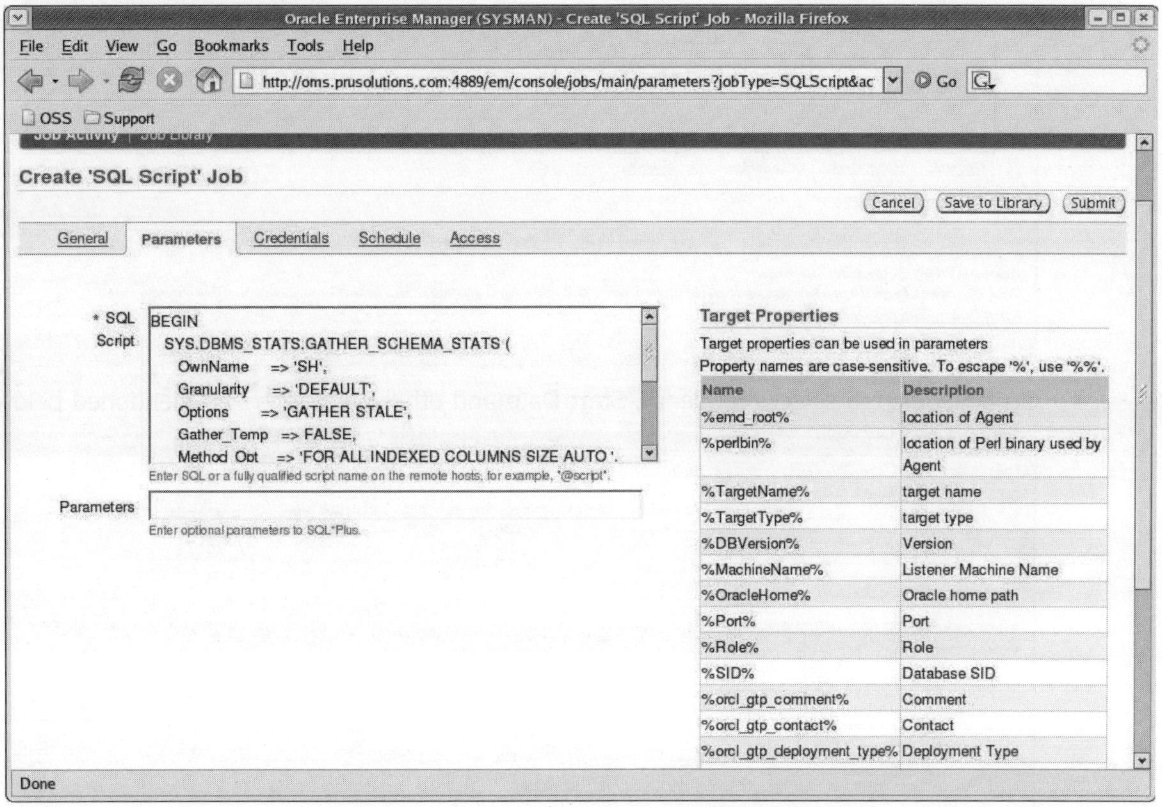

- On Credential tab: Enter Host and Database Username/Password

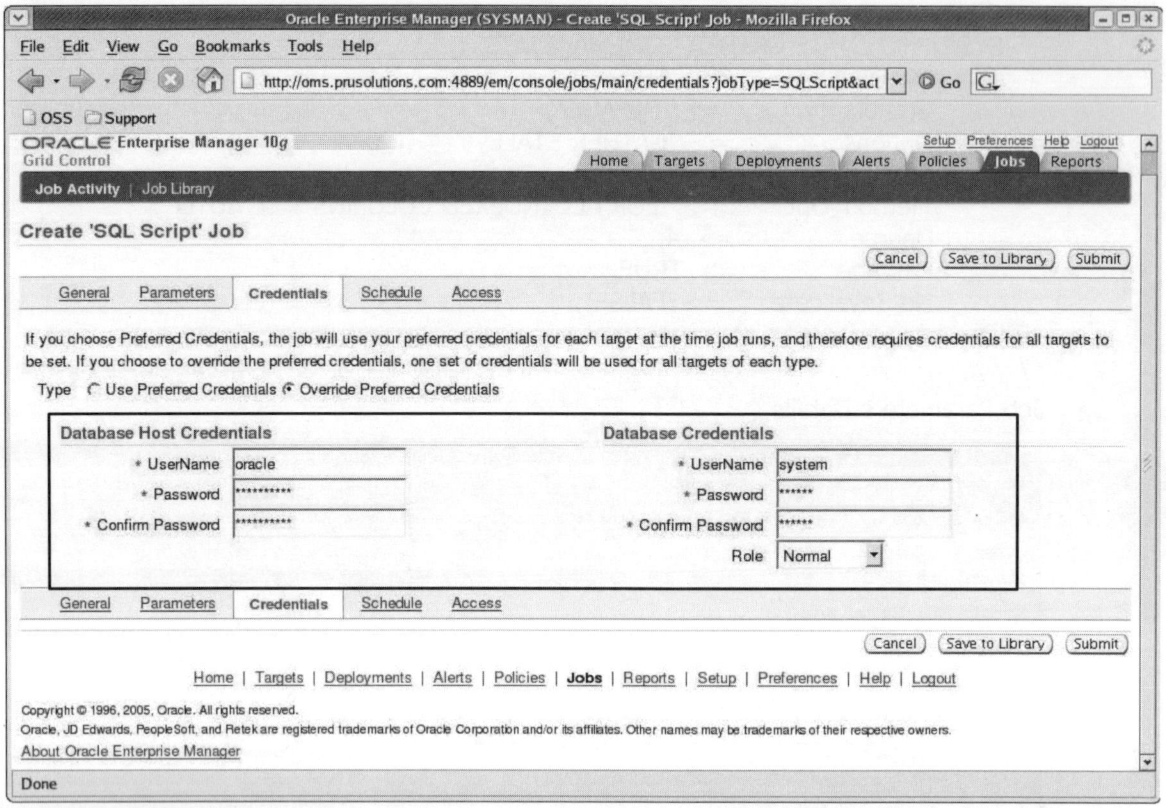

- On Schedule tab select Frequency, Start Date and other parameters as mentioned below

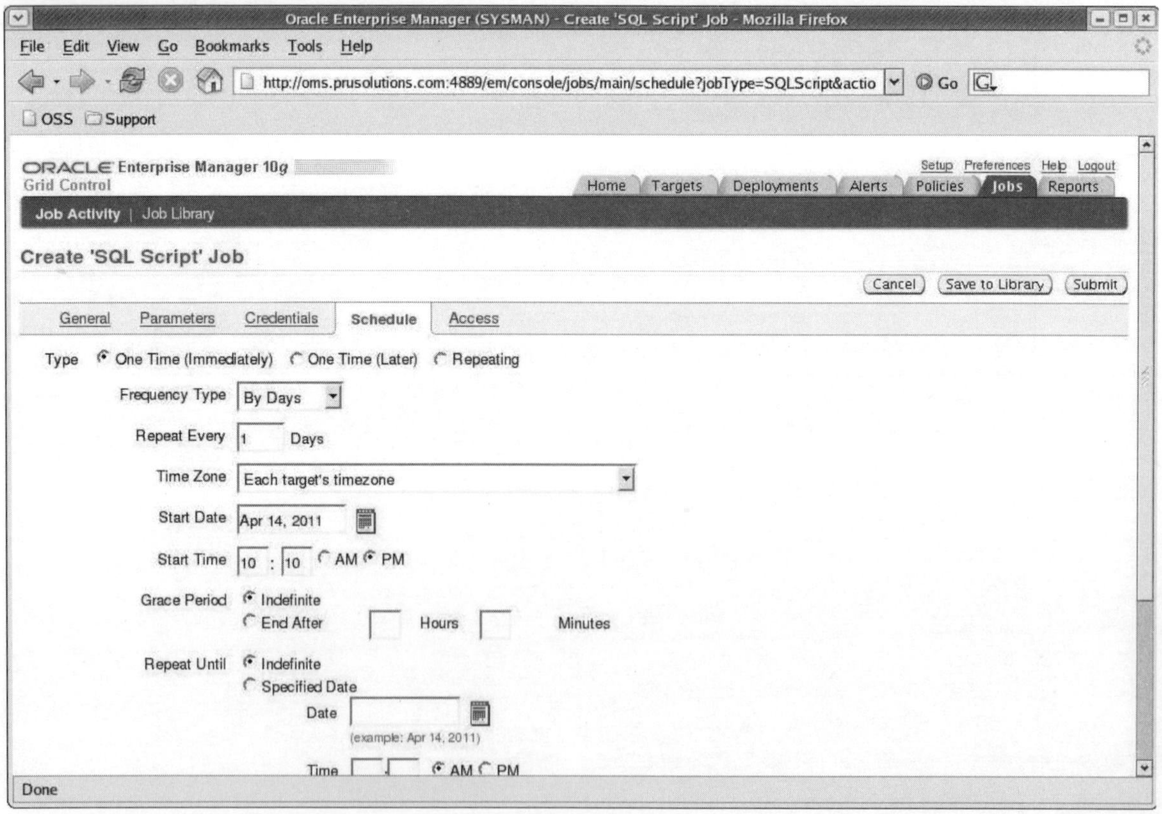

- On Access tab grant access to view jobs to different users and submit

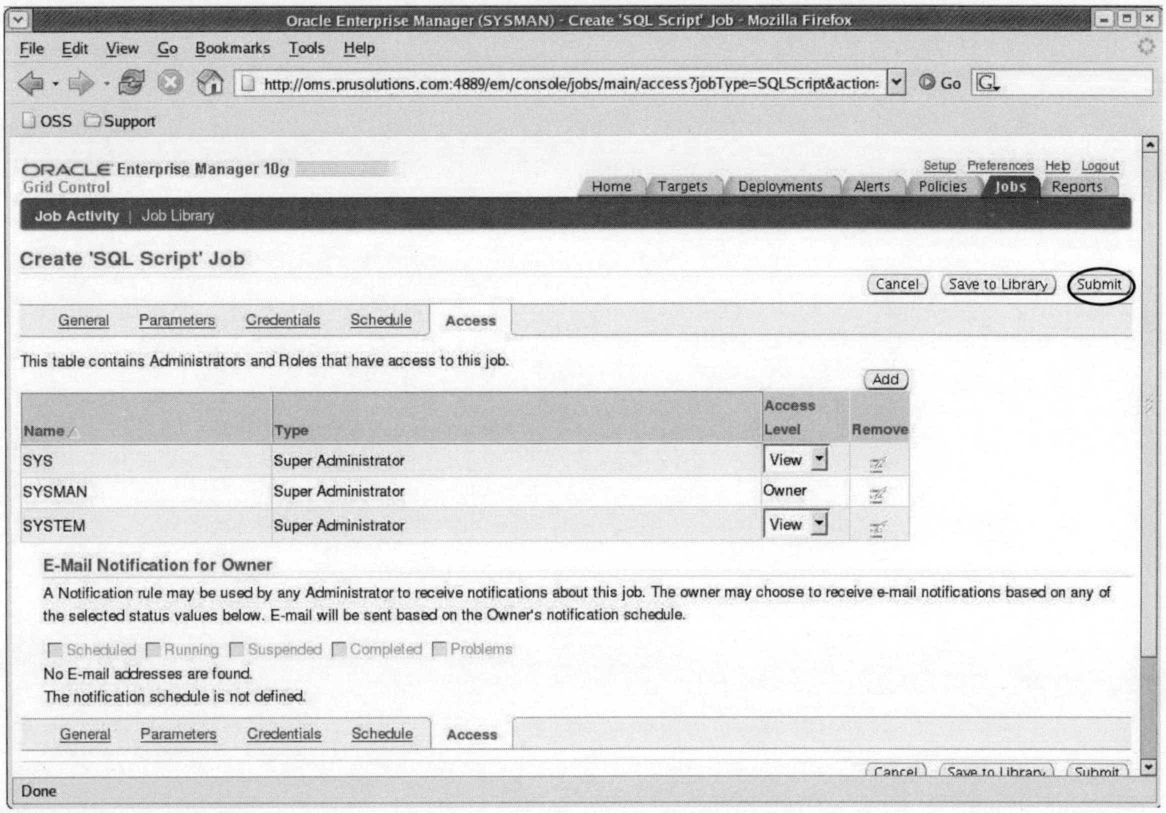

4

Managing Database Availability

- Create a recovery catalog database
- Configure Recovery Manager
- Use Recovery Manager to perform database backups
- Use Recover Manager to perform complete database restore and recovery operations
- Set Flashback Database parameters
- Monitor Flashback Database logs and statistics
- Perform a Flashback Database operation
- Configure a flash recovery area

4.1 Check database is in Archivelog Mode

```
SQL> archive log list
     Database log mode              Archive Mode
     Automatic archival             Enabled
     Archive destination            USE_DB_RECOVERY_FILE_DEST
     Oldest online log sequence     42
     Next log sequence to archive   44
     Current log sequence           44
```

4.2 Check Flash Recovery Area is configured

SQL> show parameter recovery

If recovery parameters are not set use following command

SQL> ALTER SYSTEM SET db_recovery_file_dest_size =10G scope=spfile;

SQL> ALTER SYSTEM SET db_recovery_file_dest='/u01/app/oracle/flash_recovery_area' scope=spfile;

4.3 Add OCMDB default port 1521 tnsnames entry

Add OCMDB default port 1521 tnsnames entry in oem.prusolutions.com server tnsnames.ora

```
OCMDB =
  (DESCRIPTION =
    (ADDRESS = (PROTOCOL = TCP)(HOST = ocm.prusolutions.com)(PORT = 1521))
    (CONNECT_DATA =
      (SERVER = DEDICATED)
      (SERVICE_NAME = ocmdb)
    )
  )
```

4.4 RMAN, connect to target using controlfile

- Perform steps mentioned below on ocm.prusolutions.com to connect to rman using controlfile. There are 3 ways to connect locally

[oracle@ocm ~]$ export ORACLE_SID=ocmdb

i. **[oracle@ocm ~]$ rman target /**

   Recovery Manager: Release 10.2.0.1.0 - Production on Thu Jan 27 07:42:48 2011

   Copyright (c) 1982, 2005, Oracle. All rights reserved.

   connected to target database: OCMDB (DBID=4083722939)
   RMAN> exit

   Recovery Manager complete

ii. **[oracle@ocm ~]$ rman target / nocatalog**

   Recovery Manager: Release 10.2.0.1.0 - Production on Thu Jan 27 07:43:06 2011

   Copyright (c) 1982, 2005, Oracle. All rights reserved.

   connected to target database: OCMDB (DBID=4083722939)
   using target database control file instead of recovery catalog

   RMAN> exit

   Recovery Manager complete

iii. [oracle@ocm ~]$ rman target sys/oracle@ocmdb

Recovery Manager: Release 10.2.0.1.0 - Production on Thu Jan 27 07:43:48 2011

Copyright (c) 1982, 2005, Oracle. All rights reserved.

connected to target database: OCMDB (DBID=4083722939)

- Check all the rman configuration parameters

RMAN> show all;

```
using target database control file instead of recovery catalog
RMAN configuration parameters are:
CONFIGURE RETENTION POLICY TO REDUNDANCY 1; # default
CONFIGURE BACKUP OPTIMIZATION OFF; # default
CONFIGURE DEFAULT DEVICE TYPE TO DISK; # default
CONFIGURE CONTROLFILE AUTOBACKUP OFF; # default
CONFIGURE CONTROLFILE AUTOBACKUP FORMAT FOR DEVICE TYPE DISK TO '%F'; # default
CONFIGURE DEVICE TYPE DISK PARALLELISM 1 BACKUP TYPE TO BACKUPSET; # default
CONFIGURE DATAFILE BACKUP COPIES FOR DEVICE TYPE DISK TO 1; # default
CONFIGURE ARCHIVELOG BACKUP COPIES FOR DEVICE TYPE DISK TO 1; # default
CONFIGURE MAXSETSIZE TO UNLIMITED; # default
CONFIGURE ENCRYPTION FOR DATABASE OFF; # default
CONFIGURE ENCRYPTION ALGORITHM 'AES128'; # default
CONFIGURE ARCHIVELOG DELETION POLICY TO NONE; # default
CONFIGURE SNAPSHOT CONTROLFILE NAME TO '/u01/app/oracle/product/10.2.0/db_1/dbs/
snapcf_ocmdb.f'; # default
```

- Writing output to log file and invoking rman script

File names specified on the command line that do not start with an alphabetic character should be enclosed in single quotation marks

  - Writing to logfile

    [oracle@ocm ~]$ rman target sys/oracle@ocmdb LOG=$HOME/rman/log/rman.log APPEND

  - Invoking rman script and writing to logfile

    [oracle@ocm ~]$ rman target sys/oracle@ocmdb CMDFILE=$HOME/rman/scripts/rman_backup_script.rcv LOG=$HOME/rman/log/rman_backup_ocmdb.log APPEND

Always note the DBID of database being backed up as it will save time in complete database recovery when spfile, controlfiles and all datafiles are lost. If you create rman logfile DBID is captured in that.

- For incremental backup, first we have to enable **BLOCK CHANGE TRACKING** in database

SQL> ALTER DATABASE ENABLE BLOCK CHANGE TRACKING USING FILE '/u01/app/oracle/oradata/disk3/ocmdb/rman_change_track.f' REUSE;

SQL> SELECT * FROM V$BLOCK_CHANGE_TRACKING;

- Example rman_backup_script.rcv for cumulative incremental rman backup script to backup as copy

```
run
{
recover copy of database with tag 'INCR_DAILY_UPD';
backup incremental level 1
for recover of copy with tag 'INCR_DAILY_UPD'
cumulative database plus archivelog;
}
```

- Immediately backup of both ocmdb and oemdb database

```
[oracle@ocm ~]$ rman target sys/oracle@ocmdb CMDFILE=$HOME/rman/scripts/rman_backup_script.rcv
LOG=$HOME/rman/log/rman_backup_ocmdb.log APPEND
```

```
[oracle@oem ~]$ rman target sys/oracle@oemdb CMDFILE=$HOME/rman/scripts/rman_backup_script.rcv
LOG=$HOME/rman/log/rman_backup_oemdb.log APPEND
```

4.5 Steps to set up Recovery Catalog

Steps to set up Recovery Catalog and modify RMAN parameters in oemdb database

- Create recovery catalog tablespace rcat_ts

```
SQL> CREATE TABLESPACE rcat_ts DATAFILE '/u01/app/oracle/oradata/oemdb/rcat_ts.dbf'
     SIZE 100M AUTOEXTEND ON NEXT 1M MAXSIZE 1024M EXTENT MANAGEMENT LOCAL
     UNIFORM SIZE 1M;
```

- Create recover catalog owner rman and grant privileges

```
SQL> CREATE USER rman IDENTIFIED BY rman DEFAULT TABLESPACE rcat_ts
     TEMPORARY TABLESPACE temp;
SQL> ALTER USER rman QUOTA UNLIMITED ON rcat_ts;
SQL> GRANT RECOVERY_CATALOG_OWNER TO rman;
```

- User rman to connect to oemdb database

```
[oracle@oem ~]$ rman catalog rman/rman@oemdb
```

- Create catalog in oemdb database

```
RMAN> CREATE CATALOG TABLESPACE rcat_ts;
      recovery catalog created
```

- Exit from rman session and again connect to target and catalog through rman

```
[oracle@oem ~]$ rman target sys/oracle@ocmdb catalog rman/rman@oemdb
```

- Register target database in rman catalog

```
RMAN> register database;
      database registered in recovery catalog
      starting full resync of recovery catalog
      full resync complete
```

- Check all the rman configuration parameters

```
RMAN> show all;

RMAN configuration parameters are:
CONFIGURE RETENTION POLICY TO REDUNDANCY 1; # default
CONFIGURE BACKUP OPTIMIZATION OFF; # default
CONFIGURE DEFAULT DEVICE TYPE TO DISK; # default
CONFIGURE CONTROLFILE AUTOBACKUP OFF; # default
CONFIGURE CONTROLFILE AUTOBACKUP FORMAT FOR DEVICE TYPE DISK TO '%F'; # default
CONFIGURE DEVICE TYPE DISK PARALLELISM 1 BACKUP TYPE TO BACKUPSET; # default
CONFIGURE DATAFILE BACKUP COPIES FOR DEVICE TYPE DISK TO 1; # default
CONFIGURE ARCHIVELOG BACKUP COPIES FOR DEVICE TYPE DISK TO 1; # default
CONFIGURE MAXSETSIZE TO UNLIMITED; # default
CONFIGURE ENCRYPTION FOR DATABASE OFF; # default
```

CONFIGURE ENCRYPTION ALGORITHM 'AES128'; # default
CONFIGURE ARCHIVELOG DELETION POLICY TO NONE; # default
CONFIGURE SNAPSHOT CONTROLFILE NAME TO '/u01/app/oracle/product/10.2.0/db_1/dbs/snapcf_ocmdb.f'; # default

- Modify rman configurations parameters
  - Configure default device type to disk

    RMAN> CONFIGURE DEFAULT DEVICE TYPE TO DISK;
  - Configure default device type to tape

    RMAN> CONFIGURE DEFAULT DEVICE TYPE TO sbt;
  - Configure channel device type disk

    RMAN> CONFIGURE CHANNEL DEVICE TYPE DISK FORMAT '/u01/app/oracle/flash_recovery_area/OCMDB/DB_%U';
  - Configure Controlfile auto backup on and controlfile auto backup format

    RMAN> CONFIGURE CONTROLFILE AUTOBACKUP ON;

    RMAN> CONFIGURE CONTROLFILE AUTOBACKUP FORMAT FOR DEVICE TYPE DISK TO '/u01/app/oracle/flash_recovery_area/OCMDB/cf_%F';
  - Configure backup Optimization on. Optimization does not back up a file to a device type if the identical file already backed up on the device type. For two files to be identical, their content must be the same.

    RMAN> CONFIGURE BACKUP OPTIMIZATION ON;
  - Configure Retention Policy to redundancy

    RMAN> CONFIGURE RETENTION POLICY TO REDUNDANCY 2;
  - Configure Retention Policy to recovery window.

    You should keep the recovery window time period less than or equal to the value of the control files parameter CONTROL_FILE_RECORD_KEEP_TIME to prevent the record of older backups from being overwritten in the control file.

    RMAN> CONFIGURE RETENTION POLICY TO RECOVERY WINDOW OF 7 DAYS;
  - Configure auto allocation of channel and parallel backups sets

    RMAN> CONFIGURE DEVICE TYPE DISK PARALLELISM 3;
  - Manual allocation of channel

    RMAN> run {allocate channel c1 device type disk;
    backup datafile 1 ;}
  - Show all RMAN current configuration parameters

    RMAN> show all;

    RMAN configuration parameters are:
    CONFIGURE RETENTION POLICY TO RECOVERY WINDOW OF 7 DAYS;
    CONFIGURE BACKUP OPTIMIZATION ON;
    CONFIGURE DEFAULT DEVICE TYPE TO 'SBT_TAPE';
    CONFIGURE CONTROLFILE AUTOBACKUP ON;
    CONFIGURE CONTROLFILE AUTOBACKUP FORMAT FOR DEVICE TYPE DISK TO '/u01/app/oracle/flash_recovery_area/OCMDB/cf_%F';
    CONFIGURE CONTROLFILE AUTOBACKUP FORMAT FOR DEVICE TYPE SBT_TAPE TO '%F'; # default
    CONFIGURE DEVICE TYPE DISK PARALLELISM 3 BACKUP TYPE TO BACKUPSET;
    CONFIGURE DEVICE TYPE SBT_TAPE PARALLELISM 1 BACKUP TYPE TO BACKUPSET; # default
    CONFIGURE DATAFILE BACKUP COPIES FOR DEVICE TYPE DISK TO 1; # default
    CONFIGURE DATAFILE BACKUP COPIES FOR DEVICE TYPE SBT_TAPE TO 1; # default

```
CONFIGURE ARCHIVELOG BACKUP COPIES FOR DEVICE TYPE DISK TO 1; # default
CONFIGURE ARCHIVELOG BACKUP COPIES FOR DEVICE TYPE SBT_TAPE TO 1; # default
CONFIGURE CHANNEL DEVICE TYPE DISK FORMAT   '/u01/app/oracle/flash_recovery_area/OCMDB/
DB_%U';
CONFIGURE MAXSETSIZE TO UNLIMITED; # default
CONFIGURE ENCRYPTION FOR DATABASE OFF; # default
CONFIGURE ENCRYPTION ALGORITHM 'AES128'; # default
CONFIGURE ARCHIVELOG DELETION POLICY TO NONE; # default
CONFIGURE SNAPSHOT CONTROLFILE NAME TO '/u01/app/oracle/product/10.2.0/db_1/dbs/
snapcf_ocmdb.f'; # default
```

- To make device type default again

  Either use commands in modify rman configurations parameters as shown above

  OR

  RMAN> CONFIGURE DEFAULT DEVICE TYPE CLEAR;

  In same way, we can reset all RMAN configuration parameters to their default value

  RMAN> CONFIGURE BACKUP OPTIMIZATION CLEAR;

  RMAN> CONFIGURE MAXSETSIZE CLEAR;

  RMAN> CONFIGURE RETENTION POLICY CLEAR;

- Using various parameters, we can control default behavior of allocated channels

  MAXOPENFILES parameter specifies the maximum number of files that a backup command can open at any given time. The default value is eight.

  MAXPIECESIZE parameter specifies the maximum size of a backup piece created on allocated channel. It can be specified in bytes (default), K, M, and G.

  DURATION parameter specifies the amount of allocated time to run the backup job in hours and minutes.

  PARTIAL parameter is to suppress errors messages if backup is not complete in specified duration.

  MINIMIZE TIME parameter specifies to run backup in full speed to try to complete within allocated time.

  MINIMIZE LOAD parameter monitors the backup speed and reduces the processing speed if it finds that backup will finish in less than allocated times. The option is valid only for disk not on tape drives.

  FORMAT parameter is used to give backup piece names and location path on channel allocated.

- Catalog any backups in flash_recovery_area

  RMAN> CATALOG RECOVERY AREA;

4.6 Sample RMAN Backup Commands

i. Connect to Recovery Catalog and Target database.

   [oracle@oem ~]$ rman target sys/oracle@ocmdb catalog rman/rman@oemdb

   Recovery Manager: Release 10.2.0.1.0 - Production on Sat Jan 29 05:55:10 2011

   Copyright (c) 1982, 2005, Oracle. All rights reserved.

   connected to target database: OCMDB (DBID=4083722939)

   connected to recovery catalog database

ii. Configure Redundancy Policy.

```
RMAN> CONFIGURE RETENTION POLICY TO REDUNDANCY 2;
```

iii. Backup Database Plus Archive Log.

```
RMAN> backup database plus archivelog;
```

iv. Compressed Backups Set.

```
RMAN> backup as compressed backupset database plus archivelog;
```

v. Backup as Copy.

```
RMAN> backup as copy database plus archivelog;
```

vi. Keep checking space in flash_recovery_area and on hard disk and delete old backups if required.

```
[oracle@ocm ~]$ df –h
SQL> SELECT  file_type,
             percent_space_used  used,
             percent_space_reclaimable  reclaimable,
             number_of_files
     FROM  v$flash_recovery_area_usage;
```

vii. Backup of Datafile as Copy

```
RMAN>  BACKUP AS COPY DATAFILE
       '/u01/app/oracle/oradata/disk3/ocmdb/users01.dbf'  format
       '/u01/app/oracle/flash_recovery_area/OCMDB/users01.dbf';
```

viii. Backup Format.

```
RMAN>  BACKUP FORMAT
       '/u01/app/oracle/flash_recovery_area/OCMDB/archivelog/2011_01_29/ar_%t_%s_%p'
       ARCHIVELOG FROM SEQUENCE=48 DELETE INPUT;
```

ix. Backup as Backupset

```
RMAN>  RUN {
       BACKUP AS BACKUPSET
       FORMAT '/u01/app/oracle/flash_recovery_area/OCMDB/%d_%s_%p'
       DURATION 1:00 MINIMIZE LOAD
       (DATABASE);
       SQL 'alter system archive log current';
       }
```

x. Incremental level 0 backup

```
RMAN>  BACKUP WITH TAG 'INCR_DAILY_UPD' INCREMENTAL LEVEL 0 DATABASE;
```

xi. Incremental level 1 backup

```
RMAN>  run
       {
       RECOVER COPY OF DATABASE WITH TAG 'INCR_DAILY_UPD';
       BACKUP INCREMENTAL LEVEL 1
       FOR RECOVER OF COPY WITH TAG INCR_UPD_DAILY' DATABASE PLUS ARCHIVELOG;
       }
```

xii. Incremental level 1 cumulative

```
RMAN>  run
       {
       recover copy of database with tag 'INCR_DAILY_UPD';
```

```
backup incremental level 1
for recover of copy with tag 'INCR_DAILY_UPD'
cumulative database plus archivelog;
}
```

xiii. Backup using media manager

```
RMAN> run
{
allocate channel c1 device type sbt;
backup datafile 2;
}
```

xiv. Backup Recovery Area

```
RMAN> backup recovery area;
```

xv. Backup Recovery Files

```
RMAN> backup recovery files;
```

4.7 RMAN Reporting Commands

```
RMAN> CROSSCHECK BACKUP;
RMAN> CROSSCHECK ARCHIVELOG ALL;
RMAN> BACKUP VALIDATE DATABASE;
RMAN> BACKUP CHECK LOGICAL DATABASE;
RMAN> RESTORE DATABASE VALIDATE;
RMAN> LIST INCARNATION;
RMAN> LIST BACKUP SUMMARY;
RMAN> LIST BACKUP OF DATABASE;
RMAN> LIST COPY OF TABLESPACE USERS;
RMAN> LIST COPY OF DATABASE ARCHIVELOG FROM TIME='SYSDATE-7';
RMAN> REPORT NEED BACKUP;
RMAN> REPORT OBSOLETE;
RMAN> REPORT UNRECOVERABLE;
RMAN> REPORT NEED BACKUP incremental 2;
RMAN> REPORT NEED BACKUP redundancy 2;
RMAN> REPORT NEED BACKUP recovery window of 7 days;
RMAN> LIST INCARNATION;
RMAN> REPORT SCHEMA;
```

4.8 RMAN Dynamic Views

Go through Oracle Documentation to get details of following views

i. V$ARCHIVED_LOG
ii. V$BACKUP_CORRUPTION
iii. V$BACKUP_SET
iv. V$BACKUP_SPFILE
v. V$COPY_CORRUPTION
vi. V$BACKUP_DATAFILE
vii. V$BACKUP_DEVICE
viii. V$BACKUP_FILES
ix. V$BACKUP_PIECE

x. V$BACKUP_REDOLOG
xi. V$DATABASE_BLOCK_CORRUPTION
xii. V$RMAN_CONFIGURATION
xiii. V$PROXY_ARCHIVEDLOG
xiv. V$PROXY_DATAFILE
xv. V$BACKUP_SYNC_IO
xvi. V$BACKUP_ASYNC_IO

4.9 Recovery Scenarios using RMAN

- Complete Recovery when SYSTEM tablespace is missing.

Problem Generation

Delete system tablespace datafile from operating system when database is up and running.

[oracle@ocm ocmdb]$ rm -i /u01/app/oracle/oradata/disk3/ocmdb/system01.dbf

Solution

i. [oracle@ocm ocmdb]$ sqlplus / as sysdba
ii. **SQL>** SHUTDOWN abort;
iii. **SQL>** STARTUP mount;
iv. **SQL>** SELECT file#, name FROM v$datafile;
v. Using rman connect to target database and catalog database or directly to target database.
[oracle@oem scripts]$ rman target sys/oracle@ocmdb catalog rman/rman@oemdb
vi. **RMAN>** run

```
{
restore datafile 1;
recover datafile 1;
sql ' alter database open ';
}
```

- Complete Recovery when NON-SYSTEM tablespace is missing and database is open and restoring datafile to different location.

Problem Generation

i. Delete USERS tablespace datafile from operating system
[oracle@ocm ocmdb]$ rm -i users01.dbf
ii. Connect as user sh/sh and create a table in users tablespace

```
SQL>   CREATE TABLE sales_test
       TABLESPACE users
       AS
       SELECT *
       FROM sales
       WHERE ROWNUM < 10;

ERROR at line 3:
ORA-01116: error in opening database file 4
ORA-01110: data file 4: '/u01/app/oracle/oradata/disk3/ocmdb/users01.dbf'
ORA-27041: unable to open file
Linux Error: 2: No such file or directory
Additional information: 3
```

Solution

i. As DBA user make datafile users01.dbf off line

SQL> SELECT file#, name FROM v$datafile;

SQL> ALTER DATABASE DATAFILE 4 OFFLINE;

ii. Restoring and recovering datafile 4 at new location

```
RMAN> run
      {
      set newname for datafile 4 to '/u01/app/oracle/oradata/disk5/ocmdb/users01.dbf';
      restore datafile 4;
      switch datafile 4;
      recover datafile 4;
      sql ' alter database datafile 4 online';
      }
```

iii. Connect as user sh/sh and create a table in users tablespace

```
SQL> CREATE TABLE sales_test
     TABLESPACE users
     AS
     SELECT *
     FROM sales
     WHERE ROWNUM < 10;
```

Table created.

- Complete Recovery when NON-SYSTEM tablespace is missing and database is closed and restoring datafile to different location.

Problem Generation

i. Shutdown the database.

SQL> SHUTDOWN immediate;

ii. Delete USERS tablespace datafile from operating system

[oracle@ocm ocmdb]$ rm -i users01.dbf

iii. Start the database

SQL> STARTUP;

```
ORACLE instance started.

Total System Global Area  536870912 bytes
Fixed Size                  1220460 bytes
Variable Size             213909652 bytes
Database Buffers          318767104 bytes
Redo Buffers                2973696 bytes
Database mounted.
ORA-01157: cannot identify/lock data file 4 - see DBWR trace file
ORA-01110: data file 4: '/u01/app/oracle/oradata/disk5/ocmdb/users01.dbf'
```

Solution

i. Make datafile 4 offline

SQL> ALTER DATABASE DATAFILE 4 OFFLINE;

ii. Open the database with datafile 4 oflfine

SQL> ALTER DATABASE OPEN;

iii. Using RMAN again connect to target database

[oracle@oem scripts]$ rman target sys/oracle@ocmdb catalog rman/rman@oemdb

iv. Restoring and recovering datafile 4 at new location

```
RMAN> run
      {
      set newname for datafile 4 to '/u01/app/oracle/oradata/disk3/ocmdb/users01.dbf';
      restore datafile 4;
      switch datafile 4;
      recover datafile 4;
      sql ' alter database datafile 4 online';
      }
```

- Recovery of datafile which has no backups

Problem Generation

i. Create Oracle Managed File tablespace

```
SQL> CREATE TABLESPACE reco_test;
```

ii. Create table sh_sales on tablespace reco_test.

```
SQL> CREATE TABLE sh_sales
     TABLESPACE reco_test
     AS
     SELECT *
     FROM sh.sales
     WHERE ROWNUM < 10;
```

iii. Delete RECO_TEST tablespace datafile from operating system.

[oracle@ocm ~]$ rm –i /u01/app/oracle/oradata/disk5/OCMDB/datafile/o1_mf_reco_tes_6n8dnc7z_.dbf

iv. Select from table sh_sales.

```
SQL> SELECT COUNT (*) FROM sh_sales;
                *

     ERROR at line 1:
     ORA-01116: error in opening database file 5
     ORA-01110: data file 5:
     '/u01/app/oracle/oradata/disk5/OCMDB/datafile/o1_mf_reco_tes_6n8dnc7z_.dbf'
     ORA-27041: unable to open file
     Linux Error: 2: No such file or directory
     Additional information: 3
```

Solution

i. Recover Datafile 5.

```
RMAN> run {
      sql ' alter database datafile 5 offline ';
      restore datafile 5;
      recover datafile 5;
      sql ' alter database datafile 5 online ';
      }
```

ii. Select from table sh_sales.

```
SQL> SELECT COUNT (*) FROM sh_sales;
```

- Recovery of missing controlfile (Copy other controlfile and mount database).

Problem Generation

i. Shutdown the Database

SQL> SHUTDOWN immediate;

ii. Delete Control file control01.ctl from operating system

[oracle@ocm ocmdb]$ rm -i /u01/app/oracle/oradata/disk1/ocmdb/control01.ctl

iii. Startup Database.

```
SQL> STARTUP;
     ORACLE instance started.
     Total System Global Area  536870912 bytes
     Fixed Size                  1220460 bytes
     Variable Size             218103956 bytes
     Database Buffers          314572800 bytes
     Redo Buffers                2973696 bytes
     ORA-00205: error in identifying control file, check alert log for more info
```

Solution

i. Check the control file location

SQL> SHOW PARAMETER control

NAME	TYPE	VALUE
control_file_record_keep_time	integer	7
control_files	string	/u01/app/oracle/oradata/disk1/ocmdb/control01.ctl, /u01/app/oracle/admin/ocmdb/control/control02.ctl

ii. Copy control01.ctl from control02.ctl

[oracle@ocm ocmdb]$ cp /u01/app/oracle/admin/ocmdb/control/control02.ctl /u01/app/oracle/oradata/disk1/ocmdb/control01.ctl

iii. Mount the Database and Open it.

SQL> ALTER DATABASE MOUNT;

SQL> ALTER DATABASE OPEN;

- Incomplete recovery is required when archived log, redo log is missing, then recovery can only be made until the previous sequence, or when an important object was dropped and recovery needs to be made until before the object was dropped. Use until sequence or until time or until cancel for incomplete recovery.

Problem Generation

i. Shutdown Database.

SQL> SHUTDOWN immediate;

ii. Delete redo log files from operating system

[oracle@ocm ocmdb]$ rm -i /u01/app/oracle/oradata/disk4/ocmdb/redo01b.log

[oracle@ocm ocmdb]$ rm -i /u01/app/oracle/oradata/disk2/ocmdb/redo01a.log

If redo log file is lost when database is up, always switch logfile few times until sql statement hangs to archive the available redo logfiles, which are still not archived.

iii. Startup the Database.

```
SQL> STARTUP;
     ORACLE instance started.
     Total System Global Area  536870912 bytes
     Fixed Size                  1220460 bytes
     Variable Size             218103956 bytes
     Database Buffers          314572800 bytes
     Redo Buffers                2973696 bytes
     Database mounted.
     ORA-00313: open failed for members of log group 1 of thread 1
     ORA-00312: online log 1 thread 1:
     '/u01/app/oracle/oradata/disk2/ocmdb/redo01a.log'
     ORA-00312: online log 1 thread 1:
     '/u01/app/oracle/oradata/disk4/ocmdb/redo01b.log'
```

Solution

i. Complete database restore is required, execute sql below to get latest sequence# archived, add 1 to last sequence and then use in RMAN to recover database.

```
SQL> SELECT  thread#,
             resetlogs_change#,
             archived,
             sequence#,
             TO_CHAR (completion_time, 'YYYY-MM-DD:HH24:MI:SS') completion_time
     FROM    v$archived_log
     WHERE   archived = 'YES'
     AND     completion_time = (SELECT MAX (completion_time)
                                      FROM v$archived_log
                                     WHERE archived = 'YES');
```

THREAD#	RESETLOGS_CHANGE#	ARC	SEQUENCE#	COMPLETION_TIME
1	1	YES	58	2011-01-29:21:02:46

ii. Connect to target database using RMAN catalog

[oracle@oem scripts]$ rman target sys/oracle@ocmdb catalog rman/rman@oemdb

iii. RMAN command to recover database.

```
RMAN> run
      {
      restore database;
      recover database until sequence 59 thread 1;
      sql ' alter database open resetlogs ';
      }
```

iv. After database is open switch logfile few times

```
SQL> ALTER SYSTEM SWITCH LOGFILE;
SQL> ALTER SYSTEM SWITCH LOGFILE;
SQL> ALTER SYSTEM SWITCH LOGFILE;
```

- Recover, if all controlfiles are missing

Problem Generation

i. Shutdown Database.

```
SQL> SHUTDOWN immediate;
```

ii. Delete all Control files from operating system

[oracle@ocm ocmdb]$ rm -i /u01/app/oracle/oradata/disk1/ocmdb/control01.ctl

[oracle@ocm ocmdb]$ rm -i /u01/app/oracle/admin/ocmdb/control/control02.ctl

iii. Connect as sysdba and startup Database.

[oracle@ocm ocmdb]$ sqlplus / as sysdba

```
SQL> STARTUP;
     ORACLE instance started.
     Total System Global Area  536870912 bytes
     Fixed Size                  1220460 bytes
     Variable Size             222298260 bytes
     Database Buffers          310378496 bytes
     Redo Buffers                2973696 bytes
     ORA-00205: error in identifying control file, check alert log for more info
```

Solution

i. Using RMAN restore contolfile from Autobackup and Recover Database

```
RMAN> run
      {
      restore controlfile from autobackup;
      sql ' alter database mount';
      recover database;
      sql ' alter database open resetlogs';
      }
```

ii. List Database Incarnation

```
RMAN> list incarnation;
      List of Database Incarnations
      DB Key  Inc Key  DB Name  DB ID        STATUS  Reset SCN  Reset Time
      ------- -------- -------- ------------ -- -------- ---------
      1       2        OCMDB    4083722939   PARENT  1          15-JAN-11
      1       1415     OCMDB    4083722939   PARENT  503961     29-JAN-11
      1       1867     OCMDB    4083722939   CURRENT 519078     29-JAN-11
```

iii. After database is open switch logfile few times

```
SQL> ALTER SYSTEM SWITCH LOGFILE;
SQL> ALTER SYSTEM SWITCH LOGFILE;
SQL> ALTER SYSTEM SWITCH LOGFILE;
```

iv. Always backup controlfile after open resetlogs even if CONTROLFILE AUTOBACKUP ON. Let us NOT BACKUP controlfile and see what happens in next scenario.

RMAN> backup current controlfile; — For now do not execute this command

- Recover if all controlfiles,datafiles,spfile,redologs are lost

Problem Generation

i. Shutdown Database.

SQL> SHUTDOWN immediate;

ii. Delete all the datafiles,controlfiles,redo logfiles,spfile,initocmdb.ora files from Operating System

iii. Startup Database

```
SQL> STARTUP;
ORA-01078: failure in processing system parameters
LRM-00109: could not open parameter file '/u01/app/oracle/product/10.2.0/db_1/dbs/
```

initocmdb.ora'

Make sure you have lost all the files not just spfile, if only spfile is lost , then too you will get above error you need to create only spfile.

Solution

i. Using RMAN connect to target database using catalog

[oracle@oem scripts]$ rman target sys/oracle@ocmdb catalog rman/rman@oemdb

Recovery Manager: Release 10.2.0.1.0 - Production on Sun Jan 30 06:02:44 2011

Copyright (c) 1982, 2005, Oracle. All rights reserved.

connected to target database **(not started)**
connected to recovery catalog database

ii. Set Database DBID

RMAN> set dbid <dbid> — dbid 4083722939

iii. Startup Database in Nomount State

RMAN> startup nomount;

iv. Restore spfile from Autobackup

RMAN> restore spfile from autobackup;

v. Again start the Database in Nomount State

RMAN> startup force nomount;

vi. Restore controlfile from Autobackup

RMAN> restore controlfile from autobackup;

vii. Mount Database

RMAN> alter database mount;

viii. Open a terminal in OCMDB machine and check archive log completion time

[oracle@ocm ~]$ sqlplus / as sysdba

```
SQL> SELECT  thread#,
             resetlogs_change#,
             archived,
             sequence#,
             TO_CHAR (completion_time, 'YYYY-MM-DD:HH24:MI:SS')
             completion_time
     FROM    v$archived_log
     WHERE   archived = 'YES'
     AND     completion_time = (SELECT MAX (completion_time)
                                  FROM v$archived_log
                                WHERE archived = 'YES');
```

THREAD#	RESETLOGS_CHANGE#	ARC	SEQUENCE#	COMPLETION_TIME
1	519078	YES	1	2011-01-29:23:18:17

ix. By executing the command below we may not be able to recover database because control file is from older incarnation. This is because we have not taken backup of controlfile after reset logs and immediately crashed the database after recovery in previous scenario.

```
RMAN> run
      {
```

```
restore database;
recover database until  sequence 1 thread 1;
sql ' alter database open resetlogs';
}
```

x. Now, you have to reset database to older incarnation and recover the database.

xi. List Database Incarnation.

RMAN> list incarnation;

List of Database Incarnations

DB Key	Inc Key	DB Name	DB ID	STATUS	Reset SCN	Reset Time
1	2	OCMDB	4083722939	PARENT	1	15-JAN-11
1	1415	OCMDB	4083722939	PARENT	**503961**	29-JAN-11
1	1867	OCMDB	4083722939	CURRENT	519078	29-JAN-11

xii. Open a terminal in OCMDB machine and check archive log completion time.

```
SQL> SELECT   thread#,
              resetlogs_change#,
              archived,
              sequence#,
              TO_CHAR  (completion_time,  'YYYY-MM-DD:HH24:MI:SS')
              completion_time
     FROM     v$archived_log
     WHERE    archived  =  'YES'
     ORDER  BY  completion_time;
```

THREAD#	RESETLOGS_CHANGE#	ARC	SEQUENCE#	COMPLETION_TIME
1	**503961**	YES	**4**	2011-01-29:22:18:18

Add 1 to the latest sequence of last incarnation i.e. 4+1 =5

xiii. Reset the Database to old incarnation and recover.

```
RMAN>  reset DATABASE TO incarnation 1415;
RMAN>  run
       {
       restore database;
       recover database until  sequence 5 thread 1;
       sql ' alter database open resetlogs';
       }
```

- Recover if Temporary tablespace is lost

  Recreate the temporary tablespace.

- For other backup recovery scenarios, please refer to Oracle Documentation.

4.10 Flashback Database

- **Configuring Flashback Database**

  i. Check if Database is in Flashback Mode.

  SQL> SELECT db_unique_name, flashback_on FROM v$database;

DB_UNIQUE_NAME	FLASHBACK_ON
ocmdb	NO

ii. Shutdown the Database

SQL> SHUTDOWN IMMEDIATE;

iii. Start the Database in exclusive Mode.

SQL> STARTUP MOUNT EXCLUSIVE;

iv. Set Flashback Retention

SQL> ALTER SYSTEM SET DB_FLASHBACK_RETENTION_TARGET=2880 SCOPE=BOTH;

v. Set Database in Flashback Mode

SQL> ALTER DATABASE FLASHBACK ON;

vi. Open the Database in Normal Mode.

SQL> ALTER DATABASE OPEN;

vii. Make Recyclebin ON

SQL> ALTER SYSTEM SET RECYCLEBIN=ON;

viii. Check Database Flashback Mode

SQL> SELECT db_unique_name, flashback_on FROM v$database;

DB_UNIQUE_NAME	FLASHBACK_ON
ocmdb	YES

ix. Change tablespace Flashback Mode.

SQL> SELECT name, flashback_on FROM v$tablespace;

x. ALTER TABLESPACE <ts_name> flashback {on| off};

- Flashback Table Examples

i. Drop table and flashback it before drop.

SQL> DROP TABLE sh.costs;

SQL> FLASHBACK TABLE sh.costs TO BEFORE DROP;

ii. Drop table and again flashback to new name

SQL> DROP TABLE pm.print_media;

SQL> FLASHBACK TABLE pm.print_media TO BEFORE DROP RENAME TO print_media_old;

SQL> CONNECT pm/pm

SQL> RENAME print_media_old TO print_media;

iii. Flash back table from multiple version in recyclebin

Problem Generation

SQL> CONNECT oe/oe

SQL> CREATE TABLE order_items_keep
AS
    SELECT * FROM order_items;

SQL> SELECT COUNT (*) FROM order_items;

COUNT(*)
665

```
SQL> DELETE FROM order_items
     WHERE ROWNUM <= 65;
65 rows deleted.
SQL> COMMIT;
SQL> DROP TABLE order_items;
Table dropped.
SQL> show recyclebin;

ORIGINAL NAME   RECYCLEBIN NAME                  OBJECT TYPE   DROP TIME
-------------   ------------------------------   -----------   -------------------
ORDER_ITEMS     BIN$mxC30WJTOUPgQKjAeQIElA==$0   TABLE         2011-01-30:09:05:15

SQL> CREATE TABLE order_items
     AS
     SELECT * FROM order_items_keep;
Table created.
SQL> DROP TABLE order_items;
Table dropped.
SQL> show recyclebin;

ORIGINAL NAME   RECYCLEBIN NAME                  OBJECT TYPE   DROP TIME
-------------   ------------------------------   -----------   -------------------
ORDER_ITEMS     BIN$mxC30WJWOUPgQKjAeQIElA==$0   TABLE         2011-01-30:09:07:52
ORDER_ITEMS     BIN$mxC30WJTOUPgQKjAeQIElA==$0   TABLE         2011-01-30:09:05:15

SQL> CREATE TABLE order_items
     AS
     SELECT * FROM order_items_keep;
Table created.
SQL> DELETE FROM order_items;
665 rows deleted.
SQL> COMMIT;
SQL> DROP TABLE order_items;
Table dropped.
SQL> show recyclebin;
ORIGINAL NAME   RECYCLEBIN NAME                  OBJECT TYPE   DROP TIME
-------------   ------------------------------   -----------   -------------------
ORDER_ITEMS     BIN$mxC30WJZOUPgQKjAeQIElA==$0   TABLE         2011-01-30:09:11:33
ORDER_ITEMS     BIN$mxC30WJWOUPgQKjAeQIElA==$0   TABLE         2011-01-30:09:07:52
ORDER_ITEMS     BIN$mxC30WJTOUPgQKjAeQIElA==$0   TABLE         2011-01-30:09:05:15
```

Now you have 3 tables in recyclebin and you have to recover order_items table, which should have all 665 rows.

Solution

```
SQL> SELECT   original_name,
              object_name,
              TYPE,
              ts_name,
              droptime,
              related,
              space
     FROM     user_recyclebin
     WHERE    can_undrop = 'YES';
```

Based on time the table mentioned below is the table that has all 665 rows.

```
ORDER_ITEMS     BIN$mxC30WJWOUPgQKjAeQIElA==$0 TABLE          2011-01-30:09:07:52
SQL> SELECT COUNT (*) FROM "BIN$mxC30WJWOUPgQKjAeQIElA==$0";

  COUNT(*)
----------
       665
SQL> FLASHBACK TABLE "BIN$mxC30WJWOUPgQKjAeQIElA==$0" TO BEFORE DROP;
Flashback complete.
SQL> SELECT COUNT (*) FROM order_items;

  COUNT(*)
----------
       665
```

- Manual Space Reclamation from Recyclebin

```
PURGE    {TABLE <table_name>|INDEX <index_name>};
PURGE TABLESPACE <ts_name> [USER <user_name>];
PURGE    [USER_|DBA_]RECYCLEBIN;
```

- Bypass Recyclebin

```
DROP TABLE <table_name> [PURGE];
DROP TABLESPACE <ts_name> [INCLUDING CONTENTS];
DROP USER <user_name> [CASCADE];
```

- Flashback Database commands that can be practiced after finishing all the exercises in book.

```
RMAN> FLASHBACK DATABASE TO TIME = "to_date('2011-01-29 20:00:00','YYYY-MM-DD HH24:MI:SS')";
RMAN> FLASHBACK DATABASE TO SCN=40000;
RMAN> FLASHBACK DATABASE TO SEQUENCE=60 THREAD=1;
SQL> FLASHBACK DATABASE  TO TIMESTAMP(SYSDATE-1/24);
SQL> FLASHBACK DATABASE TO SCN 40000;
SQL> CREATE RESTORE POINT before_insert GUARANTEE FLASHBACK DATABASE;
SQL> FLASHBACK DATABASE TO RESTORE POINT before_insert;
```

- Monitor Flashback Database commands

```
SQL> SELECT estimated_flashback_size, flashback_size FROM V$FLASHBACK_DATABASE_LOG;
SQL> SELECT oldest_flashback_scn, oldest_flashback_time
     FROM   V$FLASHBACK_DATABASE_LOG;
```

```
SQL> SELECT * FROM V$FLASHBACK_DATABASE_STAT;
SQL> SELECT NAME,
            space_limit QUOTA,
            space_used used,
            space_reclaimable reclaimable,
            number_of_files files
     FROM   v$recovery_file_dest;
```

- Block Corruption: dbverify

  - The select statement below gives error

```
SQL> SELECT * FROM sh.sales;
     select * from sh.sales
       *
     ERROR at line 1:
     ORA-01578: ORACLE data block corrupted (file # 10, block # 1324)
     ORA-01110: data file 10: '/u01/app/oracle/oradata/disk5/ocmdb/example01.dbf'
     ORA-26040: Data block was loaded using the NOLOGGING option
```

  - Use dbverify to find block corruption

    dbv file=/u01/app/oracle/oradata/disk5/ocmdb/example01.dbf blocksize=8192

    Output from dbv command

```
DBVERIFY - Verification complete

Total Pages Examined         : 13184
Total Pages Processed (Data) : 7224
Total Pages Failing   (Data) : 0
Total Pages Processed (Index): 799
Total Pages Failing   (Index): 0
Total Pages Processed (Other): 3801
Total Pages Processed (Seg)  : 0
Total Pages Failing   (Seg)  : 0
Total Pages Empty            : 1360
Total Pages Marked Corrupt   : 2287
Total Pages Influx           : 0
Highest block SCN            : 582419 (0.582419)
```

  - Check the status of latest backup file of example tablespace. In this case it also has corrupted blocks.

    dbv file=/u01/app/oracle/flash_recovery_area/OCMDB/DB_2fm3aiot_1_1 blocksize=8192

  - Checked further old backups and verified good backups file for example datafile

    dbv file=/u01/app/oracle/flash_recovery_area/OCMDB/DB_data_D-OCMDB_I-4083722939_TS-EXAMPLE_FNO-10_1gm3a8tu blocksize=8192

  - Used above file to restore example tablespace

  - Other commands to validate structure of Database Segments

```
ANALYZE TABLE table_name VALIDATE STRUCTURE CASCADE;

ANALYZE INDEX index_name VALIDATE STRUCTURE;

ANALYZE TABLE partitioned_table PARTITION <partition_name> VALIDATE STRUCTURE INTO invalid_rows;
```

4.11 Managing Backups from Grid Control

- Click on Targets tab, then on Databases subtab choose ocmdb database, and go to Maintenance page. In High Availability section, you can schedule, manage, configure, report and recover the database. Below are Backup/Recovery pages from Oracle's OEM Grid.

  High Availability

  Backup/Recovery
  Schedule Backup
  Perform Recovery
  Manage Current Backups
  Manage Restore Points
  Backup Reports

  Backup/Recovery Settings

  Backup Settings
  Recovery Settings
  Recovery Catalog Setting

- **Navigate through all the High Availability section pages and learn detail of every page.**
- Below are few sample screen shots of Oracle's OEM Grid Control for Backup and Recovery
- Maintenance Page

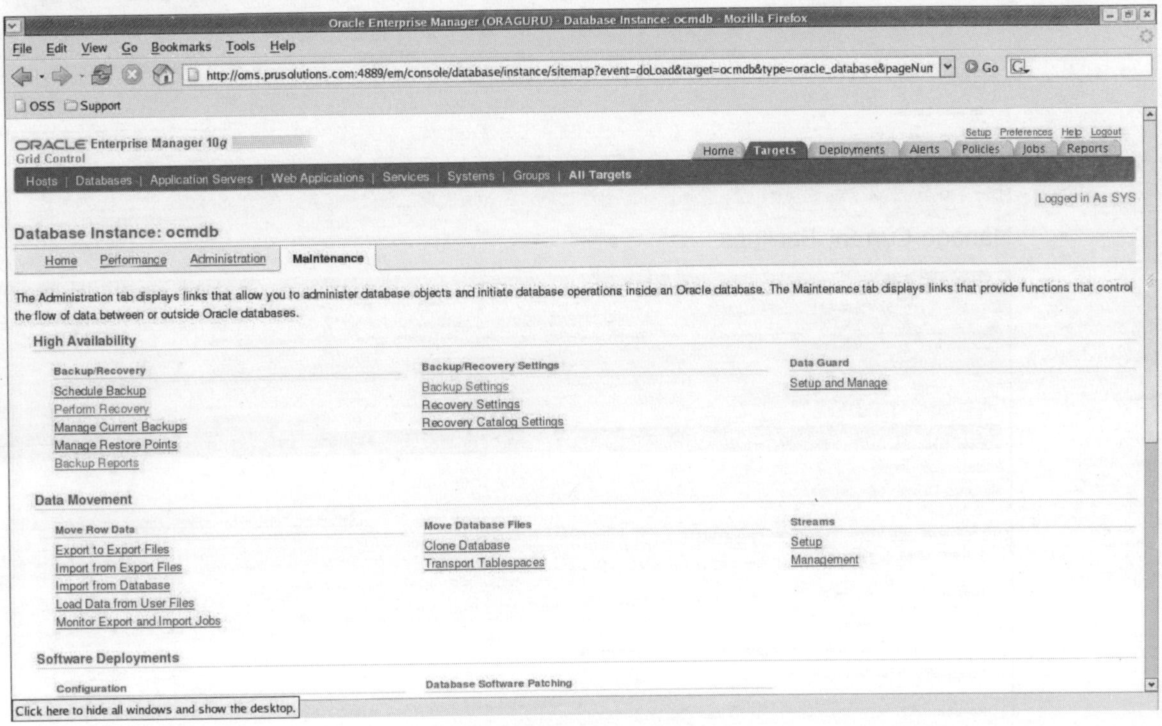

- View Backup Report

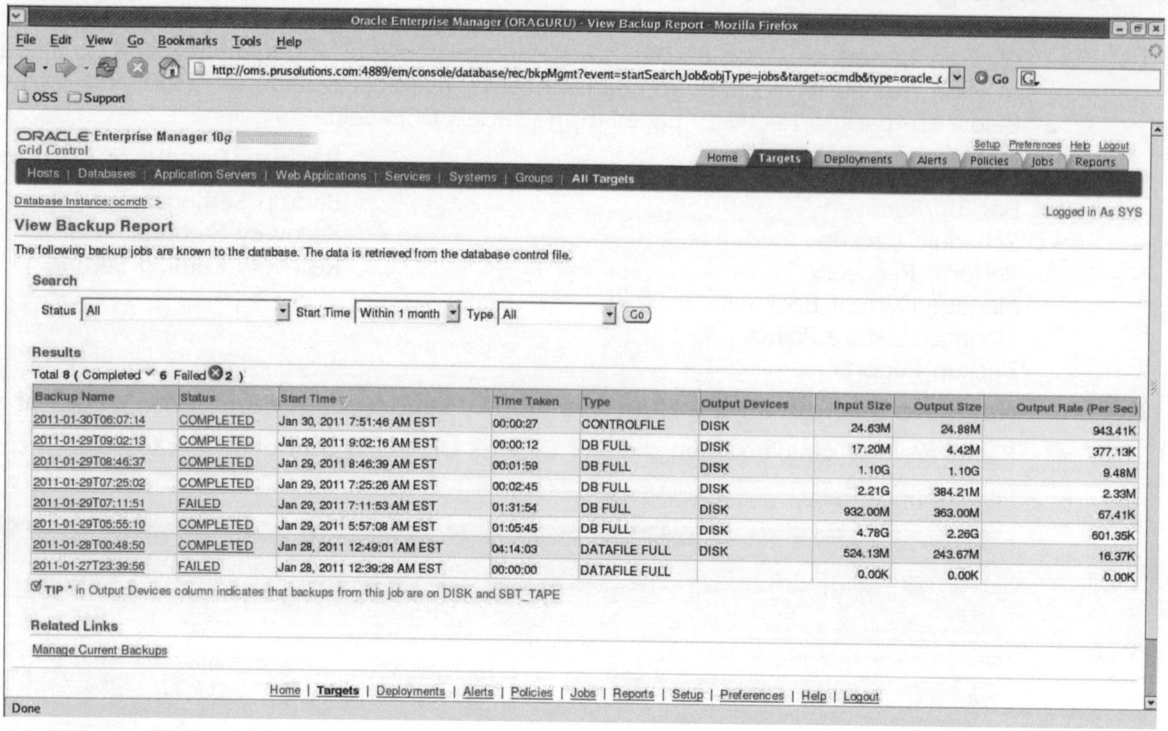

- Manage Current Backups.

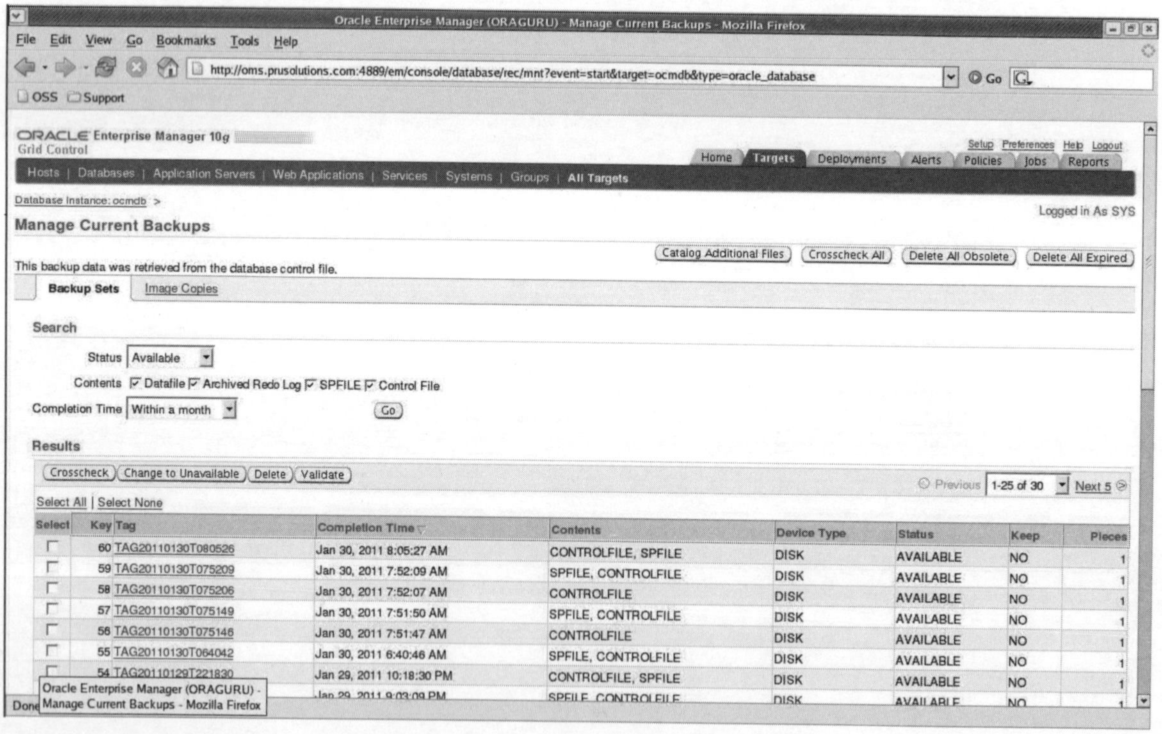

- Crosscheck, Change to Unavailable, Validate, and Delete Backups.

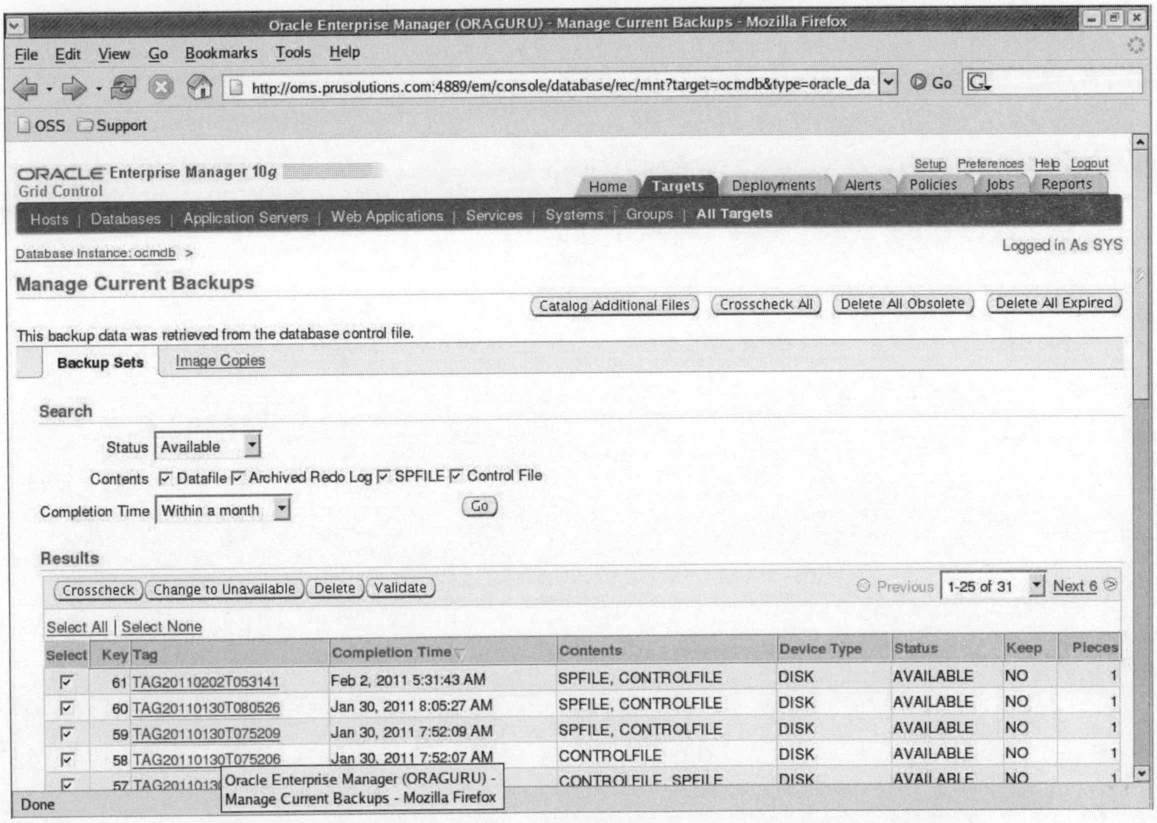

- Navigate through Oracle Documentation to get to RMAN Commands without search tab

  Oracle Database Documentation Library > Books > BAC > Backup and Recovery Reference > HTML

  On contents page Ctrl f and search for *"Commands"* you will reach RMAN Commands.

5

Data Management

- Implement fine-grained auditing
- Create a secure application role
- Grant specific privileges for a Flashback Query
- Set parameters for retaining undo
- Implement fine-grained access control
- Create and manage contexts
- Use SQL*Loader
- Implement transportable tablespaces between homogeneous and heterogeneous systems (using different methods of moving files)
- Choose the appropriate partition method (range, hash, list, and composite)
- Choose the appropriate partition key
- Choose appropriate indexing methods (local, global, prefixed, and nonprefixed)
- Perform partition maintenance operations
- Maintain indexes on a partitioned table
- Create and manage LOB segments
- Apply parallelism appropriately
- Tune memory for parallel operations
- Set parallel parameters

5.1 Implement fine-grained auditing and Virtual Private Database (VPD)

- Using Secure Session-Based Application Context

```
SQL> connect sys@ocmdb as sysdba
```

- Create user scott.

```
SQL> GRANT CREATE SESSION TO scott IDENTIFIED BY tiger;
SQL> ALTER USER scott DEFAULT TABLESPACE USERS TEMPORARY TABLESPACE temp;
SQL> GRANT CONNECT, RESOURCE TO scott;
```

- Test SYS_CONTEXT

```
SQL> SET serveroutput ON
SQL> SET serveroutput ON
SQL> BEGIN
          DBMS_OUTPUT.put_line (SYS_CONTEXT ('userenv','current_user'));
     END;
     /
     SCOTT
     PL/SQL PROCEDURE successfully completed.
SQL> BEGIN
          DBMS_OUTPUT.put_line(SYS_CONTEXT('userenv','session_user'));
     END;
     /
     SCOTT
     PL/SQL PROCEDURE successfully completed
SQL> EXEC DBMS_OUTPUT.put_line(SYS_CONTEXT('userenv','session_user'));
     SCOTT
     PL/SQL PROCEDURE successfully completed.
SQL> SELECT SYS_CONTEXT('userenv','ip_address') FROM DUAL;
```

- Grant Privileges for Secure Session-Based Application Context

```
SQL> CONNECT SYS@ocmdb AS SYSDBA
SQL> GRANT CREATE ANY CONTEXT TO scott;
SQL> GRANT ADMINISTER DATABASE TRIGGER TO scott;
SQL> GRANT SELECT_CATALOG_ROLE TO scott
SQL> GRANT SELECT ON hr.employees TO scott;
SQL> GRANT SELECT ON oe.orders TO scott;
SQL> CONNECT scott/tiger@ocmdb
```

- **Implement VPD Policy that junior Sale Rep can see only their own Orders.**
  - For secure session-based application context, following tasks are performed.
    i. Create a PL/SQL Package that Sets the Secure Context for Your Application
    ii. Create a Unique Secure Context and Associate It with the PL/SQL Package
    iii. Set the Secure Context Before the User Retrieves Data
    iv. Use the Secure Context in a VPD Policy Function

```
SQL> CREATE CONTEXT sales_rep_user USING cur_sales_rep;
```

```
SQL> CREATE OR REPLACE PACKAGE cur_sales_rep
     IS
            PROCEDURE set_sales_rep;
     END;
     /
SQL> CREATE OR REPLACE PACKAGE BODY cur_sales_rep
     IS
             PROCEDURE set_sales_rep
     IS
             v_rep_id          hr.employees.employee_id%TYPE;
             v_first_name      hr.employees.first_name%TYPE;
             v_last_name       hr.employees.last_name%TYPE;
     BEGIN
             SELECT employee_id, first_name, last_name
             INTO v_rep_id, v_first_name, v_last_name
             FROM hr.employees
             WHERE email = SYS_CONTEXT ('USERENV', 'SESSION_USER');
             DBMS_SESSION.SET_CONTEXT ('sales_rep_user', 'rep_id', v_rep_id);
             DBMS_SESSION.SET_CONTEXT ('sales_rep_user', 'rep_name',
                                       v_first_name || ' ' || v_last_name);
             DBMS_SESSION.SET_CONTEXT ('sales_rep_user', 'rep_email',
                                       SYS_CONTEXT ('USERENV', 'SESSION_USER'));
             EXCEPTION
             WHEN NO_DATA_FOUND
             THEN
                  NULL;
             END;
     END;
     /
SQL> CREATE OR REPLACE TRIGGER sales_rep_logon
     AFTER LOGON
     ON DATABASE
     BEGIN
     cur_sales_rep.set_sales_rep;
     END;
     /
SQL> SELECT *
     FROM dba_context
     WHERE namespace = 'SALES_REP_USER';
SQL> SELECT DISTINCT e.first_name, e.last_name, e.email
     FROM hr.employees e, oe.orders o
     WHERE e.employee_id = o.sales_rep_id;
```

FIRST_NAME	LAST_NAME	EMAIL
Janette	King	JKING
Louise	Doran	LDORAN
Allan	McEwen	AMCEWEN
Sarath	Sewall	SSEWALL
Oliver	Tuvault	OTUVAULT
Lindsey	Smith	LSMITH
Christopher	Olsen	COLSEN
Nanette	Cambrault	NCAMBRAU
Danielle	Greene	DGREENE

- The junior Sales Rep can see only their Orders from oe.orders table
- Create few of above users with logging id as email above

```
SQL> GRANT CONNECT,RESOURCE TO JKING IDENTIFIED BY JKING;
SQL> GRANT CONNECT,RESOURCE TO LDORAN IDENTIFIED BY LDORAN;
SQL> GRANT CONNECT,RESOURCE TO LSMITH IDENTIFIED BY LSMITH;
SQL> GRANT CONNECT,RESOURCE TO COLSEN IDENTIFIED BY COLSEN;
SQL> GRANT CONNECT,RESOURCE TO DGREENE IDENTIFIED BY DGREENE;
SQL> GRANT SELECT ON hr.employees TO JKING,LDORAN,LSMITH,COLSEN,DGREENE;
SQL> GRANT SELECT ON oe.orders TO JKING,LDORAN,LSMITH,COLSEN,DGREENE;
SQL> CONNECT jking/jking
     Connected.
SQL> SET serveroutput ON
SQL> SELECT SYS_CONTEXT('sales_rep_user','rep_id') FROM DUAL;
     SYS_CONTEXT('SALES_REP_USER','
     ----------------------------------------------------------
     156
SQL> EXEC DBMS_OUTPUT.put_line(SYS_CONTEXT('sales_rep_user','rep_name'));
     Janette King
SQL> BEGIN
             DBMS_OUTPUT.put_line (SYS_CONTEXT ('sales_rep_user', 'rep_email'));
     END;
     /
     JKING
```

- Grant privileges to scott.

```
SQL> CONNECT SYS@ocmdb AS SYSDBA
SQL> GRANT EXECUTE ON DBMS_RLS TO scott;
SQL> GRANT EXEMPT ACCESS POLICY TO scott;
```

- Create package.

```
SQL> CREATE OR REPLACE PACKAGE pkg_sales_rep_policy
     IS
     FUNCTION view_rep_orders (object_schema IN VARCHAR2, object_name  VARCHAR2)
     RETURN VARCHAR2;
     END;
     /
     Package created.
SQL> CREATE OR REPLACE PACKAGE BODY pkg_sales_rep_policy
     IS
     FUNCTION view_rep_orders (object_schema IN VARCHAR2, object_name VARCHAR2)
     RETURN VARCHAR2
     IS
     v_emp_id     NUMBER;
        BEGIN
         RETURN 'employee_id = SYS_CONTEXT(''sales_rep_user'',''rep_id'')';
        END;
     END;
     /
```

```
SQL> SELECT pkg_sales_rep_policy.view_rep_orders('x', 'y') FROM DUAL;
     PKG_SALES_REP_POLICY.VIEW_REP_
     --------------------------------------------------------------
     employee_id = SYS_CONTEXT('sales_rep_user','rep_id')
SQL> BEGIN
             DBMS_RLS.add_policy  ('HR',
                                   'EMPLOYEES',
                                   'SALES_REP_POL',
                                   'SCOTT',
                                   'pkg_sales_rep_policy.view_rep_orders',
                                   'SELECT');
     END;
     /
SQL> CONNECT  jking/jking
SQL> SELECT  employee_id,
             first_name,
             last_name,
             email
     FROM    hr.employees;
SQL> SELECT  e.first_name,
             e.last_name,
             o.order_id,
             o.order_date,
             o.customer_id,
             o.order_total
     FROM    hr.employees  E,  oe.orders  o
     WHERE   e.employee_id  =  o.sales_rep_id;
SQL> CONNECT  scott/tiger
SQL> EXEC  DBMS_RLS.drop_policy('HR',  'EMPLOYEES','SALES_REP_POL');
```

5.2 Managing Undo Tablespace

- Navigate through Oracle Documentation to get to Undo tablespace without search tab

Oracle Database Documentation Library > Books > ADM > Administrator's Guide > HTML

On contents page Ctrl f and search for *"Undo Tablespaces"* you will reach Managing Undo Tablespaces.

Parameter	Value	Description
undo_management	AUTO	Undo Management AUTO/MANUAL
undo_retention	900	Time in seconds for Undo Retention
undo_tablespace	undotbs1	Name to use multiple undo tablespace

5.3 Use SQL*Loader

- Navigate through Oracle Documentation to get to SQL*Loader Commands without search tab

Oracle Database Documentation Library > Books > UTI > **Utilities**> ***HTML***

On contents page Ctrl f and search for "SQL*Loader Case Studies" you will reach SQL*Loader Case Studies which will give location of sqlldr files in $ORACLE_HOME/rdbms/demo

On contents page Ctrl f and search for "Assembling " you will reach "Assembling Logical Records from Physical Records" which will give examples for assembling logical records from Physical records.

- Special case controlfiles samples are mentioned below.
  - Loading Fixed-Format Fields

```
LOAD DATA
INFILE '$sqlload/item.dat'
BADFILE '$sqlload/item.bad'
DISCARDFILE '$sqlload/item.dsc'
DISCARDMAX 0
INTO TABLE ITM024T
(
 ITEM_CODE   POSITION (01:04)   CHAR,
 ITEM_TEXT   POSITION(06:25)   CHAR,
 ITEM_NBR    POSITION (27:30)   INTEGER EXTERNAL
)
```

  - Loading LOB data using external lob file.

```
load data
infile *
into table PRODUCT
append
fields terminated by '|'
optionally enclosed by '"'
( PRODUCT_ID           integer external,
  PRODUCT_NAME         CHAR,
  MANUFACTURED_DT  DATE,
   DISPLAYDATA" LOBFILE ('/u01/app/oracle/data/displaydata") TERMINATED BY EOF
   NULLIF RES_FILE = 'NONE'
)
begindata
7000|"APPLE"|09-JUN-01|/u01/app/oracle/data/displaydata.dat
```

  - Using CONTINUEIF to Assemble Logical Records

```
LOAD DATA
INFILE          'items.dat'
BADFILE         'items.bad'
DISCARDFILE   'items.dsc'
INSERT
CONTINUEIF NEXT (1:1)! = "|"
INTO TABLE items
fields terminated by '|'
TRAILING NULLCOLS
(
  item_type               CHAR,
  item_number             CHAR,
  active_flag             CHAR,
  descriptipon            CHAR,
  last_update_ts          CHAR,
  last_update_userid    CHAR
)
```

5.4 Implement Transportable Tablespaces using SQLPLUS and Data Pump Utility

RMAN Catalog was created in oemdb database, using oracle transportable feature , move some tables belong to rman user in oemdb database to ocmdb database.

Tables to be moved from rman@oemdb to rman@ocmdb

DB	TABLE
NODE	TABLE

- Find out all the table tablespaces and index tablespaces for above tables.

```
SQL> SELECT  DISTINCT  dt.owner,
             dt.table_name,
             dt.tablespace_name  table_tablespace_name,
             di.tablespace_name  index_tablespace_name
     FROM dba_tables  dt,  dba_indexes  di
     WHERE dt.table_name  IN  ('DB',  'NODE')
     AND     dt.owner  =  'RMAN'
     AND     dt.table_name  =  di.table_name
     AND     dt.owner  =  di.owner;
```

OWNER	TABLE_NAME	TABLE_TABLESPACE_NAME	INDEX_TABLESPACE_NAME
RMAN	NODE	RCAT_TS	RCAT_TS
RMAN	DB	RCAT_TS	RCAT_TS

- Get details of all other tables on above tablespaces. All the tables and indexes on tablespace RCAT_TS will be transported.

```
SQL> SELECT owner, table_name
     FROM dba_tables
     WHERE tablespace_name IN
             (SELECT DISTINCT dt.tablespace_name table_tablespace_name
             FROM dba_tables dt
               WHERE dt.table_name IN ('DB', 'NODE') AND dt.owner = 'RMAN');
37 rows selected.
```

- Check if any of above tables are on snapshots.

```
SQL> SELECT  owner,  name
     FROM    dba_snapshots
     WHERE  (owner,  table_name)  IN
             (SELECT  owner,  table_name
             FROM  dba_tables
             WHERE  tablespace_name  IN
                     (SELECT  DISTINCT
                              dt.tablespace_name  table_tablespace_name
                     FROM  dba_tables  dt
                     WHERE  dt.table_name  IN  ('DB',  'NODE')
                     AND  dt.owner  =  'RMAN'));
     no rows selected
```

- Check if any of above tables are partition tables

```
SQL> SELECT *
     FROM DBA_TAB_PARTITIONS
     WHERE (TABLE_owner, table_name) IN
           (SELECT owner, table_name
           FROM dba_tables
           WHERE tablespace_name IN
                 (SELECT DISTINCT
                         dt.tablespace_name table_tablespace_name
                 FROM dba_tables dt
                 WHERE dt.table_name IN ('DB', 'NODE')
                 AND dt.owner = 'RMAN'));
     no rows selected
```

- Check if there are any snapshots whose indexes are on above tablespace

```
SQL> SELECT owner, name
     FROM dba_snapshots
     WHERE (owner, table_name) IN
           (SELECT DISTINCT owner, table_name
           FROM dba_indexes
           WHERE tablespace_name IN
                 (SELECT DISTINCT
                         di.tablespace_name index_tablespace_name
                 FROM dba_tables dt, dba_indexes di
                 WHERE     dt.table_name IN ('DB', 'NODE')
                 AND dt.owner = 'RMAN'
                 AND dt.table_name = di.table_name
                 AND dt.owner = di.owner));
no rows selected
```

- Check are there any partitions whose indexes belong to above tablespaces

```
SQL> SELECT *
     FROM DBA_TAB_PARTITIONS
     WHERE (TABLE_owner, table_name) IN
           (SELECT DISTINCT owner, table_name
           FROM dba_indexes
           WHERE tablespace_name IN
                 (SELECT DISTINCT
                         di.tablespace_name index_tablespace_name
                 FROM dba_tables dt, dba_indexes di
                 WHERE   dt.table_name IN ('DB', 'NODE')
                 AND dt.owner = 'RMAN'
                 AND dt.table_name = di.table_name
                 AND dt.owner = di.owner));
     no rows selected
```

If any rows selected then move those tables, snapshots and indexes to different tablespace and then the above tablespace is ready for transportation.

Conclusion: The RCAT_TS tablespace can be transported in set without any problems.

Suggestions: We can only transport TABLE TABLESPACES and can rebuild Indexes directly on target

OR

- You can use the method below to find out if any violations in rcat_ts tablespace set

- Check for any Violations in above Tablespaces Set

  After all the indexes mentioned above are dropped, execute the package below passing all the tablespaces in **Self Contained Set of Tablespaces**

  This check violation for transportable tablespaces. The script should be executed as SYS AS SYSDBA user.

  SQL> EXECUTE DBMS_TTS.TRANSPORT_SET_CHECK('RCAT_TS',TRUE);
  PL/SQL procedure successfully completed.

  Use the select statement below to find any violation and it should not show any violations.

  SQL> SELECT * FROM TRANSPORT_SET_VIOLATIONS;

  no rows selected

- Make all the tablespaces in the set in Read only mode.

  SQL> ALTER TABLESPACE rcat_ts READ ONLY;

- Invoke Data pump utility on source system to export metadata for the above tablespaces.

  [oracle@oem ~]$ expdp system/oracle@oemdb DUMPFILE=transport.dmp DIRECTORY=DATA_PUMP_DIR TRANSPORT_TABLESPACES=RCAT_TS TRANSPORT_FULL_CHECK=Y

- Use OS copy command to copy all the files for above tablespaces on USB Drive.

Use sql script below to get details of all the files exercise caution when using Unix utility dd to copy from raw devices

```
SQL> SELECT file_name
     FROM   dba_data_files
     WHERE  tablespace_name IN ('RCAT_TS');

FILE_NAME
--------------------------------------------------------------
/u01/app/oracle/oradata/oemdb/rcat_ts.dbf
```

While copying the data files we have to make sure the data files are copied in the respective mount points

- Make all the tablespaces on source back again in read/write mode.

  SQL> ALTER TABLESPACE rcat_ts READ WRITE;

- Plug-in the table space on target and integrate structural information using Data Pump Import utility impdp on target

  All the users which owns the objects in above transportable tablespaces must exists on target database

$ impdp system/oracle@ocmdb dumpfile=transport.dmp DIRECTORY=DATA_PUMP_DIR TRANSPORT_DATAFILES=/u01/app/oracle/oradata/oemdb/rcat_ts.dbf

5.5 Implement Transportable Tablespaces using Oracle's OEM Grid Control

- Click on Targets tab, then on Databases subtab choose ocmdb database, and go to Maintenance page. Click Transport Tablespaces.

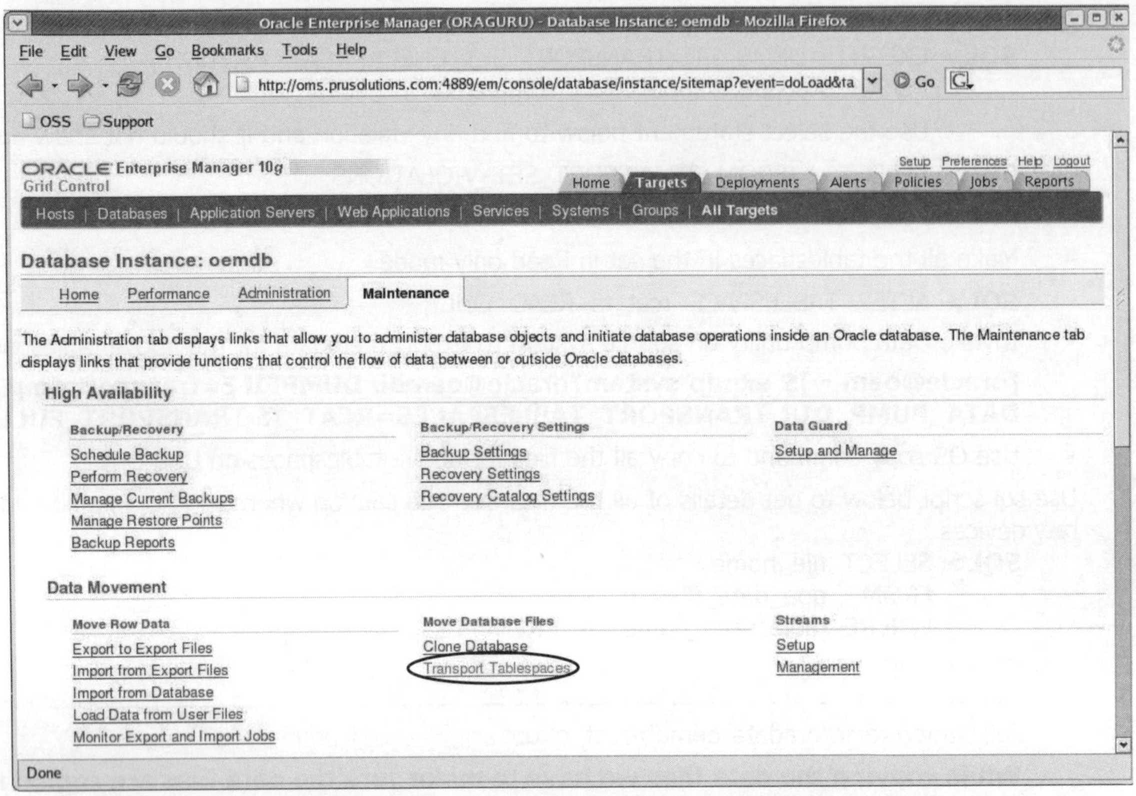

- On Transport Tablespace Page: Select Generate a transport tablespace set. Click Continue.

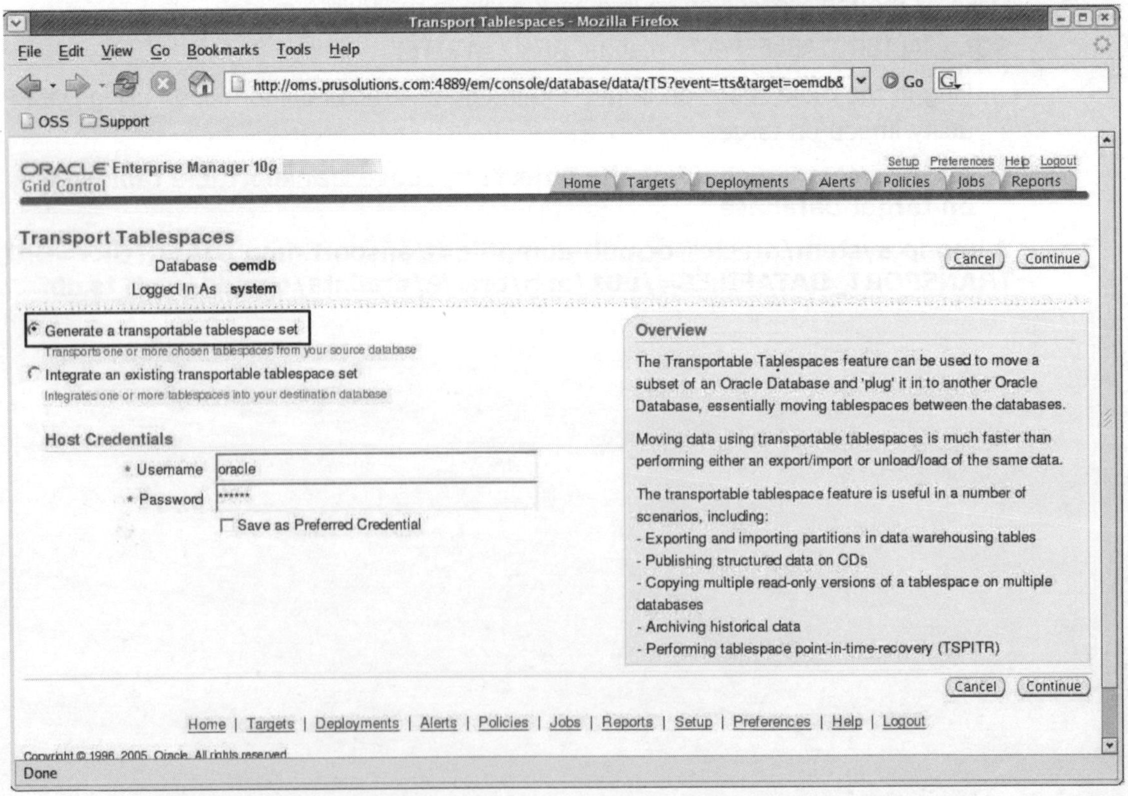

- Select tablespace RCAT_TS and Choose Containment Type Full.

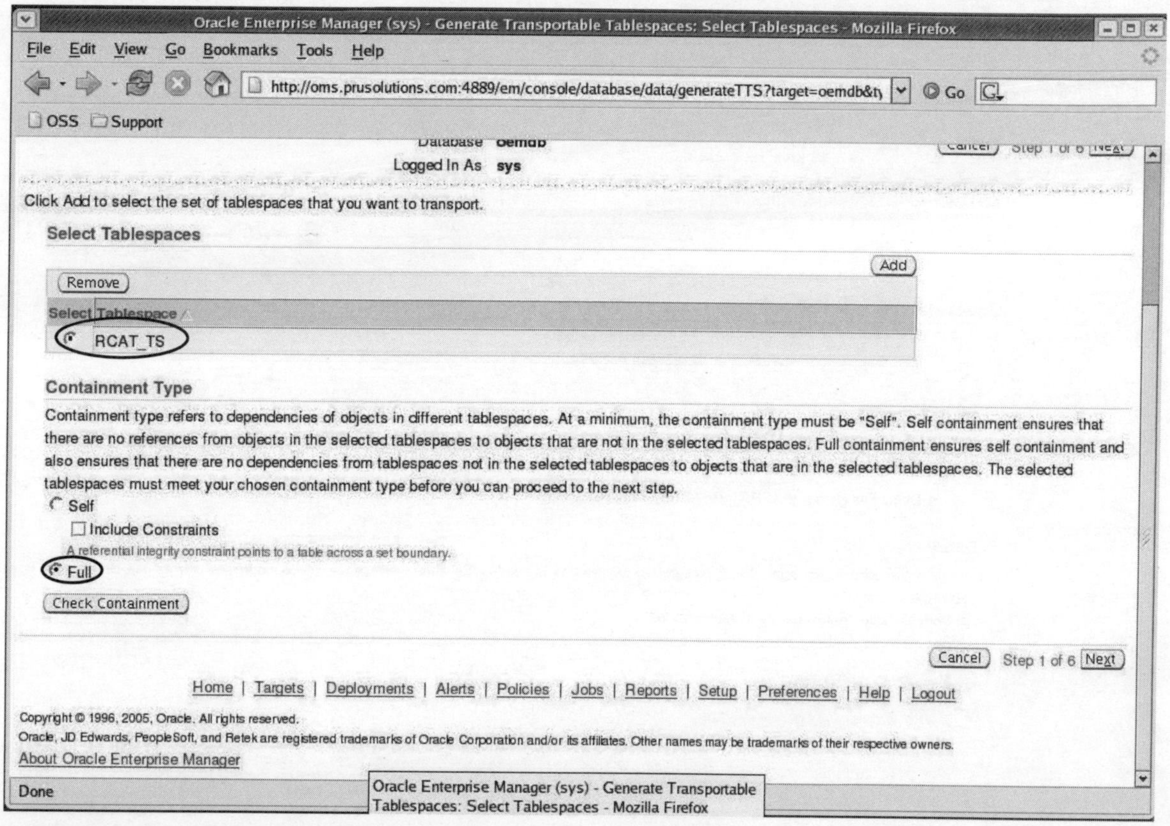

- Generate Transportable Tablespaces: Destination Characteristics.

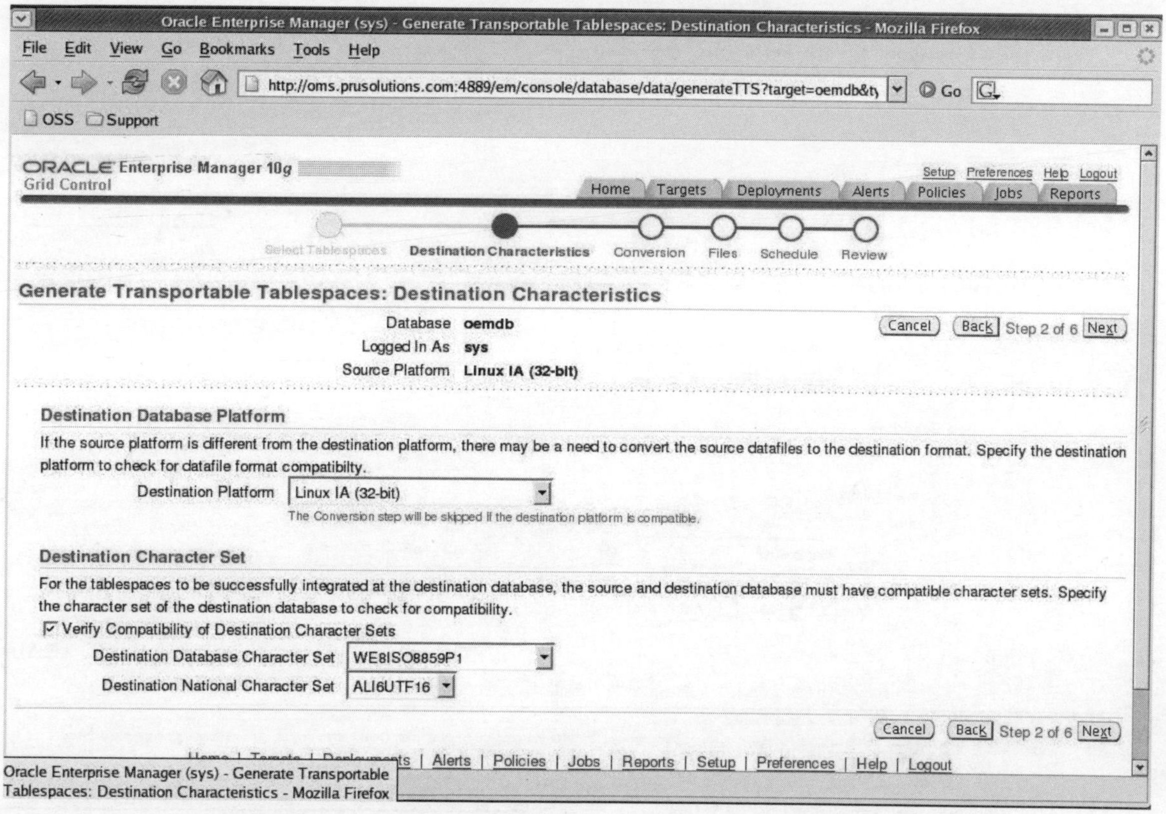

- Select Dump File and Manually Copy Datafile.

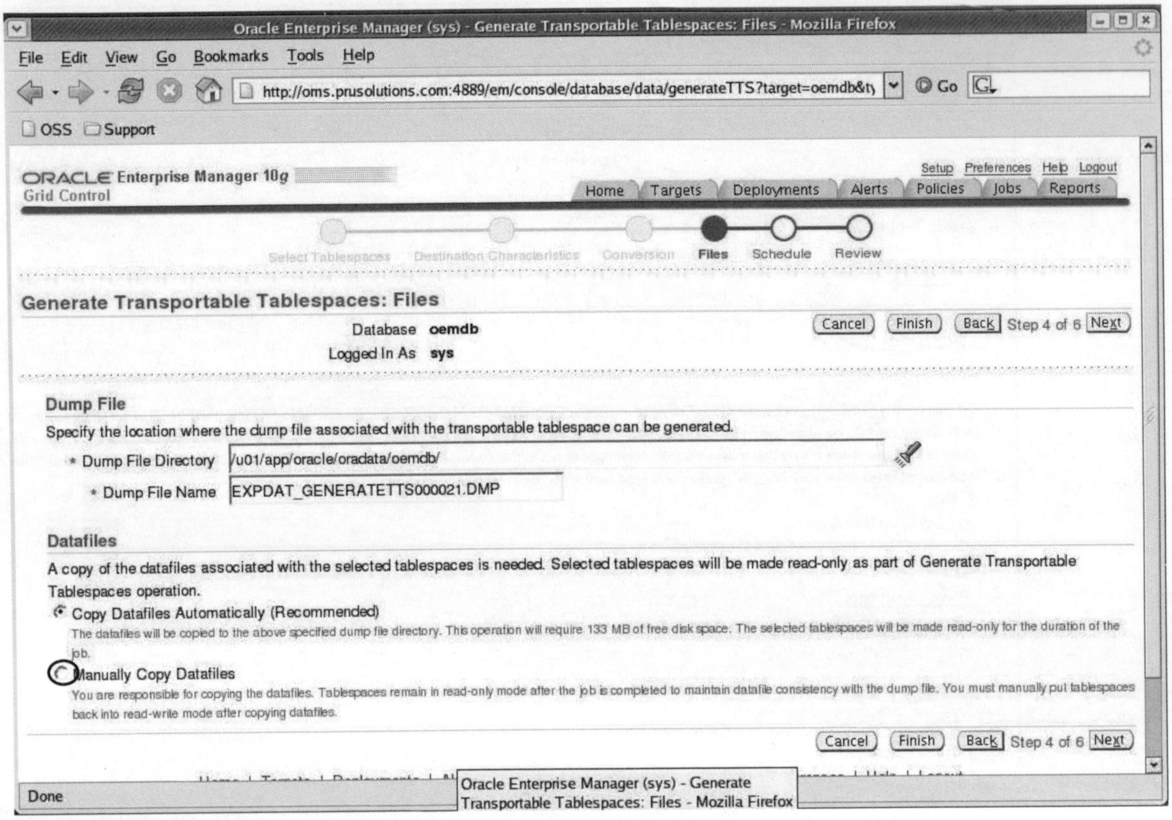

- Generate Transportable Tablespace: Schedule.

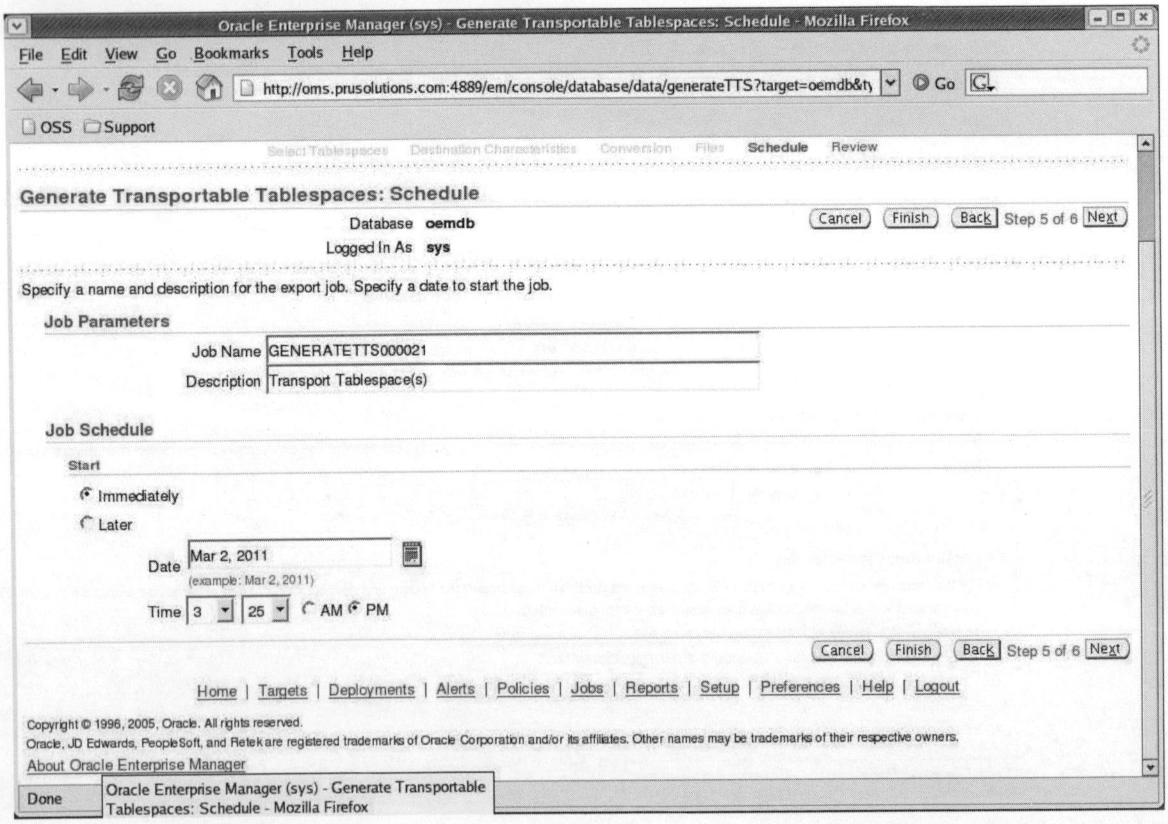

- Generate Transportable Tablespaces: Review

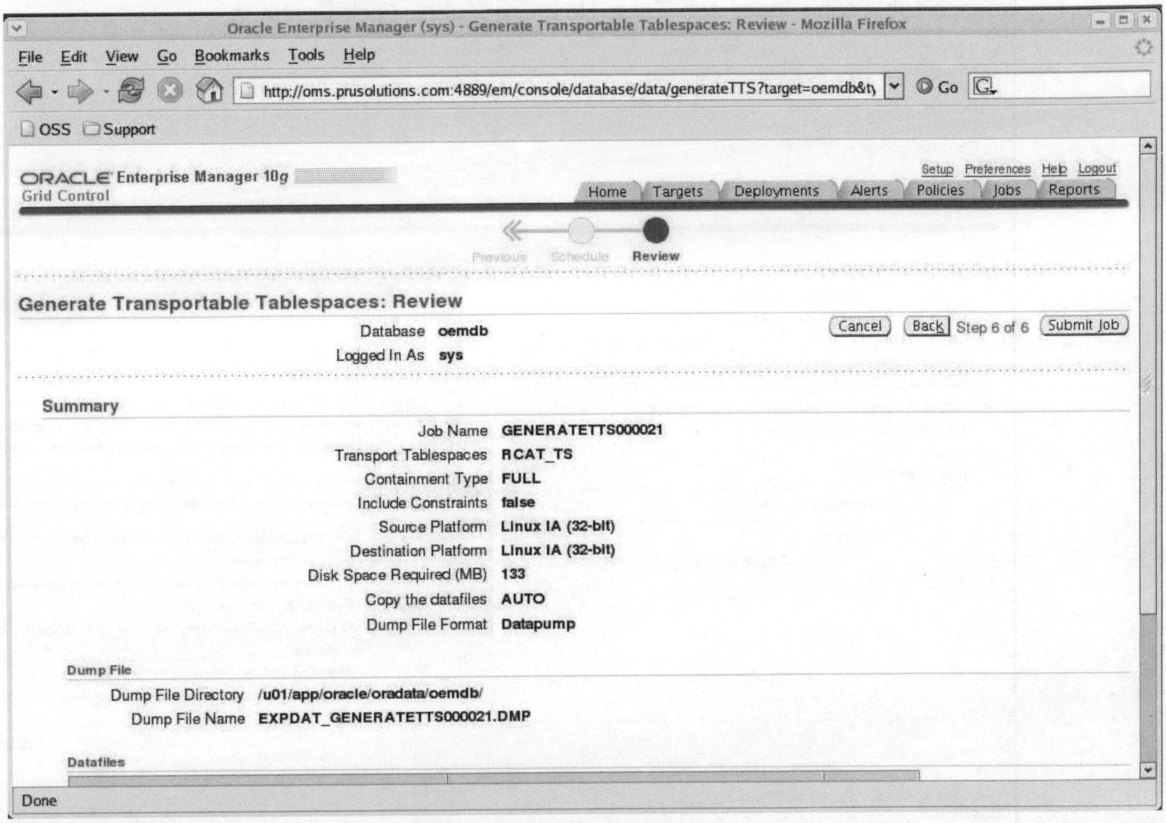

- Secure copy dumpfile from oem machine to ocm machine

  [oracle@oem oemdb]$ scp EXPDAT_GENERATETTS000021.DMP ocm:/u01/app/oracle/
  The authenticity of host 'ocm (192.168.2.121)' can't be established.
  RSA key fingerprint is f4:ac:d2:7e:05:e8:4e:47:a9:6f:80:99:46:f9:f7:58.
  Are you sure you want to continue connecting (yes/no)? yes
  Warning: Permanently added 'ocm,192.168.2.121' (RSA) to the list of known hosts.
  oracle@ocm's password:
  EXPDAT_GENERATETTS000021.DMP 100% 944KB
  944.0KB/s 00:00

- Secure copy datafile rcat_ts.dbf from oem machine to ocm machine

  [oracle@oem oemdb]$ scp rcat_ts.dbf ocm:/u01/app/oracle/oradata/oemdb/
  oracle@ocm's password:
  rcat_ts.dbf 100% 133MB 6.7MB/s 00:20

- Create user RMAN in ocmdb database

  [oracle@ocm ~]$ sqlplus / as sysdba

  SQL> CREATE USER RMAN PROFILE DEFAULT IDENTIFIED BY RMAN DEFAULT TABLESPACE USERS TEMPORARY TABLESPACE TEMP QUOTA UNLIMITED ON USERS ACCOUNT UNLOCK;

  SQL> GRANT RECOVERY_CATALOG_OWNER TO RMAN;

- Connect to Target Database ocmdb. On Transport Tablespace Page. Select Integrate as existing transportable tablespace set. Enter Host Credential. Click Continue.

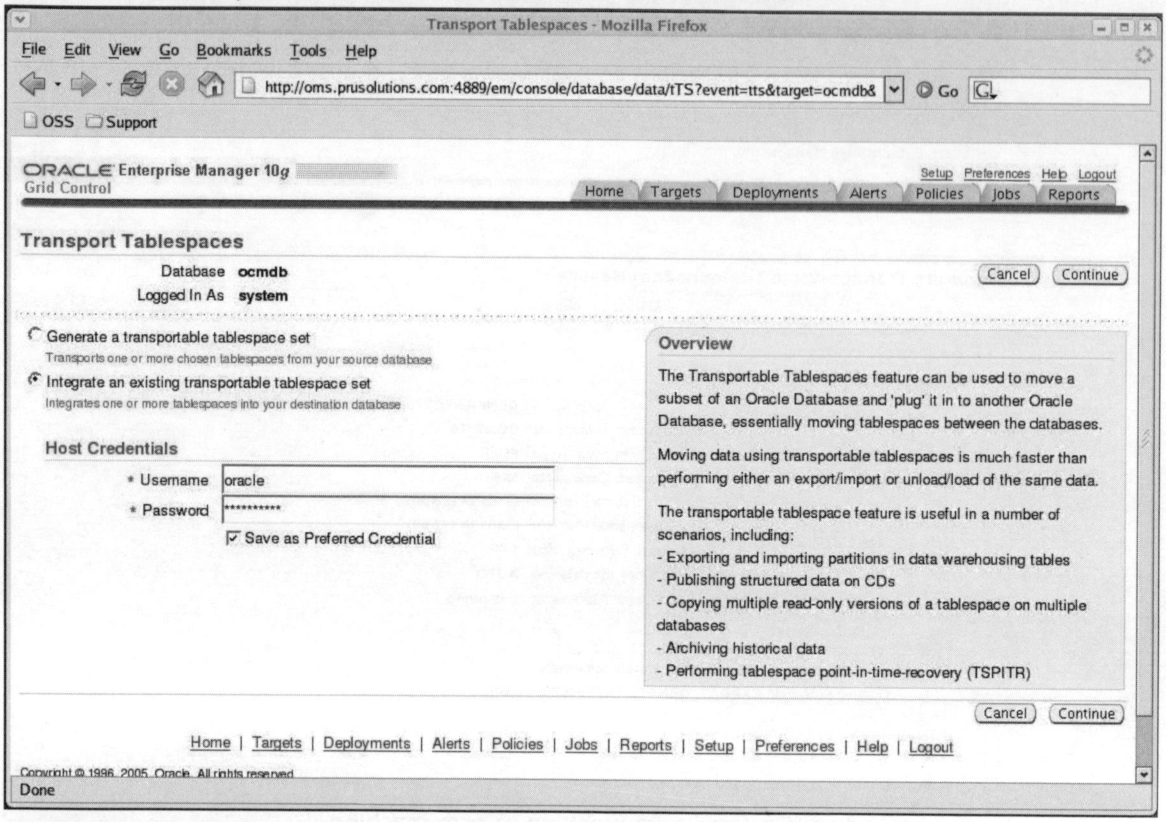

- Select Do not Copy the Datafiles. Click Next.

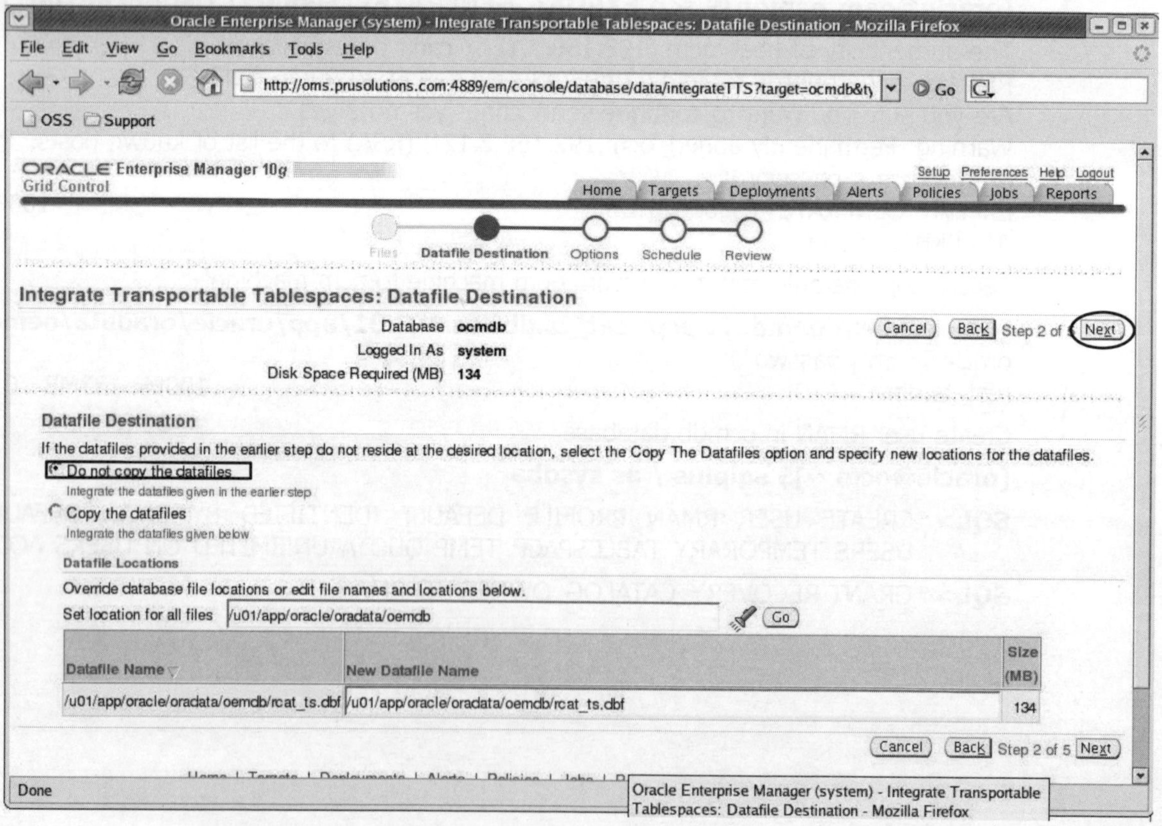

- On Re-Map Schema: Add and Select RMAN

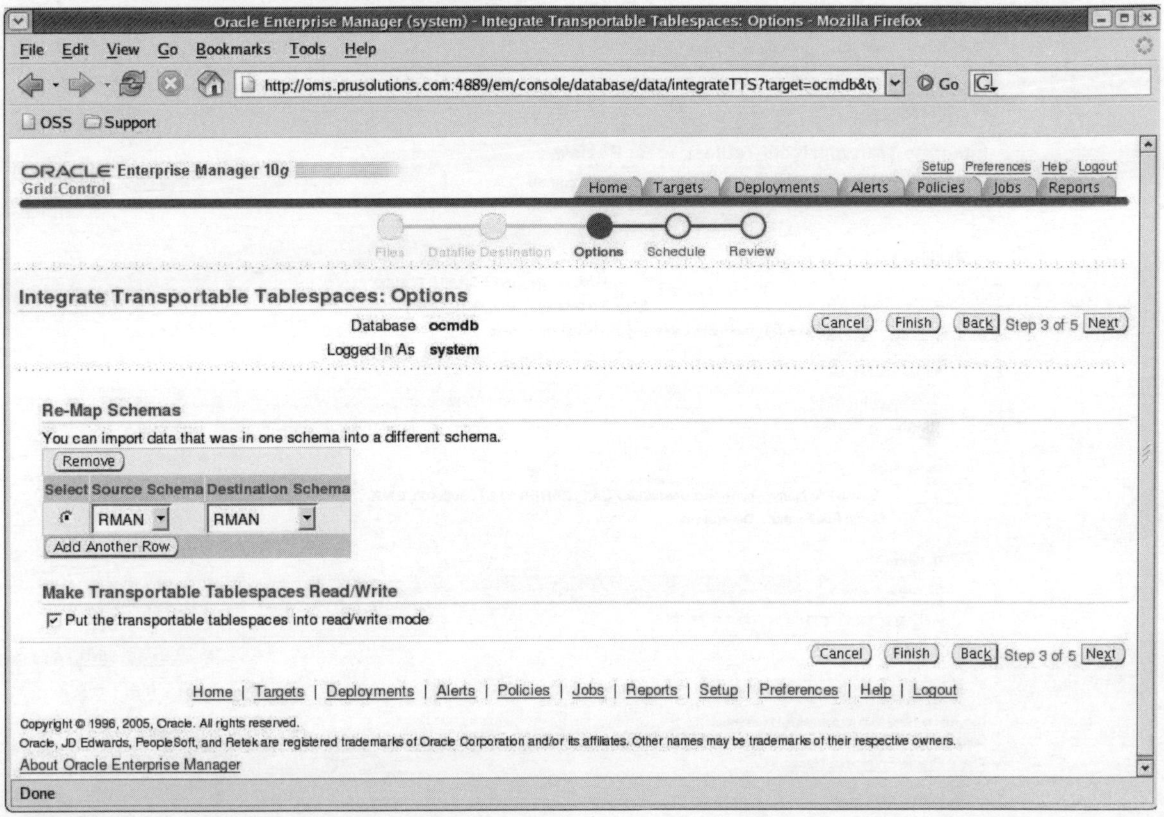

- Integrate Transportable Tablespaces: Schedule

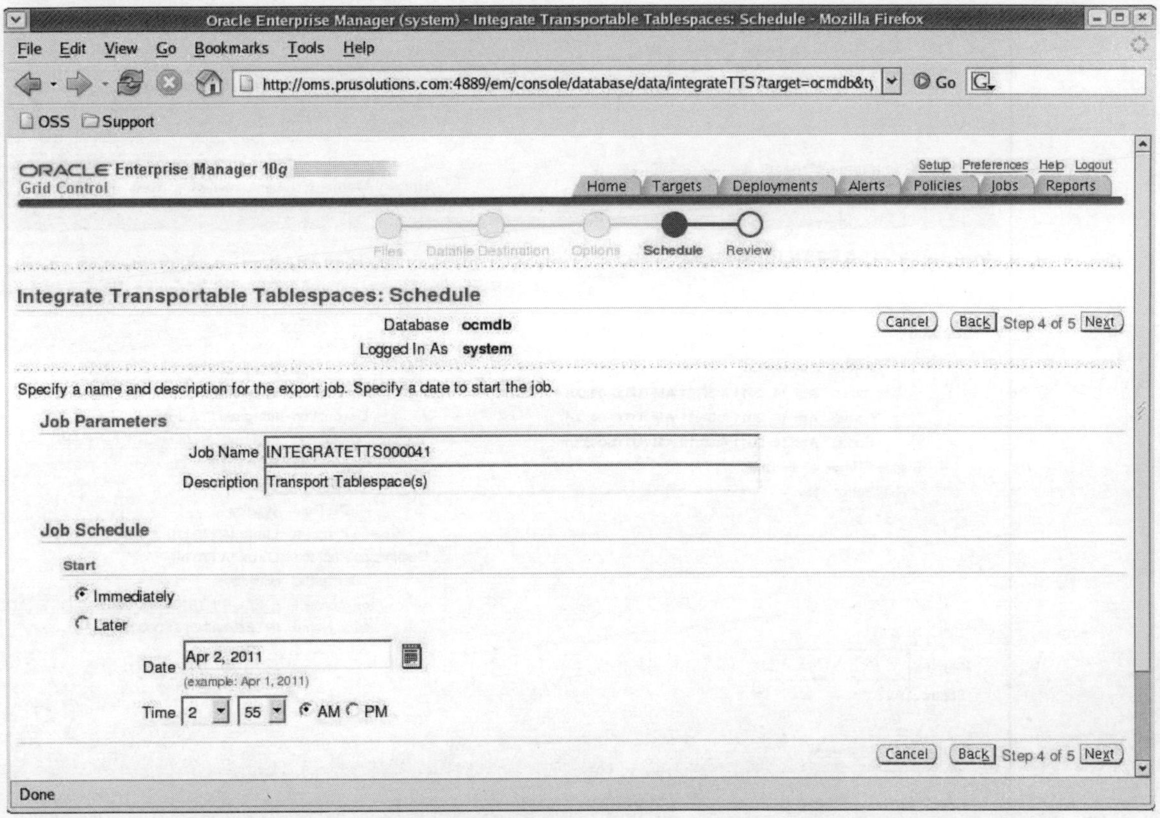

- Integrate Transportable Tablespaces: Review. Submit Job

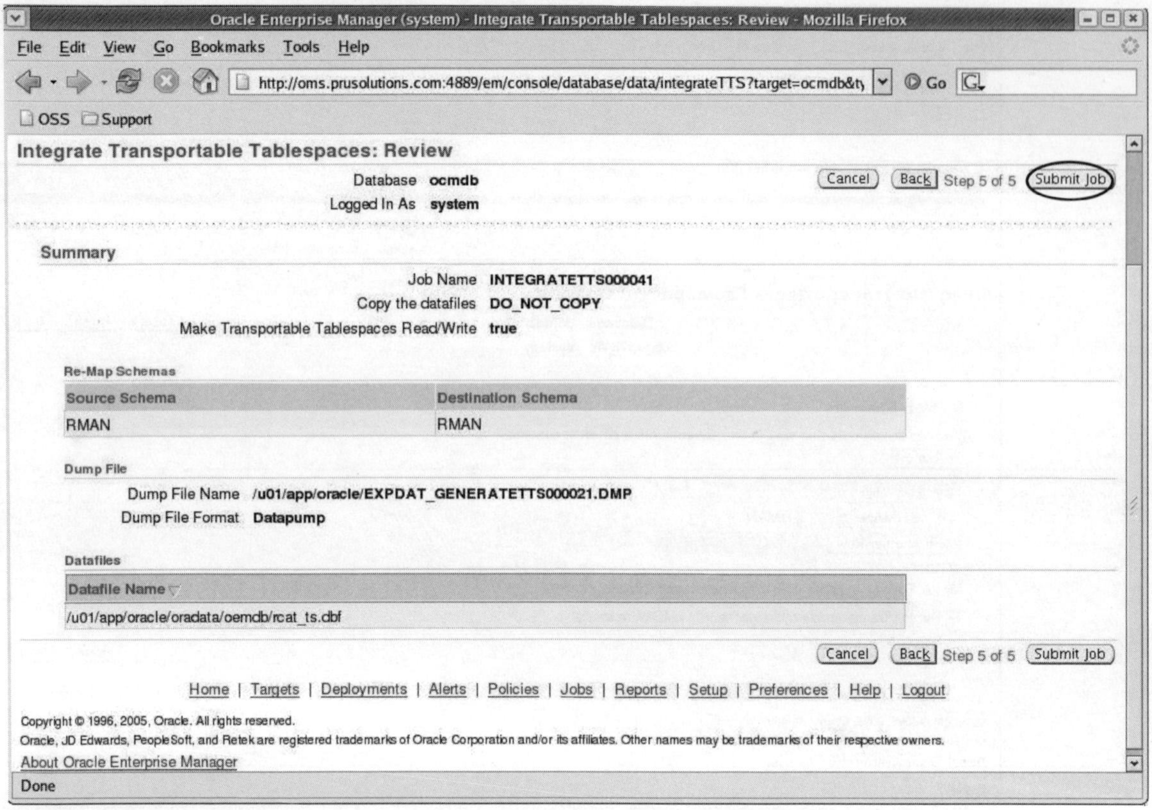

- Job Execution Summary

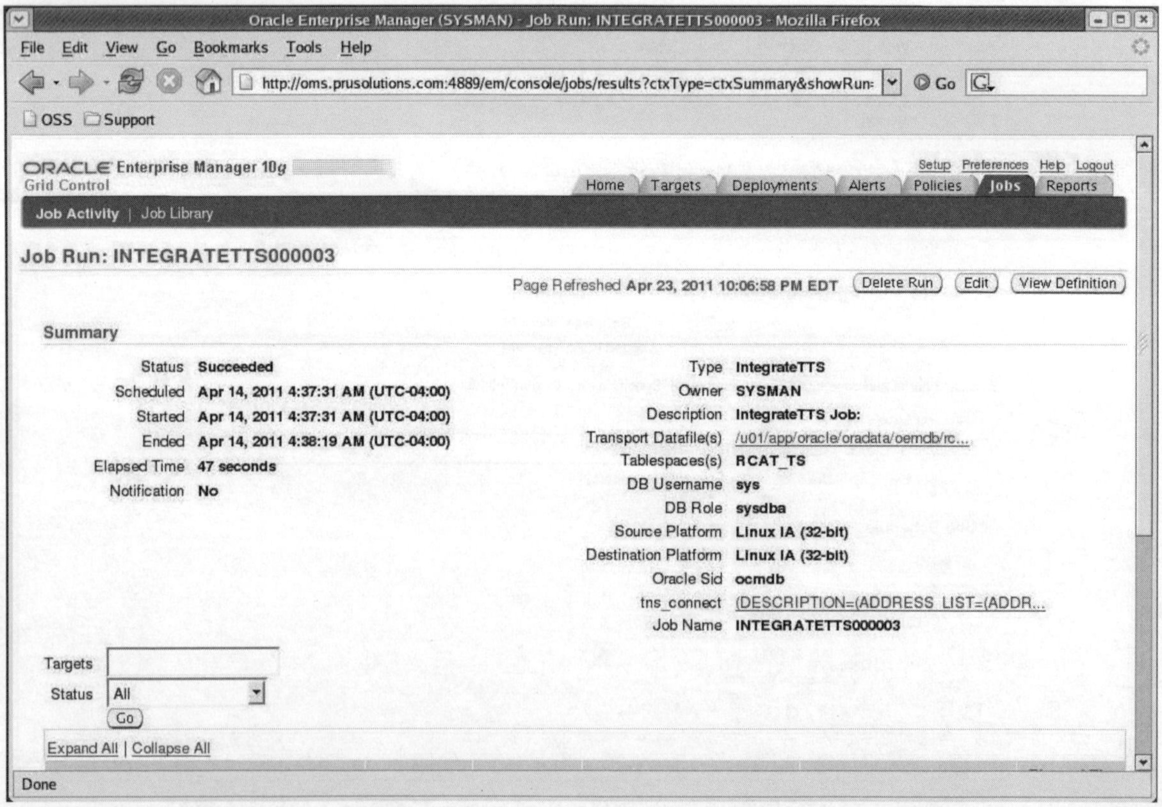

5.6 Partition Tables

- Navigate through Oracle Documentation to get to Partitioning in Data Warehouses without search tab.

  Oracle Database Documentation Library > Books > DAT > Data Warehousing Guide> HTML

  On contents page Ctrl f and search for "Partitioning in Data Warehouses" you will reach Partitioning in Data Warehouses, which will give details for all partition types.

- Range Partition: Range partitions are based on separating data on ranges of value. This is most commonly used with dates range.

```
SQL> CREATE TABLE sales_date_range
     (
     salesman_id       NUMBER (5),
     salesman_name     VARCHAR2 (30),
     sales_amount      NUMBER (10),
     sales_date        DATE
     )
     COMPRESS
     PARTITION BY RANGE (sales_date)
     ( PARTITION sales_2000
               VALUES LESS THAN (TO_DATE ('01/01/2001', 'DD/MM/YYYY')),
       PARTITION sales_2001
               VALUES LESS THAN (TO_DATE ('01/01/2002', 'DD/MM/YYYY')),
       PARTITION sales_2002
               VALUES LESS THAN (TO_DATE ('01/01/2003', 'DD/MM/YYYY')),
       PARTITION sales_2003
               VALUES LESS THAN (TO_DATE ('01/01/2004', 'DD/MM/YYYY')));
SQL> CREATE TABLE sales_name_range
     ( salesman_id       NUMBER (5),
       salesman_name     VARCHAR2 (30),
       sales_amount      NUMBER (10),
       sales_date        DATE
     )
     COMPRESS
     PARTITION BY RANGE (salesman_name)
     (PARTITION sales_name_e
               VALUES LESS THAN ('F'),
      PARTITION sales_name_m
               VALUES LESS THAN ('N'),
      PARTITION sales_name_s
               VALUES LESS THAN ('T'),
      PARTITION sales_name_max
               VALUES LESS THAN (maxvalue));
```

- Hash Partition: Hash partitions are used to partition the table for even distribution of data across devices. The rows are mapped on hash value of partition key.

```
SQL> CREATE TABLE emp_hashed
     (
         EMPNO          NUMBER (4),
         ENAME          VARCHAR2 (10),
         JOB            VARCHAR2 (9),
         MGR            NUMBER (4),
         HIREDATE       DATE,
         SAL            NUMBER (7, 2),
         COMM           NUMBER (7, 2),
         DEPTNO         NUMBER (2)
     )
         TABLESPACE USERS
         LOGGING
         PARTITION BY HASH (EMPNO)
                PARTITIONS 10;
SQL> CREATE INDEX idx1_ename ON emp_hashed (ename)
     GLOBAL PARTITION BY RANGE (ename)
     (   PARTITION VALUES LESS THAN ('F'),
         PARTITION VALUES LESS THAN ('M'),
         PARTITION VALUES LESS THAN ('T'),
         PARTITION VALUES LESS THAN (MAXVALUE));
```

- List Partition: List partition has list of discrete values in each partition column. It gives complete control over how rows maps to each partition.

```
SQL> CREATE TABLE sales_list
     (
         salesman_id       NUMBER (4),
         salesman_name     VARCHAR2 (30),
         sales_state       VARCHAR2 (2),
         sales_amount      NUMBER (10, 2),
         sales_ts          TIMESTAMP
     )
     PARTITION BY LIST (sales_state)
         (PARTITION sales_west
                VALUES ('CA', 'HI')
                COMPRESS,
         PARTITION sales_east
                VALUES ('NY', 'VA', 'FL'),
         PARTITION sales_central
                VALUES ('TX', 'IL'),
         PARTITION sales_other
         VALUES (DEFAULT));
```

- Composite Partition: Composite partition combines range and hash or list partitioning.

  Oracle Database first distributes data into partitions according to boundaries established by the partition ranges. Then, for range-hash partitioning, Oracle uses a hashing algorithm to further divide the data into subpartitions within each range partition. For range-list partitioning, Oracle divides the data into subpartitions within each range partition based on the explicit list you chose.

```
SQL> CREATE TABLE sales_range_list
     (
        salesman_id       NUMBER (4),
        salesman_name     VARCHAR2 (30),
        sales_state       VARCHAR2 (2),
        sales_amount      NUMBER (10, 2),
        sales_date        DATE
     )
     PARTITION BY RANGE (sales_date)
        SUBPARTITION BY LIST (sales_state)
        (PARTITION sales_2000
              VALUES LESS THAN (TO_DATE ('01/01/2001', 'DD/MM/YYYY')) (
              SUBPARTITION sales_2000_west VALUES ('CA', 'HI'),
              SUBPARTITION sales_2000_east VALUES ('NY', 'VA', 'FL'),
              SUBPARTITION sales_2000_central VALUES ('TX', 'IL'),
              SUBPARTITION sales_2000_other VALUES (DEFAULT)),
     PARTITION sales_2001
              VALUES LESS THAN (TO_DATE ('01/01/2002', 'DD/MM/YYYY')) (
              SUBPARTITION sales_2001_west VALUES ('CA', 'HI'),
              SUBPARTITION sales_2001_east VALUES ('NY', 'VA', 'FL'),
              SUBPARTITION sales_2001_central VALUES ('TX', 'IL'),
              SUBPARTITION sales_2001_other VALUES (DEFAULT)),
     PARTITION sales_2002
              VALUES LESS THAN (TO_DATE ('01/01/2003', 'DD/MM/YYYY')) (
              SUBPARTITION sales_2002_west VALUES ('CA', 'HI'),
              SUBPARTITION sales_2002_east VALUES ('NY', 'VA', 'FL'),
              SUBPARTITION sales_2002_central VALUES ('TX', 'IL'),
              SUBPARTITION sales_2002_other VALUES (DEFAULT)),
     PARTITION sales_2003
              VALUES LESS THAN (TO_DATE ('01/01/2004', 'DD/MM/YYYY')) (
              SUBPARTITION sales_2003_west VALUES ('CA', 'HI'),
              SUBPARTITION sales_2003_east VALUES ('NY', 'VA', 'FL'),
              SUBPARTITION sales_2003_central VALUES ('TX', 'IL'),
              SUBPARTITION sales_2003_other VALUES (DEFAULT)));

SQL> CREATE TABLE sales_range_hash
     (
        salesman_id       NUMBER (5),
        salesman_name     VARCHAR2 (30),
        sales_amount      NUMBER (10),
        sales_date        DATE
     )
     COMPRESS
     PARTITION BY RANGE (sales_date)
        SUBPARTITION BY HASH (salesman_id)
              SUBPARTITIONS 4
     (PARTITION sales_2000
        VALUES LESS THAN (TO_DATE ('01/01/2001', 'DD/MM/YYYY')),
     PARTITION sales_2001
        VALUES LESS THAN (TO_DATE ('01/01/2002', 'DD/MM/YYYY')),
     PARTITION sales_2002
        VALUES LESS THAN (TO_DATE ('01/01/2003', 'DD/MM/YYYY')),
     PARTITION sales_2003
        VALUES LESS THAN (TO_DATE ('01/01/2004', 'DD/MM/YYYY')));
```

- Truncating Partition having Global Indexes

  If partition table is having global index, when truncating the partition, you should use UPDATE INDEXES clause, partitions are truncated causes the global index to be truncated at the time the partition is truncated.

  SQL> ALTER TABLE sales_range_list TRUNCATE PARTITION sales_2000 UPDATE INDEXES;

- Navigate through Oracle Documentation to get to Managing Partitioned Tables and Indexes without search tab to learn partition exchange methods.

  Oracle Database Documentation Library > Books > ADM > Administrator's Guide > HTML

  On contents page Ctrl f and search for "Managing Partitioned" you will reach Managing Partitioned Tables and Indexes, which will give details for Managing Partitioned Tables and Indexes.

- Create and Manage Partition tables from Oracle's OEM Grid Control.
  - On Oracle's OEM Grid Control, Administration Page, in Schema Section, Click "Tables" link to create partition Table
  - General Tab: Enter Name, Schema, Tablespace and Columns detail.

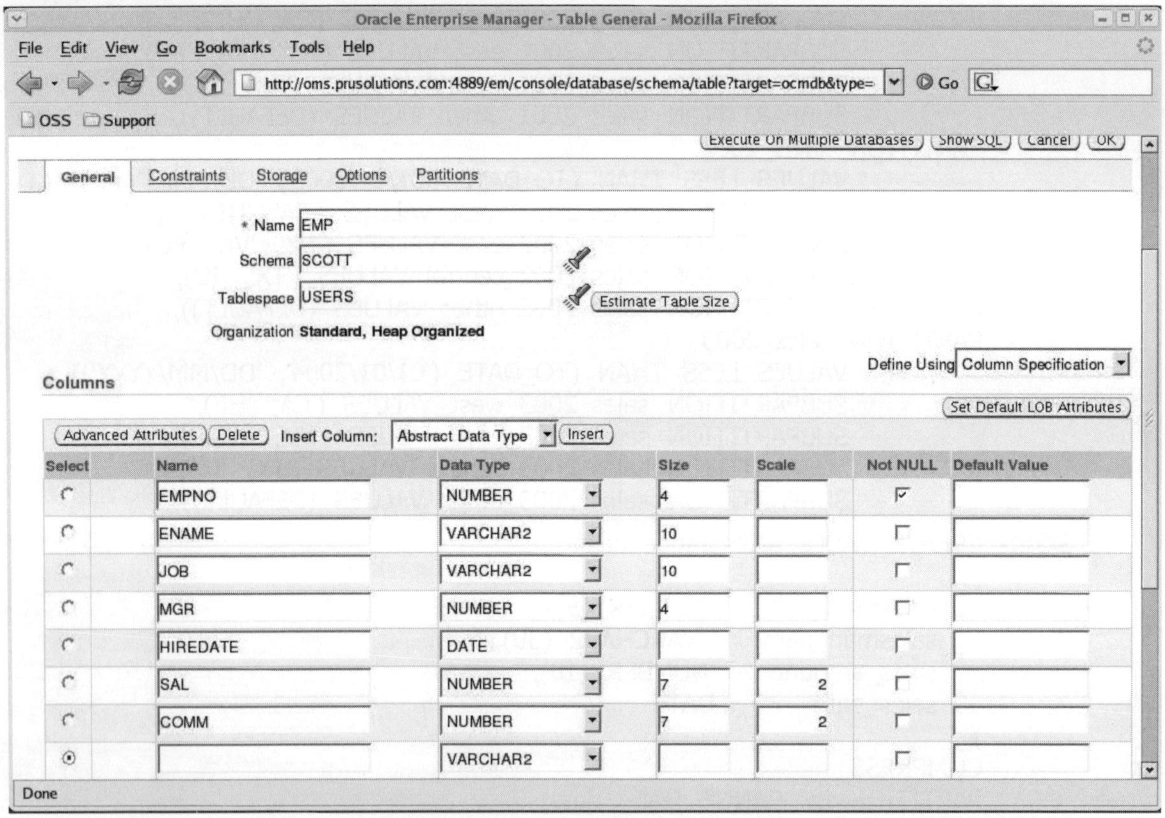

- Specify Partition Columns

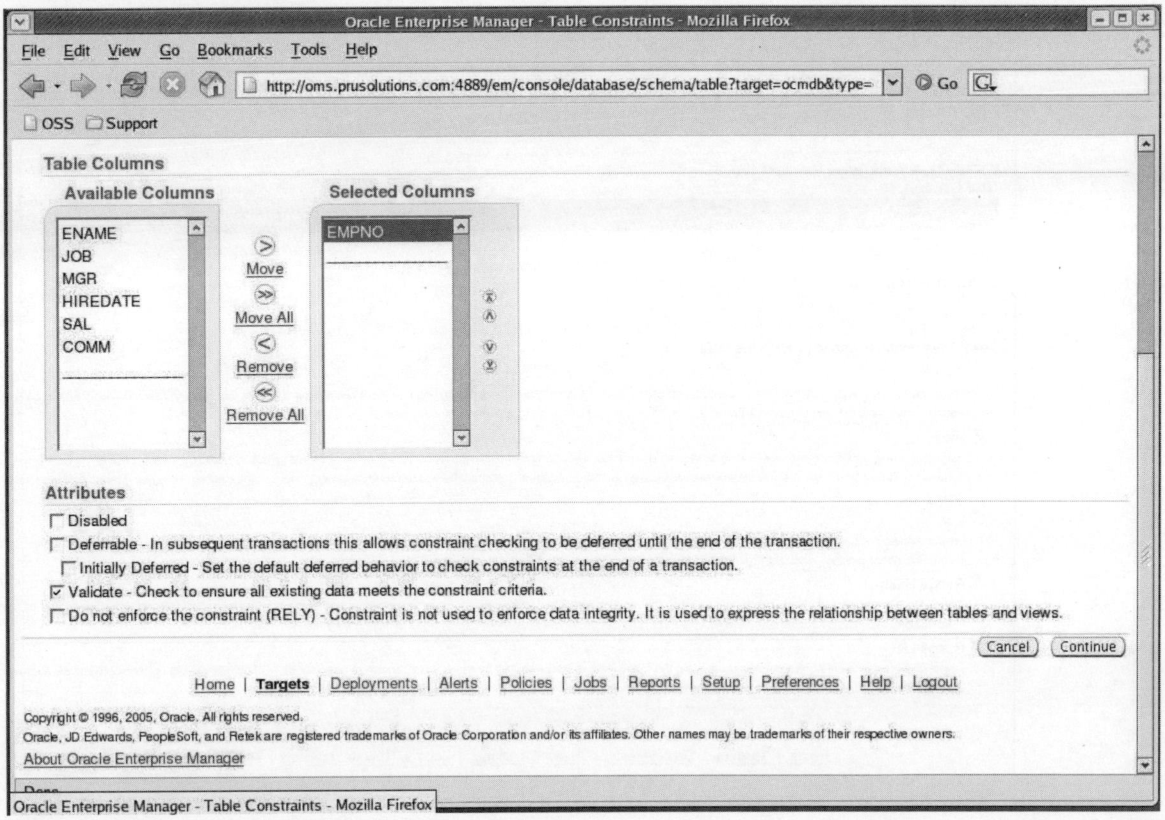

- Specify Storage Parameters

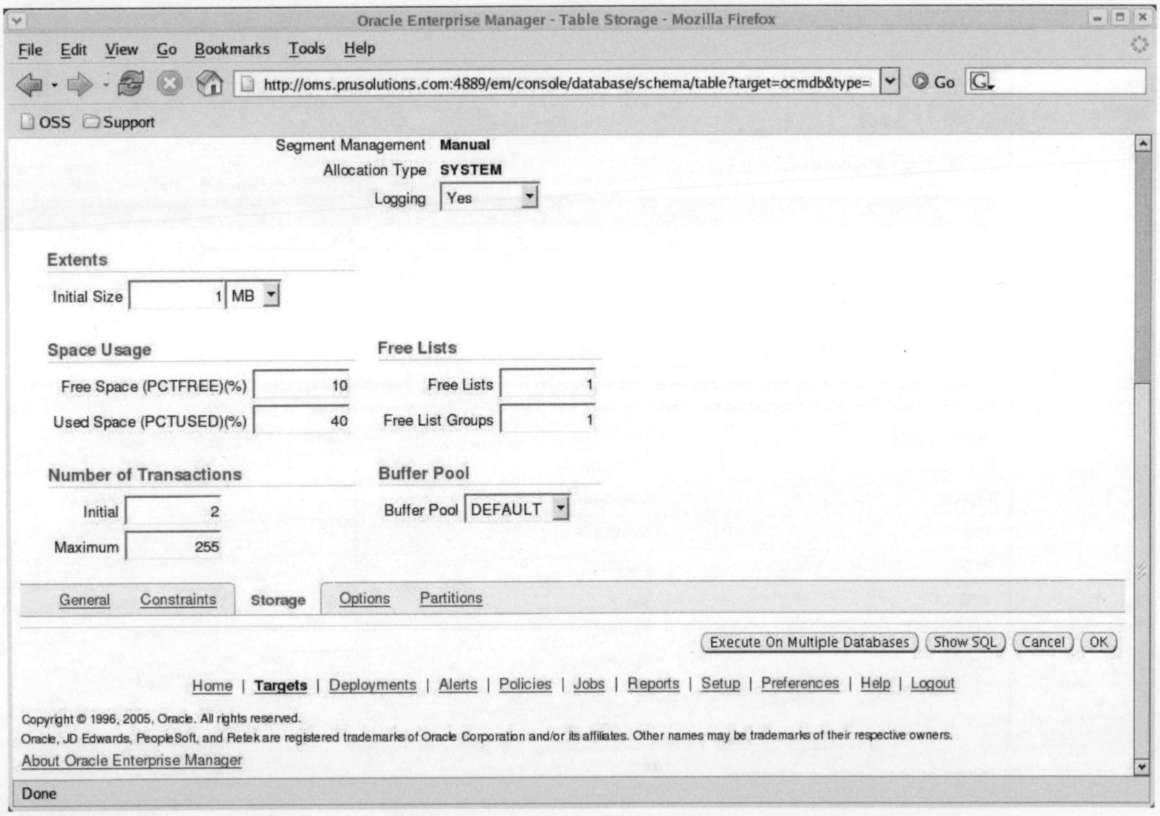

- Specify Partition Type

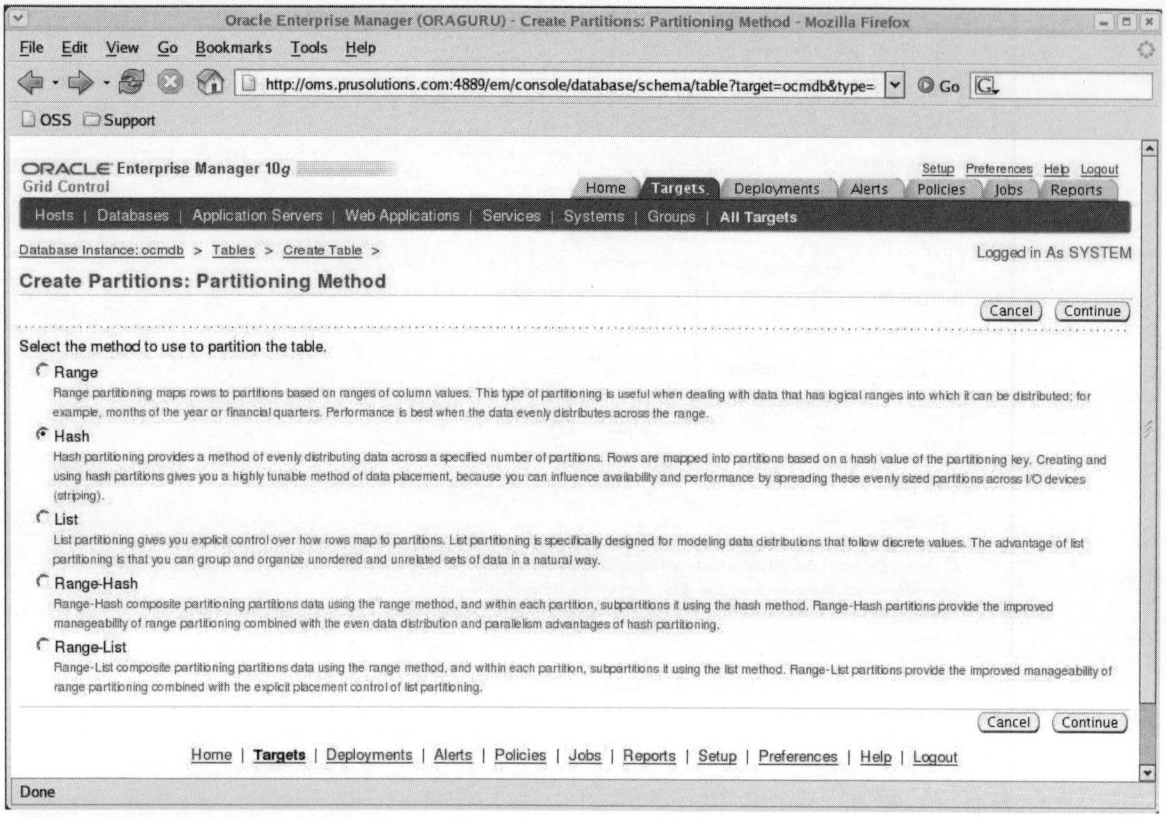

- Specify Partition Column Order

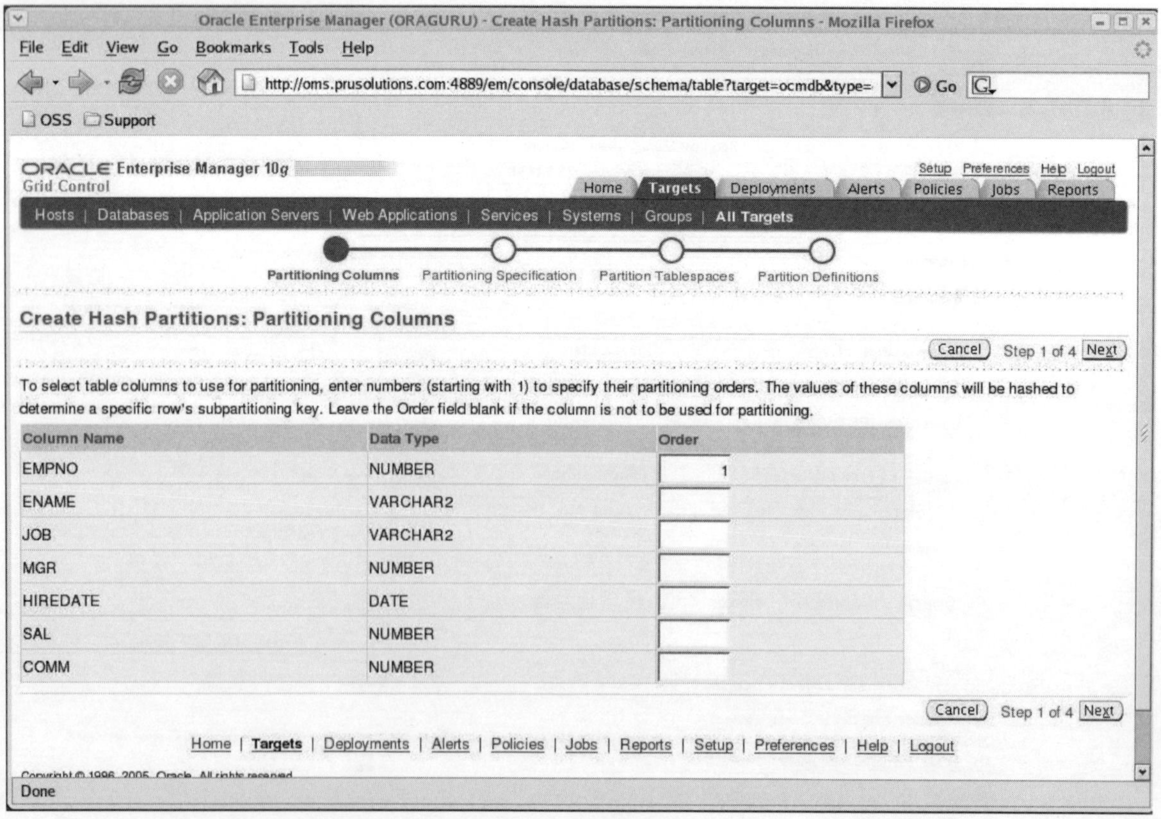

- Specify Number of Partitions

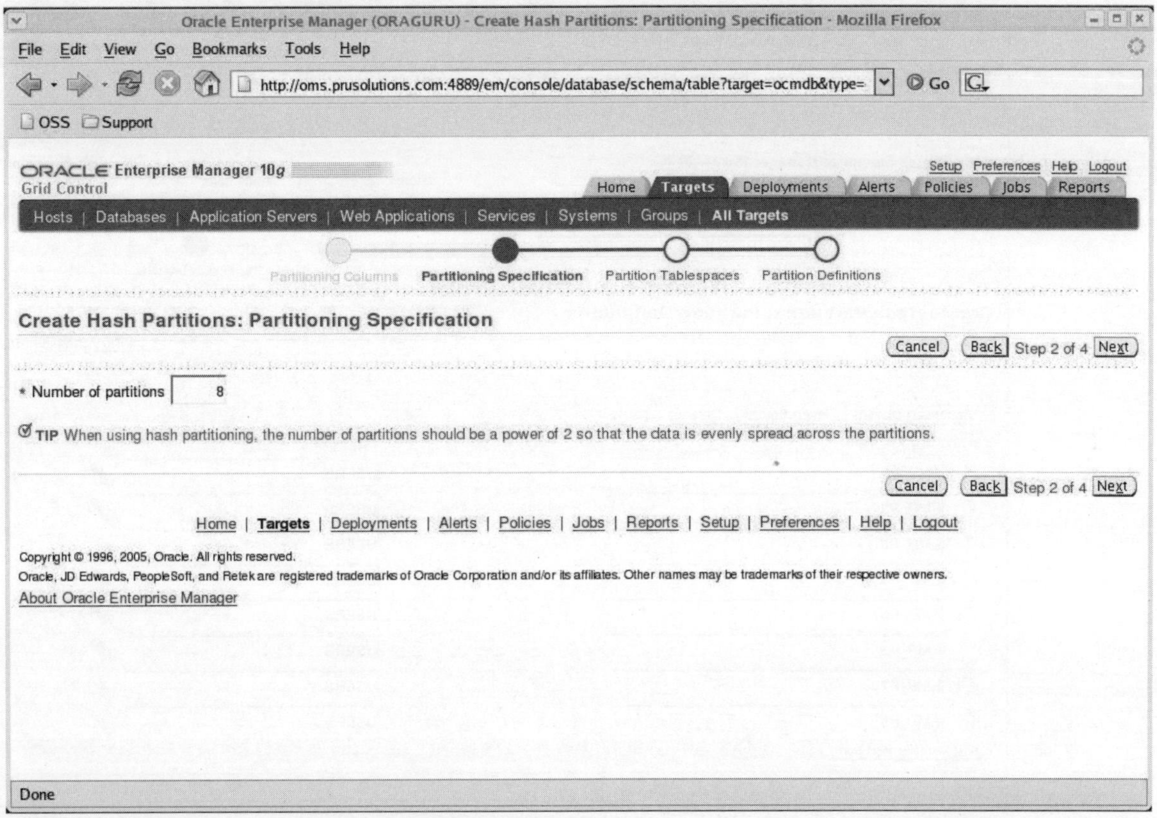

- Specify Tablespace for Partition Table

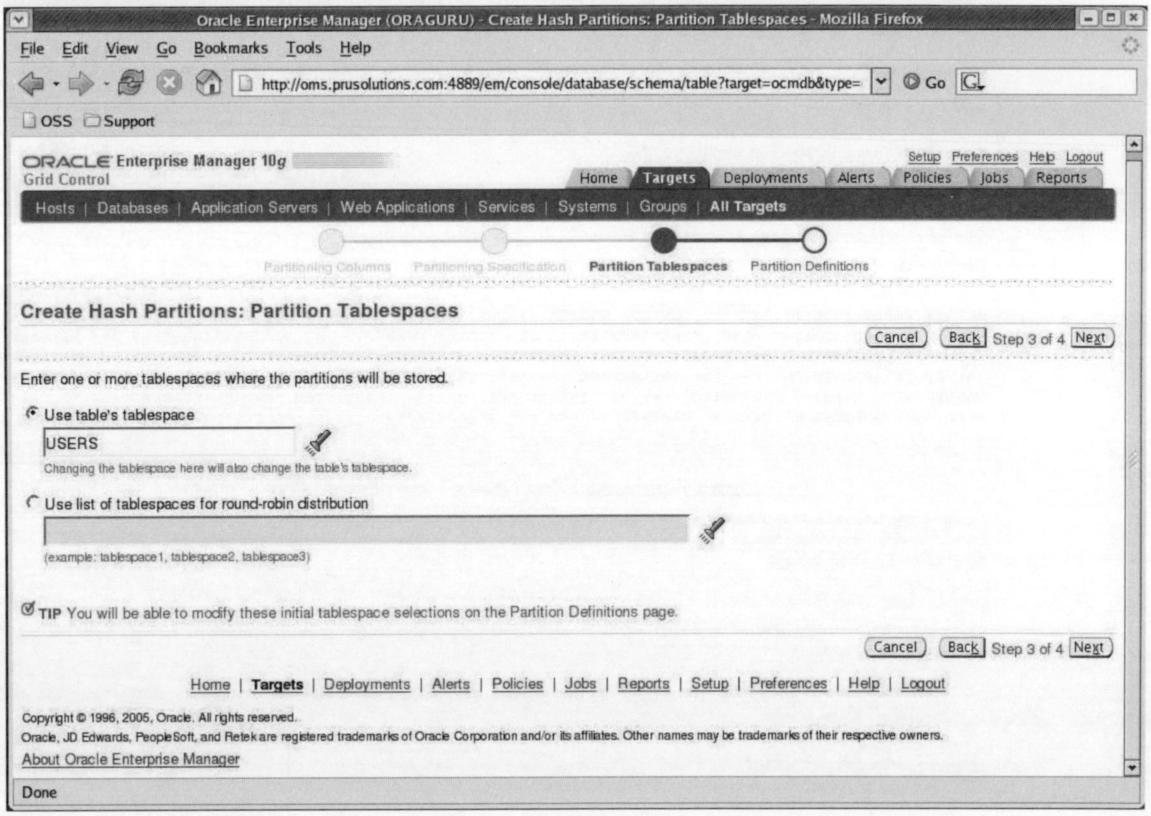

- Partitions Definitions

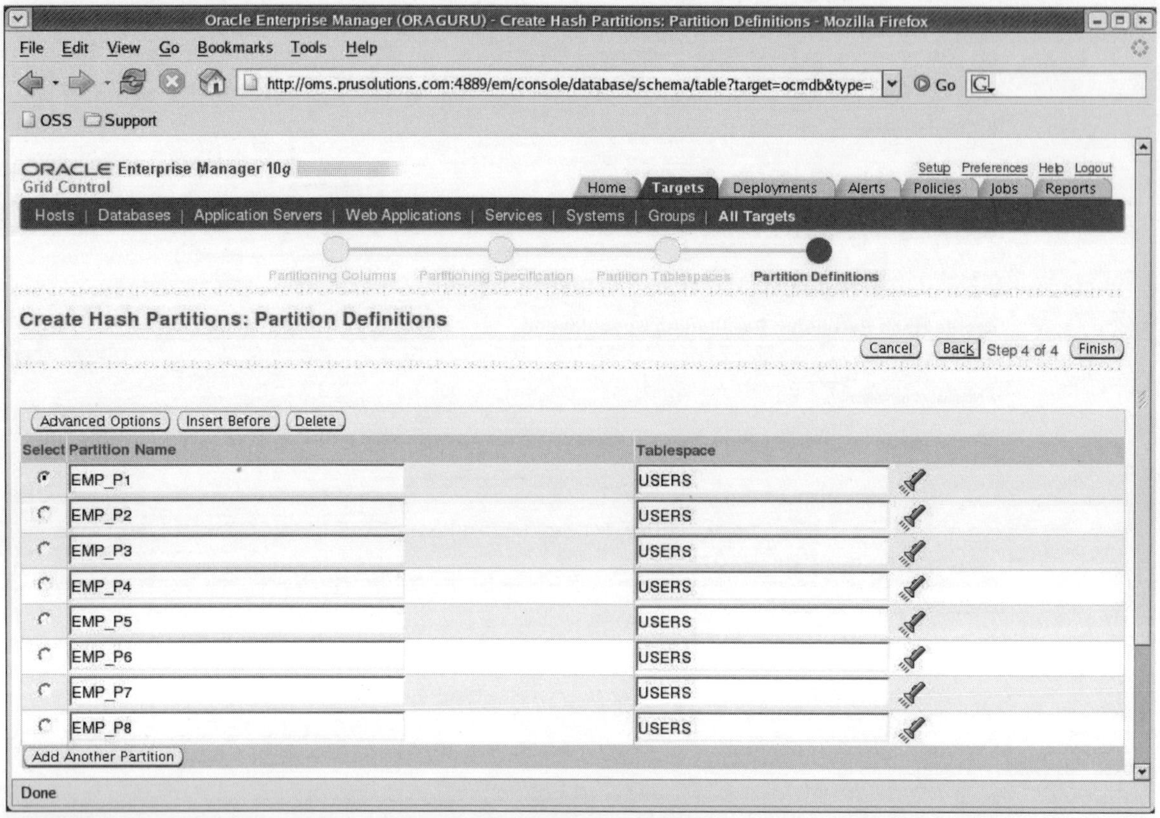

- Capture the script generated by Oracle's OEM Grid Control

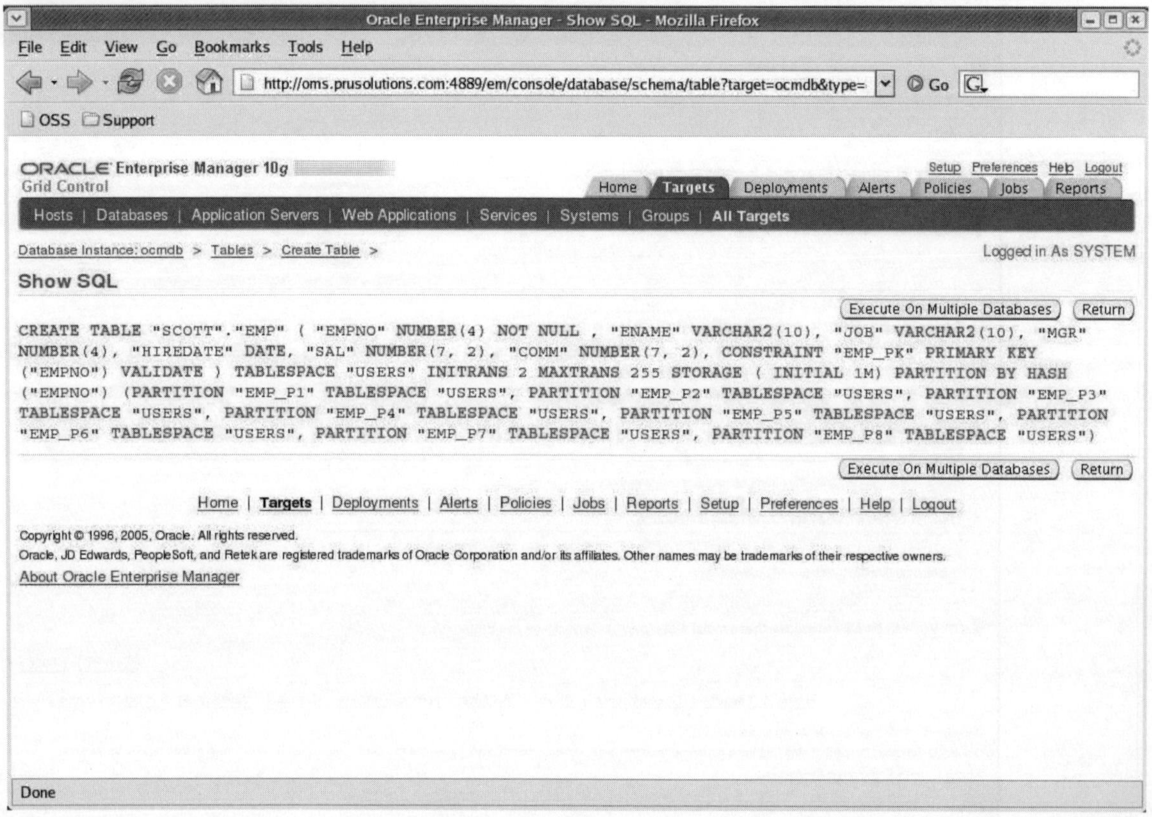

- In the same way, create index and capture the sql generated from Oracle's OEM Grid Control.

SQL> CREATE INDEX emp_idx1 ON scott.emp(ename) GLOBAL PARTITION BY RANGE (ename) (PARTITION VALUES LESS THAN ('F'), PARTITION VALUES LESS THAN ('M'), PARTITION VALUES LESS THAN ('T'), PARTITION VALUES LESS THAN (MAXVALUE));

5.7 Create and Manage LOB Segments

- Navigate through Oracle Documentation to get to PL/SQL LOB Demonstration Files

  Oracle Database Documentation Library > Books > ADM > Application Developer's Guide - Large Objects > HTML

  On contents page Ctrl f and search for *"PL/SQL LOB Demonstration Files"* you will reach PL/SQL LOB Demonstration Files

- In this practice, we will create lob segments and manipulate them.

  - Create table PM.PRINT_MEDIA_TEST same as PM.PRINT_MEDIA.

```
SQL> CREATE TABLE "PM"."PRINT_MEDIA_TEST"
     (
       "PRODUCT_ID"          NUMBER (6),
       "AD_ID"               NUMBER (6),
       "AD_COMPOSITE"        BLOB,
       "AD_SOURCETEXT"       CLOB,
       CONSTRAINT "PRINTMEDIA_TEST_FK" FOREIGN KEY
             ("PRODUCT_ID")
             REFERENCES "OE"."PRODUCT_INFORMATION" ("PRODUCT_ID")
             VALIDATE,
       CONSTRAINT "PRINTMEDIA__TEST_PK" PRIMARY KEY
             ("PRODUCT_ID", "AD_ID")
             VALIDATE
     )
       TABLESPACE "EXAMPLE"
       PCTFREE 10
       INITRANS 1
       MAXTRANS 255
       STORAGE (INITIAL 64 K BUFFER_POOL DEFAULT)
       LOGGING
       LOB (
             "AD_COMPOSITE")
             STORE AS
             (
             TABLESPACE "EXAMPLE"
             CHUNK 8192
             STORAGE (INITIAL 64 K BUFFER_POOL DEFAULT)
             NOCACHE LOGGING)
     LOB (
             "AD_SOURCETEXT")
             STORE AS
           (
             TABLESPACE "EXAMPLE"
             CHUNK 8192
             STORAGE (INITIAL 64 K BUFFER_POOL DEFAULT)
             NOCACHE LOGGING;
```

```
SQL> DESC print_media_test
Name                              Null?     Type
--------------------------------- --------- ------------
PRODUCT_ID                        NOT NULL  NUMBER (6)
AD_ID                             NOT NULL  NUMBER (6)
AD_COMPOSITE                                BLOB
AD_SOURCETEXT                               CLOB
```

- Create LOB Segment from Oracle's OEM Grid Control.

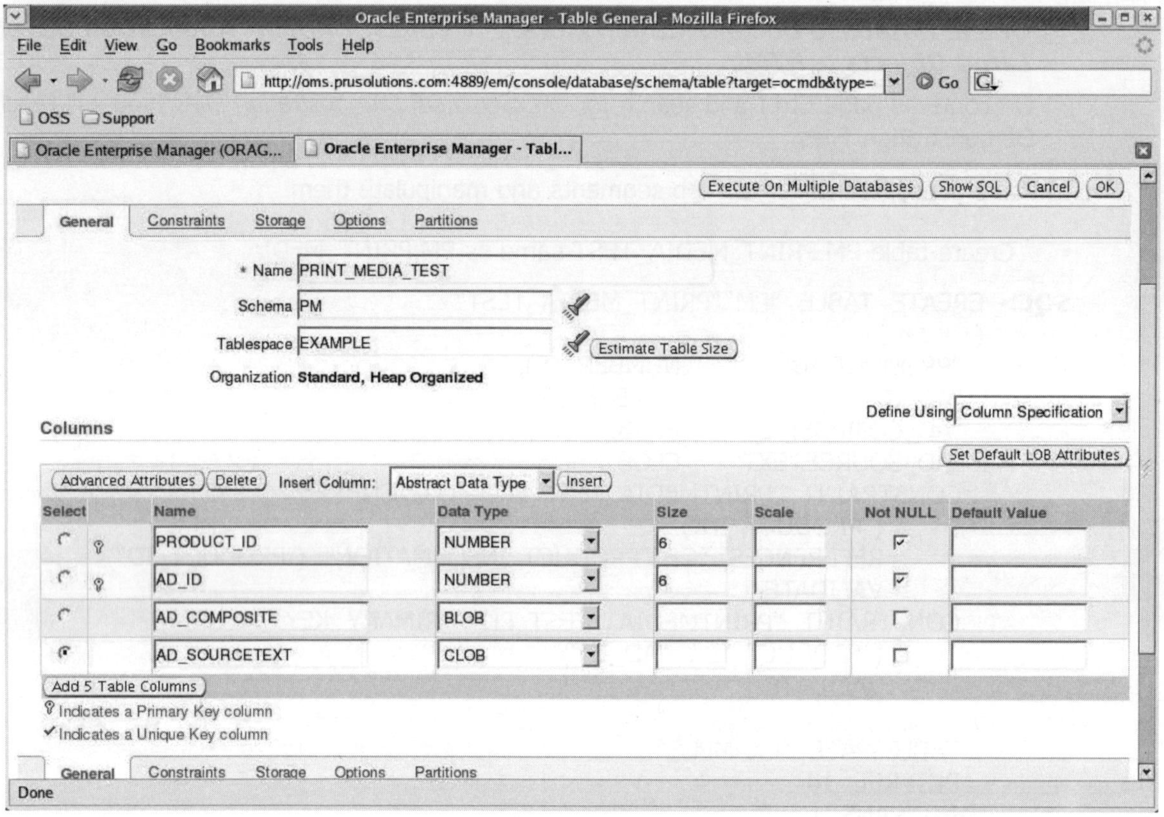

- Add Constraints to LOB Segment

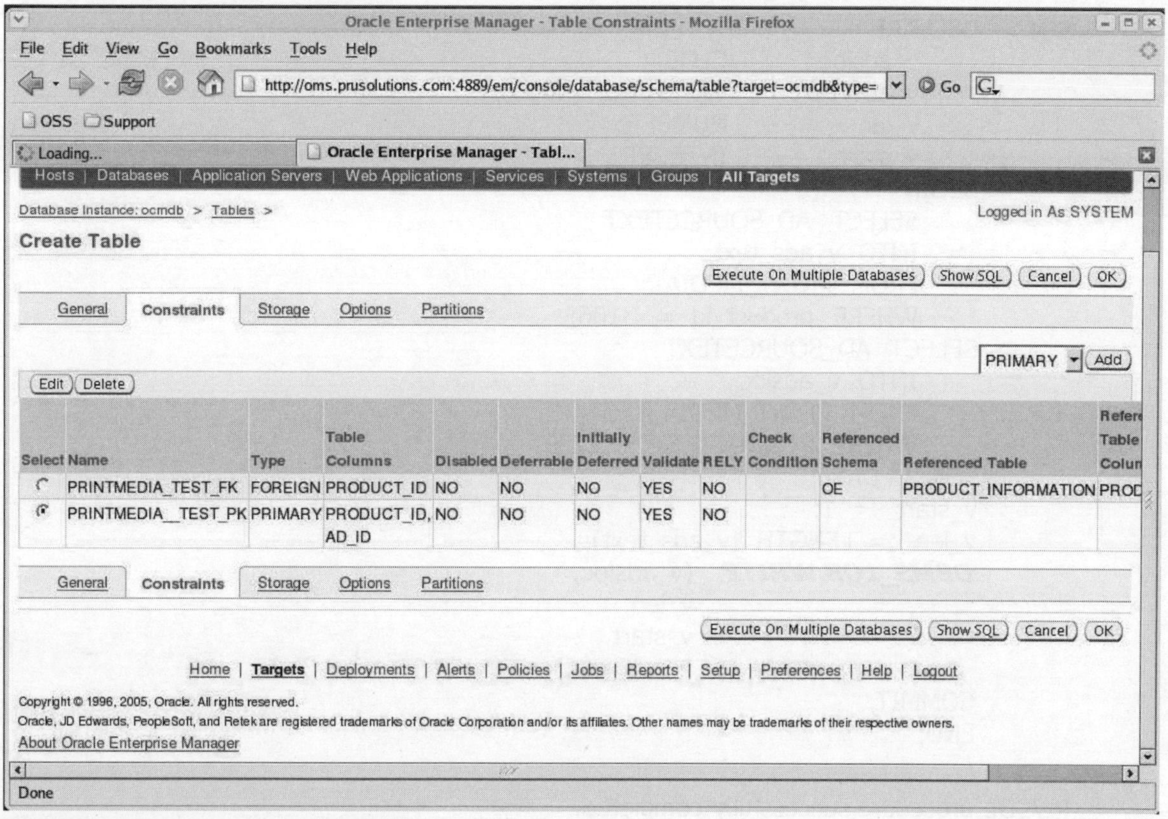

- Add two rows as mentioned below

```
SQL> INSERT INTO PRINT_MEDIA_TEST (PRODUCT_ID,
                                   AD_ID,
                                   AD_COMPOSITE,
                                   AD_SOURCETEXT)
     VALUES      (1726,
                  20001,
                  NULL,
                  EMPTY_CLOB ());
     1 row created.
SQL> INSERT INTO PRINT_MEDIA_TEST (PRODUCT_ID,
                                   AD_ID,
                                   AD_COMPOSITE,
                                   AD_SOURCETEXT)
     VALUES      (1729,
                  20002,
                  NULL,
                  EMPTY_CLOB ());
     1 row created.
```

- Update one row in PRINT_MEDIA_TEST using update statement

```
SQL> UPDATE PRINT_MEDIA_TEST
        SET (AD_COMPOSITE, AD_SOURCETEXT) =
        (SELECT AD_COMPOSITE, AD_SOURCETEXT
        FROM PRINT_MEDIA
        WHERE product_id = 3060)
     WHERE PRODUCT_ID = 1726;
     1 row updated.
```

- Updating CLOB columns using DBMS_LOB.WRITE

```
SQL> DECLARE
        v_adsloc        CLOB;
        v_ads_text      VARCHAR2 (4000);
        v_len           NUMBER;
        v_start         INTEGER;
     BEGIN
        SELECT AD_SOURCETEXT
        INTO v_ads_text
        FROM PRINT_MEDIA
        WHERE product_id = 3106;
     SELECT AD_SOURCETEXT
        INTO v_adsloc
        FROM PRINT_MEDIA_TEST
        WHERE PRODUCT_ID = 1729
     FOR UPDATE;
     v_start := 1;
     v_len := LENGTH (v_ads_text);
     DBMS_LOB.WRITE   (v_adsloc,
                       v_len,
                       v_start,
                       v_ads_text);
     COMMIT;
     END;
     /
PL/SQL procedure successfully completed.
```

- Updating BLOB columns using DBMS_LOB.WRITE

```
     DECLARE
        v_adcloc        BLOB;
        v_adc_text      RAW (10);
        v_start         INTEGER := 1;
        v_len           BINARY_INTEGER := 10;
     BEGIN
        SELECT AD_COMPOSITE
        INTO v_adcloc
        FROM PRINT_MEDIA_TEST
        WHERE PRODUCT_ID = 1726
        FOR UPDATE;
        v_adc_text := '1234567890123456789';
        DBMS_LOB.write          (v_adcloc,
                                 v_len,
                                 v_start,
                                 v_adc_text);
        COMMIT;
     END;
     /
PL/SQL procedure successfully completed.
```

- Parallel Tuning Parameters
  - Navigate through Oracle Documentation to get to Parallel Execution in Data Warehouses without search tab
    Oracle Database Documentation Library > Books > DAT > Data Warehousing Guide> HTML

On contents page Ctrl f and search for "Using Parallel Execution " you will reach Using Parallel Execution, which will give details for Parallel Execution

- Dynamic Views for Parallel Queries
  i. V$PQ_SESSTAT
  ii. V$PX_BUFFER_ADVICE
  iii. V$PX_PROCESS
  iv. V$PX_PROCESS_SYSSTAT
  v. V$PX_SESSION
  vi. V$PX_SESSTAT
- Parallel Tuning Parameter Details

Parameter	**Default**	**Comments**
PARALLEL_ADAPTIVE_ MULTI_USER	TRUE	This parameter causes parallel execution SQL to throttle DOP requests to prevent system overload.
PARALLEL_MAX_SERVERS	CPU_COUNT x PARALLEL_ THREADS_PER_ CPU x (2 if PGA_AGGREGATE_ TARGET > 0; otherwise 1) x 5	This specifies the maximum number of parallel execution processes and parallel recovery processes for an instance. As demand increases, Oracle increases the number of processes from the number created at instance startup up to this value. If this parameter is set too low, some queries may not have a parallel execution process available to them during query processing. If set it too high, memory resource shortages may occur during peak periods, which can degrade performance.
PARALLEL_EXECUTION_ MESSAGE_SIZE	2 KB (port specific)	Increase to 4k or 8k to improve parallel execution performance if sufficient SGA memory exists.

6

Data Warehouse Management

- Create external tables (Data Loader and Data Pump drivers)
- Implement Data Pump export and import jobs for data transfer
- Implement Data Pump to and from remote databases
- Implement Replication/Streams
- Configure and manage master replication
- Configure and manage distributed materialized views
- Configure and manage Streams for replication

6.1 Create External Tables

- Create external table using ORACLE_LOADER Driver.
  - Navigate through Oracle Documentation to get to External Tables without search tab

    Oracle Database Documentation Library > Books > ADM > Administrator's Guide > HTML

    On contents page Ctrl f and search for "External Tables" *you* will reach External Tables, which will give details of External Tables
  - Execute following sql statement to create directory

    SQL> CONNECT SYS@ocmdb AS SYSDBA

    SQL> CREATE OR REPLACE DIRECTORY admin_dat_dir AS '/u01/app/oracle/stage';

    SQL> CREATE OR REPLACE DIRECTORY admin_log_dir AS '/u01/app/oracle/stage';

    SQL> CREATE OR REPLACE DIRECTORY admin_bad_dir AS '/u01/app/oracle/stage';

    SQL> GRANT READ,WRITE ON DIRECTORY admin_dat_dir TO hr,pm;

    SQL> GRANT READ,WRITE ON DIRECTORY admin_log_dir TO hr,pm;

    SQL> GRANT READ,WRITE ON DIRECTORY admin_bad_dir TO hr,pm;
  - Create ext_data.dat file to load data into table

    SQL> CONNECT hr/hr

    Connected.

    SQL> spool /u01/app/oracle/stage /ext_data.dat

    SQL> SELECT employee_id||','||start_date||','||end_date||','||job_id||','||department_id FROM job_history;

    SQL> spool OFF;
  - Divide the ext_data.dat file in two files ext_data1.dat and ext_data2.dat

    [oracle@ocm stage]$ cp ext_data.dat ext_data1.dat

    [oracle@ocm stage]$ cp ext_data.dat ext_data2.dat

    [oracle@ocm stage]$ cat ext_data1.dat

    102,13-JAN-93,24-JUL-98,IT_PROG,60
    101,21-SEP-89,27-OCT-93,AC_ACCOUNT,110
    101,28-OCT-93,15-MAR-97,AC_MGR,110
    201,17-FEB-96,19-DEC-99,MK_REP,20
    114,24-MAR-98,31-DEC-99,ST_CLERK,50

    [oracle@ocm stage]$ cat ext_data2.dat

    122,01-JAN-99,31-DEC-99,ST_CLERK,50
    200,17-SEP-87,17-JUN-93,AD_ASST,90
    176,24-MAR-98,31-DEC-98,SA_REP,80
    176,01-JAN-99,31-DEC-99,SA_MAN,80
    200,01-JUL-94,31-DEC-98,AC_ACCOUNT,90
  - If there is huge amount of data to load then enable parallel dml

    SQL> ALTER SESSION ENABLE PARALLEL DML;

- Create table command using ORACLE_LOADER

```
SQL> CREATE TABLE job_history_ext_load
    (EMPLOYEE_ID          NUMBER(6),
     START_DATE           DATE,
     END_DATE             DATE,
     JOB_ID               VARCHAR2(10),
     DEPARTMENT_ID        NUMBER(4)
    )
    ORGANIZATION EXTERNAL
  (
         TYPE ORACLE_LOADER
         DEFAULT DIRECTORY admin_dat_dir
         ACCESS PARAMETERS
    (
     RECORDS DELIMITED BY NEWLINE
     BADFILE admin_bad_dir:'ext_data%a_%p.bad'
     LOGFILE admin_log_dir:'ext_data%a_%p.log'
     FIELDS TERMINATED BY ','
     MISSING FIELD VALUES ARE NULL
      ( EMPLOYEE_ID, START_DATE CHAR DATE_FORMAT DATE MASK "DD-MON-YY",
       END_DATE CHAR DATE_FORMAT DATE MASK "DD-MON-YY",
       JOB_ID, DEPARTMENT_ID
      )
    )
     LOCATION ('ext_data1.dat', 'ext_data2.dat')
  )
        PARALLEL
  REJECT LIMIT UNLIMITED;
```

- Open a new terminal, connect a hr/hr and select from job_history_ext_load

```
SQL> CONNECT hr/hr
SQL> SELECT * FROM job_history_ext_load;
```

- Create external table using ORACLE_DATAPUMP Driver.

  - Navigate through Oracle Documentation to get to ORACLE_DATAPUMP without search tab

    Oracle Database Documentation Library > Books > UTI >* Utilities>** ***HTML

    On contents page Ctrl f and search for "14 The ORACLE_DATAPUMP Access Driver " you will reach The ORACLE_DATAPUMP Access Driver which will give location of ORACLE_DATAPUMP.

  - Create external table from existing table

```
SQL> CREATE TABLE JOB_HISTORY_EXT_PUMP
    ORGANIZATION EXTERNAL
      (TYPE ORACLE_DATAPUMP
           DEFAULT DIRECTORY ADMIN_DAT_DIR LOCATION ('ext_data.dmp'))
    AS
      SELECT * FROM job_history_ext_load;
```

The select clause above can have WHERE clause also.

```
SQL> SELECT * FROM JOB_HISTORY_EXT_PUMP;
```

  - You can use the dump file 'ext_data.dmp' created for the external table for another external table in the same or different database.

```
SQL> CREATE TABLE JOB_HISTORY_EXT_PUMP2
     (EMPLOYEE_ID          NUMBER(6),
      START_DATE          DATE,
      END_DATE            DATE,
      JOB_ID            VARCHAR2(10),
      DEPARTMENT_ID         NUMBER(4)
     )
      ORGANIZATION EXTERNAL
        (TYPE ORACLE_DATAPUMP
         DEFAULT DIRECTORY ADMIN_DAT_DIR LOCATION ('ext_data.dmp'));
SQL> SELECT COUNT(*) FROM JOB_HISTORY_EXT_PUMP2;
```

- Supported Datatypes

  The database character set and the database national character set may be different between the two platforms.

  The "endianness" of the platforms for the two databases may be different.

  The ORACLE_DATAPUMP access driver automatically resolves some of these situations.

  Following Datatypes are automatically converted during loads and unloads.

  i. Character (CHAR, NCHAR, VARCHAR2, NVARCHAR2)
  ii. RAW
  iii. NUMBER
  iv. Date/Time
  v. BLOB
  vi. CLOB and NCLOB
  vii. ROWID and UROWID

- Unsupported Datatypes

  An external table supports a subset of all possible Datatypes for columns. In particular, it supports character Datatypes (except LONG), the RAW Datatypes, all numeric Datatypes, and all date, timestamp, and interval Datatypes.

  This section describes how you can use the ORACLE_DATAPUMP access driver to unload and reload data for some of the unsupported Datatypes, specifically

  i. BFILE
  ii. LONG and LONG RAW
  iii. Final object types
  iv. Tables of final object types

- External Table having BFILE datatype column

```
SQL> CONNECT pm/pm
```

i. Function to get directory for a BFILE column.

```
SQL> CREATE FUNCTION get_dir (bf BFILE)
              RETURN VARCHAR2
     IS
     dir_name   VARCHAR2 (512);
     file_name  VARCHAR2 (512);
     BEGIN
         IF bf IS NULL
         THEN
              RETURN NULL;
         ELSE
              DBMS_LOB.FILEGETNAME (bf, dir_name, file_name);
              RETURN dir_name;
         END IF;
     END;
     /
```

ii. Function to get the filename for a BFILE column.

```
SQL> CREATE FUNCTION get_file (bf BFILE)
              RETURN VARCHAR2
     IS
     dir_name   VARCHAR2 (512);
     file_name  VARCHAR2 (512);
     BEGIN
         IF bf IS NULL
         THEN
              RETURN NULL;
         ELSE
              DBMS_LOB.FILEGETNAME (bf, dir_name, file_name);
              RETURN file_name;
         END IF;
     END;
     /
```

iii. External table as select data from the print_media table

```
SQL> CREATE TABLE print_media_ext_bfile
     ORGANIZATION EXTERNAL
     (     TYPE oracle_datapump
     DEFAULT DIRECTORY admin_dat_dir LOCATION ('pm_ext_bfile.dmp'))
     AS
     SELECT  product_id,
             ad_id,
             get_dir (ad_graphic) ad_graphic_dir,
             get_file (ad_graphic) ad_graphic_file
     FROM    print_media;
```

iv. Function to load bfile column from the data that is in the external table

```
SQL> CREATE FUNCTION get_bfile (dir VARCHAR2, file VARCHAR2)
             RETURN BFILE
     IS
     bf  BFILE;
     BEGIN
         IF dir IS NULL
         THEN
             RETURN NULL;
         ELSE
             RETURN BFILENAME (dir, file);
         END IF;
     END;
     /
```

v. Create table print_media_bfile_test having a bfile column

```
SQL> CREATE TABLE print_media_bfile_test
     AS
     SELECT  product_id,
             ad_id,
             get_bfile (ad_graphic_dir, ad_graphic_file) ad_graphic
     FROM    print_media_ext_bfile;
```

vi. Check the data in table print_media_bfile_test is same as in print_media

```
SQL> SELECT  product_id,
             ad_id,
             get_dir (ad_graphic),
             get_file (ad_graphic)
     FROM    print_media_bfile_test
     MINUS
     SELECT  product_id,
             ad_id,
             get_dir (ad_graphic),
             get_file (ad_graphic)
     FROM    print_media;
```

- External Table having LONG and LONG RAW column

  i. Connect as hr user.

```
SQL> CONNECT hr/hr
```

  ii. Execute sql below to get table views, which have LONG column

```
SQL> SELECT ' select count(*) from '
            || table_name
            || ' where '
            || column_name
            || ' is not null ;'
     FROM   all_tab_columns
     WHERE  data_type = 'LONG';
```

  iii. Create external table created having LOB column to get data from LONG column

  The USER_VIEWS is used to create external table.

```
SQL> CREATE TABLE user_views_ext_long
     ORGANIZATION EXTERNAL
      (TYPE ORACLE_DATAPUMP
     DEFAULT DIRECTORY admin_dat_dir LOCATION ('user_views_ext_long.dmp'))
     AS
     SELECT VIEW_NAME, TO_LOB (TEXT) TEXT FROM USER_VIEWS;
```

iv. Select from external table user_views_ext_long

```
SQL> SELECT * FROM user_views_ext_long;
```

- **Refer Oracle Documentation for External tables on Types**
  i. Final object types
  ii. Tables of final object types

- Implement Data Pump export and import jobs for data transfer

  Below are few examples

  - Export schema both metadata and data.

expdp_schema.sh

```
#!/usr/bin/ksh
set -x
dt=`date +%y%m%d%H%M`
export ORACLE_SID=ocmdb
export ORACLE_HOME='/u01/app/oracle/product/10.2.0/db_1'
echo `date`
expdp system directory=DATA_PUMP_DIR schemas=scott logfile= scott_expdp_${dt}.log
dumpfile=scott_${dt}.dmp
```

  - Export tables using parfile only metadata having exclude parameter.

expdp_parfile.par

```
directory=data_pump_dir
content=metadata_only
tables=scott.emp, scott.dept
exclude=statistics
logfile=ocmdb_scott_tables_expdp_test.log
dumpfile=ocmdb_scott_teable_test.dmp
```

expdp_using_parfile.sh

```
#!/bin/bash
set -x
dt=`date=%y%m%d%H%M`
export ORACLE_SID=ocmdb;
export ORACLE_HOME=/u01/app/oracle/product/10.2.0/db_1;
echo `date`
echo $ORACLE_HOME
expdp system PARFILE=expdp_parfile.par
```

  - Export tables data in parallel of 8, having multiple dump files on multiple disks

```
expdp system parallel=8 directory=DATA_PUMP_DIR EXCLUDE=STATISTICS TABLES=SH.SALES
CONTENT=DATA_ONLY \
logfile=sales_data_expdp_${dt}.log dumpfile= DATA_PUMP_DIR:sales_data%U_${dt}.dmp,
EXPORT_DIR:sales_data%U_${dt}.dmp
```

- Import tables data in parallel of 8, having multiple dump files on multiple disks.

  impdp system parallel=8 directory= DATA_PUMP_DIR TABLES= SH.SALES CONTENT=DATA_ONLY logfile=sales_data_impdp_${dt}.log dumpfile= DATA_PUMP_DIR:sales_data%U_0804241211.dmp, EXPORT_DIR:sales_data%U_0804241211.dmp

- Import schema SH metadata and then data in oemdb from ocmdb using network link.

  Create Database link in oemdb Database.

  SQL> CREATE PUBLIC DATABASE LINK OCMDB CONNECT TO SYSTEM IDENTIFIED BY oracle USING ocmdb;

  impdp system parallel=4 directory= DATA_PUMP_DIR EXCLUDE=STATISTICS NETWORK_LINK=OCMDB SCHEMAS=SH CONTENT=METADATA_ONLY logfile=sh_metadata_impdp_${dt}.log

  impdp system parallel=4 directory= DATA_PUMP_DIR EXCLUDE=STATISTICS
  NETWORK_LINK=OCMDB SCHEMAS=SH CONTENT=DATA_ONLY TABLE_EXISTS_ACTION=APPEND \
  logfile=sh_data_impdp_${dt}.log

- Import schema HR oemdb from ocmdb remap tablespace and schema

  impdp system directory=DATA_PUMP_DIR EXCLUDE=STATISTICS SCHEMAS=hr
  CONTENT=METADATA_ONLY \
  REMAP_TABLESPACE=EXAMPLE:USERS \
  REMAP_SCHEMA=hr:oemhr dumpfile=hr_ocmdb.dmp logfile=oemhr_impdp.log

6.2 Implement Replication/Streams

- As Oracle Streams is very vast, topic and it will take hundreds of pages to explain every aspect of it, which is out of scope of this book. In this book, only CHANGE DATA CAPTURE (CDC) Synchronous Publishing portion is explained.

Sr.No.	Change Sources. Modes of Change Data Capture	Description
1	Synchronous Change Data Capture	The synchronous mode uses triggers on the source database to capture change data. It has zero latency because the change data is captured regularly and in real time on the source database. The change tables are populated when DML operations on the source table are committed
2	Asynchronous HotLog Mode	In the asynchronous HotLog mode, change data is captured from the online redo log file on the source database. There is a short latency ad mist the act of committing source table transactions and the arrival of change data
3	Asynchronous Distributed HotLog Mode	In the asynchronous Distributed HotLog mode, change data is captured from the online redo log file on the source database.
4	Asynchronous AutoLog Mode	There is no predefined Distributed HotLog change source. In contrast to other modes of Change Data Capture, the Distributed HotLog mode splits change data capture activities and objects across the source and staging database. Change sources are clearly defined on the source database by the staging database publisher

- Synchronous Publishing.

  - 1 Create Change Table

```
SQL> BEGIN
     DBMS_CDC_PUBLISH.create_change_table (
     owner             => 'cdc',        — Owner of CDC Publisher
     change_table_name => 'emp_cdc',    — Name of Change Table
     change_set_name   => 'SYNC_SET',   — Change set
     source_schema     => 'scott',      — Source Schema
     source_table      => 'emp',
     — Column Identifies Columns Captured by Changed Table
     column_type_list  => ' empno number, ename varchar2 (10),job varchar2(9),
                          mgr number, hiredate date,deptno number',
     — Captures values both Before Update and After Update
     capture_values    => 'both',
     rs_id             => 'y',          — Unique row sequence ID
     row_id            => 'n',
     user_id           => 'n',
     timestamp         => 'n',
     object_id         => 'n',
     source_colmap     => 'y',
     target_colmap     => 'y',
     options_string    => NULL);
   END;
   /
```

  - 2 Obtain a Subscription Handle

```
SQL> SET SERVEROUTPUT ON
SQL> VARIABLE subhandle NUMBER;
SQL> BEGIN
   DBMS_CDC_SUBSCRIBE.get_subscription_handle (
     change_set          => 'SYNC_SET',
     description         => ' Change for scott.emp',
     subscription_handle => :subhandle);
   DBMS_OUTPUT.put_line ('Subhandle = ' || :subhandle);
   END;
   /
   PRINT subhandle
```

  - 3 Subscribe to a Source Table and Columns in the Source Table

```
SQL> BEGIN
   DBMS_CDC_SUBSCRIBE.subscribe (
    subscription_handle => :subhandle,
     source_schema      => 'scott',
     source_table       => 'emp',
     subscriber_view    => 'emp_cdc',
     column_list        => 'empno,ename,job,mgr,hiredate,deptno');
   END;
   /
```

  - 4 Activate the Subscription

```
SQL> BEGIN
     DBMS_CDC_SUBSCRIBE.activate_subscription (
      subscription_handle => :subhandle);
   END;
   /
```

- 5 Set the Boundaries to See New Data

```
SQL> BEGIN
      DBMS_CDC_SUBSCRIBE.extend_window (subscription_handle =>
:subhandle);
END;
/
```

- 6 Prepare a Subscriber View

```
SQL> DECLARE
v_name   VARCHAR2 (30);
BEGIN
  DBMS_CDC_SUBSCRIBE.prepare_subscriber_view (
    subscription_handle => :subhandle,
    source_schema       => 'scott',
    source_table        => 'emp',
    view_name           => v_name);
  DBMS_OUTPUT.put_line ('View Name = ' || v_name);
END;
/
```

The output for this was CDC#CV$150404 which can be seen in data dictionary.

- 7 Read and Query the Contents of the Change Tables

```
SQL> DESC CDC#CV$150404;
```

NAME	NULL?	TYPE
OPERATION$		CHAR(2)
CSCN$		NUMBER
COMMIT_TIMESTAMP$		DATE
RSID$		NUMBER
SOURCE_COLMAP$		RAW(128)
TARGET_COLMAP$		RAW(128)
DEPTNO		NUMBER
EMPNO		NUMBER
ENAME		VARCHAR2(10)
HIREDATE		DATE
JOB		VARCHAR2(9)
MGR		NUMBER

- 8 Drop the Subscribe View

```
SQL> BEGIN
     DBMS_CDC_SUBSCRIBE.drop_subscriber_view (
       subscription_handle => :subhandle,
       source_schema       => 'scott',
       source_table        => ' emp');
END;
/
```

- 9 Empty the Old Data from the Subscription Window

```
SQL> BEGIN
      DBMS_CDC_SUBSCRIBE.purge_window (subscription_handle => :subhandle);
END;
/
```

- 10 Repeat 5 through 9 for additional change data
  i. Set the Boundaries to See New Data
  ii. Prepare a Subscriber View
  iii. Read and Query the Contents of the Change Tables
  iv. Drop the Subscribe View
  v. Empty the Old Data from the Subscription Window
- 11 End the Subscription
  i. Use the DBMS_LOGMNR_CDC_SUBSCRIBE.DROP_SUBSCRIPTION procedure to end the subscription
  ii. This is necessary to prevent the change tables from growing without bound

```
SQL> BEGIN
          SYS.DBMS_LOGMNR_CDC-SUBSCRIBE.DROP_SUBSCRIPTION (
          SUBSCRIPTION_HANDLE => :SUBHANDLE );
     END;
```

- CDC Data Dictionary Views
  i. CHANGE_SOURCES
  ii. CHANGE_SETS
  iii. CHANGE_TABLES
  iv. DBA_SOURCE_TABLES
  v. DBA_SOURCE_TAB_COLUMNS
  vi. DBA_PUBLISHED_COLUMNS
  vii. DBA_SUBSCRIPTIONS
  viii. DBA_SUBSCRIBED_TABLES
  ix. DBA_SUBSCRIBED_COLUMNS

7

Performance Management

- Install Statspack
- Adjust the default interval for statistics collection
- Customize the events that are monitored
- Use ADDM to analyze statistics and to identify performance bottlenecks and fix them
- Implement automatic shared memory management
- Tune memory using manual memory management
- Monitor and tune SGA areas that are not automatically tuned
- Implement automatic SQL execution memory management
- Tune the PGA using work area size parameters
- Use the PGA Advisor
- Create a Database Resource Manager plan with directives (active session count, max execution time)
- Create consumer groups
- Configure consumer group mappings
- Manage Services
- Create and manage objects to accommodate different data access methods (schema tuning)
- Use the SQL Tuning Advisor
- Use the SQL Access Advisor
- Gather Optimizer statistics
- Interpret execution plan
- Use SQL tuning tools and features

7.1 Statspack Setup

- Oracle parameters need for Statspack statistics collection

  Parameter   Value
  statistics_level   TYPICAL
  timed_statistics   TRUE

- Statspack is installed using spcreate.sql script available in $ORACLE_HOME/rdbms/admin/spcreate.sql
  - To install Statspack we need following

    i. PERFSTAT PASSWORD   ORACLE
    ii. DEFAULT TABLESPACE   SYSAUX
    iii. TEMPORARY TABLESPACE   TEMP

    SQL> @$ORACLE_HOME/rdbms/admin/spcreate.sql

    i. Enter value for perfstat_password: ORACLE
    ii. Enter value for default_tablespace: SYSAUX
    iii. Enter value for temporary_tablespace: TEMP

- Automation of statistics collection is done by $ORACLE_HOME/rdbms/admin/spauto.sql

  [oracle@ocm admin]$ sqlplus perfstat@ocmdb

  SQL> @$ORACLE_HOME/rdbms/admin/spauto.sql

  spauto.sql sets Oracle job that executes Statspack snapshot ever hour on the hour
  You can schedule statistics collection through Oracle scheduler also

- Manual statistics collection and modifying Statspack parameters
  - Manual statistics collection is done by perfstat.statspack.snap package. The default snap level is 5. You can change the snap level while collecting the stats
  - Collecting statistics manually at default level

    SQL> EXECUTE statspack.snap;
  - Collecting statistics manually at different level

    SQL> EXECUTE statspack.snap(i_snap_level=>7);
  - Collecting statistics manually at different level and making it default level for future statistics collection

    SQL> EXECUTE statspack.snap (i_snap_level=>7, i_modify_parameter=>'TRUE');
  - Stats collection parameters can be modified using procedure modify_statspack_parameter

    SQL> EXECUTE statspack.modify_statspack_parameter (i_snap_level=>7, i_disk_reads_th=>2000,i_buffer_gets_th=>20000);

- Statspack Snapshot Levels

Level	Statistics Captured
4	General Performance statistics on all memory areas, pools, latches and events.
5	All in level 4 plus resource intensive SQL statements.
6	All in level 5 plus SQL plans.
7	ALL in level 6 plus segment level statistics.
10	All in above level plus parent and child latches.

- Creating statistics baseline

You can create Statspack base line for normal database performance and later compare the baseline with high activity time or worst performance time, statspack.make_baseline is used to create and delete baseline.

- Create baseline using snap_id

  SQL> EXEC statspack.make_baseline (i_begin_snap => 2, i_end_snap => 5);

- Deleting baseline using snap_id

  SQL> EXEC statspack.make_baseline (2, 5, FALSE);

- Creating base line using snap time.

  SQL> EXEC statspack.make_baseline (to_date(’01-FEB-2011 19:00',’DD-MON-YYYY HH24:MI’),to_date(’01-FEB-2011 20:00',’DD-MON-YYYY HH24:MI’));

- Deleting baseline using snap time.

  SQL> EXEC statspack.clear_baseline (TO_DATE(’01-FEB-2011 19:00',’DD-MON-YYYY HH24:MI’),TO_DATE(’01-FEB-2011 20:00',’DD-MON-YYYY HH24:MI’));

- Purging Snapshots Dropping and exporting Statspack repository user perfstat

- Snapshots can be purged using statspack.purge procedure ,sppurge.sql and sptrunc.sql to truncate all Statspack tables.

  SQL> EXEC statspack.purge (i_begin_date=>to_date(’01-FEB-2011 19:00',’DD-MON-YYYY HH24:MI’),i_end_date =>to_date(’01-FEB-2011 20:00',’DD-MON-YYYY HH24:MI’),i_extended_purge=>true);

  SQL> @$ORACLE_HOME/rdbms/admin/sppurge.sql

  You have to provide value of losnapid and hisnapid range for sppurge.sql

  SQL> @$ORACLE_HOME/rdbms/admin/sptrunc.sql

- Drop Statspack repository

  SQL> @$ORACLE_HOME/rdbms/admin/spdrop.sql

- Export Statspack user perfstat use script

  [oracle@ocm admin]$ exp system@ocmdb parfile=spuexp.par

- Statspack Reports

- Statspack reports are created using $ORACLE_HOME/rdbms/admin/spreport.sql

  SQL> $ORACLE_HOME/rdbms/admin/spreport.sql

  i. Entering the number of days (n) will result in the most recent (n) days of snapshots being listed. Pressing <return> without specifying a number lists all completed snapshots.

  ii. You have to provide 3 values mentioned below.
  Enter value for begin_snap:
  Enter value for end_snap:
  Enter value for report_name:

  iii. When spreport.sql is executed, it executes two more scripts.
  sprepins.sql
  sprepcon.sql

  iv. You can also copy the above 3 scripts in any oracle client machine and execute spreport.sql as perfstat, Statspack report will be generated on that machine.

7.2 Statspack Sample Report

Below is sample Statspack report that depicts problem, details and recommendations.

- **Load Profile**
  - **Physical reads** 18234.49

    For high physical reads look into section SQL ordered by Reads for DB
- **Instance Efficiency Percentages**
  - **Recursive Call %:** 25.90

    This type of call occurs for a few reasons such as misses in the dictionary cache; dynamic storage extension; and when PL/SQL statements are executed. Generally, if number of recursive calls is more than four per process, one should check dictionary cache hit ratio and see if there are tables and indexes with large number on extents.

    Recommendation:

    Rebuild tables and indexes with large extent size so that number of extents is small.

    Ideally, one should keep all the data in a table or index in one extent, which is not possible in real life scenarios. The more extents a segment has, the more work is involved in retrieving data and administering it.

    "Many Oracle GURUS call this as myth"

    But, if you work in VLDB Oracle Data warehouse where FACT partition tables are more than Terabyte size; each partition is more than 200GB; there are lots of simultaneous parallel processing with parallel=8/16; and multiple processes are inserting hundreds of thousands rows, having large extent size is really beneficial. The only negative of this change is for 'Full Table Scans' FTS that reads complete last extent, which may **NOT** be full.

    If any query is doing FTS for more than terabyte of data then there is problem with query or system design itself.
  - **Buffer Hit %:** 72.52

    This is the ratio of hits request for a specific buffer and buffer was memory instead of needing to do physical I/O.

    Recommendation:

    Tune all sql in SQL ordered by Reads for DB section and then increase db_cache_size till the ratio is above 95% in EDW and above 99% in OLTP.
  - **Latch Hit Ratio %** - 92.47

    The details of latch contention due to Hot Blocks are detailed in the Top 5 Timed Events for DB section.
  - **Execute to Parse %** - 64.83

    DBA's are often afraid of implementing the recommendation for above problem, so they do not try even in test databases. In my experience where there are hundreds of similar sql running, having hard coded literals, and every time running with different values, the changes suggested works very fine in Oracle 10.2.0.4.

    Possible reasons why this would occur are

    i. SQL statements not using bind variables.

    ii. Opening of cursor once, repeating parse with bind variables, execute (fetch) for each SQL statement.

    iii. Cursor open, parse with bind variables, execute (fetch) and close for each SQL statement.

    iv. Cursor open and parse with bind variables once, repeated executes (fetch)

Recommendation:

The parameters that affect the points above are:

Parameter	Default Value	Suggestions
SESSION_CACHED_CURSORS	20	200
CURSOR_SPACE_FOR_TIME	FALSE	TRUE
CURSOR_SHARING	EXACT	SIMILAR

SIMILAR causes the statements to share to SQL statements but checks are still used to determine whether the executable SQL area can be shared or not. In Oracle, 9i there was bind peeking problem caused poor execution plan when using this parameter. If we have proper histograms on tables, there are no issues with bind peeking in Oracle 10.2.0.4.

If changing parameter CURSOR_SHARING starts giving bind peaking problem in 10.2.0.4 then you should delete all the database statistics and again collect stats with histograms only on INDEXED columns.

Method_Opt => 'FOR ALL INDEXED COLUMNS SIZE AUTO '

```
SQL> BEGIN
        SYS.DBMS_STATS.GATHER_SCHEMA_STATS (
                OwnName         => 'APP_USER',
                Granularity     => 'DEFAULT',
                Options         => 'GATHER',
                Gather_Temp     => FALSE,
                Method_Opt      => 'FOR ALL INDEXED COLUMNS SIZE AUTO ',
                DEGREE          => 4,
                CASCADE         => TRUE,
                No_Invalidate   => FALSE);
     END;
```

Changing **SESSION_CACHED_CURSORS** to high value gives memory leak errors

ORA-600 [729] in some Oracle 10g version, but issue is fixed in Oracle version 10.2.0.4.0.

It also uses some extra memory at OS session level.

Setting **CURSOR_SPACE_FOR_TIME** parameter to TRUE also retains the private SQL area allocated for each cursor between executes instead of discarding it after cursor execution. If there is a "cursor leak" in the application, when set to TRUE, it can quickly lead to ORA-4031 errors or severe shared pool performance problems.

The above parameters are very good for performance provided, they do not give any memory leak errors in your database version. You can test your applications by changing above parameters to make sure there is no Memory Leak error.

■ Oracle Database Timed Events

Below are most common wait events from multiple Statspack reports. If top 5 Timed Events are fixed then 90% of database problems get resolved.

- db file sequential read

  Check top sql in db file sequential read section by running an explain plan and then modify them as needed. Check Gets per execution and whether the same sql have high disk reads or not. If disk reads are not high, it may be using wrong join order and/or bad indexes.

- db file scattered read

  The db file scattered read is due to many full table scans because of Indexes missing on tables for queries in SQL ordered by Reads for DB. If high physical reads are present, check if indexes are not being used along with low cardinality columns. If low cardinality columns are used in where clause of query, then create bitmap indexes on those columns instead of btree indexes.

- db file parallel write

  The db file parallel write event shows that the DBWR is performing a parallel write to files and blocks. The parameter request depicts real number of I/Os being performed on disk. After the last I/O is completed to disk, the wait event ends.

- control file parallel write

  For control, file parallel write wait event use Asynchronous I/O, if available on your platform. Move the control file copies to less saturated storage locations.

- direct path write

  The direct path write Oracle wait event occurs when a server process is writing buffers directly from PGA instead of DBWR writing buffers from the buffer cache to disk. The server process waits on this event for the write call to complete.

- direct path read

  For SQL having clause like order by, group by, sort are too large to fit in memory and they go to disk. If a sort does not fit into memory, then some of the sort data is written out directly to disk. This data is later read back in, using direct reads. The server process is processing buffers faster than the I/O system can return the buffers. This wait event show I/O system is overloaded. Increasing PGA will reduce this wait event.

- log file parallel write

  For log file parallel write wait event, practice following

  i. Ensure tablespaces are NOT left in HOT BACKUP mode longer than needed.
     Tablespaces in HOT BACKUP mode cause more redo to be generated for each change that can vastly increase the rate of redo generation.

  ii. Redo log members should ideally be on high-speed disks

     e.g.: RAID5 is not a good candidate for redo log members.

  iii. Redo log members should be on disks with little/no IO activity from other sources.

     (Including low activity from other sources against the same disk controller)

  iv. RAW devices can be faster than file system files.

  v. NOLOGGING/UNRECOVERABLE operations may be possible for certain operations to reduce the overall rate of redo generation.

- log file sync

  The log file sync wait event occurs when process is waiting for LGWR to finish flushing the log buffer to disk. This occurs when a user commits a transaction. (A transaction is not considered committed until all of the redo to recover the transaction has been successfully written to disk.). Try to do less frequent commits in application, if possible.

- CPU time

  It is the amount of CPU time used during the snapshot window. In a heavily loaded system, if the CPU time event is the biggest event, that could point to some CPU-intensive processing (for example, forcing the use of an index when a full scan would have been better), which could be the cause of the bottleneck.

- SQL*Net break/reset to client

  The underlying network is very slow.

- log file sequential read

  The log file sequential read occurs when process is waiting for blocks to be read from the online redo log into memory. This primarily occurs at instance startup and when the ARCH process archives filled online redo logs.

- log file switch (archiving needed).

  Archive destination slow or full. Add more or larger Redo logs.

- read by other session

  Excessive waits for this event are typically due to several server processes repeatedly reading the same blocks, e.g. many sessions scanning the same index blocks or performing full-table scans on the same table. Tuning Db file sequential read, db file scattered read will fix this wait even.

- Buffer Busy Waits

  Check the tablespace segment space management is AUTO and extent management is LOCAL.

  In conjunction with above parameter, you are getting Latch wait: cache buffers then check further details in v$waitstat using query below.

```
SQL> SELECT   class, COUNT
     FROM     v$waitstat
     WHERE    COUNT > 0
     ORDER BY COUNT DESC;
```

  STATS$ENQUEUE_STAT.TOTAL_REQ# - 9.0 is the total number of requests for an enqueue + the number of enqueue conversions. This statistic is incremented at the beginning of a get request.

  STATS$ENQUEUE_STAT.TOTAL_WAIT# - 9.0 is the total number of times a session waited for any enqueue operation. This statistic is incremented at the beginning of the wait.

  If count is greater > 0 for following and undo, management is MANUAL.

  i. Segment Header: Increase freelist group, Increase pctused/pctfree gap.
  ii. Undo Header: Add more rollback segments
  iii. Undo Block/Data Block: Reduce the density of block by moving table to smaller block size.

  For this find out the hot block from query mentioned below.

  Execute the query below few times to get SADDR which has highest sleep count (get first few rows)

```
SQL> SELECT   CHILD# cCHILD,
              ADDR sADDR,
              GETS sGETS,
              MISSES sMISSES,
              SLEEPS sSLEEPS
     FROM     v$latch_children
     WHERE    name = 'cache buffers chains'
     ORDER BY SLEEPS,
              CHILD#,
              ADDR,
              GETs;
```

  The output of this query

```
CCHILD   SADDR              SGETS       SMISSES   SSLEEPS
______   ________________   _________   _______   _______

 840     C000000AB2C744C8   855300091   8279956   202851
```

  The above latch address can be used to get more details about the blocks, currently in the buffer cache protected by this latch. Run the query below immediately using ADDR from above query to find HOT block.

```
SQL> SELECT   e.owner || '.' || e.segment_name segment_name,
              e.extent_id extent#,
              x.dbablk - e.block_id + 1 block#,
              x.tch,
              l.child#
     FROM     sys.v$latch_children l, sys.x$bh x, sys.dba_extents e
     WHERE    x.hladdr = '&ADDR'
     AND      e.file_id = x.file#
     AND      x.hladdr = l.addr
     AND      x.dbablk BETWEEN e.block_id AND e.block_id + e.blocks - 1
    ORDER BY x.tch DESC;
```

Depending on the TCH column (The number of times the block is hit by a SQL statement), you can identify a hot block. The higher the value of the TCH column, the more frequent the block is accessed by SQL statements.

In order to reduce contention for this object the following mechanisms can be put in place:

i. Examine the application to see if the execution of certain DML and SELECT statements can be reorganized to eliminate contention on the object.
ii. Decrease the buffer cache -although this may only help in a small amount of cases.
iii. DBWR throughout may have a factor in this as well. If using multiple DBWRs then increase the number of DBWRs.
iv. Increase the PCTFREE for the table storage parameters via ALTER TABLE or rebuild. This will result in fewer rows per block.
v. Consider implementing reverse key indexes (if range scans aren't commonly used against the segment).

- enq: TX - row lock contention

  This enqueue type wait event occurs if user wants to change a data record but cannot do this because a transaction is running in parallel. For example, the transaction changed the same data record because a unique or primary constraint cannot be guaranteed or because a free ITL slot is no longer available in the block header.

  Find out sessions, which are having this wait event and check if the transactions are running very long.

```
SQL> SELECT   S.SID ORACLE_SID, S.PROCESS CLIENT_PID
     FROM     V$SESSION S, V$LOCK L1
     WHERE    L1.TYPE = 'TX'
     AND      L1.LMODE = 6
     AND      S.SID = L1.SID
     AND      L1.BLOCK = 1
     AND NOT EXISTS
              (SELECT *
              FROM V$LOCK L2
              WHERE L2.TYPE = 'TX' AND L2.REQUEST > 0 AND L1.SID = L2.SID);
```

- dbwr checkpoint buffers written

  Number of buffers that were written for checkpoints

- dbwr checkpoints

  Number of times the DBWR was asked to scan the cache and write all blocks marked for a checkpoint or the end of recovery. This statistic is always larger than "background checkpoints completed".

- dbwr revisited being-written buffer

  It is number of times that DBWR tried to save a buffer for writing and found that it was already in the write batch. This statistic measures the amount of "useless" work that DBWR had to do in trying to fill the batch. Many sources contribute to a write batch. If the same buffer from different sources is considered for adding to the write batch, then all but the first attempt will be "useless" because the buffer is already marked as being written.

i. dbwr transaction table writes
Number of rollback segment headers written by DBWR. This statistic indicates how many "hot" buffers were written, causing a user process to wait while the write completed.
ii. dbwr undo block writes
Number of rollback segment blocks written by DBWR.
iii. table fetched Count row
Check for row chaining and row migrations.
iv. free Buffer Inspected – dirty Buffer inspected = pinned Count.
This shows latch contention due to hot block.

7.3 Parameter Changes to Tune I/O on Intel x86 machine

i. Comment parameter CPU_COUNT in init.ora to let Oracle set it automatically.
ii. Comment parameter DB_FILE_MULTIBLOCK_READ_COUNT in init.ora to let Oracle set it automatically.
iii. Comment parameter DBWR_IO_SLAVES in init.ora and let Oracle set it default to 0.
iv. Comment parameter DISK_ASYNCH_IO in init.ora and let Oracle set it default to TRUE.
v. Set parameter FILESYSTEMIO_OPTIONS = setall in init.ora (to allow ASYNC and DIRECTIO)
vi. Check how i/o is setup at UNIX level using **mount –p**
*rw,suid,mincache=**direct,**convosync=direct,nodatainlog,delaylog,largefiles,ioerror=mwdisable*

7.4 AWR, ADDM and ASH Reports

- The two Oracle parameters need for ADDM/AWR

Parameter	**Value**
statistics_level	TYPICAL
timed_statistics	TRUE

- ADDM,AWR Snapshot Settings/Report Generations from SQLPLUS
  - Create Baseline

SQL> EXECUTE dbms_workload_repository.create_baseline(start_snap_id =>83,end_snap_id=> 85,baseline_name=>'OCMDB_NORMAL_LOAD');

  - Drop Baseline

SQL> EXECUTE dbms_workload_repository.drop_baseline('OCMDB_NORMAL_LOAD');

  - Modify Snapshot settings Retention in minutes, Interval in minutes

SQL> EXECUTE DBMS_WORKLOAD_REPOSITORY.modify_snapshot_settings (RETENTION => 4320, INTERVAL=> 60, topnsql=> 1000);

```
SQL> SELECT dbid,
            snap_interval interval_hours,
            RETENTION retention_days,
            topnsql
     FROM dba_hist_wr_control;
```

  - Create Snapshot Manually

SQL> EXECUTE DBMS_WORKLOAD_REPOSITORY.create_snapshot();

  - Drop Snapshot Range

SQL> EXECUTE DBMS_WORKLOAD_REPOSITORY.drop_snapshot_range(low_snap_id => 80,high_snap_id => 82,dbid => 4083722939);

- Generating ADDM Analysis report using sqlplus
  i. Make directory on Linux.
  [oracle@ocm ~]$ mkdir -p /u01/app/oracle/admin/ocmdb/work
  ii. Create directory in the Database.
  SQL> CREATE OR REPLACE DIRECTORY WORK_DIR AS '/u01/app/oracle/admin/ocmdb/work';
  iii. Check statistics name and its current value
  SQL> SELECT stat_name,VALUE FROM v$sys_time_model;
  iv. Below is pl/sql block which will generate ADDM Report

```
SQL> DECLARE
        db_adv_task_id       NUMBER (10);
        db_adv_taskname      VARCHAR2 (50);
     BEGIN
        db_adv_taskname := 'ADDM_SNAP_89_90';
        — Create new task name 'ADDM_SNAP_89_90' for snapshots 89-90
        DBMS_ADVISOR.create_task ('ADDM', db_adv_task_id, db_adv_taskname);
        — SET task snapshots to analyze
        DBMS_ADVISOR.set_task_parameter (db_adv_taskname, 'START_SNAPSHOT', 89);
        DBMS_ADVISOR.set_task_parameter (db_adv_taskname, 'END_SNAPSHOT', 90);
        — Execute task
        DBMS_ADVISOR.execute_task  (db_adv_taskname);
        DBMS_ADVISOR.create_file  (
        DBMS_ADVISOR.get_task_report (db_adv_taskname, 'TEXT', 'ALL'),
        'WORK_DIR',
        'addmrpt_snap_89_90.txt');
     END;
     /
```

  v. You can view /u01/app/oracle/admin/ocmdb/work/addmrpt_snap_89_90.txt to get recommendations for database activities during snapshot 89-90
- Navigate through Oracle Documentation to get to DBMS_ADVISOR Package without search tab
  Oracle Database Documentation Library > Books >PL/> PL/SQL Packages and Types Reference > HTLM
  On contents page Ctrl f and search for "DBMS_ADVISOR" you will reach DBMS_ADVISOR section
- Below are sql to generate ADDM/AWR Report
  i. ADDM report are created using $ORACLE_HOME/rdbms/admin/addmrpt.sql
  SQL> $ORACLE_HOME/rdbms/admin/addmrpt.sql
  You have to provide 3 values mentioned below:
  Enter value for begin_snap::
  Enter value for end_snap:
  Enter value for report_name:
  When addmrpt.sql is executed, it executes one more scripts addmrpt.sql
  ii. You can also copy the above 2 scripts in any oracle client machine and execute addmrpt.sql ADDM report will be generated on that machine.
  iii. AWR report are created using $ORACLE_HOME/rdbms/admin/awrrpt.sql
  SQL> $ORACLE_HOME/rdbms/admin/awrrpt.sql
  You have to provide 4 values mentioned below:
  Enter value for report_type: text/html
  Enter value for num_days: Number of days snapshots to be listed

```
Enter value for begin_snap:
Enter value for end_snap:
Enter value for report_name:
```

iv. When awrrpt.sql is executed, it executes 3 more scripts

awrrpti.sql
awrinpnm.sql
awrinput.sql

You can also copy the above 4 scripts in any oracle client machine and execute awrrpt.sql. AWR report will be generated on that machine.

- Changing ADDM Attributes

```
SQL> SELECT  advisor_name,
             parameter_name,
             parameter_value,
             is_default
     FROM  dba_advisor_def_parameters
     WHERE advisor_name = 'ADDM';
```

ADVISOR_NAME	PARAMETER_NAME	PARAMETER_VALUE	IS_DEFAULT
ADDM	DB_ID	0	Y
ADDM	ANALYSIS_TYPE	PERIOD	Y
ADDM	SCOPE_TYPE	UNUSED	Y
ADDM	SCOPE_VALUE	UNUSED	Y
ADDM	HISTORY_TABLE	UNUSED	Y
ADDM	DBIO_EXPECTED	10000	Y
ADDM	DB_ELAPSED_TIME	0	Y

If I/O subsystem speed is faster, then we can decrease DBIO_EXPECTED value.

```
SQL> EXECUTE dbms_advisor.set_default_task_parameter (advisor_name=>'ADDM',
     parameter=>'DBIO_EXPECTED', value=>9000);
```

- ADDM, AWR Snapshot Settings/Report Generations from dbcontrol/Oracle's OEM Grid Control
  - On Database Administration Automatic Workload Repository Page, Click Snapshots

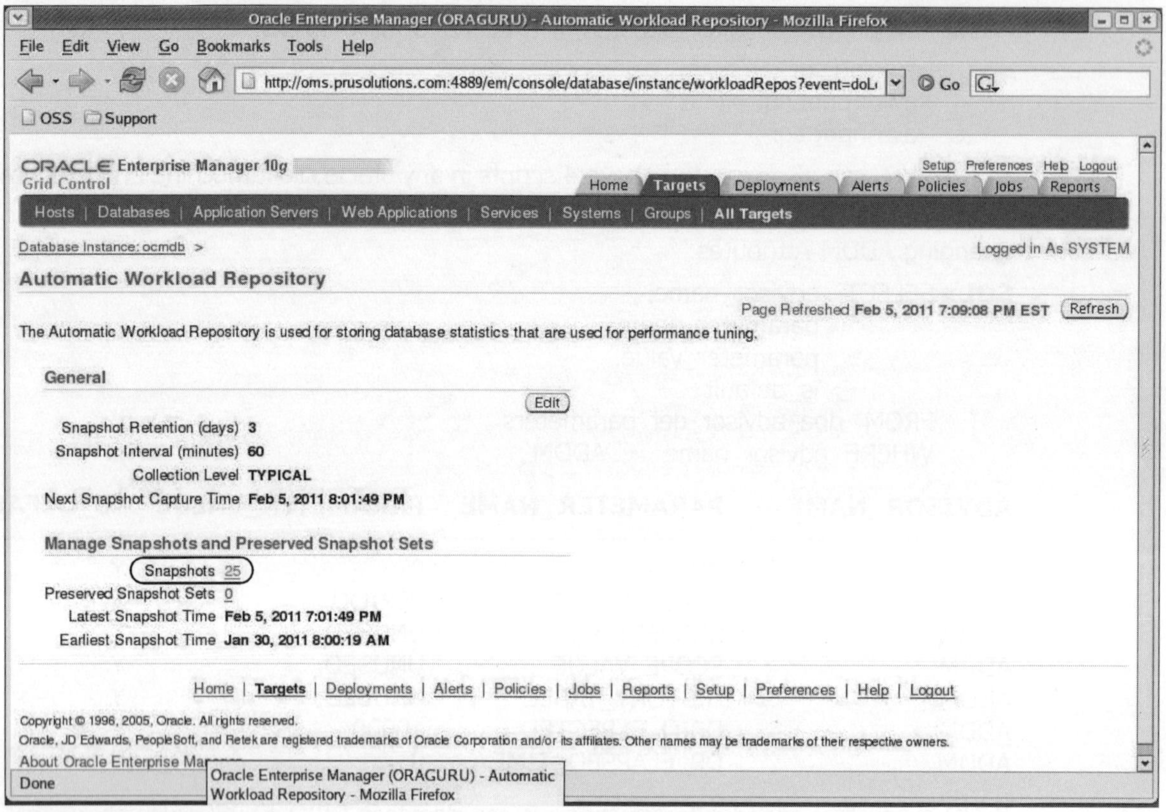

- On Snapshots Page

  Choose Snapshot-beginning date and time and click go.

  Choose Beginning Snapshot (e.g.89) from Actions drop down list choose type of action (View report) from one of following and Click Go.

  Practice all the Actions mentioned below.

  Create Preserved Snapshot Set
  Create SQL Tuning Set
  View Report
  Run ADDM
  Delete Snapshot Range
  Compare Periods

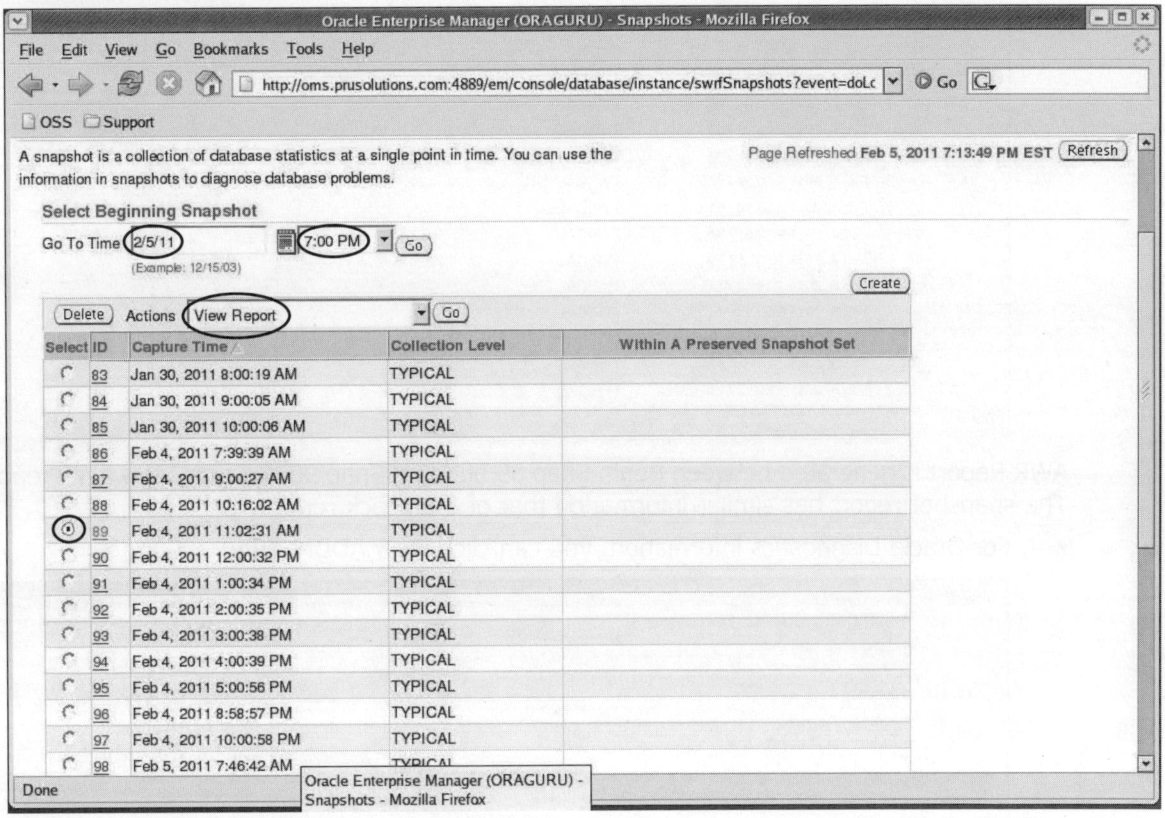

- Choose Ending Snapshot (90) and click OK

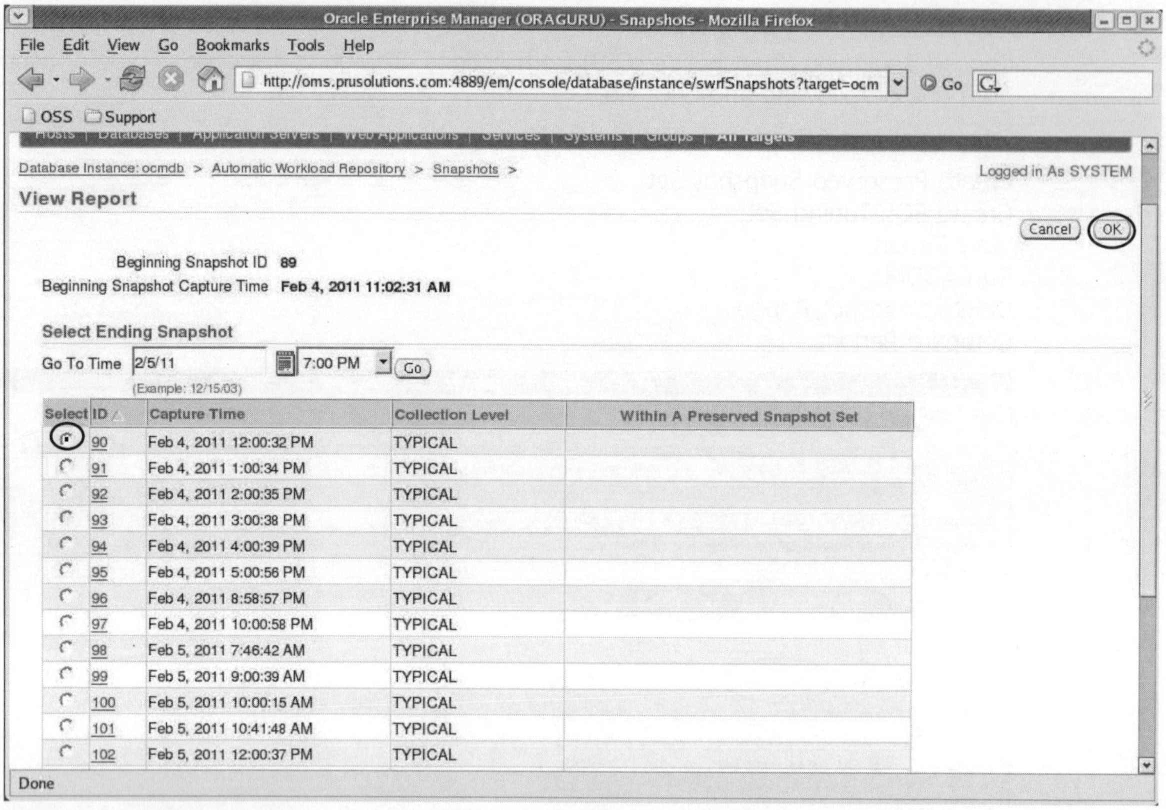

AWR Report is generated between Begin Snap 89 and End Snap 90. You can view AWR report or save to file. The snapshot report has similar information that of Statspack report.

- For Oracle Diagnostics information, you can click View ADDM Run.

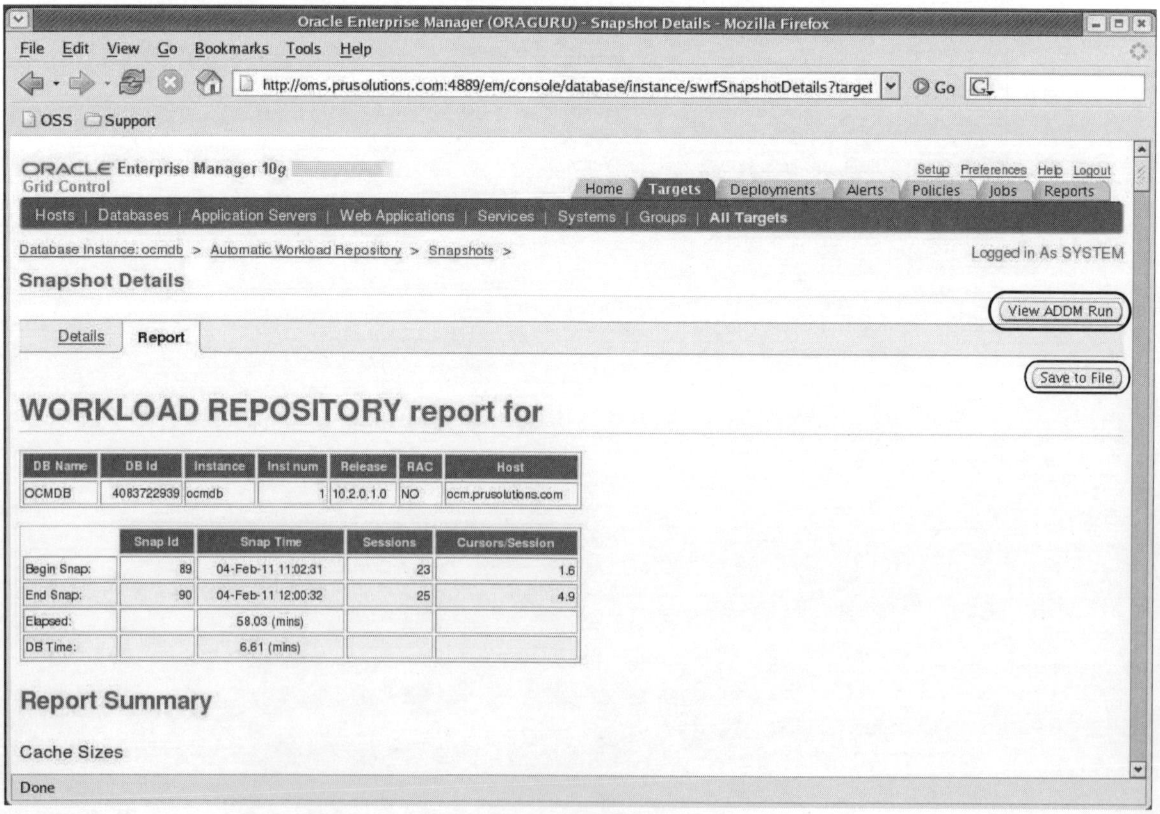

- Automatic Database Diagnostic Monitor (ADDM). On this Page, Click Run ADDM

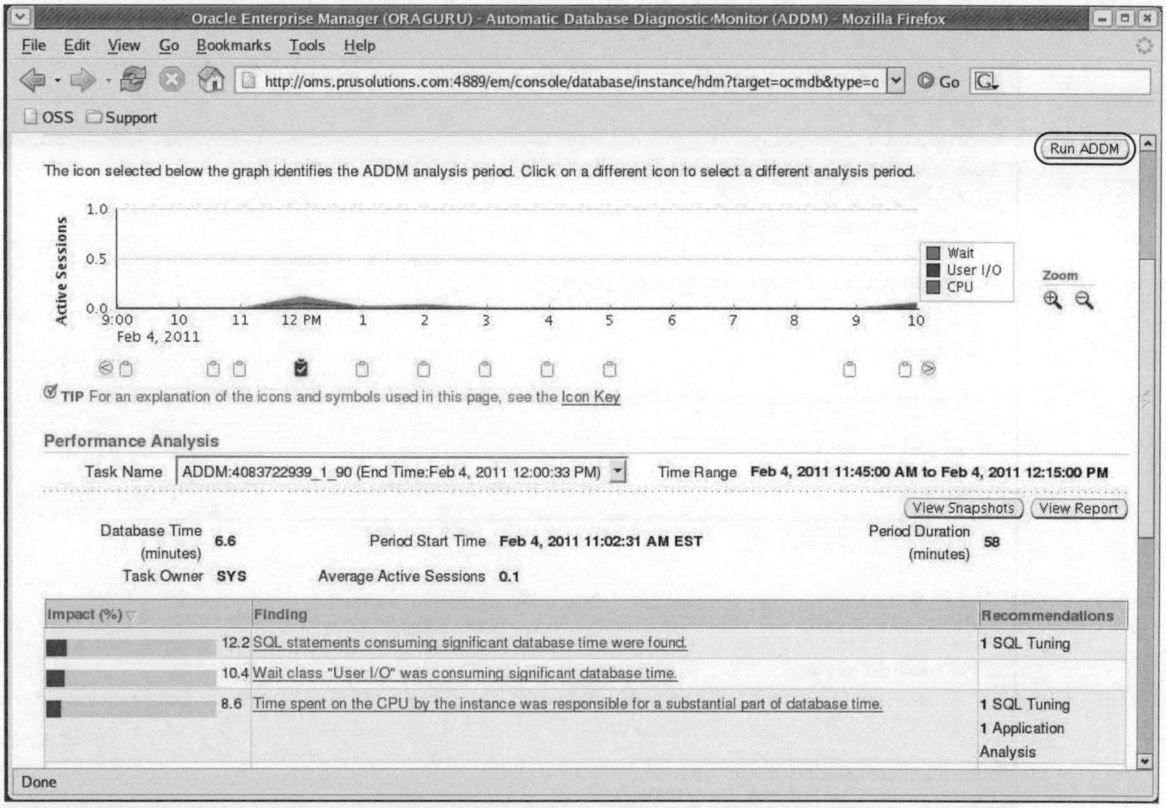

- Select Run ADDM to analyze past instance performance and Click OK

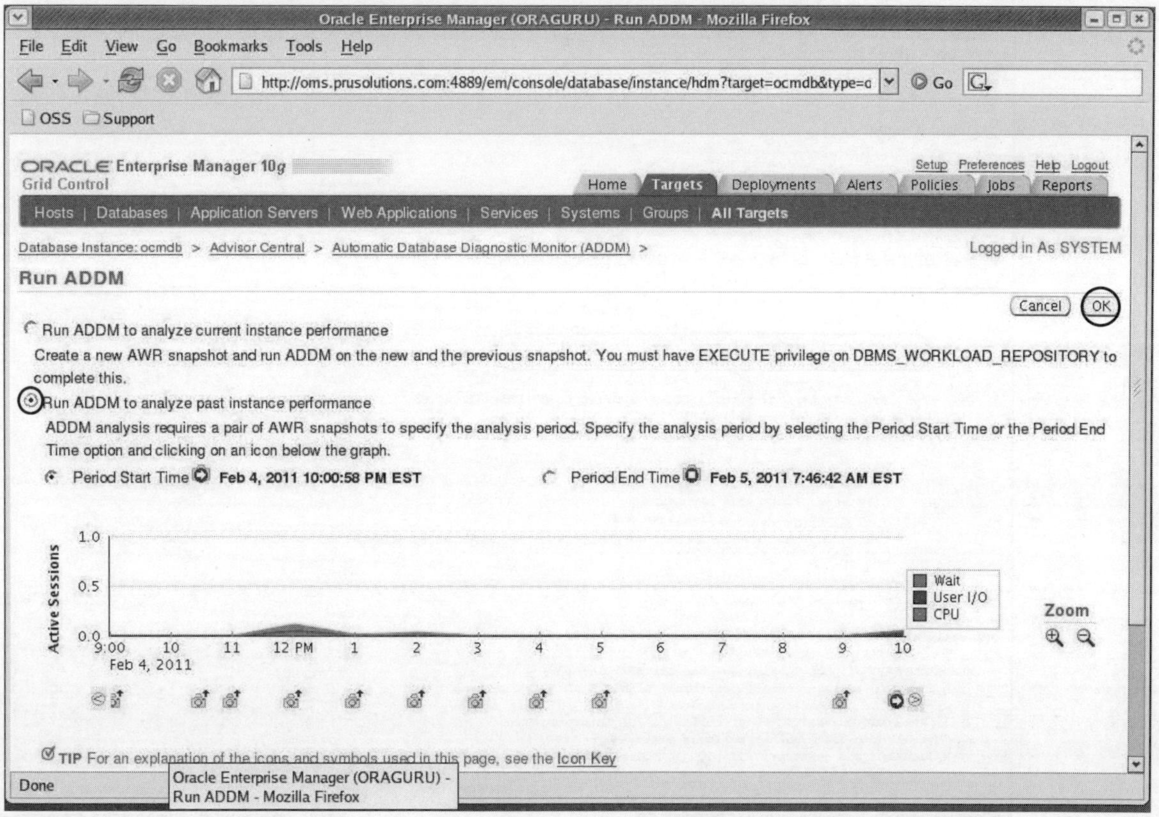

- Click View Report to get detail ADDM Report

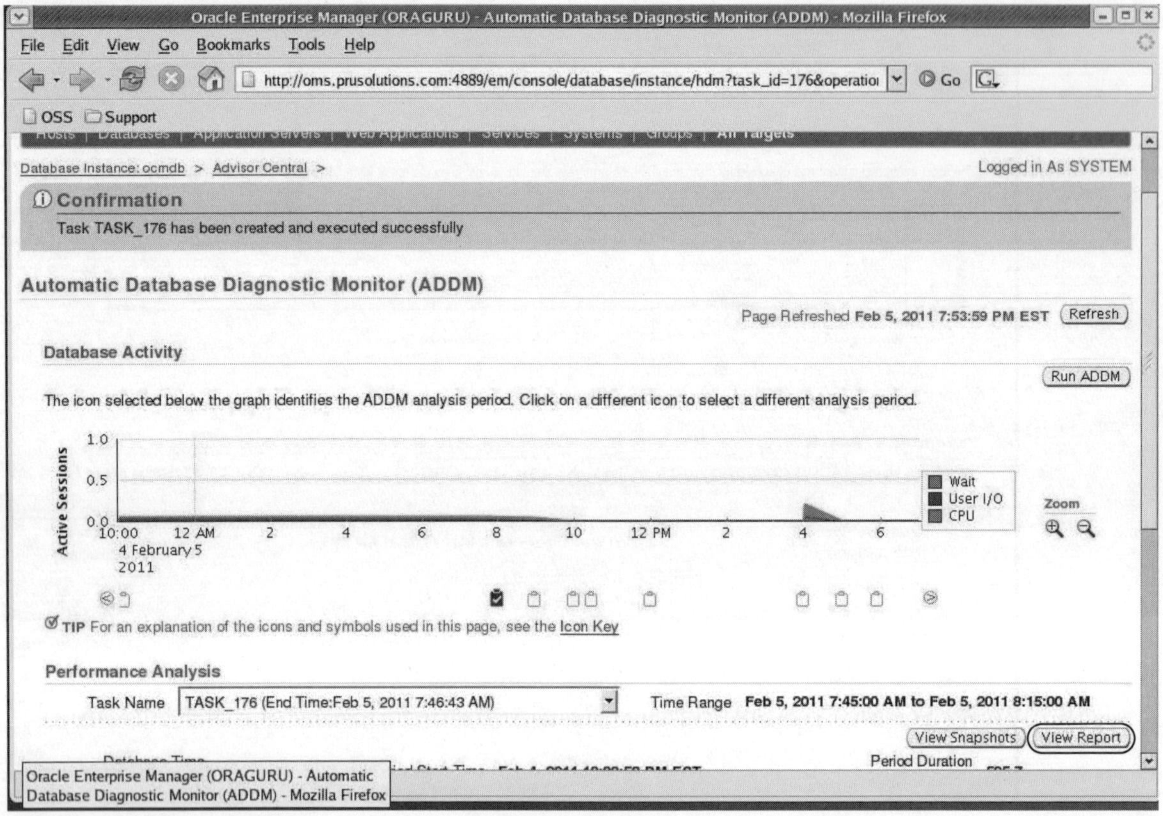

- Detail ADDM Report :You can save ADDM Report to file

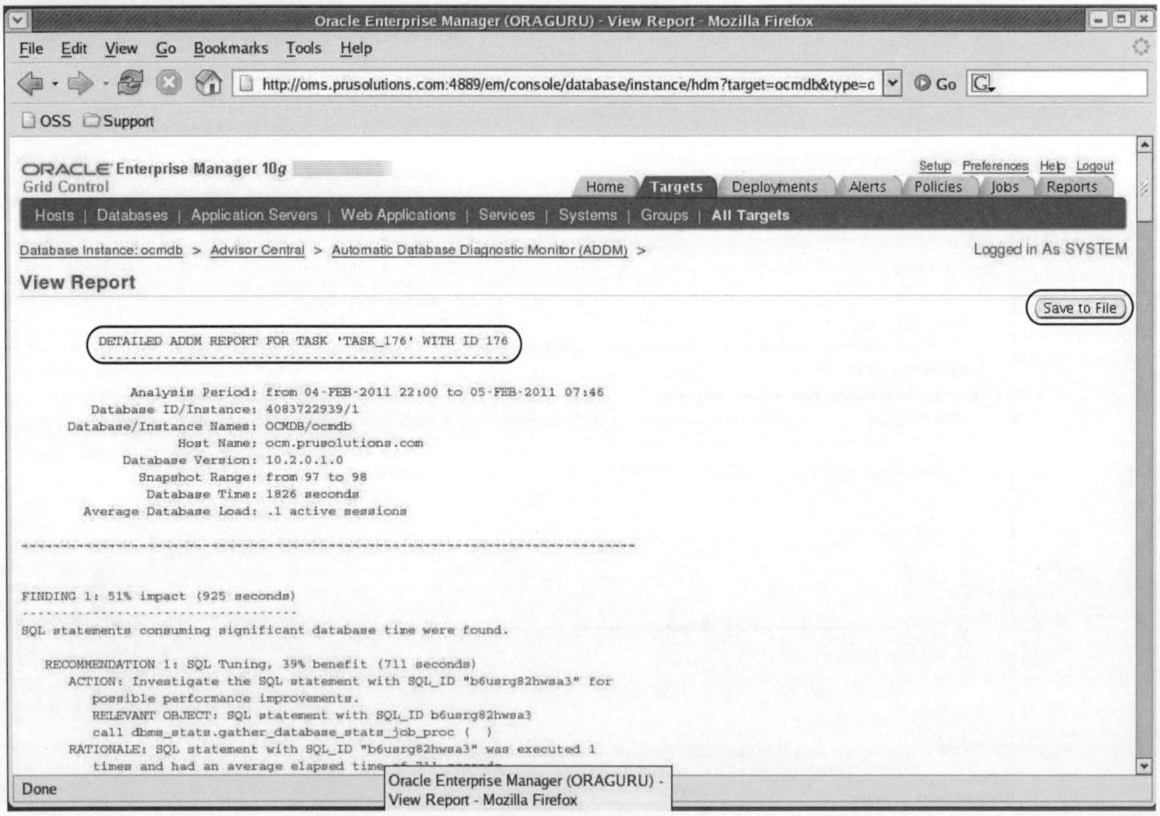

- ADDM Recommendations

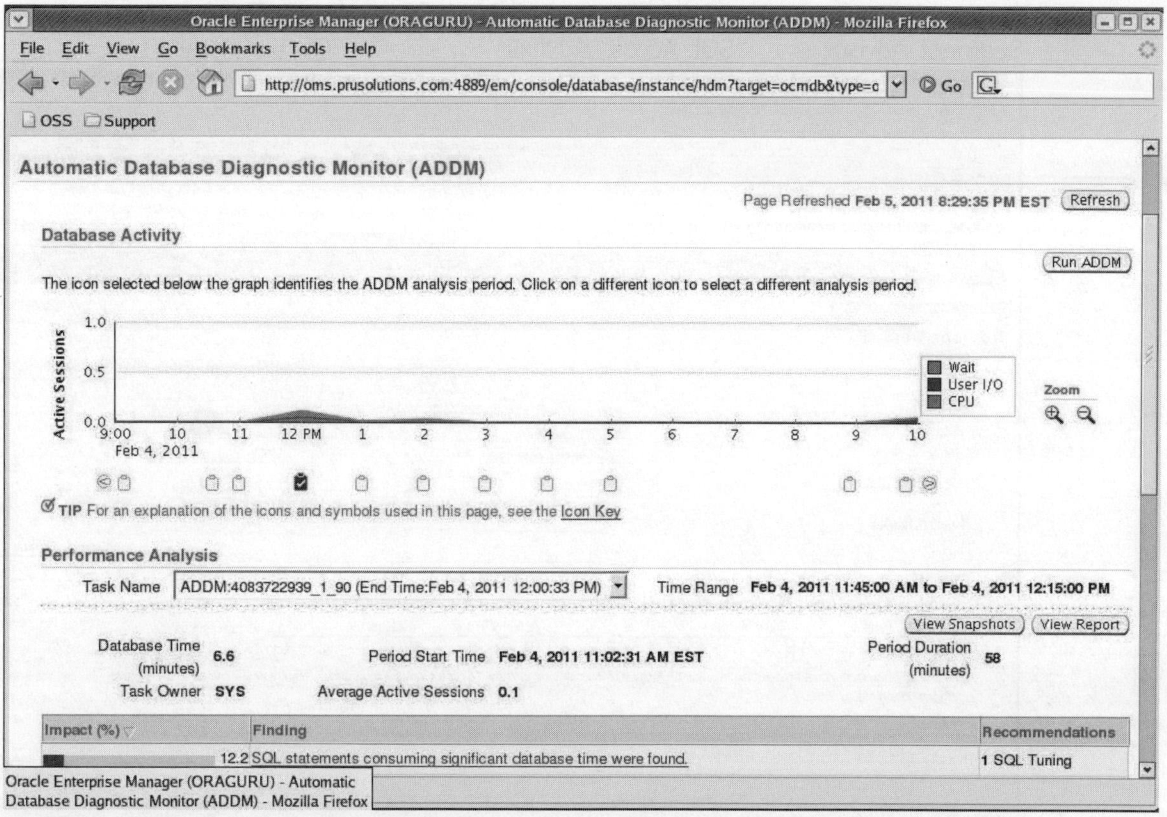

- ADDM Findings on Database Home Page

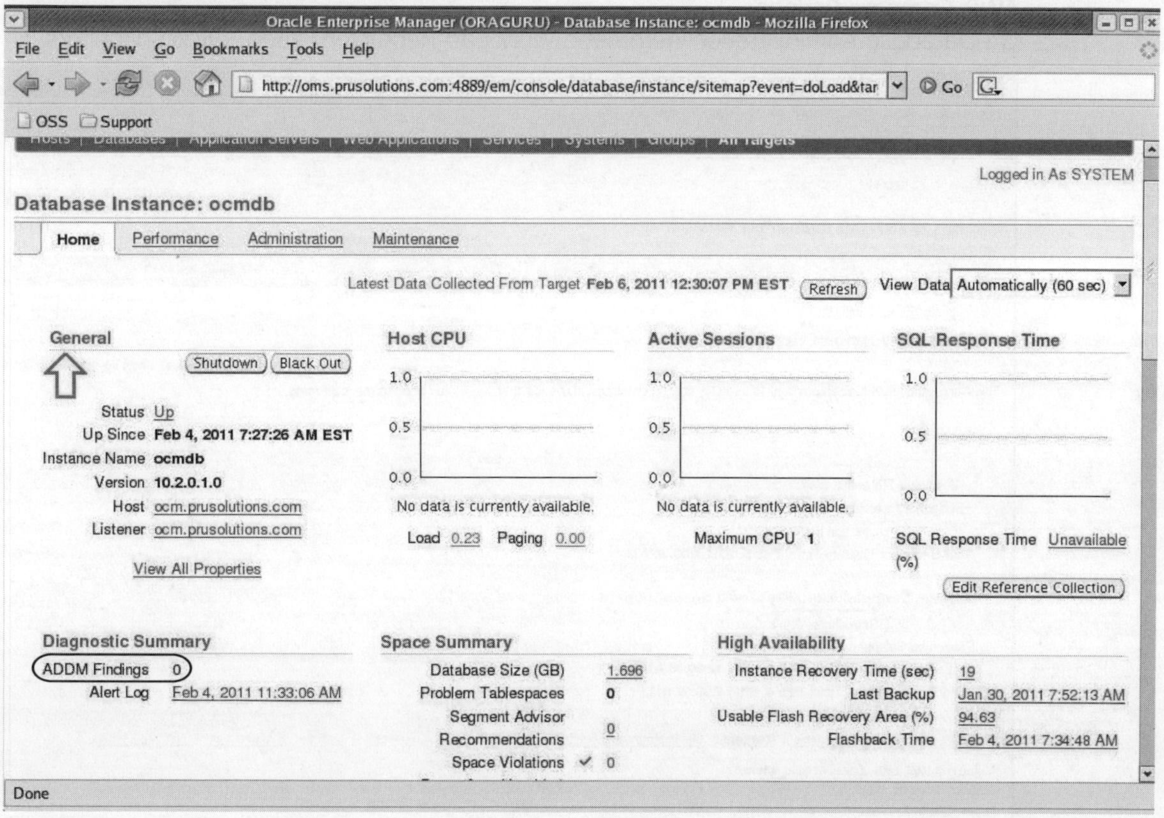

- Advisor Central Page to get Oracle Advices for following

ADDM	Memory Advisor	MTTR Advisor
Segment Advisor	SQL Access Advisor	SQL Tuning Advisor

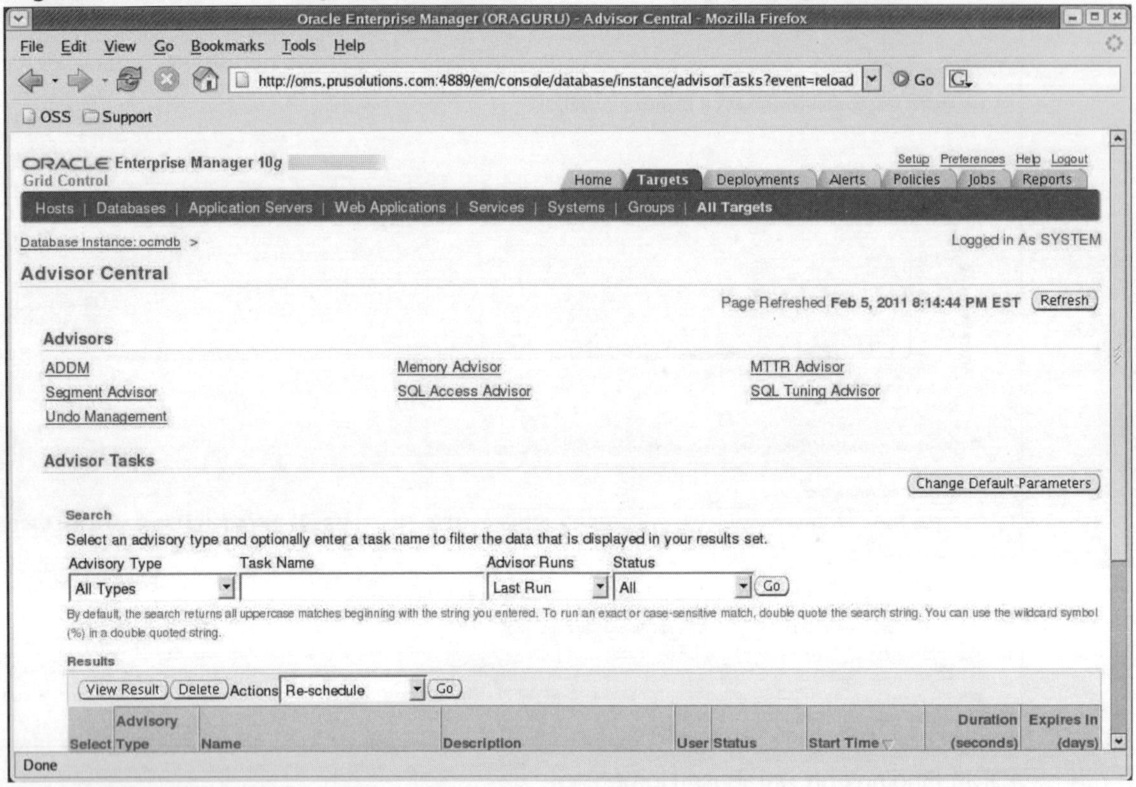

- AWR Compare Periods
  On Database Administration Automatic Workload Repository Page, Click Snapshots.

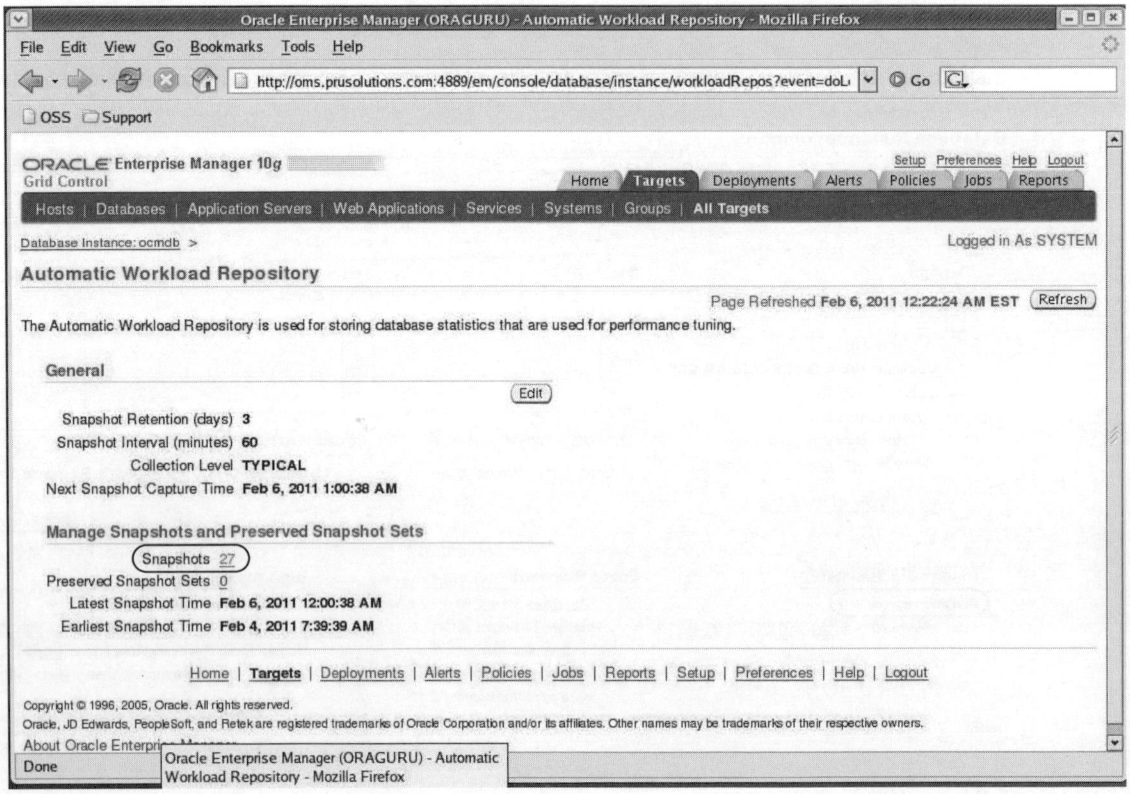

- On Snapshots Page
  Choose Snapshot-beginning date and time and Click go
  Choose Beginning Snapshot (e.g.89) from Actions drop down list choose type of action (Compare Periods) from one of following and click Go.

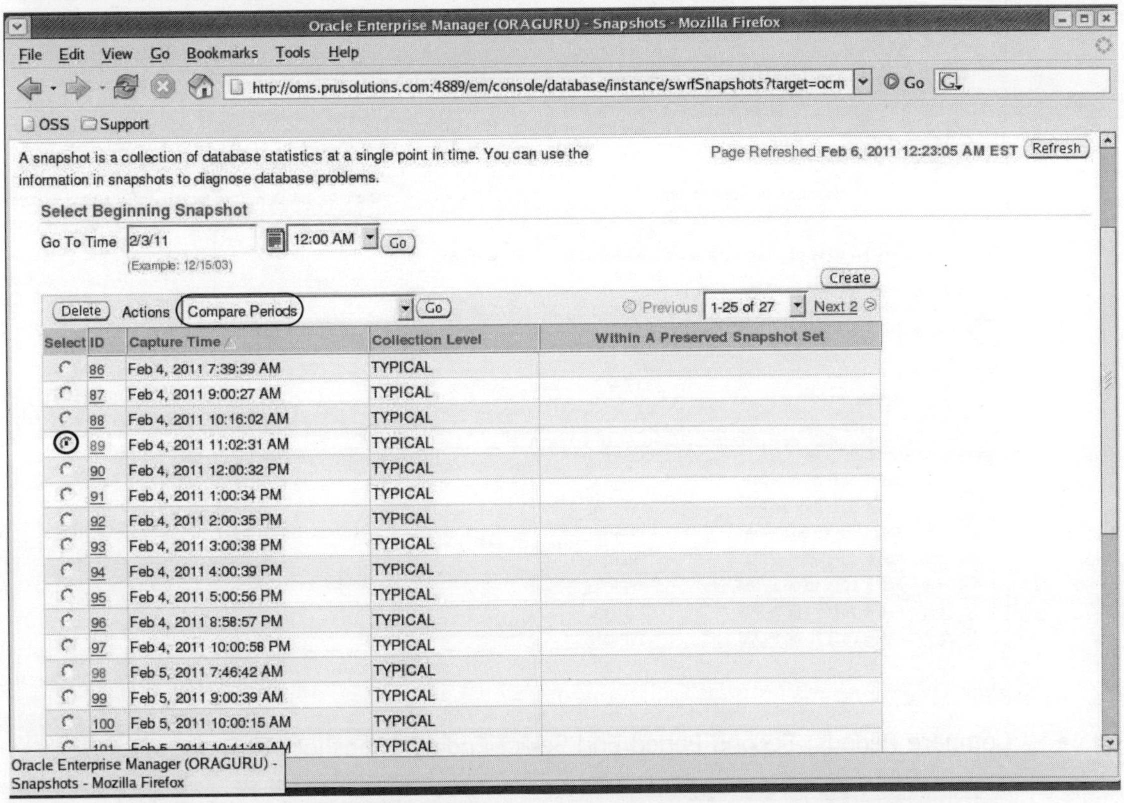

- Compare Periods: First Period End Select Ending Snapshot (90) and Click Next

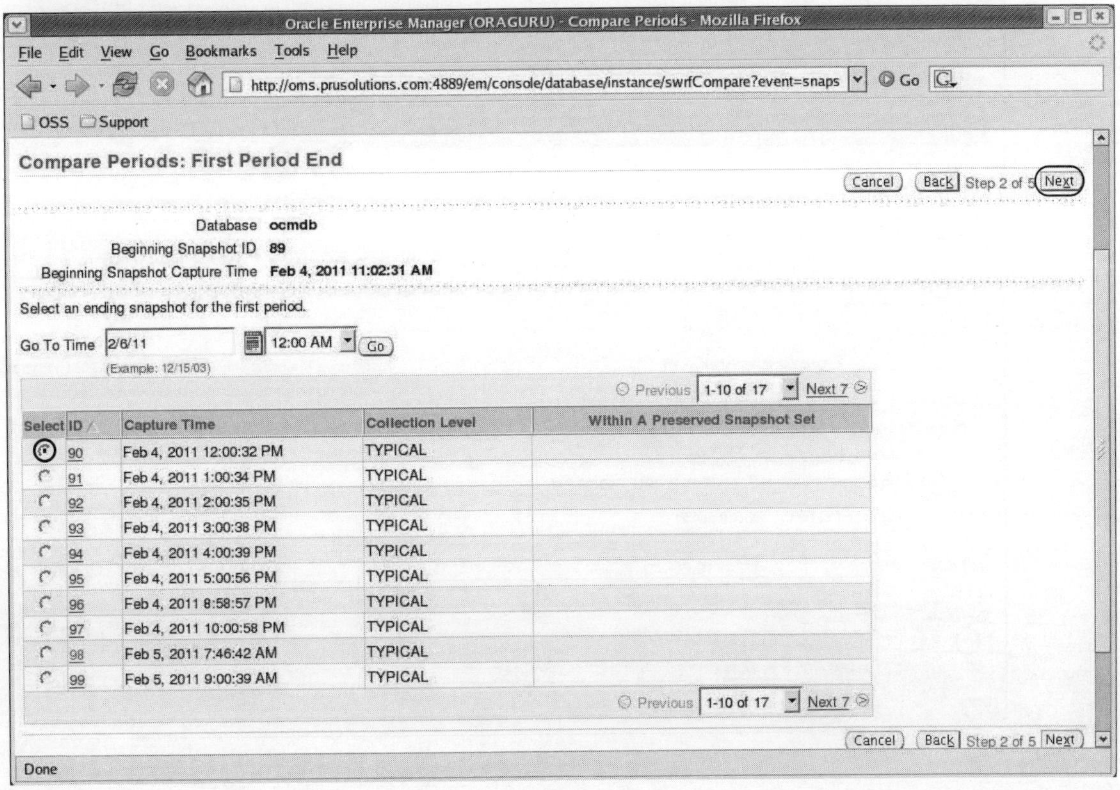

- Compare Periods: Second Period Start Choose Snap Id 107

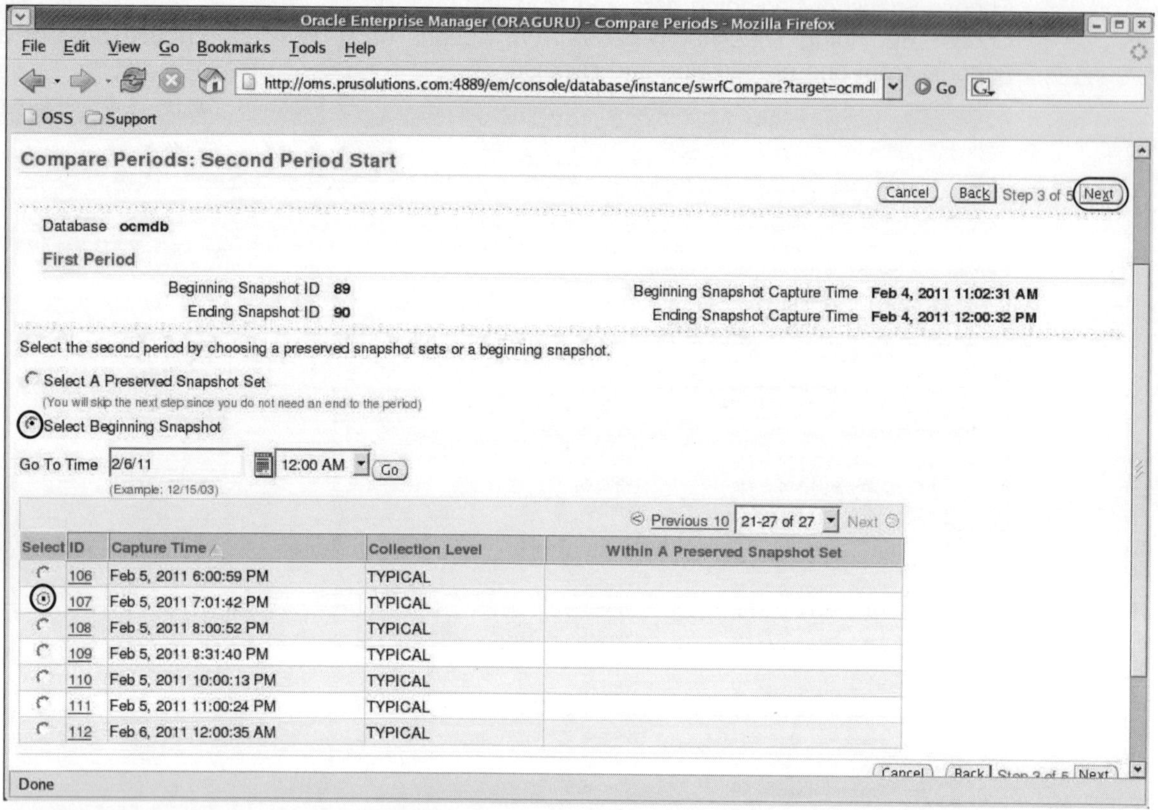

- Compare Periods: Second Period End Select Ending Snapshot (108) and Click Next

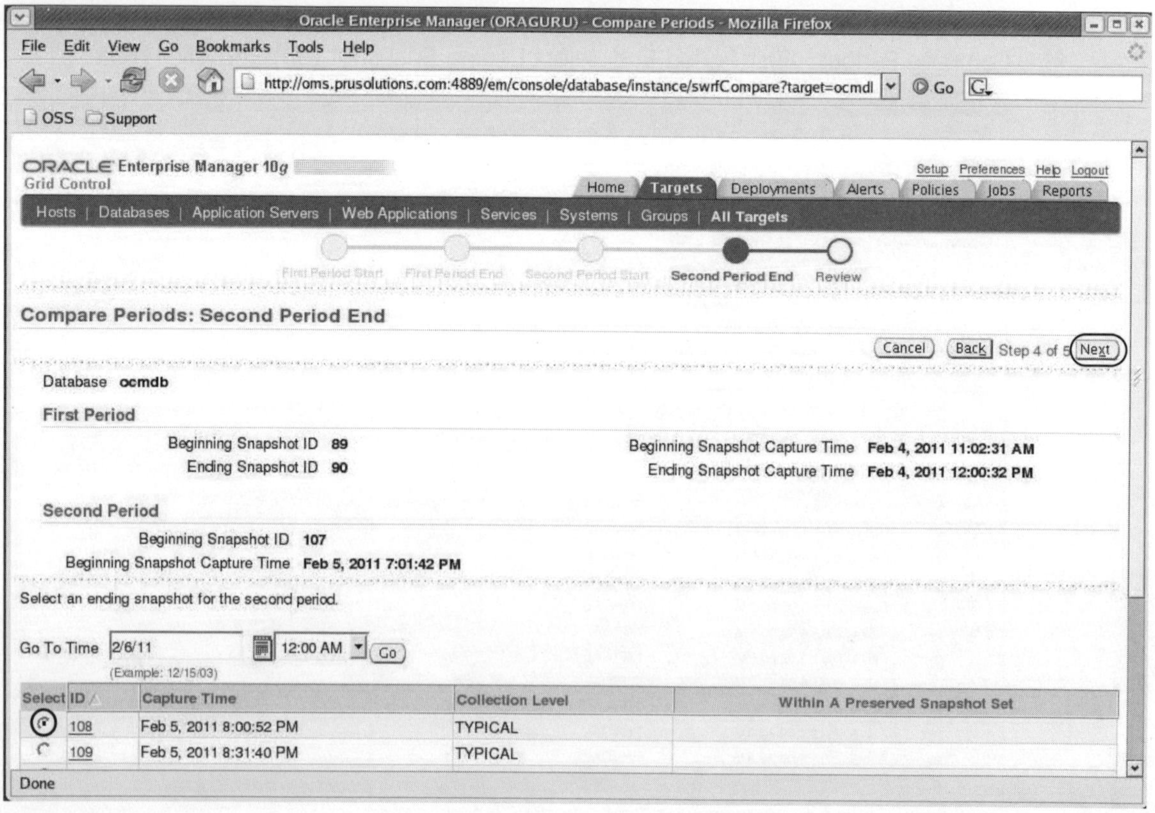

- Compare Periods: Review and Finish

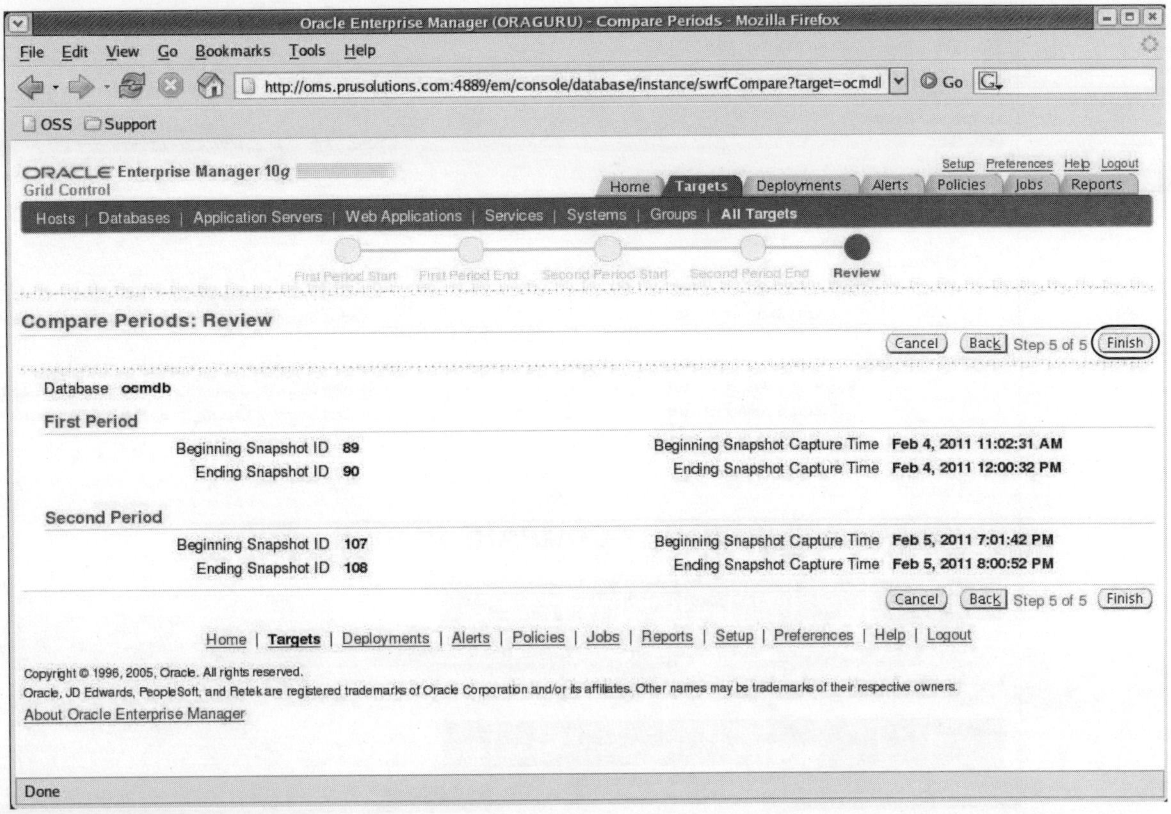

- Compare Periods: Results

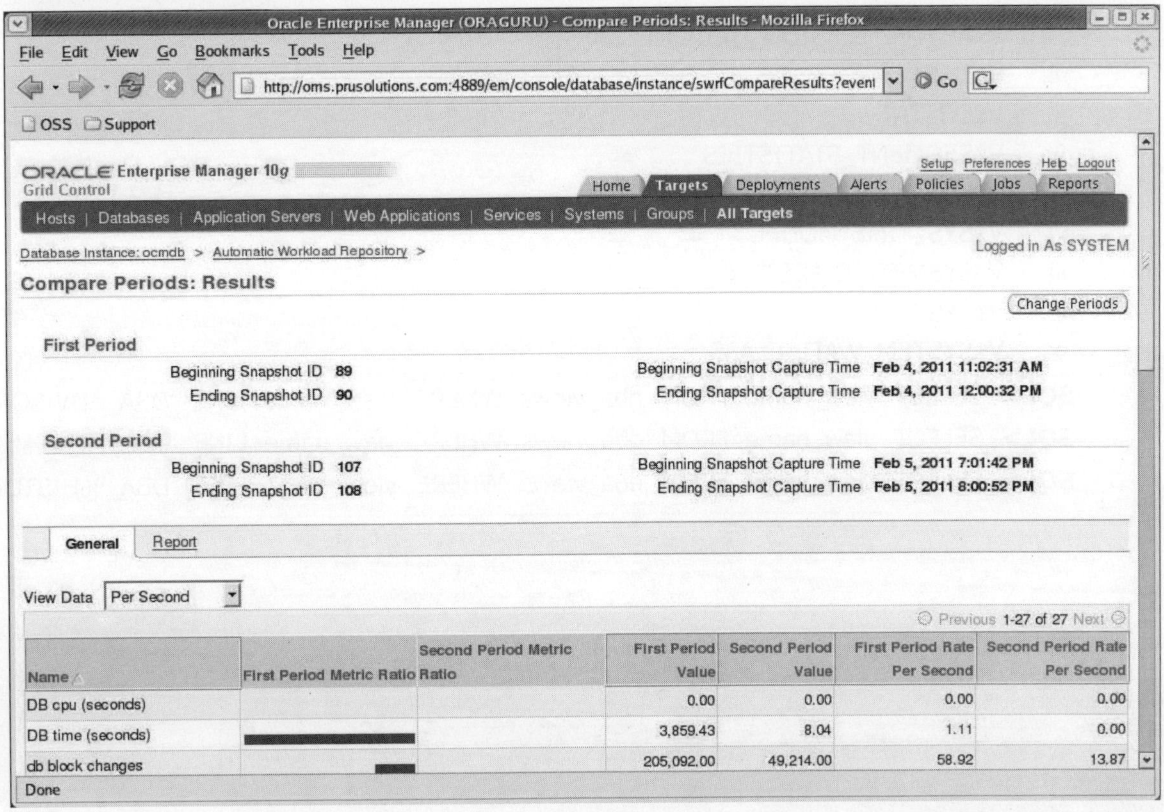

- Compare Periods: Report

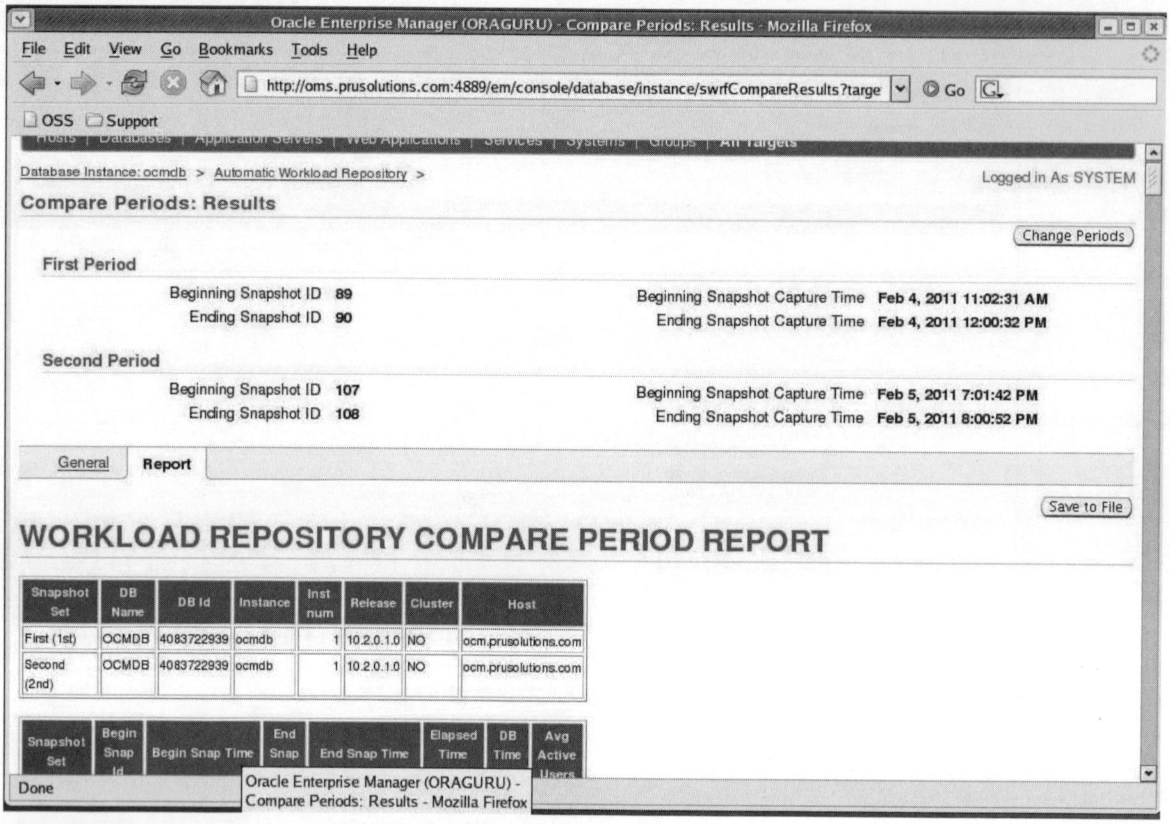

- Views for AWR and ASH

  i. V$ACTIVE_SESSION_HISTORY
  ii. V$OSSTAT
  iii. V$OSSTAT
  iv. V$SEGMENT_STATISTICS
  v. V$SQL
  vi. V$SYS_TIME_MODEL
  vii. V$SYSMETRIC_HISTORY
  viii. V$SYSSTAT
  ix. V$SYSTEM_WAIT_CLASS

```
SQL> SELECT view_name FROM dba_views WHERE view_name LIKE 'DBA_ADVISOR%';
SQL> SELECT view_name FROM dba_views WHERE view_name LIKE 'DBA_HIST%';
SQL> SELECT view_name FROM dba_views WHERE view_name LIKE 'DBA_%HISTORY';
```

- ASH Settings/Report Generations from OEM Grid Control
    - ASH reports tab is available on Performance Page

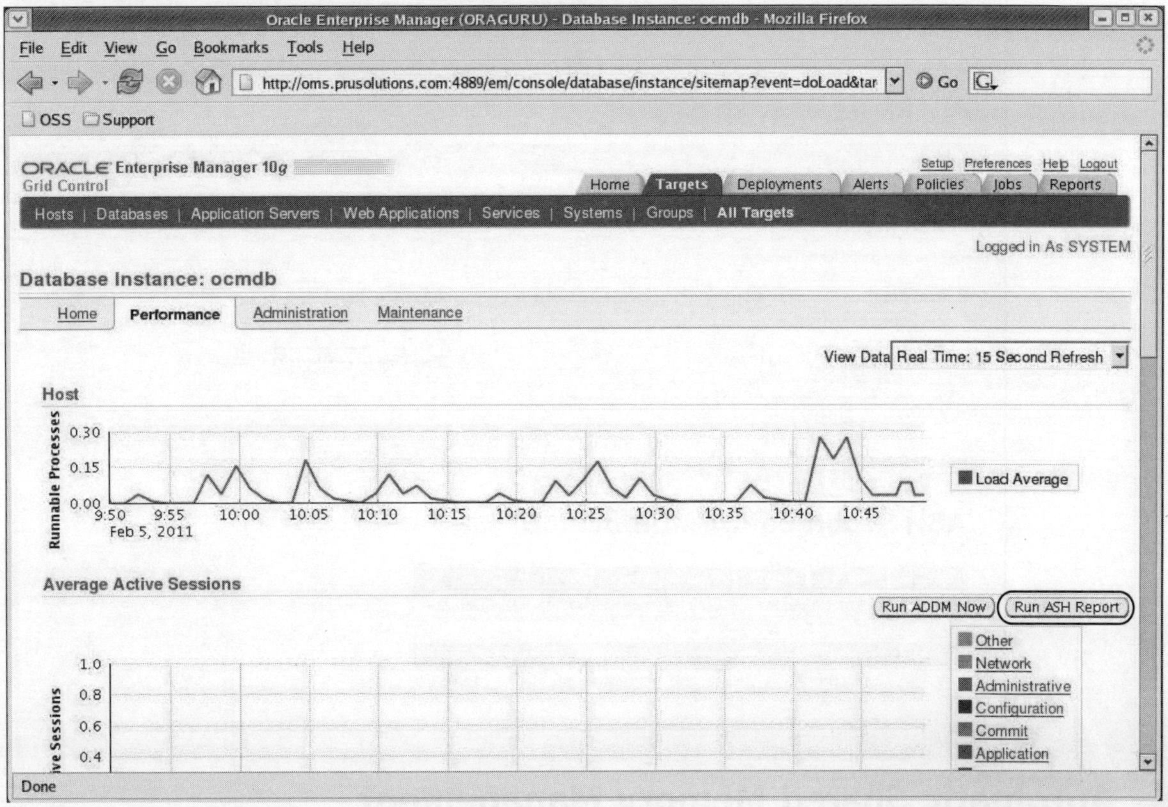

Choose the Start Date and Time and End Date and Time for ASH Report and click Generate Report.

ASH report tells about following in relation with active session during the period

Top Events
Load Profile
Top SQL
Top Sessions
Top Objects/Files/Latches
Activity Over Time

- ASH Report

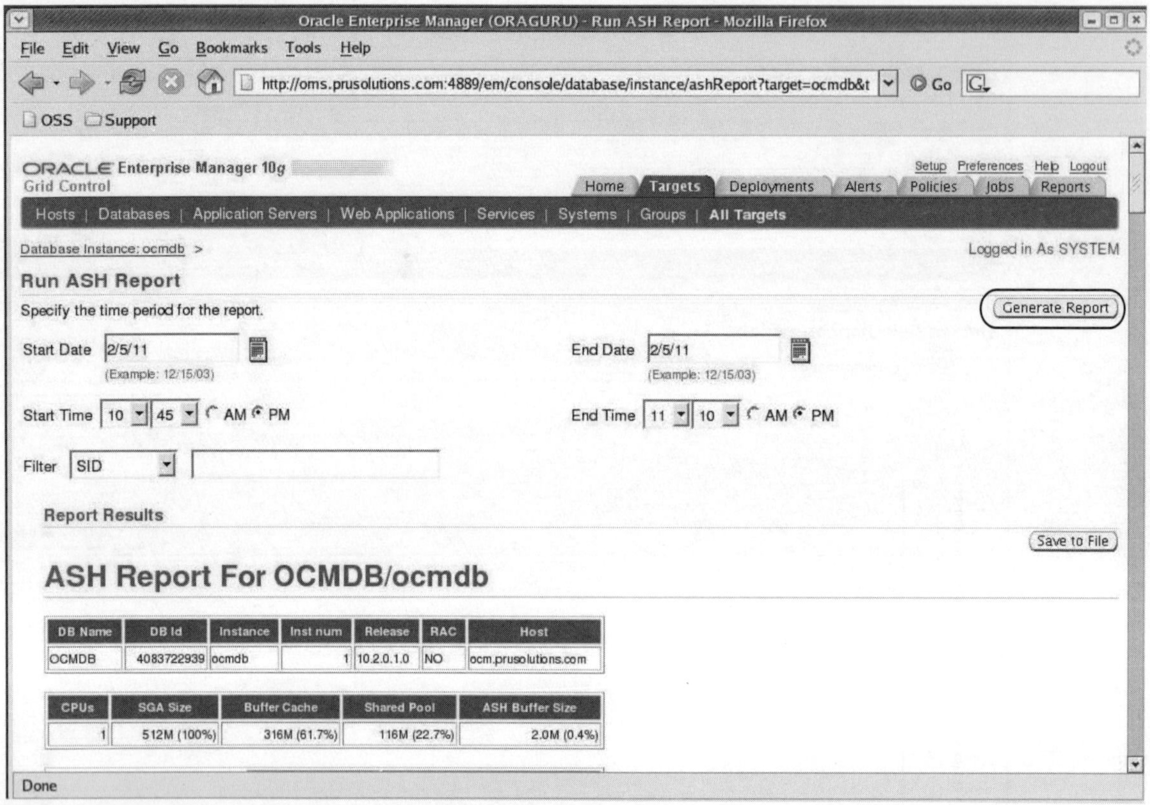

7.5 Automatic Shared Memory Management

The memory for dynamic components in the SGA is allocated in units of contiguous memory chunks called granules. The maximum size of SGA is limited by parameter SGA_MAX_SIZE. By defining SGA_MAX_SIZE Oracle **DOES NOT** take that memory from operating system immediately, but it takes memory from operating system defined by SGA_TARGET and it grows up to parameter SGA_MAX_SIZE without database recycle, provided free memory available in operating system.

Below are few queries useful for memory management

```
SQL> SELECT  BYTES
     FROM  v$sgainfo
     WHERE  NAME  =  'Granule Size';

SQL> SELECT  BYTES
     FROM  v$sgainfo
     WHERE  NAME  =  'Free SGA Memory Available';

SQL> SELECT   NAME,
              DECODE (TYPE,1, 'boolean',2, 'string',3, 'integer',4, 'file',5, 'number',6,
              'big integer','unknown')  TYPE,display_value
     FROM  v$parameter
     WHERE  NAME  LIKE  '%size%'
     ORDER  BY  NAME,  ROWNUM;
```

- Implement Automatic Shared Memory Management from OEM Grid Control
  - On Database Administration Page in Database Configuration section, Click Memory Parameters. It will take to Memory Management page.

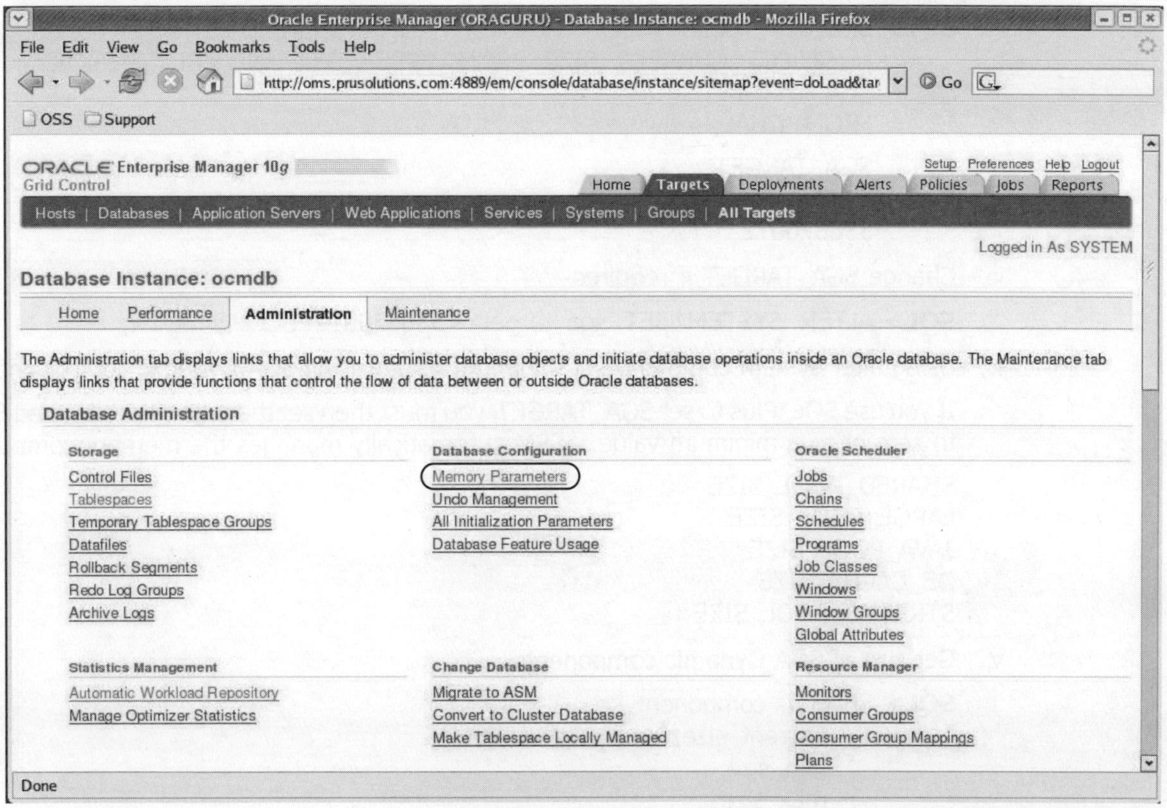

  - On this page, you can have a look into SGA/PGA Advice, Enable /Disable Automatic Memory Management

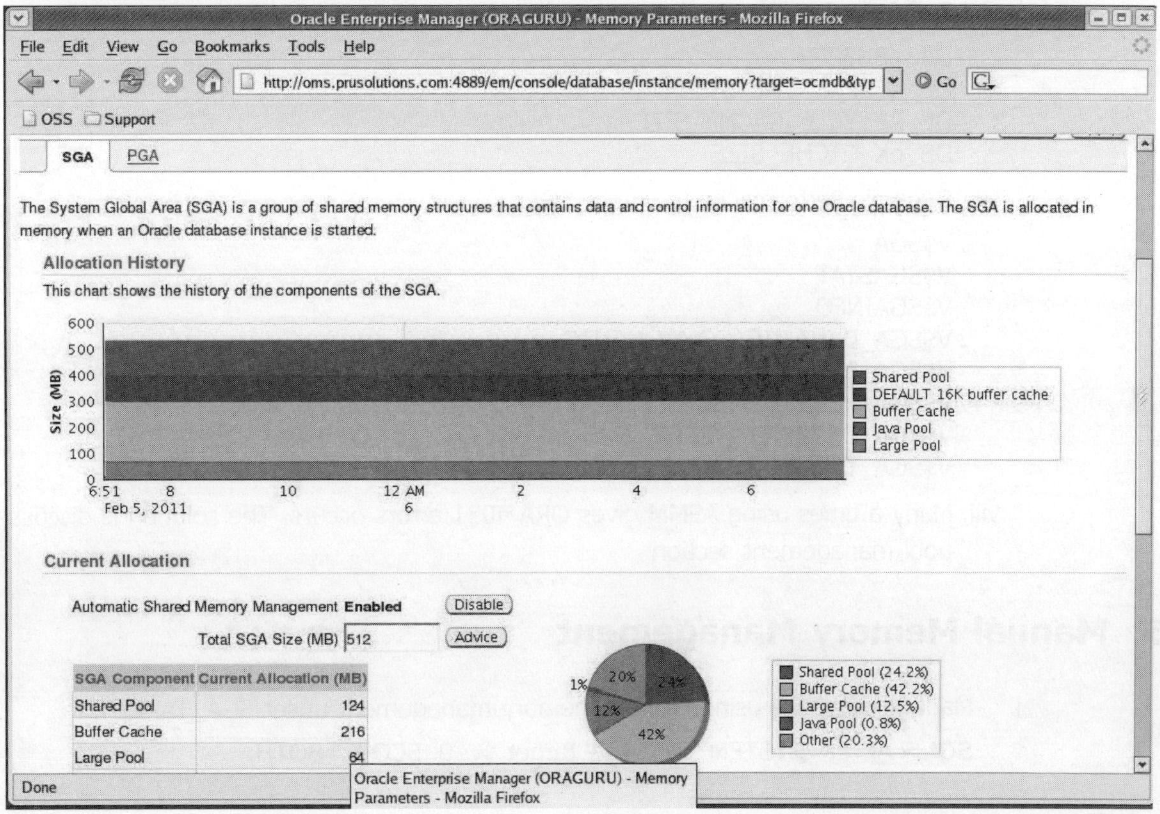

- Implement Automatic Shared Memory Management from SQLPLUS

  i. Find out if Database has ASMM set or not if SGA_TARGET=0 then ASMM is NOT set

  ii. Get Current SGA_TARGET Memory used

```
SQL> SELECT ((SELECT SUM (VALUE) FROM V$SGA)
     - (SELECT CURRENT_SIZE FROM V$SGA_DYNAMIC_FREE_MEMORY))
     SGA_TARGET
     FROM DUAL;

     SGA_TARGET
     ---------------
     536870912
```

  iii. Change SGA_TARGET if required

```
SQL> ALTER SYSTEM SET sga_target =536870912 SCOPE=BOTH;
```

  iv. Using alter system command set minimum value for all SGA Dynamic components

  If you use SQL*Plus to set SGA_TARGET, you must then set the automatically sized SGA components to zero or to a minimum value. ASSM automatically manages the memory component itself.

  SHARED_POOL_SIZE
  LARGE_POOL_SIZE
  JAVA_POOL_SIZE
  DB_CACHE_SIZE
  STREAMS_POOL_SIZE

  v. Get size of SGA Dynamic components.

```
SQL> SELECT component,
            current_size,
            min_size,
            max_size
     FROM V$SGA_DYNAMIC_COMPONENTS;
```

  vi. The following parameters are tuned and managed manually even if ASSM is set.

  LOG_BUFFER
  DB_KEEP_CACHE_SIZE
  DB_RECYCLE_CACHE_SIZE
  DB_nK_CACHE_SIZE

  vii. Dynamic Performance views for SGA.

  V$SGA
  V$SGASTAT
  V$SGAINFO
  V$SGA_DYNAMIC_COMPONENTS
  V$SGA_DYNAMIC_FREE_MEMORY
  V$SGA_RESIZE_OPS
  V$SGA_CURRENT_RESIZE_OPS
  V$SGA_TARGET_ADVICE

  viii. Many a times using ASMM gives ORA-4031 errors occurs. The solution is discussed in shared pool management section.

7.6 Manual Memory Management

i. Manage database using manual memory management unset SGA_TARGET.

```
SQL> ALTER SYSTEM SET sga_target = 0 SCOPE=BOTH;
```

If set database in manual memory management then you have to set the following parameters manually.

SHARED_POOL_SIZE
LARGE_POOL_SIZE
JAVA_POOL_SIZE
DB_CACHE_SIZE
STREAMS_POOL_SIZE

ii. Manage above parameters manually you can use following sql to get Advice.

```
SQL> SELECT * FROM V$DB_CACHE_ADVICE;
SQL> SELECT * FROM V$SHARED_POOL_ADVICE;
SQL> SELECT * FROM V$JAVA_POOL_ADVICE;
SQL> SELECT * FROM V$STREAMS_POOL_ADVICE;
```

iii. Set value of any above parameters you can use ALTER SYSTEM command

```
SQL> ALTER SYSTEM SET shared_pool_size=124 m SCOPE= MEMORY|spfile|both;
```

7.7 Monitor and Tune SGA Areas that are Not Automatically Tuned

- LOG_BUFFER

```
SQL> SELECT NAME, VALUE
     FROM v$sysstat
     WHERE NAME = 'redo log space requests';
```

If the value of **redo log space requests** is greater than 0 and is keep increasing then we have to tune LOG_BUFFER. If redo log space requests increases consistently then processes are waiting for space in redo buffer. If the value doesn't come down over a period of time then we have to increase LOG_BUFFER in increments (generally of 10%) until redo log space requests comes to 0. This parameter requires database recycle, so make proper analysis of LOG_BUFFER value to be increased and then modify the parameters.

```
SQL> ALTER SYSTEM SET LOG_BUFFER=10485760 SCOPE=SPFILE;
     Restart the DATABASE
```

Other sqls to analyze LOG_BUFFER parameter are mentioned below.

```
SQL> SELECT name, VALUE
     FROM v$sysstat
     WHERE name = 'redo buffer allocation retries';

SQL> SELECT 100 * (a.VALUE / b.VALUE) " retries ratio < 1% "
     FROM v$sysstat a, v$sysstat b
     WHERE a.name = 'redo buffer allocation retries' AND b.name = 'redo entries';

SQL> SELECT sid,
            event,
            seconds_in_wait,
            state
     FROM v$session_wait
     WHERE event = 'log buffer space';

SQL> SELECT name, VALUE
     FROM v$sysstat
     WHERE name LIKE 'change write time';
```

- DB_nK_CACHE_SIZE,DB_KEEP_CACHE_SIZE,DB_RECYCLE_CACHE_SIZE

  Execute the sql below and look for advice

```
SQL> SELECT * FROM v$db_cache_advice;
```

7.8 Keeping Tables and their Indexes in DB_KEEP_CACHE_SIZE

In Data Warehouse environment, many times Dimension tables and their indexes are kept in DB_KEEP_CACHE_SIZE as they are readily accessed by different applications. Below are details to keep tables and indexes in DB_KEEP_CACHE_SIZE.

```
SQL> ALTER SYSTEM SET db_keep_cache_size=100M SCOPE=BOTH;
SQL> ALTER TABLE hr.jobs STORAGE (BUFFER_POOL KEEP);
SQL> SELECT * FROM hr.jobs;
SQL> ALTER INDEX hr.job_id_pk STORAGE (BUFFER_POOL KEEP);
SQL> SELECT COUNT (*) FROM hr.jobs;
SQL> SELECT name,
            physical_reads,
            db_block_gets,
            consistent_gets
     FROM v$buffer_pool_statistics;
```

7.9 Tuning Shared Pool

- Tuning Shared Pool from SQLPLUS
  - The Library Cache Hit Ratio should be greater than 99.0%. Reload Ratio should be less than 1%.

```
SQL> SELECT SUM (pins - reloads) / SUM (pins) * 100 " Library Cache Hit Ratio "
     FROM v$librarycache;
SQL> SELECT SUM (pins) "Executions",
            SUM (reloads) "Misses",
            SUM (reloads) / SUM (pins) * 100 "Reload Ratio"
     FROM   v$librarycache;
```

  - Namespace vice hit ratio and invalidations.

```
SQL> SELECT namespace,
            gets,
            pins,
            reloads,
            invalidations,
            gethitratio
     FROM v$librarycache;
```

  - Sizing Shared Pool,get Shared Pool Advice from sql below see if there is need to increase shared_pool_size

```
SQL> SELECT *
     FROM v$sgastat
     WHERE name = 'free memory' AND pool = 'shared pool';
SQL> SELECT shared_pool_size_for_estimate, estd_lc_size, estd_lc_time_saved
     FROM v$shared_pool_advice;
```

  - Check, which sql statements can be shared

```
SQL> SELECT plan_hash_value, COUNT (*) COUNT
     FROM v$sql
     GROUP BY plan_hash_value
     HAVING COUNT (*) > 1
     ORDER BY COUNT DESC;
```

- Get the plan_hash_value from above statement and substitute in statement below

```
SQL> SELECT sql_text, executions
     FROM v$sqlarea
     WHERE plan_hash_value = '&1';
```

- Check if literals are used in sql statements

```
SQL> SELECT SUBSTR (sql_text, 1, 150) "SQL",
            COUNT (*),
            SUM (executions) "TOTAL EXECUTIONS"
     FROM v$sqlarea
     WHERE executions < 5
     GROUP BY SUBSTR (sql_text, 1, 150)
     HAVING COUNT (*) > 20
     ORDER BY 2;
```

- Parameters that effect execute to parse ratio, you should always avoid hard parses

  See section 7.2 Execute to Parse %

- Data Dictionary Cache Hit Ratio to check if application is using dictionary cache efficiently

```
SQL> SELECT ((1-(SUM (getmisses)/(SUM (gets) + SUM (getmisses)))) * 100)
     FROM v$rowcache
     WHERE gets + getmisses <> 0;

SQL> SELECT parameter,
            SUM (gets),
            SUM (getmisses),
            100 * SUM (gets - getmisses) / SUM (gets) "Pct Success Gets",
            SUM (modifications) updates
     FROM v$rowcache
     WHERE gets > 0
     GROUP BY parameter;
```

- Resolving ORA-04031 Errors, many a times when ASMM is configured, we get ORA-04031 errors due to memory resize operations between shared pool and database buffer cache.

  - Check how fast the resize ops is taking place

```
SQL> SELECT component,
            oper_type,
            oper_mode,
            parameter,
            initial_size,
            target_size,
            final_size,
            status,
            TO_CHAR (start_time, 'dd-mon-yyyy:hh24:mi:ss') started,
            TO_CHAR (end_time, 'dd-mon-yyyy:hh24:mi:ss') ended
     FROM v$sga_resize_ops
     ORDER BY started;
```

  - Check Shared Pool Advice how much extra memory is needed

```
SQL> SELECT shared_pool_size_for_estimate, estd_lc_size, estd_lc_time_saved
     FROM v$shared_pool_advice;
```

- Check Shared Pool Reserved Size

```
SQL> SELECT free_space,
            avg_free_size,
            free_count,
            max_free_size,
            request_misses,
            request_failures
     FROM  v$shared_pool_reserved;
```

The inference of the output from above sql will be one of the following

Request Misses =0 shows Reserved Area may be too big.

Request Misses is increasing always and Request Failures are not increasing can mean the Reserved Area is too small.

Keeps flushing shared pool at regular intervals using Oracle Jobs to satisfy the memory needs.

```
SQL> ALTER SYSTEM FLUSH SHARED_POOL;
```

Request Misses and Request Failures always increasing which means the Reserved Area is too small and flushing the Shared Pool are not helping and you get ORA-04031.

- Check number of sub pool in shared pool.

The script below on X$ tables to show the value of this **kghdsidx** parameter.

```
SQL> SELECT * FROM x$ksmss WHERE ksmssnam='free memory';
```

Pass the value **kghdsidx** to query below to get details of subpools

```
SQL> SELECT n.ksppinm pd_name, c.ksppstvl pd_value, n.ksppdesc pd_descr
     FROM x$ksppi n, x$ksppcv c
     WHERE n.indx = c.indx
          AND (LOWER (n.ksppinm) LIKE LOWER ('%&1%') — kghdsidx
               OR LOWER (n.ksppdesc) LIKE LOWER ('%&1%'));

SQL> SELECT COUNT (DISTINCT kghluidx) subpools_cnt
     FROM x$kghlu
     WHERE kghlushrpool = 1;
```

- Solution Change Oracle Hidden Parameters mentioned below

_memory_broker_stat_interval = 1800 — 30 minutes

_kghdsidx_count = 2 — (2 Sub Pools) or (1 for one Pool)

- Keeping Large Objects in Memory

  i. Find out the packages which are larger than 10000 bytes

```
SQL> SELECT OWNER,
            NAME,
            TYPE,
            sharable_mem,
            executions,
            kept
     FROM v$db_object_cache
     WHERE sharable_mem > 10000
            AND TYPE IN
                ('PACKAGE',
                 'PACKAGE BODY',
                 'PROCEDURE',
                 'FUNCTION',
                 'TRIGGER',
                 'VIEW')
            AND kept = 'NO'
            ORDER BY sharable_mem DESC;
```

ii. Pin any objects in shared pool dbmspool.sql script must be executed

SQL>@$ORACLE_HOME/rdbms/ADMIN/dbmspool.sql

SQL> EXEC SYS.DBMS_SHARED_POOL.KEEP ('OWNER.PACKAGE_NAME');

Example: **SQL>**EXEC SYS.DBMS_SHARED_POOL.KEEP ('SYS.STANDARD');

iii. Unpin the objects from shared pool

SQL> EXEC SYS.DBMS_SHARED_POOL.UNKEEP ('SYS.STANDARD');

iv. Find objects greater than particular value X in KB , it will return all object in shared pool greater than size x in kb

SQL> EXEC SYS.DBMS_SHARED_POOL.SIZES(X);

v. Pin the anonymous block find out its hash value and pin.

```
SQL> SELECT address, hash_value, sql_text
     FROM v$sqlarea
     WHERE command_type = 47 AND LENGTH (sql_text) > 500;
```

Pass address, hash_value from above query to package below

SQL> EXEC SYS.DBMS_SHARED_POOL.KEEP ('address,hash_value');

- Java Pool and Large Pool Details

SQL> SELECT * FROM v$sgastat WHERE pool LIKE '%java%';

SQL> SELECT * FROM v$sgastat WHERE pool = 'large pool';

- SGA Memory Advisory Page on Oracle's OEM Grid Control

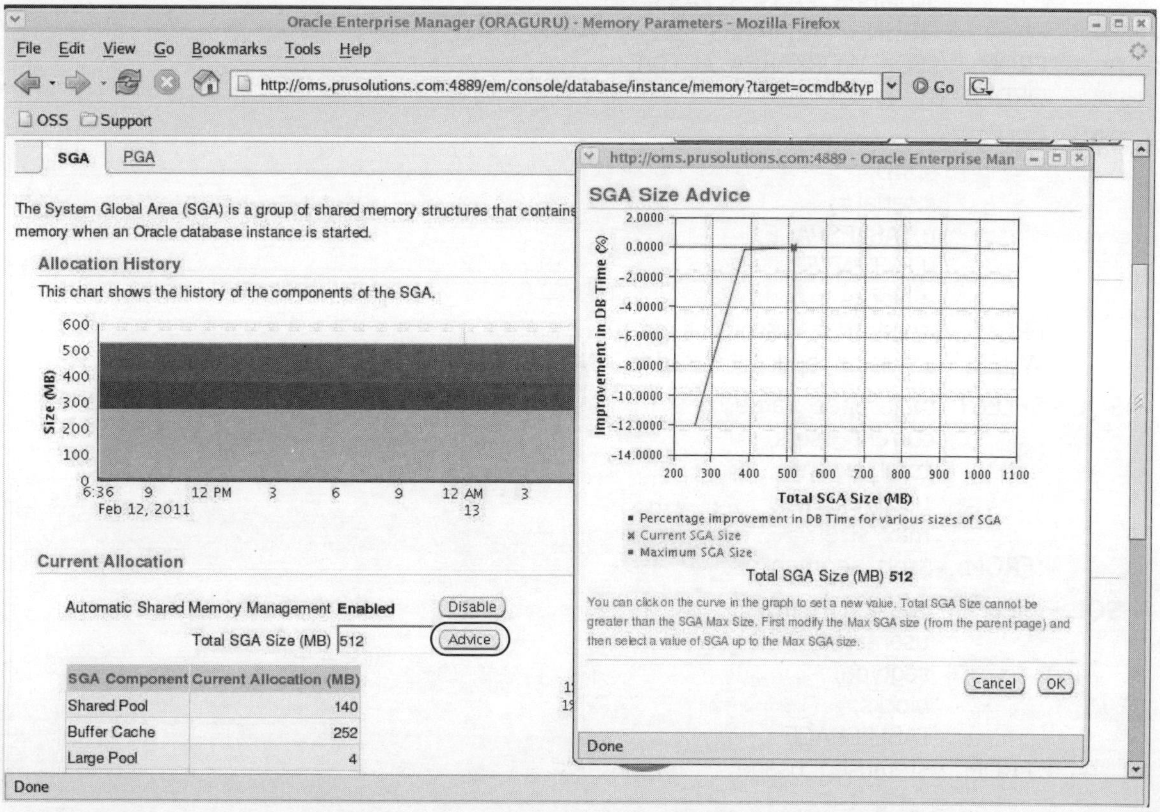

7.10 Tuning Program Global Area (PGA)

- Parameters for PGA
  - For DSS Applications
    PGA_AGGREGATE_TARGET= (TOTAL_MEMORY*80%)*50%
  - For OLTP Applications
    PGA_AGGREGATE_TARGET= (TOTAL_MEMORY*80%)*20%
  - WORKAREA_SIZE_POLICY= AUTO
- Memory Usage for SQL Queries and session sorts and sort segment Usage

```
SQL> SELECT sql_text,
            SUM (ONEPASS_EXECUTIONS) onepass_cnt,
             SUM (MULTIPASSES_EXECUTIONS) mpass_cnt
     FROM V$SQL s, V$SQL_WORKAREA wa
     WHERE s.address = wa.address
     GROUP BY sql_text
     HAVING SUM (ONEPASS_EXECUTIONS + MULTIPASSES_EXECUTIONS) > 0;

SQL> SELECT TO_NUMBER (DECODE (SID, 65535, NULL, SID)) SID,
            operation_type OPERATION,
            TRUNC (EXPECTED_SIZE / 1024) ESIZE,
            TRUNC (ACTUAL_MEM_USED / 1024) MEM,
            TRUNC (MAX_MEM_USED / 1024) "MAX MEM",
            NUMBER_PASSES PASS,
            TRUNC (TEMPSEG_SIZE / 1024) TSIZE
     FROM V$SQL_WORKAREA_ACTIVE
     ORDER BY 1, 2;

SQL> SELECT s.username,
            s.SID,
            s.serial#,
            u.TABLESPACE,
            u.EXTENTS,
            u.blocks
     FROM v$session s, v$sort_usage u
     WHERE u.session_addr = s.saddr AND u.CONTENTS = 'TEMPORARY';

SQL> SELECT tablespace_name,
            current_users,
            total_extents,
            used_extents,
            max_size
     FROM v$sort_segment;

SQL> SELECT session_num,
            username,
            segtype,
            blocks,
            TABLESPACE
     FROM v$tempseg_usage;
```

■ **PGA advisor Page on Oracle's OEM Grid Control**

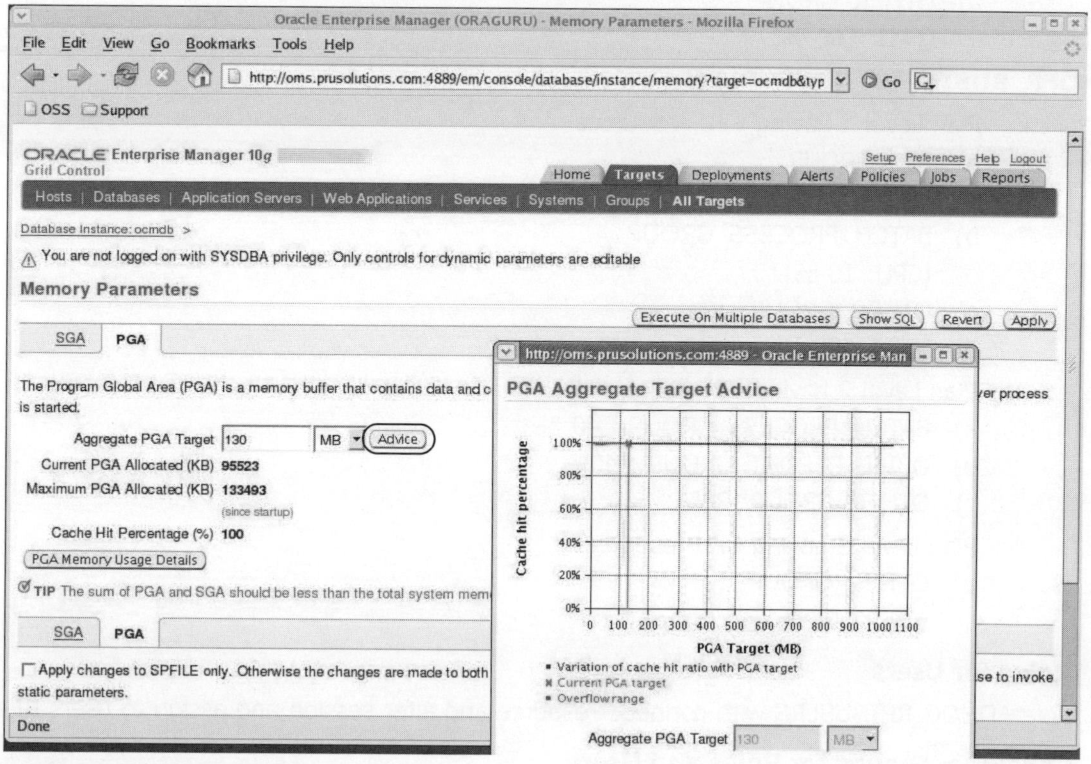

7.11 Resource Manager

■ **Resource Manager Scenario**

You have requirement to create BUSINESS_HOUR_PLAN and OFF_BUSINESS_HOUR_PLAN having resources mentioned below. Create a role ADHOC_RPT_USERS and assign it to users. Assign Consumer Groups to Users/Roles and use schedule to activate plans.

- **Resource Plans**

  BUSINESS_HOUR_PLAN

  i. Plan Level 1 having following
     a) SYS_GROUP (CPU: 60%)
     b) OTHER_GROUP (CPU: 10%)
     c) TRANSACTION_PLAN (CPU: 30%)

  ii. Plan Level 2 having following
     a) TRANSACTION_PLAN (CPU: 100%)
        1. Sub Level 1
           - OLTP_GROUP
           (CPU: 85%)
           - ADHOC_RPT_GROUP
           (CPU: 15 %, PARALLEL 2, MAX_SESSION: 20 TIMEOUT: 300, UNDO_POOL: 1 GB MAX_EXECUTION_TIME: 30 Minutes, SWITCH_OVER_TIME:5 Minutes, SWITCH_OVER_GROUP: Low Group, Estimate: YES, MAX_IDEL_TIME:30 Minutes, MAX_IDLE_TIME (if blocking other session: 1 minute).
        2. Sub Level 2
           - OTHER_GROUP
           (CPU: 100 %)

iii. Plan Level 3 having following
   a) OTHER_GROUP
      (CPU: 100 %)

OFF_BUSINESS_HOUR_PLAN

i. Plan Level 1 having CPU resources
   a) SYS_GROUP
      (CPU: 80 %)
   b) BATCH_PROCESS_GROUP
      (CPU: 10 %)
   c) OTHER_GROUP
      (CPU: 10%)

ii. Plan Level 2 having CPU resources
   a) BATCH_PROCESS_GROUP : 40 %
   b) OBIEE_REPORT_GROUP : 40%
   c) OTHER_GROUP: 20%

iii. Plan Level 3 having CPU resources
   a) OTHER_GROUP
      (CPU: 100 %)

- **Roles for Users**

  Role ADHOC_RPT_USERS with connect, resource and alter session and assign to users BI and SCOTT.

- **Consumer Groups for Roles and Users**

	Consumer Groups	Users/Roles
i.	ADHOC_RPT_GROUP	ADHOC_RPT_USERS
ii.	OLTP_GROUP	HR,OE
iii.	BATCH_PROCESS_GROUP	BI,SH,PM
iv.	OBIEE_REPORT_GROUP	BI

- **Resource Consumer Group Mapping**

	Consumer Group	Oracle Users
i.	ADHOC_RPT_GROUP	BI, SCOTT
ii.	OLTP_GROUP	HR, OE
iii.	BATCH_PROCESS_GROUP	SH
iv.	OBIEE_REPORT_GROUP	PM

- **Schedules for Resource Manager Plan**

  i. BUSINESS_HOUR_PLAN should be active from 8:00 AM to 7:00 PM every day including weekends

  ii. OFF_BUSINESS_HOUR_PLAN should be active from 7:00PM to 8:00 AM everyday including weekends

Solution for Resource Manager Scenario

This problem will be solved using Oracle's OEM Grid Control and from SQLPLUS. Capture all the SQL while configuring Resource Manager using Oracle's OEM Grid Control and the same sqls can be used to create resource manager through sql.

Pending Area is created first and then Consumer Resource group is created. Then you create the Resource Plan and finally Resource Plan Directive is created to link them all together.

- Resource Manager Plan using Oracle's OEM Grid Control
  - On Database Administration Page in Resource Manager Section, click Consumer Groups. It will take to Resource Consumer Groups Page

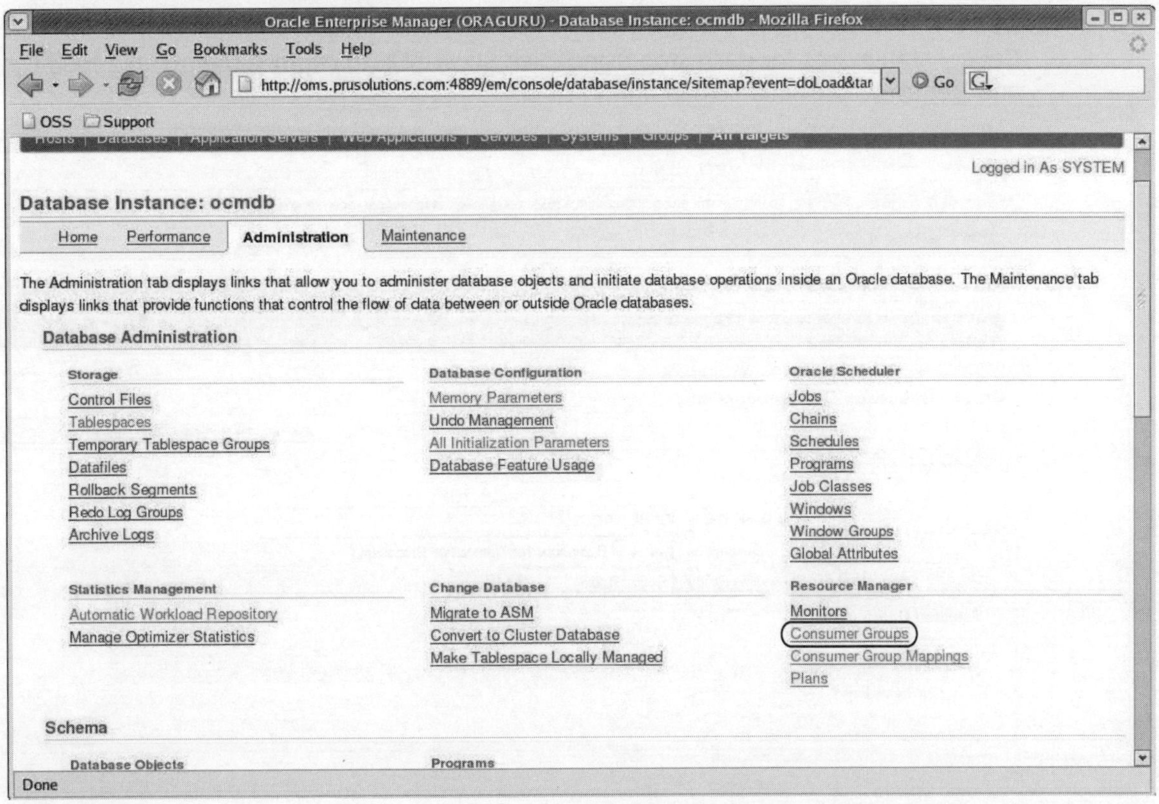

  - Click Create

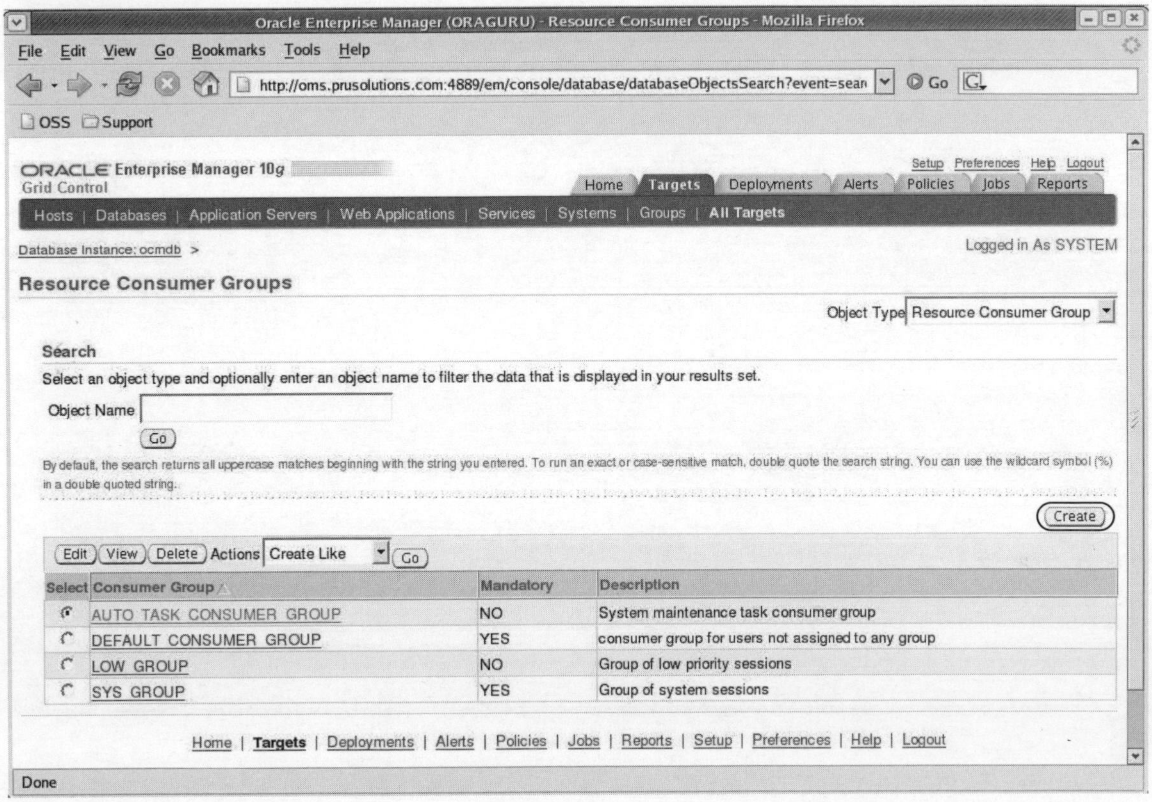

- Create Consumer Group

  Consumer Group: OLTP_GROUP

  Description: Manages Resources for Transaction Processing

  Scheduling Policy: Round Robin

  Get sql statements for each step using Click Show SQL to capture them in notepad for future reference and Return to previous screen and Click OK.

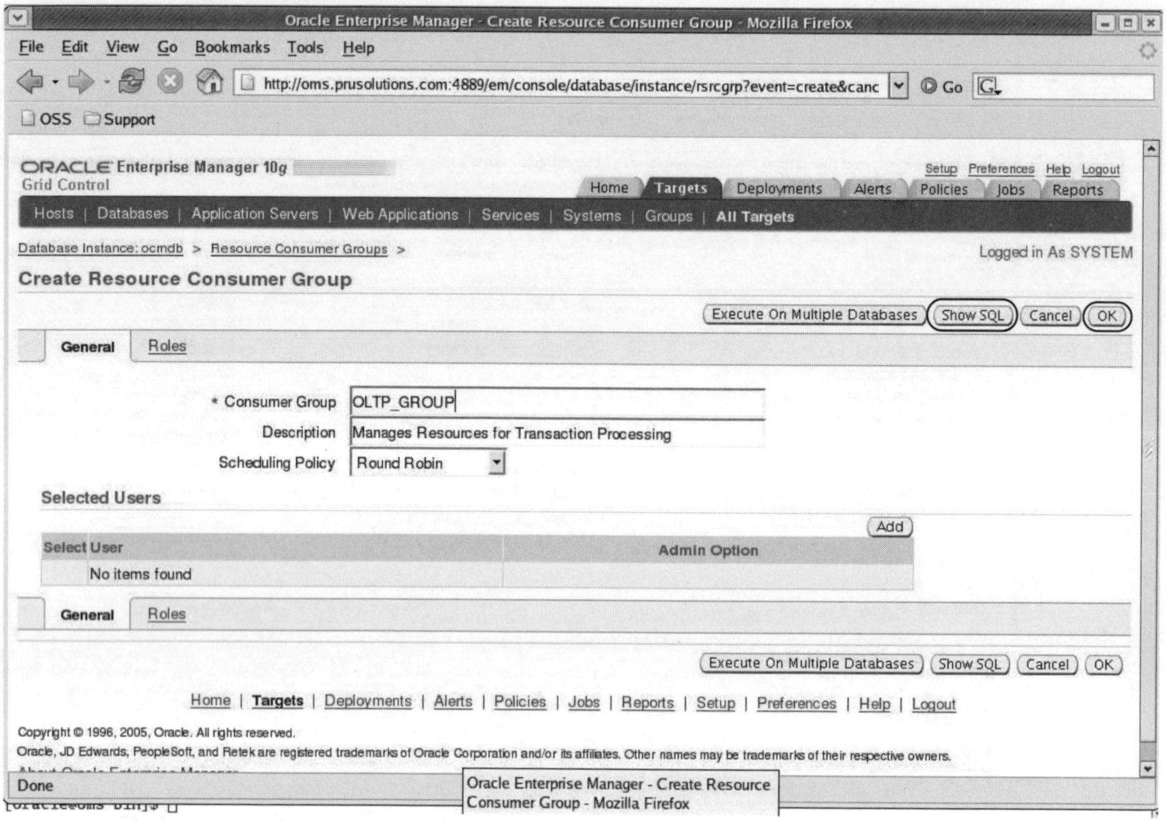

- Create all the group required, as OLTP_GROUP was created
  ADHOC_RPT_GROUP
  BATCH_PROCESS_GROUP
  OBIEE_REPORT_GROUP
  The SYS_GROUP and OTHER_GROUP are already created in database by default.
  Below is the screen shot for all the Consumer Groups Created.

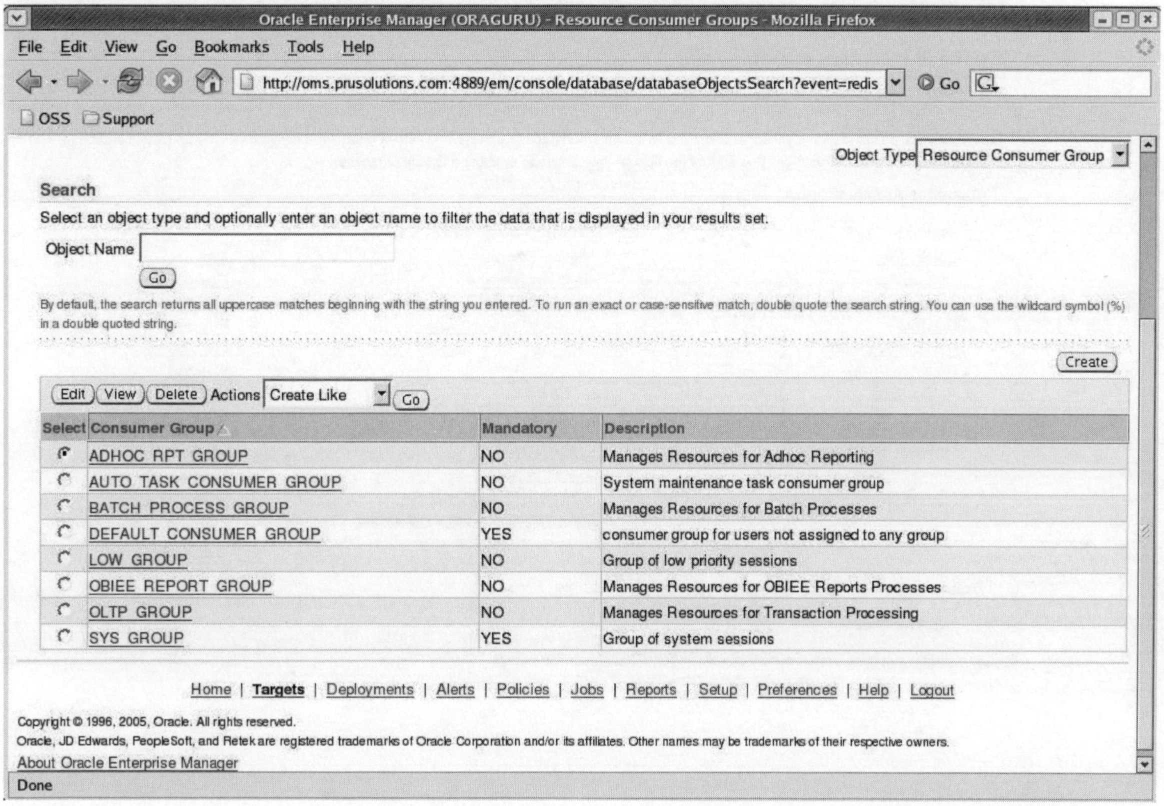

- Now all the Consumer Groups are created, proceed to next step of creating Resource Plan
- On Database Administration Page in Resource Manager Section, Click Plans. It will take to Resource Plans page

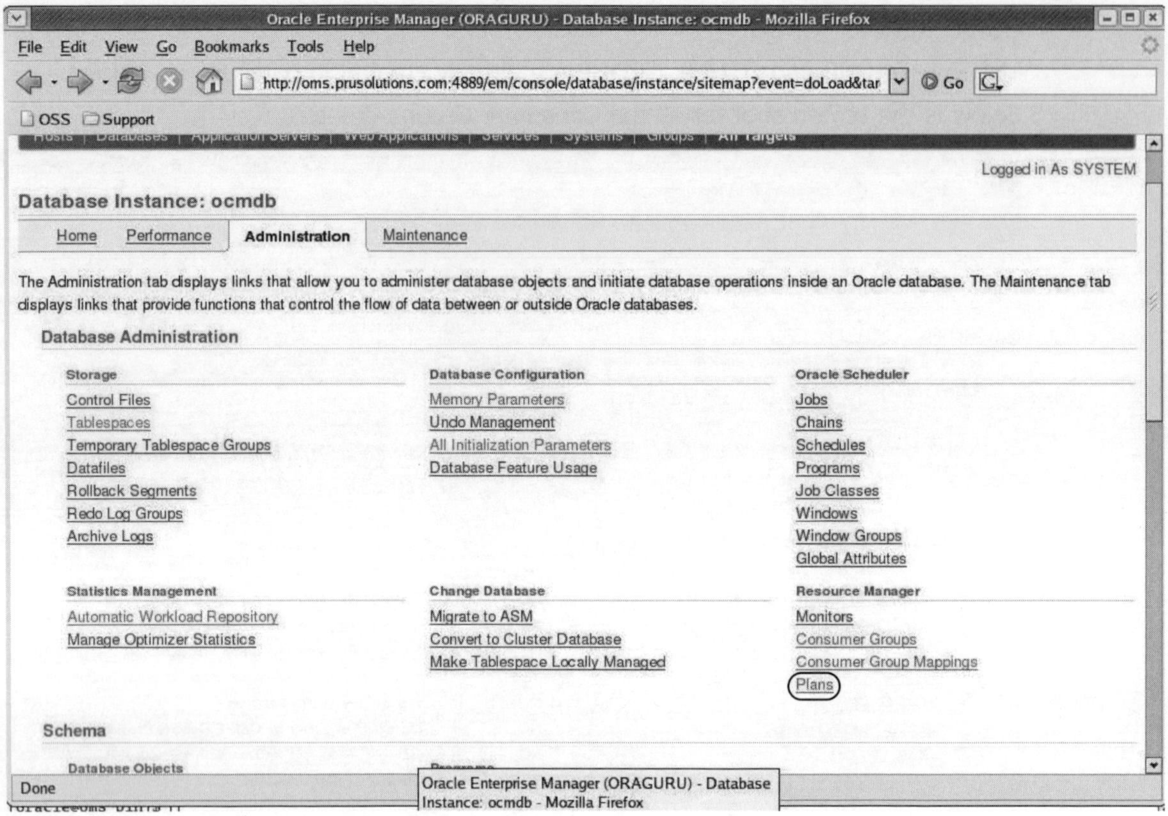

- Click Create on Resource Plan page to create a New Plan. By default, OTHER_GROUP will be part of any new plan created

  First, you should create inner level plan in this example it is TRANSACTION_PLAN

  Plan: TRANSACTION_PLAN

  Description: Plan to manage resources for Transaction Processing

  Select: Automatic Plan Switching Enabled

  Click Modify

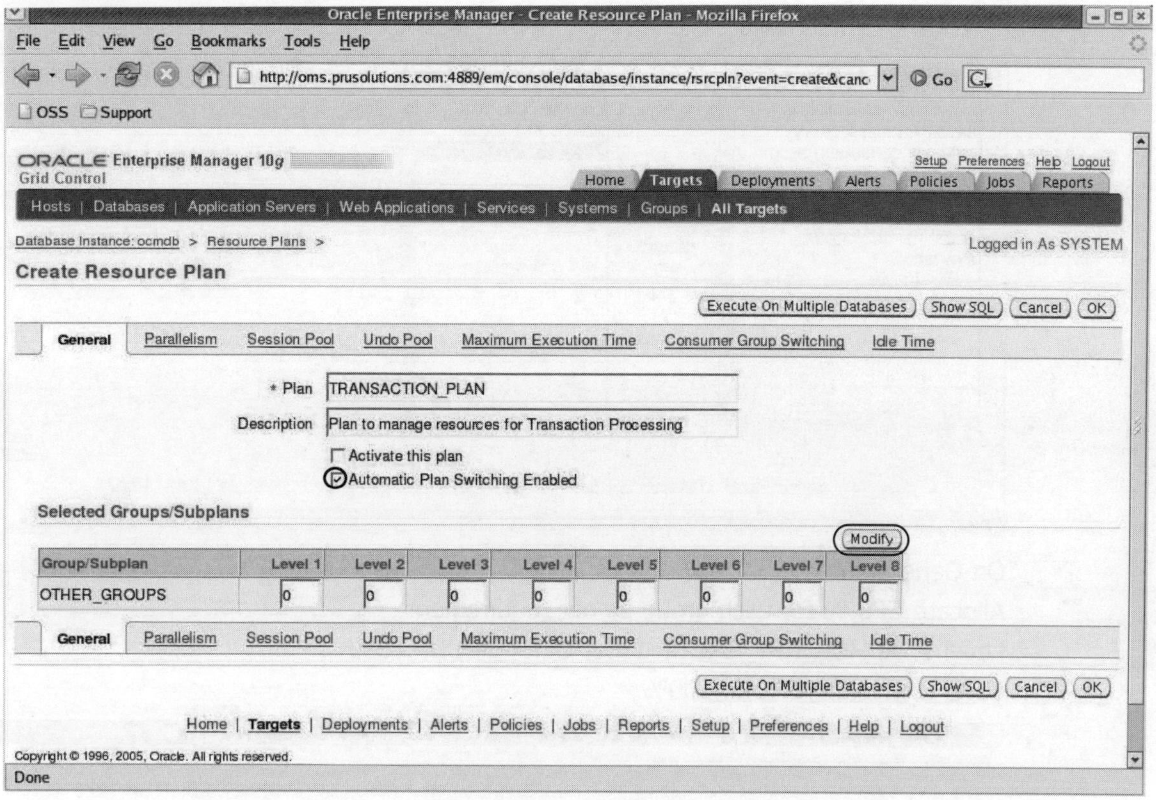

- Choose Resource Groups belong to TRANSACTION_PLAN in the requirement that are OLTP_GROUP and ADHOC_RPT_GROUP and click OK

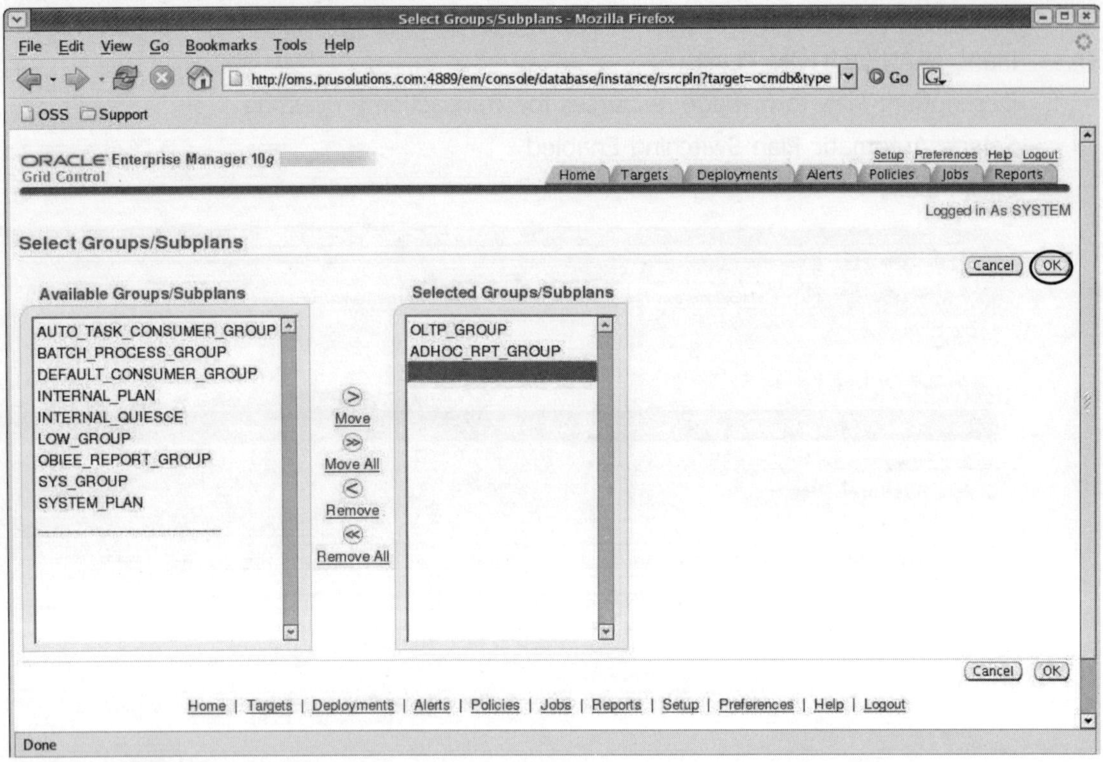

- On General tab

  Allocate CPU % for each group as per requirement

  Level 1: ADHOC_RPT_GROUP 15%, OLTP_GROUP 85%

  Level 2: OTHER_GROUP 100%

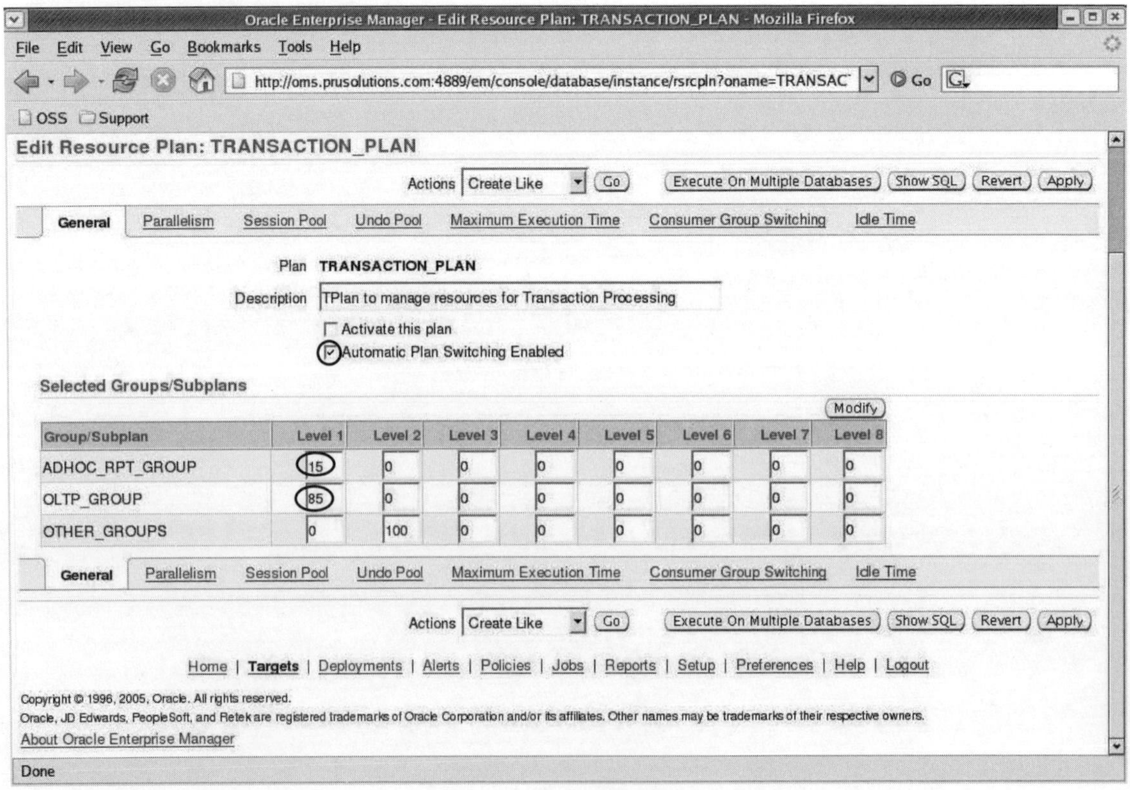

- On Parallelism tab
  Maximum Degree of Parallelism for ADHOC_RPT_GROUP to 2

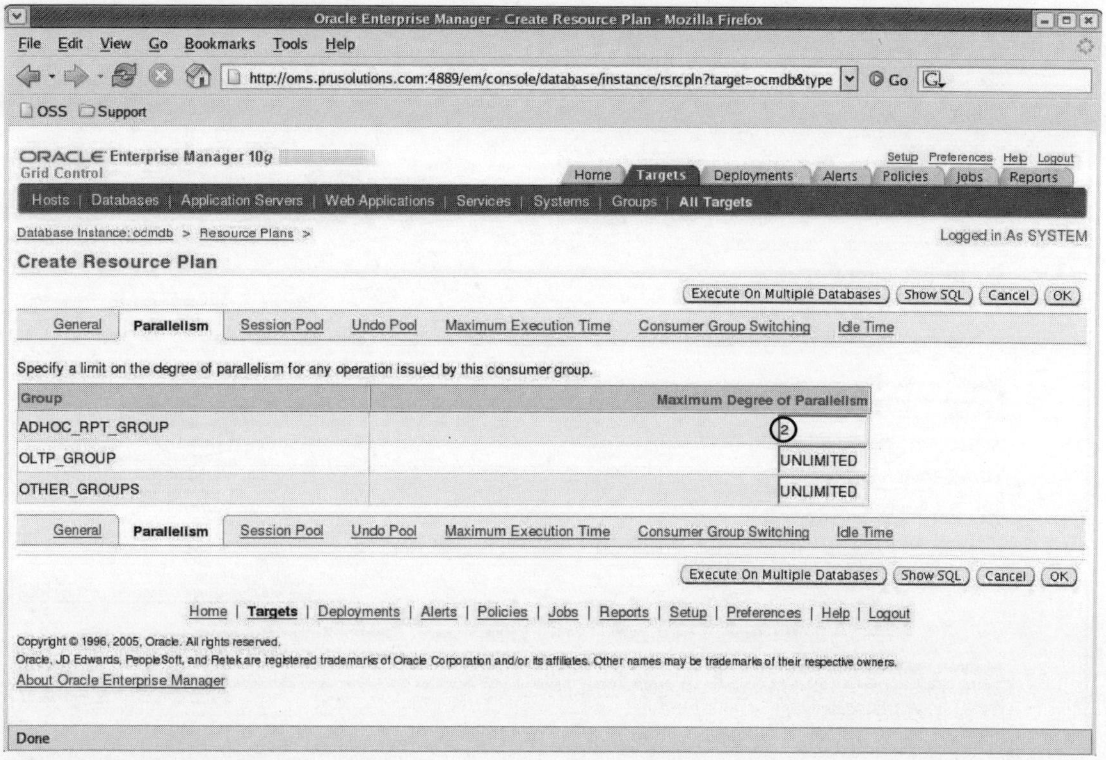

- On Session Pool Tab.
  For ADHOC_RPT_GROUP
  Maximum Number of Active Session: 20
  Activation Queue Timeout: 6 minutes

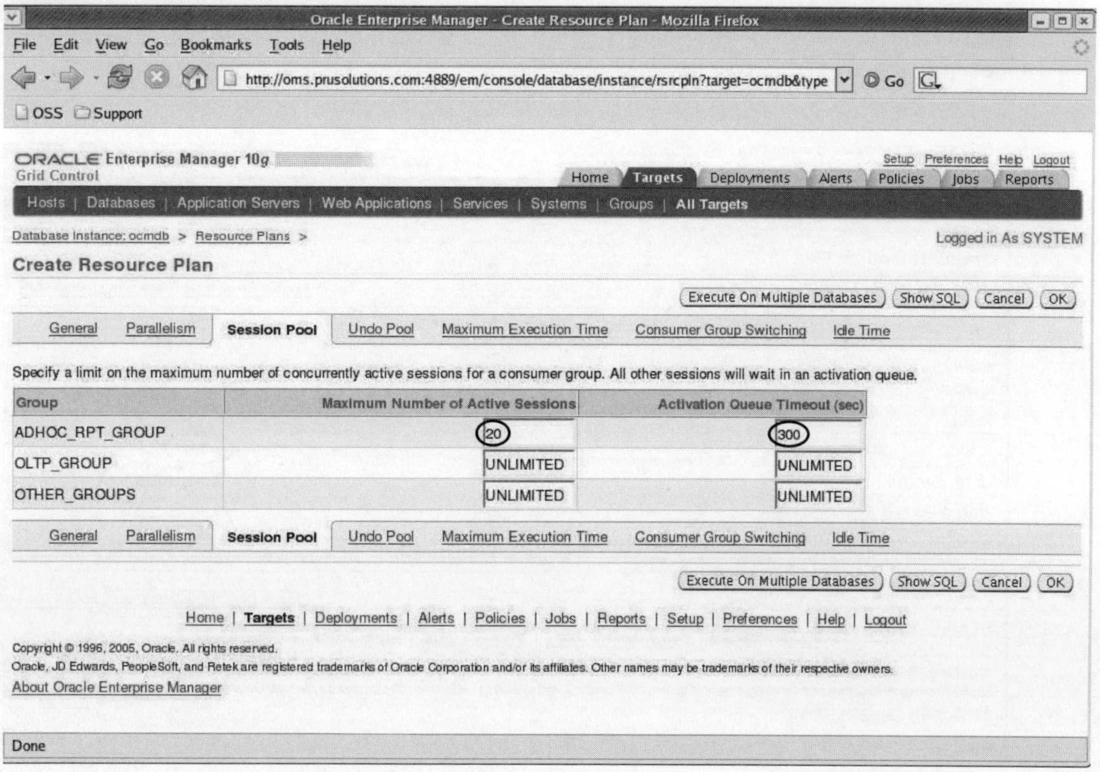

- On Undo Pool tab
  Maximum Undo Space (KB):10240

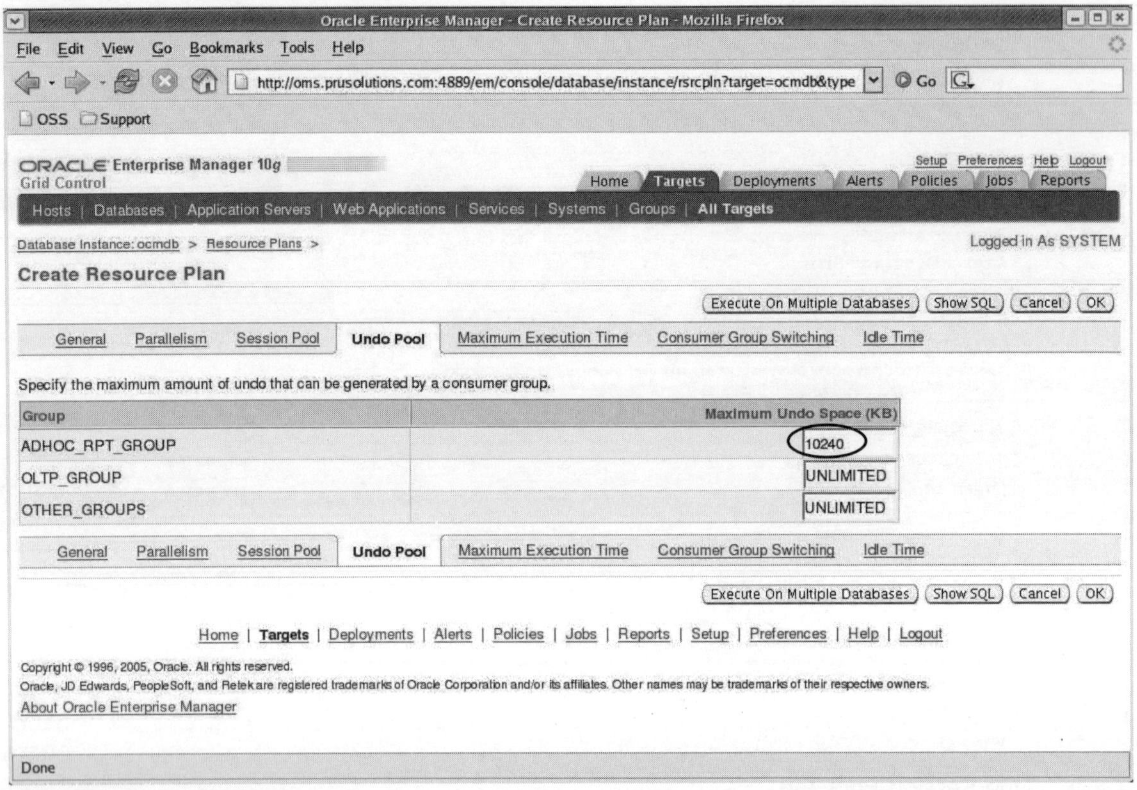

- On Maximum Execution Time, tab
  Maximum Estimated Execution Time: 30 minutes. The sql will not execute if the maximum estimated time is beyond 30 minutes and it will give ORA-07455.

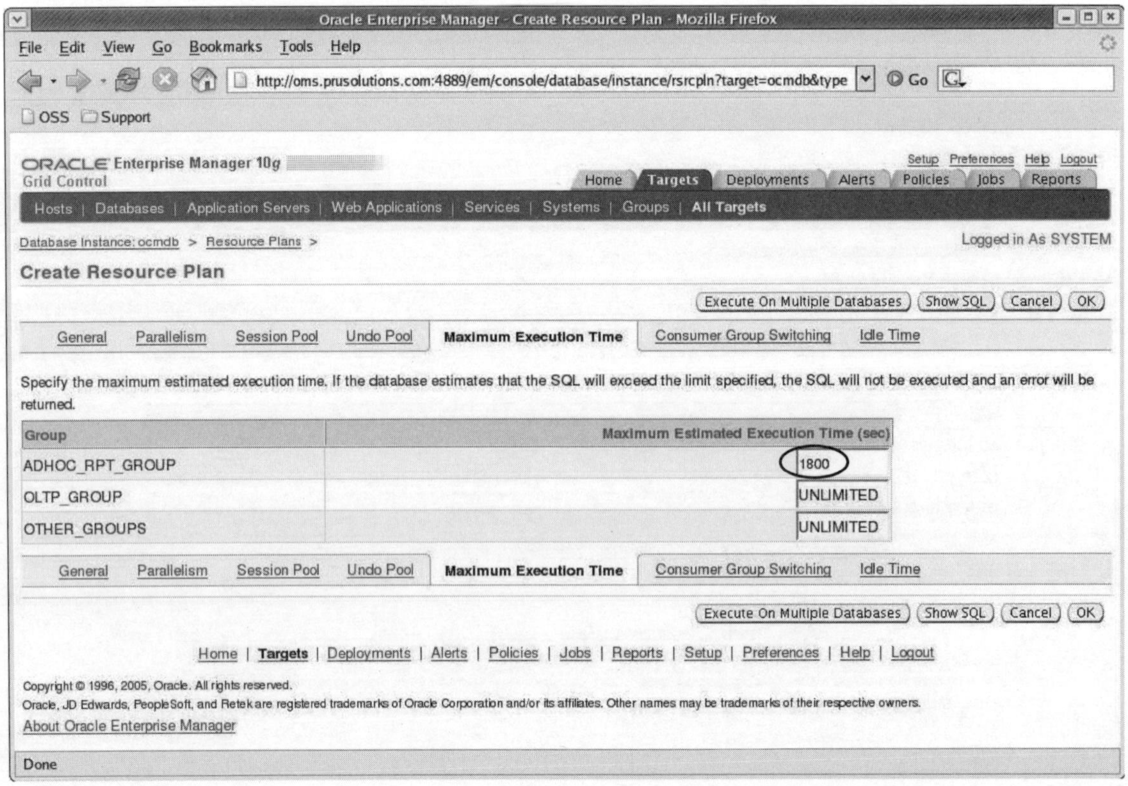

- On Consumer Group Switching
  Maximum Execution Time: 5 minutes
  Action to Take: Switch to Group LOW_GROUP
  Use Estimate: YES

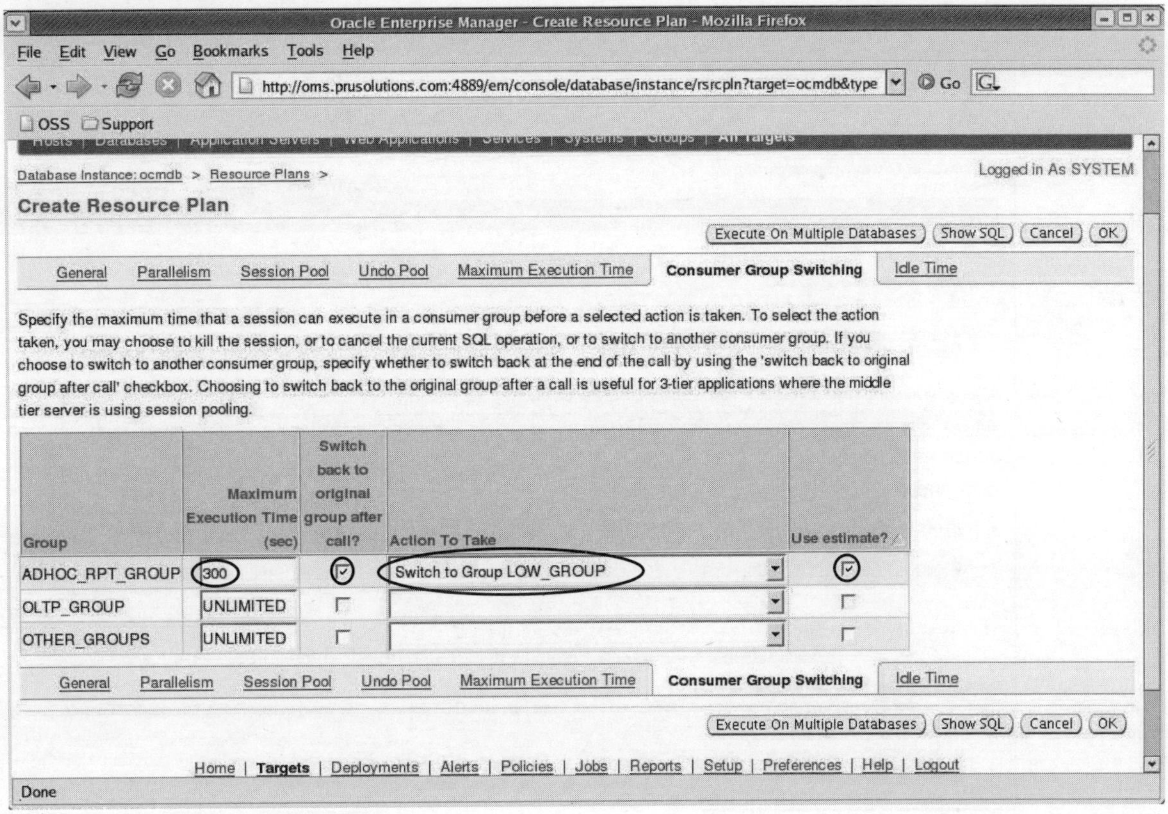

- On Idle Time tab
  Max idle Time: 30 Minutes
  Max Idle Time if Blocking another Session: 1 Minute
  Click Show SQL to capture the sql click OK to create TRANSACTION_PLAN

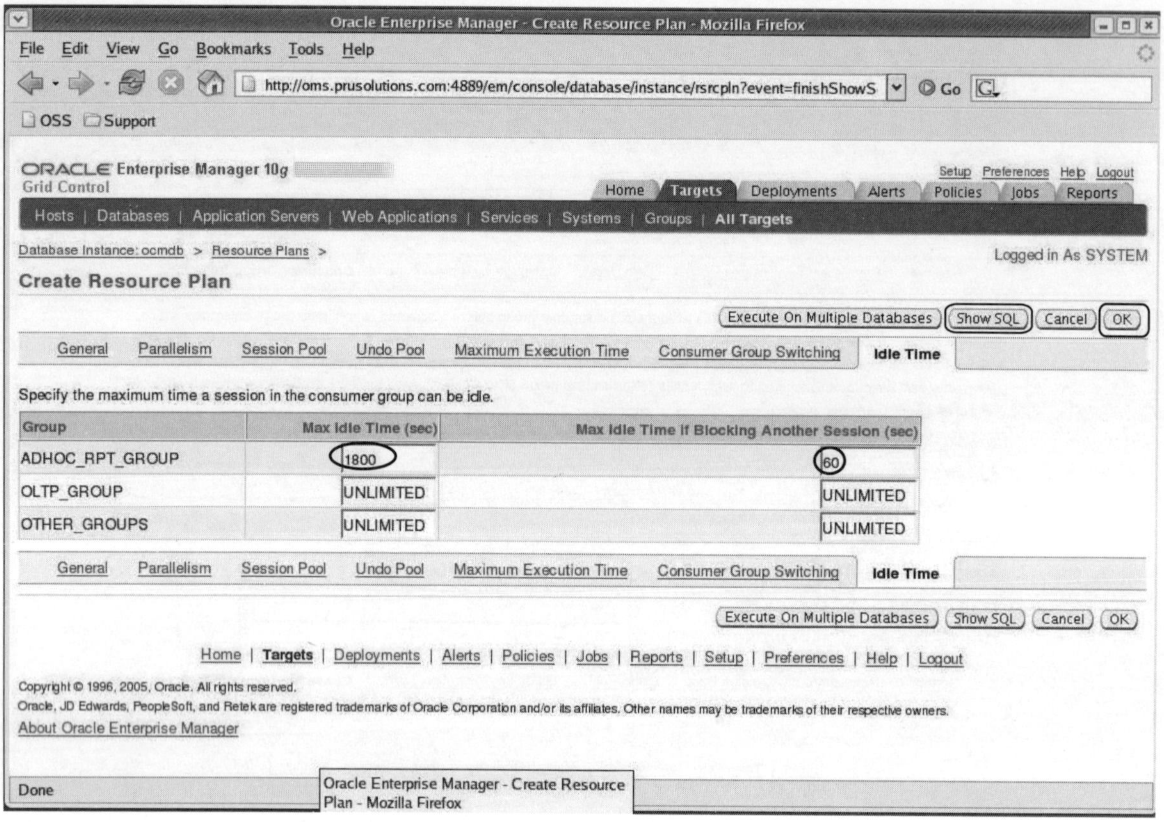

- In the same way as TRANSACTION_PLAN was created, create BUSINESS_HOUR_PLAN.
The TRANSACTION_PLAN will be part of BUSINESS_HOUR_PLAN
Example screen shot show below.

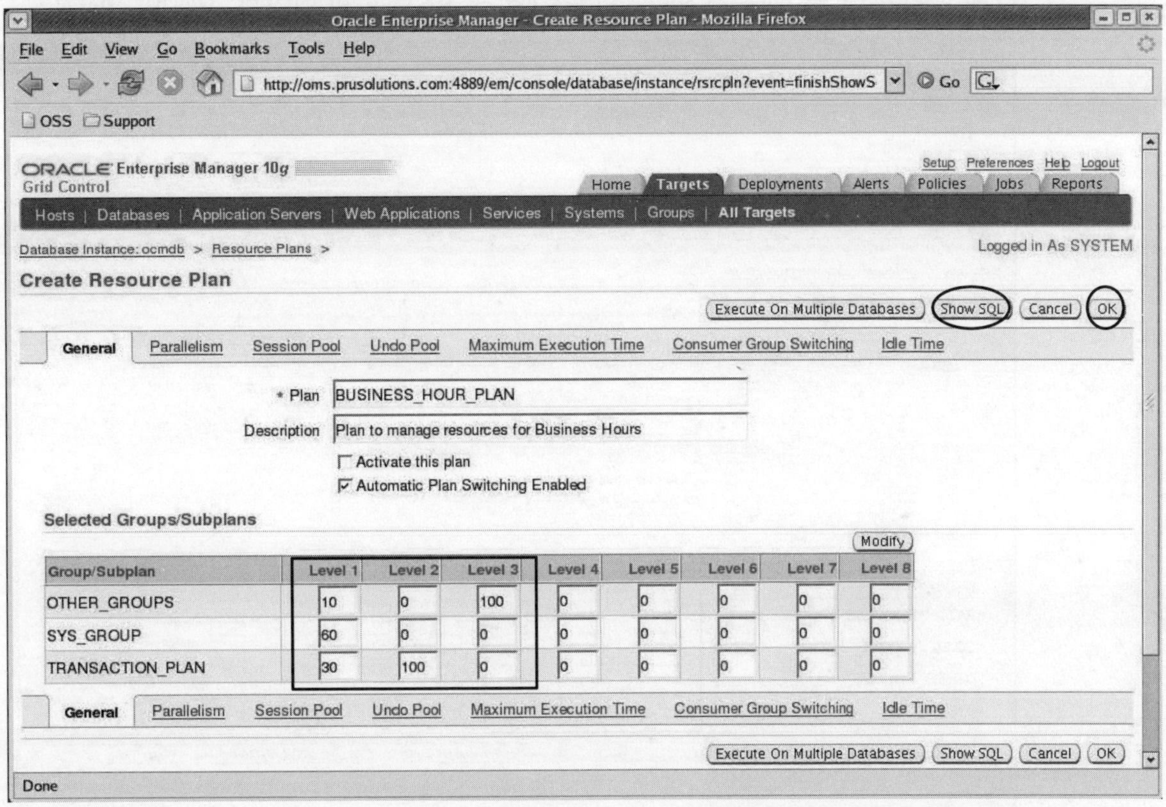

- Details for OFF_BUSINESS_HOURS_PALN

  Create OFF_BUSINESS_HOURS_PALN as BUSINESS_HOURS_PALN was created, the changes shown below

  Click Show SQL to capture sql and Click OK create OFF_BUSINESS_HOURS_PALN.

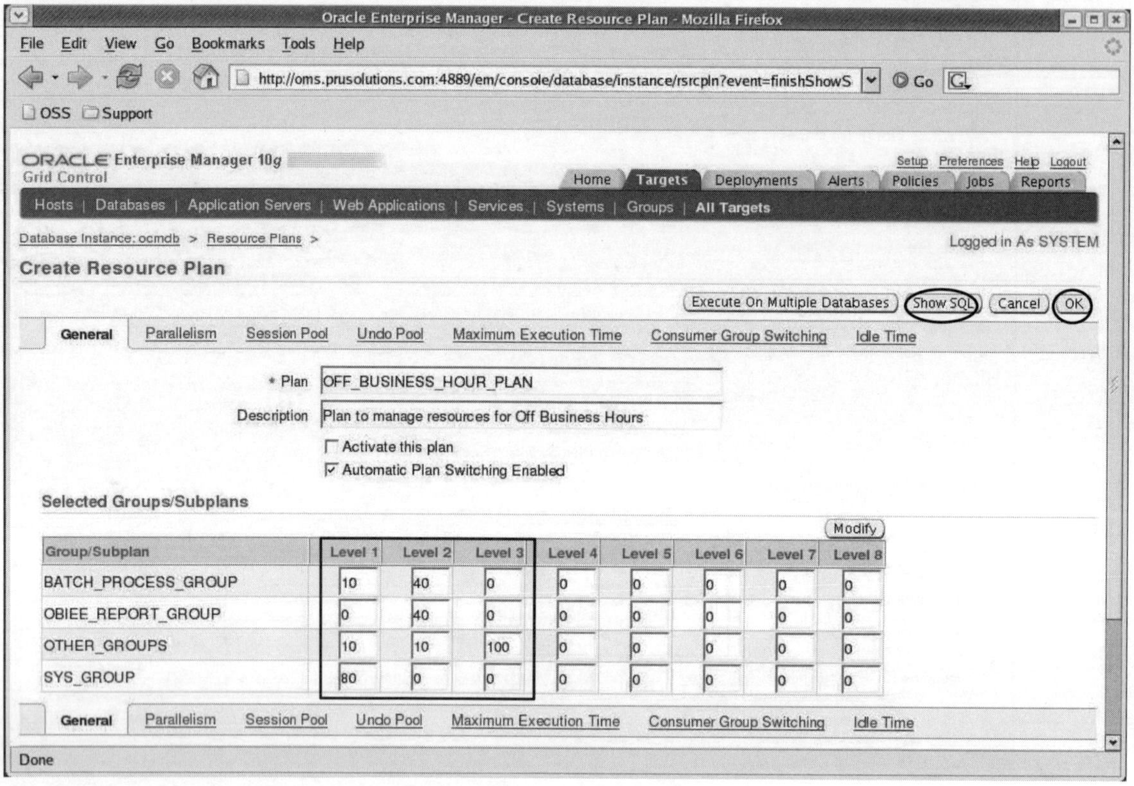

- Now all the plans have been created

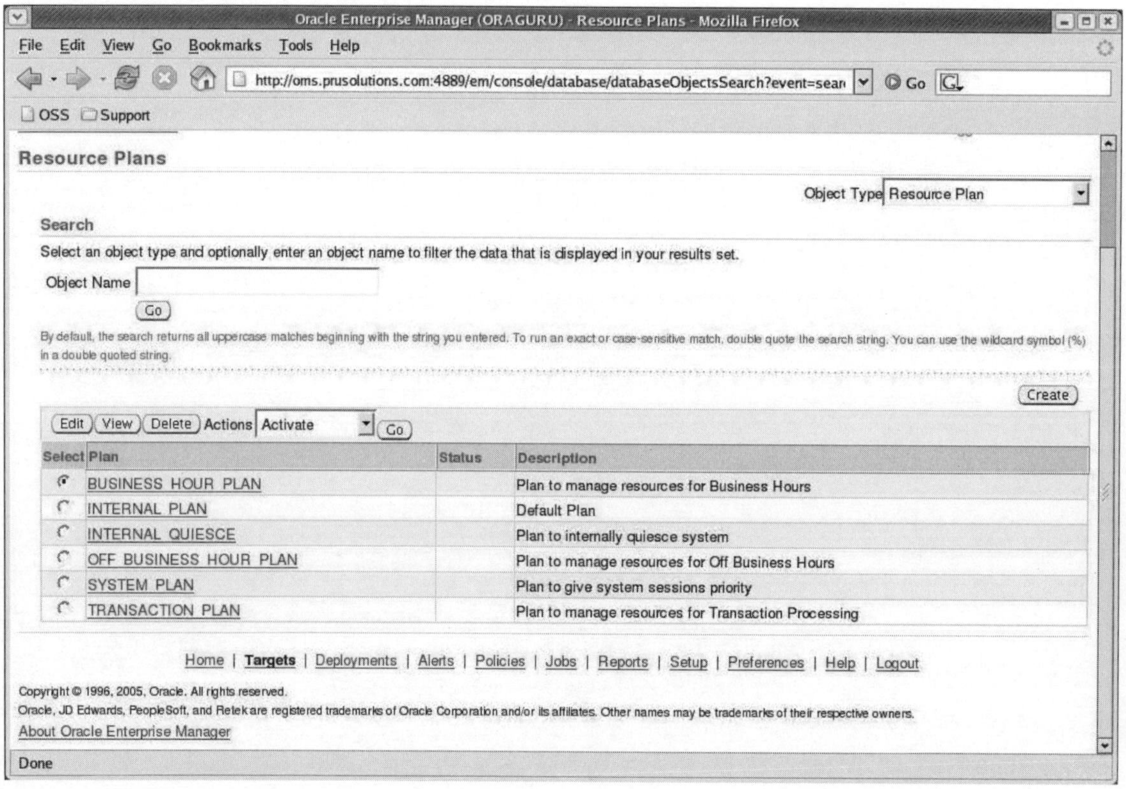

- We can assign Consumer Group to Users/Roles and activate plans using Oracle Scheduler and at a time, only one plan can be activated.
  - Create a role ADHOC_RPT_USERS and assign the role to user BI and SCOTT, you can create this using Oracle's OEM Grid Control also.

    SQL> CREATE ROLE ADHOC_RPT_USERS NOT IDENTIFIED;

    SQL> GRANT ALTER SESSION TO ADHOC_RPT_USERS;

    SQL> GRANT CONNECT TO ADHOC_RPT_USERS;

    SQL> GRANT RESOURCE TO ADHOC_RPT_USERS;

    SQL> GRANT ADHOC_RPT_USERS TO BI;

    SQL> ALTER USER "BI" DEFAULT ROLE ALL;

    SQL> GRANT ADHOC_RPT_USERS TO SCOTT;

    SQL> ALTER USER SCOTT DEFAULT ROLE ALL;
  - Assign Consumer Groups to Roles

    One Role can belong to multiple Consumer Groups, Below is example of assign a Consumer Group users BI and SCOTT through role ADHOC_RPT_USERS.

    On Database Administration Page in Users & Privileges Section, click Roles. It will take to Roles Management page. Edit role ADHOC_RPT_USERS role.

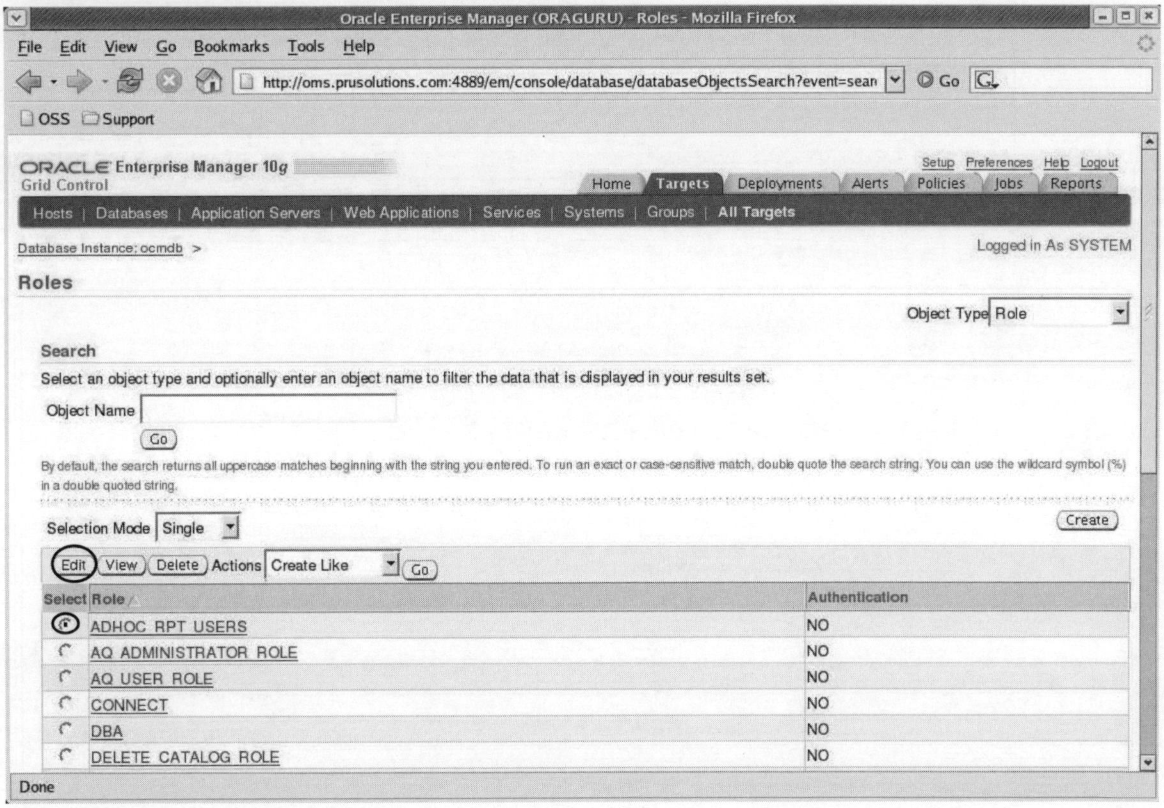

- Edit Role ADHOC_RPT_USERS, in Consumer Groups Switching Privileges, Edit List, and assign it ADHOC_RPT_GROUP, Show SQL to see the sql and then apply the changes

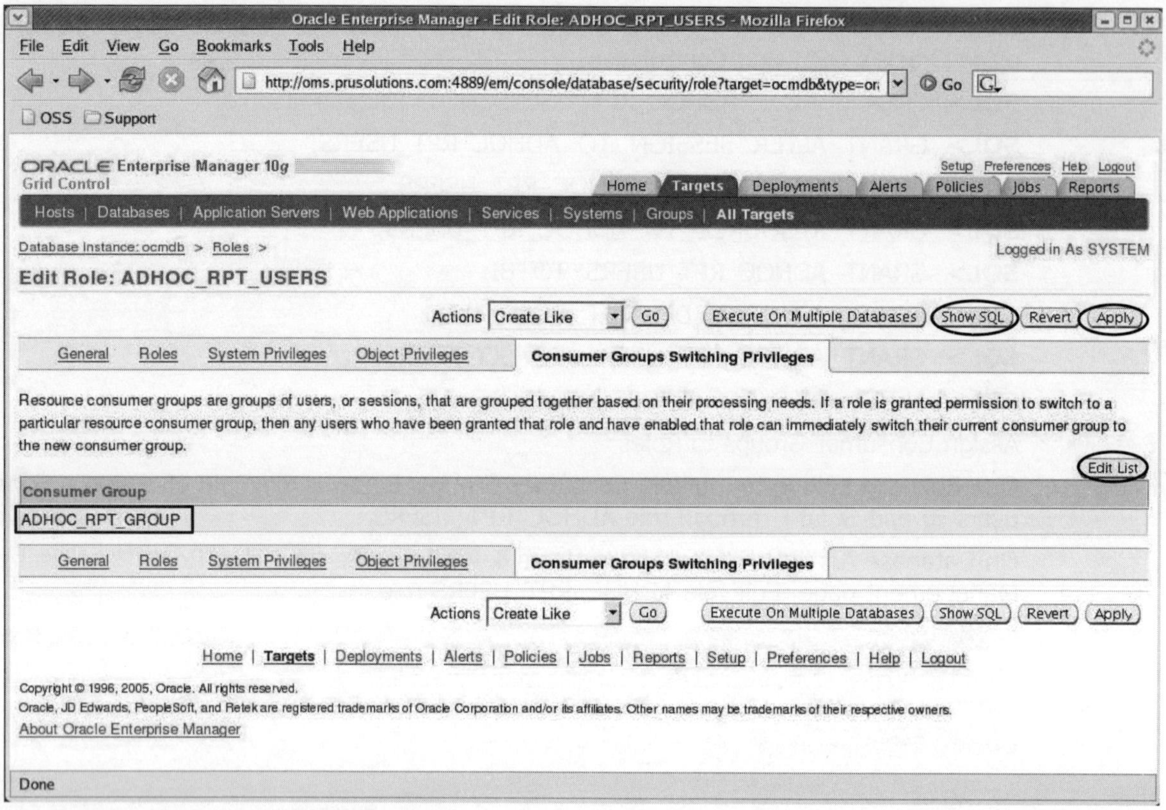

- Assign Consumer Groups to Users

  One User can belong to multiple Consumer Groups, Below is example of assign multiple Consumer Group BATCH_PROCESS_GROUP and OBIEE_REPORT_GROUP to user BI.

  On Database Administration Page in Users & Privileges Section, click Users. It will take to Users Management page. Edit user BI and in Consumer Groups Switching Privileges Edit List and assign it BATCH_PROCESS_GROUP and OBIEE_REPORT_GROUP, Show SQL to see the sql and then apply the changes.

In same way, assign consumer group to all other users

i. OLTP_GROUP HR, OE

ii. BATCH_PROCESS_GROUP SH, PM

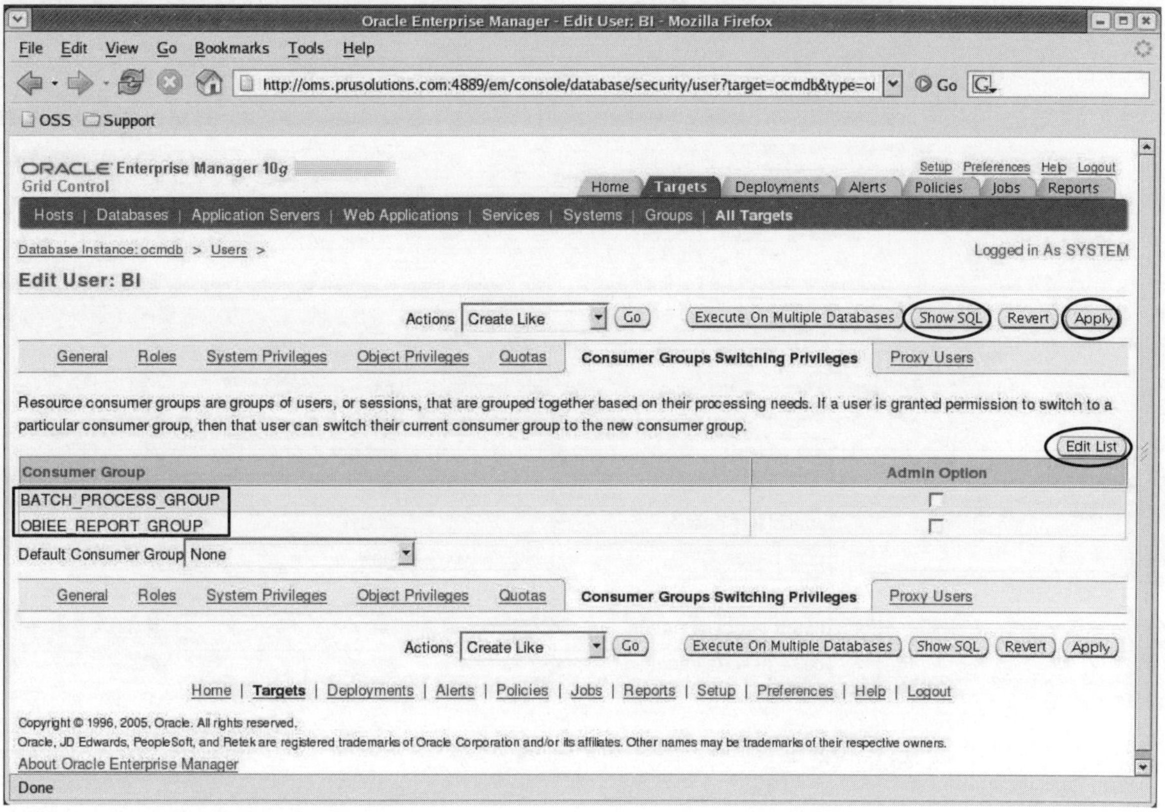

- On Database Administration Page in Resource Manager Section, click Resource Consumer Group Mapping. It will take to Resource Consumer Group Mapping page.

  Assign following users the consumer groups mentioned below as default, Click Show SQL to Capture SQL and Return then Apply.

	Consumer Group	Oracle Users
i.	ADHOC_RPT_GROUP	BI, SCOTT
ii.	OLTP_GROUP	HR, OE
iii.	BATCH_PROCESS_GROUP	SH
iv.	OBIEE_REPORT_GROUP	PM

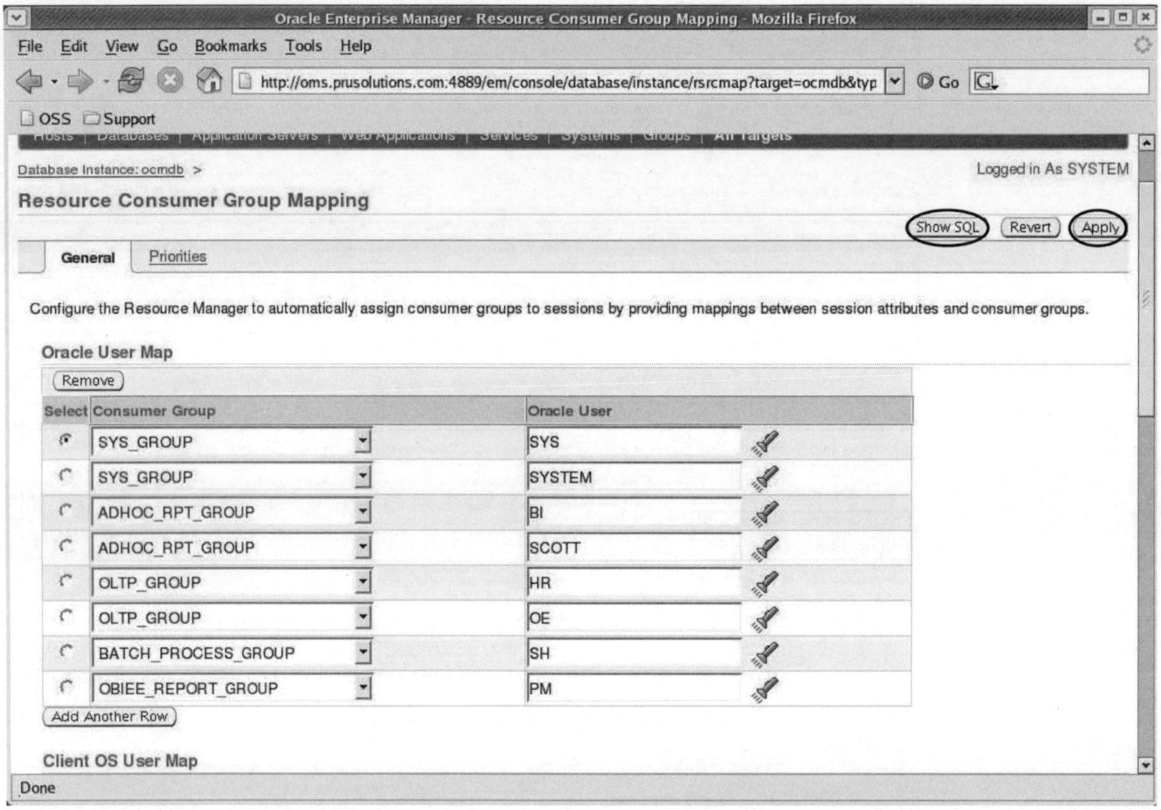

- In the same way you can practice mappings for following and assign priorities to them
  i. Client OS User Map
  ii. Client Program Map
  iii. Client Machine Map
  iv. Service Map
  v. Module Map
  vi. Module and Action

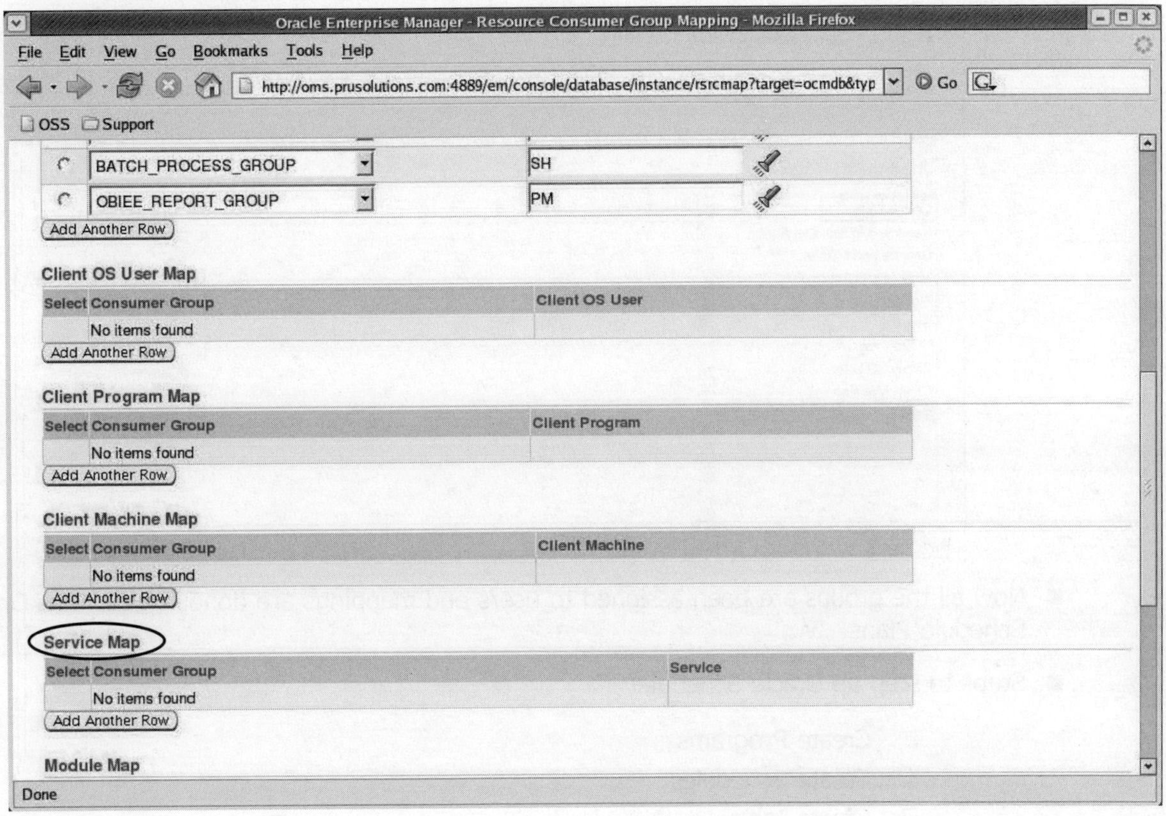

- Modify the priorities and Set Oracle User priority at highest level

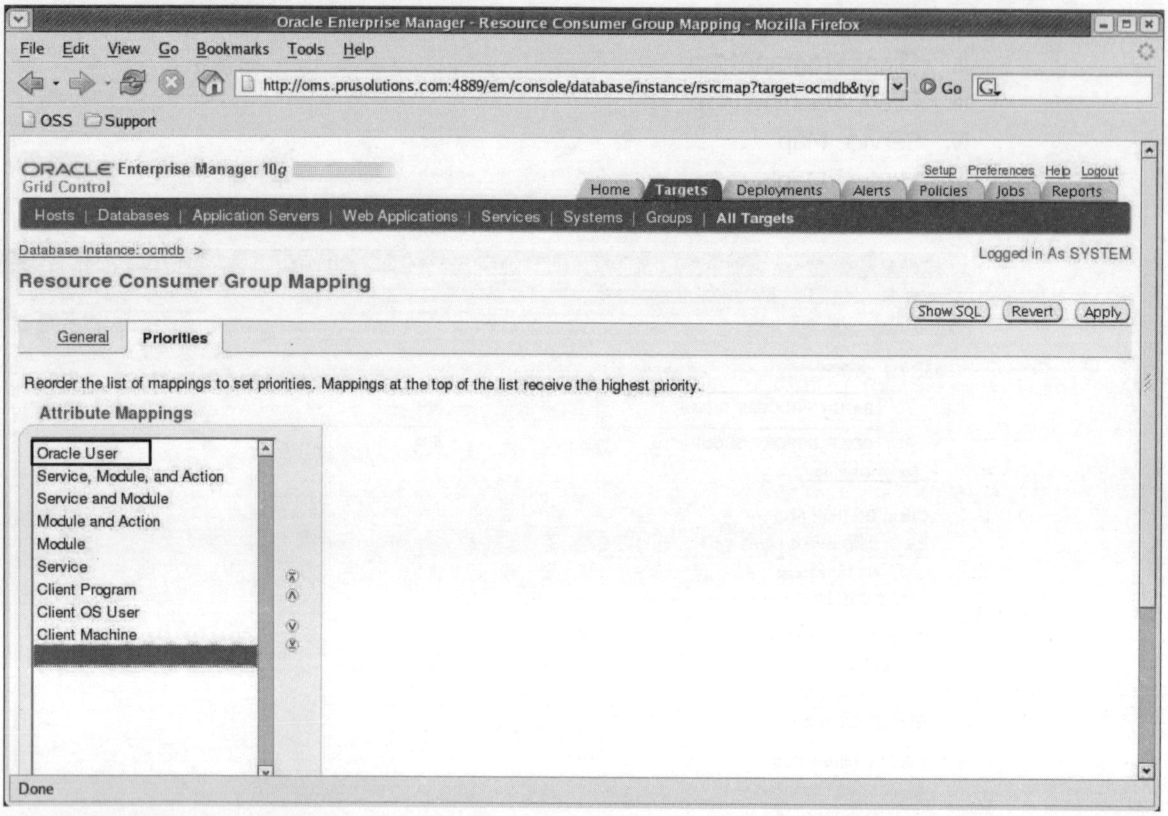

- Now all the groups are been assigned to users and mappings are done, we can use Oracle scheduler to Schedule Plans

- Steps to step up Oracle Scheduler

    i. Create Programs
    ii. Create Schedules
    iii. Create Jobs
    iv. Monitor Jobs

- Create Programs

  On Database Administration Page in Oracle Scheduler Section, Click Programs. It will take to Scheduler Programs page. Click Create

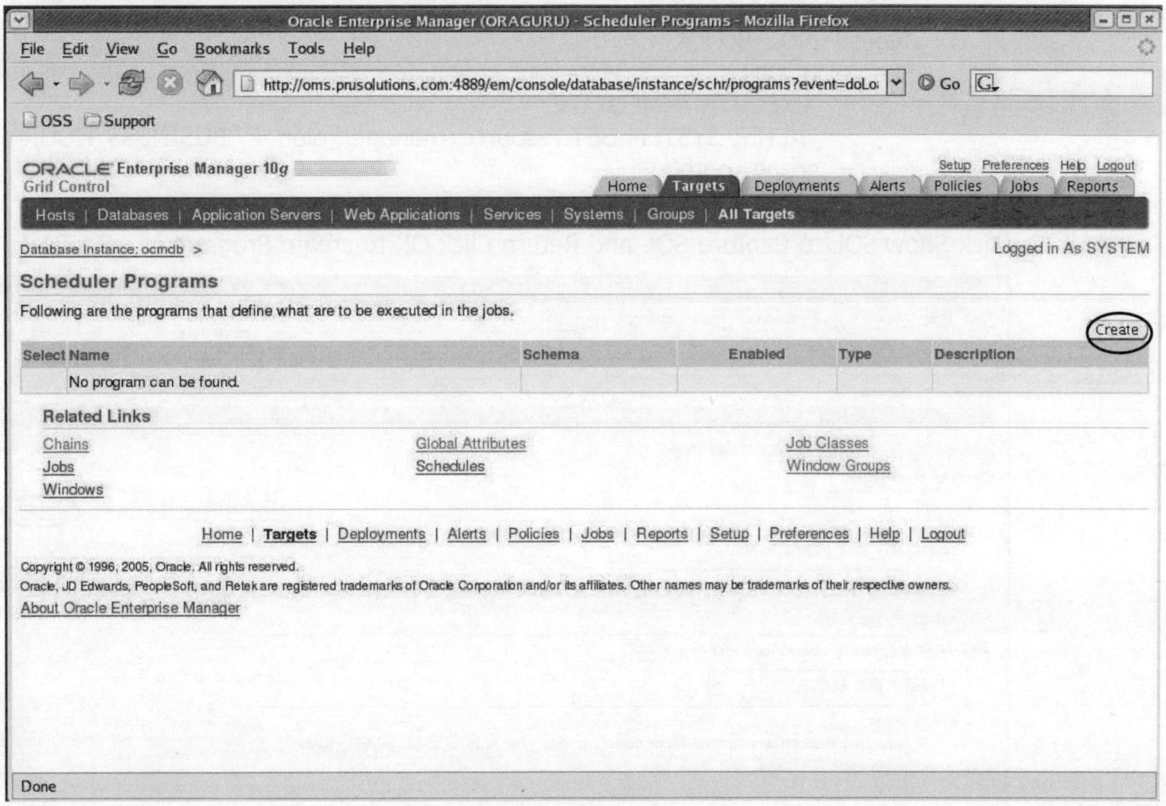

- On Create Program page, create Program ACT_BUS_HOUR_PLAN

  Name: ACTIVATE_BUSINESS_HOUR_PLAN
  Description: Activate Business Hours Plan at 8:00 AM
  Enabled: Select Yes
  Type: PLSQL_BLOCK
  Source: BEGIN
  EXECUTE IMMEDIATE
  'ALTER SYSTEM SET resource_manager_plan = ''BUSINESS_HOUR_PLAN ''
  scope=both';
  END;

  Click Show SQL to Capture SQL and Return Click OK to create Program

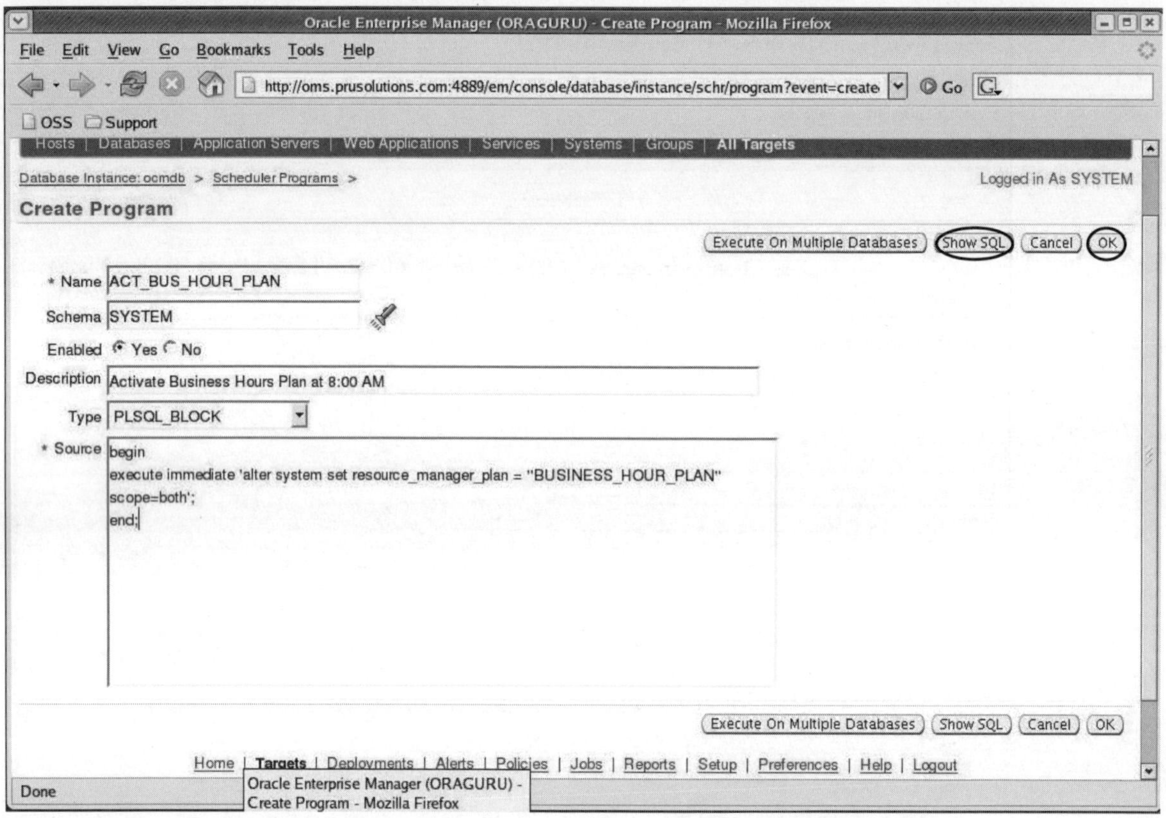

- On Create Program page, create Program ACT_OFF_BUS_HOUR_PLAN

  Name: ACT_OFF_BUS_HOUR_PLAN

  Description: Activate Off Business Hours Plan at 7:00 PM

  Enabled: Select Yes

  Type: PLSQL_BLOCK

  Source: BEGIN

```
EXECUTE  IMMEDIATE
'ALTER SYSTEM SET resource_manager_plan = ''OFF_BUSINESS_HOUR_PLAN''
scope=both';
END;
```

Click Show SQL to Capture SQL and Return and Click OK to create Program

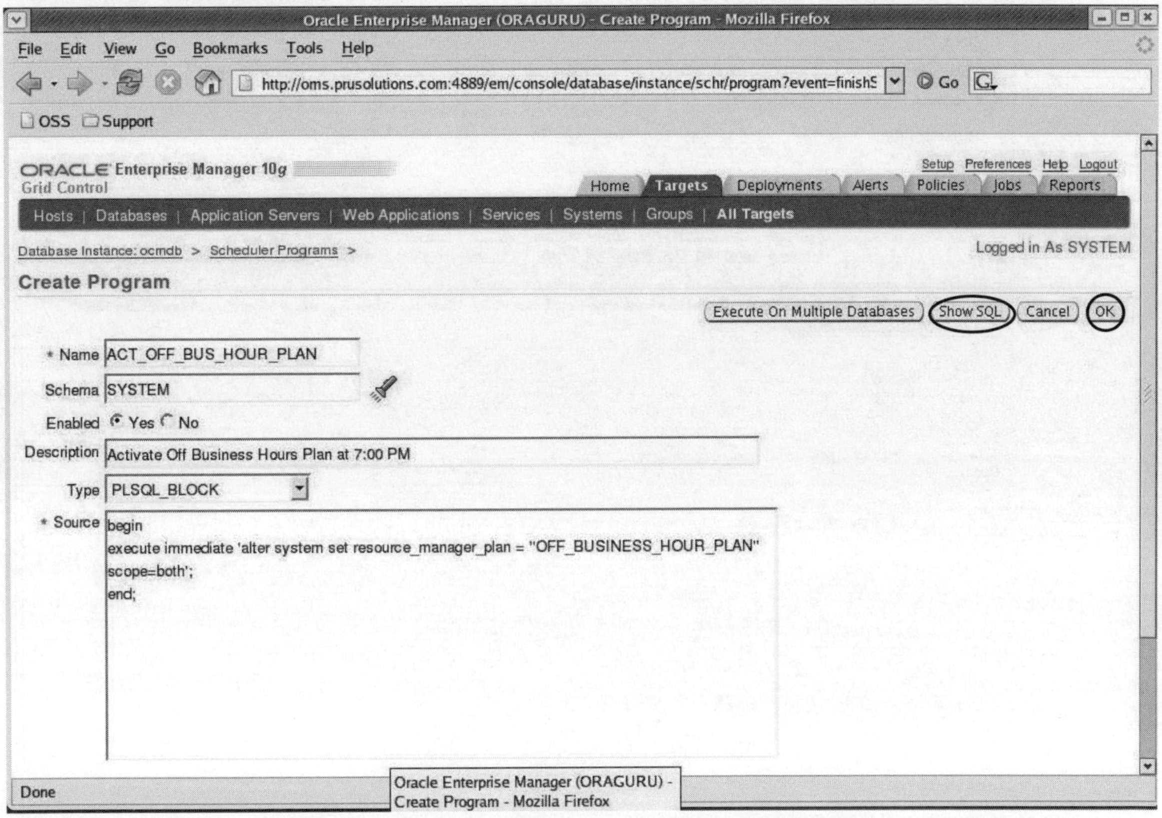

- Create Schedules.

  On Database Administration Page in Oracle Scheduler Section , click Schedule. It will take to Scheduler Schedules Page. Click Create

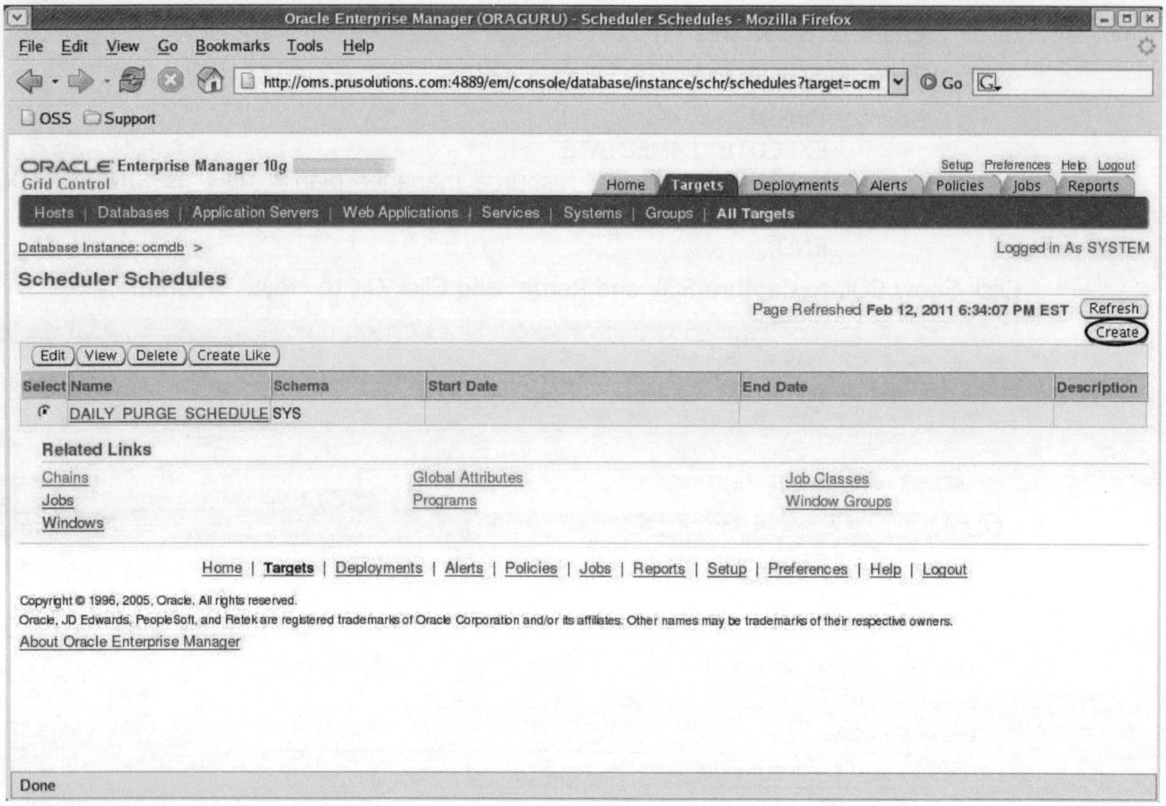

- Create a schedule having following.

  Name: ACTIVATE_BUS_HOUR_PLAN

  Schema: SYSTEM

  Description: Activate Business Hours Resource Manager Plan

  Time Zone: America/New York

  Schedule Type: Standard

  Repeat: By Days

  Interval: 1

  Time : 8:00:00 AM

  Later Date : <DATE>

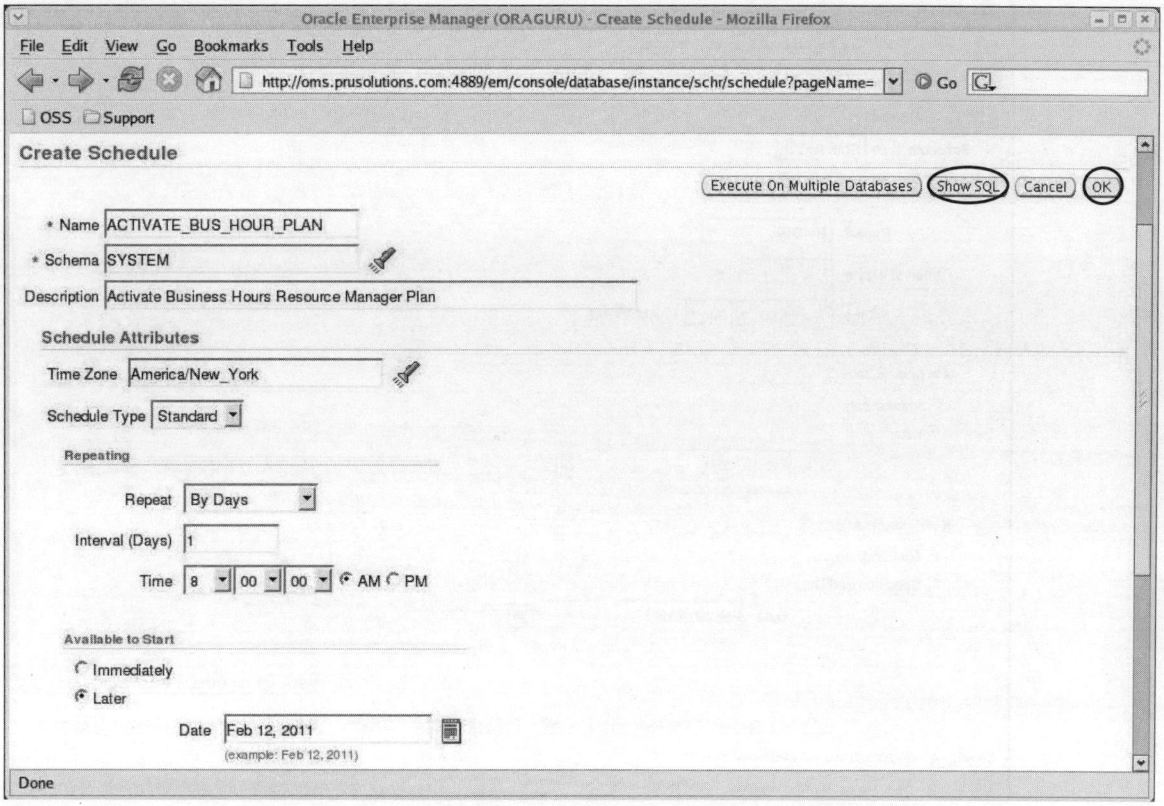

- Create another schedule having following.
  Name: ACTIVATE_OFF_BUS_HOUR_PLAN
  Schema: SYSTEM
  Description: Activate Off Business Hours Resource Manager Plan
  Time Zone: America/New York
  Schedule Type: Standard
  Repeat: By Days
  Interval: 1
  Time : 7:00:00 PM
  Later Date : <DATE>

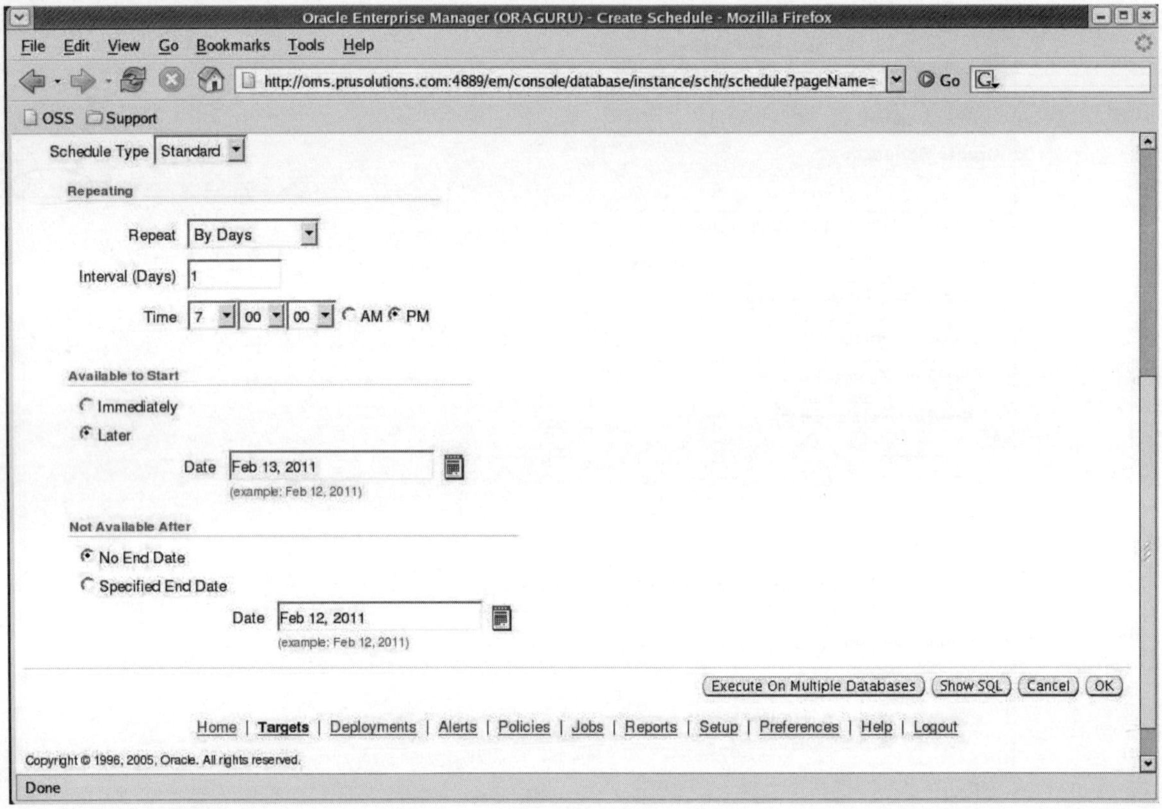

- Create Jobs

  On Database Administration Page in Oracle Scheduler Section, click Jobs. It will take to Scheduler Jobs Page.

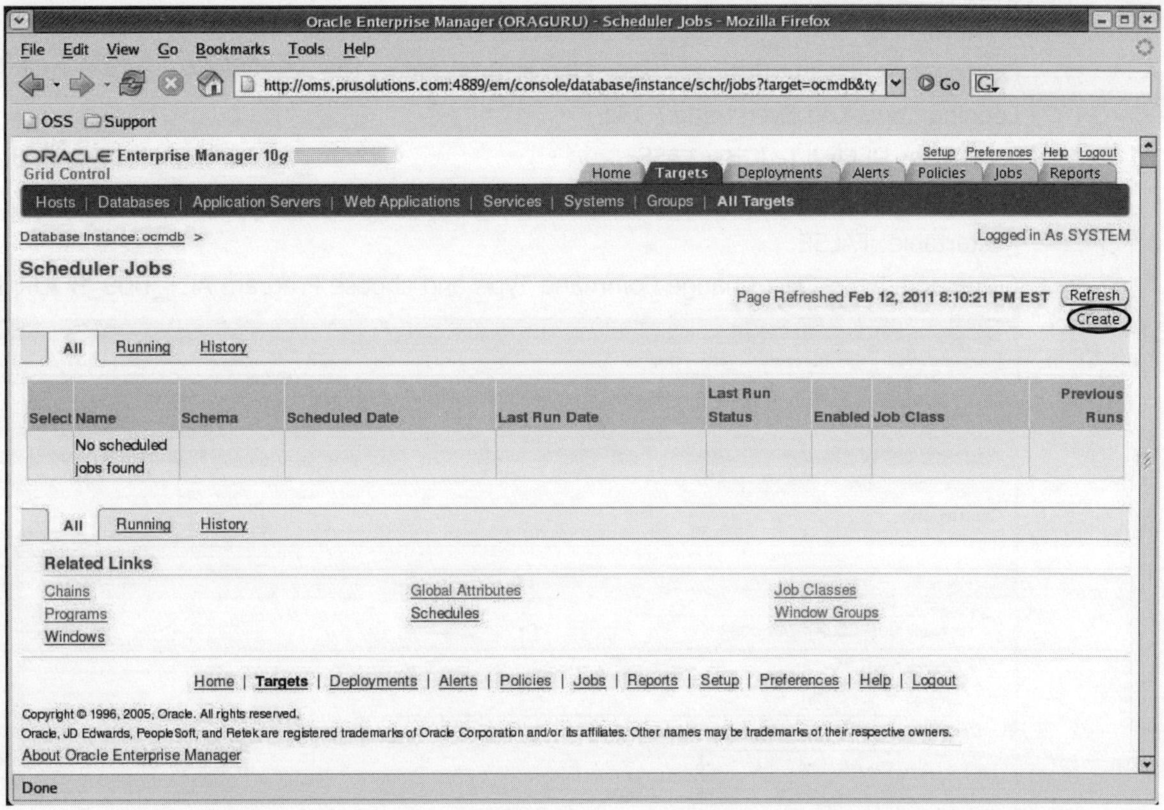

- On General tab of Create Job Page
  Name: BUS_HOUR_PLAN_JOB
  Schema: SYSTEM
  Enabled: Yes
  Description: Activate Business Hour Plan at 8:00 AM
  Logging Level Log Everything (FULL)
  Job Class: DEFAULT_JOB_CLASS
  Auto Drop: FALSE
  Restartable: FALSE
  Command Type: Click Change Command Type and choose Program ACT_BUS_HOUR_PLAN

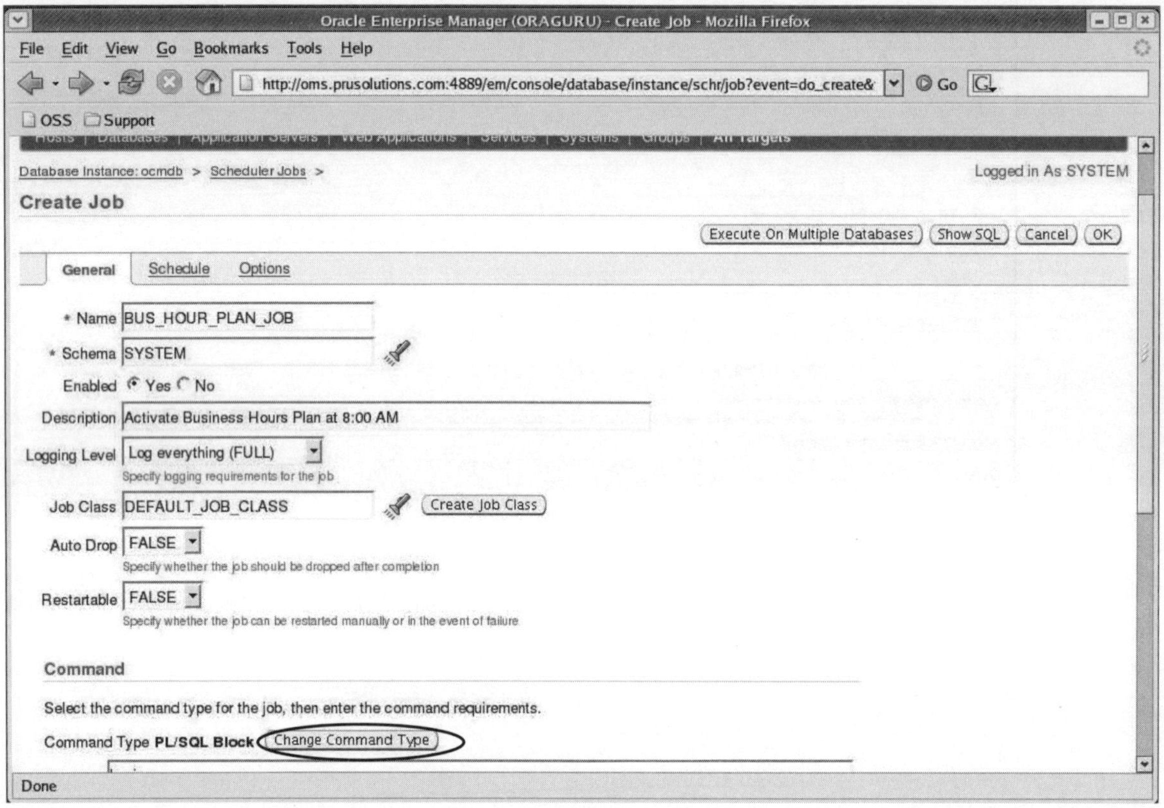

- Select Command Option.

Program Name: SYSTEM ACT_BUS_HOUR_PLAN

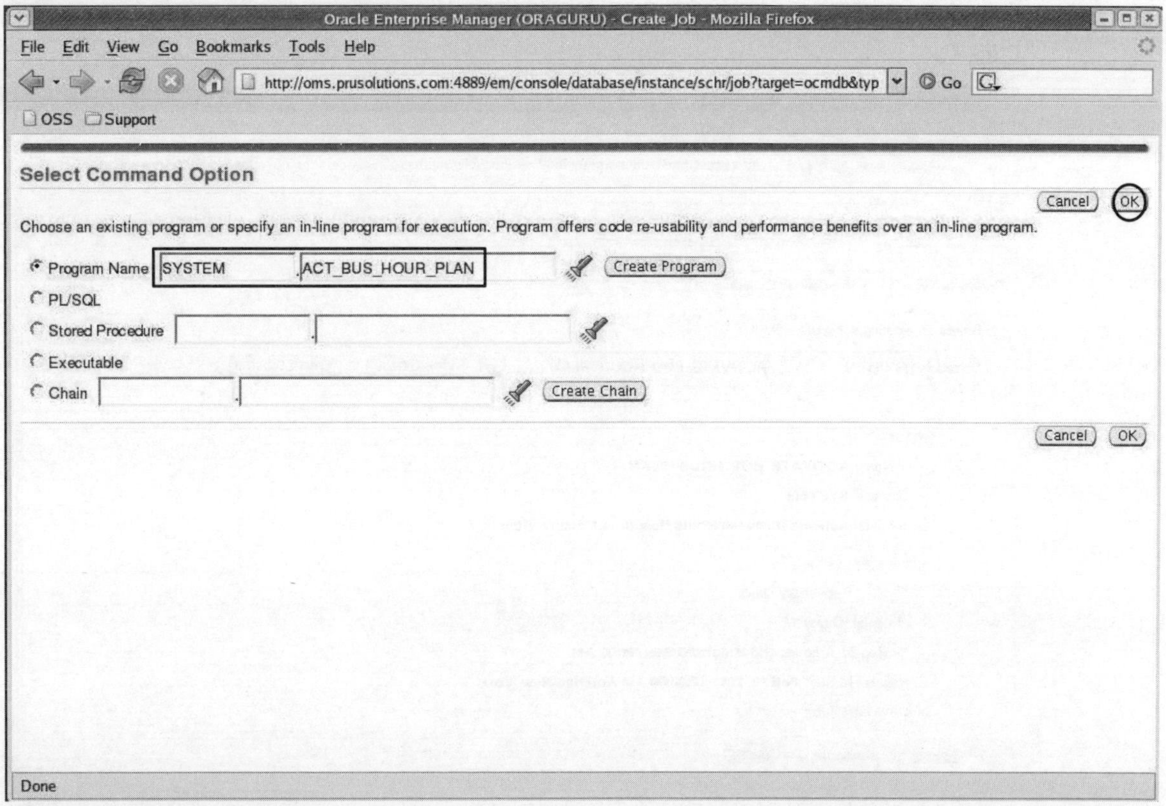

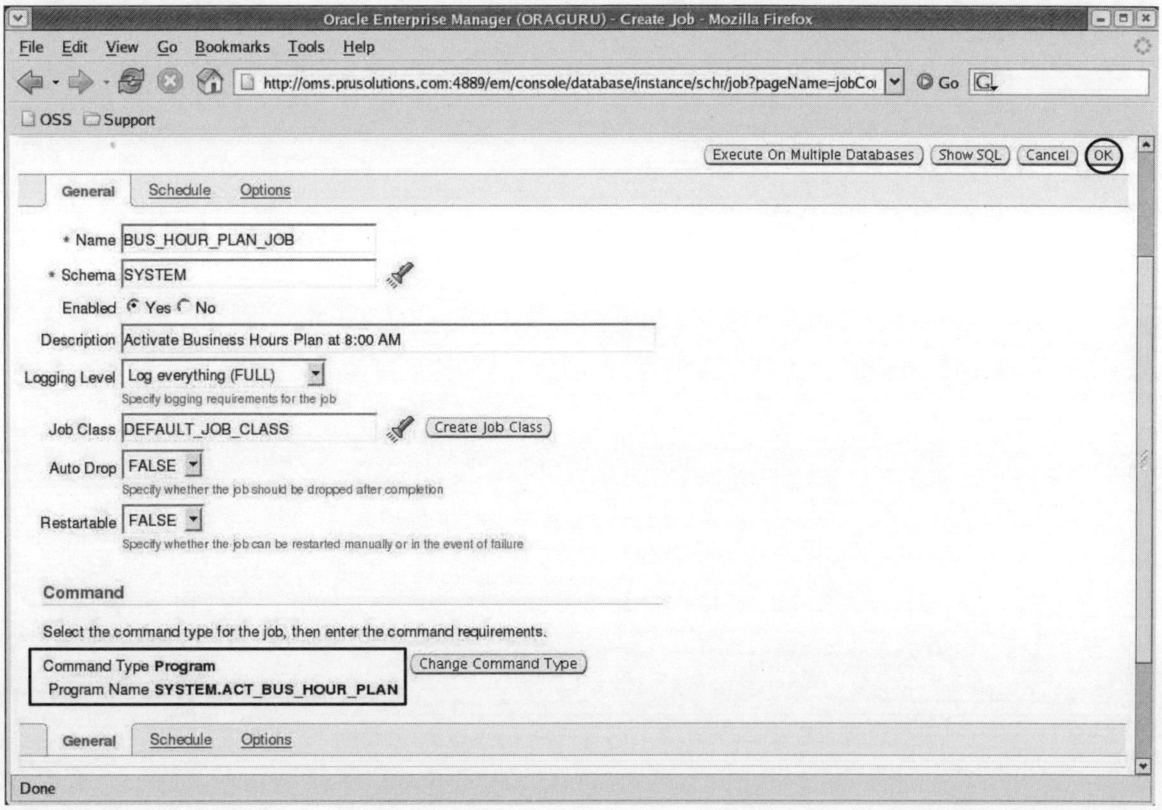

- Go to Schedule tab
  Schedule Type: Use Pre-defined Schedule
  Schedule: SYSTEM ACTIVATE_BUS_HOUR_PLAN
  Click OK

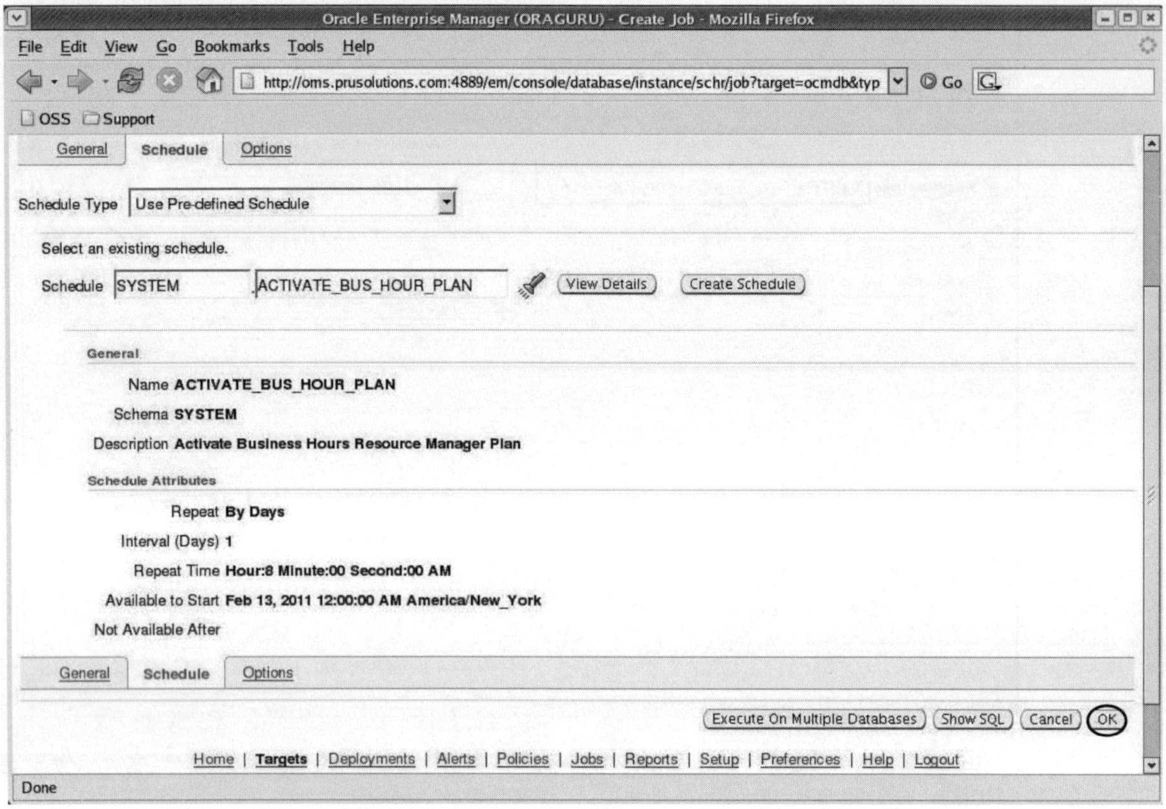

- On Option tab

  Raise Events: Select all Click Show SQL to Capture SQL and Return

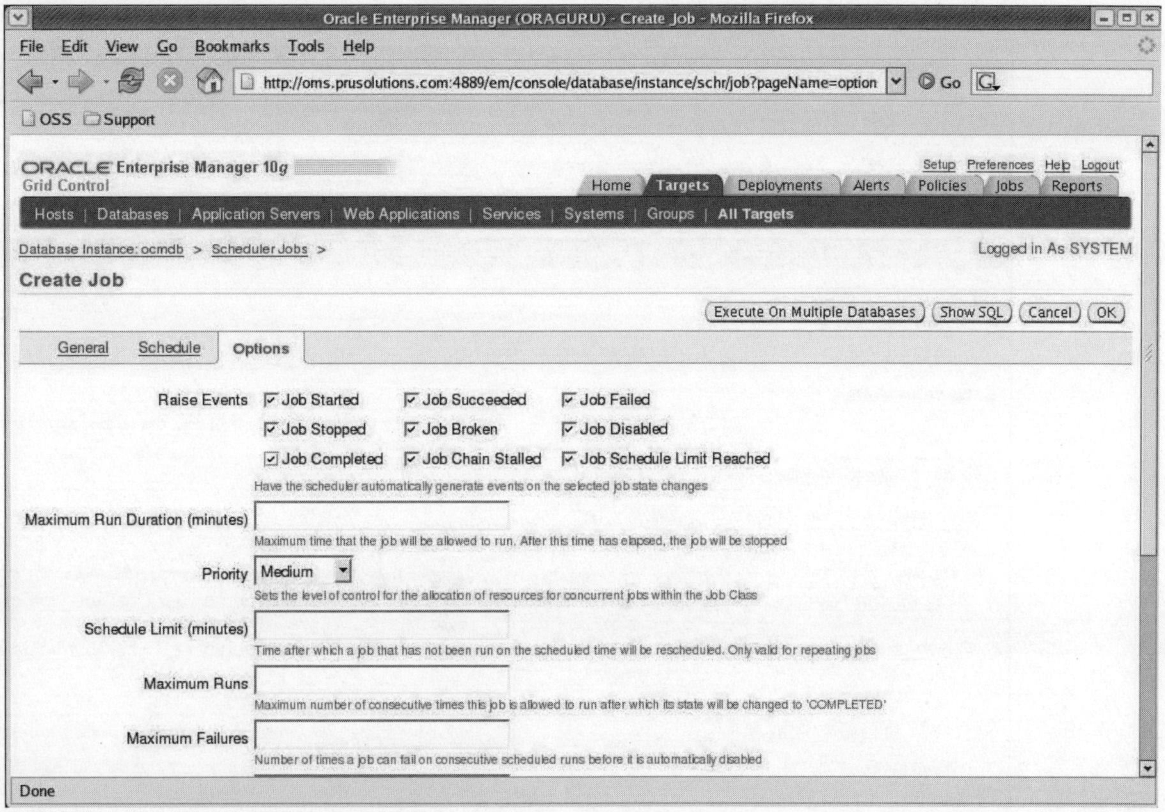

- Create job for Off Business Hour Plan

  On General tab of Create Job Page

  Name: OFF_BUS_HOUR_PLAN_JOB
  Schema: SYSTEM
  Enabled: Yes
  Description: Activate Business Hour Plan at 8:00 AM
  Logging Level Log Everything (FULL)
  Job Class: DEFAULT_JOB_CLASS
  Auto Drop: FALSE
  Restartable: FALSE
  Command Type: Click Change Command Type and choose Program ACT_OFF_BUS_HOUR_PLAN
- On Schedule tab

  Schedule Type: Use Pre-defined Schedule
  Schedule: SYSTEM ACTIVATE_OFF_BUS_HOUR_PLAN

- On Option tab

  Raise Events: Select all Click Show SQL to Capture SQL and Return

  Both the jobs are schedule as shown below

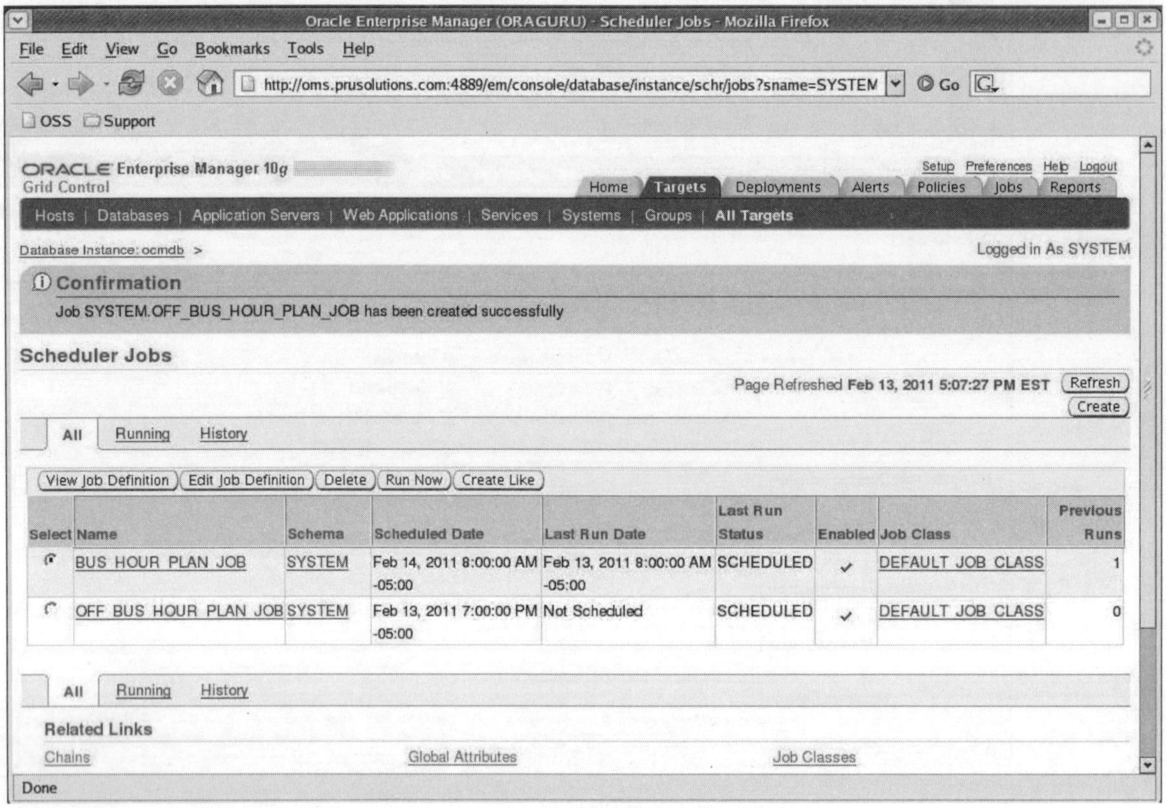

- Resource Manager Plan using SQLPLUS

All the sqls were captured using Show SQL while creating resource manager and jobs using Oracle's OEM Grid Control are mentioned below.

- Create Groups and PLANS

OLTP_GROUP

```
BEGIN
        dbms_resource_manager.clear_pending_area();
        dbms_resource_manager.create_pending_area();
        dbms_resource_manager.create_consumer_group(consumer_group => 'OLTP_GROUP',
        comment => 'Manages Resources for Transaction Processing', cpu_mth => 'ROUND-
        ROBIN');
        dbms_resource_manager.submit_pending_area();
END;
/
```

ADHOC_RPT_GROUP

```
BEGIN
        dbms_resource_manager.clear_pending_area();
        dbms_resource_manager.create_pending_area();
        dbms_resource_manager.create_consumer_group(consumer_group =>
        'ADHOC_RPT_GROUP', comment => 'Manages Resources for Adhoc Reporting', cpu_mth =>
        'ROUND-ROBIN');
        dbms_resource_manager.submit_pending_area();
END;
/
```

BATCH_PROCESS_GROUP

```
BEGIN
        dbms_resource_manager.clear_pending_area();
        dbms_resource_manager.create_pending_area();
        dbms_resource_manager.create_consumer_group(consumer_group =>
        'BATCH_PROCESS_GROUP', comment => 'Manages Resources for Batch Processes', cpu_mth
        => 'ROUND-ROBIN');
        dbms_resource_manager.submit_pending_area();
END;
/
```

OBIEE_REPORT_GROUP

```
BEGIN
        dbms_resource_manager.clear_pending_area();
        dbms_resource_manager.create_pending_area();
        dbms_resource_manager.create_consumer_group(consumer_group =>
        'OBIEE_REPORT_GROUP', comment => 'Manages Resources for OBIEE Reports Processes',
        cpu_mth => 'ROUND-ROBIN');
        dbms_resource_manager.submit_pending_area();
END;
/
```

TRANSACTION_PLAN

```
BEGIN
        dbms_resource_manager.clear_pending_area();
        dbms_resource_manager.create_pending_area();
        dbms_resource_manager.create_plan( 'TRANSACTION_PLAN', 'Plan to manage resources for
        Transaction Processing');
        dbms_resource_manager.create_plan_directive(
            plan => 'TRANSACTION_PLAN',
            group_or_subplan => 'ADHOC_RPT_GROUP',
            comment => '',
            cpu_p1 => 15, cpu_p2 => NULL, cpu_p3 => NULL, cpu_p4 => NULL,
            cpu_p5 => NULL, cpu_p6 => NULL, cpu_p7 => NULL, cpu_p8 => NULL,
            parallel_degree_limit_p1 => 2,
            active_sess_pool_p1 => 20,
            queueing_p1 => 300,
            switch_group => 'LOW_GROUP',
            switch_time => 300,
            switch_estimate => true,
            max_est_exec_time => 1800,
            undo_pool => 10240,
            max_idle_time => 1800,
            max_idle_blocker_time => 60,
            switch_time_in_call => NULL
        );
        dbms_resource_manager.create_plan_directive(
            plan => 'TRANSACTION_PLAN',
            group_or_subplan => 'OLTP_GROUP',
            comment => '',
            cpu_p1 => 85, cpu_p2 => 0, cpu_p3 => NULL, cpu_p4 => NULL,
            cpu_p5 => NULL, cpu_p6 => NULL, cpu_p7 => NULL, cpu_p8 => NULL,
            parallel_degree_limit_p1 => NULL,
            active_sess_pool_p1 => NULL,
            queueing_p1 => NULL,
            switch_group => NULL,
```

```
            switch_time => NULL,
            switch_estimate => false,
            max_est_exec_time => NULL,
            undo_pool => NULL,
            max_idle_time => NULL,
            max_idle_blocker_time => NULL,
            switch_time_in_call => NULL
        );
        dbms_resource_manager.create_plan_directive(
            plan => 'TRANSACTION_PLAN',
            group_or_subplan => 'OTHER_GROUPS',
            comment => '',
            cpu_p1 => NULL, cpu_p2 => 100, cpu_p3 => NULL, cpu_p4 => NULL,
            cpu_p5 => NULL, cpu_p6 => NULL, cpu_p7 => NULL, cpu_p8 => NULL,
            parallel_degree_limit_p1 => NULL,
            active_sess_pool_p1 => NULL,
            queueing_p1 => NULL,
            switch_group => NULL,
            switch_time => NULL,
            switch_estimate => false,
            max_est_exec_time => NULL,
            undo_pool => NULL,
            max_idle_time => NULL,
            max_idle_blocker_time => NULL,
            switch_time_in_call => NULL
        );
        dbms_resource_manager.submit_pending_area();
END;
/
```

BUSINESS_HOUR_PLAN

```
BEGIN
        dbms_resource_manager.clear_pending_area();
        dbms_resource_manager.create_pending_area();
        dbms_resource_manager.create_plan( 'BUSINESS_HOUR_PLAN', 'Plan to manage resources
        for Business Hours');
        dbms_resource_manager.create_plan_directive(
            plan => 'BUSINESS_HOUR_PLAN',
            group_or_subplan => 'OTHER_GROUPS',
            comment => '',
            cpu_p1 => 10, cpu_p2 => NULL, cpu_p3 => 100, cpu_p4 => NULL,
            cpu_p5 => NULL, cpu_p6 => NULL, cpu_p7 => NULL, cpu_p8 => NULL,
            parallel_degree_limit_p1 => NULL,
            active_sess_pool_p1 => NULL,
            queueing_p1 => NULL,
            switch_group => '',
            switch_time => NULL,
            switch_estimate => false,
            max_est_exec_time => NULL,
            undo_pool => NULL,
            max_idle_time => NULL,
            max_idle_blocker_time => NULL,
            switch_time_in_call => NULL
        );
```

```
        dbms_resource_manager.create_plan_directive(
            plan => 'BUSINESS_HOUR_PLAN',
            group_or_subplan => 'SYS_GROUP',
            comment => '',
            cpu_p1 => 60, cpu_p2 => NULL, cpu_p3 => NULL, cpu_p4 => NULL,
            cpu_p5 => NULL, cpu_p6 => NULL, cpu_p7 => NULL, cpu_p8 => NULL,
            parallel_degree_limit_p1 => NULL,
            active_sess_pool_p1 => NULL,
            queueing_p1 => NULL,
            switch_group => '',
            switch_time => NULL,
            switch_estimate => false,
            max_est_exec_time => NULL,
            undo_pool => NULL,
            max_idle_time => NULL,
            max_idle_blocker_time => NULL,
            switch_time_in_call => NULL
        );
        dbms_resource_manager.create_plan_directive(
            plan => 'BUSINESS_HOUR_PLAN',
            group_or_subplan => 'TRANSACTION_PLAN',
            comment => '',
            cpu_p1 => 30, cpu_p2 => 100, cpu_p3 => NULL, cpu_p4 => NULL,
            cpu_p5 => NULL, cpu_p6 => NULL, cpu_p7 => NULL, cpu_p8 => NULL
        );
        dbms_resource_manager.submit_pending_area();
END;
/
```

OFF_BUSINESS_HOUR_PLAN

```
BEGIN
        dbms_resource_manager.clear_pending_area();
        dbms_resource_manager.create_pending_area();
        dbms_resource_manager.create_plan( 'OFF_BUSINESS_HOUR_PLAN', 'Plan to manage
        resources for Off Business Hours');
        dbms_resource_manager.create_plan_directive(
            plan => 'OFF_BUSINESS_HOUR_PLAN',
            group_or_subplan => 'BATCH_PROCESS_GROUP',
            comment => '',
            cpu_p1 => 10, cpu_p2 => 40, cpu_p3 => NULL, cpu_p4 => NULL,
            cpu_p5 => NULL, cpu_p6 => NULL, cpu_p7 => NULL, cpu_p8 => NULL,
            parallel_degree_limit_p1 => NULL,
            active_sess_pool_p1 => NULL,
            queueing_p1 => NULL,
            switch_group => '',
            switch_time => NULL,
            switch_estimate => false,
            max_est_exec_time => NULL,
            undo_pool => NULL,
            max_idle_time => NULL,
            max_idle_blocker_time => NULL,
            switch_time_in_call => NULL
        );
```

```
        dbms_resource_manager.create_plan_directive(
            plan => 'OFF_BUSINESS_HOUR_PLAN',
            group_or_subplan => 'OBIEE_REPORT_GROUP',
            comment => '',
            cpu_p1 => NULL, cpu_p2 => 40, cpu_p3 => NULL, cpu_p4 => NULL,
            cpu_p5 => NULL, cpu_p6 => NULL, cpu_p7 => NULL, cpu_p8 => NULL,
            parallel_degree_limit_p1 => NULL,
            active_sess_pool_p1 => NULL,
            queueing_p1 => NULL,
            switch_group => '',
            switch_time => NULL,
            switch_estimate => false,
            max_est_exec_time => NULL,
            undo_pool => NULL,
            max_idle_time => NULL,
            max_idle_blocker_time => NULL,
            switch_time_in_call => NULL
        );
        dbms_resource_manager.create_plan_directive(
            plan => 'OFF_BUSINESS_HOUR_PLAN',
            group_or_subplan => 'OTHER_GROUPS',
            comment => '',
            cpu_p1 => 10, cpu_p2 => 10, cpu_p3 => 100, cpu_p4 => NULL,
            cpu_p5 => NULL, cpu_p6 => NULL, cpu_p7 => NULL, cpu_p8 => NULL,
            parallel_degree_limit_p1 => NULL,
            active_sess_pool_p1 => NULL,
            queueing_p1 => NULL,
            switch_group => '',
            switch_time => NULL,
            switch_estimate => false,
            max_est_exec_time => NULL,
            undo_pool => NULL,
            max_idle_time => NULL,
            max_idle_blocker_time => NULL,
            switch_time_in_call => NULL
        );
        dbms_resource_manager.create_plan_directive(
            plan => 'OFF_BUSINESS_HOUR_PLAN',
            group_or_subplan => 'SYS_GROUP',
            comment => '',
            cpu_p1 => 80, cpu_p2 => NULL, cpu_p3 => NULL, cpu_p4 => NULL,
            cpu_p5 => NULL, cpu_p6 => NULL, cpu_p7 => NULL, cpu_p8 => NULL,
            parallel_degree_limit_p1 => NULL,
            active_sess_pool_p1 => NULL,
            queueing_p1 => NULL,
            switch_group => '',
            switch_time => NULL,
            switch_estimate => false,
            max_est_exec_time => NULL,
            undo_pool => NULL,
            max_idle_time => NULL,
            max_idle_blocker_time => NULL,
            switch_time_in_call => NULL
        );
        dbms_resource_manager.submit_pending_area();
    END;
    /
```

ALL ABOVE GROUPS AND PLANS CAN BE CREATED IN ONE PENDING AREA ALSO

```
BEGIN
        dbms_resource_manager.create_pending_area();
        :
        :
        dbms_resource_manager.submit_pending_area();
END;
```

- Create ROLE

SQL> CREATE ROLE ADHOC_RPT_USERS NOT IDENTIFIED;
SQL> GRANT ALTER SESSION TO ADHOC_RPT_USERS;
SQL> GRANT CONNECT TO ADHOC_RPT_USERS;
SQL> GRANT RESOURCE TO ADHOC_RPT_USERS;
SQL> GRANT ADHOC_RPT_USERS TO BI;
SQL> ALTER USER "BI" DEFAULT ROLE ALL;
SQL> GRANT ADHOC_RPT_USERS TO SCOTT;
SQL> ALTER USER SCOTT DEFAULT ROLE ALL;

- Grant GRANT_SWITCH_CONSUMNER_GROUP

User can switch consumer group only if grant_switch_consumer_group granted to it either directly or through role.

```
BEGIN
        dbms_resource_manager_privs.grant_switch_consumer_group(
        grantee_name => 'ADHOC_RPT_USERS',
        consumer_group => 'ADHOC_RPT_GROUP',
        grant_option => FALSE
        );
END;
/
BEGIN
        dbms_resource_manager_privs.grant_switch_consumer_group(
        grantee_name => 'BI',
        consumer_group => 'BATCH_PROCESS_GROUP',
        grant_option => FALSE
        );
END;
/
BEGIN
        dbms_resource_manager_privs.grant_switch_consumer_group(
        grantee_name => 'BI',
        consumer_group => 'OBIEE_REPORT_GROUP',
        grant_option => FALSE
        );
END;
/
BEGIN
        dbms_resource_manager_privs.grant_switch_consumer_group(
        grantee_name => 'HR',
        consumer_group => 'OLTP_GROUP',
        grant_option => FALSE
        );
END;
/
```

```
BEGIN
     dbms_resource_manager_privs.grant_switch_consumer_group(
     grantee_name => 'OE',
     consumer_group => 'OLTP_GROUP',
     grant_option => FALSE
     );
END;
/
BEGIN
     dbms_resource_manager_privs.grant_switch_consumer_group(
     grantee_name => 'SH',
     consumer_group => 'BATCH_PROCESS_GROUP',
     grant_option => FALSE
     );
END;
/
BEGIN
     dbms_resource_manager_privs.grant_switch_consumer_group(
     grantee_name => 'PM',
     consumer_group => 'BATCH_PROCESS_GROUP',
     grant_option => FALSE
     );
END;
/
```

- Create Consumer group mappings and set attributes priorities

  Before you enable the Database Resource Manager, you must assign resource consumer groups to users. This can be done manually, or you can provide mappings that enable the database to automatically assign user sessions to consumer groups depending upon session attributes.

  Create Consumer Group Mappings

```
BEGIN
       dbms_resource_manager.clear_pending_area();
       dbms_resource_manager.create_pending_area();
       dbms_resource_manager.set_consumer_group_mapping(
           dbms_resource_manager.oracle_user,
           'BI',
           'ADHOC_RPT_GROUP'
       );
       dbms_resource_manager.set_consumer_group_mapping(
           dbms_resource_manager.oracle_user,
           'SCOTT',
           'ADHOC_RPT_GROUP'
       );
       dbms_resource_manager.set_consumer_group_mapping(
           dbms_resource_manager.oracle_user,
           'HR',
           'OLTP_GROUP'
       );
       dbms_resource_manager.set_consumer_group_mapping(
           dbms_resource_manager.oracle_user,
           'OE',
           'OLTP_GROUP'
       );
```

```
        dbms_resource_manager.set_consumer_group_mapping(
            dbms_resource_manager.oracle_user,
            'SH',
            'BATCH_PROCESS_GROUP'
        );
        dbms_resource_manager.set_consumer_group_mapping(
            dbms_resource_manager.oracle_user,
            'PM',
            'OBIEE_REPORT_GROUP'
        );
        dbms_resource_manager.submit_pending_area();
END;
/
```

Set Consumer Groups attributes Priorities (ORACLE_USER => 2

```
BEGIN
        dbms_resource_manager.clear_pending_area();
        dbms_resource_manager.create_pending_area();
        dbms_resource_manager.set_consumer_group_mapping_pri(
            EXPLICIT => 1,
            ORACLE_USER => 2,
            SERVICE_MODULE_ACTION => 3,
            SERVICE_MODULE => 4,
            MODULE_NAME_ACTION => 5,
            MODULE_NAME => 6,
            SERVICE_NAME => 7,
            CLIENT_PROGRAM => 8,
            CLIENT_OS_USER => 9,
            CLIENT_MACHINE => 10
        );
        dbms_resource_manager.submit_pending_area();
END;
/
```

- Create Oracle Scheduler

Create Programs (ACT_BUS_HOUR_PLAN & ACT_OFF_BUS_HOUR_PLAN)

ACT_BUS_HOUR_PLAN

```
BEGIN
        DBMS_SCHEDULER.CREATE_PROGRAM(
        program_name=>'"SYSTEM"."ACT_BUS_HOUR_PLAN"',
        program_action=>'begin
        execute immediate ''alter system set resource_manager_plan = ''"BUSINESS_HOUR_PLAN"''
        scope=both'';
        end;',
        program_type=>'PLSQL_BLOCK',
        number_of_arguments=>0,
        comments=>'Activate Business Hours Plan at 8:00 AM',
        enabled=>TRUE);
END;
/
```

ACT_OFF_BUS_HOUR_PLAN

```
BEGIN
    DBMS_SCHEDULER.CREATE_PROGRAM(
    program_name=>'"SYSTEM"."ACT_OFF_BUS_HOUR_PLAN"',
    program_action=>'begin
    execute immediate ''alter system set resource_manager_plan =
    '''"OFF_BUSINESS_HOUR_PLAN"''' scope=both'';
    end;',
    program_type=>'PLSQL_BLOCK',
    number_of_arguments=>0,
    comments=>'Activate Off Business Hours Plan at 7:00 PM',
    enabled=>TRUE);
END;
/
```

Create Schedule (Daily 8:00 AM & 7:00 PM)

ACTIVATE_BUS_HOUR_PLAN

```
BEGIN
    sys.dbms_scheduler.create_schedule(
    repeat_interval => 'FREQ=DAILY;BYHOUR=8;BYMINUTE=0;BYSECOND=0',
    start_date => to_timestamp_tz('2011-02-13 America/New_York', 'YYYY-MM-DD TZR'),
    comments => 'Activate Business Hours Resource Manager Plan',
    schedule_name => '"SYSTEM"."ACTIVATE_BUS_HOUR_PLAN"');
END;
/
```

ACTIVATE_OFF_BUS_HOUR_PLAN

```
BEGIN
    sys.dbms_scheduler.create_schedule(
    repeat_interval => 'FREQ=DAILY;BYHOUR=19;BYMINUTE=0;BYSECOND=0',
    start_date => to_timestamp_tz('2011-02-13 America/New_York', 'YYYY-MM-DD TZR'),
    comments => 'Activate Off Business Hours Resource Manager Plan',
    schedule_name => '"SYSTEM"."ACTIVATE_OFF_BUS_HOUR_PLAN"');
END;
/
```

Create Jobs and assign programs jobs class and schedule to jobs

BUS_HOUR_PLAN_JOB

```
BEGIN
    sys.dbms_scheduler.create_job(
    job_name => '"SYSTEM"."BUS_HOUR_PLAN_JOB"',
    program_name => '"SYSTEM"."ACT_BUS_HOUR_PLAN"',
    schedule_name => '"SYSTEM"."ACTIVATE_BUS_HOUR_PLAN"',
    job_class => '"DEFAULT_JOB_CLASS"',
    comments => 'Activate Business Hours Plan at 8:00 AM',
    auto_drop => FALSE,
    enabled => FALSE);
    sys.dbms_scheduler.set_attribute( name => '"SYSTEM"."BUS_HOUR_PLAN_JOB"', attribute =>
    'raise_events', value => dbms_scheduler.job_started + dbms_scheduler.job_succeeded +
    dbms_scheduler.job_failed + dbms_scheduler.job_broken + dbms_scheduler.job_completed +
    dbms_scheduler.job_stopped + dbms_scheduler.job_sch_lim_reached +
    dbms_scheduler.job_disabled + dbms_scheduler.job_chain_stalled);
    sys.dbms_scheduler.set_attribute( name => '"SYSTEM"."BUS_HOUR_PLAN_JOB"', attribute
    => 'logging_level', value => DBMS_SCHEDULER.LOGGING_FULL);
    sys.dbms_scheduler.enable( '"SYSTEM"."BUS_HOUR_PLAN_JOB"' );
END;
/
```

OFF_BUS_HOUR_PLAN_JOB

```
BEGIN
        sys.dbms_scheduler.create_job(
        job_name => '"SYSTEM"."OFF_BUS_HOUR_PLAN_JOB"',
        program_name => '"SYSTEM"."ACT_OFF_BUS_HOUR_PLAN"',
        schedule_name => '"SYSTEM"."ACTIVATE_OFF_BUS_HOUR_PLAN"',
        job_class => '"DEFAULT_JOB_CLASS"',
        comments => 'Activate Off Business Hours Plan at 7:00 PM',
        auto_drop => FALSE,
        enabled => FALSE);
        sys.dbms_scheduler.set_attribute( name => '"SYSTEM"."OFF_BUS_HOUR_PLAN_JOB"',
        attribute => 'raise_events', value => dbms_scheduler.job_started +
        dbms_scheduler.job_succeeded + dbms_scheduler.job_failed + dbms_scheduler.job_broken
        + dbms_scheduler.job_completed + dbms_scheduler.job_stopped +
        dbms_scheduler.job_sch_lim_reached + dbms_scheduler.job_disabled +
        dbms_scheduler.job_chain_stalled);
        sys.dbms_scheduler.set_attribute( name => '"SYSTEM"."OFF_BUS_HOUR_PLAN_JOB"',
        attribute => 'logging_level', value => DBMS_SCHEDULER.LOGGING_FULL);
        sys.dbms_scheduler.enable( '"SYSTEM"."OFF_BUS_HOUR_PLAN_JOB"' );
END;
/
```

7.12 Manage Schema Objects

All Schema objects are managed from OEM GRID Control Administration Page. Navigate through all the sections, links on this page, and create various objects

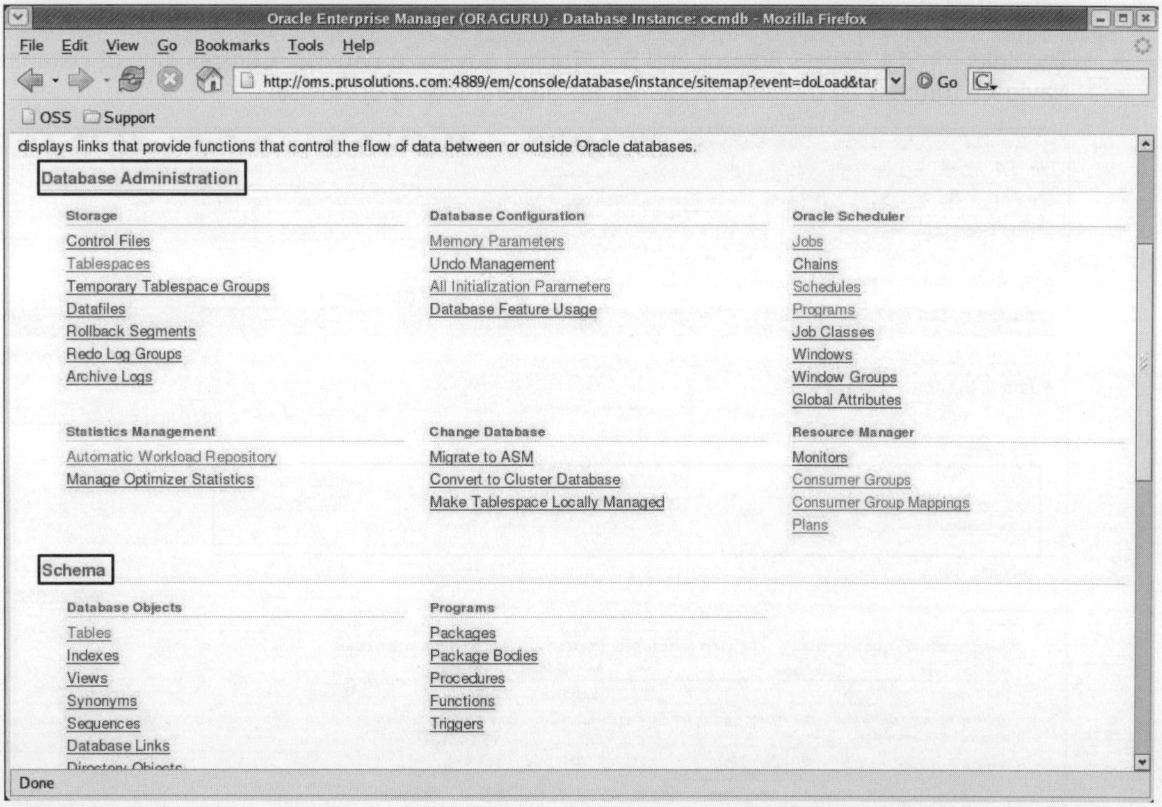

7.13 SQL Access Advisor and SQL Tuning Advisor

- On Database Home Page in Related Links Section, click Advisor Central link

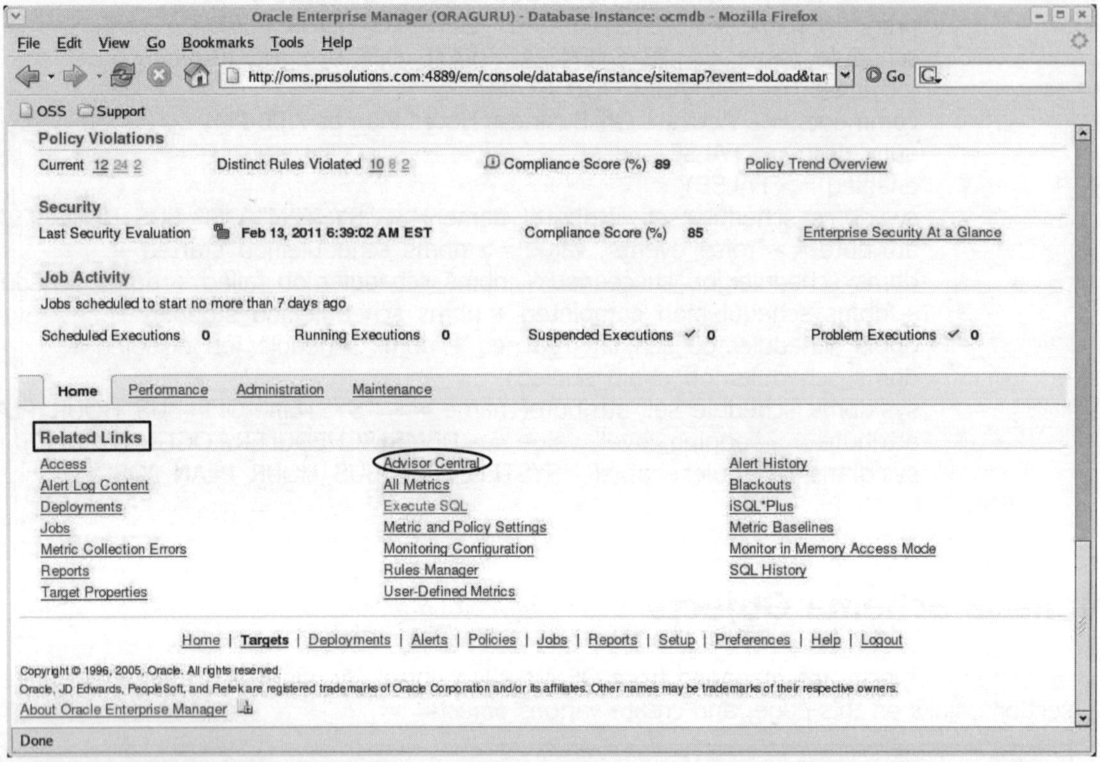

- The links for SQL Access Advisor and SQL Tuning Advisor on Advisor Central Page of Database Instance. Navigate through all the links below to get understanding of Advisor

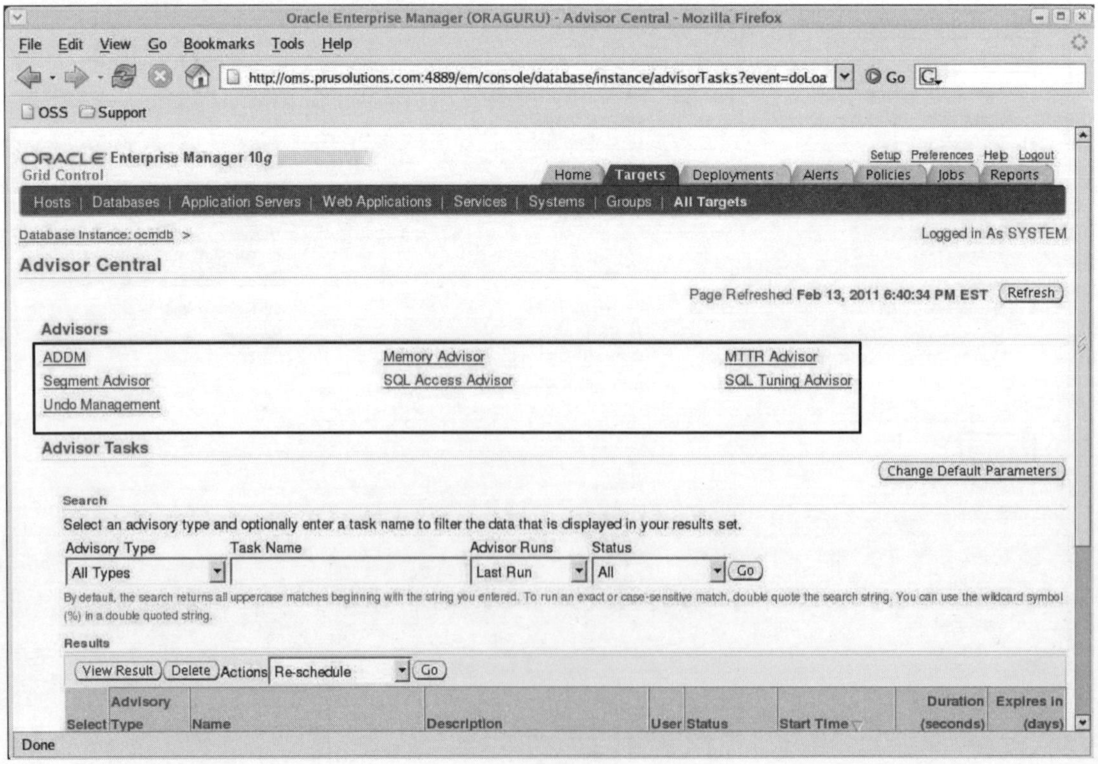

- SQL Tuning sets using Oracle's SQL Developer

  i. Connect as SYSTEM.

  ii. Create Tuning Task.

```
SQL> DECLARE
        my_task_name      VARCHAR2 (30);
        my_sqltext     CLOB;
     BEGIN
        my_sqltext  :=  'select * from sales where prod_id ="136'";
        my_task_name  :=
           DBMS_SQLTUNE.CREATE_TUNING_TASK  (
              sql_text               =>  my_sqltext,
              user_name              =>  'SH',
              scope                  =>  'COMPREHENSIVE',
              time_limit             =>  900,
              task_name              =>  'sh_sales_sqltune_1',
              description            =>  'Task to tune a query on a SALES Query');
     END;
     /
```

  iii. Query to see all Tuning Tasks

```
SQL> SELECT task_name
     FROM DBA_ADVISOR_LOG
     WHERE OWNER = 'SYSTEM';
```

  iv. Perform Tuning

```
SQL> BEGIN
        DBMS_SQLTUNE.EXECUTE_TUNING_TASK  (task_name  =>  'sh_sales_sqltune_1');
     END;
     /
```

  v. Get Output of the Query Tuning

```
SQL>  SELECT  DBMS_SQLTUNE.REPORT_TUNING_TASK
     ('sh_sales_sqltune_1')  FROM  DUAL;
```

  vi. Accept Profile if Suggested by Oracle

```
SQL>  EXECUTE  dbms_sqltune.accept_sql_profile(task_name
     =>'sh_sales_sqltune_1',  replace  =>  TRUE);
```

  vii. Drop the Tuning Task

```
SQL>BEGIN
        DBMS_SQLTUNE.drop_TUNING_TASK ('sh_sales_sqltune_1');
     END;
     /
```

  viii. Dropping a profile

```
SQL>  SELECT  *  FROM  dba_profiles;
SQL>  BEGIN
         DBMS_SQLTUNE.drop_sql_profile ('SYS_SQLPROF_014baffb92768000');
      END;
      /
```

- Few Tips for Tuning SQL

  - **Scenario 1**

In large Data Warehouse, where there are FACT tables with hundreds of columns and millions of rows. If you want to select only few **NOT NULL** columns from that table then you should have index on all columns in where clause and select list.

When select is executed on these columns Oracle will retrieve data only from Index and it will not visit table. The number of blocks on index will be far less than the number of blocks on table and query will be much faster.

Below is the example for above test We will create a new table SH.PROD_SALES by combining two tables in SH schema PRODUCTS and SALES_TRANSACTIONS_EXT the join will be between PROD_ID and indexes.

i. Create a new table PROD_SALES

```
SQL> CREATE TABLE sh.prod_sales
     TABLESPACE example AS
     SELECT p.prod_id, p.prod_name, p.prod_desc, p.prod_subcategory,
            p.prod_subcategory_id, p.prod_subcategory_desc, p.prod_category,
            p.prod_category_id, p.prod_category_desc, p.prod_weight_class,
            p.prod_unit_of_measure, p.prod_pack_size, p.supplier_id, p.prod_status,
            p.prod_list_price, p.prod_min_price, p.prod_total, p.prod_total_id,
            p.prod_src_id, p.prod_eff_from, p.prod_eff_to, p.prod_valid, s.cust_id,
            s.time_id, s.channel_id, s.promo_id, s.quantity_sold, s.amount_sold,
            s.unit_cost, s.unit_price
     FROM   sh.products p, sh.sales_transactions_ext s
     WHERE  p.prod_id = s.prod_id
     /
```

ii. Create an index on column PROD_ID

```
SQL> CREATE INDEX sh.prod_sales_idx1 ON sh.prod_sales (prod_id)
     TABLESPACE example COMPUTE STATISTICS
     /
```

iii. Analyze table PROD_SALES

```
SQL> BEGIN
            SYS.DBMS_STATS.GATHER_TABLE_STATS (
            OwnName        => 'SH'
            ,TabName       => 'PROD_SALES'
            ,Method_Opt        => 'FOR ALL INDEXED COLUMNS SIZE AUTO '
            ,Degree        => 2
            ,Cascade       => TRUE
            ,No_Invalidate     => FALSE);
     END;
     /
```

iv. Set AUTO TRACE and LINESIZE

```
SQL> set autotrace traceonly
SQL> set linesize 200
```

v. Execute the select statement below and check the execution plan below

```
SQL> SELECT prod_id, quantity_sold, amount_sold
     FROM  sh.prod_sales
     WHERE prod_id IN ('30', '40');
55910 rows selected.
```

Execution Plan

```
----------------------------------------------------------
Plan hash value: 1455011100

-----------------------------------------------------------------------------------------------
-
| Id  | Operation                    | Name              | Rows  | Bytes | Cost (%CPU)| Time     |
-----------------------------------------------------------------------------------------------
-
|   0 | SELECT STATEMENT             |                   | 24956 |   731K|   823   (1)| 00:00:10 |
|   1 |  INLIST ITERATOR             |                   |       |       |            |          |
|   2 |   TABLE ACCESS BY INDEX ROWID| PROD_SALES        | 24956 |   731K|   823   (1)|
00:00:10 |
|*  3 |    INDEX RANGE SCAN          | PROD_SALES_IDX1   | 24956 |       |    54   (0)| 00:00:01 |
-----------------------------------------------------------------------------------------------
-

Predicate Information (identified by operation id):
---------------------------------------------------

   3 - access("PROD_ID"=30 OR "PROD_ID"=40)
```

Statistics

```
----------------------------------------------------------
          1  recursive calls
          0  db block gets
       9049  consistent gets
          0  physical reads
          0  redo size
     767257  bytes sent via SQL*Net to client
      41382  bytes received via SQL*Net from client
       3729  SQL*Net roundtrips to/from client
          0  sorts (memory)
          0  sorts (disk)
      55910  rows processed
```

vi. Create one more index on two columns in select list and one column in where clause of select statement

```
SQL> CREATE INDEX sh.prod_sales_idx2 ON sh.prod_sales
     (prod_id,quantity_sold,amount_sold)
     TABLESPACE example COMPUTE STATISTICS
     /
```

vii. Analyze table PROD_SALES

```
SQL> BEGIN
              SYS.DBMS_STATS.GATHER_TABLE_STATS (
              OwnName        => 'SH'
              ,TabName       => 'PROD_SALES'
              ,Method_Opt    => 'FOR ALL INDEXED COLUMNS SIZE AUTO '
              ,Degree        => 2
              ,Cascade       => TRUE
              ,No_Invalidate => FALSE);
     END;
      /
```

viii. Execute the same select statement again and check the execution plan below

```
SQL> SELECT prod_id, quantity_sold, amount_sold
       FROM  sh.prod_sales
      WHERE  prod_id IN ('30', '40');

55910 rows selected.
```

Execution Plan

```
Plan hash value: 2061759593

-------------------------------------------------------------------------------
| Id | Operation          | Name              | Rows  | Bytes | Cost (%CPU)| Time     |
-------------------------------------------------------------------------------
|  0 | SELECT STATEMENT   |                   | 57652 |  675K|   180  (2)| 00:00:03 |
|  1 |  INLIST ITERATOR   |                   |       |      |           |          |
|* 2 |   INDEX RANGE SCAN | PROD_SALES_IDX2   | 57652 |  675K|   180  (2)| 00:00:03 |
-------------------------------------------------------------------------------

Predicate Information (identified by operation id):
---------------------------------------------------

  2 - access("PROD_ID"=30 OR "PROD_ID"=40)
```

Statistics

```
----------------------------------------------------------
        1  recursive calls
        0  db block gets
     3887  consistent gets
        2  physical reads
        0  redo size
   753845  bytes sent via SQL*Net to client
    41382  bytes received via SQL*Net from client
     3729  SQL*Net roundtrips to/from client
        0  sorts (memory)
        0  sorts (disk)
    55910  rows processed
```

ix. **Inference** : After creating second index the query only uses index to retrieve data table is NOT accessed and cost is very less

- **Scenario 2**

  Avoid using "NOT IN" and "<>" in where clause , Oracle never uses indexes when where condition is one of above, Instead of that create a lookup table for that where clause and use not in lookup table.

  i. Create index on table PROD_SALES column PROD_CATEGORY

```
SQL> set autotrace off

SQL> CREATE INDEX sh.prod_sales_idx3
     ON sh.prod_sales (prod_category)
     TABLESPACE example
     COMPUTE STATISTICS;
```

```
SQL> BEGIN
            SYS.DBMS_STATS.GATHER_TABLE_STATS (
            OwnName        => 'SH'
            ,TabName       => 'PROD_SALES'
            ,Method_Opt    => 'FOR ALL INDEXED COLUMNS SIZE AUTO '
            ,Degree        => 2
            ,Cascade       => TRUE
            ,No_Invalidate => FALSE);
     END;
     /
```

ii. Execute the select statement below and check the execution plan below

```
SQL> set autotrace traceonly
SQL> set linesize 200
SQL> SELECT *
     FROM prod_sales
     WHERE prod_category NOT IN
     ('Software/Other', 'Peripherals and Accessories', 'Electronics');

110862 rows selected.

Execution Plan
----------------------------------------------------------
Plan hash value: 2351929797
----------------------------------------------------------------------------------
| Id | Operation         | Name       | Rows | Bytes | Cost (%CPU)| Time     |
----------------------------------------------------------------------------------
|  0 | SELECT STATEMENT  |            | 310K|   61M|  6158   (2)| 00:01:14 |
|* 1 | TABLE ACCESS FULL| PROD_SALES |  310K|   61M|  6158   (2)| 00:01:14 |
----------------------------------------------------------------------------------

Predicate Information (identified by operation id):
---------------------------------------------------
   1 - filter("PROD_CATEGORY"<>'Software/Other' AND
          "PROD_CATEGORY"<>'Peripherals and Accessories' AND
          "PROD_CATEGORY"<>'Electronics')
Statistics
----------------------------------------------------------
        1   recursive calls
        0   db block gets
    34621   consistent gets
    20077   physical reads
        0   redo size
  2714592   bytes sent via SQL*Net to client
    81675   bytes received via SQL*Net from client
     7392   SQL*Net roundtrips to/from client
        0   sorts (memory)
        0   sorts (disk)
   110862   rows processed
```

iii. Create lookup table on column prod_category

```
SQL> create table prod_category_lkp
     TABLESPACE example
     as select distinct prod_category from prod_sales
     /
```

```
SQL> BEGIN
             SYS.DBMS_STATS.GATHER_TABLE_STATS (
             OwnName        => 'SH'
             ,TabName       => 'PROD_CATEGORY_LKP'
             ,Method_Opt    => 'FOR ALL INDEXED COLUMNS SIZE AUTO '
             ,Degree        => 2
             ,Cascade       => TRUE
             ,No_Invalidate => FALSE);
     END;
     /
```

iv. Execute the similar modified select statement again and check the execution plan below

```
SQL> SELECT *
     FROM prod_sales
     WHERE prod_category IN
          (SELECT prod_category
          FROM prod_category_lkp
          WHERE prod_category NOT IN
               ('Software/Other',
               'Peripherals and Accessories',
               'Electronics'))
     /

110862 rows selected.

Execution Plan
----------------------------------------------------------
Plan hash value: 2501610635

-----------------------------------------------------------------------------------------------
---
| Id  | Operation                    | Name              | Rows  | Bytes | Cost (%CPU)| Time     |
-----------------------------------------------------------------------------------------------
---
|   0 | SELECT STATEMENT             |                   |  158K|   33M|  5264   (1)| 00:01:04 |
|   1 |  TABLE ACCESS BY INDEX ROWID| PROD_SALES        | 62000 |   12M|  2630   (1)|
00:00:32 |
|   2 |   NESTED LOOPS               |                   |  158K|   33M|  5264   (1)| 00:01:04 |
|   3 |    SORT UNIQUE               |                   |     3 |   42 |     3   (0)| 00:00:01 |
|*  4 |     TABLE ACCESS FULL        | PROD_CATEGORY_LKP |     3 |   42 |     3   (0)| 00:00:01 |
|*  5 |    INDEX RANGE SCAN          | PROD_SALES_IDX3   | 62000 |       |   738   (1)| 00:00:09 |
-----------------------------------------------------------------------------------------------
---

Predicate Information (identified by operation id):
---------------------------------------------------

   4 - filter("PROD_CATEGORY"<>'Software/Other' AND "PROD_CATEGORY"<>'Peripherals and
              Accessories' AND "PROD_CATEGORY"<>'Electronics')
   5 - access("PROD_CATEGORY"="PROD_CATEGORY")
       filter("PROD_CATEGORY"<>'Software/Other' AND "PROD_CATEGORY"<>'Peripherals and
              Accessories' AND "PROD_CATEGORY"<>'Electronics')
```

Statistics

```
       175  recursive calls
         0  db block gets
     17854  consistent gets
         0  physical reads
         0  redo size
   2714395  bytes sent via SQL*Net to client
     81675  bytes received via SQL*Net from client
      7392  SQL*Net roundtrips to/from client
         5  sorts (memory)
         0  sorts (disk)
    110862  rows processed
```

- **Scenario 3**

  If the table column data type is DATE, don't pass TIMESTAMP data type in where clause. Oracle will never use index it will always do FTS, instead of that either pass value as DATE data type in where clause or change table column to TIMESTAMP data type.

- **Scenario 4**

  Where using LIKE in where clause NEVER use % in beginning of where condition. Oracle will not use index. Always put some value in beginning then use %.

  ename like '%CO%' ; — Index will not be used.

  ename like 'SC%'; — Index will be used.

- **SQL Hints**

  In Data Warehouse two sql hints are very useful /*+ DRIVING_SITE */ and /*+ PUSH_SUBQ */

- Index Monitoring

  Monitor all the indexes in database over the period and drop the indexes that are not used

  ```
  SQL> ALTER INDEX <schema_name>.<index_name> MONITORING USAGE;
  ```

  Query to find which indexes are being used

  ```
  SQL> SELECT u.NAME,
              io.NAME,
              to.NAME,
              DECODE (BITAND (i.flags, 65536), 0, 'NO', 'YES') INDEX_MONITORED,
              DECODE (BITAND (ou.flags, 1), 0, 'NO', 'YES') INDEX_USED,
              ou.start_monitoring,
              ou.end_monitoring
       FROM SYS.obj$ io,
              SYS.obj$ to,
              SYS.user$ u,
              SYS.ind$ i,
              SYS.object_usage ou
       WHERE  i.obj# = ou.obj#
       AND    io.obj# = ou.obj#
       AND    to.obj# = i.bo#
       AND    u.user# = io.owner#;
  ```

7.14 Gather Optimizer Statistics

Optimizer statistics are a collection of data that describes more details about the database and the objects in the database. These statistics are used by the query optimizer to choose the best execution plan for each SQL statement.

- Optimizer Statistics using SQLPLUS
  - Manually statistics can be gathered using DBMS_STATS Package

    i. Gather Table Statistics

```
SQL> BEGIN
     SYS.DBMS_STATS.GATHER_TABLE_STATS (
           OwnName          => 'SH',
           TabName          => 'SALES',
           Method_Opt       => 'FOR ALL INDEXED COLUMNS SIZE AUTO ',
           Degree           => 4,
           Cascade          => TRUE,
           No_Invalidate    => FALSE);
     END;
     /
```

    ii. Gather Schema Statistics

```
SQL> BEGIN
     SYS.DBMS_STATS.GATHER_SCHEMA_STATS  (
           OwnName          =>  'SH',
           Granularity      =>  'DEFAULT',
           Options          =>  'GATHER STALE',
           Gather_Temp      =>  FALSE,
           Method_Opt       =>  'FOR ALL INDEXED COLUMNS SIZE AUTO ',
           Degree           =>  4,
           Cascade          =>  TRUE,
           No_Invalidate    =>  FALSE);
     END;
     /
```

    iii. Gather Database Statistics

```
SQL> BEGIN
     SYS.DBMS_STATS.GATHER_DATABASE_STATS  (
           Granularity      =>  'OCMDB',
           Options          =>  'GATHER STALE',
           Gather_Temp      =>  FALSE,
           Gather_Sys       =>  FALSE,
           Method_Opt       =>  'FOR ALL INDEXED COLUMNS SIZE AUTO ',
           Degree           =>  4,
           Cascade          =>  TRUE,
           No_Invalidate    =>  FALSE);
     END;
     /
```

    iv. Delete Table Statistics

```
SQL> BEGIN
       DBMS_STATS.DELETE_TABLE_STATS ('SH', 'SALES');
     END;
     /
```

v. Lock Table Statistics

```
SQL> BEGIN
         DBMS_STATS.LOCK_TABLE_STATS ('SH', 'SALES');
     END;
     /
```

- Practice all other DBMS_STATS commands from Oracle Documentation

■ Optimizer Statistics can be managed through Oracle's OEM Grid Control page

Navigate through all the sections of the page mentioned below

- On Database Administration Page in Statistics Management Section, click Manage Optimizer Statistics. It will take to Manage Optimizer Statistics Page.

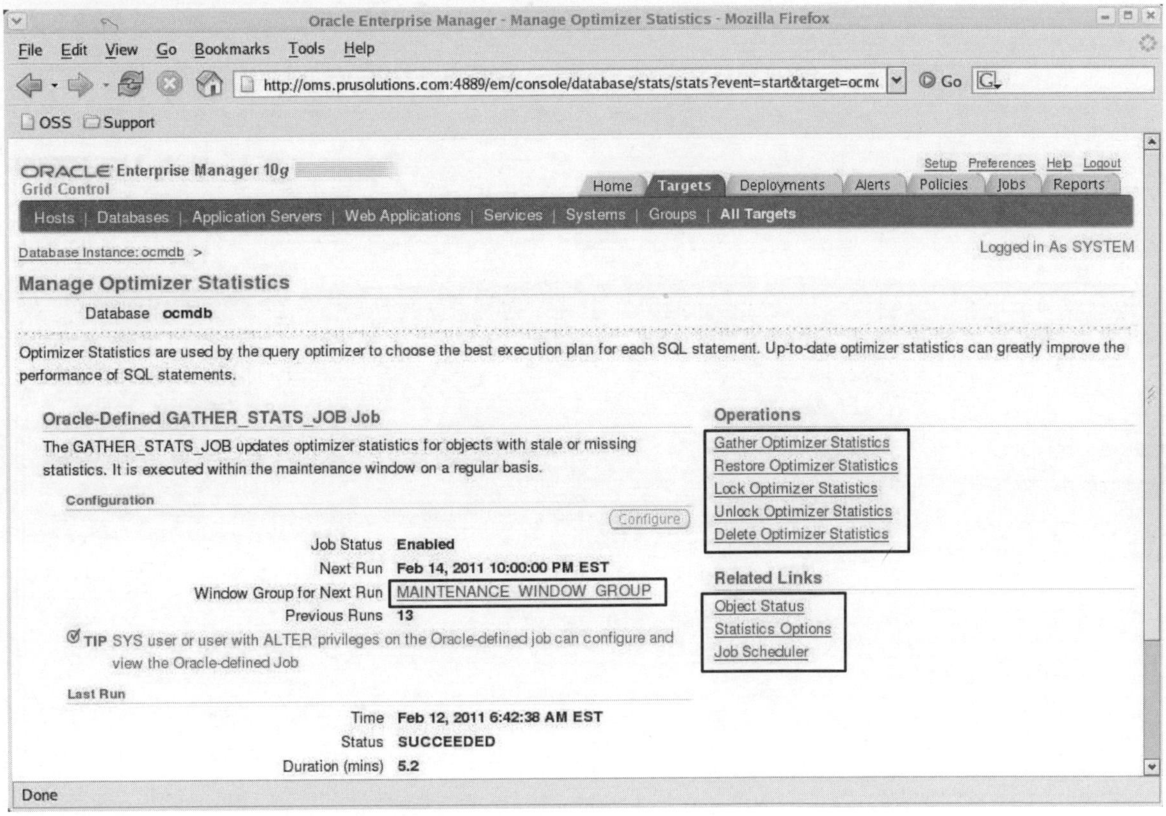

8

Real Application Clusters

- Install Oracle Clusterware
- Install the Oracle Database 10g software
- Implement ASM failure groups
- Create and manage as ASM instance
- Create and manage ASM disk groups
- Configure ASM for the shared disks, and create a clustered database
- Configure archiving
- Configure Services with a preferred instance and an available instance

8.1 Start machines CRS1 and CRS2

- Shutdown machines OMS, OCM and OEM and Start machines CRS1and CRS2 and ftp Oracle Software mentioned below to crs1 and crs2 machines.
- Ftp and unzip Oracle 10g Database software and JDK

Start "crs1,crs2" machines on VMware, logon to oracle user then create folder /u01/software.

ftp Oracle 10g Database software and JDK mentioned below to crs1,crs2 Linux guest machine from Windows host. Unzip the oracle database 10g software files.

10201_clusterware_linux32.zip
10201_database_linux32.zip
oracleasmlib-2.0.2-1.i386.rpm

Sometimes while creating zip file some of the oracle install files becomes read only. Using user oracle on Linux change the permission to read, write, execute (chmod 755 <filename>) on those files if you get any error during install of any Oracle software on VMware.

8.2 OS Configuration checks to install Oracle Clusterware Software

- Following checks are to be made both on crs1 and crs2 nodes
- Check hosts names, files option should be the first

```
# cat /etc/nsswitch.conf | grep hosts
make sure it has file option first then dns
```

- Check Kernel Parameters are set properly (Converted into kb, mb, gb to remember easily)

  - **/etc/sysctl.conf**

```
kernel.shmall = 2097152                    # (2mb)
kernel.shmmax = 2147483648                 # (2g)
kernel.shmmni = 4096                       # (4k)
kernel.sem = 250 32000 100 128
fs.file-max = 65536                        # (64k)
net.ipv4.ip_local_port_range = 1024 65000
net.core.rmem_default = 1048576            # (1mb)
net.core.rmem_max = 1048576                # (1mb)
net.core.wmem_default = 262144             # (256k)
net.core.wmem_max = 262144                 # (256k)
```

  - **/etc/security/limits.conf**

```
oracle    soft   nproc 2047
oracle    hard   nproc 16384
oracle    soft   nofile 1024
oracle    hard   nofile 65536
```

  - **/etc/pam.d/login**

```
session   required   /lib/security/pam_limits.so
session   required   pam_limits.so
```

- **/etc/profile**

```
if [ $USER = "oracle" ]; then
        if [ $SHELL = "/bin/ksh" ]; then
                ulimit -p 16384
                ulimit -n 65536
        else
                ulimit -u 16384 -n 65536
        fi
fi
```

- Check /etc/hosts for following values are set

```
127.0.0.1          localhost
# Oracle Database ip addresses
192.168.2.121      ocm.prusolutions.com            ocm
# Oracle Enterprise Manager ip addresses
192.168.2.161      oem.prusolutions.com            oem
192.168.2.162      oms.prusolutions.com            oms
# Oracle RAC ip addresses
192.168.2.131      crs1.prusolutions.com           crs1
192.168.2.31       crs1-vip.prusolutions.com       crs1-vip
10.10.10.31        crs1-priv.prusolutions.com      crs1-priv
192.162.2.132      crs2.prusolutions.com           crs2
192.168.2.32       crs2-vip.prusolutions.com       crs2-vip
10.10.10.32        crs2-priv.prusolutions.com      crs2-priv
# Oracle RAC Dataguard ip addresses
192.168.2.141      crsdg1.prusolutions.com         crsdg1
192.168.2.41       crsdg1-vip.prusolutions.com     crsdg1-vip
10.10.10.41        crsdg1-priv.prusolutions.com    crsdg1-priv
192.162.2.142      crsdg2.prusolutions.com         crsdg2
192.168.2.42       crsdg2-vip.prusolutions.com     crsdg2-vip
10.10.10.42        crsdg2-priv.prusolutions.com    crsdg2-priv
```

- Check user oracle and nobody for software Install

```
# cat /etc/passwd
```

- Check following parameters swap should be 3G, memory 1G and temp at least 512M

```
# grep MemTotal /proc/meminfo
# grep SwapTotal /proc/meminfo
# df -k /tmp
```

- Check Linux required packages are installed

```
binutils-2.15.92.0.2-21
compat-db-4.1.25-9
compat-libstdc++-33-3.2.3-47.3
gcc-3.4.6-3.1
gcc-c++-3.4.6-3.1
glibc-2.3.4-2.25
glibc-common-2.3.4-2.25
gnome-libs-1.4.1.2.90-44.2
libstdc++-3.4.6-3.1
```

libstdc++-devel-3.4.6-3.1
make-3.80-6.EL4
pdksh-5.2.14-30.3
sysstat-5.0.5-11.rhel4
xscreensaver-4.18-5.rhel4.12
setarch-1.6-1
libaio-0.3.105-2.i386.rpm
openmotif21-2.1.30-11.RHEL4.6.i386.rpm

If the different version of Linux is installed then packages may be as mentioned below or combination of both

binutils-2.15.92.0.2-13.EL4
compat-db-4.1.25-9
compat-libstdc++-296-2.96-132.7.2
control-center-2.8.0-12
gcc-3.4.3-22.1.EL4
gcc-c++-3.4.3-22.1.EL44
glibc-2.3.4-2.9
glibc-common-2.3.4-2.9
gnome-libs-1.4.1.2.90-44.1
libstdc++-3.4.3-22.1
libstdc++-devel-3.4.3-22.1
make-3.80-5
pdksh-5.2.14-30
sysstat-5.0.5-1
xscreensaver-4.18-5.rhel4.2
setarch-1.6-1
libaio-0.3.105-2.i386.rpm
openmotif21-2.1.30-11.RHEL4.6.i386.rpm

- Check iptables are disabled on both nodes

  [root@crs2 oracle]# system-config-services

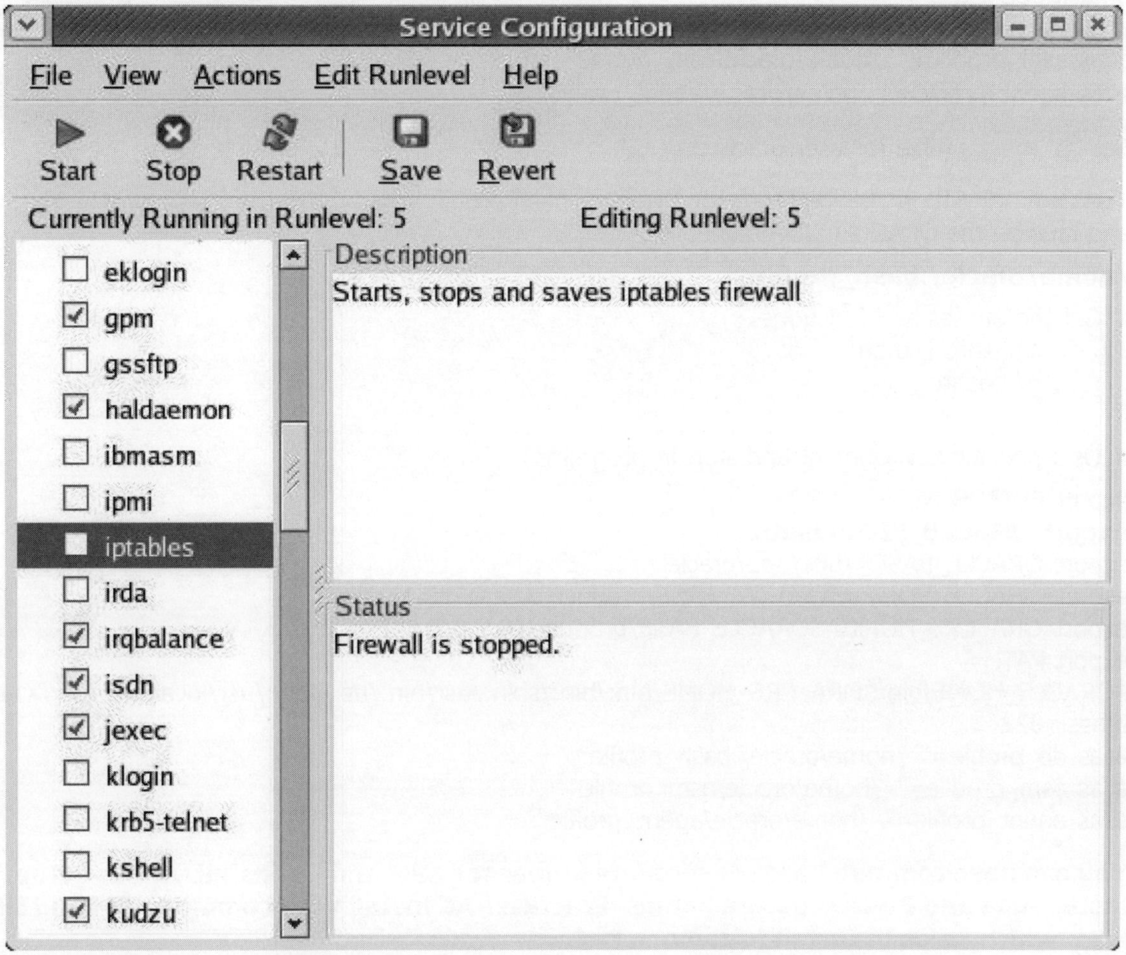

8.3 Remaining OS Configuration on both nodes crs1, crs2

- Set up .bash_profile for user oracle on crs1

  Database name crsdb. The ORACLE_SID name on crs1 node will be crsdb1. The ORACLE_HOME, ORA_CRS_HOME path can be customized to any Unix directory.

  The setup of all 3 profile files mentioned below on both crs1 and crs2 should not take more than 5 minutes.

  - You can create these profile files in vi editor when you are practicing other Oracle's OEM Grid install

  /home/oracle/.bash_profile

```
# Get the aliases and functions
if [ -f ~/.bashrc ]; then
        . ~/.bashrc
fi

# User specific environment and startup programs
export EDITOR=vi
export ORACLE_SID=crsdb1
export ORACLE_BASE=/u01/app/oracle
export ORACLE_HOME=$ORACLE_BASE/product/10.2.0/db_1
export ORA_CRS_HOME=$ORACLE_BASE/product/10.2.0/crs_1
```

```
export PATH=$ORACLE_HOME/bin:$ORA_CRS_HOME/bin:/bin:/sbin:/usr/bin:/usr/sbin:/usr/local/bin:/usr/
X11R6/bin
umask 022
alias db_profile=". /home/oracle/.bash_profile"
alias asm_prodile=". /home/oracle/asm_profile"
alias agent_profile=". /home/oracle/agent_profile"
```

- Set up .bash_profile for user oracle on crs2

  The ORACLE_SID is changed to crsdb2 rest of .bash profile is same, ftp the .bash_profile from crs1 to crs2 and change the ORACLE_SID name.

  /home/oracle/.bash_profile

```
# Get the aliases and functions
if [ -f ~/.bashrc ]; then
      . ~/.bashrc
fi

# User specific environment and startup programs

export EDITOR=vi
export ORACLE_SID=crsdb2
export ORACLE_BASE=/u01/app/oracle
export ORACLE_HOME=$ORACLE_BASE/product/10.2.0/db_1
export ORA_CRS_HOME=$ORACLE_BASE/product/10.2.0/crs_1
export PATH=
$ORACLE_HOME/bin:$ORA_CRS_HOME/bin:/bin:/sbin:/usr/bin:/usr/sbin:/usr/local/bin:/usr/X11R6/bin
umask 022
alias db_profile=". /home/oracle/.bash_profile"
alias asm_prodile=". /home/oracle/asm_profile"
alias agent_profile=". /home/oracle/agent_profile"
```

You can have common home or separate homes for ASM and DB install. In this setup, we will install ASM and DB in separate homes. Practice RAC install with common ASM and DB home also, which helps to install RAC much faster.

- Set up asm_profile on crs1

  Copy .bash_profile to asm_profile and make OARCLE_HOME and ORACLE_SID changes as mentioned below.

  /home/oracle/asm_profile (Permission on file chmod 755 asm_profile)

```
# Get the aliases and functions
if [ -f ~/.bashrc ]; then
      . ~/.bashrc
fi

# User specific environment and startup programs

export EDITOR=vi
export ORACLE_SID=+ASM1
export ORACLE_BASE=/u01/app/oracle
export ORACLE_HOME=$ORACLE_BASE/product/10.2.0/asm_1
export ORA_CRS_HOME=$ORACLE_BASE/product/10.2.0/crs_1
export DBCA_RAW_CONFIG=$ORACLE_BASE/oradata/crsdb
export PATH=$ORACLE_HOME/bin:$ORA_CRS_HOME/bin:/bin:/sbin:/usr/bin:/usr/sbin:/usr/local/bin:/usr/
X11R6/bin
umask 022
alias db_profile=". /home/oracle/.bash_profile"
alias asm_prodile=". /home/oracle/asm_profile"
alias agent_profile=". /home/oracle/agent_profile"
```

- Set up asm_profile on crs2

/home/oracle/asm_profile (Permission on file chmod 755 asm_profile)

```
# Get the aliases and functions
if [ -f ~/.bashrc ]; then
        . ~/.bashrc
fi
# User specific environment and startup programs
export EDITOR=vi
export ORACLE_SID=+ASM2
export ORACLE_BASE=/u01/app/oracle
export ORACLE_HOME=$ORACLE_BASE/product/10.2.0/asm_1
export ORA_CRS_HOME=$ORACLE_BASE/product/10.2.0/crs_1
export DBCA_RAW_CONFIG=$ORACLE_BASE/oradata/crsdb
export PATH=$ORACLE_HOME/bin:$ORA_CRS_HOME/bin:/bin:/sbin:/usr/bin:/usr/sbin:/usr/local/bin:/usr/
X11R6/bin
umask 022
alias db_profile=". /home/oracle/.bash_profile"
alias asm_prodile=". /home/oracle/asm_profile"
alias agent_profile=". /home/oracle/agent_profile"
```

- Set up agent_profile on both crs1 and crs2

/home/oracle/agent_profile (Permission on file chmod 755 agent_profile)

Copy .bash_profile to agent_profile and make OARCLE_HOME change as mentioned below)

```
# agent_profile
# Get the aliases and functions
if [ -f ~/.bashrc ]; then
        . ~/.bashrc
fi
# User specific environment and startup programs
export EDITOR=vi
export ORACLE_BASE=/u01/app/oracle
export ORACLE_HOME=$ORACLE_BASE/product/10.2.0/agent10g
export PATH=$ORACLE_HOME/bin:/bin:/sbin:/usr/bin:/usr/sbin:/usr/local/bin:/usr/X11R6/bin
umask 022
alias db_profile=". /home/oracle/.bash_profile"
alias asm_prodile=". /home/oracle/asm_profile"
alias agent_profile=". /home/oracle/agent_profile"
```

- To change environment variable use following

```
$. /home/oracle/.bash_profile
$. /home/oracle/agent_profile
$. /home/oracle/asm_profile
$ echo $ORACLE_HOME
```

- Make following directories for Oracle Install on both nodes crs1 and crs2

```
[oracle@crs1 ~]$ . /home/oracle/agent_profile
[oracle@crs1 ~]$ mkdir -p $ORACLE_HOME
[oracle@crs1 ~]$ . /home/oracle/asm_profile
[oracle@crs1 ~]$ mkdir -p $ORACLE_HOME
[oracle@crs1 ~]$ . /home/oracle/.bash_profile
```

```
[oracle@crs1 ~]$ mkdir -p $ORACLE_HOME
[oracle@crs1 ~]$ mkdir –p $ORA_CRS_HOME
[oracle@crs1 ~]$ mkdir –p $ORA_CRS_HOME
[oracle@crs1 ~]$ mkdir –p $ORACLE_BASE/admin
[oracle@crs1 ~]$ mkdir –p $ORACLE_BASE/oradata/crsdb
[oracle@crs1 ~]$ mkdir -p $ORACLE_BASE/admin/crsdb/adump
[oracle@crs1 ~]$ mkdir -p $ORACLE_BASE/admin/crsdb/bdump
[oracle@crs1 ~]$ mkdir -p $ORACLE_BASE/admin/crsdb/cdump
[oracle@crs1 ~]$ mkdir -p $ORACLE_BASE/admin/crsdb/udump
[oracle@crs1 ~]$ mkdir -p $ORACLE_BASE/admin/crsdb/scripts
```

- Create /dev/timedev

  As root user Device on each node for performance for gettimeofday() calls

  # mknod /dev/timedev c 15 0

  # chmod 644/dev/timedev

- Install following package from Linux cdrom iso image.

  # rpm -Uvh libaio-0.3.105-2.i386.rpm

  # rpm -Uvh openmotif21-2.1.30-11.RHEL4.6.i386.rpm

- Install Oracle ASM Libraries from Oracle Download

  # rpm -Uvh oracleasmlib-2.0.2-1.i386.rpm

- Install jdk-6u21-linux-i586-rpm.bin on crs1, crs2 as root user

  # /u01/software/jdk/jdk-6u21-linux-i586-rpm.bin

- Format disk partitions as root user to be used by ocr, voting disk and ASM

  - Logon as root user on crs1 and list disks partition details

    ```
    [root@crs1 ~]# fdisk -l | grep -i disk
    Disk /dev/sdb doesn't contain a valid partition table
    Disk /dev/sdc doesn't contain a valid partition table
    Disk /dev/sdd doesn't contain a valid partition table
    Disk /dev/sde doesn't contain a valid partition table
    Disk /dev/sdf doesn't contain a valid partition table
    Disk /dev/sdg doesn't contain a valid partition table
    Disk /dev/sdh doesn't contain a valid partition table
    Disk /dev/sdi doesn't contain a valid partition table
    Disk /dev/sdj doesn't contain a valid partition table
    Disk /dev/sdk doesn't contain a valid partition table
    Disk /dev/sdl doesn't contain a valid partition table
    Disk /dev/sdm doesn't contain a valid partition table
    Disk /dev/sdn doesn't contain a valid partition table
    Disk /dev/sdo doesn't contain a valid partition table
    Disk /dev/sda: 21.4 GB, 21474836480 bytes
    Disk /dev/sdb: 536 MB, 536870912 bytes
    Disk /dev/sdc: 536 MB, 536870912 bytes
    Disk /dev/sdd: 536 MB, 536870912 bytes
    Disk /dev/sde: 536 MB, 536870912 bytes
    ```

Disk /dev/sdf: 536 MB, 536870912 bytes
Disk /dev/sdg: 4294 MB, 4294967296 bytes
Disk /dev/sdh: 4294 MB, 4294967296 bytes
Disk /dev/sdi: 536 MB, 536870912 bytes
Disk /dev/sdj: 536 MB, 536870912 bytes
Disk /dev/sdk: 536 MB, 536870912 bytes
Disk /dev/sdl: 536 MB, 536870912 bytes
Disk /dev/sdm: 536 MB, 536870912 bytes
Disk /dev/sdn: 536 MB, 536870912 bytes
Disk /dev/sdo: 536 MB, 536870912 bytes

- Format all the partitions shown above /dev/sdb... /dev/sdo using command fdisk

  [root@crs1 ~]# fdisk /dev/sdb

  Device contains neither a valid DOS partition table, nor Sun, SGI or OSF disklabel
  Building a new DOS disklabel. Changes will remain in memory only,
  until you decide to write them. After that, of course, the previous
  content won't be recoverable.

  Warning: invalid flag 0x0000 of partition table 4 will be corrected by w(rite)

  Command (m for help): **n**
  Command action
  e extended
  p primary partition (1-4)
  p
  Partition number (1-4): **1**
  First cylinder (1-512, default 1):
  Using default value 1
  Last cylinder or +size or +sizeM or +sizeK (1-512, default 512):
  Using default value 512

  Command (m for help): **w**
  The partition table has been altered!

  Calling ioctl() to re-read partition table.
  Syncing disks.

- **In same way, format all the disk /dev/sdb... /dev/sdo with following input**

  i. Command (m for help): **n**
  ii. Command action
     e extended
     p primary partition (1-4)
     p
  iii. Partition number (1-4): **1**
  iv. First cylinder (1-512, default 1): **< press enter>**
  v. Last cylinder or +size or +sizeM or +sizeK (1-512, default 512): **< press enter>**
  vi. Command (m for help): **w**

- Below are format details of last disk /dev/sd0

  [root@crs1 ~]# fdisk /dev/sdo

  Device contains neither a valid DOS partition table, nor Sun, SGI or OSF disklabel
  Building a new DOS disklabel. Changes will remain in memory only,
  until you decide to write them. After that, of course, the previous
  content won't be recoverable.

Warning: invalid flag 0x0000 of partition table 4 will be corrected by w(rite)

Command (m for help): **n**
Command action
  e extended
  p primary partition (1-4)
p
Partition number (1-4): **1**
First cylinder (1-512, default 1):
Using default value 1
Last cylinder or +size or +sizeM or +sizeK (1-512, default 512):
Using default value 512

Command (m for help): **w**
The partition table has been altered!

Calling ioctl() to re-read partition table.
Syncing disks.

- Again check details of all disk partitions

  [root@crs1 ~]# fdisk -l | grep -i disk

  Disk /dev/sda: 21.4 GB, 21474836480 bytes
  Disk /dev/sdb: 536 MB, 536870912 bytes
  Disk /dev/sdc: 536 MB, 536870912 bytes
  Disk /dev/sdd: 536 MB, 536870912 bytes
  Disk /dev/sde: 536 MB, 536870912 bytes
  Disk /dev/sdf: 536 MB, 536870912 bytes
  Disk /dev/sdg: 4294 MB, 4294967296 bytes
  Disk /dev/sdh: 4294 MB, 4294967296 bytes
  Disk /dev/sdi: 536 MB, 536870912 bytes
  Disk /dev/sdj: 536 MB, 536870912 bytes
  Disk /dev/sdk: 536 MB, 536870912 bytes
  Disk /dev/sdl: 536 MB, 536870912 bytes
  Disk /dev/sdm: 536 MB, 536870912 bytes
  Disk /dev/sdn: 536 MB, 536870912 bytes
  Disk /dev/sdo: 536 MB, 536870912 bytes

- Verify all the disks from crs2 to make sure all the disk are visible from crs2

  [root@crs2 RPMS]# fdisk /dev/sdb

  Command (m for help): **v**
  31 unallocated sectors

  Command (m for help): **w**
  The partition table has been altered!

  Calling ioctl() to re-read partition table.
  Syncing disks.

- **In same way, verify all the disks /dev/sdc .. /dev/sdo**

- Binding raw partitions for ocr, voting disks in /etc/sysconfig/rawdevices

  5 disks /dev/sdb1... /dev/sdf1 will be used for ocr and voting disk. Add following lines on both crs1 and crs2

  # /etc/sysconfig/rawdevices

  ```
  /dev/raw/raw1        /dev/sdb1
  /dev/raw/raw2        /dev/sdc1
  /dev/raw/raw3        /dev/sdd1
  /dev/raw/raw4        /dev/sde1
  /dev/raw/raw5        /dev/sdf1
  ```

- Restart the rawdevices again and change ownership to oracle on both crs1 and crs2

[root@crs1 RPMS]# /sbin/service rawdevices restart

[root@crs1 RPMS]# chown oracle:dba /dev/raw/raw[1-5]

[root@crs1 RPMS]# chmod 660 /dev/raw/raw[1-5]

[root@crs1 RPMS]# ls -lat /dev/raw/raw*

```
crw-rw——  1 oracle dba 162, 5 Feb 19 11:20 /dev/raw/raw5
crw-rw——  1 oracle dba 162, 4 Feb 19 11:20 /dev/raw/raw4
crw-rw——  1 oracle dba 162, 3 Feb 19 11:20 /dev/raw/raw3
crw-rw——  1 oracle dba 162, 2 Feb 19 11:20 /dev/raw/raw2
crw-rw——  1 oracle dba 162, 1 Feb 19 11:20 /dev/raw/raw1
```

- Modify the permission for rawdevices in following file on both crs1 and crs2.

/etc/udev/permissions.d/50-udev.permissions

raw devices
ram*:root:disk:660
 # raw/*:root:disk:660 # comment this line and add line mentioned below
raw/*:oracle:dba:660

[root@crs1 RPMS]# cat /etc/udev/permissions.d/50-udev.permissions | grep -i raw

- Hang Check Timer Configuration

Add the following line to **/etc/modprobe.conf**

options hangcheck-timer hangcheck_tick=30 hangcheck_margin=180

OR you can add following line to **/etc/rc.d/rc.local**

modprobe hangcheck-timer hangcheck_tick=30 hangcheck_margin=180

Restart both crs1 and crs2 to check if hangcheck-timer is working or not using following

[oracle@crs2 ~]$ /sbin/lsmod | grep -i hang

hangcheck_timer 7897 0

On VMware server increase hangcheck_tick=60 and hangcheck_marging=360

- Configure SSH and user Equivalence

  - On crs1 execute following as oracle User

    [oracle@crs1 ~]$ chmod 755 /home/oracle

    [oracle@crs1 ~]$ mkdir ~/.ssh

    [oracle@crs1 ~]$ chmod 700 ~/.ssh

    Accept the default location for the key file and for pass phrase press Enter Key

    [oracle@crs1 ~]$ ssh-keygen -t rsa

    ```
    Generating public/private rsa key pair.
    Enter file in which to save the key (/home/oracle/.ssh/id_rsa):
    Enter passphrase (empty for no passphrase):
    Enter same passphrase again:
    Your identification has been saved in /home/oracle/.ssh/id_rsa.
    Your public key has been saved in /home/oracle/.ssh/id_rsa.pub.
    The key fingerprint is:
    25:d0:44:00:92:a9:85:0e:e8:46:ec:2f:5e:12:ff:cf oracle@crs1.prusolutions.com
    ```

    [oracle@crs1 ~]$ ssh-keygen -t dsa

    ```
    Generating public/private dsa key pair.
    Enter file in which to save the key (/home/oracle/.ssh/id_dsa):
    ```

```
Enter passphrase (empty for no passphrase):
Enter same passphrase again:
Your identification has been saved in /home/oracle/.ssh/id_dsa.
Your public key has been saved in /home/oracle/.ssh/id_dsa.pub.
The key fingerprint is:
cb:37:48:ee:8f:f4:cc:d0:e6:51:26:8b:10:e4:86:0e oracle@crs1.prusolutions.com
```

- On crs2 execute following as oracle User

[oracle@crs2 ~]$ chmod 755 /home/oracle

[oracle@crs2 ~]$ mkdir ~/.ssh

[oracle@crs2 ~]$ chmod 700 ~/.ssh

Accept the default location for the key file and for pass phrase press Enter Key

[oracle@crs2 ~]$ ssh-keygen -t rsa

```
Generating public/private rsa key pair.
Enter file in which to save the key (/home/oracle/.ssh/id_rsa):
Enter passphrase (empty for no passphrase):
Enter same passphrase again:
Your identification has been saved in /home/oracle/.ssh/id_rsa.
Your public key has been saved in /home/oracle/.ssh/id_rsa.pub.
The key fingerprint is:
16:5d:6d:d2:49:bf:09:d8:d3:5d:39:b1:c1:59:7c:d3 oracle@crs2.prusolutions.com
```

[oracle@crs2 ~]$ ssh-keygen -t dsa

```
Generating public/private dsa key pair.
Enter file in which to save the key (/home/oracle/.ssh/id_dsa):
Enter passphrase (empty for no passphrase):
Enter same passphrase again:
Your identification has been saved in /home/oracle/.ssh/id_dsa.
Your public key has been saved in /home/oracle/.ssh/id_dsa.pub.
The key fingerprint is:
59:bf:2c:64:d4:8d:ae:41:c1:20:a8:41:5d:e3:35:50 oracle@crs2.prusolutions.com
```

- On crs1 node set ssh

[oracle@crs1 ~]$ cat ~/.ssh/id_rsa.pub >> ~/.ssh/authorized_keys

[oracle@crs1 ~]$ cat ~/.ssh/id_dsa.pub >>~/.ssh/authorized_keys

[oracle@crs1 ~]$ ssh crs2 cat ~/.ssh/id_rsa.pub >> ~/.ssh/authorized_keys

```
The authenticity of host 'crs2 (192.168.2.132)' can't be established.
RSA key fingerprint is f4:ac:d2:7e:05:e8:4e:47:a9:6f:80:99:46:f9:f7:58.
Are you sure you want to continue connecting (yes/no)? yes
Warning: Permanently added 'crs2,192.168.2.132' (RSA) to the list of known hosts.
oracle@crs2's password:
```

[oracle@crs1 ~]$ ssh crs2 cat ~/.ssh/id_dsa.pub >> ~/.ssh/authorized_keys

```
oracle@crs2's password:
```

[oracle@crs1 .ssh]$ scp ~/.ssh/authorized_keys crs2:~/.ssh/authorized_keys

```
oracle@crs2's password:
authorized_keys                    100% 1712     1.7KB/s   00:00
```

- Test connection execute following commands twice on both crs1,crs2 and verify the password is not required when the commands are run seconds time.

```
$ ssh crs1 date
$ ssh crs1.prusolutions.com date
$ ssh crs1-priv date
$ ssh crs1-priv.prusolutions.com date
```

```
$ ssh crs2 date
$ ssh crs2.prusolutions.com date
$ ssh crs2-priv date
$ ssh crs2-priv.prusolutions.com date
```

[oracle@crs1 .ssh]$ ssh crs1 date

```
The authenticity of host 'crs1 (192.168.2.131)' can't be established.
RSA key fingerprint is f4:ac:d2:7e:05:e8:4e:47:a9:6f:80:99:46:f9:f7:58.
Are you sure you want to continue connecting (yes/no)? yes
Warning: Permanently added 'crs1,192.168.2.131' (RSA) to the list of known hosts.
Sat Feb 19 13:24:08 EST 2011
```

[oracle@crs1 .ssh]$ ssh crs1.prusolutions.com date

```
The authenticity of host 'crs1.prusolutions.com (192.168.2.131)' can't be established.
RSA key fingerprint is f4:ac:d2:7e:05:e8:4e:47:a9:6f:80:99:46:f9:f7:58.
Are you sure you want to continue connecting (yes/no)? yes
Warning: Permanently added 'crs1.prusolutions.com' (RSA) to the list of known hosts.
Sat Feb 19 13:24:23 EST 2011
```

[oracle@crs1 .ssh]$ ssh crs1-priv date

```
The authenticity of host 'crs1-priv (10.10.10.31)' can't be established.
RSA key fingerprint is f4:ac:d2:7e:05:e8:4e:47:a9:6f:80:99:46:f9:f7:58.
Are you sure you want to continue connecting (yes/no)? yes
Warning: Permanently added 'crs1-priv,10.10.10.31' (RSA) to the list of known hosts.
Sat Feb 19 13:24:39 EST 2011
```

[oracle@crs1 .ssh]$ ssh crs1-priv.prusolutions.com date

```
The authenticity of host 'crs1-priv.prusolutions.com (10.10.10.31)' can't be established.
RSA key fingerprint is f4:ac:d2:7e:05:e8:4e:47:a9:6f:80:99:46:f9:f7:58.
Are you sure you want to continue connecting (yes/no)? yes
Warning: Permanently added 'crs1-priv.prusolutions.com' (RSA) to the list of known hosts.
Sat Feb 19 13:25:09 EST 2011
```

[oracle@crs1 .ssh]$ ssh crs2 date

```
Sat Feb 19 13:25:20 EST 2011
```

[oracle@crs1 .ssh]$ ssh crs2.prusolutions.com date

```
The authenticity of host 'crs2.prusolutions.com (192.168.2.132)' can't be established.
RSA key fingerprint is f4:ac:d2:7e:05:e8:4e:47:a9:6f:80:99:46:f9:f7:58.
Are you sure you want to continue connecting (yes/no)? yes
Warning: Permanently added 'crs2.prusolutions.com' (RSA) to the list of known hosts.
Sat Feb 19 13:25:49 EST 2011
```

[oracle@crs1 .ssh]$ ssh crs2-priv date

```
The authenticity of host 'crs2-priv (10.10.10.32)' can't be established.
RSA key fingerprint is f4:ac:d2:7e:05:e8:4e:47:a9:6f:80:99:46:f9:f7:58.
Are you sure you want to continue connecting (yes/no)? yes
Warning: Permanently added 'crs2-priv,10.10.10.32' (RSA) to the list of known hosts.
Sat Feb 19 13:27:54 EST 2011
```

[oracle@crs1 .ssh]$ ssh crs2-priv.prusolutions.com date

```
The authenticity of host 'crs2-priv.prusolutions.com (10.10.10.32)' can't be established.
RSA key fingerprint is f4:ac:d2:7e:05:e8:4e:47:a9:6f:80:99:46:f9:f7:58.
Are you sure you want to continue connecting (yes/no)? yes
Warning: Permanently added 'crs2-priv.prusolutions.com' (RSA) to the list of known hosts.
Sat Feb 19 13:28:10 EST 2011
```

- The same date commands are executed twice and second time it does not ask for password

```
[oracle@crs1 .ssh]$ ssh crs1 date
Sat Feb 19 13:28:23 EST 2011
[oracle@crs1 .ssh]$ ssh crs1.prusolutions.com date
Sat Feb 19 13:28:31 EST 2011
[oracle@crs1 .ssh]$ ssh crs1-priv date
Sat Feb 19 13:28:39 EST 2011
[oracle@crs1 .ssh]$ ssh crs1-priv.prusolutions.com date
Sat Feb 19 13:29:06 EST 2011
[oracle@crs1 .ssh]$ ssh crs2 date
Sat Feb 19 13:29:20 EST 2011
[oracle@crs1 .ssh]$ ssh crs2.prusolutions.com date
Sat Feb 19 13:29:35 EST 2011
[oracle@crs1 .ssh]$ ssh crs2-priv date
Sat Feb 19 13:30:38 EST 2011
[oracle@crs1 .ssh]$ ssh crs2-priv.prusolutions.com date
Sat Feb 19 13:30:52 EST 2011
```

- **Perform the same date commands on crs2**

8.4 Configure ASM on both the nodes as root user

As /dev/sdb1 .. /dev/sdf1 will be used for ocr and voting disk, configure rest of disk from /dev/sdg1 ../dev/sdo1 for ASM

- On both crs1 and crs2 nodes execute following

```
[root@crs1 ~]# /sbin/service oracleasm configure
Configuring the Oracle ASM library driver.

This will configure the on-boot properties of the Oracle ASM library
driver.  The following questions will determine whether the driver is
loaded on boot and what permissions it will have.  The current values
will be shown in brackets ('[]').  Hitting <ENTER> without typing an
answer will keep that current value.  Ctrl-C will abort.

Default user to own the driver interface []: oracle
Default group to own the driver interface []: dba
Start Oracle ASM library driver on boot (y/n) [n]: y
Fix permissions of Oracle ASM disks on boot (y/n) [y]: y
Writing Oracle ASM library driver configuration:     [  OK  ]
Loading module "oracleasm":                          [  OK  ]
Mounting ASMlib driver filesystem:                   [  OK  ]
Scanning system for ASM disks:                       [  OK  ]

[root@crs2 ~]# /sbin/service oracleasm configure
Default user to own the driver interface []: oracle
Default group to own the driver interface []: dba
Start Oracle ASM library driver on boot (y/n) [n]: y
Fix permissions of Oracle ASM disks on boot (y/n) [y]: y
```

- Create ASM disk on any one node

```
[root@crs1 ~]# /sbin/service oracleasm createdisk VOL1 /dev/sdg1
Marking disk "/dev/sdg1" as an ASM disk:             [  OK  ]
```

```
[root@crs1 ~]# /sbin/service oracleasm createdisk VOL2 /dev/sdh1
Marking disk "/dev/sdh1" as an ASM disk:                [ OK ]
[root@crs1 ~]# /sbin/service oracleasm createdisk VOL3 /dev/sdi1
Marking disk "/dev/sdi1" as an ASM disk:                [ OK ]
[root@crs1 ~]# /sbin/service oracleasm createdisk VOL4 /dev/sdj1
Marking disk "/dev/sdj1" as an ASM disk:                [ OK ]
[root@crs1 ~]# /sbin/service oracleasm createdisk VOL5 /dev/sdk1
Marking disk "/dev/sdk1" as an ASM disk:                [ OK ]
[root@crs1 ~]# /sbin/service oracleasm createdisk VOL6 /dev/sdl1
Marking disk "/dev/sdl1" as an ASM disk:                [ OK ]
[root@crs1 ~]# /sbin/service oracleasm createdisk VOL7 /dev/sdm1
Marking disk "/dev/sdm1" as an ASM disk:                [ OK ]
[root@crs1 ~]# /sbin/service oracleasm createdisk VOL8 /dev/sdn1
Marking disk "/dev/sdn1" as an ASM disk:                [ OK ]
[root@crs1 ~]# /sbin/service oracleasm createdisk VOL9 /dev/sdo1
Marking disk "/dev/sdo1" as an ASM disk:                [ OK ]
```

- On crs1 list all the disks

```
[root@crs1 ~]# /sbin/service oracleasm listdisks
VOL1
VOL2
VOL3
VOL4
VOL5
VOL6
VOL7
VOL8
VOL9
```

- On crs2 scandisks and listdisks

```
[root@crs2 ~]# /sbin/service oracleasm scandisks
Scanning system for ASM disks:                [ OK ]
[root@crs2 ~]# /sbin/service oracleasm listdisks
VOL1
VOL2
VOL3
VOL4
VOL5
VOL6
VOL7
VOL8
VOL9
```

8.5 Install cvuqdisk rpm required for cluvfy on both nodes

```
[root@crs1 rpm]#  export CVUQDISK_GRP=dba
[root@crs1 rpm]#  rpm -Uvh /u01/software/clusterware/rpm/cvuqdisk-1.0.1-1.rpm
Preparing... ########################################### [100%]
 1:cvuqdisk  ########################################### [100%]
[root@crs2 rpm]# export CVUQDISK_GRP=dba
```

[root@crs2 rpm]# rpm -Uvh /u01/software/clusterware/rpm/cvuqdisk-1.0.1-1.rpm

```
Preparing...########################################### [100%]
1:cvuqdisk ########################################### [100%]
```

8.6 Run Oracle Cluvfy utility on both the nodes crs1 and crs2

- **Cluvfy utility post Hardware OS**

Ignore only errors for VIP interfaces and last storage disk /dev/sd0. Make sure all other checks are passed

[oracle@crs1 cluvfy]$ chmod 755 /u01/software/clusterware/cluvfy/runcluvfy.sh

[oracle@crs1 cluvfy]$ /u01/software/clusterware/cluvfy/runcluvfy.sh stage -post hwos -n crs1,crs2 –verbose

```
Performing post-checks for hardware and operating system setup
Checking node reachability...
Check: Node reachability from node "crs1"
 Destination Node                    Reachable?
 ______________________________      ________________________
crs1                                 yes
crs2                                 yes
Result: Node reachability check passed from node "crs1".
Checking user equivalence...
Check: User equivalence for user "oracle"
Node Name                            Comment
______________________________       ________________________
crs2                                 passed
crs1                                 passed
Result: User equivalence check passed for user "oracle".
Checking node connectivity...
Interface information for node "crs2"
Interface Name          IP Address               Subnet
__________________      ____________________     ________________
 eth0                   192.168.2.132            192.168.2.0
 eth1                   10.10.10.32              10.10.10.0

Interface information for node "crs1"
Interface Name          IP Address               Subnet
__________________      ____________________     ________________
eth0                    192.168.2.131            192.168.2.0
eth1                    10.10.10.31              10.10.10.0

Check: Node connectivity of subnet "192.168.2.0"
 Source                 Destination              Connected.
__________________      ____________________     ________________
crs2:eth0               crs1:eth0                yes
Result: Node connectivity check passed for subnet "192.168.2.0" with node(s) crs2,crs1.
Check: Node connectivity of subnet "10.10.10.0"
 Source                 Destination              Connected.
__________________      ____________________     ________________
crs2:eth1               crs1:eth1                yes
Result: Node connectivity check passed for subnet "10.10.10.0" with node(s) crs2,crs1.
```

Suitable interfaces for the private interconnect on subnet "192.168.2.0":
crs2 eth0:192.168.2.132
crs1 eth0:192.168.2.131

Suitable interfaces for the private interconnect on subnet "10.10.10.0":
crs2 eth1:10.10.10.32
crs1 eth1:10.10.10.31

ERROR:
Could not find a suitable set of interfaces for VIPs.

Result: Node connectivity check failed
Checking shared storage accessibility...

WARNING:
Unable to determine the sharedness of /dev/sdo on nodes:

crs2,crs2,crs2,crs2,crs2,crs2,crs2,crs2,crs2,crs2,crs2,crs2,crs2,crs2,crs2,crs1,crs1,crs1,crs1,crs1,crs1,crs1,crs1,crs1,crs1,crs1,crs1,crs1,crs1,crs1

Shared storage check failed on nodes "crs2,crs1".

Post-check for hardware and operating system setup was unsuccessful on all the nodes.

- **Cluvfy Utility Pre crsinst Install**

  [oracle@crs1 cluvfy]$ /u01/software/clusterware/cluvfy/runcluvfy.sh stage -pre crsinst -n crs1,crs2 -verbose

  Make sure all the required packages are installed on both crs1 and crs2

  On VMware some packages checks will fail and if older version of those packages are installed then you can ignore them.
  For example: if you get error for following packages then use can do rpm –qa to get details if older version of packages are installed

  compat-gcc-7.3-2.96.128".
  compat-gcc-c++-7.3-2.96.128".
  compat-libstdc++-7.3-2.96.128".
  compat-libstdc++-devel-7.3-2.96.128".
  openmotif-2.2.3".

  [oracle@crs1 ~]$ rpm -qa | grep -i compat

  compat-libgcc-296-2.96-132.7.2
  compat-gcc-32-3.2.3-47.3
  compat-libstdc++-296-2.96-132.7.2
  compat-gcc-32-c++-3.2.3-47.3
  compat-libstdc++-33-3.2.3-47.3
  compat-db-4.1.25-9
  java-1.4.2-gcj-compat-1.4.2.0-27jpp
  compat-libcom_err-1.0-5

  [oracle@crsdg2 ~]$ rpm -qa | grep -i openmotif

- Navigate through Oracle Documentation to get to Real Application Clusters Installation Guide for Linux without search tab

  Oracle Database Documentation Library > Books > DAT >

  On contents page Ctrl f and search for 'Real Application Clusters Installation Guide for Linux" you will reach Real Application Clusters Installation Guide for Linux. Click HTML to go Contents page

8.7 Reboot both crs1 and crs2 before proceeding further

8.8 Install Oracle Clusterware from any one node crs1

[oracle@crs1 ~]$ /u01/software/clusterware/runInstaller

If there any error in executing any file change its permission chmod 755 <file_name>

- Welcome Screen: Click Next
- Specify Inventory Directory and Credentials

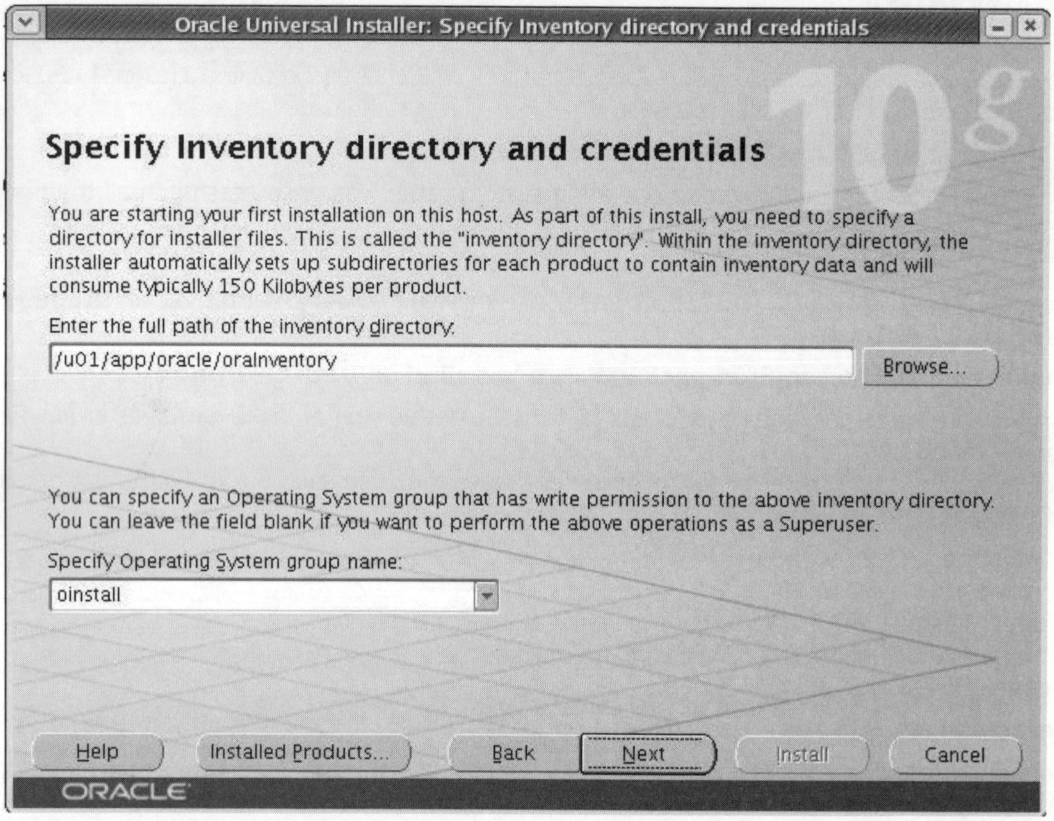

- Specify Home Details Path of CRS install directory /u01/app/oracle/product/10.2.0/crs_1

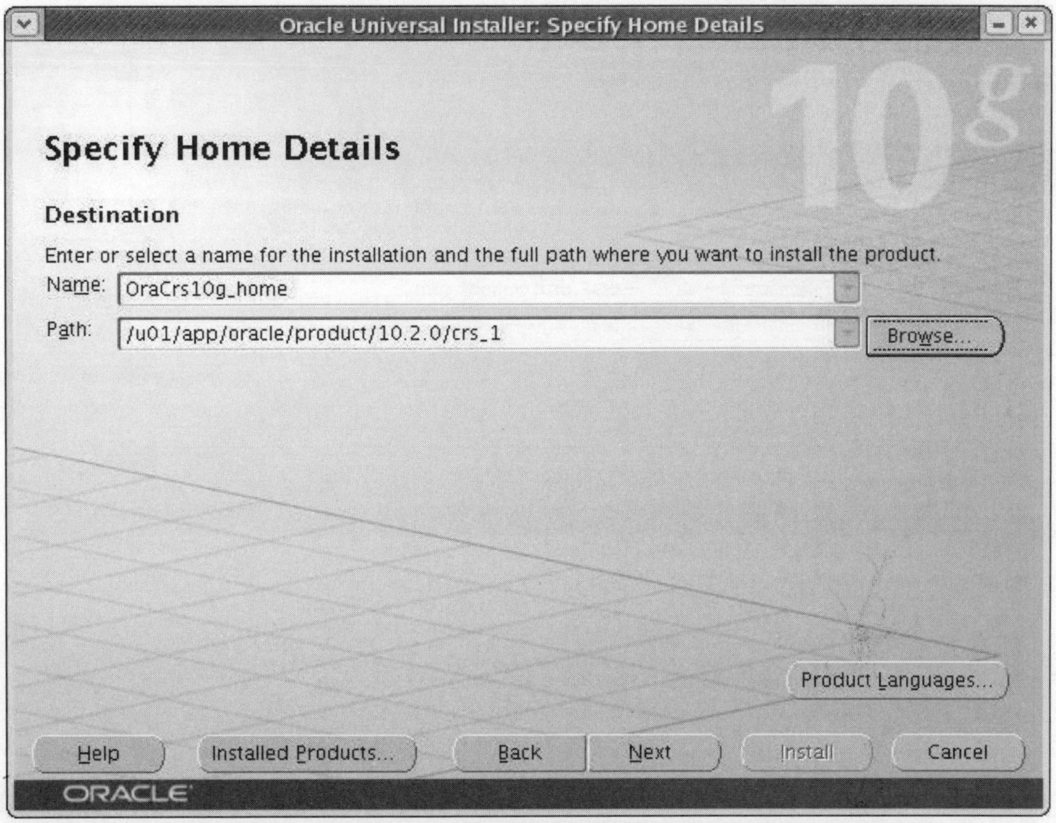

- Product – Specific Prerequisite Checks: Make sure the check result is passed

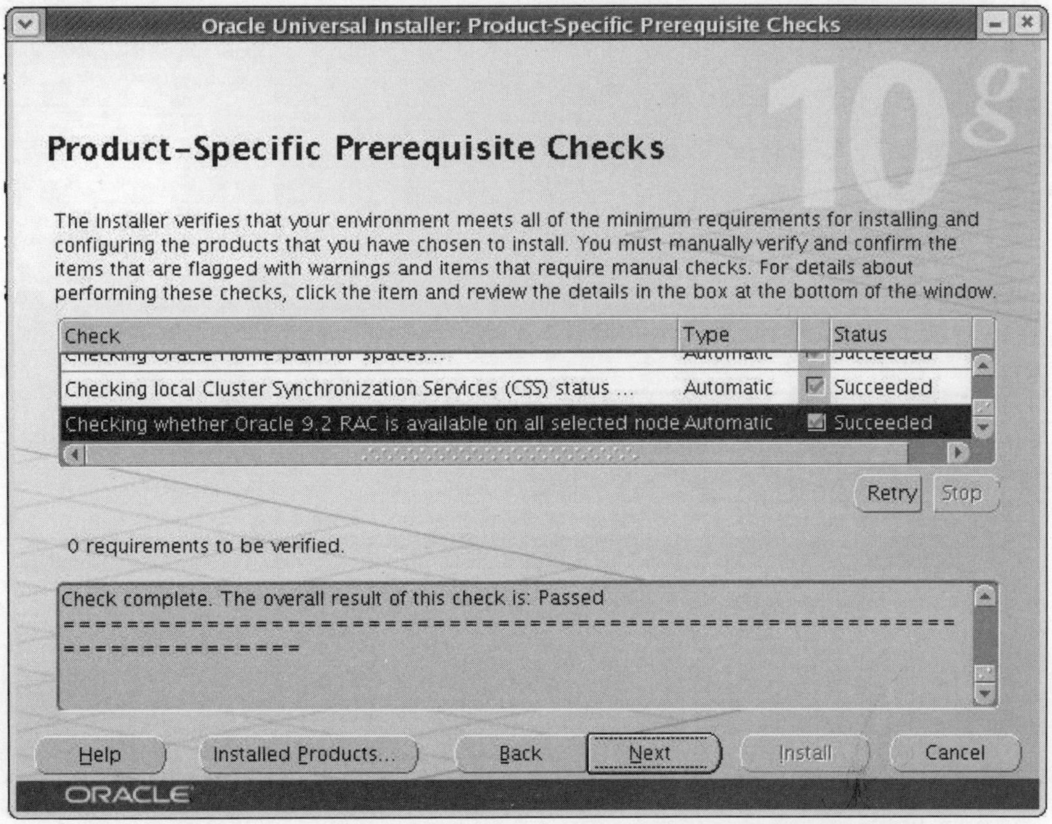

- Specify Cluster Name and ip Addresses

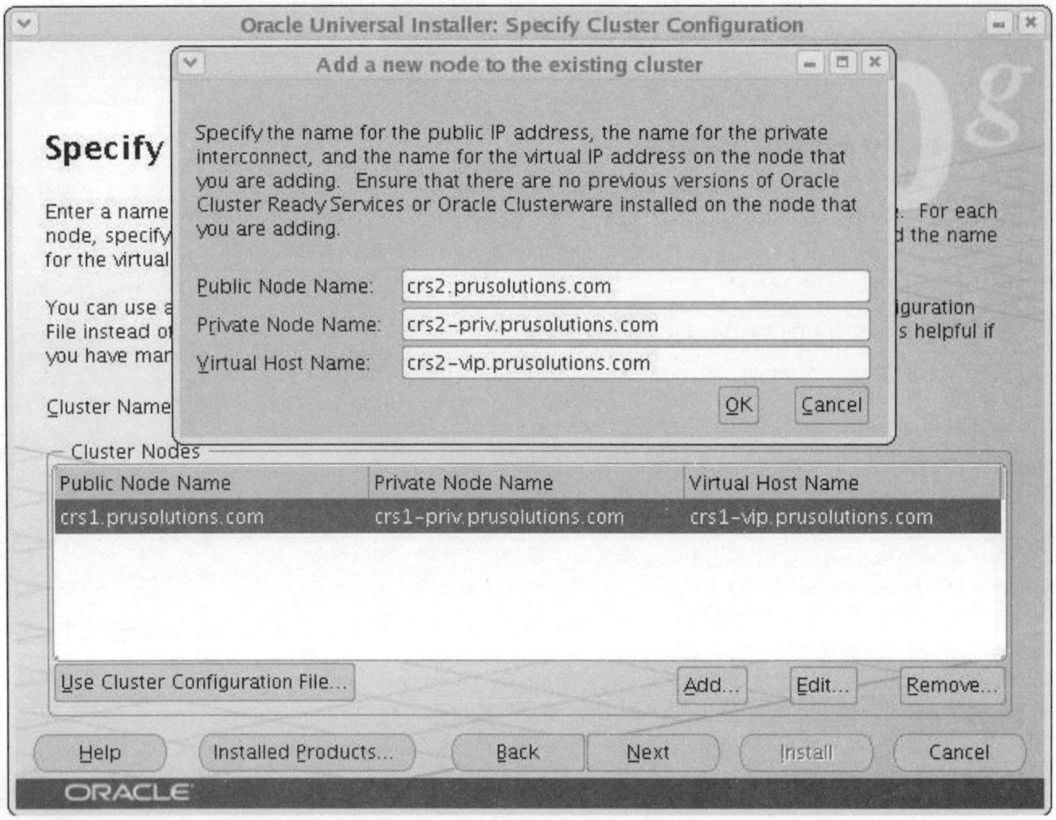

- Specify Cluster Configuration

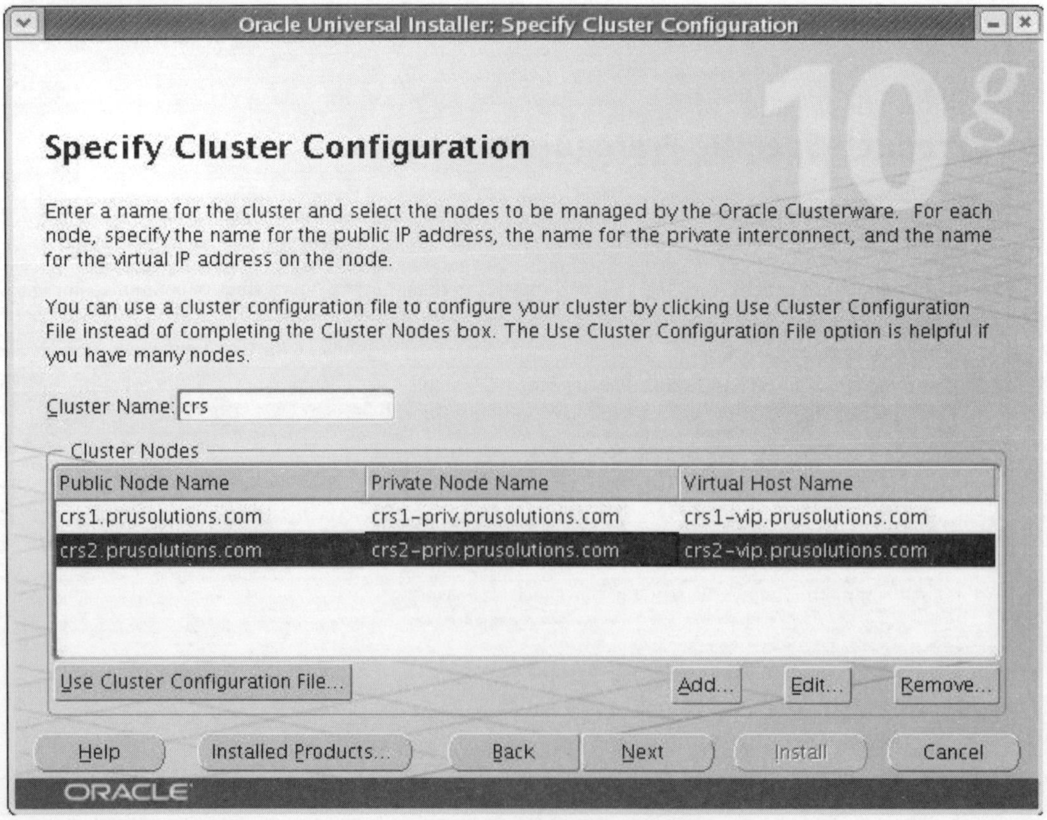

- Specify Network Interface Usage

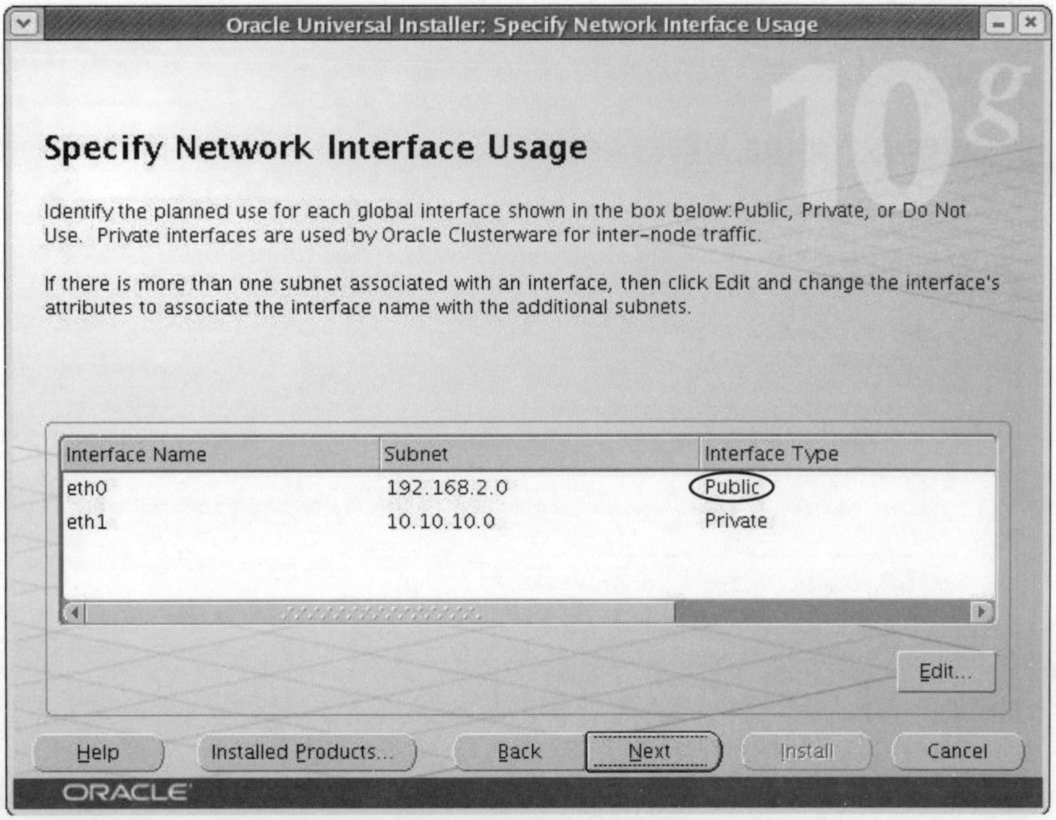

- Specify Oracle Cluster Registry (OCR) Location

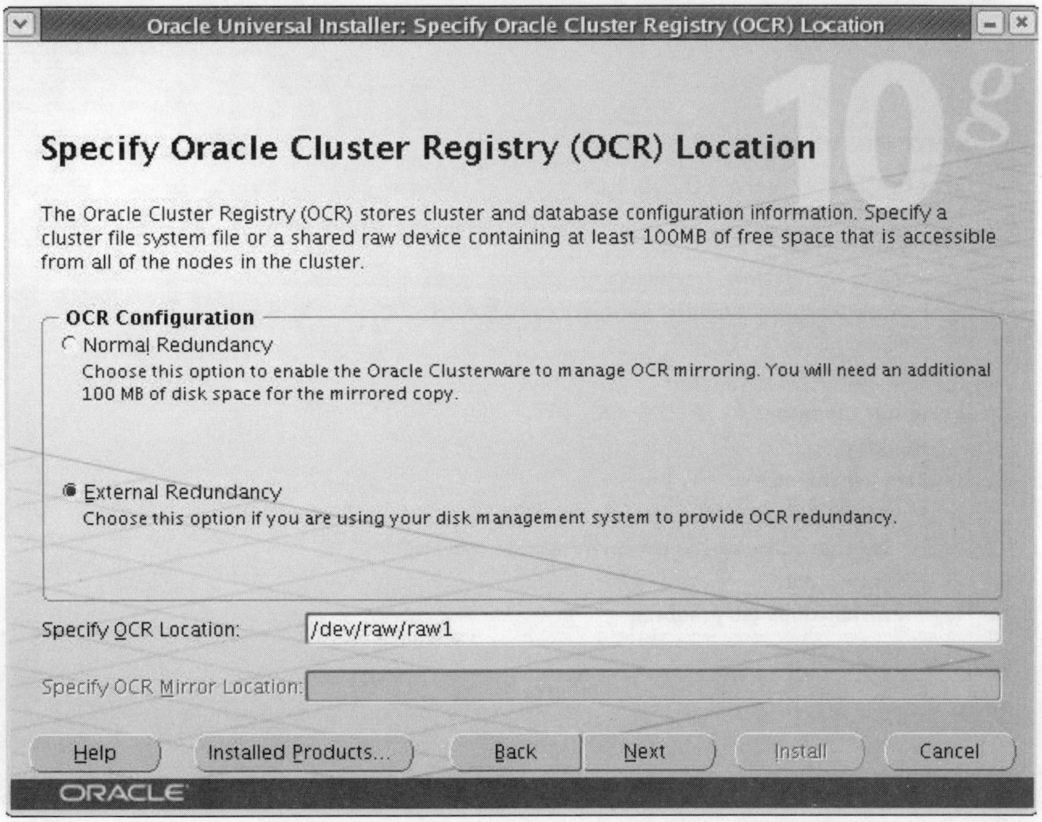

- Specify Voting Disk Location

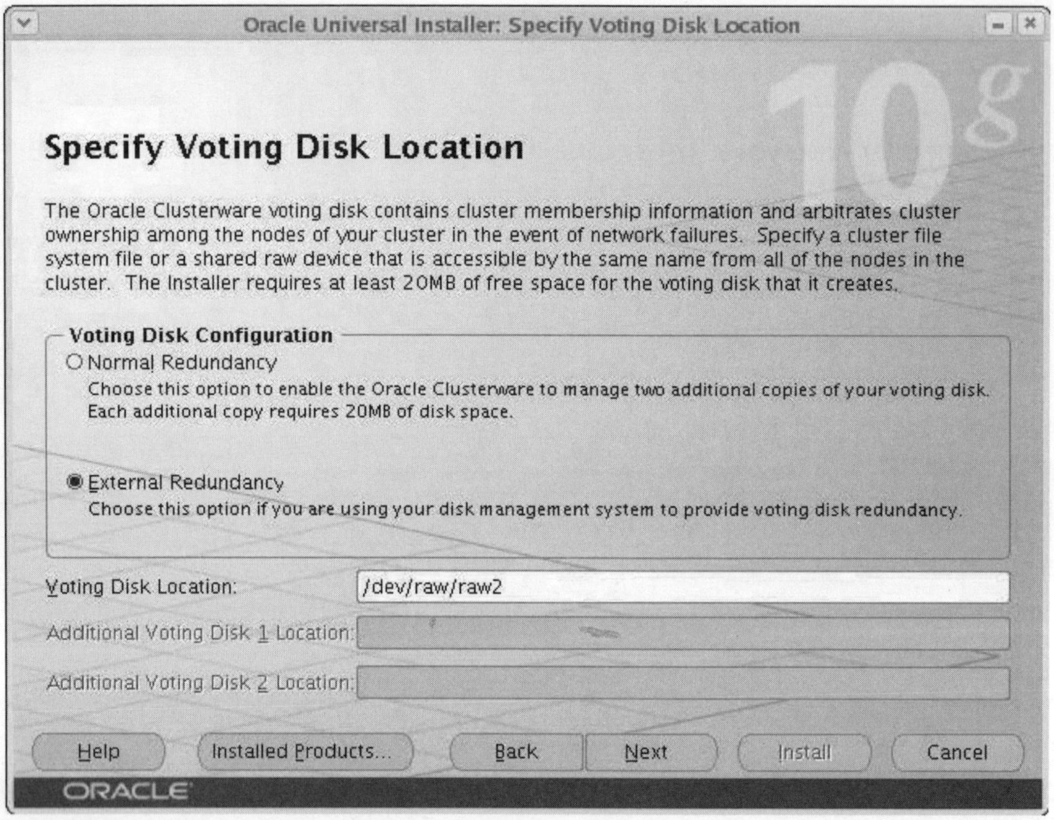

- Summary

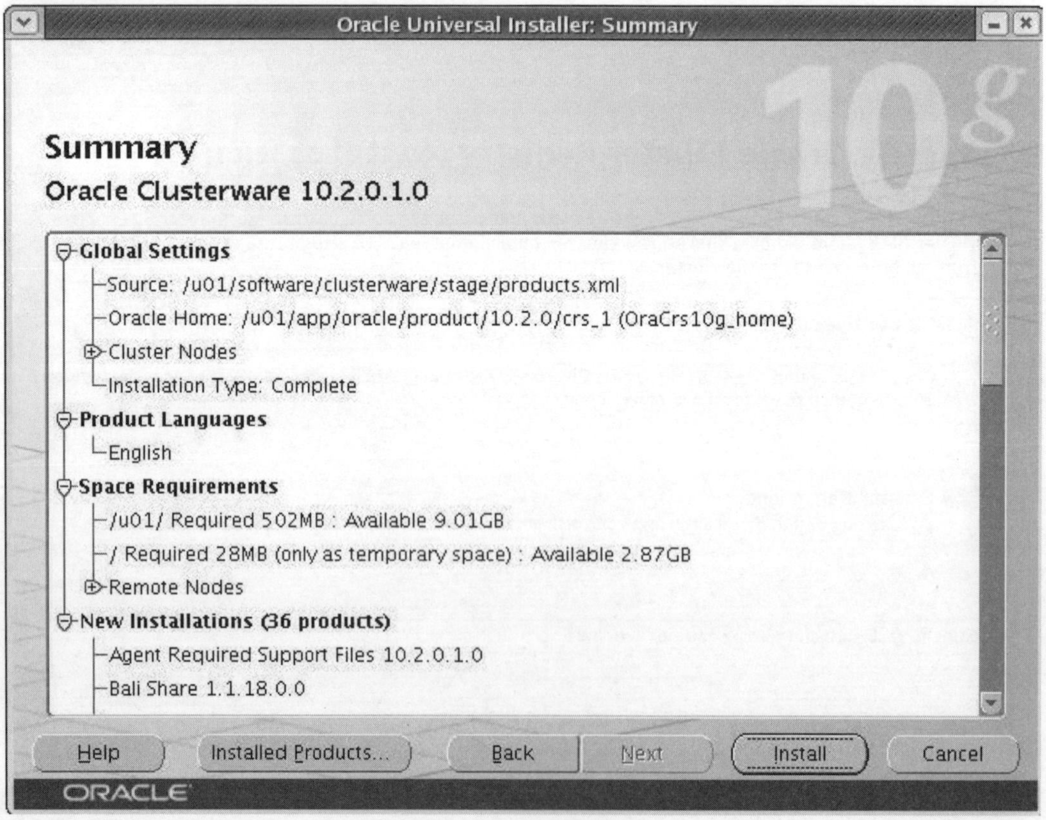

- Install

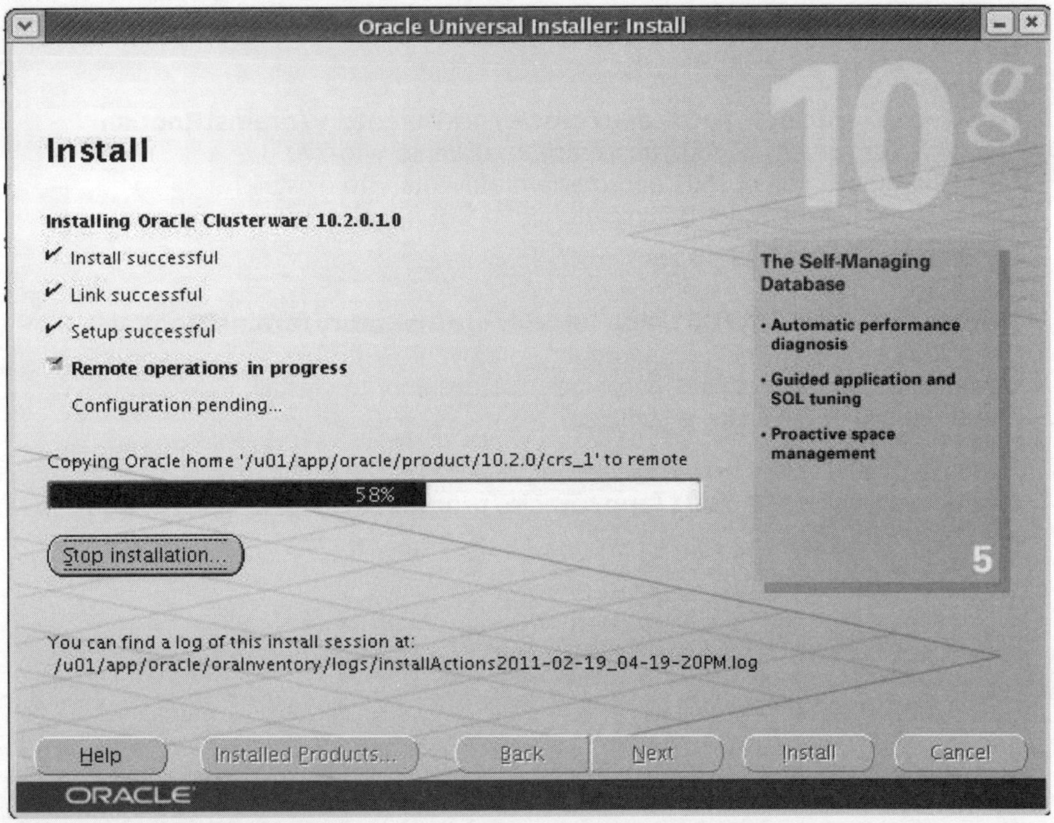

- Execute Configuration Scripts

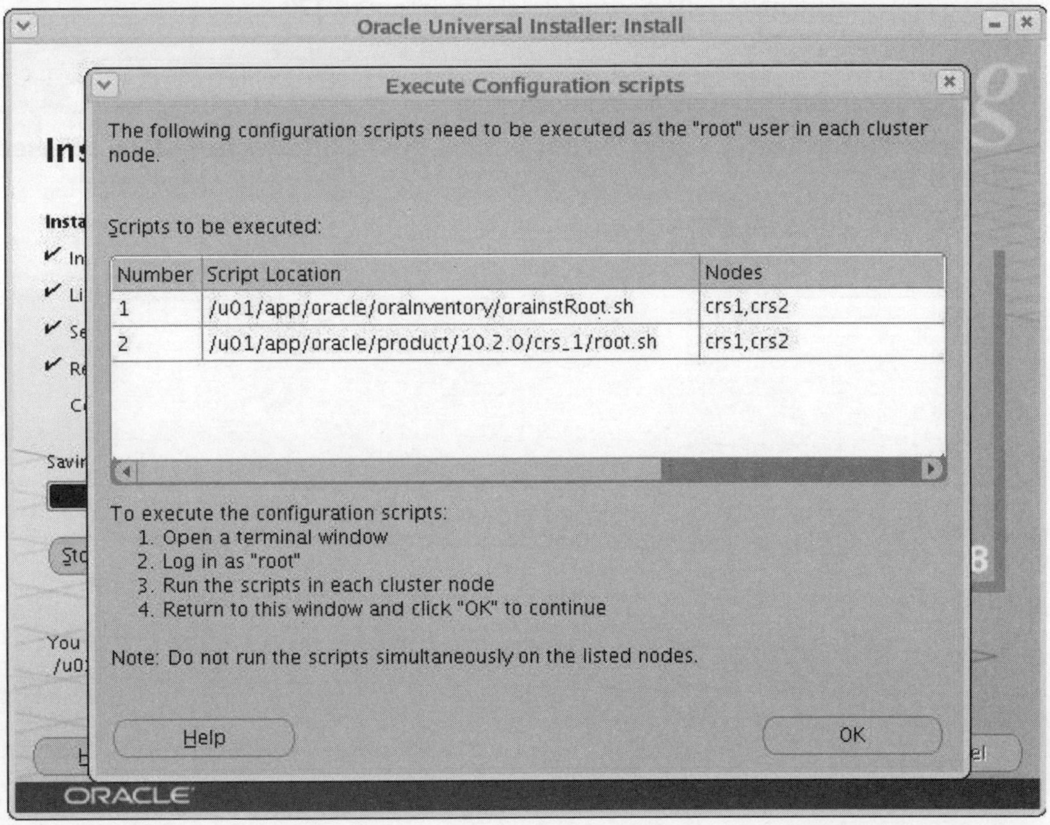

- Open a new terminal login as root and execute /u01/app/oracle/oraInventory/orainstRoot.sh on both the nodes.

[oracle@crs1 ~]$ su root
Password:
[root@crs1 oracle]# /u01/app/oracle/oraInventory/orainstRoot.sh
Changing permissions of /u01/app/oracle/oraInventory to 770.
Changing groupname of /u01/app/oracle/oraInventory to oinstall.
The execution of the script is complete.

[oracle@crs2 cluvfy]$ su root
Password:
[root@crs2 cluvfy]# /u01/app/oracle/oraInventory/orainstRoot.sh
Changing permissions of /u01/app/oracle/oraInventory to 770.
Changing groupname of /u01/app/oracle/oraInventory to oinstall.
The execution of the script is complete.

- Execute /u01/app/oracle/product/10.2.0/crs_1/root.sh on crs1 first and then on crs2

[root@crs1 oracle]# /u01/app/oracle/product/10.2.0/crs_1/root.sh

Changing permissions of /u01/app/oracle/oraInventory to 770.
:
:
CSS is active on these nodes.
        crs1
CSS is inactive on these nodes.
        crs2
Local node checking complete.
Run root.sh on remaining nodes to start CRS daemons.

[root@crs2 cluvfy]# /u01/app/oracle/product/10.2.0/crs_1/root.sh

Changing permissions of /u01/app/oracle/oraInventory to 770.
:
:
Running vipca(silent) for configuring nodeapps

The given interface(s), "eth0" is not public. Public interfaces should be used to configure virtual IPs.

[root@crs2 cluvfy]# vipca

- Welcome

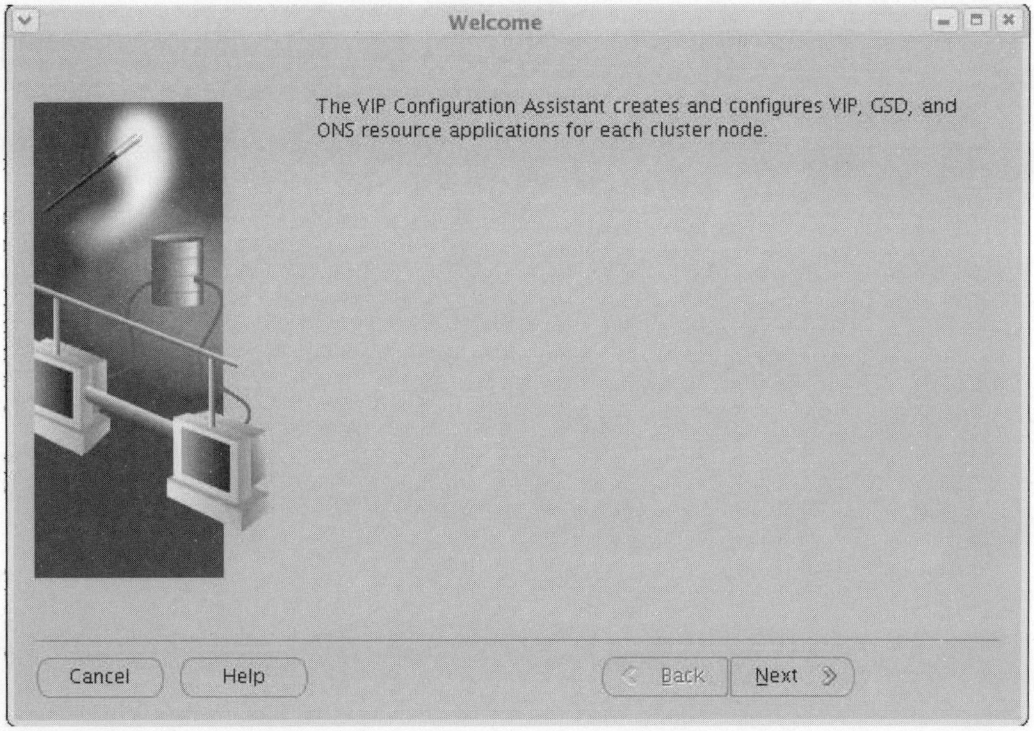

- Select eth0 only

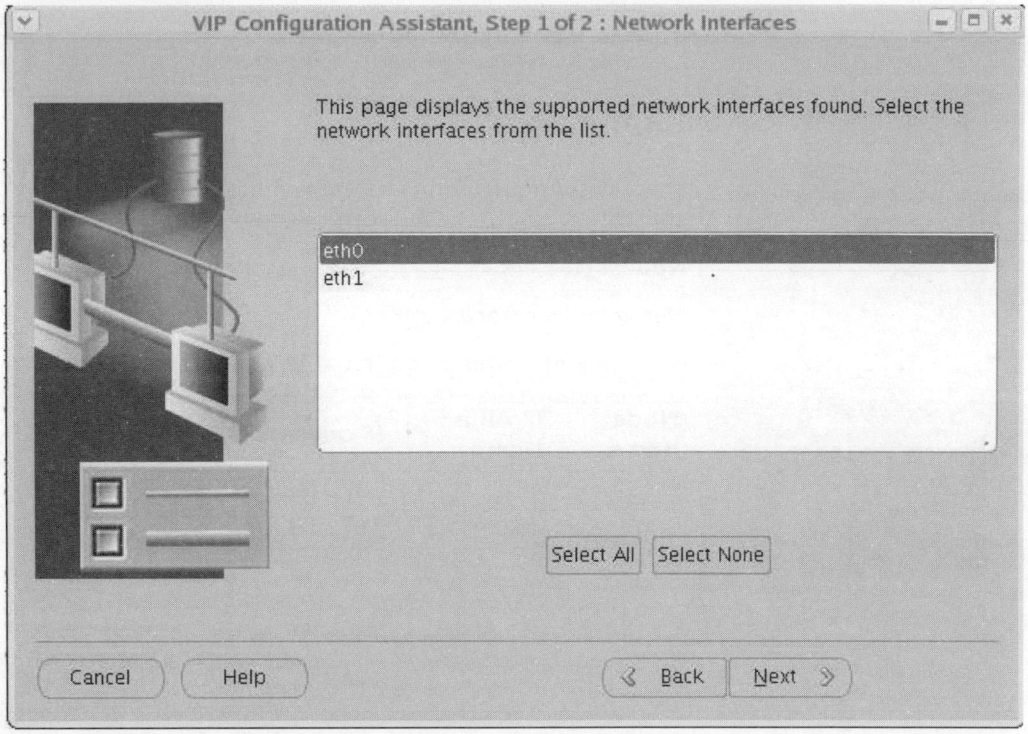

- VIP Configuration Assistant

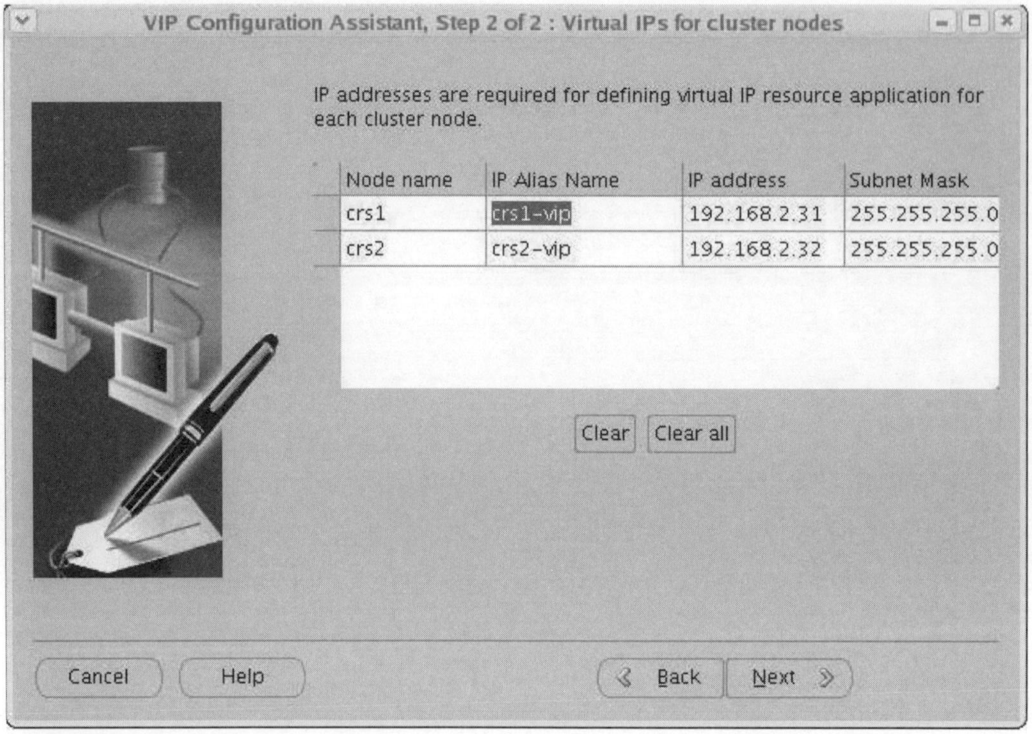

- Summary

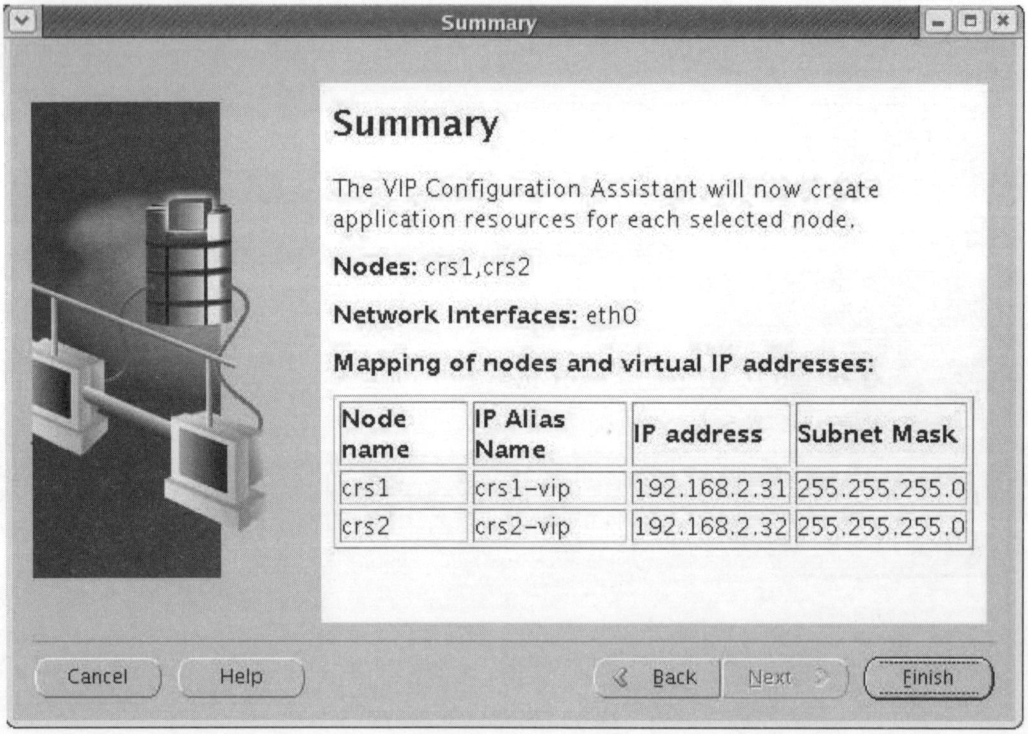

- Configuration Assistant Progress Dialog

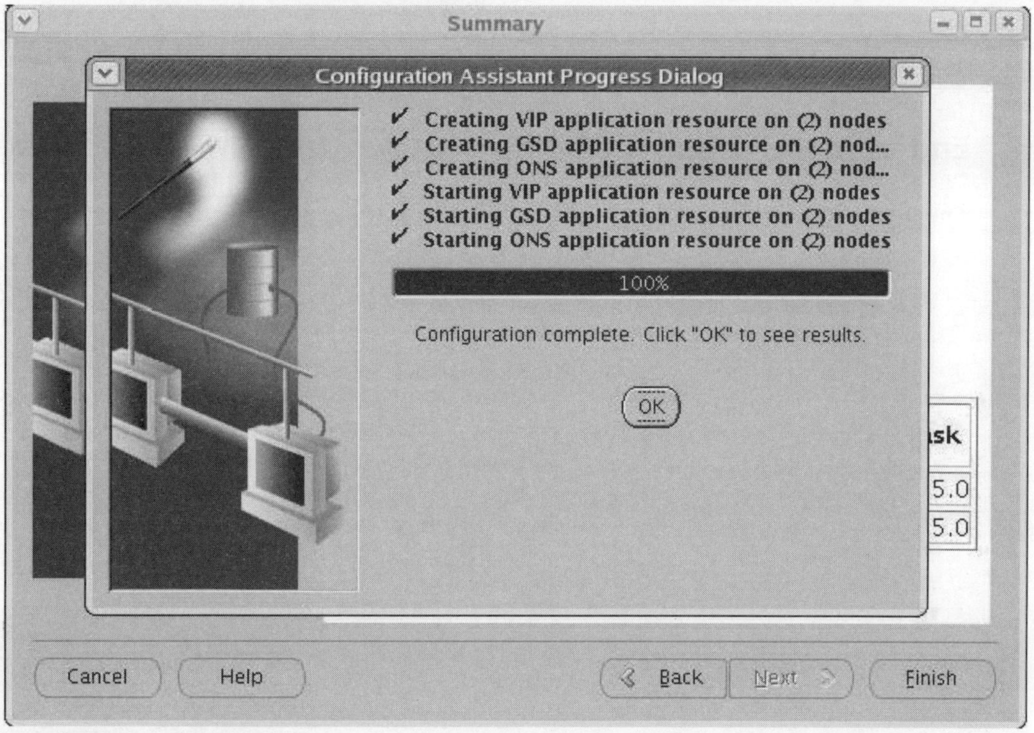

- Configuration Assistants

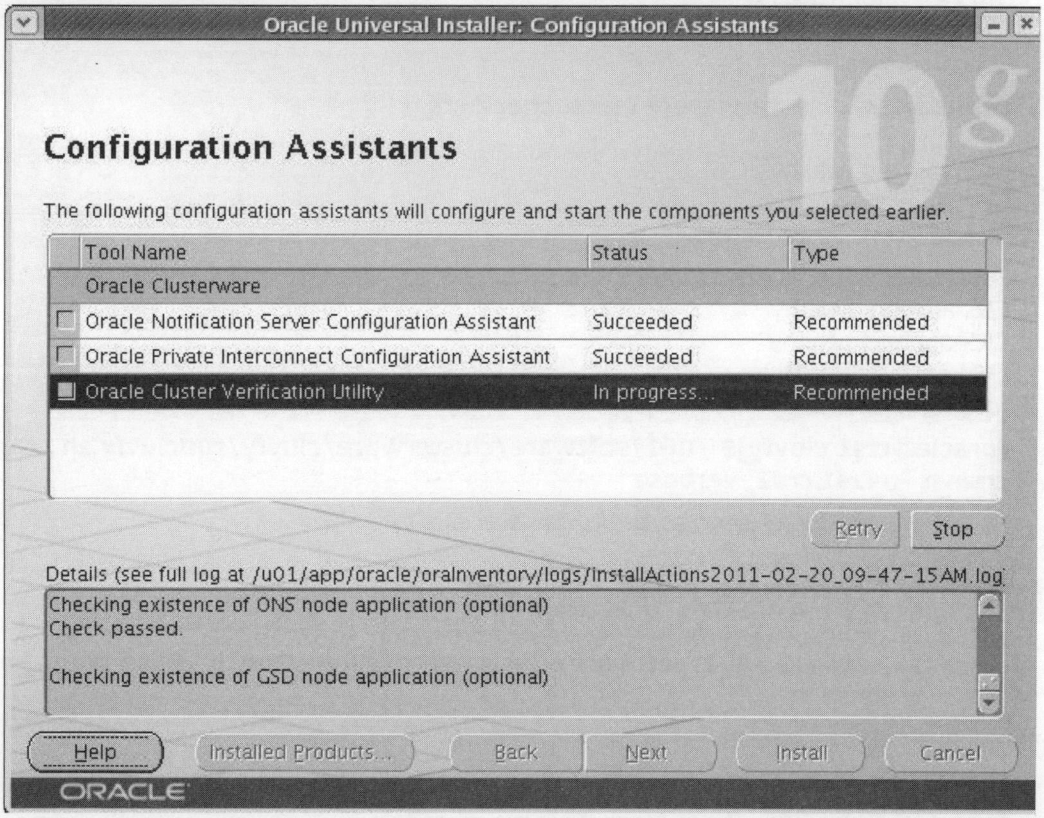

- End of Installation

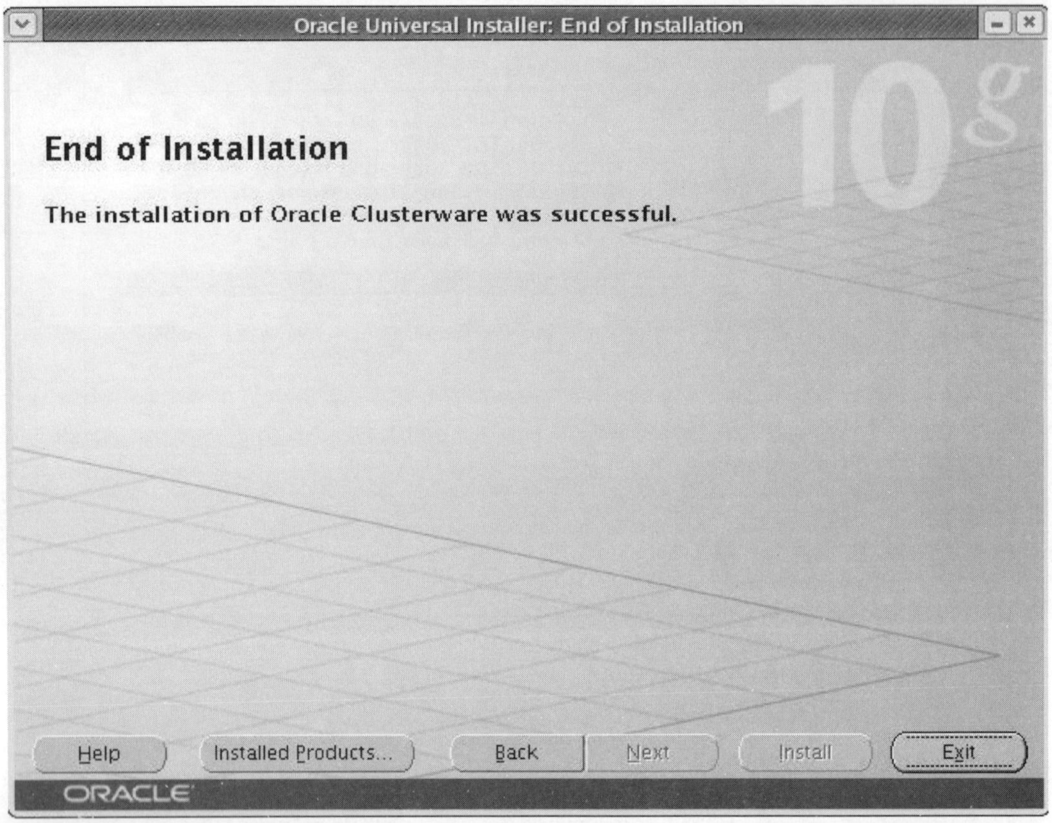

- Check crs Health

[oracle@crs1 clusterware]$ crsctl check crs
CSS appears healthy
CRS appears healthy
EVM appears healthy
[oracle@crs1 clusterware]$

[oracle@crs2 ~]$ crsctl check crs
CSS appears healthy
CRS appears healthy
EVM appears healthy
[oracle@crs2 ~]$

[oracle@crs1 cluvfy]$ /u01/software/clusterware/cluvfy/runcluvfy.sh stage -post crsinst -n crs1,crs2 -verbose

Post-check for cluster services setup was successful.

8.9 Install and Configure ASM

[oracle@crs1 cluvfy]$ /u01/software/clusterware/cluvfy/runcluvfy.sh stage -pre dbinst -n crs1,crs2 -verbose

Ignore Linux package version warnings

- Set ASM Environments

[oracle@crs1 ~]$. /home/oracle/asm_profile

[oracle@crs1 ~]$ echo $ORACLE_HOME
/u01/app/oracle/product/10.2.0/asm_1

- Install ASM Software

  [oracle@crs1 database]$. /runInstaller

- Welcome Screen: Click Next
- Select Installation Type: Enterprise Edition (1.24 GB)
- Specify Home Details

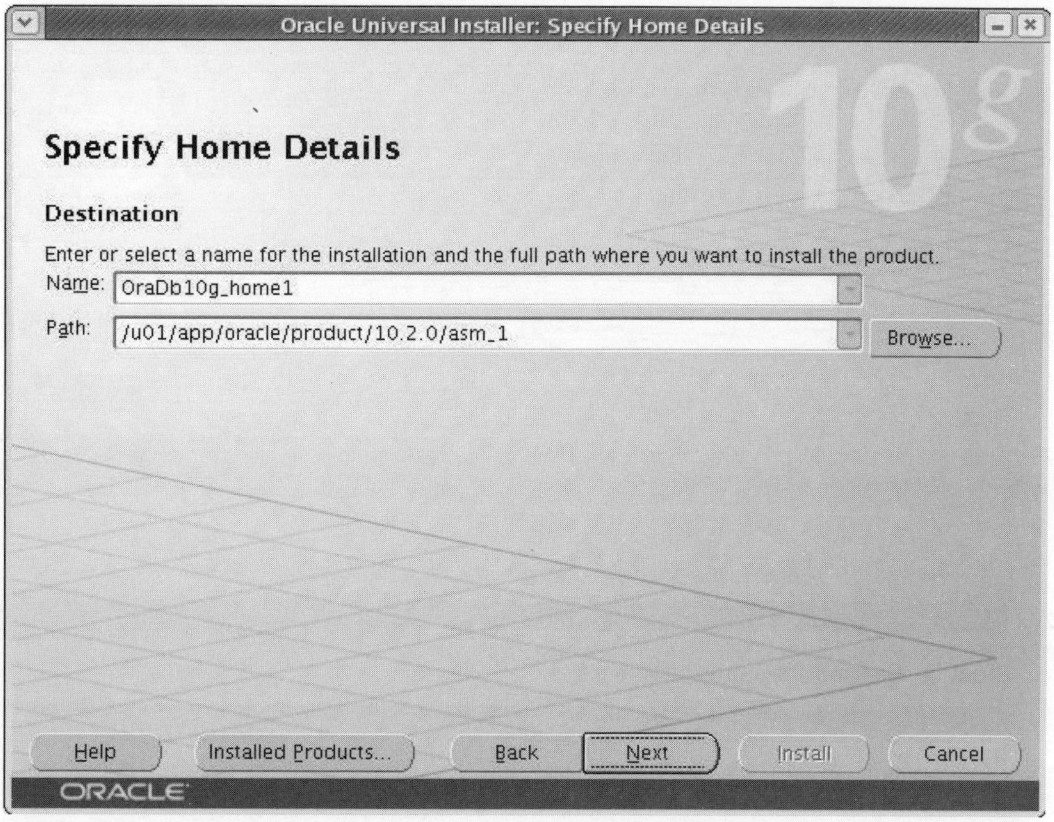

- Specify Hardware Cluster Installation Mode

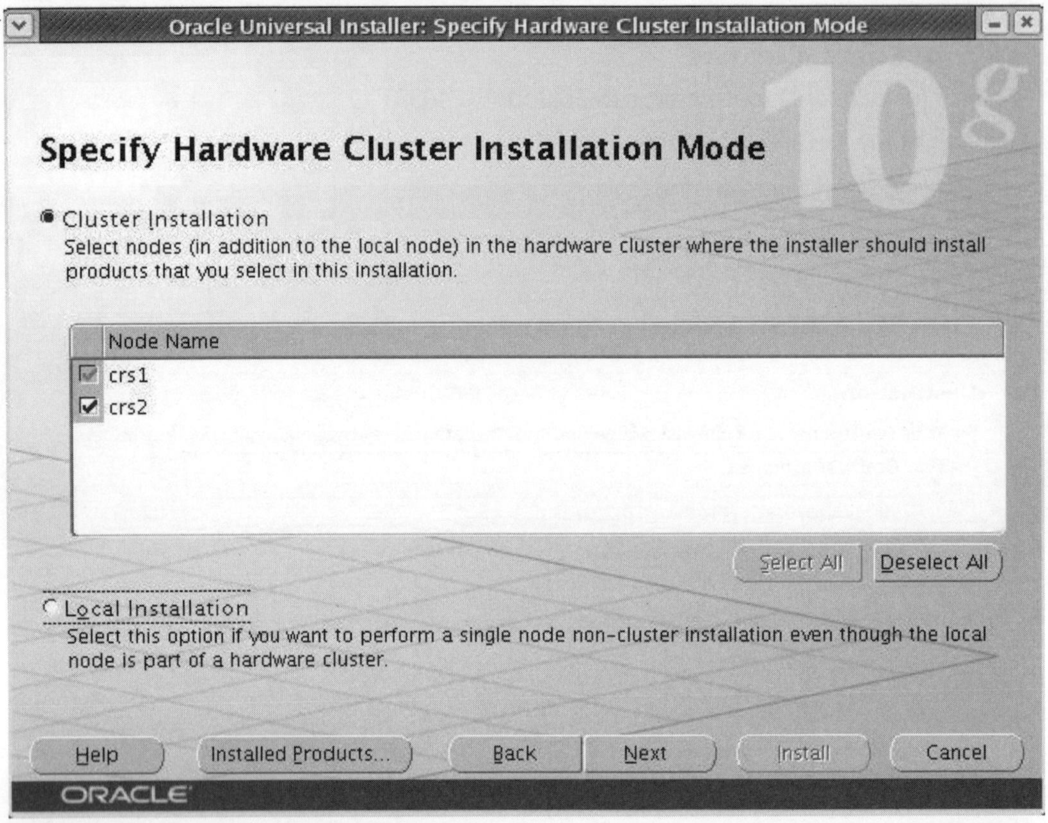

- Product- Specific Prerequisite Checks

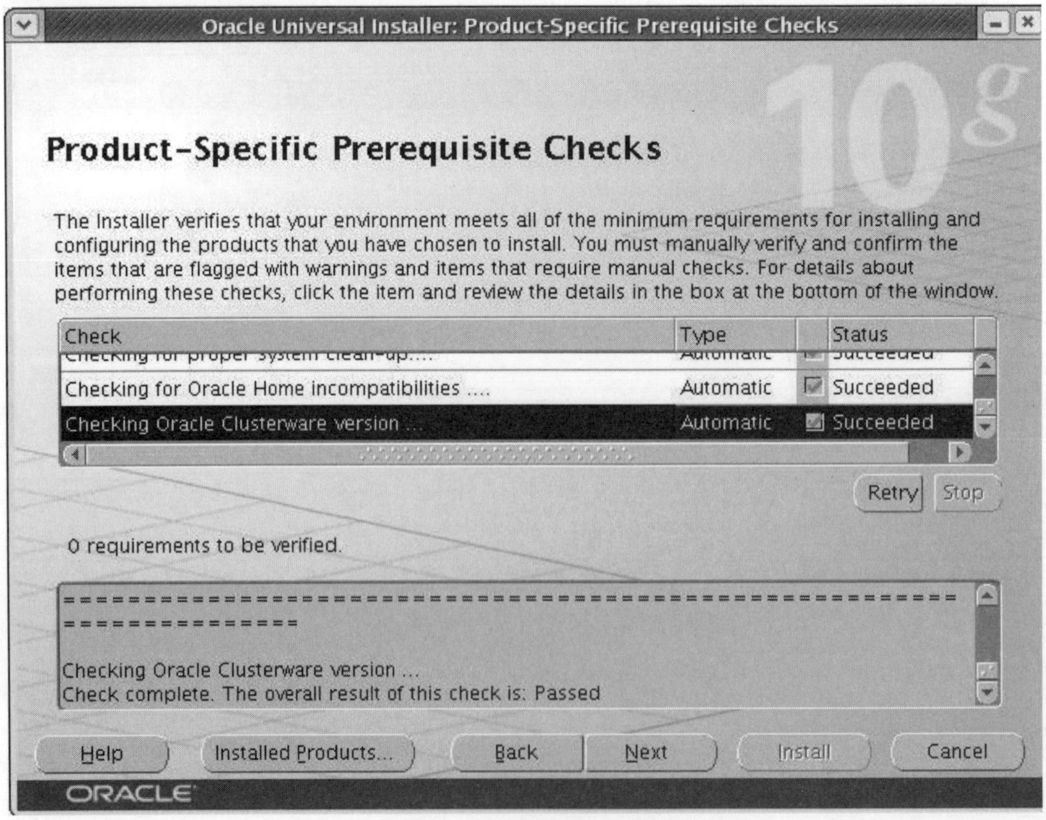

- Select Configuration Option

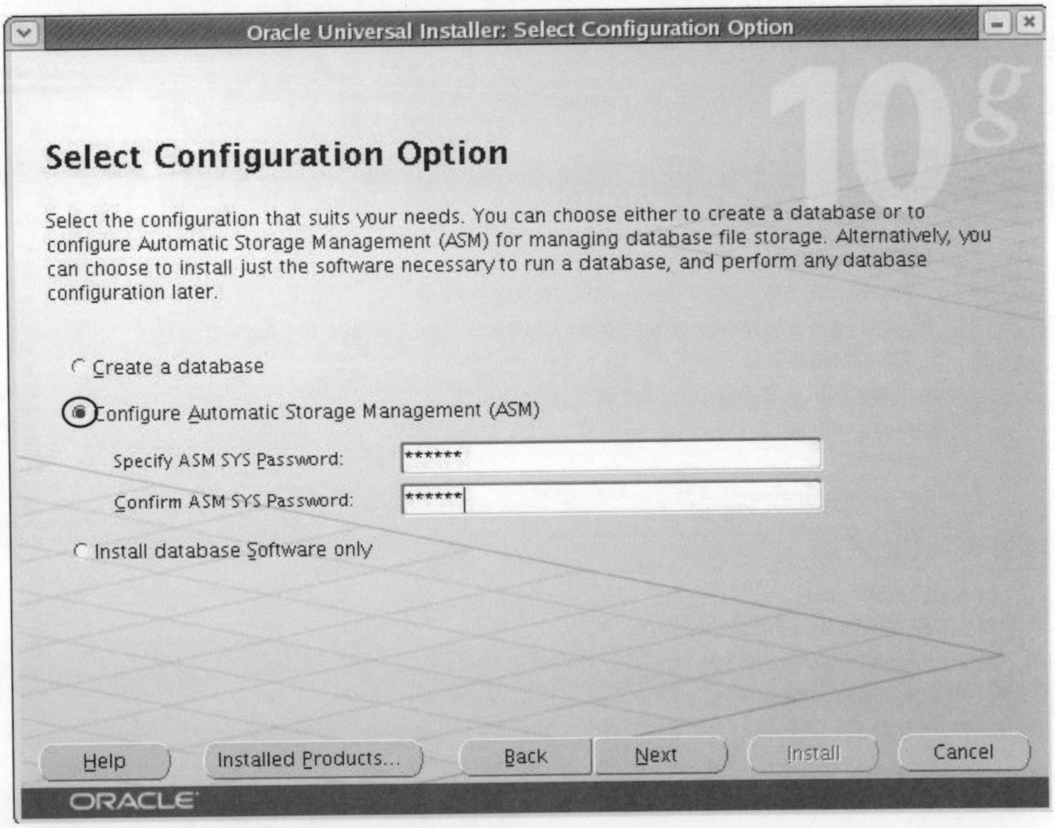

- Configure Automatic Storage Management

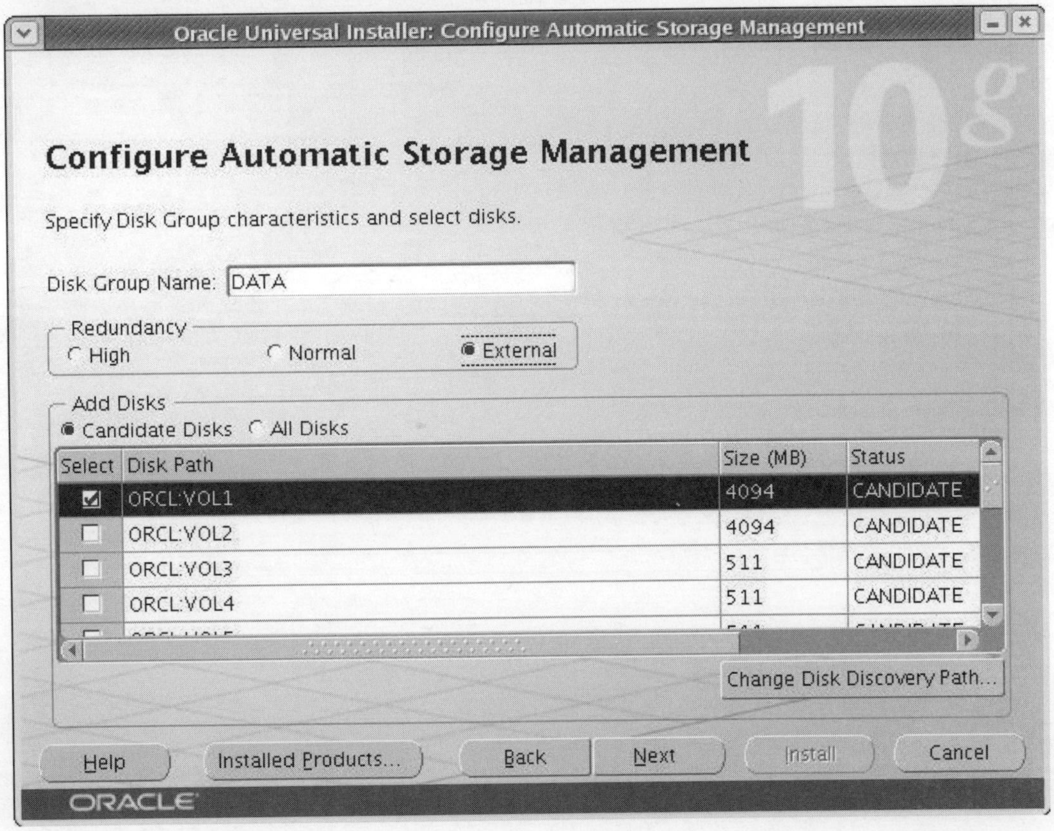

- Summary

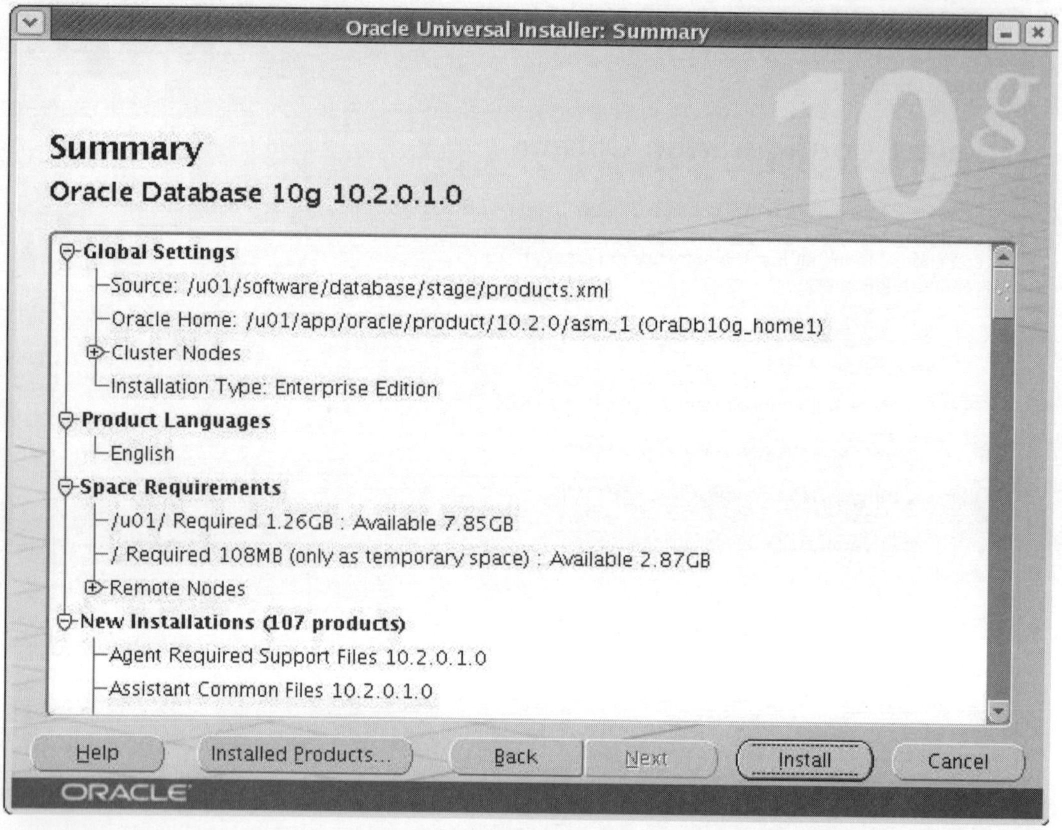

- Install

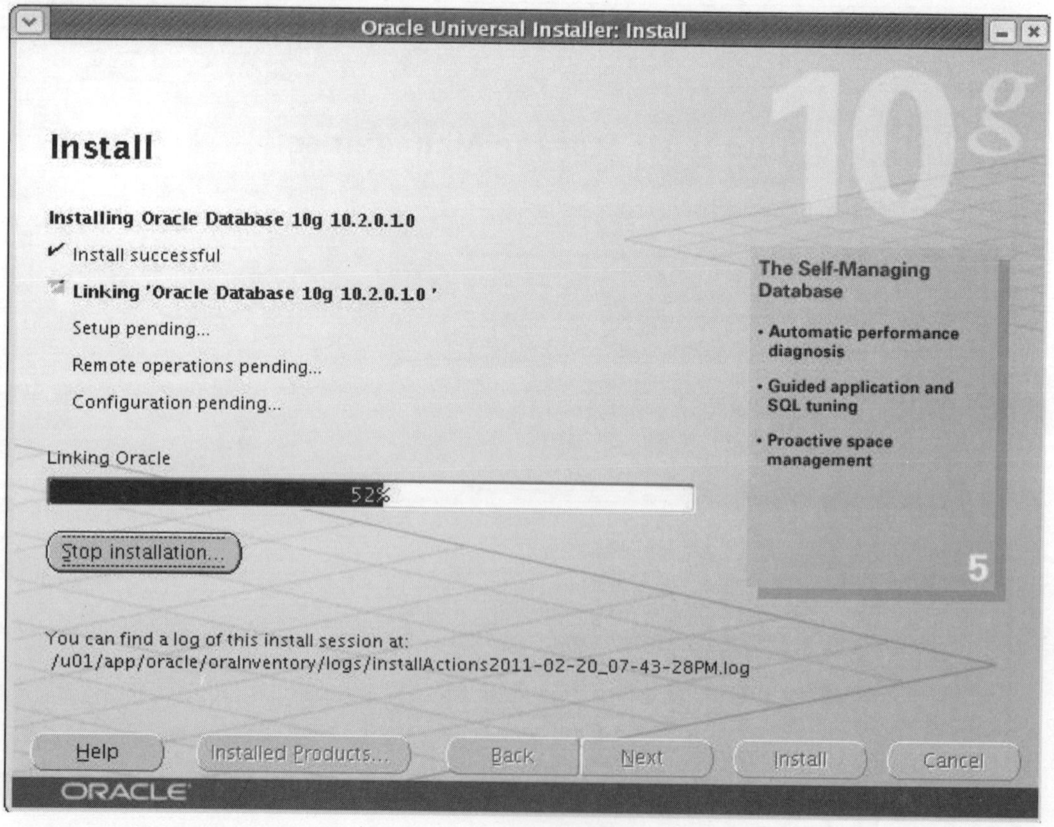

- Configuration Assistants

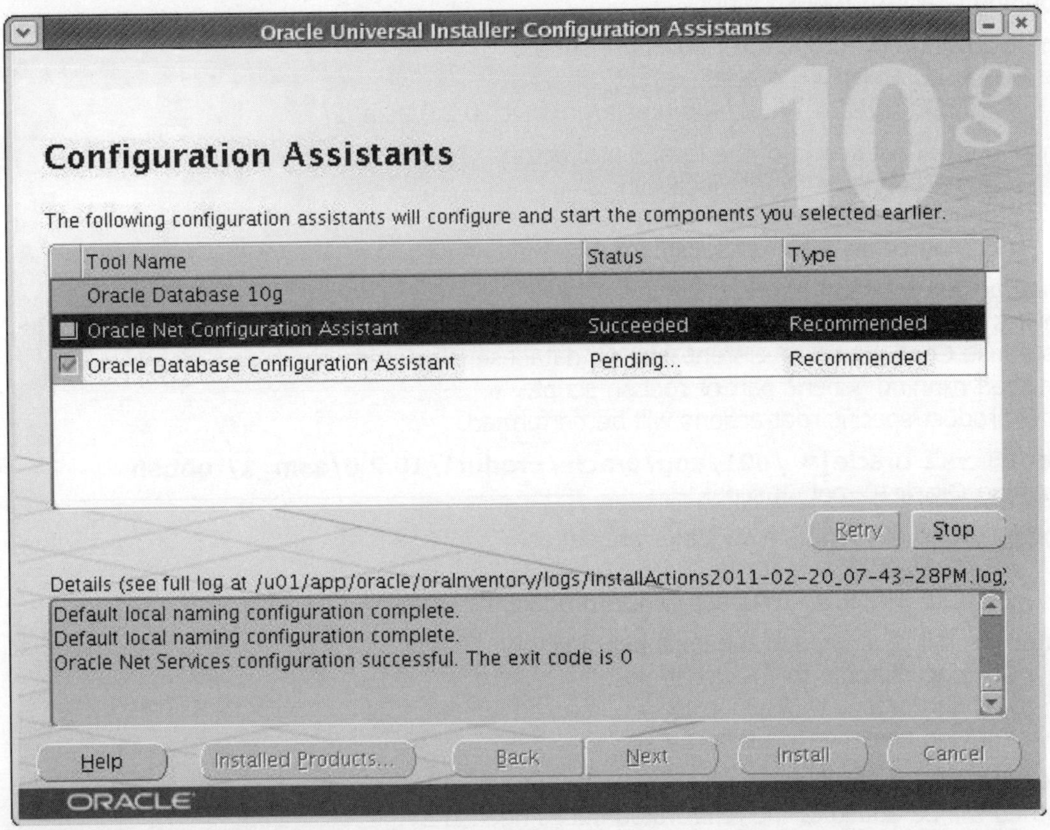

- Execute Configuration Scripts

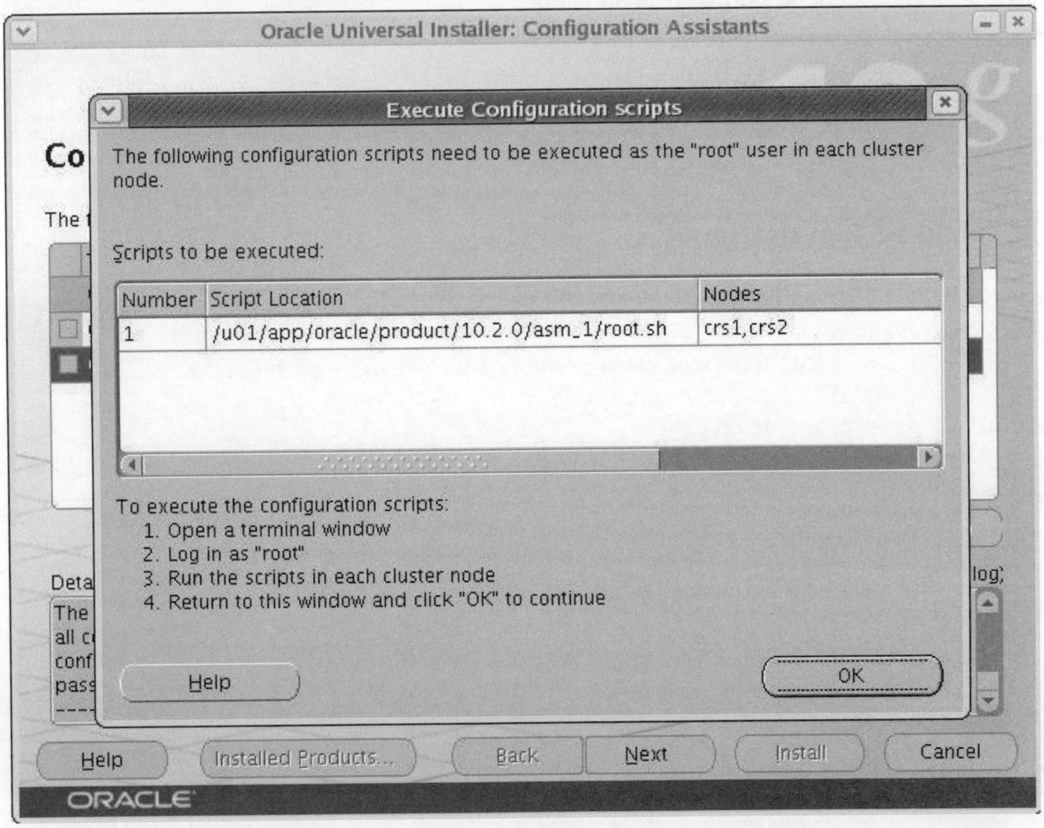

```
[root@crs1 oracle]# /u01/app/oracle/product/10.2.0/asm_1/root.sh
Running Oracle10 root.sh script...

The following environment variables are set as:
    ORACLE_OWNER= oracle
    ORACLE_HOME=  /u01/app/oracle/product/10.2.0/asm_1

Enter the full pathname of the local bin directory: [/usr/local/bin]:
    Copying dbhome to /usr/local/bin ...
    Copying oraenv to /usr/local/bin ...
    Copying coraenv to /usr/local/bin ...

Creating /etc/oratab file...
Entries will be added to the /etc/oratab file as needed by
Database Configuration Assistant when a database is created
Finished running generic part of root.sh script.
Now product-specific root actions will be performed.

[root@crs2 oracle]# /u01/app/oracle/product/10.2.0/asm_1/root.sh
Running Oracle10 root.sh script...

The following environment variables are set as:
    ORACLE_OWNER= oracle
    ORACLE_HOME=  /u01/app/oracle/product/10.2.0/asm_1

Enter the full pathname of the local bin directory: [/usr/local/bin]:
    Copying dbhome to /usr/local/bin ...
    Copying oraenv to /usr/local/bin ...
    Copying coraenv to /usr/local/bin ...

Creating /etc/oratab file...
Entries will be added to the /etc/oratab file as needed by
Database Configuration Assistant when a database is created
Finished running generic part of root.sh script.
Now product-specific root actions will be performed.
```

- End of Installation

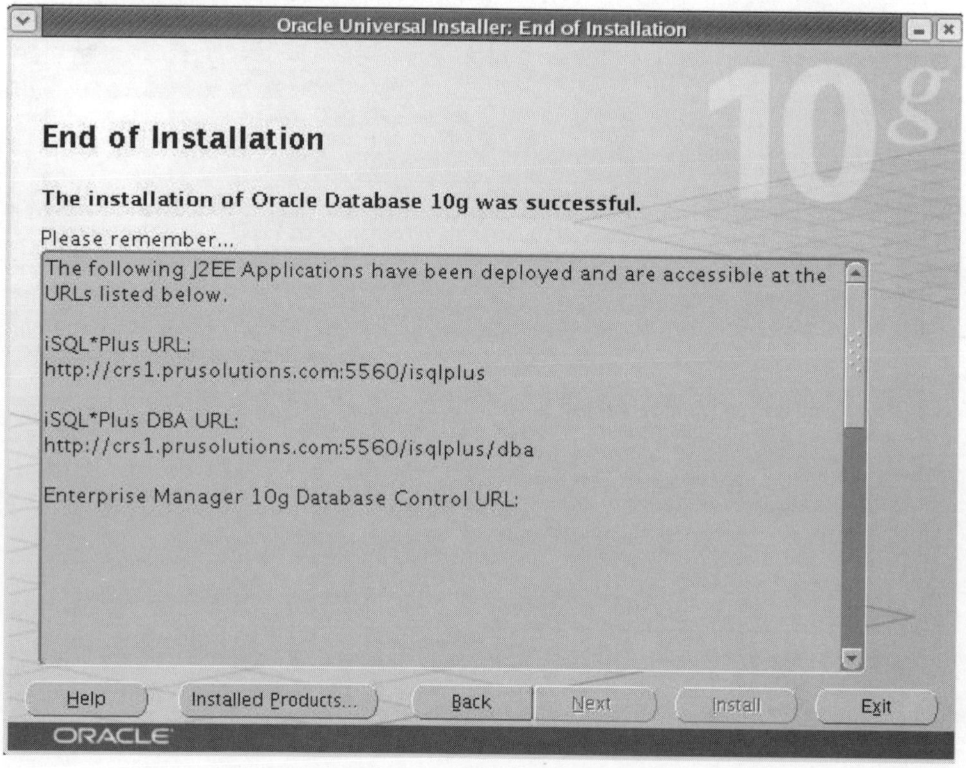

8.10 Install Database Software

[oracle@crs1 cluvfy]$ /u01/software/clusterware/cluvfy/runcluvfy.sh stage -pre dbinst -n crs1,crs2 -verbose

Ignore Linux package version warnings

[oracle@crs1 ~]$. /home/oracle/.bash_profile

[oracle@crs1 ~]$ echo $ORACLE_HOME
/u01/app/oracle/product/10.2.0/db_1

[oracle@crs1 ~]$ echo $ORACLE_SID
crsdb1

- Welcome Screen: Click Next
- Select Installation Type: Enterprise Edition (1.24GB)
- Select Configuration Option: Install database Software only

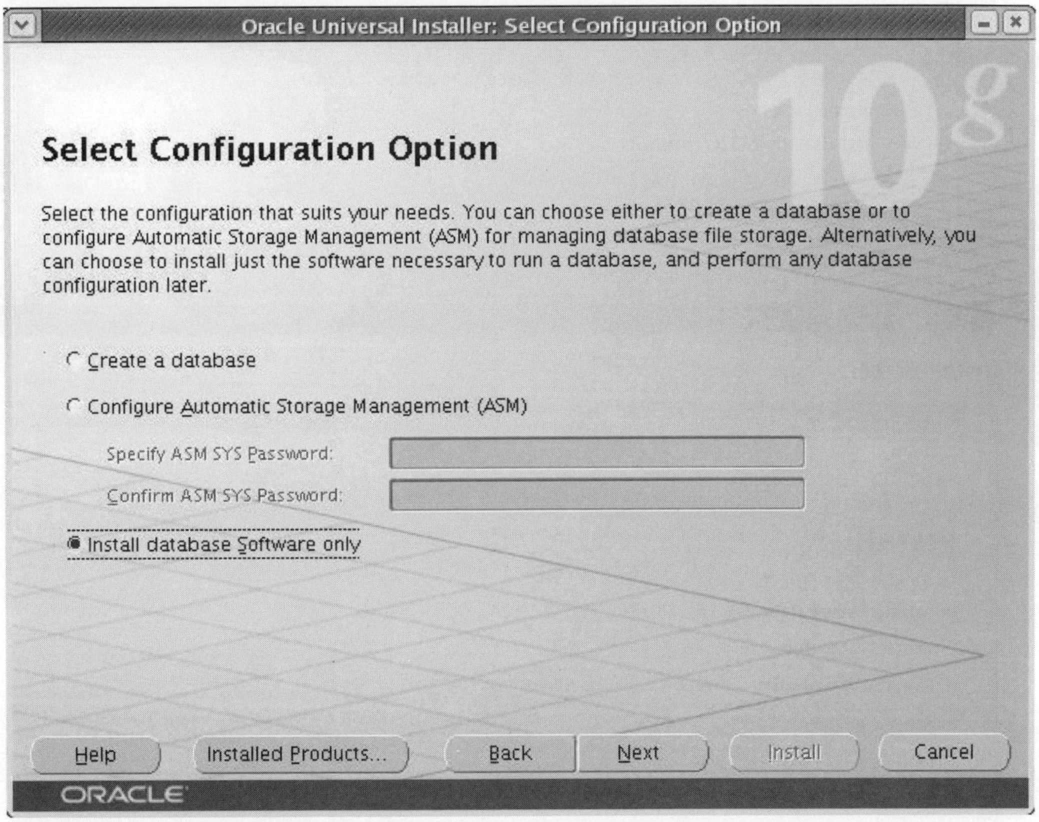

- Summary: Click Install

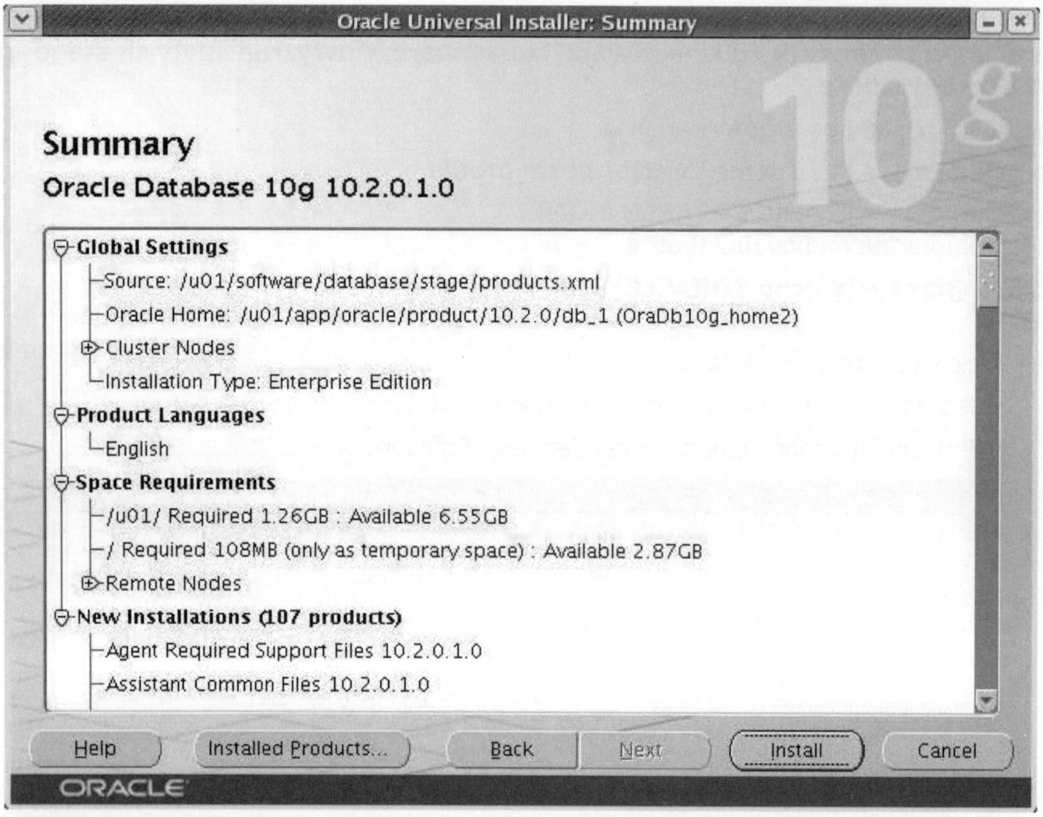

- Install Screen

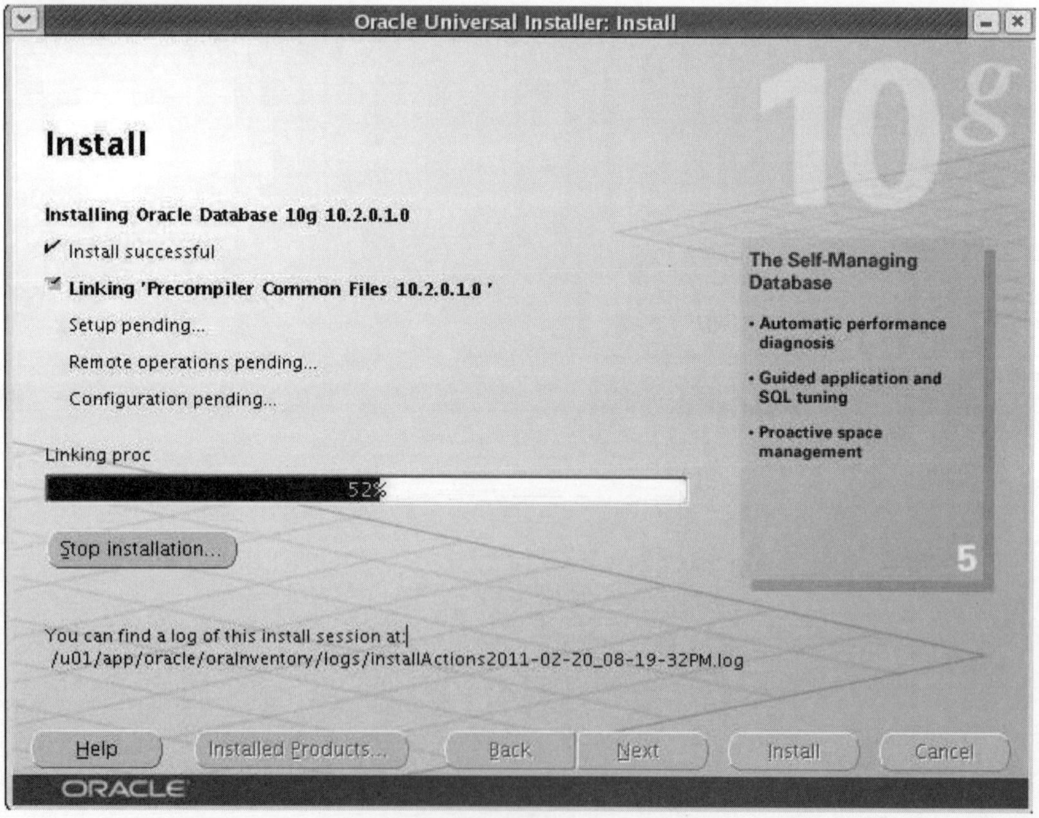

- Execute Configuration Scripts

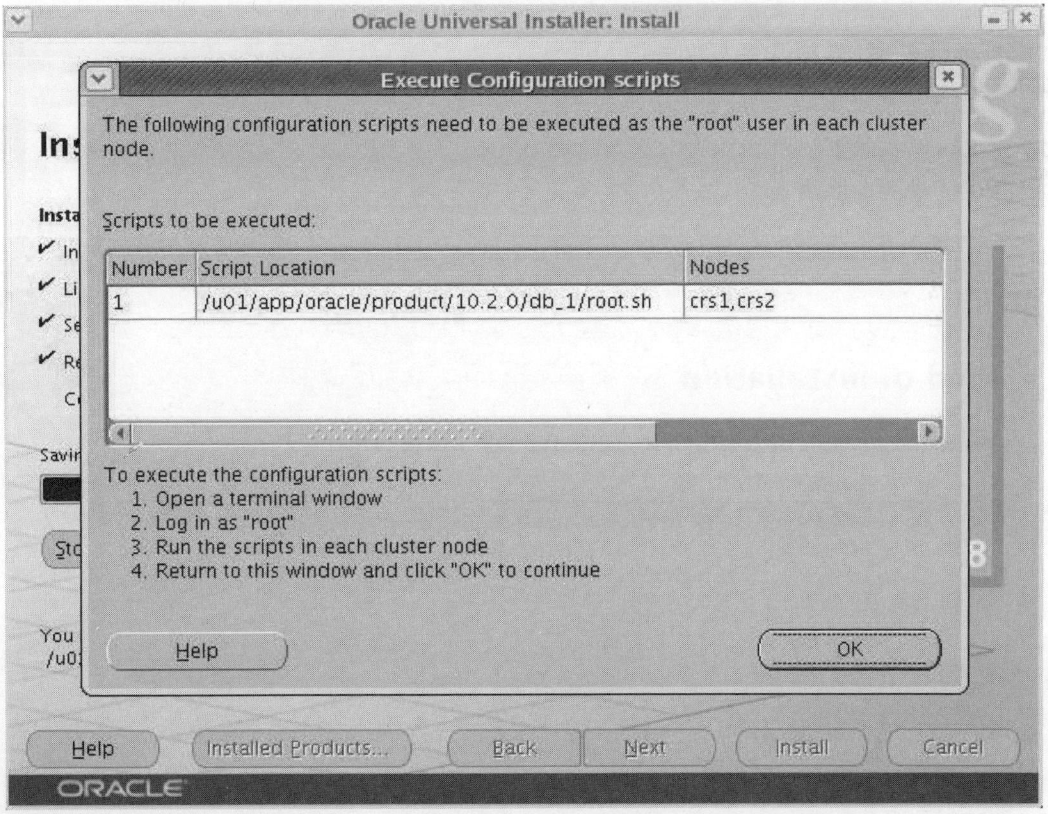

[root@crs1 oracle]# /u01/app/oracle/product/10.2.0/db_1/root.sh
Running Oracle10 root.sh script...

The following environment variables are set as:
    ORACLE_OWNER= oracle
    ORACLE_HOME= /u01/app/oracle/product/10.2.0/db_1

Enter the full pathname of the local bin directory: [/usr/local/bin]:
The file "dbhome" already exists in /usr/local/bin. Overwrite it? (y/n)
[n]:
The file "oraenv" already exists in /usr/local/bin. Overwrite it? (y/n)
[n]:
The file "coraenv" already exists in /usr/local/bin. Overwrite it? (y/n)
[n]:

Entries will be added to the /etc/oratab file as needed by
Database Configuration Assistant when a database is created
Finished running generic part of root.sh script.
Now product-specific root actions will be performed.

[root@crs2 oracle]# /u01/app/oracle/product/10.2.0/db_1/root.sh
Running Oracle10 root.sh script...

The following environment variables are set as:
    ORACLE_OWNER= oracle
    ORACLE_HOME= /u01/app/oracle/product/10.2.0/db_1

Enter the full pathname of the local bin directory: [/usr/local/bin]:
The file "dbhome" already exists in /usr/local/bin. Overwrite it? (y/n)
[n]:
The file "oraenv" already exists in /usr/local/bin. Overwrite it? (y/n)
[n]:

The file "coraenv" already exists in /usr/local/bin. Overwrite it? (y/n)
[n]:

Entries will be added to the /etc/oratab file as needed by
Database Configuration Assistant when a database is created
Finished running generic part of root.sh script.
Now product-specific root actions will be performed.

- End of Installation

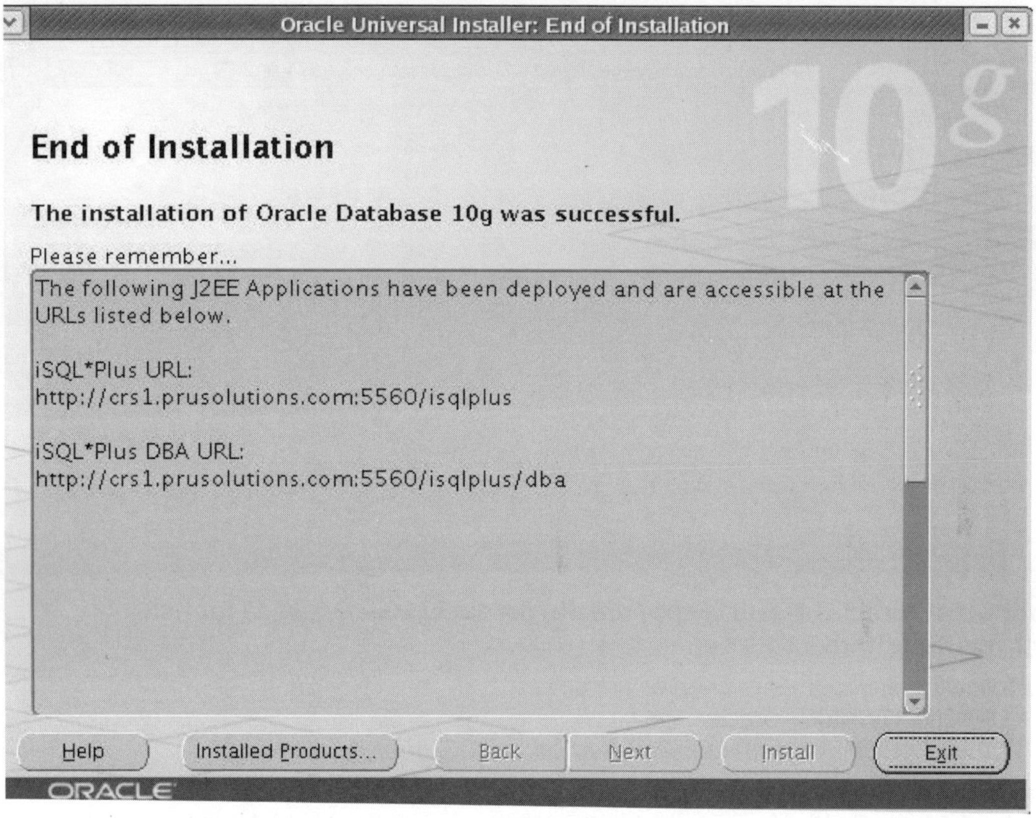

8.11 Create Database crsdb

[oracle@crs1 ~]$ dbca

- Database Configuration Assistant: Welcome

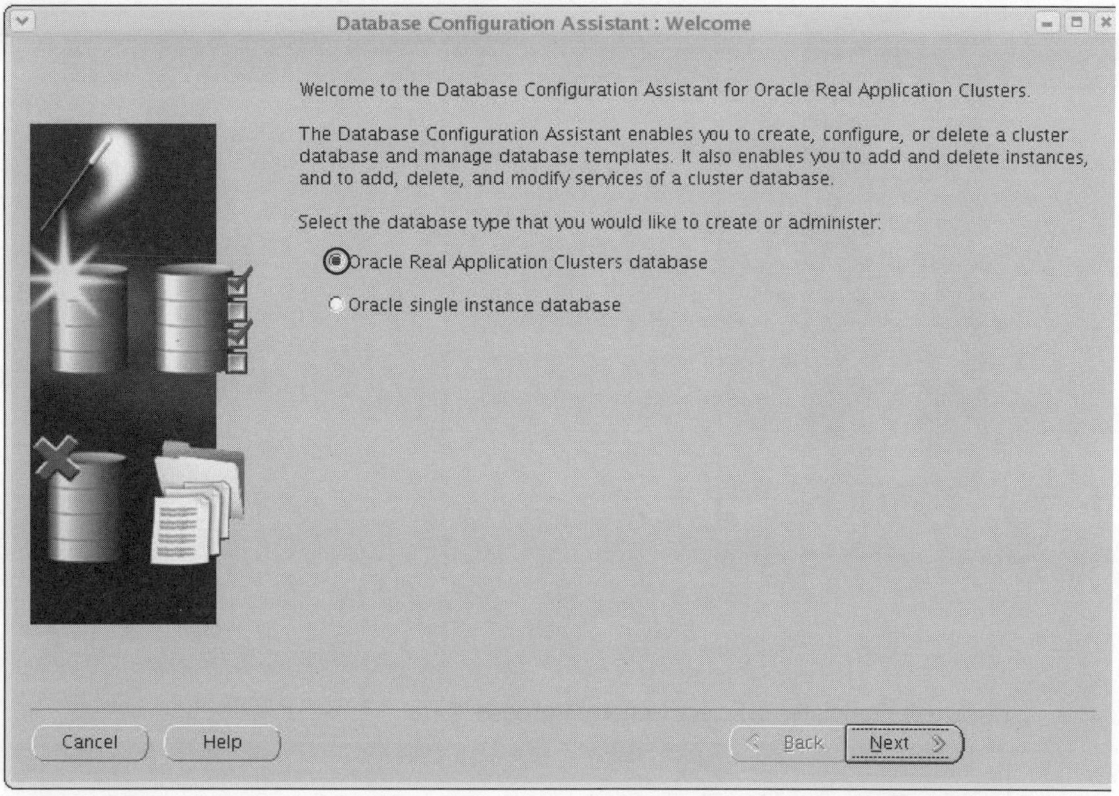

- Create a Database

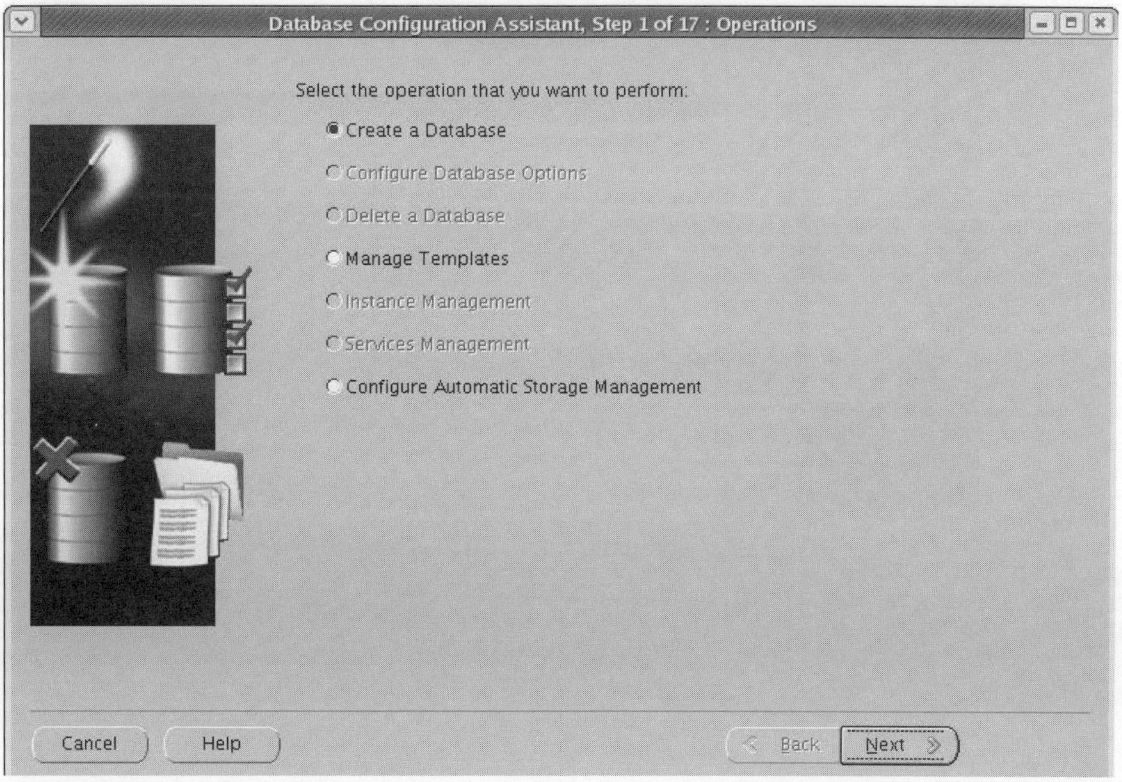

- Node Selection Screen: Select both the Nodes

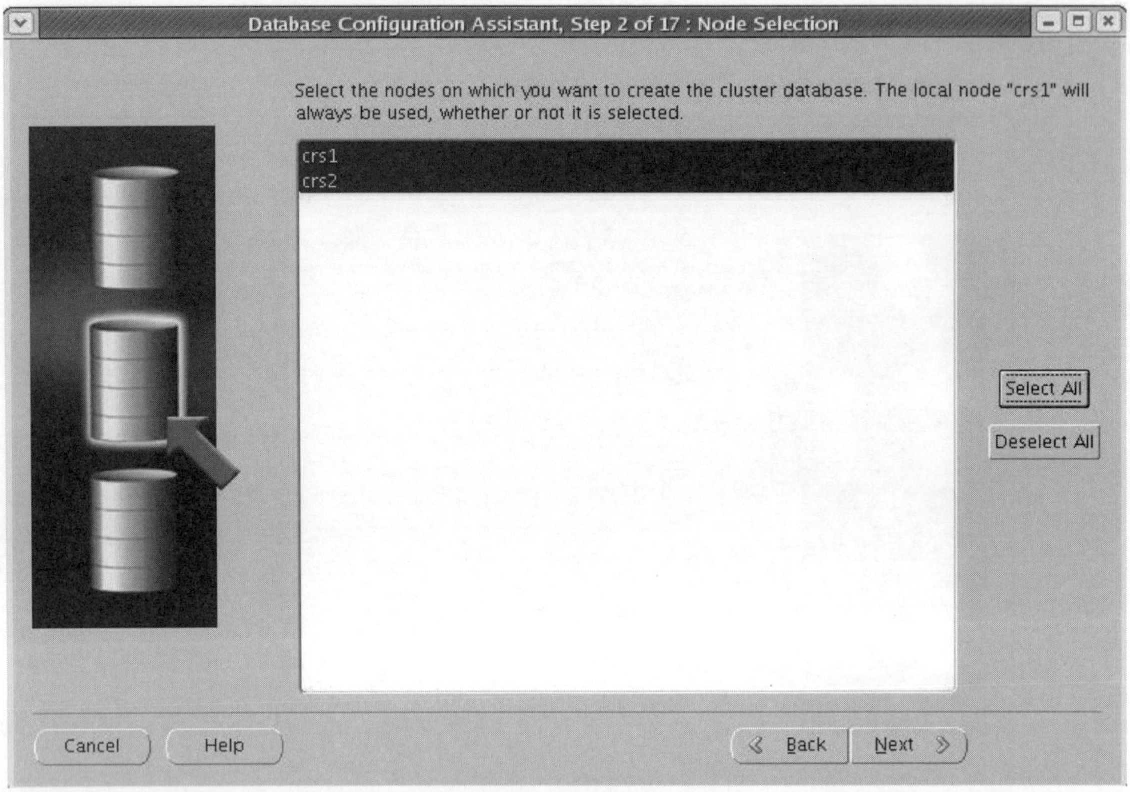

- Database Templates : Select General Purpose

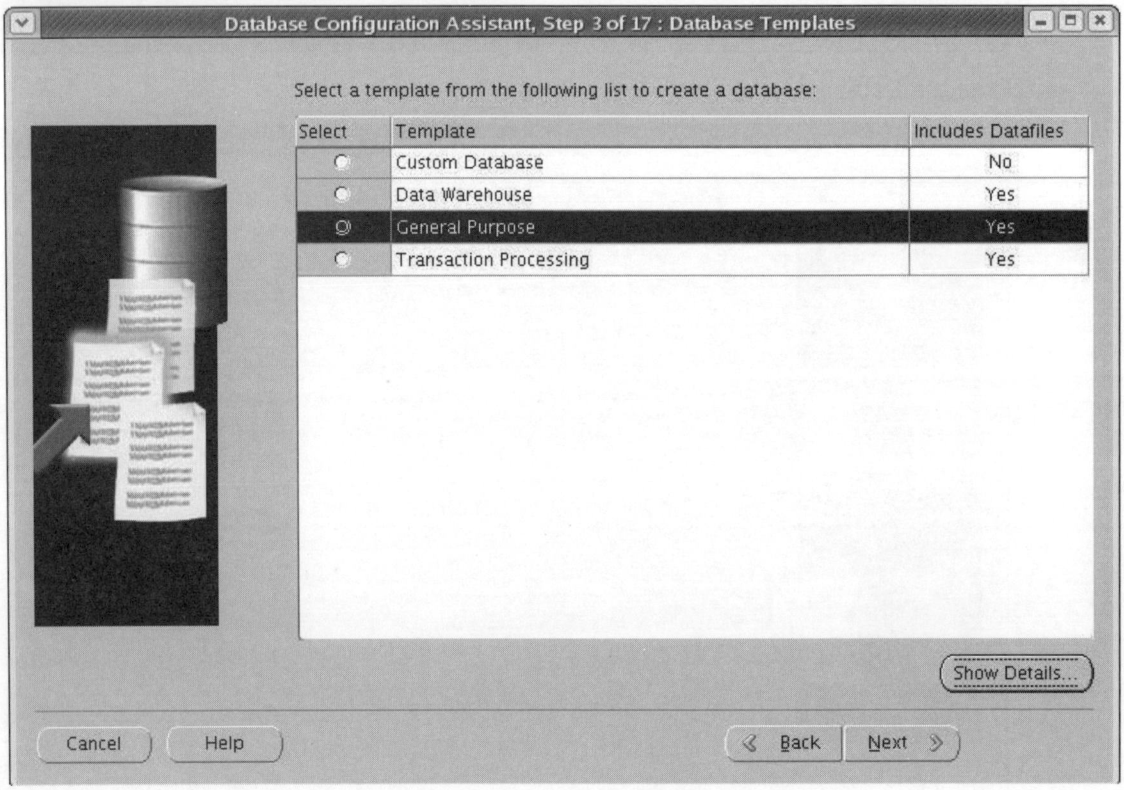

- Global Identification Screen: Global Database Name: **crsdb** SID Prefix: **crsdb**

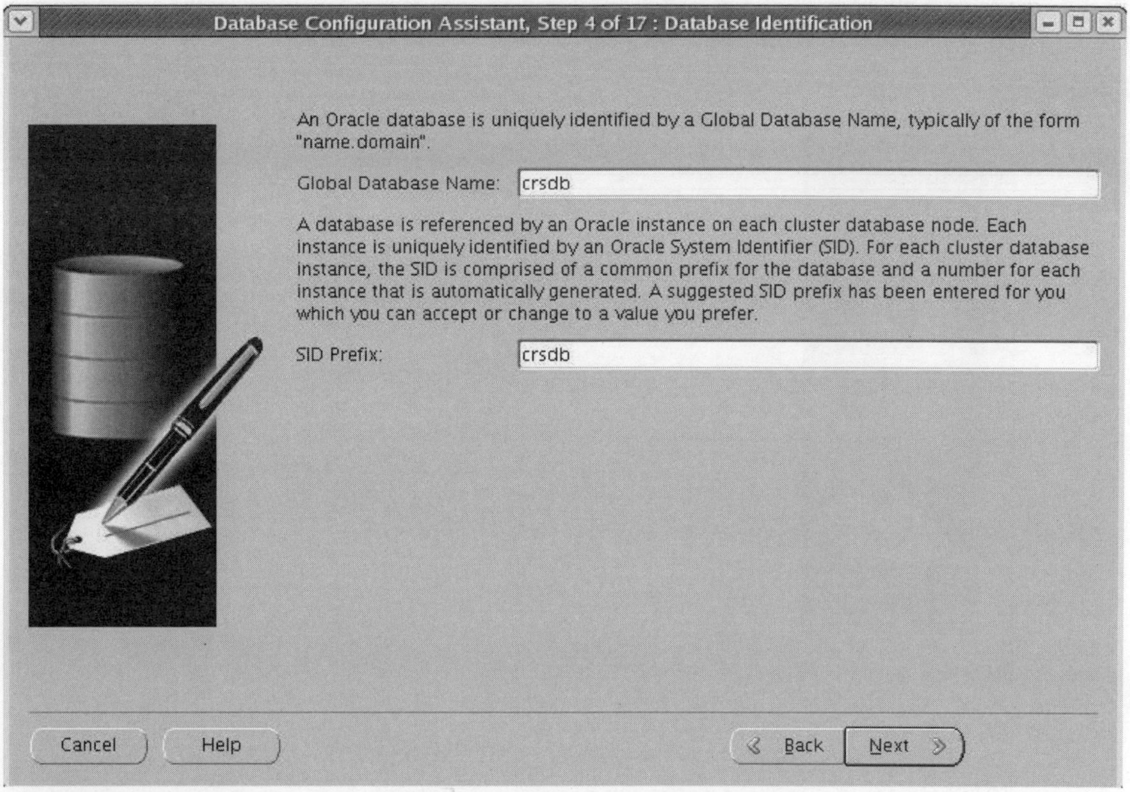

- Management Options

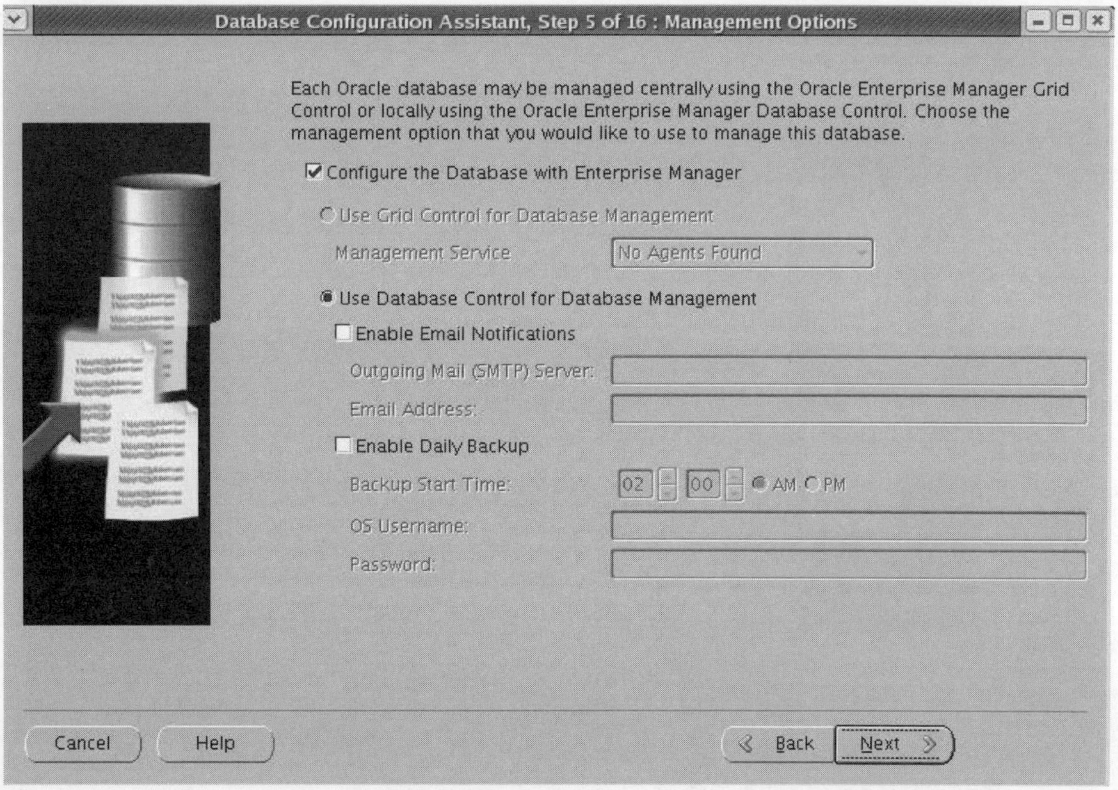

- Database Credentials: Password **oracle**

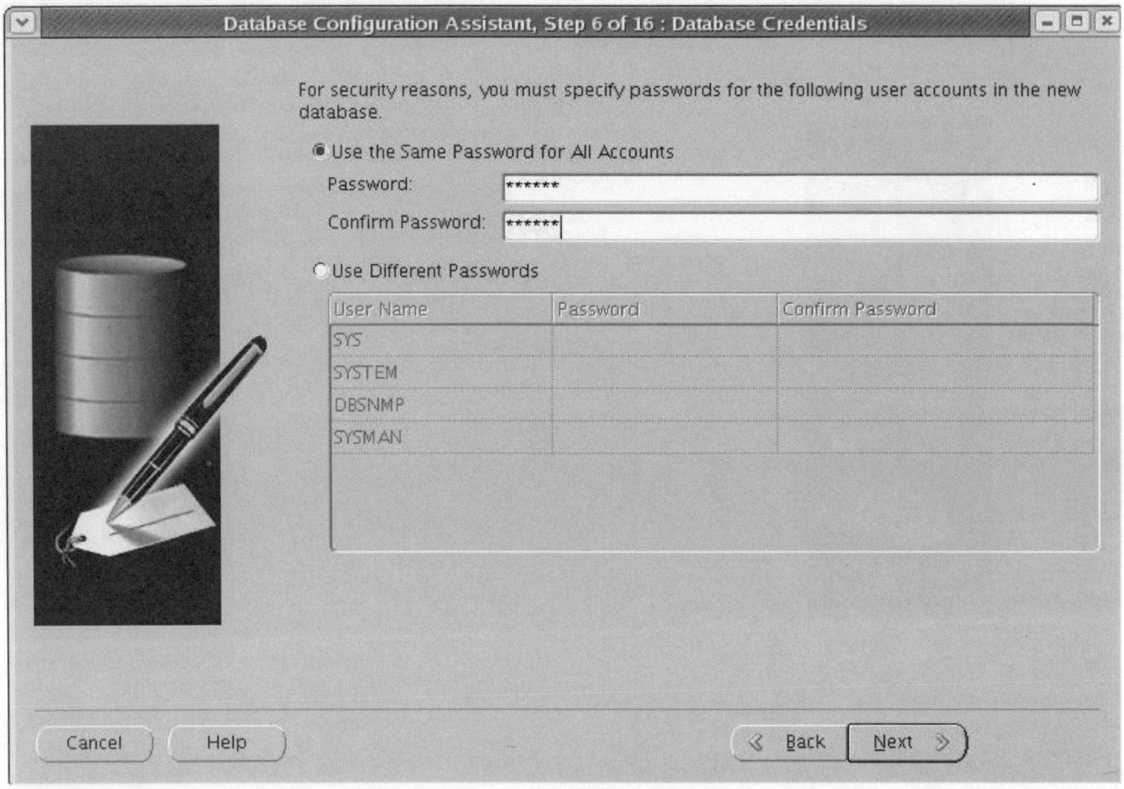

- Storage Options

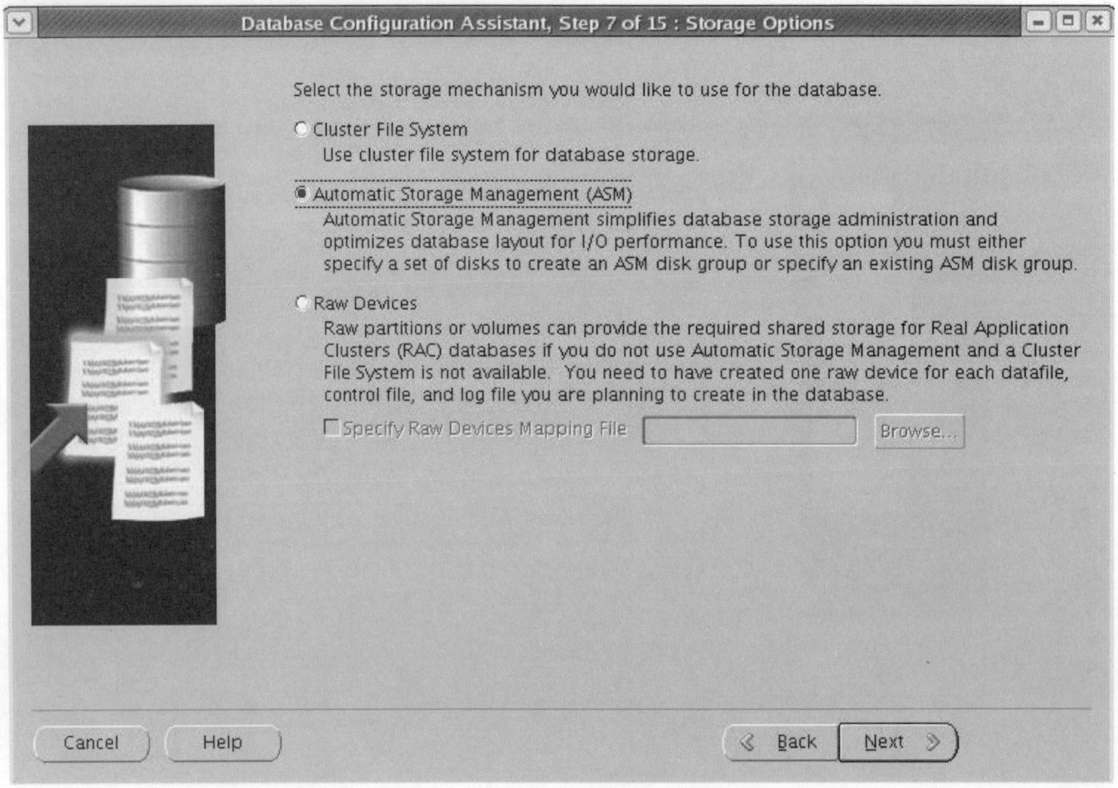

- Disk Groups: Create New

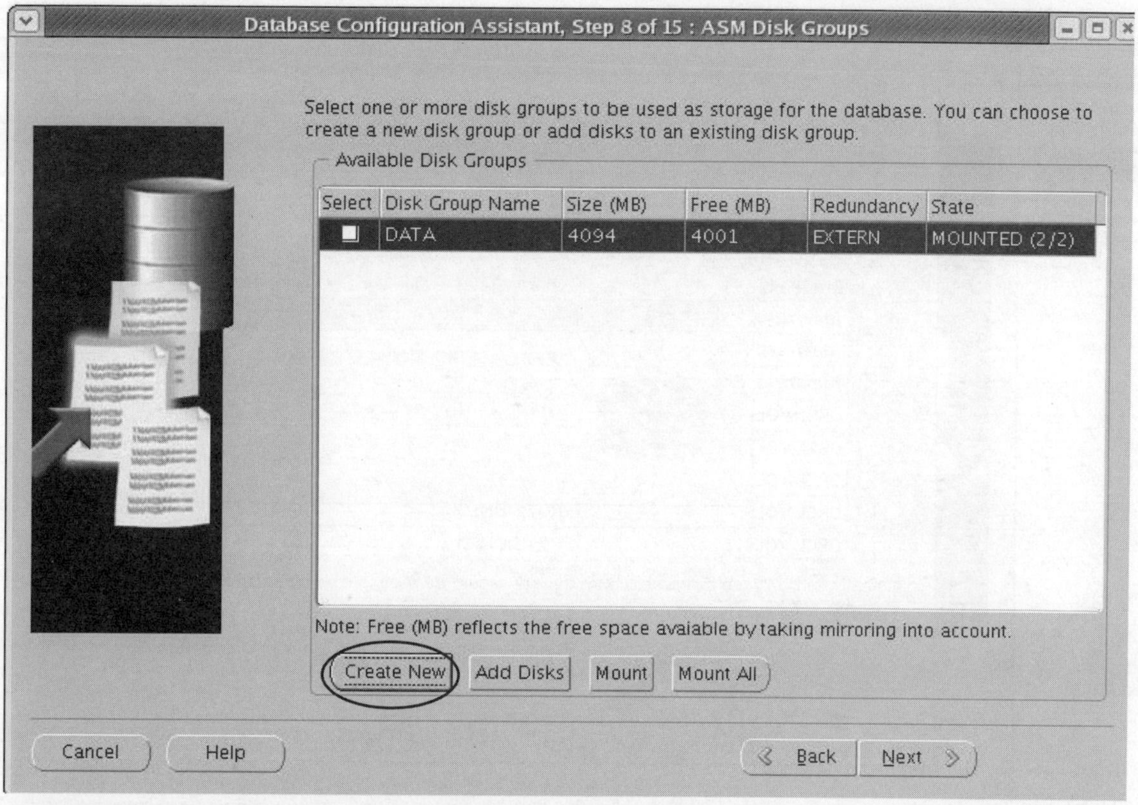

- Disk Group Name: FRA, Disk Path : ORCL: VOL2, Click OK

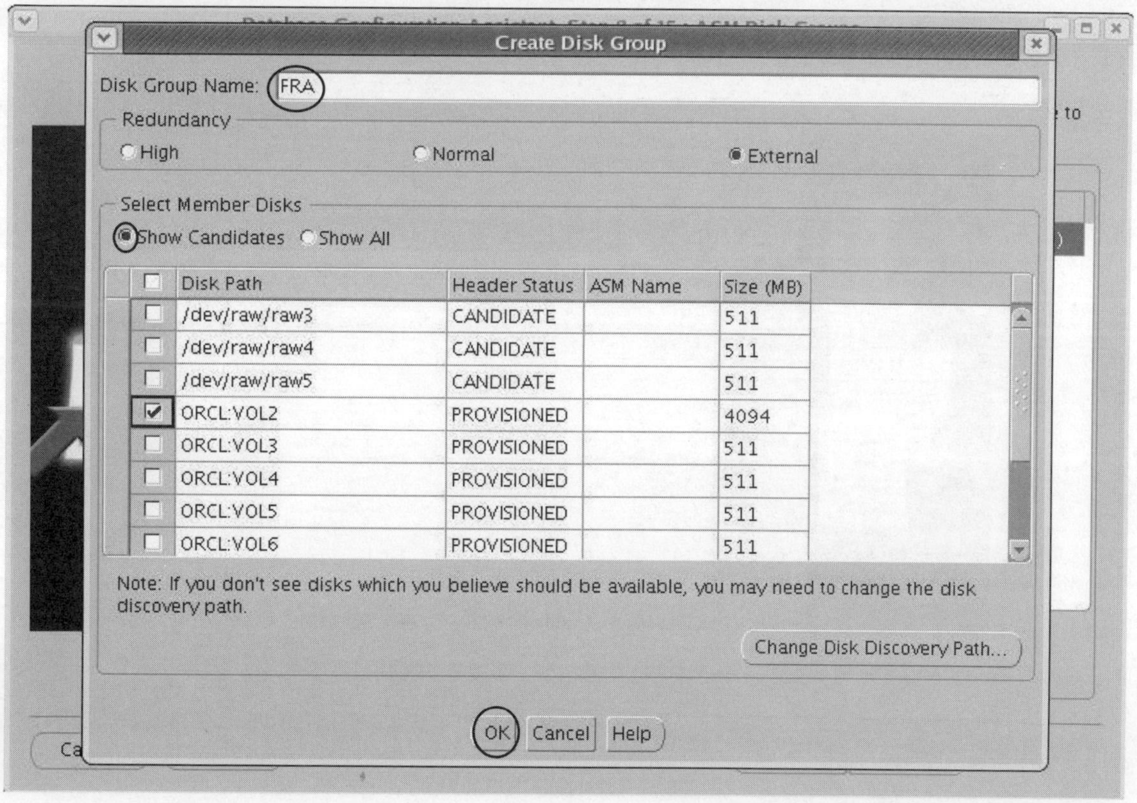

- ASM Disk Group Creation in Progress

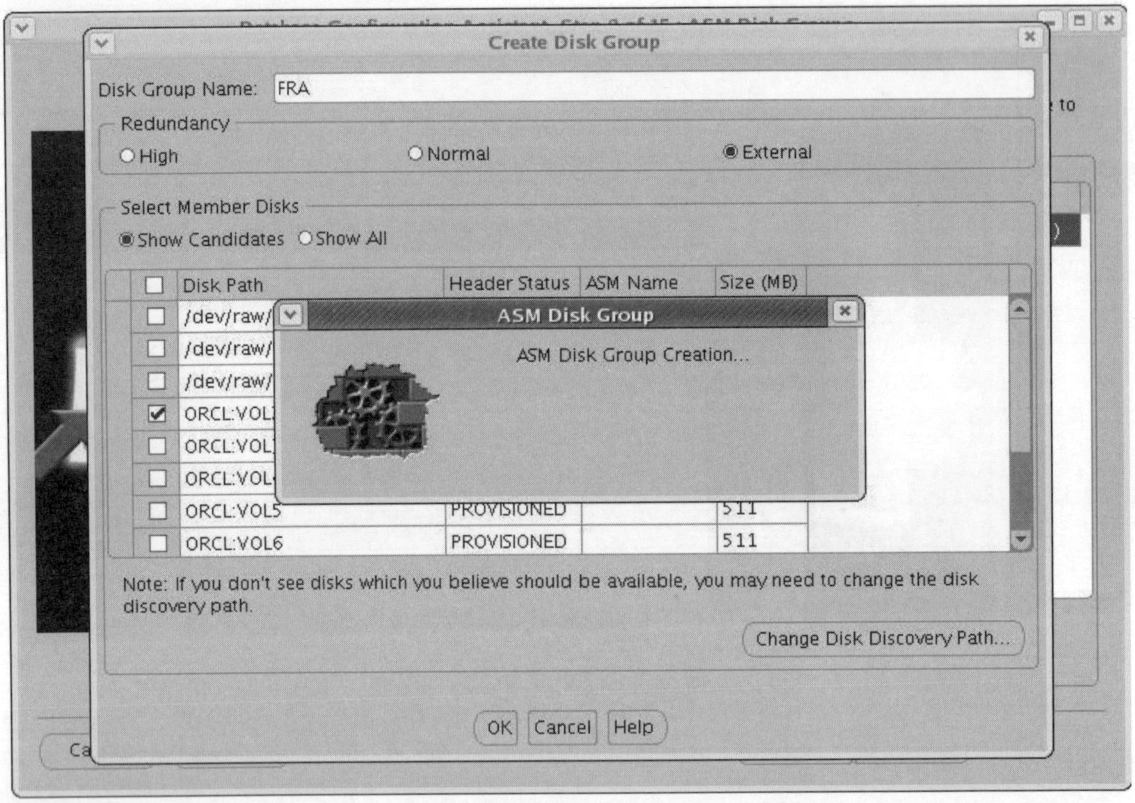

- Select Database Storage Disk Group: DATA

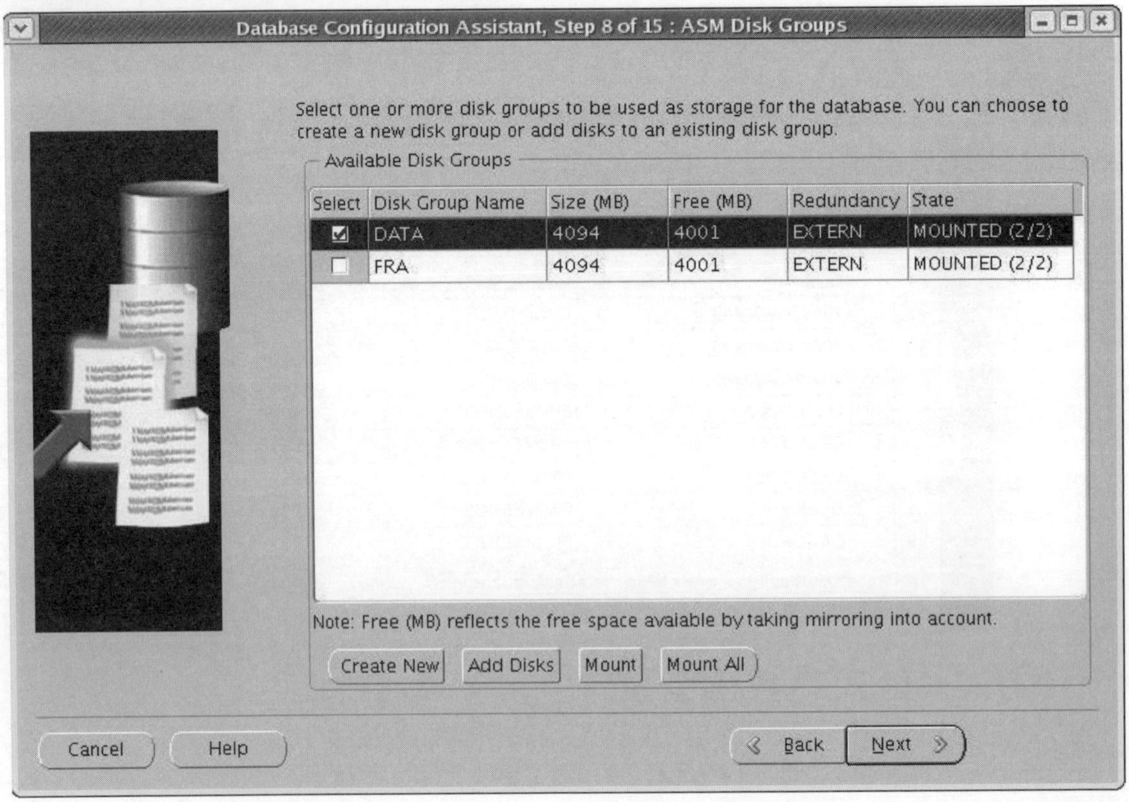

- Database File Locations: Use Oracle-Managed Files: +DATA

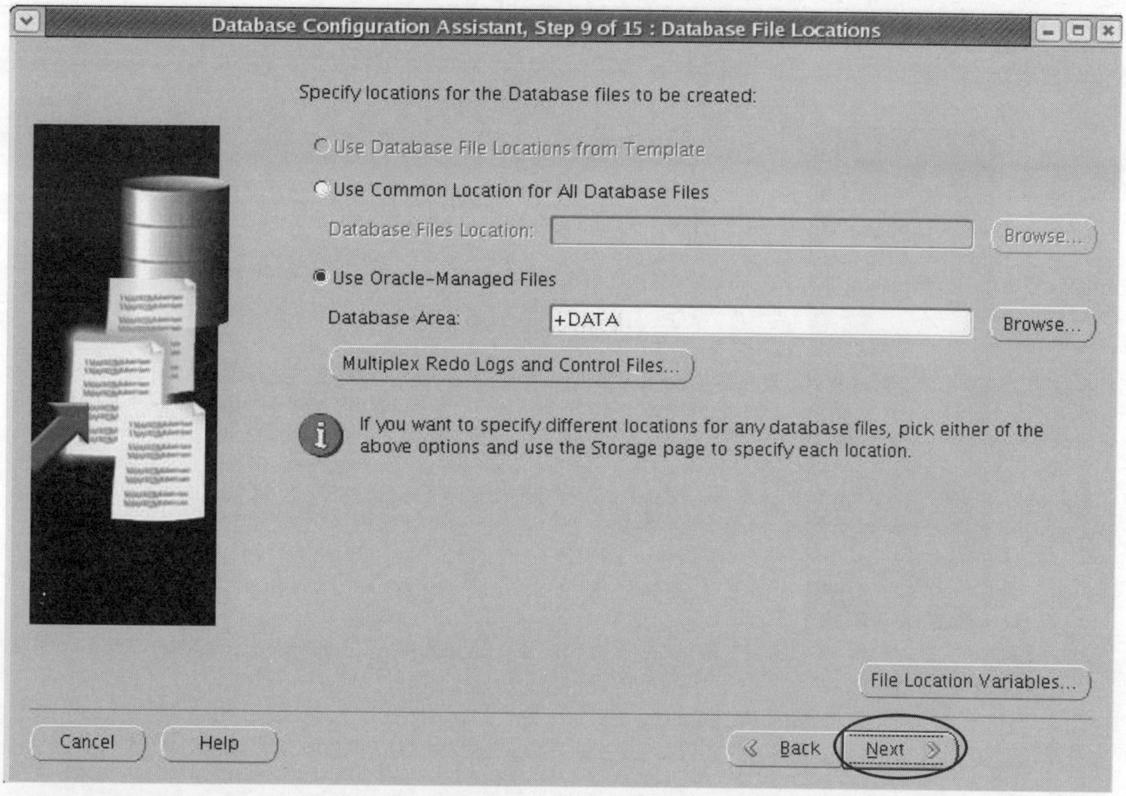

- Recovery Configuration: Specify Flash Recovery Area: + FRA , Flash Recovery Size 4096

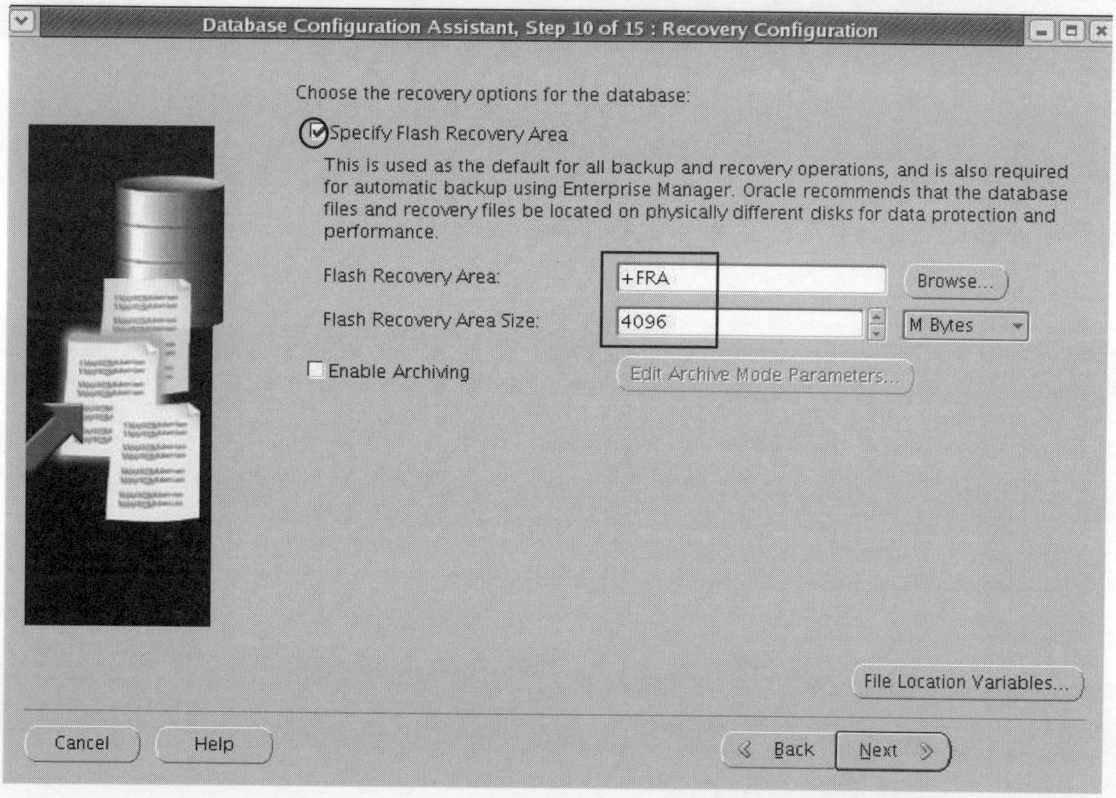

- Database Content: Sample Schemas

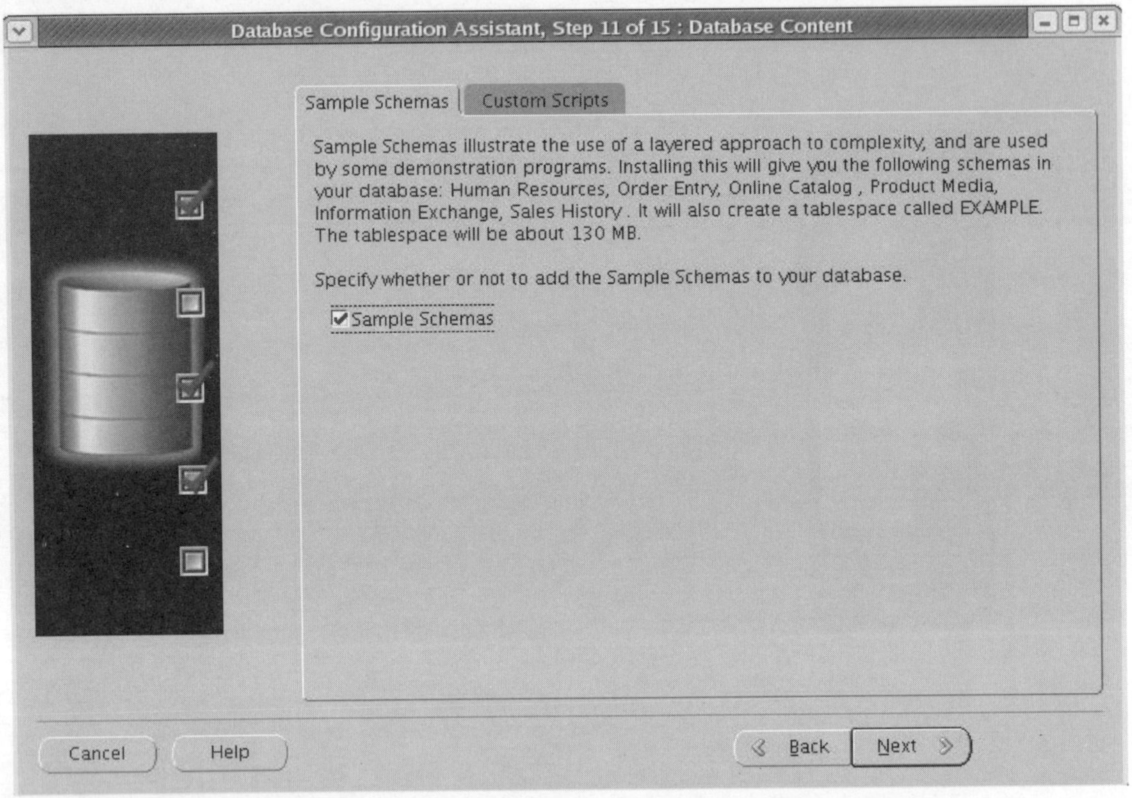

- Database Services: Click Next

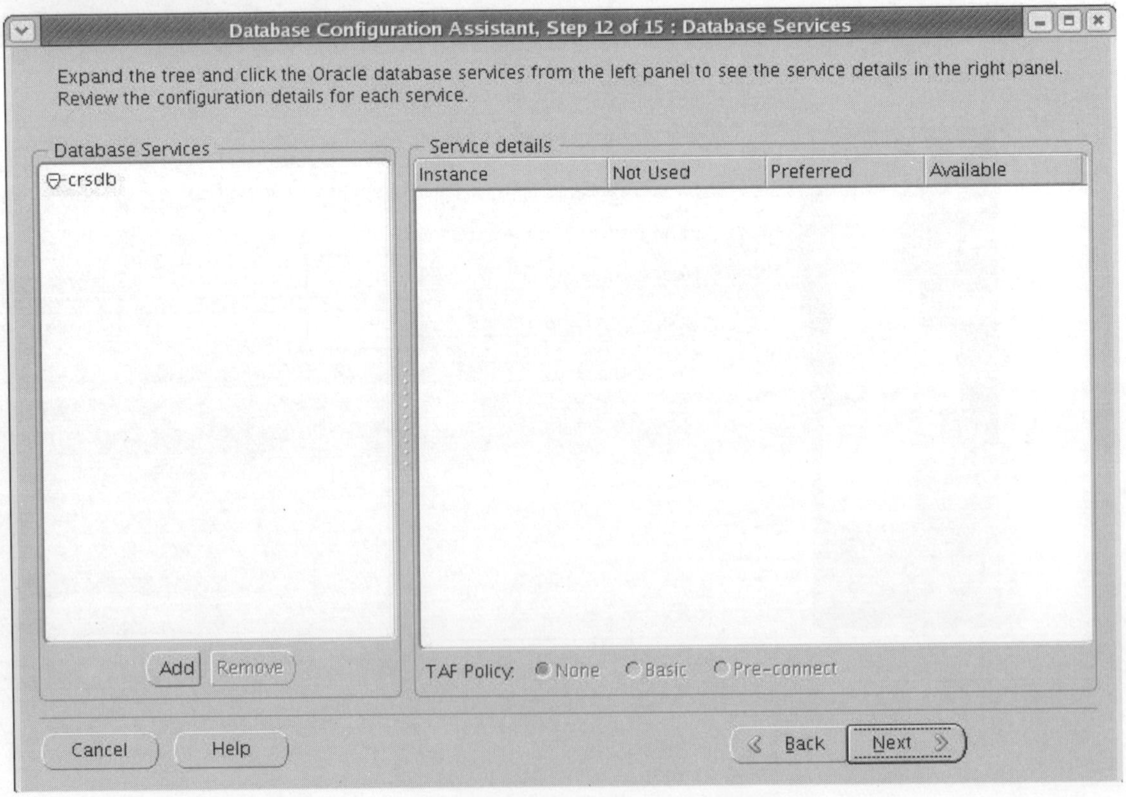

- Initialization Parameters: Typical Percentage: 40

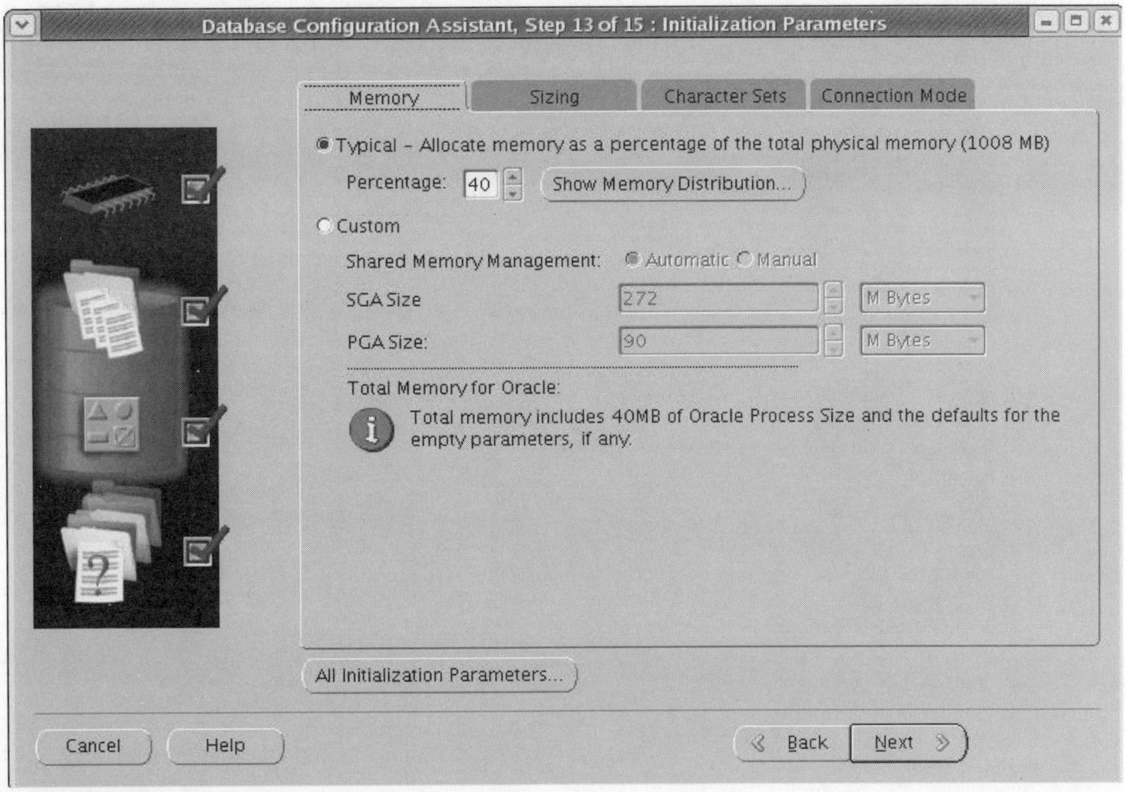

- Database Storage

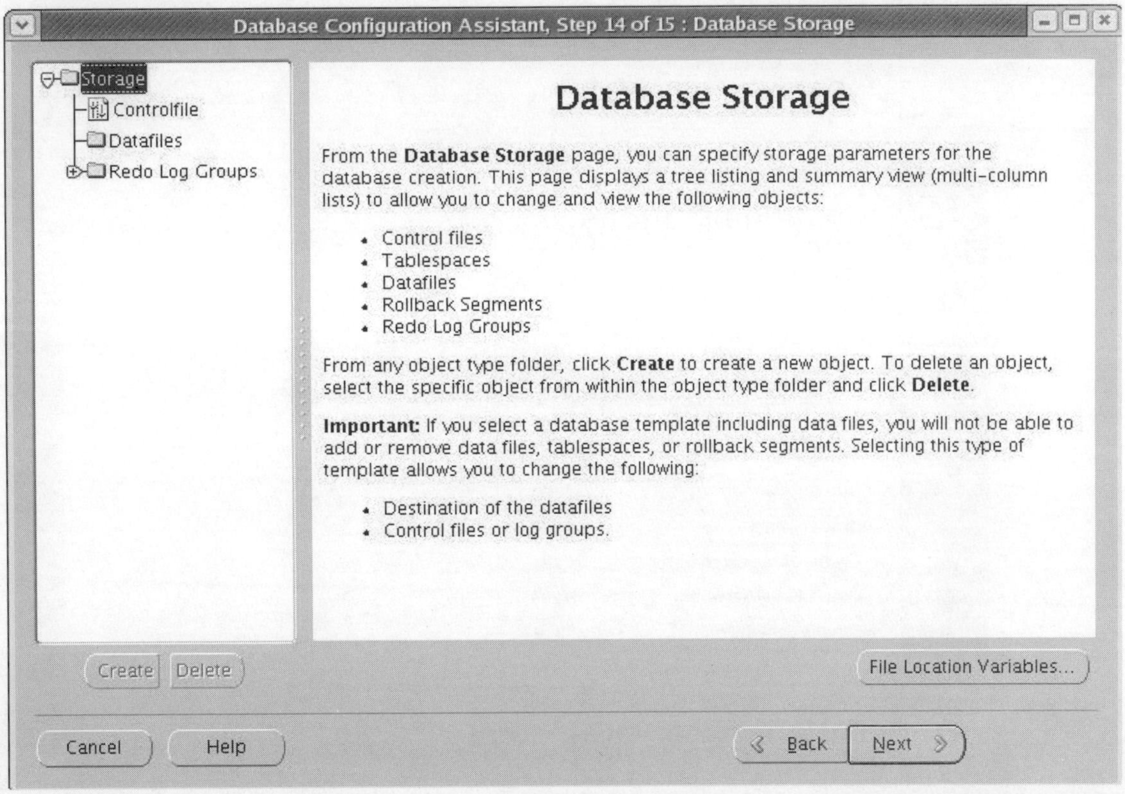

- Create Options: Create Database

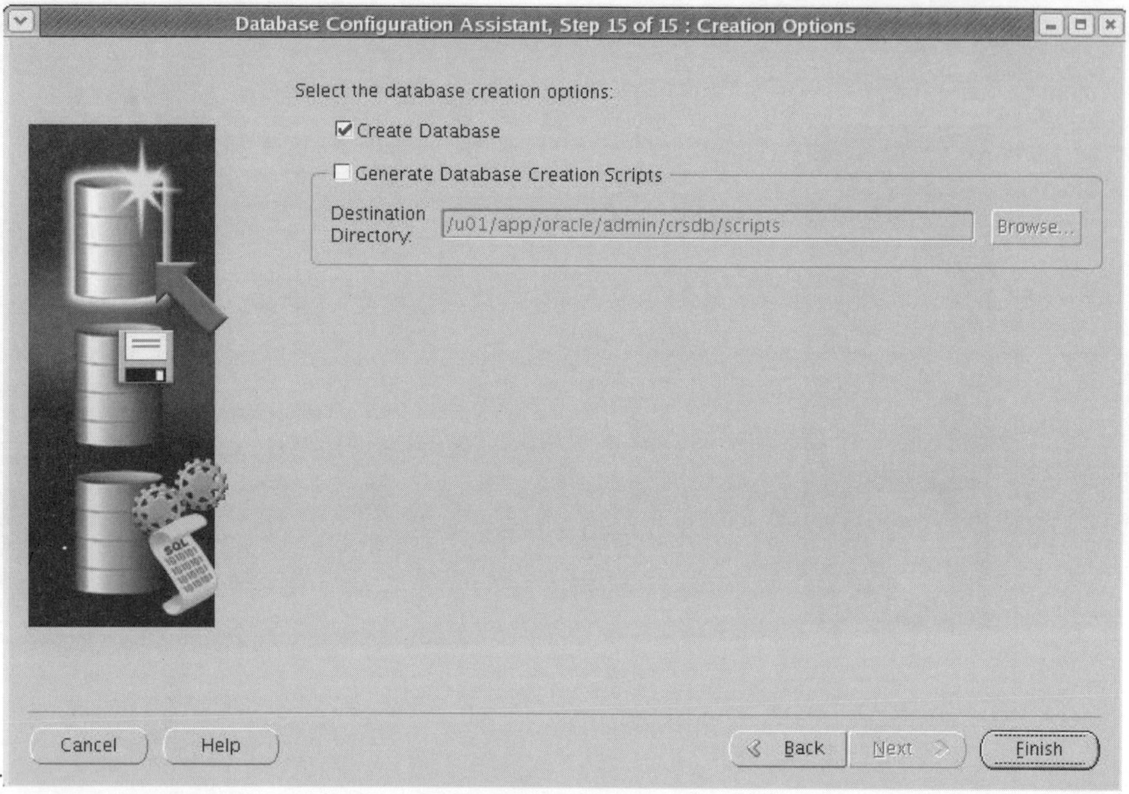

- Database Configuration Assistant: Summary

- Database Creation in Progress

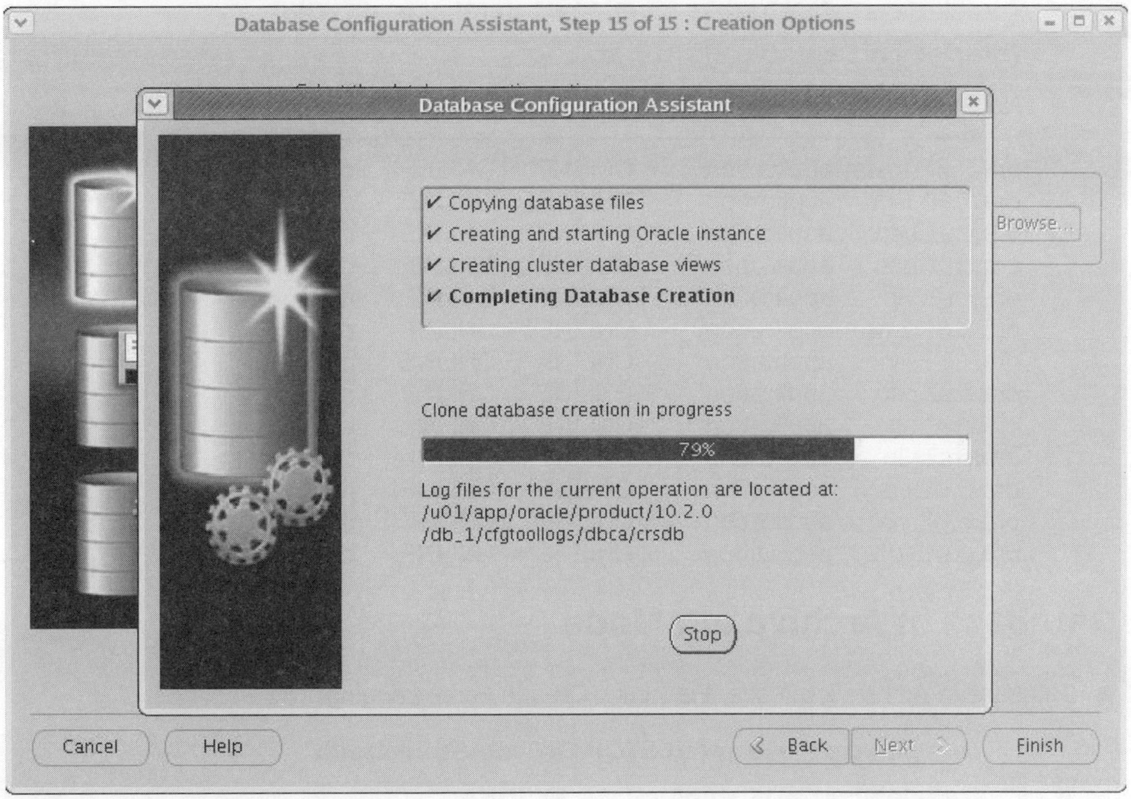

- Database Configuration Assistant: Exit

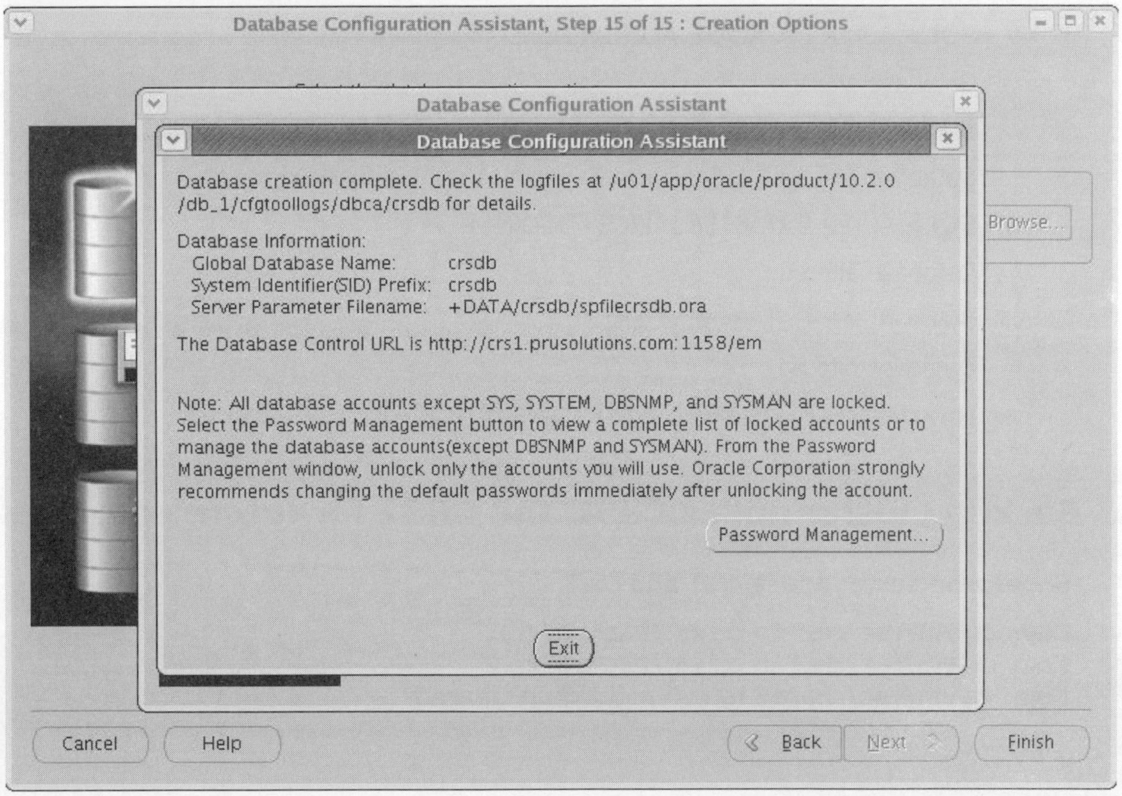

- Start Cluster Database and Check Cluster Configuration Status

  [oracle@crs1 database]$ srvctl start database -d crsdb

  [oracle@crs1 database]$ crs_stat –t

Name	Type	Target	State	Host
ora....SM1.asm	application	ONLINE	ONLINE	crs1
ora....S1.lsnr	application	ONLINE	ONLINE	crs1
ora.crs1.gsd	application	ONLINE	ONLINE	crs1
ora.crs1.ons	application	ONLINE	ONLINE	crs1
ora.crs1.vip	application	ONLINE	ONLINE	crs1
ora....SM2.asm	application	ONLINE	ONLINE	crs2
ora....S2.lsnr	application	ONLINE	ONLINE	crs2
ora.crs2.gsd	application	ONLINE	ONLINE	crs2
ora.crs2.ons	application	ONLINE	ONLINE	crs2
ora.crs2.vip	application	ONLINE	ONLINE	crs2
ora....b1.inst	application	ONLINE	ONLINE	crs1
ora....b2.inst	application	ONLINE	ONLINE	crs2
ora.crsdb.db	application	ONLINE	ONLINE	crs1

8.12 Database in Archive log Mode

- Database in Archive log Mode, Flashback On and Force Logging

  i. **[oracle@crs1 ~]$ srvctl STOP DATABASE -d crsdb**

  ii. **[oracle@crs1 ~]$ sqlplus / AS SYSDBA**

  iii. **SQL>** STARTUP MOUNT EXCLUSIVE;

  iv. **SQL>** ALTER DATABASE ARCHIVELOG;

  Database altered.

  v. **SQL>** ALTER DATABASE FLASHBACK ON;

  Database altered.

  vi. **SQL>** ALTER DATABASE FORCE LOGGING;

  Database altered.

  vii. **SQL>** ALTER DATABASE OPEN;

  Database altered.

  viii. **[oracle@crs1 ~]$ srvctl START INSTANCE -i crsdb2 -d crsdb**

8.13 Backup Cluster nodes CRS1 and CRS2 for future exercises

Shutdown cluster nodes crs1 and crs2

Copy c:/vm/rac/crs1 to c:/vm/backup/crs1
Copy c:/vm/rac/crs2 to c:/vm/backup/crs2
Copy c:/vm/rac/shared to c:/vm/backup/shared

8.14 Install agent on RAC using agent deploy

- Start oem server, listener, oemdb database oem agent and oms server to start Oracle. Enterprise Manager Grid Control
- On RAC nodes check jdk is installed or not (jdk was installed in Chapter 2)

[oracle@crs1 ~]$ which java
/usr/bin/java

- Logon to oms machine where Oracle's OEM Grid software is installed and secure copy agentDownload.linux to target machine parent directory where agent has to be deployed <OMS_HOME>/oms10g/sysman/agent_download/10.2.0.1.0/linux

[oracle@oms ~]$ cd /u01/app/oracle/OracleHomes/oms10g/sysman/agent_download/10.2.0.1.0/linux

[oracle@oms linux]$ scp agentDownload.linux crs1:/u01/app/oracle/product/10.2.0

The authenticity of host 'crs1 (192.168.2.131)' can't be established.
RSA key fingerprint is f4:ac:d2:7e:05:e8:4e:47:a9:6f:80:99:46:f9:f7:58.
Are you sure, you want to continue connecting (yes/no)? yes
Warning: Permanently added 'crs1, 192.168.2.131' (RSA) to the list of known hosts.
oracle@crs1's password:
agentDownload.linux 100% 22KB 22.3KB/s 00:00

- On node crs1, execute agent_profile

[oracle@crs1 ~]$. /home/oracle/agent_profile

[oracle@crs1 10.2.0]$ echo $ORACLE_HOME
/u01/app/oracle/product/10.2.0/agent10g

- Change directory to parent directory of <AGENT_HOME>

[oracle@crs1 10.2.0]$ cd /u01/app/oracle/product/10.2.0

[oracle@crs1 10.2.0]$ ls -ltr

- Change agentDownload.linux file permission

[oracle@crs1 10.2.0]$ chmod 755 agentDownload.linux

[oracle@crs1 10.2.0]$ ./agentDownload.linux -b /u01/app/oracle/product/10.2.0 -m oms.prusolutions.com -r 4889 -c "crs1, crs2" -n crs

Agent install will start and at the end you will get following message

End of install phases.(Thursday, February 24, 2011 7:07:00 AM EST)
WARNING:

- The following configuration scripts need to be executed as the "root" user in each cluster node

#!/bin/sh
#Root script to run
/u01/app/oracle/product/10.2.0/agent10g/root.sh
#On nodes crs1,crs2

To execute the configuration scripts:

1. Open a terminal window
2. Log in as "root"
3. Run the scripts in each cluster node

- Open a new terminal, su root and execute root.sh script

[oracle@crs1 ~]$ su root
Password:
[root@crs1 oracle]# /u01/app/oracle/product/10.2.0/agent10g/root.sh
Running Oracle10 root.sh script...

```
The following environment variables are set as:
    ORACLE_OWNER= oracle
    ORACLE_HOME= /u01/app/oracle/product/10.2.0/agent10g
Enter the full pathname of the local bin directory: [/usr/local/bin]:
The file "dbhome" already exists in /usr/local/bin.  Overwrite it? (y/n)
[n]:
The file "oraenv" already exists in /usr/local/bin.  Overwrite it? (y/n)
[n]:
The file "coraenv" already exists in /usr/local/bin.  Overwrite it? (y/n)
[n]:
Entries will be added to the /etc/oratab file as needed by
Database Configuration Assistant when a database is created
Finished running generic part of root.sh script.
Now product-specific root actions will be performed.
Finished product-specific root actions.
[root@crs1 oracle]#
```

- Execute the script on crs2

```
[oracle@crs2 ~]$ su root
Password:
[root@crs2 oracle]# /u01/app/oracle/product/10.2.0/agent10g/root.sh
```

- Return back to crs1 agent install window to check status of agent install

```
Configuration assistant "Agent Configuration Assistant" succeeded
The installation of Oracle Management Agent was successful.
Please check '/u01/app/oracle/oraInventory/logs/silentInstall2011-02-24_07-01-28AM.log' for more details.
```

- Once agent is installed, secure agent and upload agent to Oracle's OEM Grid.

Here $ORACLE_HOME is <AGENT_HOME> password for secure oms was set in chapter 4 **"oracle123"**

```
[oracle@crs1 10.2.0]$ . /home/oracle/agent_profile
[oracle@crs1 10.2.0]$ echo $ORACLE_HOME
/u01/app/oracle/product/10.2.0/agent10g
```

- Perform following steps on both crs1 and crs2

```
$ORACLE_HOME/bin/emctl stop agent
$ORACLE_HOME/bin/emctl secure agent
$ORACLE_HOME/bin/emctl clearstate agent
$ORACLE_HOME/bin/emctl start agent
$ORACLE_HOME/bin/emctl upload
[oracle@crs1 10.2.0]$ . /home/oracle/agent_profile
[oracle@crs1 10.2.0]$ echo $ORACLE_HOME
/u01/app/oracle/product/10.2.0/agent10g
[oracle@crs1 10.2.0]$ $ORACLE_HOME/bin/emctl stop agent
Oracle Enterprise Manager 10g Release 10.2.0.1.0.
Copyright (c) 1996, 2005 Oracle Corporation.  All rights reserved.
Stopping agent ... stopped.
[oracle@crs1 10.2.0]$ $ORACLE_HOME/bin/emctl secure agent
Oracle Enterprise Manager 10g Release 10.2.0.1.0.
Copyright (c) 1996, 2005 Oracle Corporation.  All rights reserved.
Enter Agent Registration password :oracle123
Agent is already stopped...   Done.
Securing agent...   Started.
```

```
Requesting an HTTPS Upload URL from the OMS...   Done.
Requesting an Oracle Wallet and Agent Key from the OMS...   Done.
Check if HTTPS Upload URL is accessible from the agent...   Done.
Configuring Agent for HTTPS in CENTRAL_AGENT mode...   Done.
EMD_URL set in /u01/app/oracle/product/10.2.0/agent10g/crs1.prusolutions.com/sysman/config/
emd.properties
Securing agent...   Successful.
[oracle@crs1 10.2.0]$ $ORACLE_HOME/bin/emctl clearstate agent
Oracle Enterprise Manager 10g Release 10.2.0.1.0.
Copyright (c) 1996, 2005 Oracle Corporation.  All rights reserved.
EMD clearstate completed successfully
[oracle@crs1 10.2.0]$ $ORACLE_HOME/bin/emctl start agent
Oracle Enterprise Manager 10g Release 10.2.0.1.0.
Copyright (c) 1996, 2005 Oracle Corporation.  All rights reserved.
Starting agent ...... started.
[oracle@crs1 10.2.0]$ $ORACLE_HOME/bin/emctl upload
Oracle Enterprise Manager 10g Release 10.2.0.1.0.
Copyright (c) 1996, 2005 Oracle Corporation.  All rights reserved.
---------------------------------------------------------------
EMD upload completed successfully
```

8.15 Configure CRSDB Database on Oracle's OEM Grid Control

- Configure crsdb database in OEM Grid Control the same way ocmdb was configured

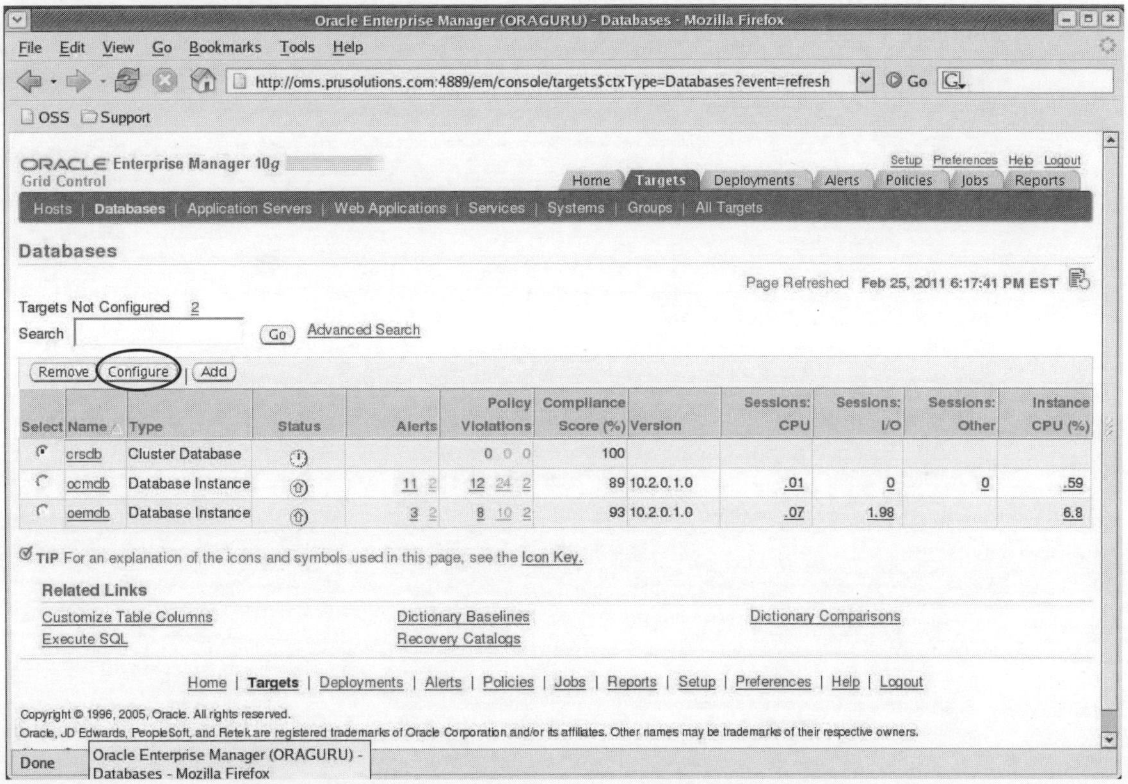

- Configure Cluster Database: Properties

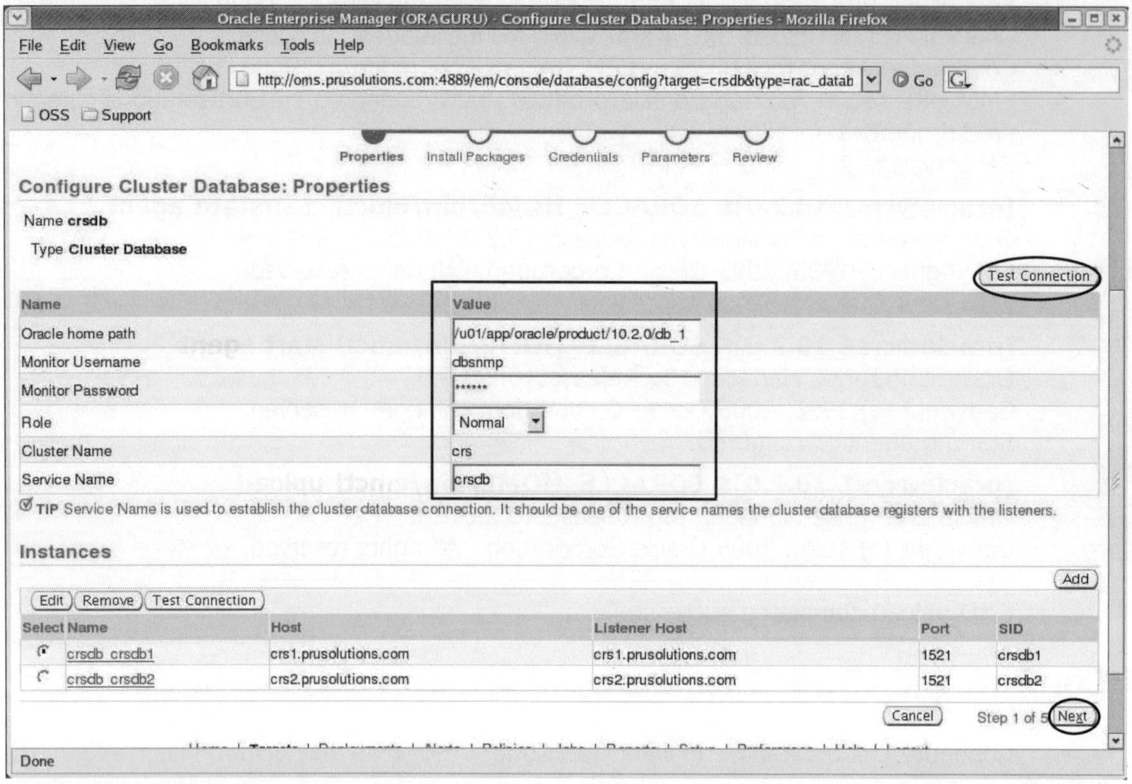

- Configure Cluster Database: Review

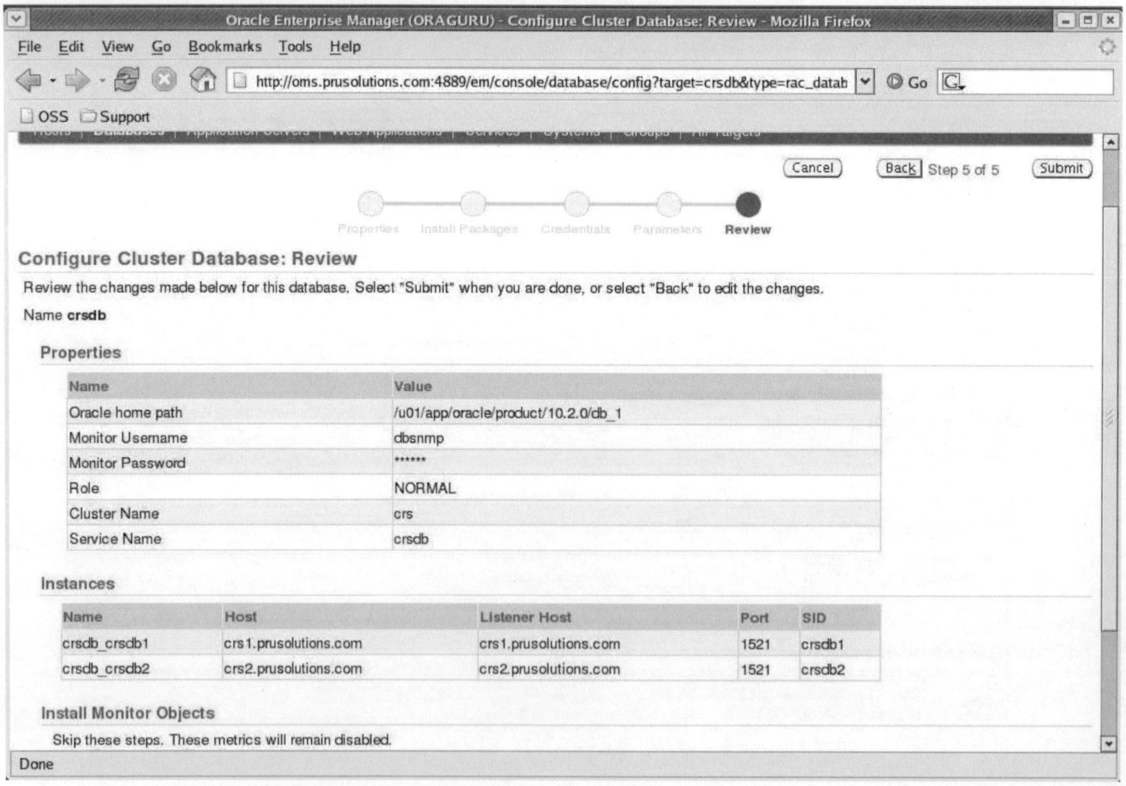

- Database Instance Configuration Result

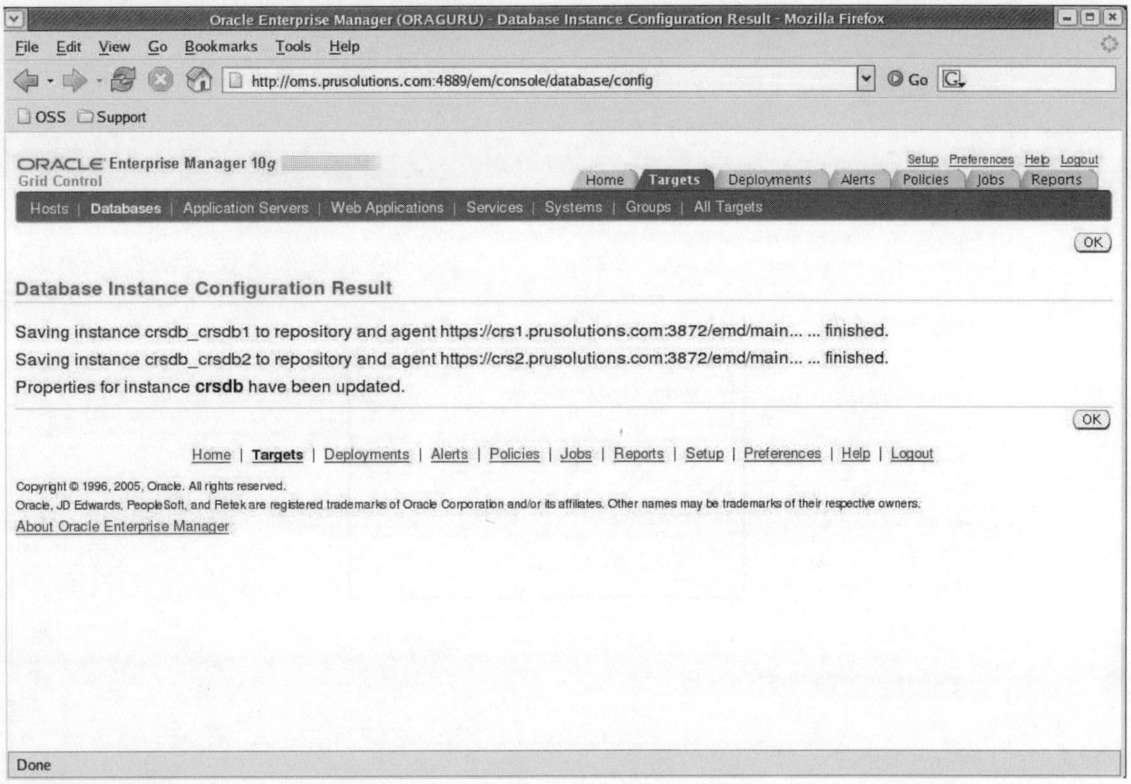

- Configure ASM

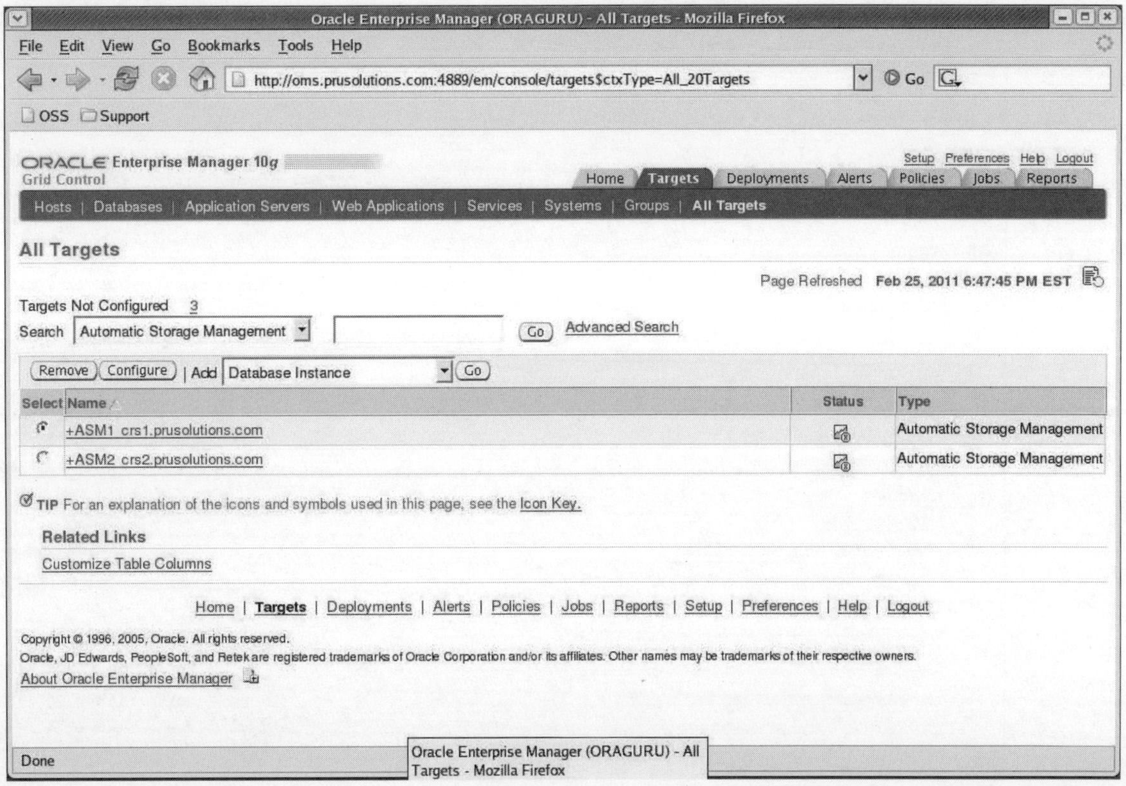

- Monitor Configuration

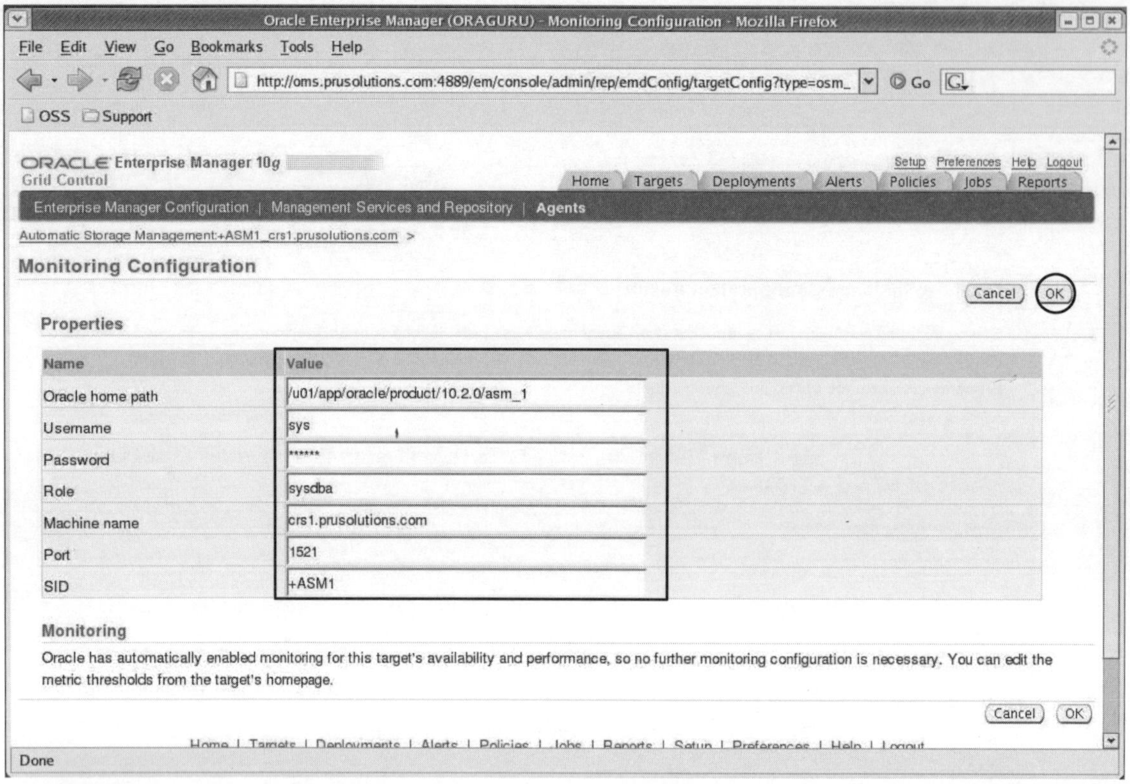

- In same way configure +ASM2

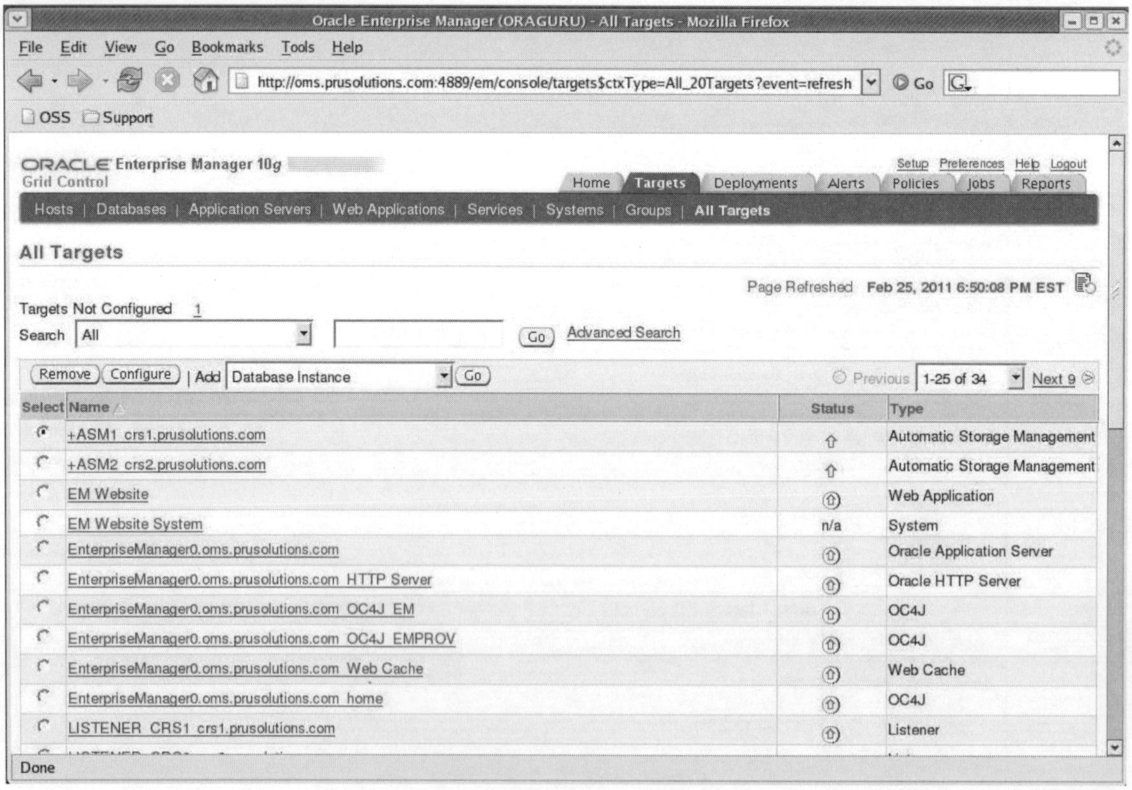

8.16 Server Control Utility

- Stop and Start Database

  [oracle@crs1 ~]$ srvctl stop database -d crsdb

  [oracle@crs1 ~]$ srvctl start database -d crsdb

- Stop and Start Instance

  [oracle@crs1 ~]$ srvctl stop instance -d crsdb -i crsdb2

  [oracle@crs1 ~]$ srvctl start instance -d crsdb -i crsdb2

- Stop and Start asm

  [oracle@crs1 ~]$ srvctl stop asm -n crs2

  [oracle@crs1 ~]$ srvctl start asm -n crs2

- Stop and Start listener

  [oracle@crs1 ~]$ srvctl stop listener -n crs2

  [oracle@crs1 ~]$ srvctl start listener -n crs2

- Stop and Start nodeapps

  [oracle@crs1 ~]$ srvctl stop nodeapps -n crs2

  [oracle@crs1 ~]$ srvctl start nodeapps -n crs2

- Add service using srvctl

  Below service, TEST1 is added having crsdb1 as preferred (-r) and crsdb2 as available (-a) instance

  [oracle@crs1 ~]$ srvctl add service -s TEST1 -d crsdb   -r crsdb1 -a crsdb2

  [oracle@crs1 ~]$ srvctl start service -s TEST1 -d crsdb

  As the service was added using srvctl command, then next step is to add TNS entry for service TEST1 in tnsnames.ora, use srvctl command to get tnsentry details

  [oracle@crs1 ~]$ srvctl config database -d crsdb -t

  Example client-side TNS entry for service TEST1:

  ```
  TEST1 =
  (DESCRIPTION=(ADDRESS=(PROTOCOL=TCP)(HOST=db_vip)(PORT=dedicated_port))(CONNECT_DATA=
  (SERVICE_NAME=TEST1)))
  ```

  OR

  Copy the default service CRSDB in tnsnames.ora file and rename for connect descriptor and service_name.

- In addition, start OCM server and add this service to OCM server try to test connection from ocmdb database to crsdb (RAC) database using service TEST1

  ```
  TEST1 =
      (DESCRIPTION =
      (ADDRESS = (PROTOCOL = TCP)(HOST = crs1-vip.prusolutions.com)(PORT = 1521))
      (ADDRESS = (PROTOCOL = TCP)(HOST = crs2-vip.prusolutions.com)(PORT = 1521))
      (LOAD_BALANCE = yes)
      (CONNECT_DATA =
          (SERVER = DEDICATED)
          (SERVICE_NAME = test1)
        )
      )
  ```

  [oracle@ocm ~]$ sqlplus /nolog

  SQL*Plus: Release 10.2.0.1.0 - Production on Wed Feb 23 22:08:05 2011

SQL> connect system@test1
Enter password:
Connected.

SQL> SELECT db_unique_name FROM v$database;

DB_UNIQUE_NAME

---

crsdb

After the test, you may shutdown "ocm" server.

- Modify Service

  Currently crsdb1 is preferred instance for service TEST1

  [oracle@crs1 ~]$ srvctl config service -s TEST1 -d crsdb

  TEST1 PREF: crsdb1 AVAIL: crsdb2

  Make crsdb2 instance also as preferred for service TEST1

  [oracle@crs1 ~]$ srvctl modify service -s TEST1 -d crsdb -i crsdb2 -r

  [oracle@crs1 ~]$ srvctl config service -s TEST1 -d crsdb
  TEST1 PREF: crsdb1 crsdb2 AVAIL:

- Stop, Start, Disable, Enable Service

  $ srvctl stop |start |enable | disable service -s TEST1 -d crsdb -i crsdb1

- Changing between manual and auto policy

  $ srvctl config database –d crsdb –a

  $ srvctl modify database –d crsdb –y MANUAL

- Srvctl database commands and options

  srvctl start | stop instance –d <db_name> -i <inst_name> [-o open | mount | nomount | normal | transactional | immediate | abort] [-c connect_str> | -q] (q is to get connect string from standard input)

  srvctl start | stop database -d <db_name> [-o open | mount | nomount | normal | transactional | immediate | abort] –c [connect_str] | -q]
  srvctl modify database -d db_unique_name [-n db_name] [-o oracle_home] [-m domain_name] [-p spfile] [-r {PRIMARY | PHYSICAL_STANDBY | LOGICAL_STANDBY}] [-s start_options]

- To get help all Server Control commands just type srvctl and press enter

  [oracle@crs2 ~]$ srvctl
  Usage: srvctl <command> <object> [<options>]
  command:
  enable|disable|start|stop|relocate|status|add|remove|modify|getenv|setenv|unsetenv|config
  objects: database | instance | service | nodeapps | asm | listener

  For detailed help on each command and object and its options use:

  srvctl <command> <object> -h

8.17 Create Service Using Oracle's OEM Grid Control

- Manage Services

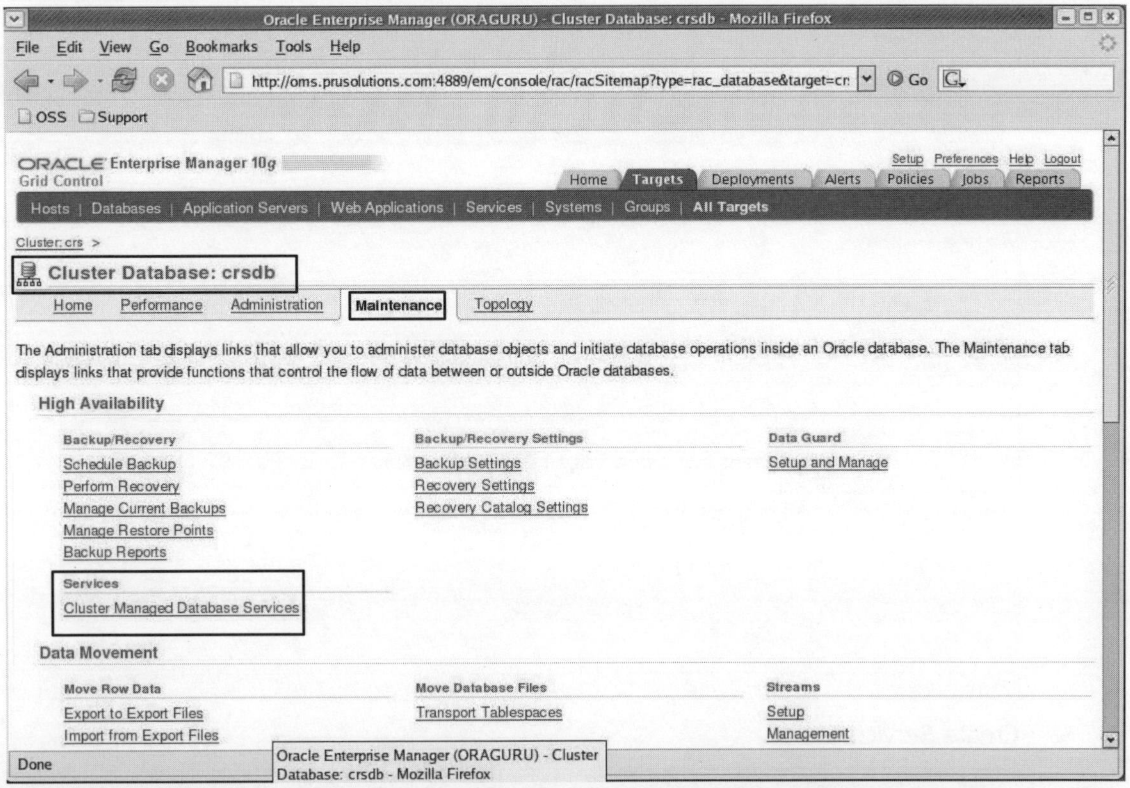

- Cluster Managed Database Services: Specify Cluster and Database Login

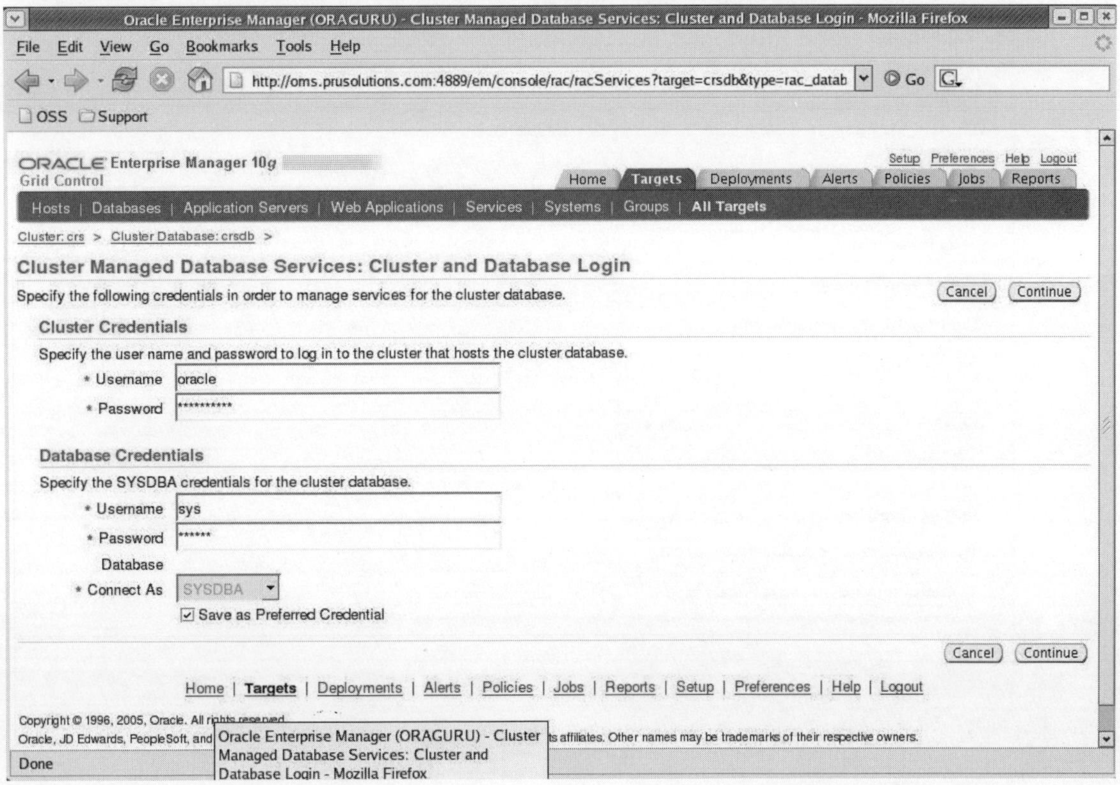

- Cluster Managed Database Services

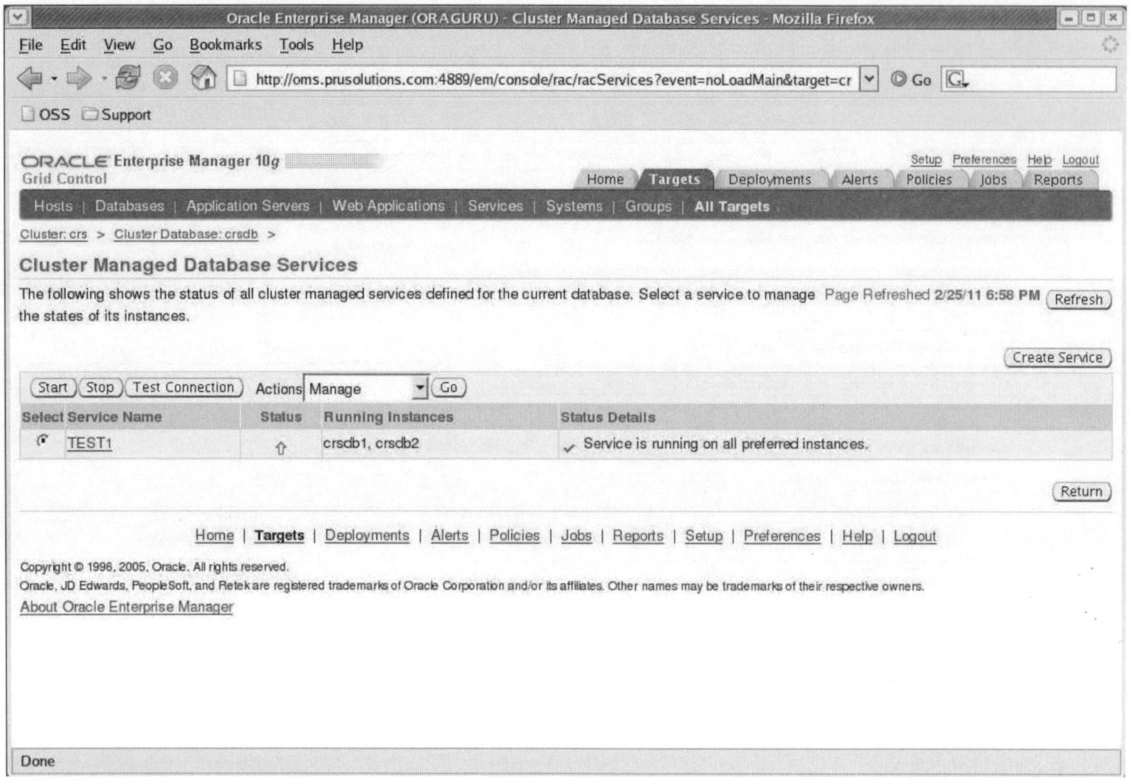

- Create Service

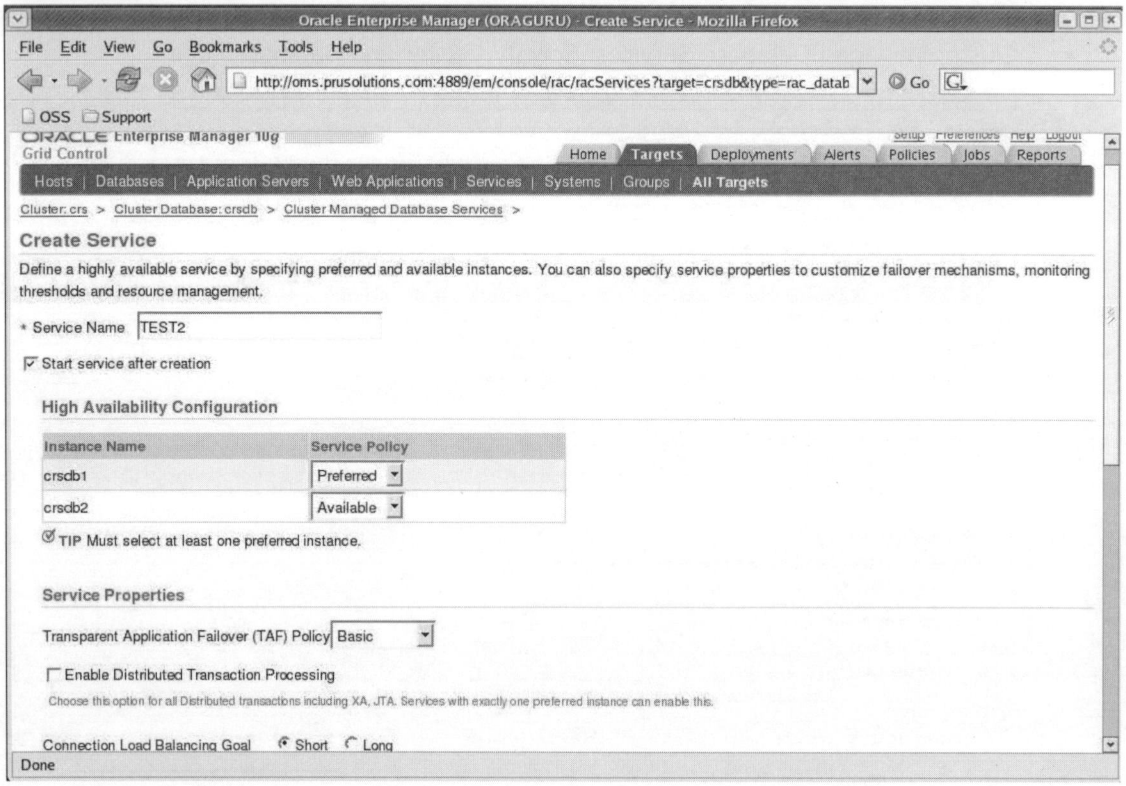

- Select Notification Resource Management Properties and Service Throughput Levels

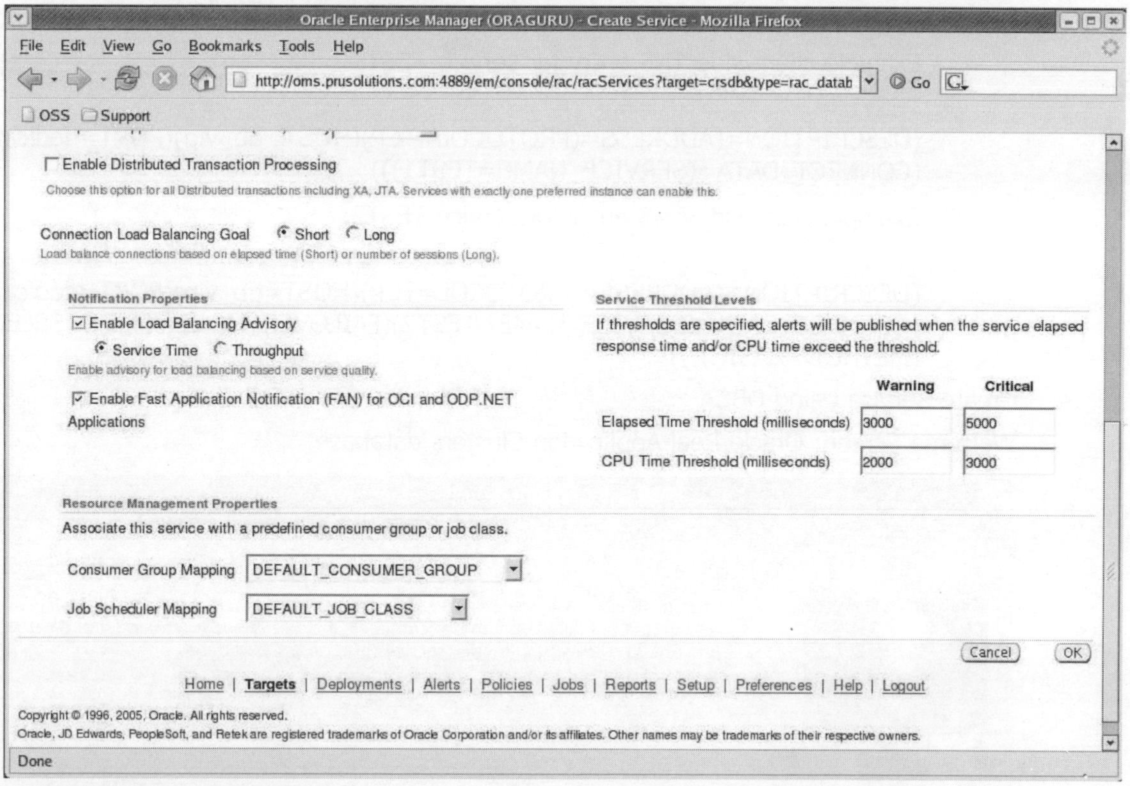

- Create Service: Successful

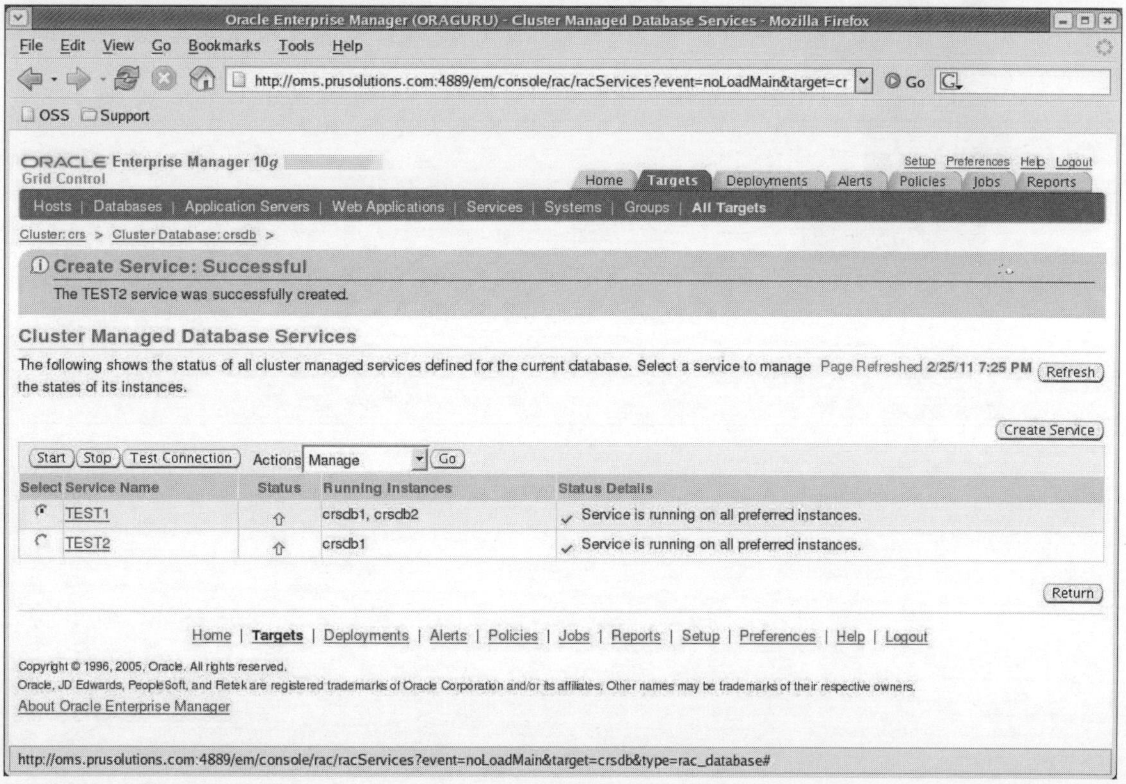

- Add tnsentry for this service in tsnnames.ora to get sample for tnsentry, use srvctl command
  [oracle@crs2 ~]$ srvctl config database -d crsdb –t
  i. Example client-side TNS entry for service TEST1:
     TEST1 =
     (DESCRIPTION=(ADDRESS=(PROTOCOL=TCP)(HOST=db_vip)(PORT=dedicated_port))
     (CONNECT_DATA=(SERVICE_NAME=TEST1)))
  ii. Example client-side TNS entry for service TEST2:
     TEST2 =
     (DESCRIPTION=(ADDRESS=(PROTOCOL=TCP)(HOST=db_vip)(PORT=dedicated_port))
     (CONNECT_DATA=(SERVICE_NAME=TEST2)(FAILOVER_MODE=(TYPE=SELECT)
     (METHOD=BASIC))))
- Create Service Using DBCA
  Welcome Screen: Oracle Real Application Clusters database

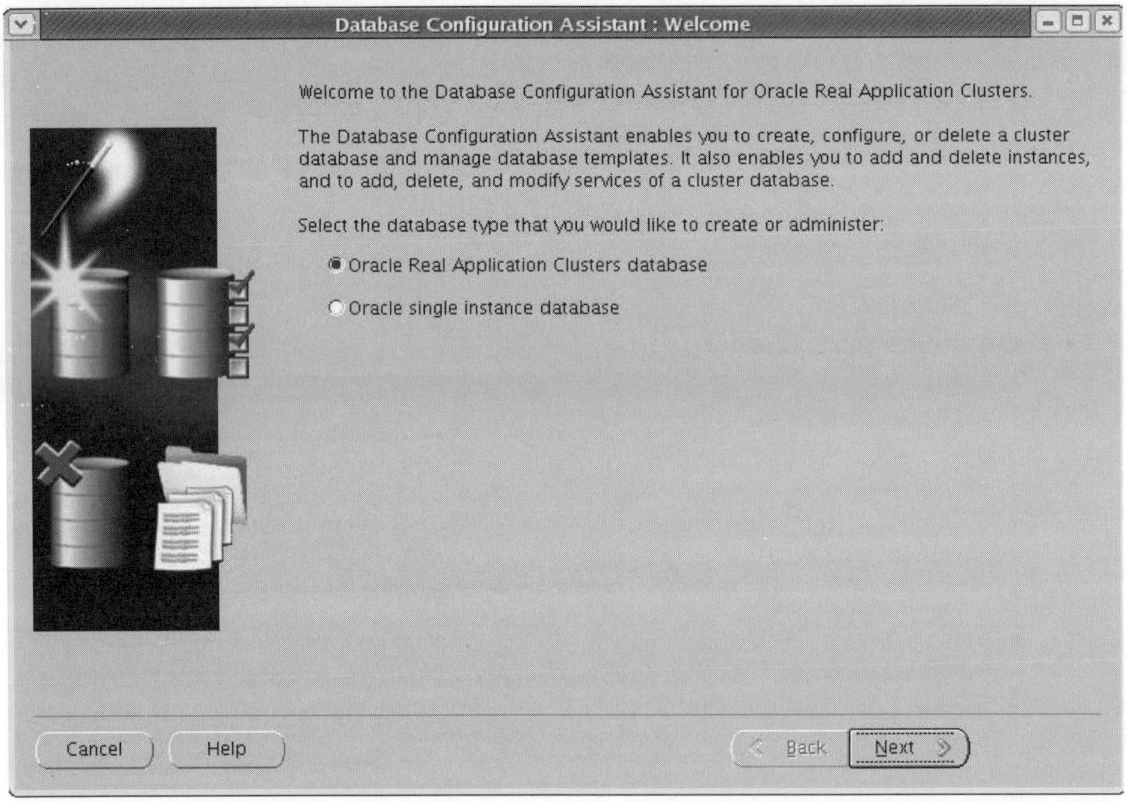

- Operations: Service Management

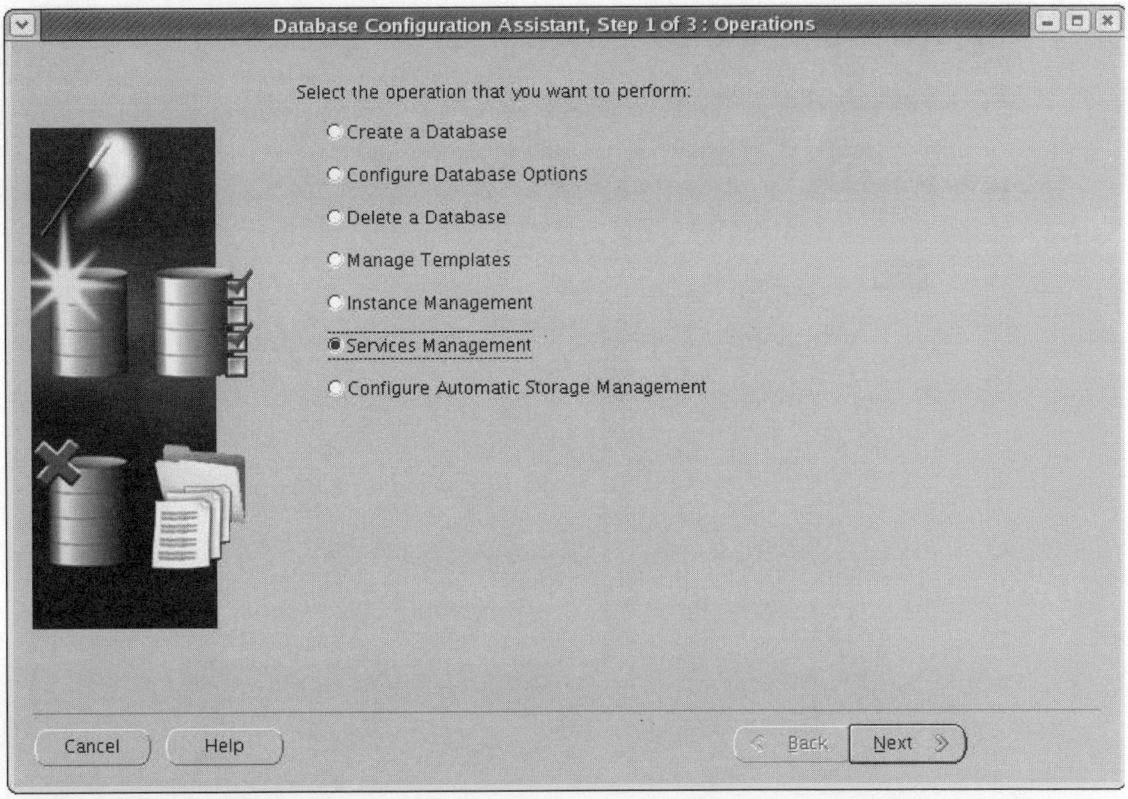

- Select Cluster Database: crsdb

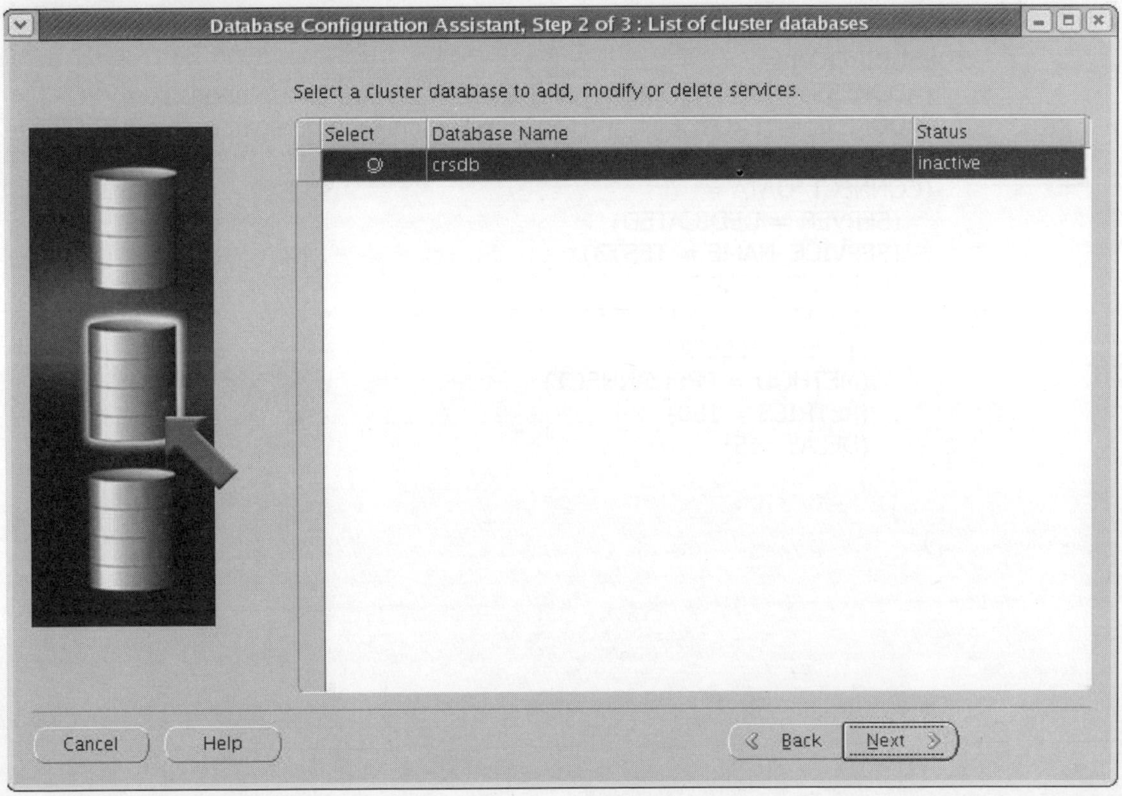

- Database Services: Select Preferred and Available Instance and Click Finish

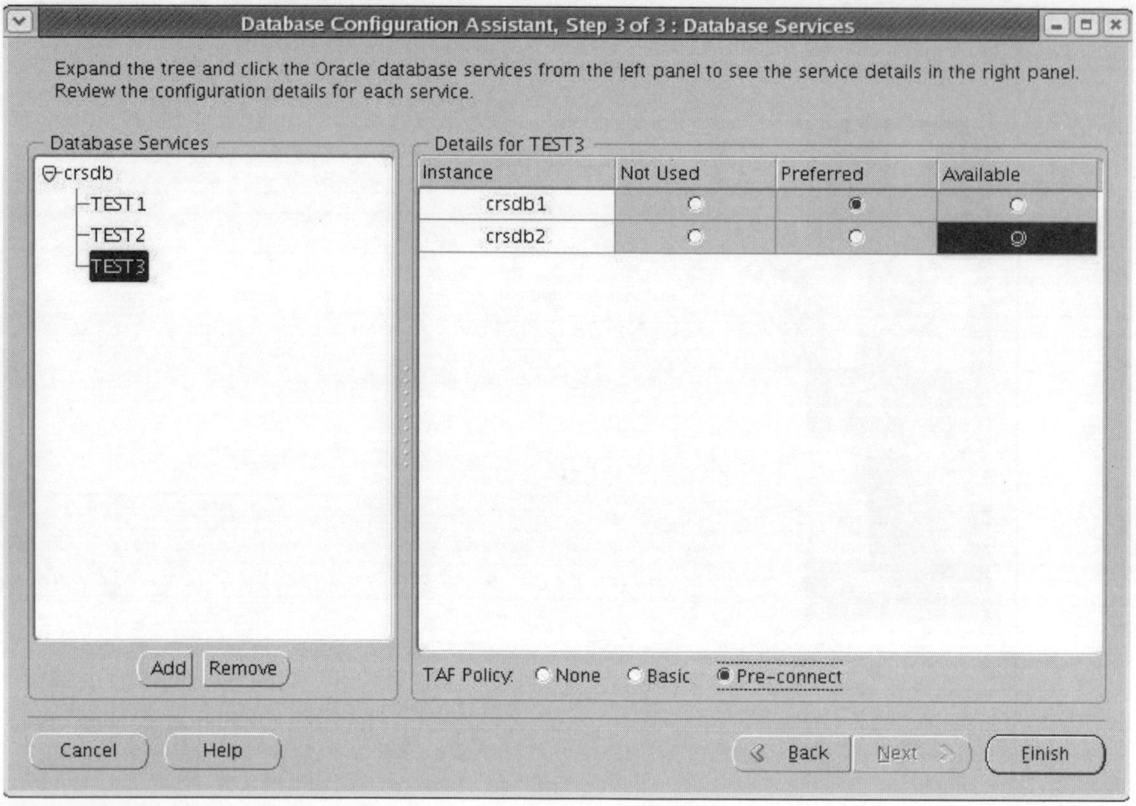

- The tnsentry for service is automatically added to tnsnames.ora

```
TEST3 =
   (DESCRIPTION =
      (ADDRESS = (PROTOCOL = TCP)(HOST = crs1-vip.prusolutions.com)(PORT = 1521))
      (ADDRESS = (PROTOCOL = TCP)(HOST = crs2-vip.prusolutions.com)(PORT = 1521))
      (LOAD_BALANCE = yes)
      (CONNECT_DATA =
         (SERVER = DEDICATED)
         (SERVICE_NAME = TEST3)
         (FAILOVER_MODE =
            (BACKUP = TEST3_PRECONNECT)
            (TYPE = SELECT)
            (METHOD = PRECONNECT)
            (RETRIES = 180)
            (DELAY = 5)
            )
         )
      )
```

- On Cluster Database Page Manage Top Services and Top Modules

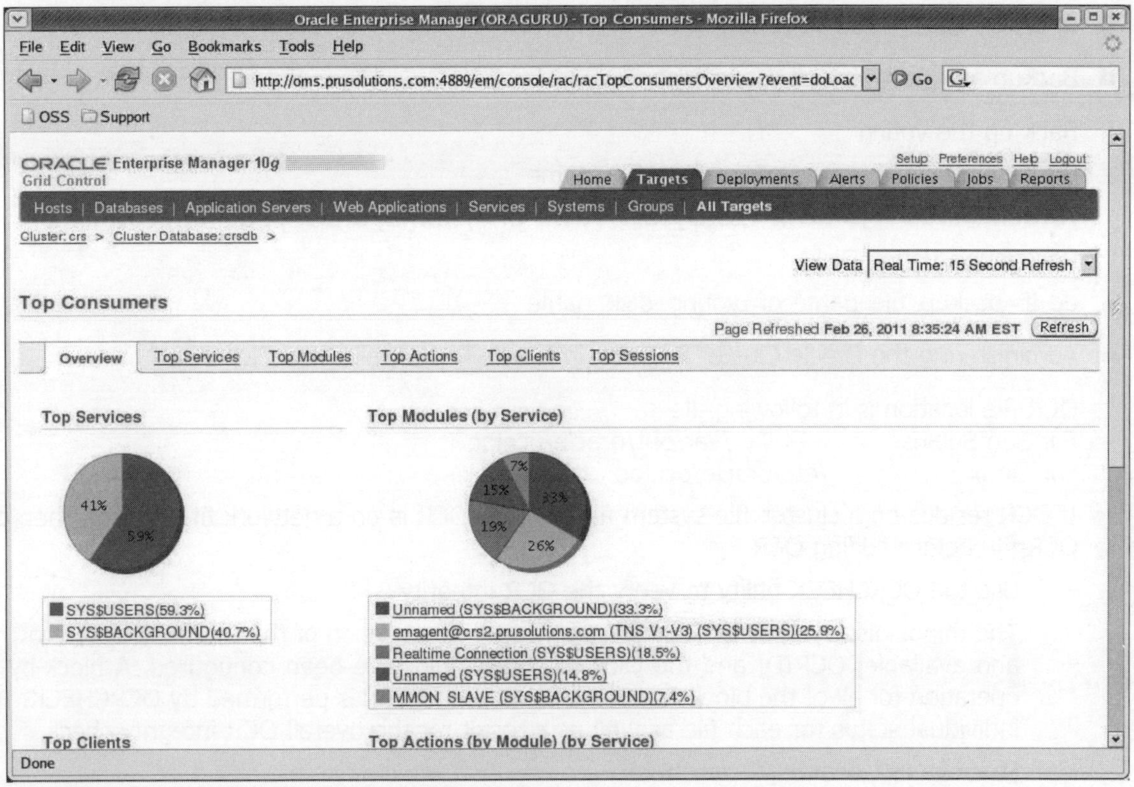

8.18 Voting Disk and OCR Management

The recommendations for the addition or removal of a voting disk is shutdown Oracle Cluster ware first on all nodes and then utilize the commands below as root user where path is completely qualified path for the additional voting disk. In the case of new voting disk over the network file system (NFS), create an empty voting disk file location with the correct owner and permissions before execute of commands mentioned below. Three extra raw partitions **/dev/raw/raw3/, dev/raw/raw4, /dev/raw/raw5** have been created in order to practice following exercises.

- Run the following command to find path of voting disks

[oracle@crs1 ~]$ crsctl query css votedisk
```
 0.    0    /dev/raw/raw2
located 1 votedisk(s).
```

- Run the following command as the root user to add a voting disk

[root@crs1 oracle]# crsctl stop crs

[root@crs2 oracle]# crsctl stop crs

[root@crs1 oracle]# crsctl add css votedisk /dev/raw/raw3 -force
```
Now formatting voting disk: /dev/raw/raw3
successful addition of votedisk /dev/raw/raw3.
```

[root@crs1 oracle]# crsctl start crs

[root@crs2 oracle]# crsctl start crs

[oracle@crs2 oracle]$ crsctl query css votedisk
```
 0.    0    /dev/raw/raw2
 1.    0    /dev/raw/raw3
located 2 votedisk(s).
```

- Run the following command as the root user to remove a voting disk

  # crsctl delete css votedisk path

- Backup and Recovery of Voting Disk

  Back up the voting

  dd if=voting_disk_name of=backup_file_name

  [oracle@crs1 ~]$ dd if=/dev/raw/raw2 of=/home/oracle/backup/votdisk1

  Recovering Voting Disks

  dd if=backup_file_name of=voting_disk_name

- Administering the Oracle Cluster Registry in Oracle Real Application Clusters

  OCR file location is in following file
  For Sun Solaris /var/opt/oracle/ocr.loc
  For Linux /etc/oracle/ocr.loc

  If OCR resides on a cluster, file system file or if the OCR is on a network file system, then create the target OCR file before adding OCR.

  - Use the OCRCHECK utility to verify the OCR integrity

    The things displayed by OCRCHECK utility are – the version of the OCR's block format; total space used and available; OCRID; and the OCR locations that have been configured. A block-by-block checksum operation for all of the blocks in all the configured OCRs is performed by OCRCHECK. It also returns an individual status for each file as well as a result for the overall OCR integrity check.

    [root@crs1 oracle]# ocrcheck

```
Status of Oracle Cluster Registry is as follows :
         Version                  :    2
         Total space (kbytes)     :    524184
         Used space (kbytes)      :      5644
         Available space (kbytes) :    518540
         ID                       :  87847809
         Device/File Name         : /dev/raw/raw1
                              Device/File integrity check succeeded

                         Device/File not configured
Cluster registry integrity check succeeded
```

    Device/File not configured means ocrmirror is not configured

    OCRCHECK creates a log file in the directory *CRS_Home*/log/*hostname*/client. To change amount of logging, edit the file *CRS_Home*/srvm/admin/ocrlog.ini.

  - Run the following command to add an OCR mirror location using either destination_file or disk to designate the target location of the additional OCR

    First, make sure you have proper backup of ocr

    [root@crs2 oracle]# ocrconfig –showbackup

  - Run the following command to add an OCR location using either destination_file or disk to designate the target location of the additional OCR

    ocrconfig -replace ocr destination_file or disk

    ocrconfig -replace ocrmirror destination_file or disk

    First zero out the raw device

    If your OCR configuration were altered while a particular node is stopped, you would be required to repair the OCR configuration on that particular node. For instance, there may be need to repair the OCR on a node that was not up at the time of removing, replacing or adding an OCR. For repairing an OCR configuration, run the following command on the node on which the Oracle Clusterware daemon was stopped.

ocrconfig –repair ocrmirror device_name

This operation only changes the OCR configuration on the node from which you run this command. For example, if the OCR mirror device name is /dev/raw1, then use the command syntax ocrconfig -repair ocrmirror /dev/raw1 on this node to repair its OCR configuration.

You **cannot** perform this operation on a node on which the Oracle Clusterware daemon is running.

- Run the following command on any node in the cluster to remove the OCR

  ocrconfig -replace ocr

- Run the following command on any node in the cluster to remove the mirrored OCR

  ocrconfig -replace ocrmirror

- The above commands update the OCR configuration on all of the nodes on which Oracle Clusterware is running.
- The ocrconfig Command Options

Option	Purpose
-backuploc	To change an OCR backup file location. For this entry, use a full path that is accessible by all of the nodes.
-downgrade	To downgrade an OCR to an earlier version.
-export	To export the contents of an OCR into a target file.
-help	To display help for the ocrconfig commands.
-import	To import the OCR contents from a previously exported OCR file.
-overwrite	To update an OCR configuration that is recorded on the OCR with the current OCR configuration information that is found on the node from which you are running this command.
-repair	To update an OCR configuration on the node from which you are running this command with the new configuration information specified by this command.
-replace	To add, replace, or remove an OCR location.
-restore	To restore an OCR from an automatically created OCR backup file.
showbackup	To display the location, timestamp, and the originating node name of the backup files that Oracle created in the past 4 hours, 8 hours, 12 hours, and in the last day and week. You do not have to be the root user to execute the -showbackup option.
-upgrade	To upgrade an OCR to a later version.

For example, to export the OCR contents to a binary file, use the ocrconfig command with the following syntax where *file_name* is the file to which you want to export the OCR contents as follows

ocrconfig -export *file_name*

- Managing Backups and Recovering the OCR Using OCR Backup Files

This section explains the two methods for the purpose of copying of OCR content and further utilizing it for recovery. The first method uses automatically generated OCR file copies and the second method uses manually created OCR export files.

The Oracle Clusterware automatically creates OCR backups every four hours. At any one time, Oracle always retains the last three backup copies of the OCR. The CRSD process that creates the backups also creates and retains an OCR backup for each full day and at the end of each week.

Restoring the Oracle Cluster Registry on UNIX-Based Systems: use ***oracheck*** to check OCR status

Use the following procedure to restore the OCR on UNIX-based systems:
Identify the OCR backups using the ocrconfig -showbackup command. Review the contents of the backup using ocrdump -backupfile *file_name* where *file_name* is the name of the backup file.

Stop Oracle Clusterware on all of the nodes in your Oracle RAC database by executing the init.crs stop command on all of the nodes.

Perform the restore by applying an OCR backup file that you identified in Step 1 using the following command where *file_name* is the name of the OCR that you want to restore. Make sure that the OCR devices that you specify in the OCR configuration exist and that these OCR devices are valid before running this command.

ocrconfig -restore *file_name*
Restart Oracle Clusterware on all of the nodes in your cluster by restarting each node or by running the init.crs start command.

Run the following command to verify the OCR integrity where the -n all argument retrieves a listing of all of the cluster nodes that are configured as part of your cluster.

cluvfy comp ocr -n all [-verbose]

Use the OCRDUMP utility to write the OCR contents to a file so that you can examine the OCR content.

ocrdump [*file_name*|-stdout] [-backupfile *backup_file_name*] [-keyname *keyname*] [-xml] [-noheader]

OCRDUMP Options and Option Descriptions

Option	Purpose
file_name	Name of a file to which you want OCRDUMP to write output.
-stdout	The predefined output location that you can redirect with, for example, a filename.
-keyname	The name of an OCR key whose subtree is to be dumped.
-xml	Writes the output in XML format.
-noheader	Does not print the time at which you ran the command and when the OCR configuration occurred.
-backupfile	Option to identify a backup file.
backup_file_name	The name of the backup file the content of which you want to view. You can query the backups using the ocrconfig -showbackup command.

- OCR Exports/Imports

ocrconfig -export *file_name*

ocrconfig -import *file_name*

Restart Oracle Clusterware on all of the nodes in your cluster by restarting each node.

Run the following Cluster Verification Utility (CVU) command to verify the OCR integrity where the -n all argument retrieves a listing of all of the cluster nodes that are configured as part of your cluster:

cluvfy comp ocr -n all [-verbose]

8.19 ASM Management

- Get details of ASM Disks

  - Execute following queries on ASM instance (+ASM1 or +ASM2)e to get details of disks

```
[oracle@crs1 ~]$ . /home/oracle/asm_profile
[oracle@crs1 ~]$ echo $ORACLE_HOME
/u01/app/oracle/product/10.2.0/asm_1
[oracle@crs1 ~]$ sqlplus / as sysdba
SQL> SELECT SUM (total_mb) total_mb, SUM (free_mb) free_mb FROM v$asm_disk;

TOTAL_MB  FREE_MB
--------  -------
   14320     6579
```

  - To find out the ASM disk details allocated by group name

```
SQL> SELECT   a.name GRP_NAME,
              a.state GRP_STATE,
              a.TYPE GRP_TYPE,
              a.total_mb GRP_TOTAL_MB,
              a.free_mb grp_free_mb,
              b.name,
              b.PATH,
              b.HEADER_STATUS,
              b.MODE_STATUS,
              b.MOUNT_STATUS,
              b.TOTAL_MB,
              b.FREE_MB
     FROM     v$asm_diskgroup a, V$ASM_DISK b
     WHERE    a.group_number (+) = b.group_number;

SQL> col NAME format a10
SQL> col PATH format a15
SQL> SELECT name,
            PATH,
            header_status,
            mode_status,
            total_mb,
            free_mb
     FROM   v$asm_disk;

NAME    PATH            HEADER_STATU  MODE_ST  TOTAL_MB  FREE_MB
------  --------------  ------------  -------  --------  -------
        /dev/raw/raw1   FOREIGN       ONLINE   511       0
        /dev/raw/raw2   FOREIGN       ONLINE   511       0
        /dev/raw/raw3   FOREIGN       ONLINE   511       0
        /dev/raw/raw4   CANDIDATE     ONLINE   511       0
        /dev/raw/raw5   CANDIDATE     ONLINE   511       0
        ORCL:VOL3       PROVISIONED   ONLINE   511       0
        ORCL:VOL4       PROVISIONED   ONLINE   511       0
        ORCL:VOL9       PROVISIONED   ONLINE   511       0
        ORCL:VOL5       PROVISIONED   ONLINE   511       0
        ORCL:VOL6       PROVISIONED   ONLINE   511       0
        ORCL:VOL7       PROVISIONED   ONLINE   511       0
        ORCL:VOL8       PROVISIONED   ONLINE   511       0
VOL1    ORCL:VOL1       MEMBER        ONLINE   4094      2819
VOL2    ORCL:VOL2       MEMBER        ONLINE   4094      3760
```

The disk having HEADER_STATUS of PROVISONED is available for ASM. The TOTAL_MB indicates the size of disk.

- Create ASM Diskgroup
  - Create new external redundancy Diskgroup TEST1 from **sqlplus**

```
SQL> CREATE DISKGROUP TEST1 EXTERNAL REDUNDANCY DISK 'ORCL:VOL3';
     Diskgroup created.
SQL> ALTER SYSTEM SET asm_diskgroups='DATA','FRA','TEST1';
```

After creating, the disk groups add it to **init.ora** file for all ASM instance (+ASM1,+ASM2) otherwise after next ASM restart that disk won't be mounted and any datafile created on that disk will give error mentioned below.

```
ERROR at line 1:
ORA-01157: cannot identify/lock data file 7 - see DBWR trace file
ORA-01110: data file 7: '+TEST1/crsdb/datafile/test1.256.744125767
```

  - Add 'TEST1' to init.ora parameter asm_diskgroup

```
[oracle@crs1 ~]$ . /home/oracle/asm_profile
[oracle@crs1 ~]$ ls -ls $ORACLE_HOME/dbs
[oracle@crs1 ~]$ vi /u01/app/oracle/admin/+ASM/pfile/init.ora
asm_diskgroups='DATA','FRA','TEST1'
```

  - Create new high redundancy Diskgroup TEST2 from sqlplus

```
SQL> CREATE DISKGROUP TEST2 NORMAL REDUNDANCY DISK
     'ORCL:VOL4','ORCL:VOL5';
     Diskgroup created.
SQL> ALTER SYSTEM SET asm_diskgroups='DATA','FRA','TEST1', 'TEST2';
[oracle@crs1 ~]$ vi /u01/app/oracle/admin/+ASM/pfile/init.ora
asm_diskgroups='DATA','FRA','TEST1', 'TEST2'
```

  - Create a new tablespace TEST1 on ASM DISKGROUP TEST1

Log on to database and execute query below

```
SQL> SELECT  a.name GRP_NAME,
             a.state  GRP_STATE,
             a.TYPE  GRP_TYPE,
             a.total_mb  GRP_TOTAL_MB,
             a.free_mb  grp_free_mb,
             b.name,
             b.PATH,
             b.HEADER_STATUS,
             b.MODE_STATUS,
             b.MOUNT_STATUS,
             b.TOTAL_MB,
             b.FREE_MB
     FROM    v$asm_diskgroup  a
             FULL  OUTER  JOIN
             V$ASM_DISK  b
             ON  a.group_number  =  b.group_number
     ORDER  BY  grp_name  NULLS  LAST;
SQL> CREATE  TABLESPACE  TEST1  DATAFILE  '+TEST1' SIZE  100M;
```

- Create new external redundancy Diskgroup from Oracle's OEM Grid Control.

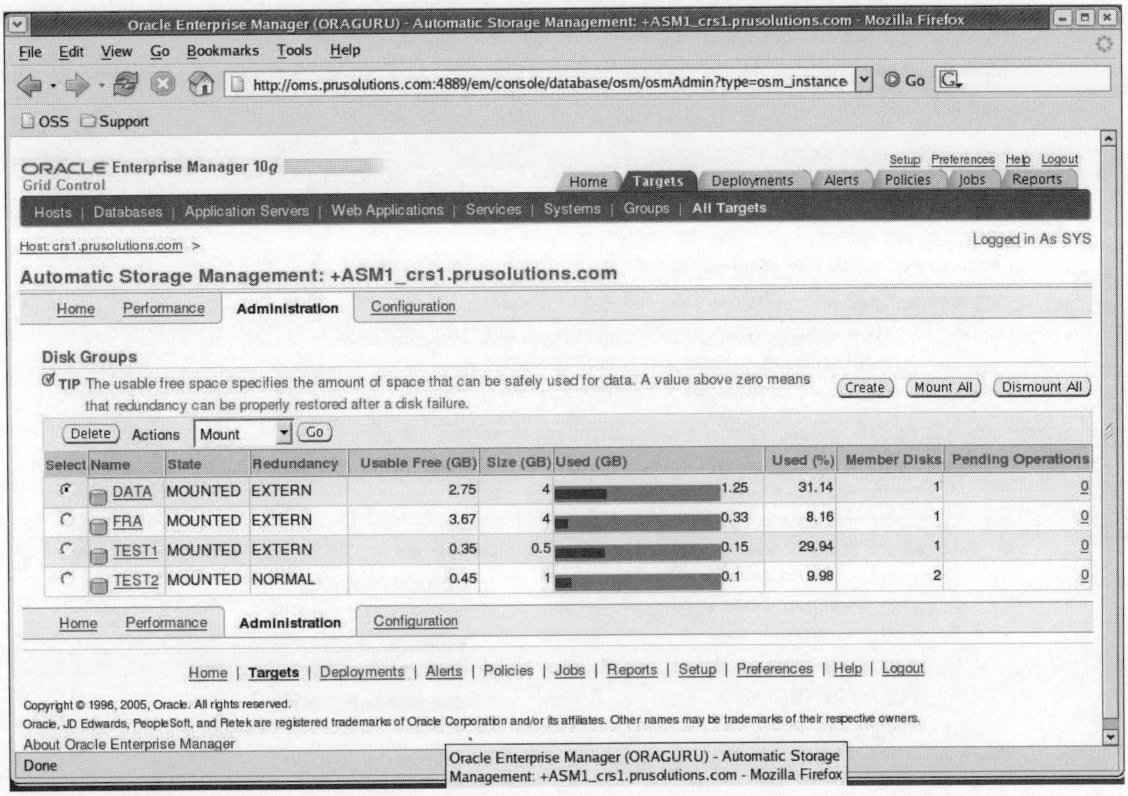

- Create Diskgroup

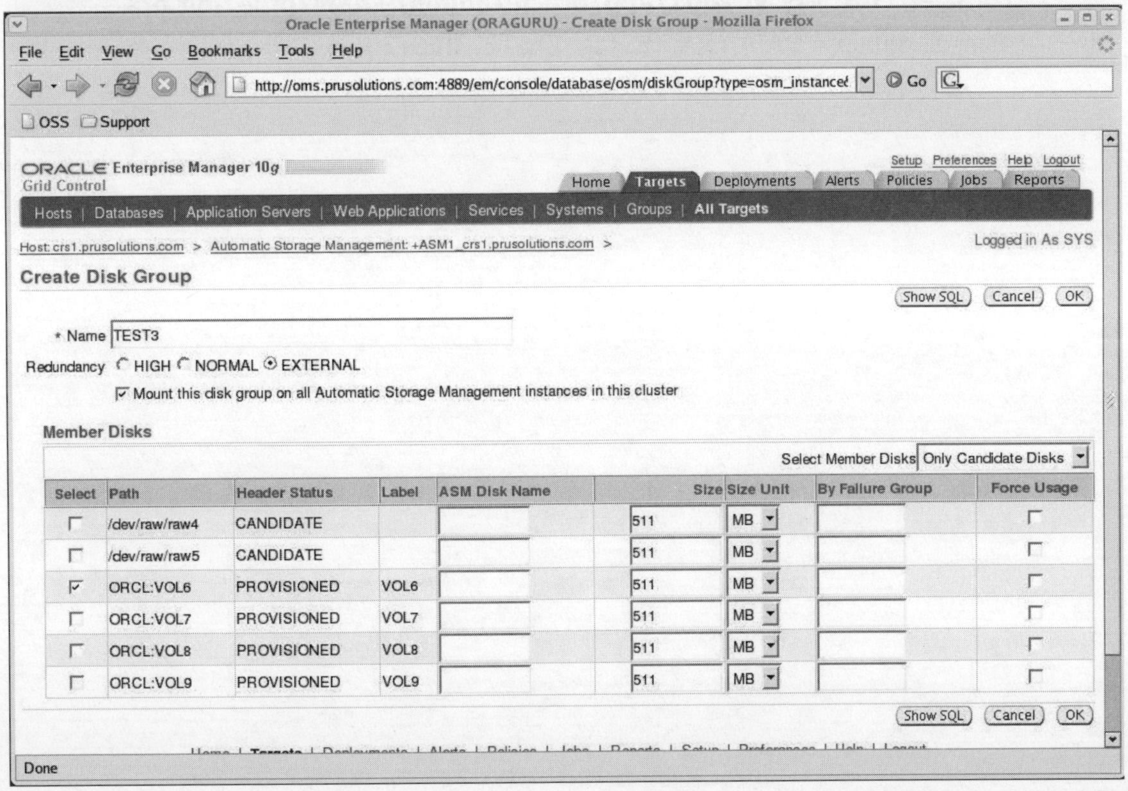

- ASM Confirmation page

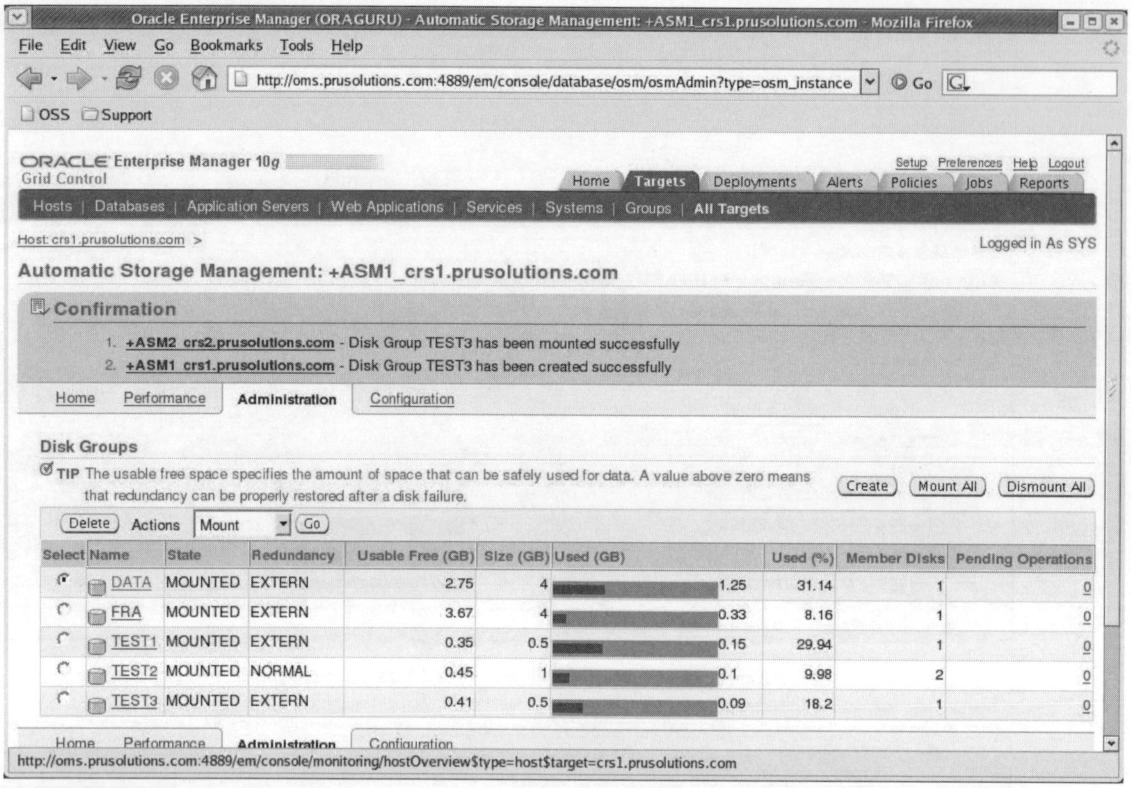

- Add Diskgroup TEST3 to ASM init.ora file

[oracle@crs1 ~]$ vi /u01/app/oracle/admin/+ASM/pfile/init.ora

asm_diskgroups='DATA','FRA','TEST1', 'TEST2', 'TEST3'

- Add a ASM Diskgroup using dbca

[oracle@crs1 ~]$ dbca

On dbca Operations page: Select Automatic Storage Management

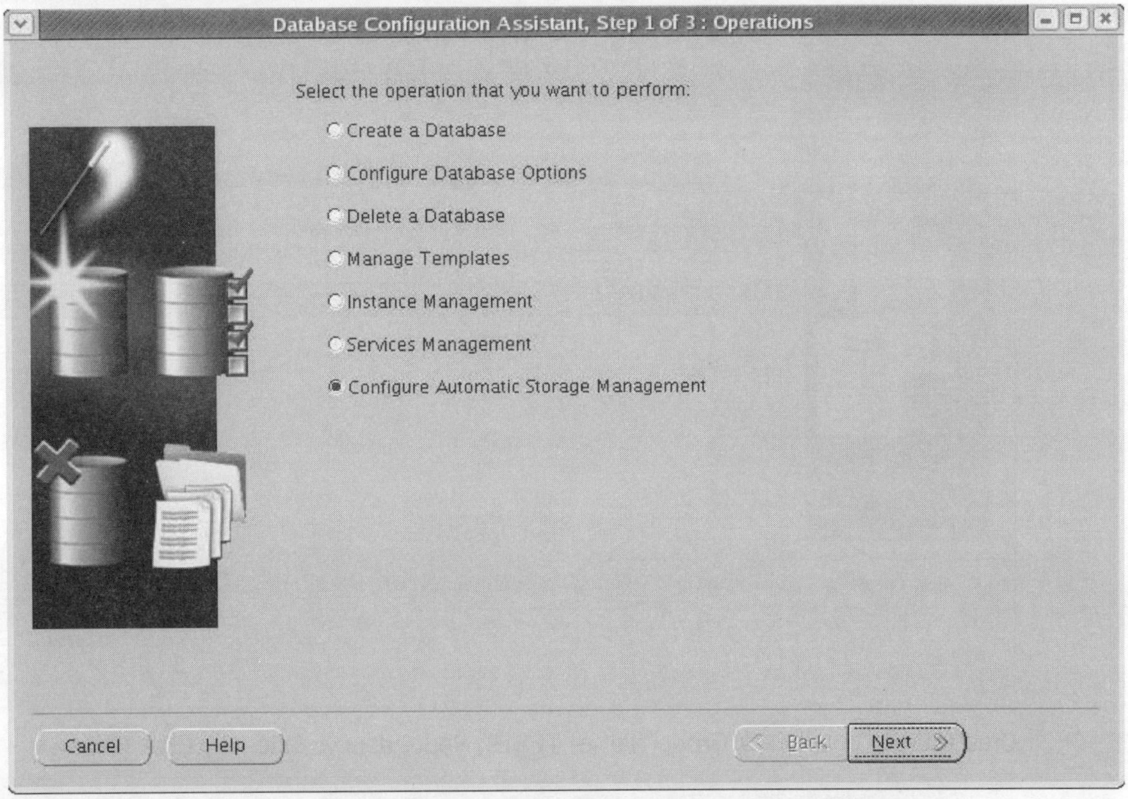

- Node Section: Select All, ASM Credential: Specify ASM SYS password < **oracle**>

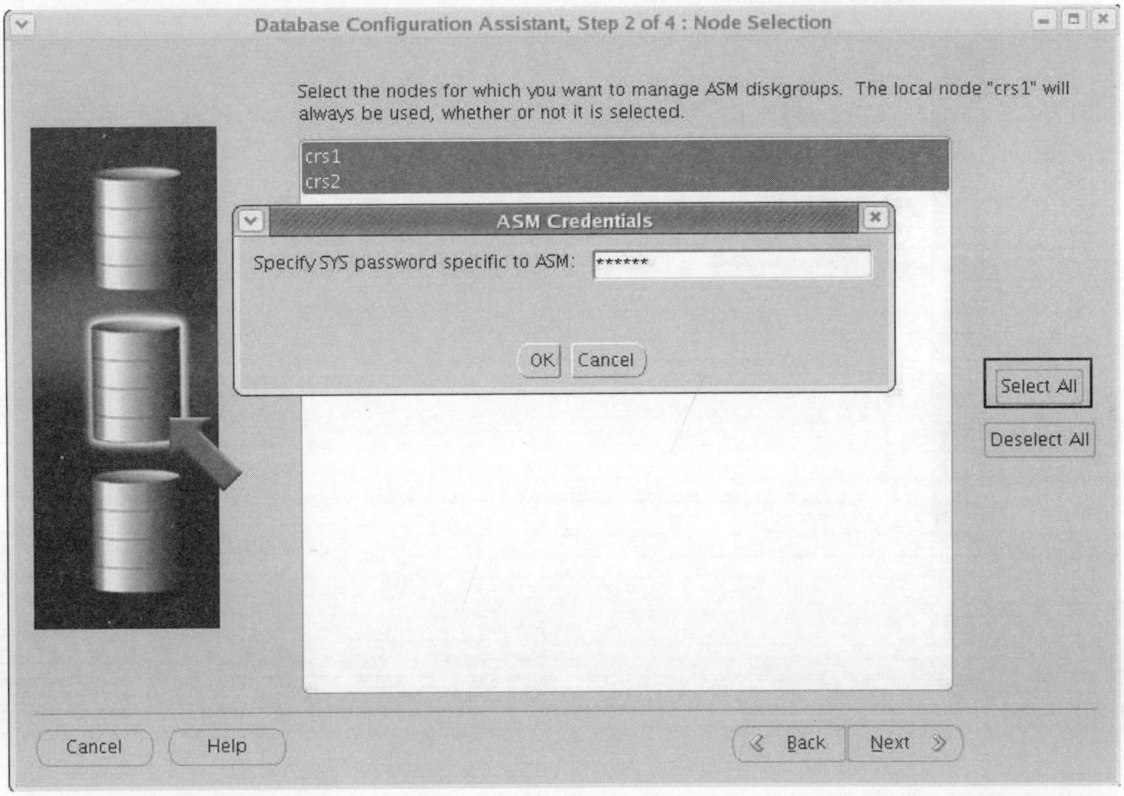

ASM Disk Groups: Create New

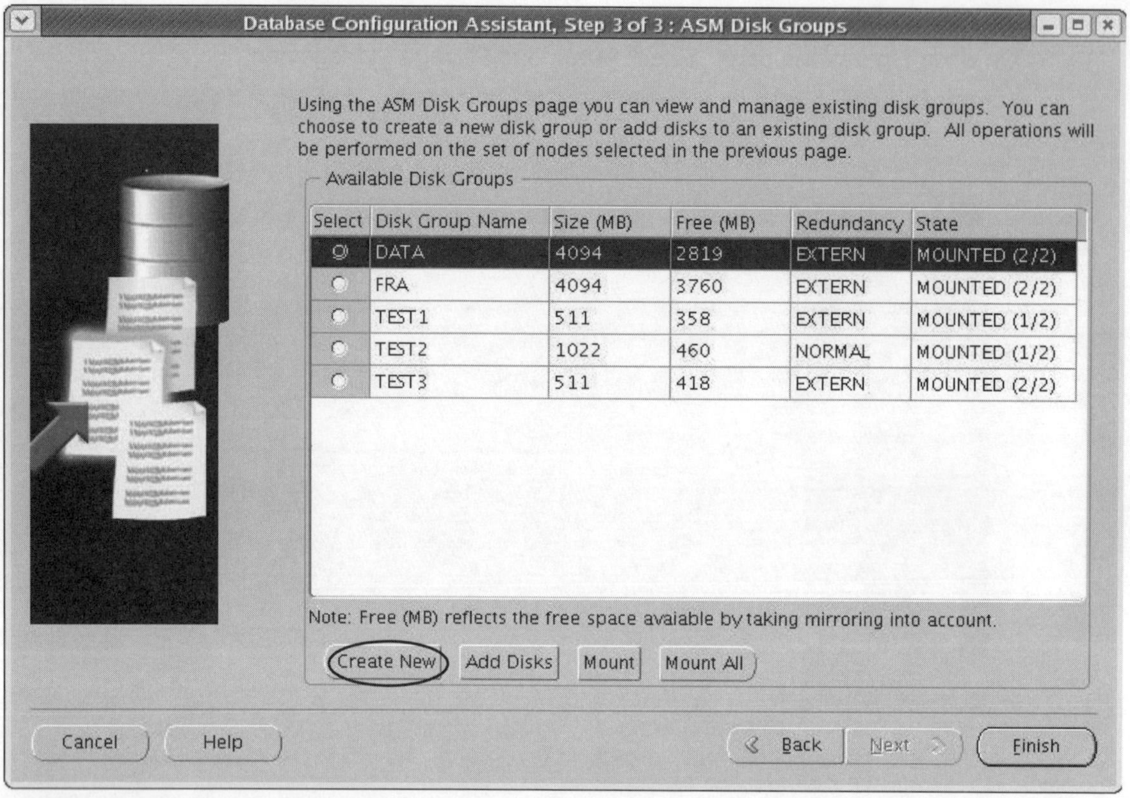

- Create Disk Group: Disk Group Name: TEST4, Redundancy: External, Click OK

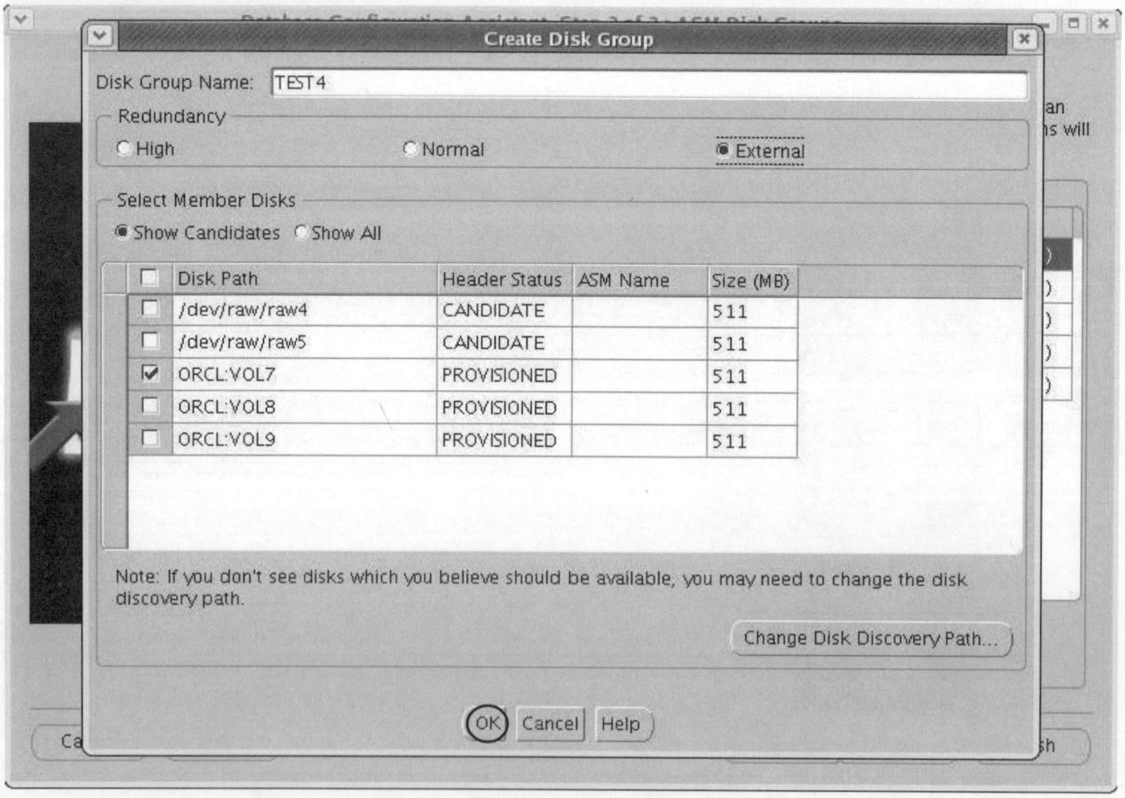

- ASM Disk Groups: Mount and Finish

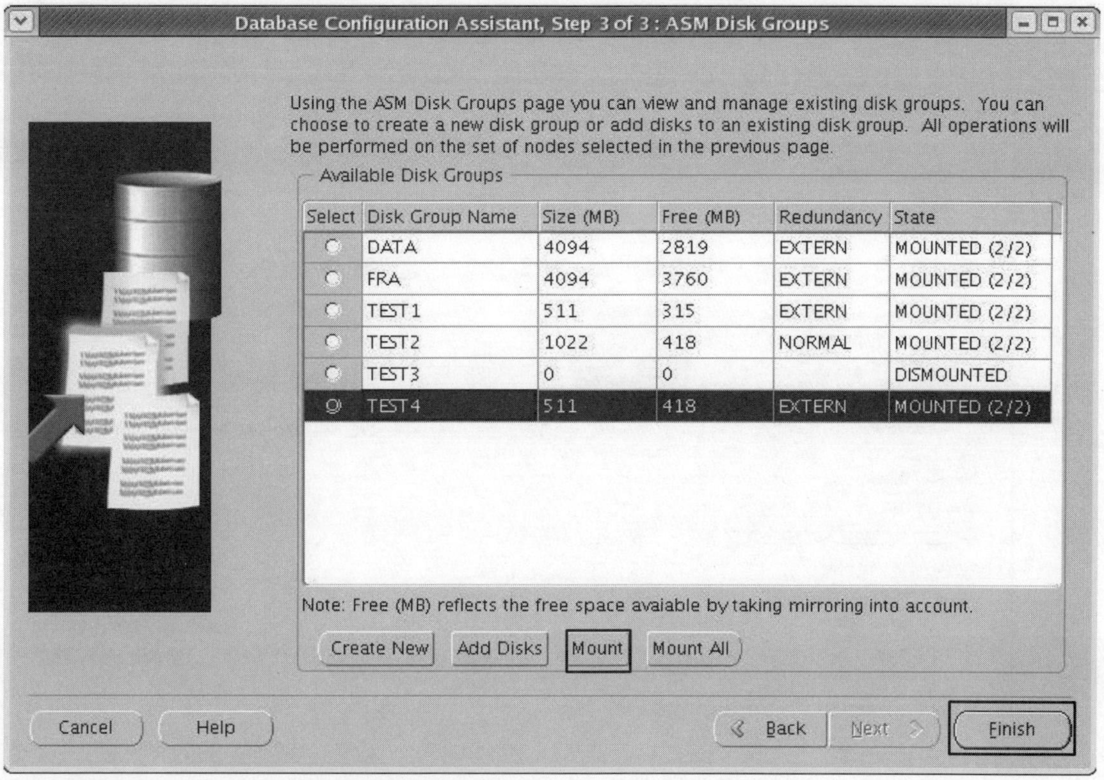

- Add new ASM disks to existing ASM Diskgroup
  - Add ASM disk to existing ASM Diskgroup from sqlplus

    SQL> ALTER DISKGROUP TEST1 ADD DISK 'ORCL: VOL8';
  - Add ASM disk to existing ASM Diskgroup from OEM Grid Control

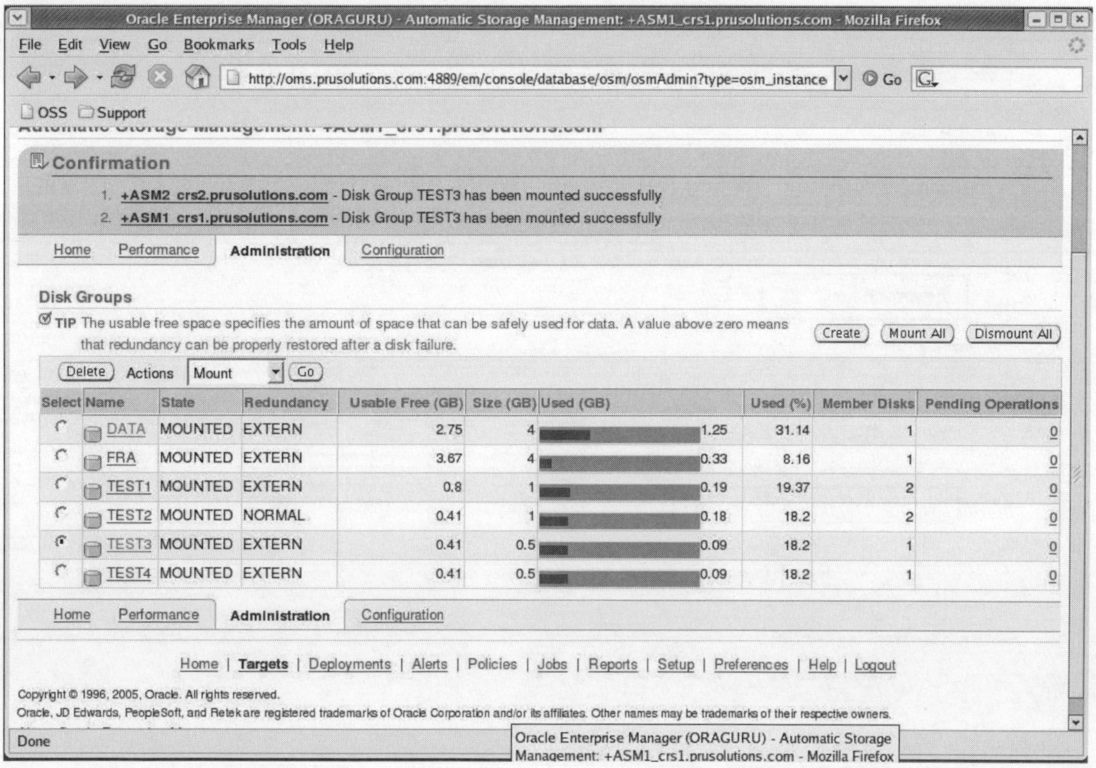

- Disk Group: TEST3

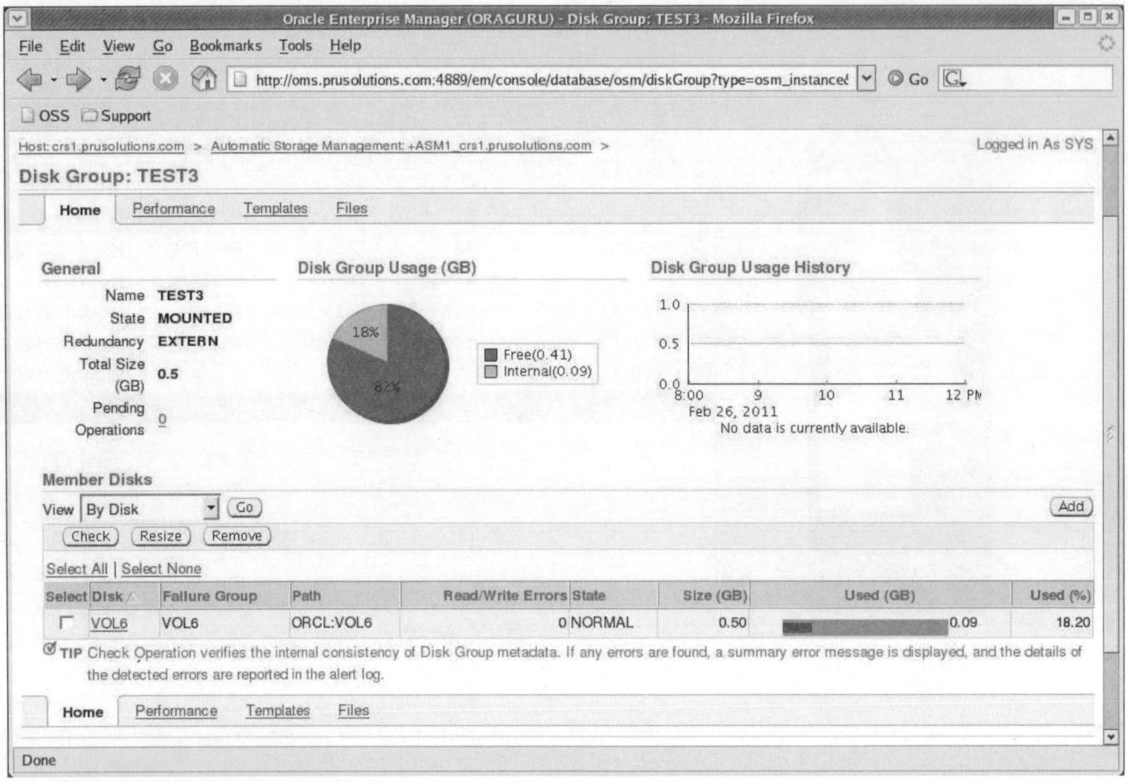

- Add Disks: Rebalance Power:2 , Member Disks ORCL:VOL9

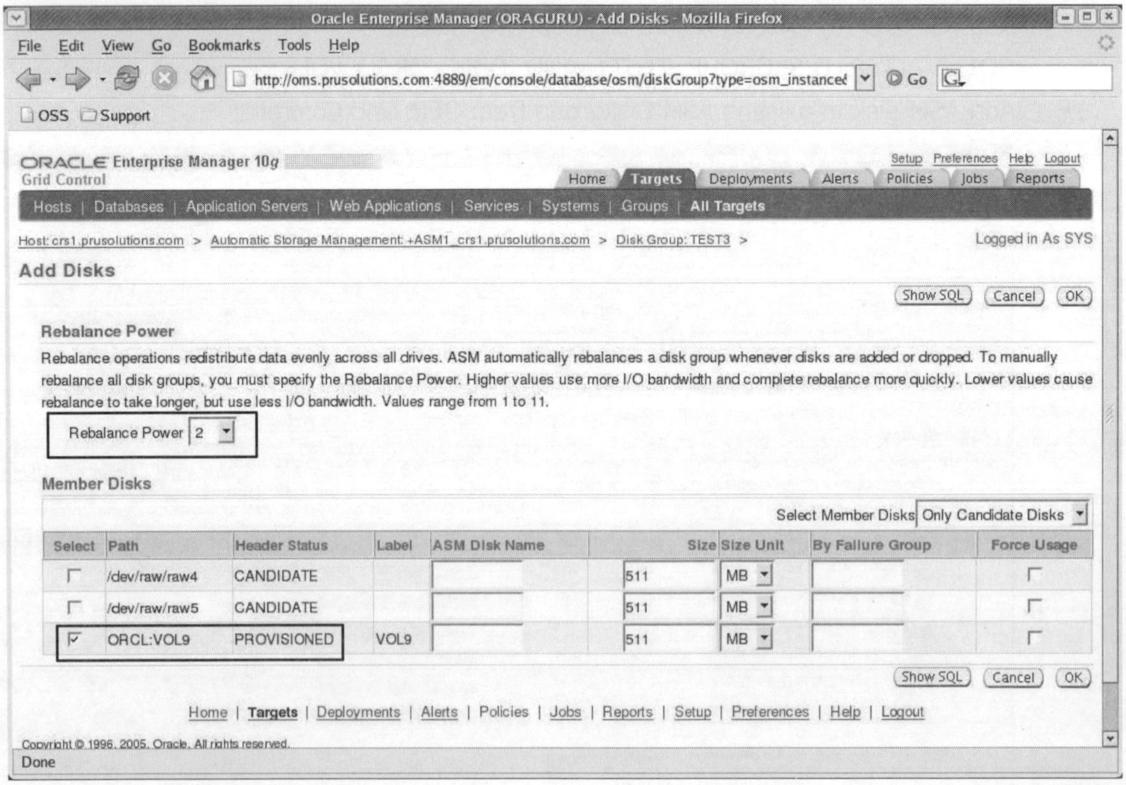

8.20 Creating Extra Controlfiles on ASM

The following procedure can be used to create additional controlfiles in the ASM Diskgroup

- Create a new directory in ASM Diskgroup

  SQL> ALTER DISKGROUP TEST4 ADD DIRECTORY '+TEST4/crsdb';

  SQL> ALTER DISKGROUP TEST4 ADD DIRECTORY '+TEST4/crsdb/controlfile';

  OR

  You can use asmcmd command to create directory (check all **asmcmd** commands)

  [oracle@crs1 ~]$. /home/oracle/asm_profile

  [oracle@crs1 ~]$ asmcmd

  ASMCMD> cd +TEST4

  ASMCMD> mkdir crsdb

  ASMCMD> cd crsdb

  ASMCMD> mkdir controlfile

- Edit the controlfile entry in spfile/init.ora to add a mirror controlfile

  SQL> SHOW PARAMETER spfile

NAME	TYPE	VALUE
spfile	string	+DATA/crsdb/spfilecrsdb.ora

  SQL> CREATE PFILE='/u01/app/oracle/product/10.2.0/db_1/dbs/initcrsdb.ora.20110226' FROM SPFILE;

  Edit pfile initcrsdb.ora.20110226 add entry for new controlfile location to it.

  *.control_files='+DATA/crsdb/controlfile/current.260.743634235','+FRA/crsdb/controlfile/current.256.743634235',**'+TEST4/crsdb/controlfile/controlfile3.ctl'**

- Cleanly shutdown all the instances of RAC (crsdb1, crsdb2)

  SQL> SHUTDOWN IMMEDIATE; (On both crsdb1, crsdb2 instances)

  OR

  [oracle@crs1 ~]$ srvctl stop database -d crsdb

- Start only one instance in NOMOUNT mode;

  SQL> STARTUP nomount;

- Use RMAN to restore controlfile from one of the existing locations to the new one.

  [oracle@crs1 ~]$ rman target /

  RMAN> restore controlfile to '+TEST4/crsdb/controlfile/controlfile3.ctl' FROM '+DATA/crsdb/controlfile/current.260.743634235';

  Starting restore at 26-FEB-11
  using target database control file instead of recovery catalog
  allocated channel: ORA_DISK_1
  channel ORA_DISK_1: sid=146 instance=crsdb1 devtype=DISK

  channel ORA_DISK_1: copied control file copy
  Finished restore at 26-FEB-11

- Shutdown database cleanly to create new spfile from pfile;

SQL> SHUTDOWN immediate;

ORA-01507: database not mounted
ORACLE instance shut down.

SQL> CREATE SPFILE='+DATA/crsdb/spfilecrsdb.ora' FROM PFILE='/u01/app/oracle/product/10.2.0/db_1/dbs/initcrsdb.ora.20110226';
File created

- Startup database again

SQL> STARTUP nomount;
SQL> SHOW PARAMETER control;

NAME	TYPE	VALUE
control_file_record_keep_time	integer	7
control_files	string	+DATA/crsdb/controlfile/current.260.743634235, +FRA/crsdb/controlfile/current.256.743634235, +TEST4/crsdb/controlfile/controlfile3.ctl

SQL> ALTER DATABASE MOUNT;

SQL> ALTER DATABASE OPEN;

8.21 Recovery Scenarios through RMAN

- For incremental backup, first we have to enable **BLOCK CHANGE TRACKING** in database

[oracle@crs1 ~]$. /home/oracle/asm_profile

[oracle@crs1 ~]$ echo $ORACLE_SID
+ASM1

[oracle@crs1 ~]$ asmcmd

ASMCMD> mkdir +FRA/CRSDB/DATAFILE

ASMCMD> cd +FRA/CRSDB/DATAFILE

[oracle@crs1 ~]$. /home/oracle/.bash_profile

[oracle@crs1 ~]$ sqlplus / as sysdba

SQL> ALTER DATABASE ENABLE BLOCK CHANGE TRACKING USING FILE '+FRA/CRSDB/DATAFILE/rman_change_track.f' REUSE;

Database altered.

SQL> SELECT * FROM V$BLOCK_CHANGE_TRACKING;

- Example rman_backup_script.rcv for cumulative incremental rman backup script to backup as copy

[oracle@crs1 ~]$ vi /home/oracle/rman/scripts/rman_backup_script.rcv

```
run
{
recover copy of database with tag 'INCR_DAILY_UPD';
backup incremental level 1
for recover of copy with tag 'INCR_DAILY_UPD'
cumulative database plus archivelog;
}
```

- Immediately backup of crsdb database

  [oracle@crs1 scripts]$ rman target / CMDFILE=$HOME/rman/scripts/rman_backup_script.rcv LOG=$HOME/rman/log/rman_backup_crsdb.log APPEND

- Complete Recovery when SYSTEM tablespace is missing.

  Problem Generation

  Delete system tablespace datafile from operating system when database is SHUTDOWN.

  [oracle@crs1 dbs]$ srvctl stop database -d crsdb

  [oracle@crs1 ~]$. /home/oracle/asm_profile

  [oracle@crs1 ~]$ asmcmd

  ASMCMD> cd +DATA/CRSDB/DATAFILE

  ASMCMD> ls

  ```
  EXAMPLE.264.743634277
  SYSAUX.257.743634153
  SYSTEM.256.743634151
  UNDOTBS1.258.743634153
  UNDOTBS2.265.743634431
  USERS.259.743634153
  ```

  ASMCMD> rm -rf SYSTEM.256.743634151

  ASMCMD> ls

  ```
  EXAMPLE.264.743634277
  SYSAUX.257.743634153
  UNDOTBS1.258.743634153
  UNDOTBS2.265.743634431
  USERS.259.743634153
  ```

  Solution

  [oracle@crs1 ~]$. /home/oracle/.bash_profile

  [oracle@crs1 ~]$ sqlplus / as sysdba

  SQL> STARTUP MOUNT EXCLUSIVE;

  ```
  ORACLE instance started.

  Total System Global Area 285212672 bytes
  Fixed Size                 1218992 bytes
  Variable Size            142607952 bytes
  Database Buffers         138412032 bytes
  Redo Buffers               2973696 bytes
  Database mounted.
  ```

  [oracle@crs1 ~]$ rman target /

  ```
  RMAN> run
  {
   restore datafile 1;
   recover datafile 1;
   sql ' alter database open ';
  }
  ```

- Practice all the recovery scenarios that are mentioned in Chapter 5 Section 8 on crsdb database

8.22 Creating Bugs and Fixing them in RAC

In next RAC practice install, add following bugs one after another and check the errors to learn more to fix bugs. **If you encounter any bug during install, you should ask for new set of machines instead of fixing bugs.**

- Before using Cluvfy utility pre crsinst install, stop eth1 on node2 crs2 and capture the error.
- Modify the localhost ip address on node2 crs2 from 127.0.0.1 to 127.1.0.0. This will give error during configuration of GSD

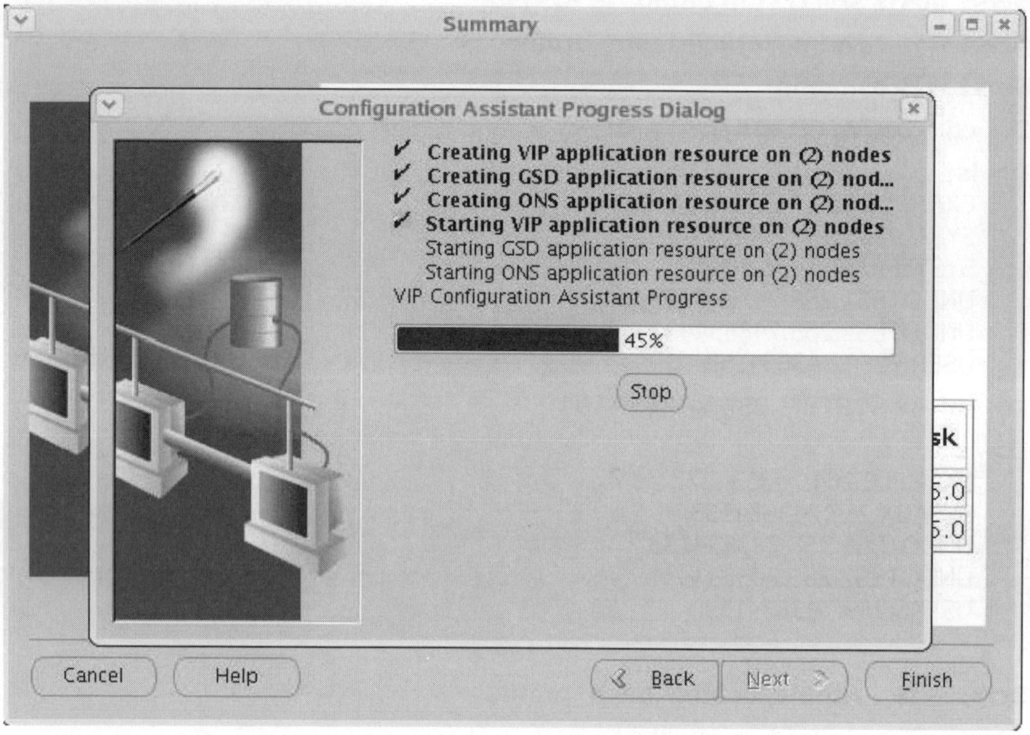

- Enable iptables on node2 crs2 using system-config-services

  [root@crs2 oracle]# system-config-services

  This will give error during configuration of VIP on second node.

- Refer Metalink Documents mentioned below for RAC

  i. SSH and Xauth Warning Before RAC 10g Installation [ID 285070.1]
  ii. How to Recreate OCR/Voting Disk Accidentally Deleted [ID 399482.1]
  iii. OUI-25023 When Trying To Install A Patchset On RAC [ID 394868.1]
  iv. RAC Assurance Support Team: RAC Starter Kit and Best Practices (Linux) [ID 811306.1]
  v. RAC: Frequently Asked Questions [ID 220970.1]

- If you encounter any bug during install, you should ask for new set of machines instead of fixing bugs

9

Data Guard

- Use Data Guard Manager and DGMGRL
- Create and utilize a physical standby database
- Create and utilize a logical standby database
- Set up log transport services for various levels or protection
- Configure the network environment to allow communication between the standby database and the primary database
- Open the physical standby database in a "ready-only" state
- Perform a switchover operation and a failover operation
- Implement Data Guard

9.1 Start Data Guard Cluster Nodes

Shutdown machines OCM, OMS and OEM and start machines CRSDG1 and CRSDG2.

- Ftp and unzip Oracle 10g Database software and JDK

Start "crsdg1, crsdg2" machines on VMware, logon to oracle user then create folder /u01/software.

ftp Oracle 10g Database software and JDK mentioned below to crsdg1, crsdg2 Linux guest machine from Windows host. Unzip the oracle database 10g software files

10201_clusterware_linux32.zip
10201_database_linux32.zip
oracleasmlib-2.0.2-1.i386.rpm

9.2 OS configuration checks to install Oracle Clusterware

Following checks are to be made both on crsdg1 and crsdg2 nodes

- Check hosts names, files option should be the first

```
# cat /etc/nsswitch.conf | grep hosts
make sure it has file option first then dns
```

- Check Kernel Parameters are set properly (Converted into kb, mb, gb to remember easily)

  - **/etc/sysctl.conf**

```
kernel.shmall = 2097152                        # (2mb)
kernel.shmmax = 2147483648                     # (2g)
kernel.shmmni = 4096                           # (4k)
kernel.sem = 250 32000 100 128
fs.file-max = 65536                            # (64k)
net.ipv4.ip_local_port_range = 1024 65000
net.core.rmem_default = 1048576                # (1mb)
net.core.rmem_max = 1048576                    # (1mb)
net.core.wmem_default = 262144                 # (256k)
net.core.wmem_max = 262144                     # (256k)
```

  - **/etc/security/limits.conf**

```
oracle     soft   nproc 2047
oracle     hard   nproc 16384
oracle     soft   nofile 1024
oracle     hard   nofile 65536
```

  - **/etc/pam.d/login**

```
session   required   /lib/security/pam_limits.so
session   required   pam_limits.so
```

  - **/etc/profile**

```
if [ $USER = "oracle" ]; then
      if [ $SHELL = "/bin/ksh" ]; then
            ulimit -p 16384
            ulimit -n 65536
      else
            ulimit -u 16384 -n 65536
      fi
fi
```

- Check /etc/hosts for following values are set

```
127.0.0.1         localhost
# Oracle Database ip addresses
192.168.2.121     ocm.prusolutions.com            ocm
# Oracle Enterprise Manager ip addresses
192.168.2.161     oem.prusolutions.com            oem
192.168.2.162     oms.prusolutions.com            oms
# Oracle RAC ip addresses
192.168.2.131     crs1.prusolutions.com           crs1
192.168.2.31      crs1-vip.prusolutions.com       crs1-vip
10.10.10.31       crs1-priv.prusolutions.com      crs1-priv
192.162.2.132     crs2.prusolutions.com           crs2
192.168.2.32      crs2-vip.prusolutions.com       crs2-vip
10.10.10.32       crs2-priv.prusolutions.com      crs2-priv
# Oracle RAC Dataguard ip addresses
192.168.2.141     crsdg1.prusolutions.com         crsdg1
192.168.2.41      crsdg1-vip.prusolutions.com     crsdg1-vip
10.10.10.41       crsdg1-priv.prusolutions.com    crsdg1-priv
192.162.2.142     crsdg2.prusolutions.com         crsdg2
192.168.2.42      crsdg2-vip.prusolutions.com     crsdg2-vip
10.10.10.42       crsdg2-priv.prusolutions.com    crsdg2-priv
```

- Check user oracle and nobody for software Install

```
# cat /etc/passwd
```

- Check following parameters swap should be 3G, memory 1G and temp at least 512M

```
# grep MemTotal /proc/meminfo
# grep SwapTotal /proc/meminfo
# df -k /tmp
```

- Check Linux required packages are installed

```
binutils-2.15.92.0.2-21
compat-db-4.1.25-9
compat-libstdc++-33-3.2.3-47.3
gcc-3.4.6-3.1
gcc-c++-3.4.6-3.1
glibc-2.3.4-2.25
glibc-common-2.3.4-2.25
gnome-libs-1.4.1.2.90-44.2
libstdc++-3.4.6-3.1
libstdc++-devel-3.4.6-3.1
make-3.80-6.EL4
pdksh-5.2.14-30.3
sysstat-5.0.5-11.rhel4
xscreensaver-4.18-5.rhel4.12
setarch-1.6-1
libaio-0.3.105-2.i386.rpm
openmotif21-2.1.30-11.RHEL4.6.i386.rpm
```

If the different version of Linux is installed then packages may be as mentioned below or combination of both

binutils-2.15.92.0.2-13.EL4
compat-db-4.1.25-9
compat-libstdc++-296-2.96-132.7.2
control-center-2.8.0-12
gcc-3.4.3-22.1.EL4
gcc-c++-3.4.3-22.1.EL44
glibc-2.3.4-2.9
glibc-common-2.3.4-2.9
gnome-libs-1.4.1.2.90-44.1
libstdc++-3.4.3-22.1
libstdc++-devel-3.4.3-22.1
make-3.80-5
pdksh-5.2.14-30
sysstat-5.0.5-1
xscreensaver-4.18-5.rhel4.2
setarch-1.6-1
libaio-0.3.105-2.i386.rpm
openmotif21-2.1.30-11.RHEL4.6.i386.rpm

- Check iptables are disabled on both nodes.

  [root@crs2 oracle]# system-config-services

9.3 Remaining OS configuration on both Data Guard nodes

- Set up .bash_profile for user oracle on crsdg1

  Database name is crsdgdb. The ORACLE_SID name on crsdg1 node will be crsdgdb1. The ORACLE_HOME, ORA_CRS_HOME path can be customized to any Unix directory.

  The setup of all 3 profile files mentioned below on both crsdg1 and crsdg2 should not take more than 5 minutes.

  - You can create these profile files in vi editor when you are practicing other Oracle's OEM Grid install

    /home/oracle/.bash_profile

```
# Get the aliases and functions
if [ -f ~/.bashrc ]; then
        . ~/.bashrc
fi
# User specific environment and startup programs
export EDITOR=vi
export ORACLE_SID=crsdgdb1
export ORACLE_BASE=/u01/app/oracle
export ORACLE_HOME=$ORACLE_BASE/product/10.2.0/db_1
export ORA_CRS_HOME=$ORACLE_BASE/product/10.2.0/crs_1
export PATH=$ORACLE_HOME/bin:$ORA_CRS_HOME/bin:/bin:/sbin:/usr/bin:/usr/sbin:/usr/local/
bin:/usr/X11R6/bin
umask 022
alias db_profile=". /home/oracle/.bash_profile"
alias asm_prodile=". /home/oracle/asm_profile"
alias agent_profile=". /home/oracle/agent_profile"
```

- Set up .bash_profile for user oracle on crsdg2

  The ORACLE_SID is changed to crsdgdb2 rest of .bash profile is same, ftp the .bash_profile from crsdg1 to crsdg2 and change the ORACLE_SID name

/home/oracle/.bash_profile

```
# Get the aliases and functions
if [ -f ~/.bashrc ]; then
      . ~/.bashrc
fi

# User specific environment and startup programs
export EDITOR=vi
export ORACLE_SID=crsdgdb2
export ORACLE_BASE=/u01/app/oracle
export ORACLE_HOME=$ORACLE_BASE/product/10.2.0/db_1
export ORA_CRS_HOME=$ORACLE_BASE/product/10.2.0/crs_1
export PATH=
$ORACLE_HOME/bin:$ORA_CRS_HOME/bin:/bin:/sbin:/usr/bin:/usr/sbin:/usr/local/bin:/usr/X11R6/bin
umask 022
alias db_profile=". /home/oracle/.bash_profile"
alias asm_prodile=". /home/oracle/asm_profile"
alias agent_profile=". /home/oracle/agent_profile"
```

- Set up asm_profile on crsdg1

  (Copy .bash_profile to asm_profile and make OARCLE_HOME and ORACLE_SID changes as mentioned below).

  You can have common home or separate homes for ASM and DB install. In this setup, we will install ASM and DB in separate home. Practice RAC install with common ASM and DB home also, which helps to install RAC much faster

/home/oracle/asm_profile (Permission on file chmod 755 asm_profile)

```
# Get the aliases and functions
if [ -f ~/.bashrc ]; then
      . ~/.bashrc
fi

# User specific environment and startup programs
export EDITOR=vi
export ORACLE_SID=+ASM1
export ORACLE_BASE=/u01/app/oracle
export ORACLE_HOME=$ORACLE_BASE/product/10.2.0/asm_1
export ORA_CRS_HOME=$ORACLE_BASE/product/10.2.0/crs_1
export PATH=$ORACLE_HOME/bin:$ORA_CRS_HOME/bin:/bin:/sbin:/usr/bin:/usr/sbin:/usr/local/bin:/usr/
X11R6/bin
umask 022
alias db_profile=". /home/oracle/.bash_profile"
alias asm_prodile=". /home/oracle/asm_profile"
alias agent_profile=". /home/oracle/agent_profile"
```

- Set up asm_profile on crsdg2

/home/oracle/asm_profile (Permission on file chmod 755 asm_profile)

```
# Get the aliases and functions
if [ -f ~/.bashrc ]; then
      . ~/.bashrc
fi
# User specific environment and startup programs
export EDITOR=vi
export ORACLE_SID=+ASM2
export ORACLE_BASE=/u01/app/oracle
```

```
export ORACLE_HOME=$ORACLE_BASE/product/10.2.0/asm_1
export ORA_CRS_HOME=$ORACLE_BASE/product/10.2.0/crs_1
export PATH=$ORACLE_HOME/bin:$ORA_CRS_HOME/bin:/bin:/sbin:/usr/bin:/usr/sbin:/usr/local/bin:/usr/
X11R6/bin
umask 022
alias db_profile=". /home/oracle/.bash_profile"
alias asm_prodile=". /home/oracle/asm_profile"
alias agent_profile=". /home/oracle/agent_profile"
```

- Set up agent_profile on both crsdg1 and crsdg2

/home/oracle/agent_profile (Permission on file chmod 755 agent_profile)
Copy .bash_profile to agent_profile and make OARCLE_HOME change as mentioned below)

```
# agent_profile
# Get the aliases and functions
if [ -f ~/.bashrc ]; then
        . ~/.bashrc
fi
# User specific environment and startup programs
export EDITOR=vi
export ORACLE_BASE=/u01/app/oracle
export ORACLE_HOME=$ORACLE_BASE/product/10.2.0/agent10g
export PATH=$ORACLE_HOME/bin:/bin:/sbin:/usr/bin:/usr/sbin:/usr/local/bin:/usr/X11R6/bin
umask 022
alias db_profile=". /home/oracle/.bash_profile"
alias asm_prodile=". /home/oracle/asm_profile"
alias agent_profile=". /home/oracle/agent_profile"
```

- To change environment variable use following

```
$. /home/oracle/.bash_profile
$. /home/oracle/agent_profile
$. /home/oracle/asm_profile
$ echo $ORACLE_HOME
```

- Make following directories for Oracle Install on both nodes crsdg1 and crsdg2

```
[oracle@crsdg1 ~]$ . /home/oracle/agent_profile
[oracle@crsdg1 ~]$ mkdir -p $ORACLE_HOME
[oracle@crsdg1 ~]$ . /home/oracle/asm_profile
[oracle@crsdg1 ~]$ mkdir -p $ORACLE_HOME
[oracle@crsdg1 ~]$ . /home/oracle/.bash_profile
[oracle@crsdg1 ~]$ mkdir -p $ORACLE_HOME
[oracle@crsdg1 ~]$ mkdir –p $ORA_CRS_HOME
[oracle@crsdg1 ~]$ mkdir –p $ORA_CRS_HOME
[oracle@crsdg1 ~]$ mkdir –p $ORACLE_BASE/admin
[oracle@crsdg1 ~]$ mkdir –p $ORACLE_BASE/oradata/crsdgdb
[oracle@crsdg1 ~]$ mkdir -p $ORACLE_BASE/admin/crsdgdb/adump
[oracle@crsdg1 ~]$ mkdir -p $ORACLE_BASE/admin/crsdgdb/bdump
[oracle@crsdg1 ~]$ mkdir -p $ORACLE_BASE/admin/crsdgdb/cdump
[oracle@crsdg1 ~]$ mkdir -p $ORACLE_BASE/admin/crsdgdb/udump
[oracle@crsdg1 ~]$ mkdir -p $ORACLE_BASE/admin/crsdgdb/scripts
```

- Create /dev/timedev on both nodes crsdg1 and crsdg2

  As root user Device on each node for performance for gettimeofday() calls

  # mknod /dev/timedev c 15 0

  # chmod 644 /dev/timedev

- Install following package from Linux cdrom iso image on both nodes crsdg1 and crsdg2

  # rpm -Uvh libaio-0.3.105-2.i386.rpm

  # rpm -Uvh openmotif21-2.1.30-11.RHEL4.6.i386.rpm

- Install Oracle ASM Libraries from Oracle Download

  # rpm -Uvh oracleasmlib-2.0.2-1.i386.rpm

- Install jdk-6u21-linux-i586-rpm.bin on crsdg1, crsdg2 as root user

  # /u01/software/jdk/ jdk-6u21-linux-i586-rpm.bin

- Format disk partitions as root user to be used by ocr, voting disk and ASM

  - Logon as root user on crsdg1 and list disks partition details

    [root@crsdg1 clusterware]# fdisk -l | grep -i disk

    Disk /dev/sdb doesn't contain a valid partition table
    Disk /dev/sdc doesn't contain a valid partition table
    Disk /dev/sdd doesn't contain a valid partition table
    Disk /dev/sde doesn't contain a valid partition table
    Disk /dev/sdf doesn't contain a valid partition table
    Disk /dev/sdg doesn't contain a valid partition table
    Disk /dev/sdh doesn't contain a valid partition table
    Disk /dev/sdi doesn't contain a valid partition table
    Disk /dev/sdj doesn't contain a valid partition table
    Disk /dev/sdk doesn't contain a valid partition table
    Disk /dev/sdl doesn't contain a valid partition table
    Disk /dev/sdm doesn't contain a valid partition table
    Disk /dev/sdn doesn't contain a valid partition table
    Disk /dev/sdo doesn't contain a valid partition table
    Disk /dev/sda: 21.4 GB, 21474836480 bytes
    Disk /dev/sdb: 536 MB, 536870912 bytes
    Disk /dev/sdc: 536 MB, 536870912 bytes
    Disk /dev/sdd: 536 MB, 536870912 bytes
    Disk /dev/sde: 536 MB, 536870912 bytes
    Disk /dev/sdf: 536 MB, 536870912 bytes
    Disk /dev/sdg: 4294 MB, 4294967296 bytes
    Disk /dev/sdh: 4294 MB, 4294967296 bytes
    Disk /dev/sdi: 536 MB, 536870912 bytes
    Disk /dev/sdj: 536 MB, 536870912 bytes
    Disk /dev/sdk: 536 MB, 536870912 bytes
    Disk /dev/sdl: 536 MB, 536870912 bytes
    Disk /dev/sdm: 536 MB, 536870912 bytes
    Disk /dev/sdn: 536 MB, 536870912 bytes
    Disk /dev/sdo: 536 MB, 536870912 bytes

  - Format all the partitions shown above /dev/sdb... /dev/sdo using command fdisk

    [root@crsdg1 ~]# fdisk /dev/sdb

Device contains neither a valid DOS partition table, nor Sun, SGI or OSF disklabel
Building a new DOS disklabel. Changes will remain in memory only,
until you decide to write them. After that, of course, the previous
content won't be recoverable.

Warning: invalid flag 0x0000 of partition table 4 will be corrected by w(rite)

Command (m for help): **n**
Command action
  e extended
  p primary partition (1-4)
p
Partition number (1-4): **1**
First cylinder (1-512, default 1):
Using default value 1
Last cylinder or +size or +sizeM or +sizeK (1-512, default 512):
Using default value 512

Command (m for help): w
The partition table has been altered!

Calling ioctl() to re-read partition table.
Syncing disks.

- **In same way, format all the disk /dev/sdb... /dev/sdo with following input**
  i. Command (m for help): **n**
  ii. Command action
     e extended
     p primary partition (1-4)
     p
  iii. Partition number (1-4): **1**
  iv. First cylinder (1-512, default 1): **< press enter>**
  v. Last cylinder or +size or +sizeM or +sizeK (1-512, default 512): **< press enter>**
  vi. Command (m for help): **w**

- Below are format details of last disk /dev/sd0

[root@crsdg1 ~]# fdisk /dev/sdo

Device contains neither a valid DOS partition table, nor Sun, SGI or OSF disklabel
Building a new DOS disklabel. Changes will remain in memory only,
until you decide to write them. After that, of course, the previous
content won't be recoverable.
Warning: invalid flag 0x0000 of partition table 4 will be corrected by w(rite)

Command (m for help): **n**
Command action
  e extended
  p primary partition (1-4)
p
Partition number (1-4): **1**
First cylinder (1-512, default 1):
Using default value 1
Last cylinder or +size or +sizeM or +sizeK (1-512, default 512):
Using default value 512

Command (m for help): **w**
The partition table has been altered!

Calling ioctl() to re-read partition table.
Syncing disks.

- Again check details of all disk partitions

[root@crsdg1 clusterware]# fdisk -l | grep -i disk

```
Disk /dev/sda: 21.4 GB, 21474836480 bytes
Disk /dev/sdb: 536 MB, 536870912 bytes
Disk /dev/sdc: 536 MB, 536870912 bytes
Disk /dev/sdd: 536 MB, 536870912 bytes
Disk /dev/sde: 536 MB, 536870912 bytes
Disk /dev/sdf: 536 MB, 536870912 bytes
Disk /dev/sdg: 4294 MB, 4294967296 bytes
Disk /dev/sdh: 4294 MB, 4294967296 bytes
Disk /dev/sdi: 536 MB, 536870912 bytes
Disk /dev/sdj: 536 MB, 536870912 bytes
Disk /dev/sdk: 536 MB, 536870912 bytes
Disk /dev/sdl: 536 MB, 536870912 bytes
Disk /dev/sdm: 536 MB, 536870912 bytes
Disk /dev/sdn: 536 MB, 536870912 bytes
Disk /dev/sdo: 536 MB, 536870912 bytes
```

- Verify all the disks from crsdg2 to make sure all the disk are visible from crsdg2

[root@crsdg2 RPMS]# fdisk /dev/sdb

Command (m for help): **v**
31 unallocated sectors

Command (m for help): **w**
The partition table has been altered!

Calling ioctl() to re-read partition table.
Syncing disks.

In same way, verify all the disks /dev/sdc .. /dev/sdo

- Binding raw partitions for ocr, voting disks in /etc/sysconfig/rawdevices

Five disks /dev/sdb1... /dev/sdf1 will be used for ocr and voting disk. Add following lines on both crsdg1 and crsdg2

 # /etc/sysconfig/rawdevices

```
/dev/raw/raw1        /dev/sdb1
/dev/raw/raw2        /dev/sdc1
/dev/raw/raw3        /dev/sdd1
/dev/raw/raw4        /dev/sde1
/dev/raw/raw5        /dev/sdf1
```

- Restart the rawdevices again and change ownership to oracle on both crsdg1 and crsdg2

[root@crsdg1 RPMS]# /sbin/service rawdevices restart

[root@crsdg1 RPMS]# chown oracle:dba /dev/raw/raw[1-5]

[root@crsdg1 RPMS]# chmod 660 /dev/raw/raw[1-5]

[root@crsdg1 clusterware]# ls -lat /dev/raw/raw*

```
crw-rw—— 1 oracle dba 162, 5 Feb 27 23:57 /dev/raw/raw5
crw-rw—— 1 oracle dba 162, 4 Feb 27 23:57 /dev/raw/raw4
crw-rw—— 1 oracle dba 162, 3 Feb 27 23:57 /dev/raw/raw3
crw-rw—— 1 oracle dba 162, 2 Feb 27 23:57 /dev/raw/raw2
crw-rw—— 1 oracle dba 162, 1 Feb 27 23:57 /dev/raw/raw1
```

Modify the permission for rawdevices in following file on both crsdg1 and crsdg2

[root@crsdg1 clusterware]# vi /etc/udev/permissions.d/50-udev.permissions

raw devices
ram*:root:disk:660
 # raw/*:root:disk:660 # comment this line and add line mentioned below
raw/*:oracle:dba:660

[root@crsdg1 RPMS]# cat /etc/udev/permissions.d/50-udev.permissions | grep -i raw

- Hang Check Timer Configuration

  Add the following line to **/etc/modprobe.conf**

  options hangcheck-timer hangcheck_tick=30 hangcheck_margin=180

  OR you can add following line to **/etc/rc.d/rc.local**

  modprobe hangcheck-timer hangcheck_tick=30 hangcheck_margin=180

  Restart both crsdg1 and crsdg2 to check if hangcheck-timer is working or not using following

  [oracle@crsdg2 ~]$ /sbin/lsmod | grep -i hang
  hangcheck_timer 7897 0

  On VMware server increase hangcheck_tick=60 and hangcheck_marging=360

- Configure SSH and user Equivalence

  - On crsdg1 execute following as oracle User

    [oracle@crsdg1 ~]$ chmod 755 /home/oracle

    [oracle@crsdg1 ~]$ mkdir ~/.ssh

    [oracle@crsdg1 ~]$ chmod 700 ~/.ssh

    Accept the default location for the key file and for pass phrase press Enter Key

    [oracle@crsdg1 ~]$ ssh-keygen -t rsa

    Generating public/private rsa key pair.
    Enter file in which to save the key (/home/oracle/.ssh/id_rsa):
    Enter passphrase (empty for no passphrase):
    Enter same passphrase again:
    Your identification has been saved in /home/oracle/.ssh/id_rsa.
    Your public key has been saved in /home/oracle/.ssh/id_rsa.pub.
    The key fingerprint is:
    f1:4d:60:a1:c4:6b:d4:f1:4c:b7:84:83:03:8e:b9:f3 oracle@crsdg1.prusolutions.com

    [oracle@crsdg1 ~]$ ssh-keygen -t dsa

    Generating public/private dsa key pair.
    Enter file in which to save the key (/home/oracle/.ssh/id_dsa):
    Enter passphrase (empty for no passphrase):
    Enter same passphrase again:
    Your identification has been saved in /home/oracle/.ssh/id_dsa.
    Your public key has been saved in /home/oracle/.ssh/id_dsa.pub.
    The key fingerprint is:
    40:68:aa:90:b6:e0:99:06:fa:16:f5:3a:7d:37:f6:a1 oracle@crsdg1.prusolutions.com

  - On crsdg2 execute following as oracle User

    [oracle@crsdg2 ~]$ chmod 755 /home/oracle

    [oracle@crsdg2 ~]$ mkdir ~/.ssh

    [oracle@crsdg2 ~]$ chmod 700 ~/.ssh

    Accept the default location for the key file and for pass phrase press Enter Key

[oracle@crsdg2 ~]$ ssh-keygen -t rsa

```
Generating public/private rsa key pair.
Enter file in which to save the key (/home/oracle/.ssh/id_rsa):
Enter passphrase (empty for no passphrase):
Enter same passphrase again:
Your identification has been saved in /home/oracle/.ssh/id_rsa.
Your public key has been saved in /home/oracle/.ssh/id_rsa.pub.
The key fingerprint is:
70:ef:e3:30:78:67:ae:30:1c:02:6b:d3:23:99:c9:15 oracle@crsdg2.prusolutions.com
```

[oracle@crsdg2 ~]$ ssh-keygen -t dsa

```
Generating public/private dsa key pair.
Enter file in which to save the key (/home/oracle/.ssh/id_dsa):
Enter passphrase (empty for no passphrase):
Enter same passphrase again:
Your identification has been saved in /home/oracle/.ssh/id_dsa.
Your public key has been saved in /home/oracle/.ssh/id_dsa.pub.
The key fingerprint is:
9f:73:02:fc:8b:eb:0b:44:bf:38:0d:8e:8f:c0:78:ad oracle@crsdg2.prusolutions.com
```

- On crsdg1 node

[oracle@crsdg1 ~]$ cat ~/.ssh/id_rsa.pub >> ~/.ssh/authorized_keys

[oracle@crsdg1 ~]$ cat ~/.ssh/id_dsa.pub >> ~/.ssh/authorized_keys

[oracle@crsdg1 ~]$ ssh crsdg2 cat ~/.ssh/id_rsa.pub >> ~/.ssh/authorized_keys

```
The authenticity of host 'crsdg2 (192.168.2.142)' can't be established.
RSA key fingerprint is f4:ac:d2:7e:05:e8:4e:47:a9:6f:80:99:46:f9:f7:58.
Are you sure you want to continue connecting (yes/no)? yes
Warning: Permanently added 'crsdg2,192.168.2.142' (RSA) to the list of known hosts.
oracle@crsdg2's password:
```

[oracle@crsdg1 ~]$ ssh crsdg2 cat ~/.ssh/id_dsa.pub >> ~/.ssh/authorized_keys

```
oracle@crsdg2's password:
```

[oracle@crsdg1 ~]$ more ~/.ssh/authorized_keys

[oracle@crsdg1 ~]$ scp ~/.ssh/authorized_keys crsdg2:~/.ssh/authorized_keys

```
oracle@crsdg2's password:
authorized_keys                                100% 1720    1.7KB/s   00:00
```

- Test connection using following commands twice on both crsdg1,crsdg2 and verify the password is not required when the commands are run seconds time.

```
$ ssh crsdg1 date
$ ssh crsdg1.prusolutions.com date
$ ssh crsdg1-priv date
$ ssh crsdg1-priv.prusolutions.com date
$ ssh crsdg2 date
$ ssh crsdg2.prusolutions.com date
$ ssh crsdg2-priv date
$ ssh crsdg2-priv.prusolutions.com date
```

[oracle@crsdg1 ~]$ ssh crsdg1 date

```
The authenticity of host 'crsdg1 (192.168.2.141)' can't be established.
RSA key fingerprint is f4:ac:d2:7e:05:e8:4e:47:a9:6f:80:99:46:f9:f7:58.
Are you sure you want to continue connecting (yes/no)? yes
Warning: Permanently added 'crsdg1,192.168.2.141' (RSA) to the list of known hosts.
Tue Mar  1 14:40:35 EST 2011
```

```
[oracle@crsdg1 ~]$ ssh crsdg1.prusolutions.com date
The authenticity of host 'crsdg1.prusolutions.com (192.168.2.141)' can't be established.
RSA key fingerprint is f4:ac:d2:7e:05:e8:4e:47:a9:6f:80:99:46:f9:f7:58.
Are you sure you want to continue connecting (yes/no)? yes
Warning: Permanently added 'crsdg1.prusolutions.com' (RSA) to the list of known hosts.
Tue Mar  1 14:40:44 EST 2011
[oracle@crsdg1 ~]$ ssh crsdg1-priv date
The authenticity of host 'crsdg1-priv (10.10.10.41)' can't be established.
RSA key fingerprint is f4:ac:d2:7e:05:e8:4e:47:a9:6f:80:99:46:f9:f7:58.
Are you sure you want to continue connecting (yes/no)? yes
Warning: Permanently added 'crsdg1-priv,10.10.10.41' (RSA) to the list of known hosts.
Tue Mar  1 14:40:52 EST 2011
[oracle@crsdg1 ~]$ ssh crsdg1-priv.prusolutions.com date
The authenticity of host 'crsdg1-priv.prusolutions.com (10.10.10.41)' can't be established.
RSA key fingerprint is f4:ac:d2:7e:05:e8:4e:47:a9:6f:80:99:46:f9:f7:58.
Are you sure you want to continue connecting (yes/no)? yes
Warning: Permanently added 'crsdg1-priv.prusolutions.com' (RSA) to the list of known hosts.
Tue Mar  1 14:41:15 EST 2011
[oracle@crsdg1 ~]$ ssh crsdg2 date
Tue Mar  1 14:41:23 EST 2011
[oracle@crsdg1 ~]$ ssh crsdg2.prusolutions.com date
The authenticity of host 'crsdg2.prusolutions.com (192.168.2.142)' can't be established.
RSA key fingerprint is f4:ac:d2:7e:05:e8:4e:47:a9:6f:80:99:46:f9:f7:58.
Are you sure you want to continue connecting (yes/no)? yes
Warning: Permanently added 'crsdg2.prusolutions.com' (RSA) to the list of known hosts.
Tue Mar  1 14:41:34 EST 2011
[oracle@crsdg1 ~]$ ssh crsdg2-priv date
The authenticity of host 'crsdg2-priv (10.10.10.42)' can't be established.
RSA key fingerprint is f4:ac:d2:7e:05:e8:4e:47:a9:6f:80:99:46:f9:f7:58.
Are you sure you want to continue connecting (yes/no)? yes
Warning: Permanently added 'crsdg2-priv,10.10.10.42' (RSA) to the list of known hosts.
Tue Mar  1 14:41:59 EST 2011
[oracle@crsdg1 ~]$ ssh crsdg2-priv.prusolutions.com date
The authenticity of host 'crsdg2-priv.prusolutions.com (10.10.10.42)' can't be established.
RSA key fingerprint is f4:ac:d2:7e:05:e8:4e:47:a9:6f:80:99:46:f9:f7:58.
Are you sure you want to continue connecting (yes/no)? yes
Warning: Permanently added 'crsdg2-priv.prusolutions.com' (RSA) to the list of known hosts.
Tue Mar  1 14:53:47 EST 2011
[oracle@crsdg1 ~]$ ssh crsdg1 date
Tue Mar  1 14:53:56 EST 2011
[oracle@crsdg1 ~]$ ssh crsdg1.prusolutions.com date
Tue Mar  1 14:54:07 EST 2011
[oracle@crsdg1 ~]$ ssh crsdg1-priv date
Tue Mar  1 14:54:14 EST 2011
[oracle@crsdg1 ~]$ ssh crsdg1-priv.prusolutions.com date
Tue Mar  1 14:54:24 EST 2011
[oracle@crsdg1 ~]$ ssh crsdg2 date
Tue Mar  1 14:54:34 EST 2011
```

[oracle@crsdg1 ~]$ ssh crsdg2.prusolutions.com date

Tue Mar 1 14:54:42 EST 2011

[oracle@crsdg1 ~]$ ssh crsdg2-priv date

Tue Mar 1 14:54:53 EST 2011

[oracle@crsdg1 ~]$ ssh crsdg2-priv.prusolutions.com date

Tue Mar 1 14:55:00 EST 2011

Configure ASM on both the nodes as root user using command below.

As /dev/sdb1 .. /dev/sdf1 will be used for ocr and voting disk, configure rest of disk from /dev/sdg1 .. /dev/sdo1 for ASM

- Configure Oracle ASM on both crsdg1 and crsdg2 nodes

[root@crsdg1 ~]# /sbin/service oracleasm configure

Configuring the Oracle ASM library driver.

This will configure the on-boot properties of the Oracle ASM library driver. The following questions will determine whether the driver is loaded on boot and what permissions it will have. The current values will be shown in brackets ('[]'). Hitting <ENTER> without typing an answer will keep that current value. Ctrl-C will abort.

Default user to own the driver interface []: **oracle**
Default group to own the driver interface []: **dba**
Start Oracle ASM library driver on boot (y/n) [n]: **y**
Fix permissions of Oracle ASM disks on boot (y/n) [y]: **y**
Writing Oracle ASM library driver configuration: [OK]
Loading module "oracleasm": [OK]
Mounting ASMlib driver filesystem: [OK]
Scanning system for ASM disks: [OK]

[root@crsdg2 ~]# /sbin/service oracleasm configure

Default user to own the driver interface []: **oracle**
Default group to own the driver interface []: **dba**
Start Oracle ASM library driver on boot (y/n) [n]: **y**
Fix permissions of Oracle ASM disks on boot (y/n) [y]: **y**

- Create ASM disk on any one node.

[root@crsdg1 oracle]# /sbin/service oracleasm createdisk VOL1 /dev/sdg1
Marking disk "/dev/sdg1" as an ASM disk: [OK]

[root@crsdg1 oracle]# /sbin/service oracleasm createdisk VOL2 /dev/sdh1
Marking disk "/dev/sdh1" as an ASM disk: [OK]

[root@crsdg1 oracle]# /sbin/service oracleasm createdisk VOL3 /dev/sdi1
Marking disk "/dev/sdi1" as an ASM disk: [OK]

[root@crsdg1 oracle]# /sbin/service oracleasm createdisk VOL4 /dev/sdj1
Marking disk "/dev/sdj1" as an ASM disk: [OK]

[root@crsdg1 oracle]# /sbin/service oracleasm createdisk VOL5 /dev/sdk1
Marking disk "/dev/sdk1" as an ASM disk: [OK]

[root@crsdg1 oracle]# /sbin/service oracleasm createdisk VOL6 /dev/sdl1
Marking disk "/dev/sdl1" as an ASM disk: [OK]

[root@crsdg1 oracle]# /sbin/service oracleasm createdisk VOL7 /dev/sdm1
Marking disk "/dev/sdm1" as an ASM disk: [OK]

```
[root@crsdg1 oracle]# /sbin/service oracleasm createdisk VOL8 /dev/sdn1
Marking disk "/dev/sdn1" as an ASM disk:                    [  OK  ]
[root@crsdg1 oracle]# /sbin/service oracleasm createdisk VOL9 /dev/sdo1
Marking disk "/dev/sdo1" as an ASM disk:                    [  OK  ]
```

- On crsdg1 list all the disks

```
[root@crsdg1 oracle]# /sbin/service oracleasm listdisks
VOL1
VOL2
VOL3
VOL4
VOL5
VOL6
VOL7
VOL8
VOL9
```

- On crsdg2 scandisks and then listdisks

```
[root@crsdg2 oracle]# /sbin/service oracleasm scandisks
Scanning system for ASM disks:                    [  OK  ]
[root@crsdg2 oracle]# /sbin/service oracleasm listdisks
VOL1
VOL2
VOL3
VOL4
VOL5
VOL6
VOL7
VOL8
VOL9
```

9.4 Install cvuqdisk rpm required for cluvfy on both the nodes

```
[root@crsdg1 oracle]# export CVUQDISK_GRP=dba
[root@crsdg1 oracle]# rpm -Uvh /u01/software/clusterware/rpm/cvuqdisk-1.0.1-1.rpm
Preparing...   ########################################### [100%]
1:cvuqdisk     ########################################### [100%]
[root@crsdg2 oracle]# export CVUQDISK_GRP=dba
[root@crsdg2 oracle]# rpm -Uvh /u01/software/clusterware/rpm/cvuqdisk-1.0.1-1.rpm
Preparing...   ########################################### [100%]
1:cvuqdisk     ########################################### [100%]
```

9.5 Run Oracle Cluvfy utility on both the nodes

- Cluvfy Utility Post Hardware OS

Ignore only errors for VIP interfaces and last storage disk /dev/sd0. Make sure all other checks are passed.

```
[oracle@crsdg1 cluvfy]$ chmod 755 /u01/software/clusterware/cluvfy/runcluvfy.sh
[oracle@crsdg1 cluvfy]$ /u01/software/clusterware/cluvfy/runcluvfy.sh stage -post hwos -
n crsdg1,crsdg2 –verbose
Performing post-checks for hardware and operating system setup
```

```
Checking node reachability...

Check: Node reachability from node "crsdg1"
  Destination Node                      Reachable?
  ------------------------------------  ------------------------
  crsdg2                                yes
  crsdg1                                yes
Result: Node reachability check passed from node "crsdg1".

Checking user equivalence...

Check: User equivalence for user "oracle"
  Node Name                             Comment
  ------------------------------------  ------------------------
  crsdg2                                passed
  crsdg1                                passed
Result: User equivalence check passed for user "oracle".

Checking node connectivity...
Interface information for node "crsdg2"
  Interface Name                  IP Address                Subnet
  ------------------------------  ------------------------  ----------------
  eth0                            192.168.2.142             192.168.2.0
  eth1                            10.10.10.42               10.10.10.0

Interface information for node "crsdg1"
  Interface Name                  IP Address                Subnet
  ------------------------------  ------------------------  ----------------
  eth0                            192.168.2.141             192.168.2.0
  eth1                            10.10.10.41               10.10.10.0

Check: Node connectivity of subnet "192.168.2.0"
  Source                          Destination               Connected?
  ------------------------------  ------------------------  ----------------
  crsdg2:eth0                     crsdg1:eth0               yes
Result: Node connectivity check passed for subnet "192.168.2.0" with node(s) crsdg2,crsdg1.

Check: Node connectivity of subnet "10.10.10.0"
  Source                          Destination               Connected?
  ------------------------------  ------------------------  ----------------
  crsdg2:eth1                     crsdg1:eth1               yes
Result: Node connectivity check passed for subnet "10.10.10.0" with node(s) crsdg2,crsdg1.

Suitable interfaces for the private interconnect on subnet "192.168.2.0":
crsdg2 eth0:192.168.2.142
crsdg1 eth0:192.168.2.141

Suitable interfaces for the private interconnect on subnet "10.10.10.0":
crsdg2 eth1:10.10.10.42
crsdg1 eth1:10.10.10.41

ERROR:
Could not find a suitable set of interfaces for VIPs.

Result: Node connectivity check failed.

Checking shared storage accessibility...

WARNING:
Unable to determine the sharedness of /dev/sdo on nodes:

crsdg2,crsdg2,crsdg2,crsdg2,crsdg2,crsdg2,crsdg2,crsdg2,crsdg2,crsdg2,crsdg2,crsdg2,crsdg2,crsdg
2,crsdg2,crsdg1,crsdg1,crsdg1,crsdg1,crsdg1,crsdg1,crsdg1,crsdg1,crsdg1,crsdg1,crsdg1,
crsdg1,crsdg1,crsdg1,crsdg1
```

Shared storage check failed on nodes "crsdg2,crsdg1".

Post-check for hardware and operating system setup was unsuccessful on all the nodes.

Ignore Errors and Warning mentioned below

ERROR:
Could not find a suitable set of interfaces for VIPs.
WARNING:
Unable to determine the sharedness of /dev/sdo on nodes

- Cluvfy Utility Pre crsinst install

  [oracle@crsdg1 cluvfy]$ /u01/software/clusterware/cluvfy/runcluvfy.sh stage -pre crsinst -n crsdg1,crsdg2 -verbose

  Make sure all the required packages are installed on both crsdg1 and crsdg2

  On VMware, some packages checks will fail and if older versions of those packages are installed then you can ignore them.
  For example: if you get error for following packages then use can do rpm –qa to get details, if older version of packages are installed

  compat-gcc-7.3-2.96.128".
  compat-gcc-c++-7.3-2.96.128".
  compat-libstdc++-7.3-2.96.128".
  compat-libstdc++-devel-7.3-2.96.128".
  openmotif-2.2.3".

  [oracle@crsdg2 ~]$ rpm -qa | grep -i compat

  compat-libgcc-296-2.96-132.7.2
  compat-gcc-32-3.2.3-47.3
  compat-libstdc++-296-2.96-132.7.2
  compat-gcc-32-c++-3.2.3-47.3
  compat-libstdc++-33-3.2.3-47.3
  compat-db-4.1.25-9
  java-1.4.2-gcj-compat-1.4.2.0-27jpp
  compat-libcom_err-1.0-5

  [oracle@crsdg2 ~]$ rpm -qa | grep -i openmotif

  openmotif21-2.1.30-11.RHEL4.6

- Navigate through Oracle Documentation to get to Data Guard without search tab

  Oracle Database Documentation Library > Books > HIG >

  On contents page Ctrl f and search for 'High Availability Best Practices" you will reach High Availability Best Practices. Click **HTML** to go Contents page

9.6 Reboot both crsdg1 and crsdg2 before proceeding further

9.7 Install Oracle Clusterware from any one node crsdg1

[oracle@crsdg1 ~]$ /u01/software/clusterware/runInstaller

If there any error in executing any file change its permission chmod 755 <file_name>

- Welcome Screen: Click Next

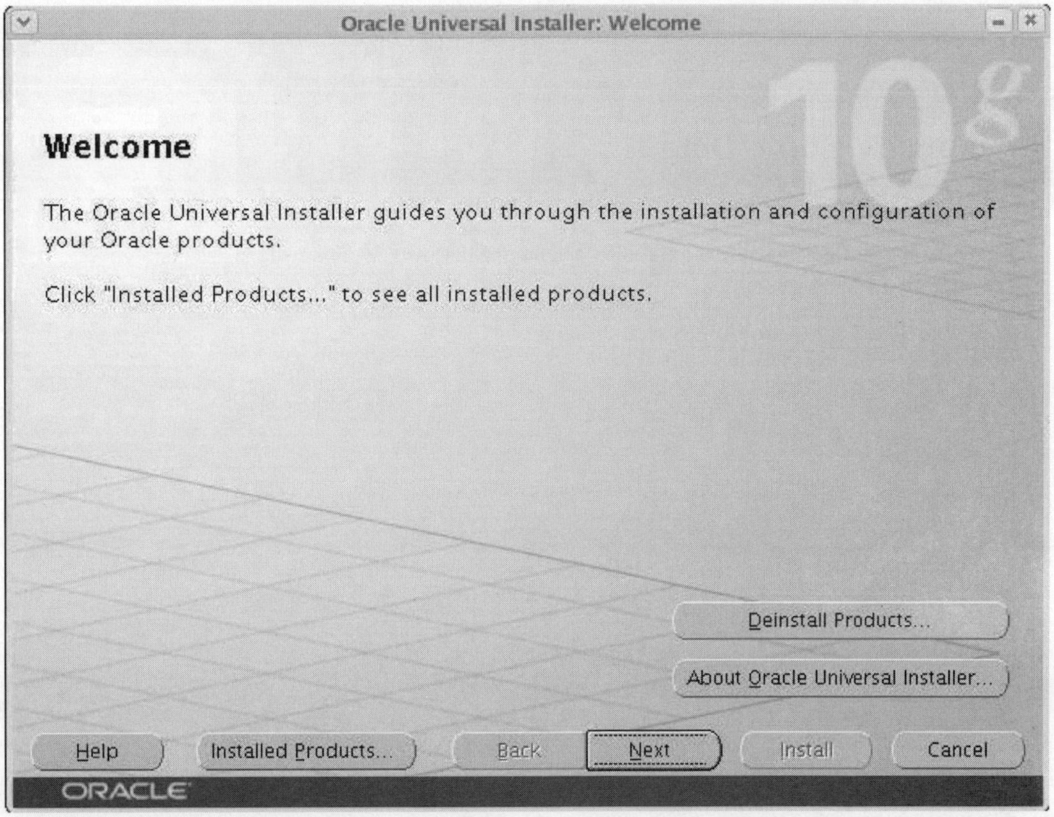

- Specify Inventory Directory and Credentials

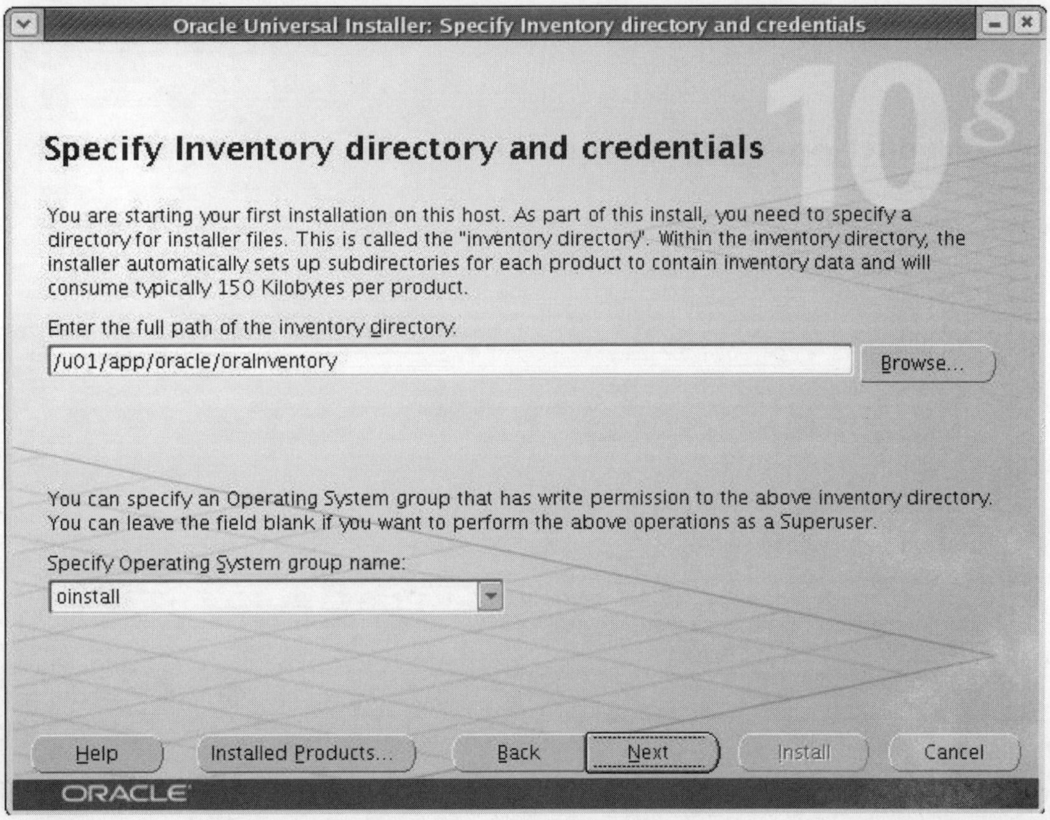

- Specify Home Details

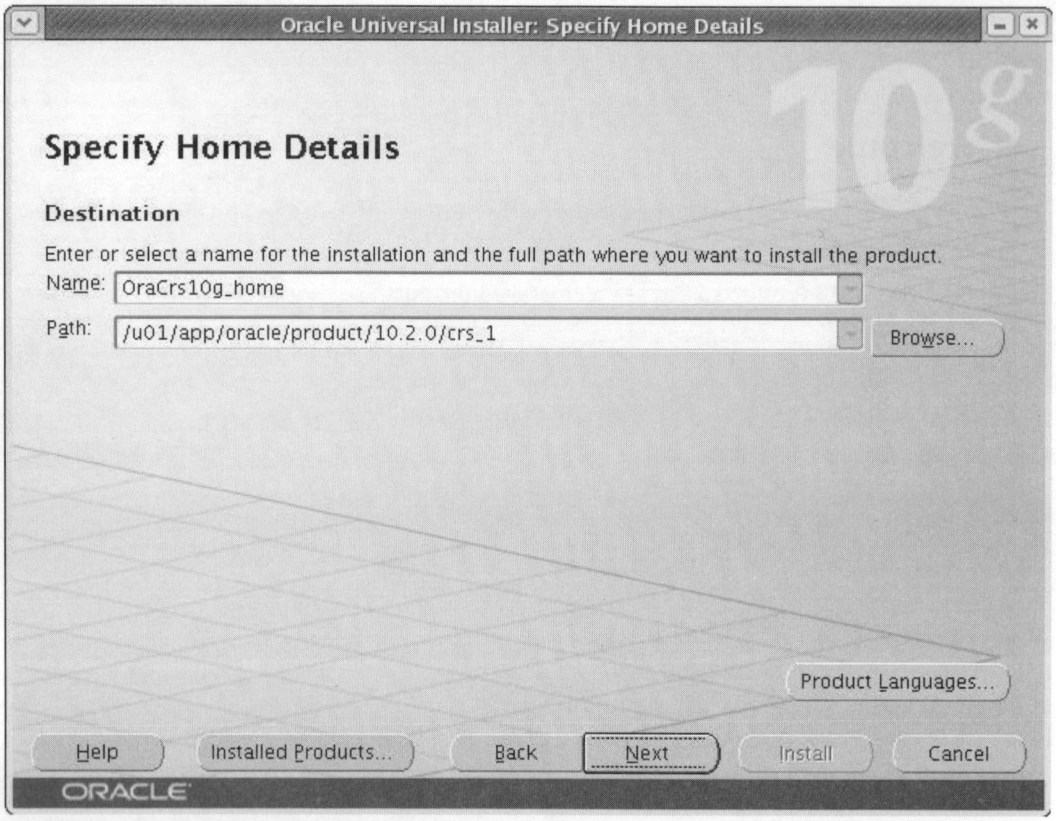

- Product-Specific Prerequisite Checks

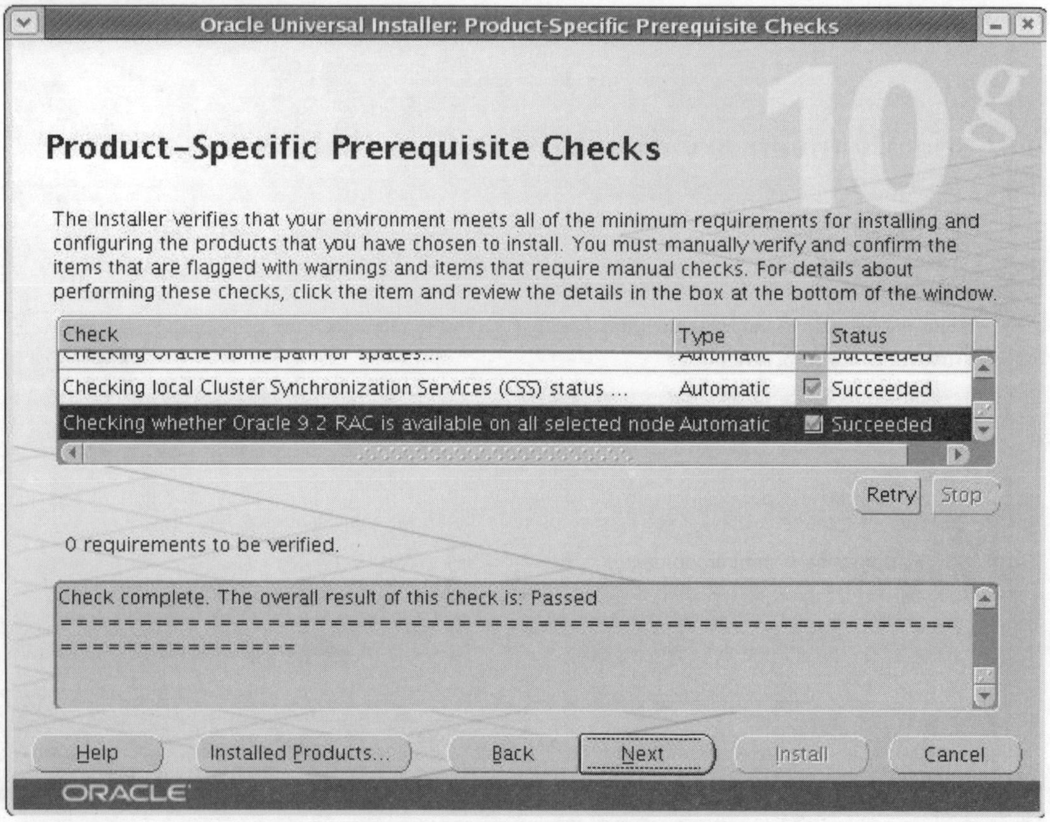

- Specify Cluster Configuration

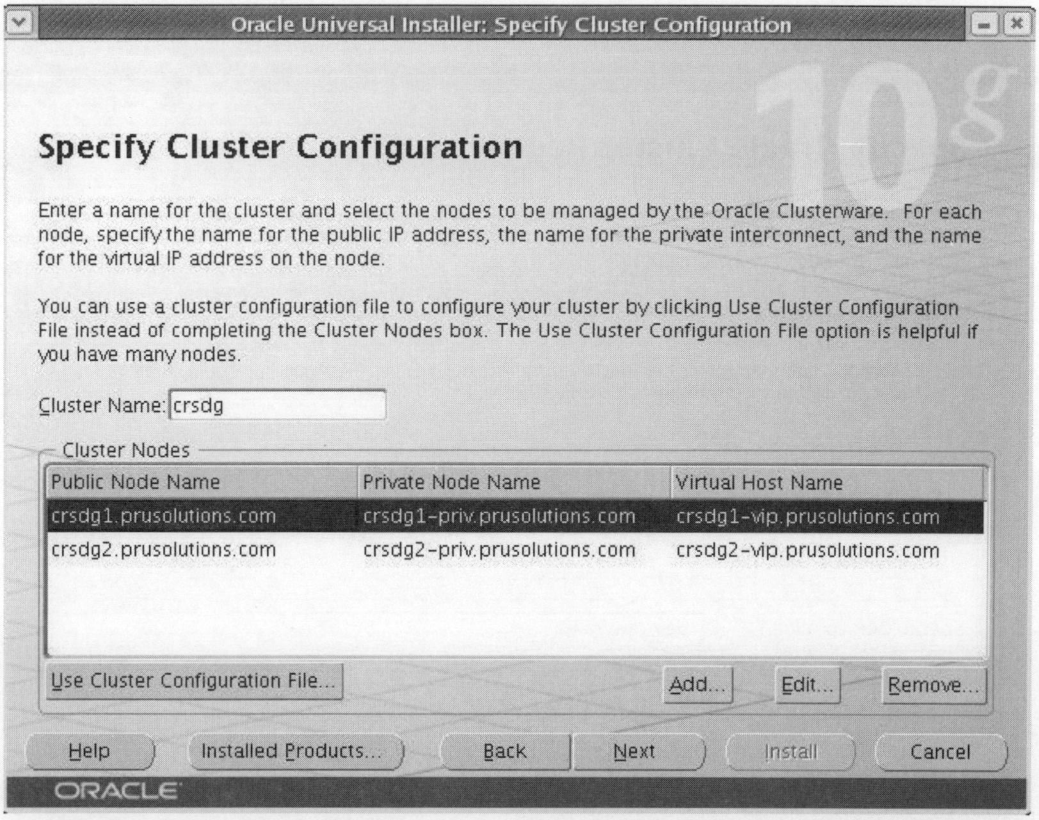

- Specify Network Interface Usage

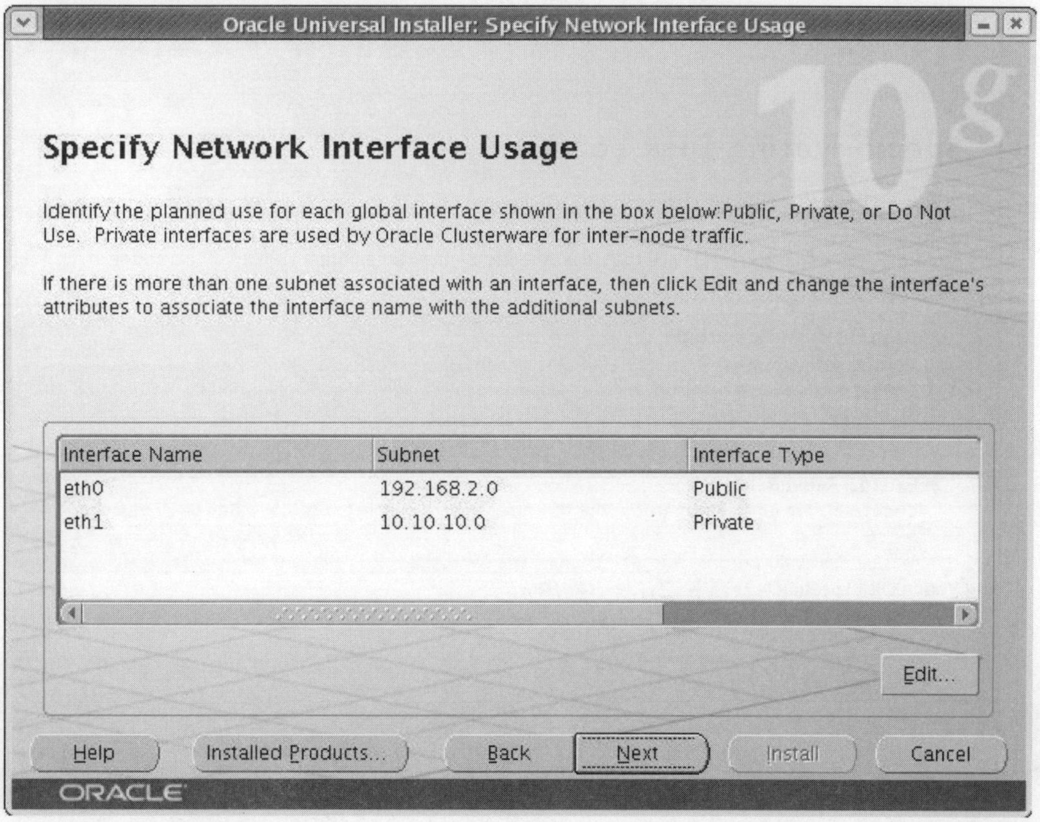

- Specify Oracle Cluster Registry (OCR) Location

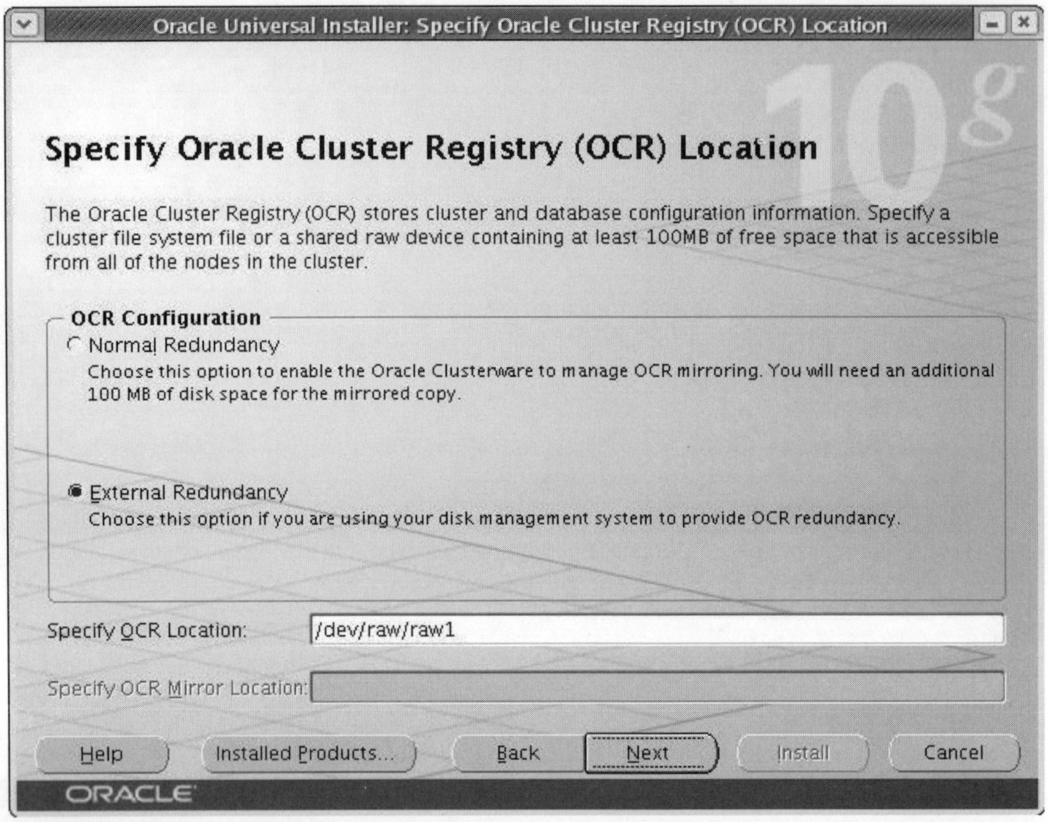

- Specify Voting Disk Location

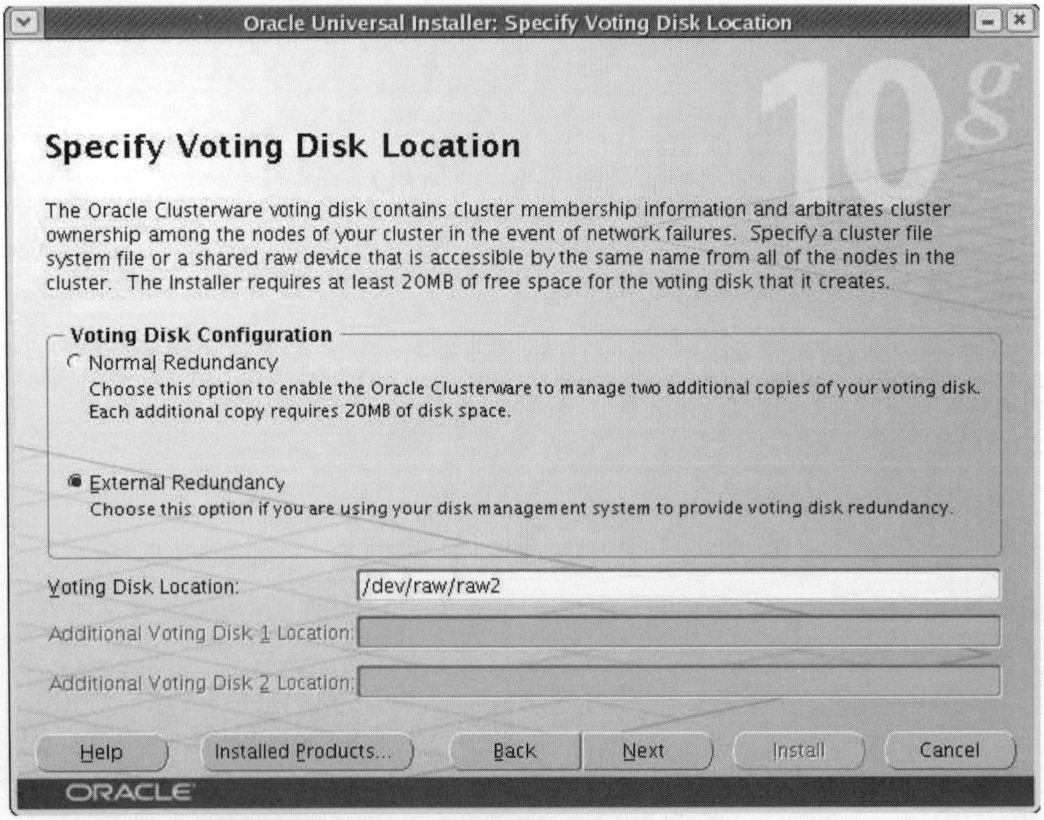

- Summary

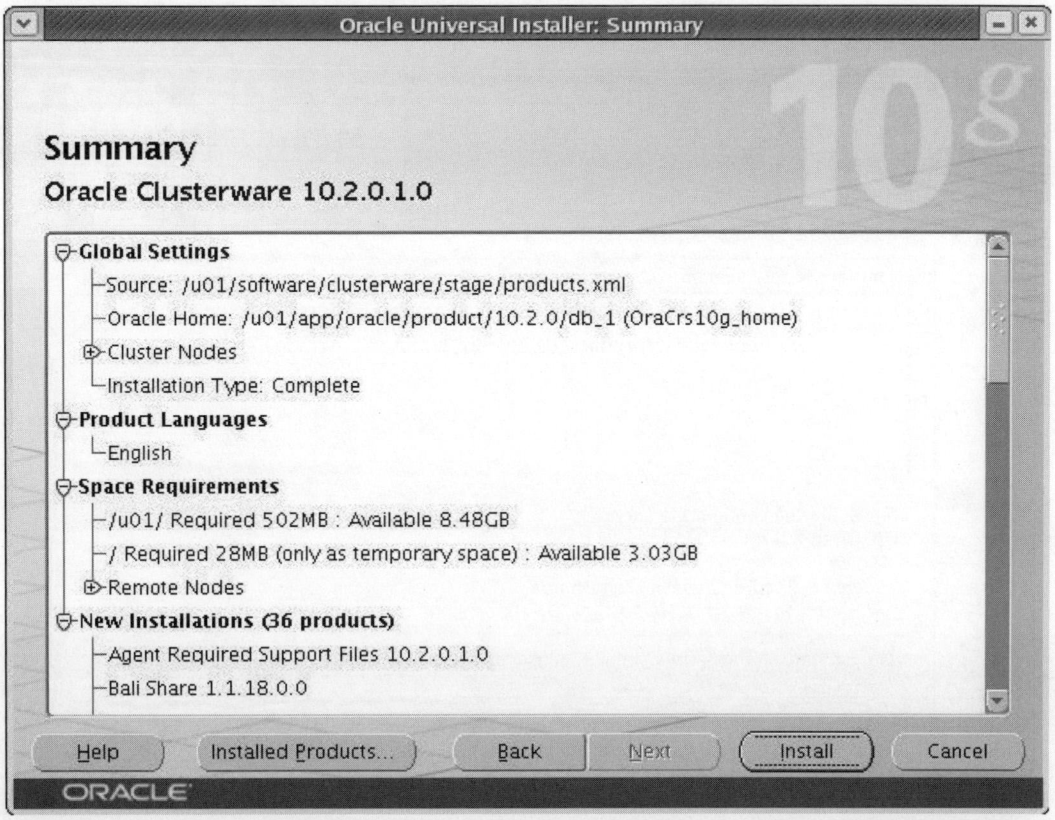

- Install

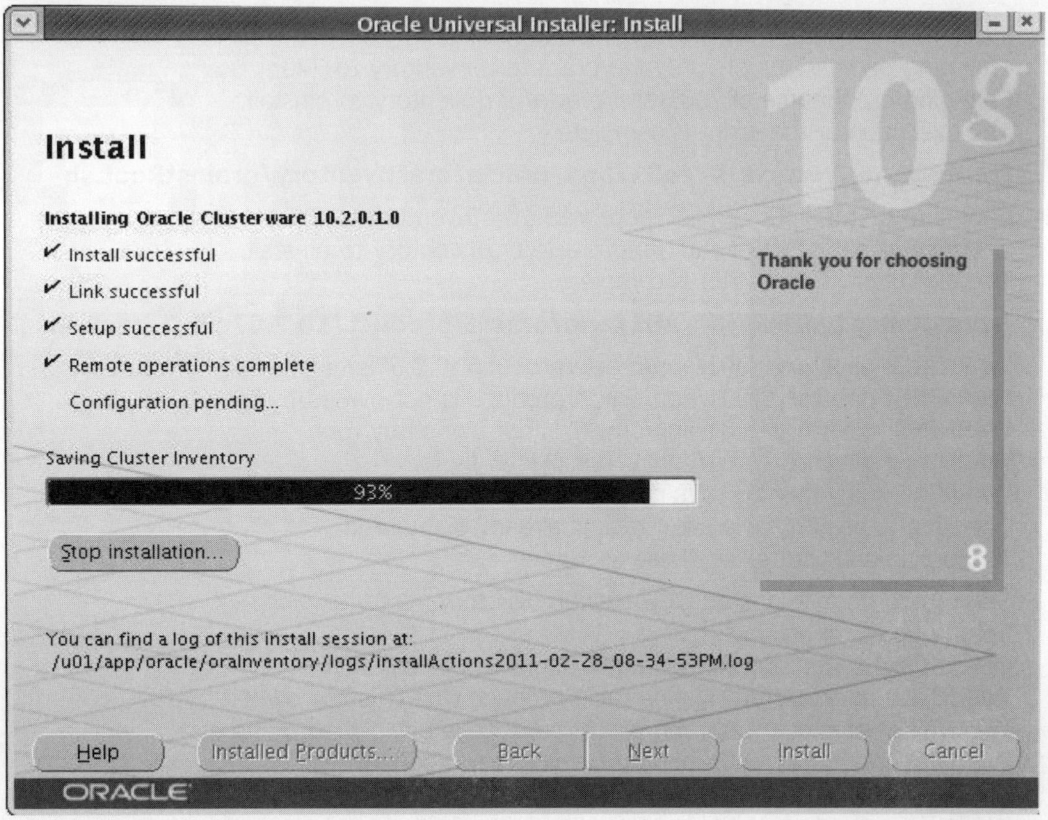

- Execute Configuration Scripts

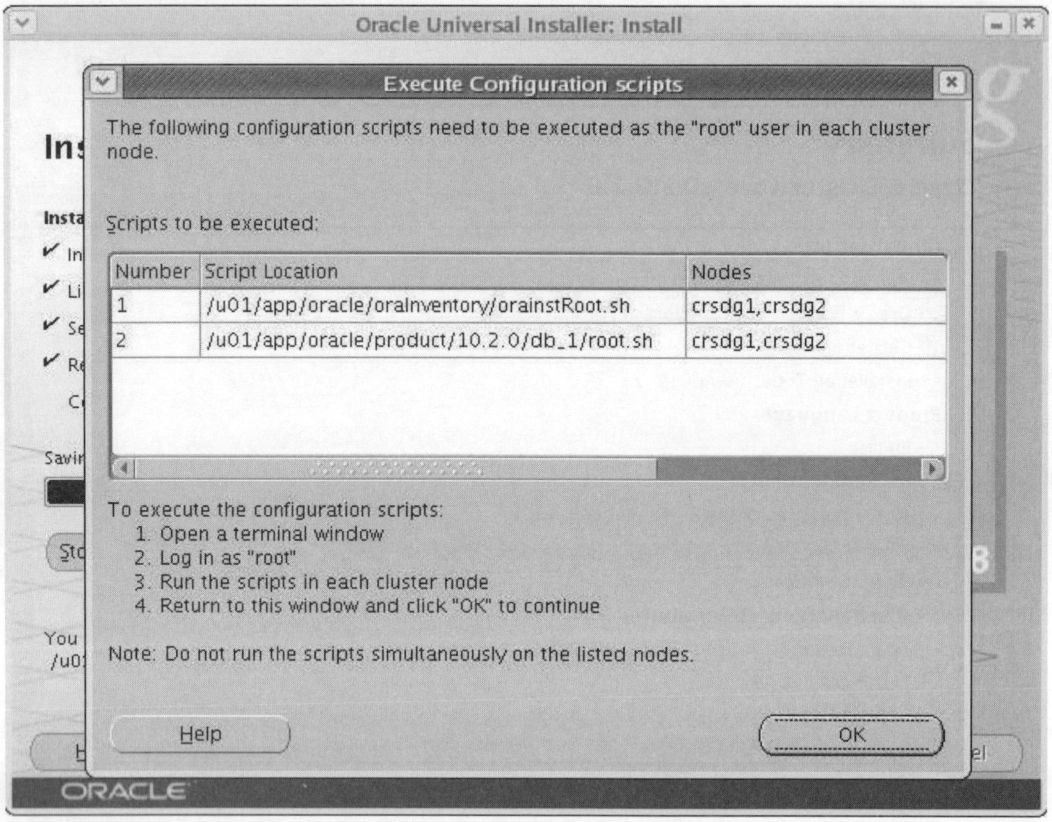

- Open a new terminal login as root and execute following configuration scripts

[root@crsdg1 oracle]# /u01/app/oracle/oraInventory/orainstRoot.sh

Changing permissions of /u01/app/oracle/oraInventory to 770.
Changing groupname of /u01/app/oracle/oraInventory to oinstall.
The execution of the script is complete

[root@crsdg2 oracle]# /u01/app/oracle/oraInventory/orainstRoot.sh

Changing permissions of /u01/app/oracle/oraInventory to 770.
Changing groupname of /u01/app/oracle/oraInventory to oinstall.
The execution of the script is complete

[root@crsdg1 oracle]# /u01/app/oracle/product/10.2.0/crs_1/root.sh

WARNING: directory '/u01/app/oracle/product/10.2.0' is not owned by root
WARNING: directory '/u01/app/oracle/product' is not owned by root
WARNING: directory '/u01/app/oracle' is not owned by root
WARNING: directory '/u01/app' is not owned by root
WARNING: directory '/u01' is not owned by root
Checking to see if Oracle CRS stack is already configured
/etc/oracle does not exist. Creating it now.

Setting the permissions on OCR backup directory
Setting up NS directories
Oracle Cluster Registry configuration upgraded successfully
WARNING: directory '/u01/app/oracle/product/10.2.0' is not owned by root
WARNING: directory '/u01/app/oracle/product' is not owned by root
WARNING: directory '/u01/app/oracle' is not owned by root
WARNING: directory '/u01/app' is not owned by root
WARNING: directory '/u01' is not owned by root
assigning default hostname crsdg1 for node 1.

```
assigning default hostname crsdg2 for node 2.
Successfully accumulated necessary OCR keys.
Using ports: CSS=49895 CRS=49896 EVMC=49898 and EVMR=49897.
node <nodenumber>: <nodename> <private interconnect name> <hostname>
node 1: crsdg1 crsdg1-priv crsdg1
node 2: crsdg2 crsdg2-priv crsdg2
Creating OCR keys for user 'root', privgrp 'root'..
Operation successful.
Now formatting voting device: /dev/raw/raw2
Format of 1 voting devices complete.
Startup will be queued to init within 90 seconds.
Adding daemons to inittab
Expecting the CRS daemons to be up within 600 seconds.
CSS is active on these nodes.
     crsdg1
CSS is inactive on these nodes.
     crsdg2
Local node checking complete.
Run root.sh on remaining nodes to start CRS daemons.
```

[root@crsdg2 oracle]# /u01/app/oracle/product/10.2.0/crs_1/root.sh

```
WARNING: directory '/u01/app/oracle/product/10.2.0' is not owned by root
WARNING: directory '/u01/app/oracle/product' is not owned by root
WARNING: directory '/u01/app/oracle' is not owned by root
WARNING: directory '/u01/app' is not owned by root
WARNING: directory '/u01' is not owned by root
Checking to see if Oracle CRS stack is already configured
/etc/oracle does not exist. Creating it now.
Setting the permissions on OCR backup directory
Setting up NS directories
Oracle Cluster Registry configuration upgraded successfully
WARNING: directory '/u01/app/oracle/product/10.2.0' is not owned by root
WARNING: directory '/u01/app/oracle/product' is not owned by root
WARNING: directory '/u01/app/oracle' is not owned by root
WARNING: directory '/u01/app' is not owned by root
WARNING: directory '/u01' is not owned by root
clscfg: EXISTING configuration version 3 detected.
clscfg: version 3 is 10G Release 2.
assigning default hostname crsdg1 for node 1.
assigning default hostname crsdg2 for node 2.
Successfully accumulated necessary OCR keys.
Using ports: CSS=49895 CRS=49896 EVMC=49898 and EVMR=49897.
node <nodenumber>: <nodename> <private interconnect name> <hostname>
node 1: crsdg1 crsdg1-priv crsdg1
node 2: crsdg2 crsdg2-priv crsdg2
clscfg: Arguments check out successfully.
NO KEYS WERE WRITTEN. Supply -force parameter to override.
-force is destructive and will destroy any previous cluster
configuration.
Oracle Cluster Registry for cluster has already been initialized
Startup will be queued to init within 90 seconds.
Adding daemons to inittab
Expecting the CRS daemons to be up within 600 seconds.
CSS is active on these nodes.
     crsdg1
```

```
    crsdg2
CSS is active on all nodes.
Waiting for the Oracle CRSD and EVMD to start
Oracle CRS stack installed and running under init(1M)
Running vipca(silent) for configuring nodeapps
```

The given interface(s), "eth0" is not public. Public interfaces should be used to configure virtual IPs.

[root@crsdg2 cluvfy]# vipca

- Welcome Screen

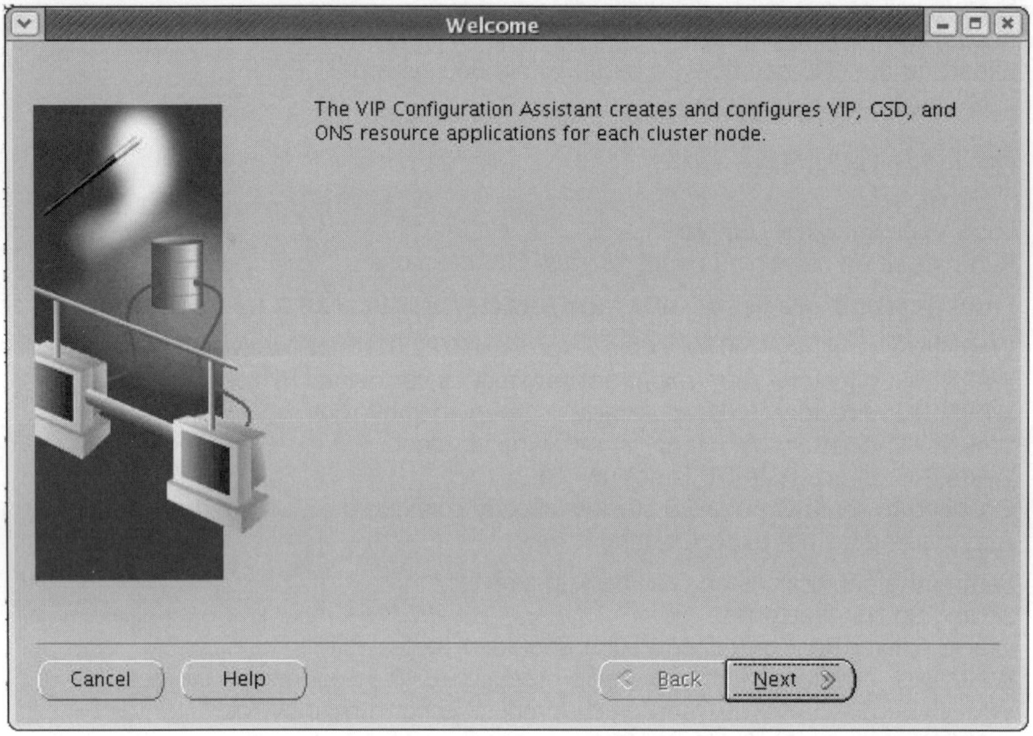

- VIP Configuration Assistant: Select eth0

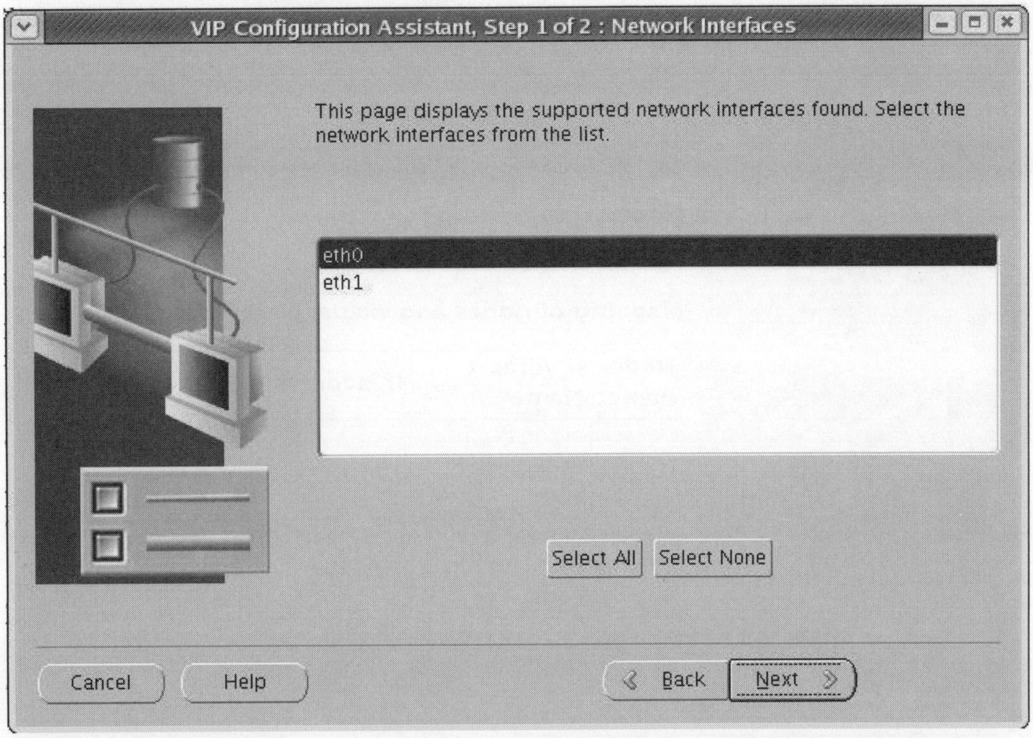

- IP address Review Page

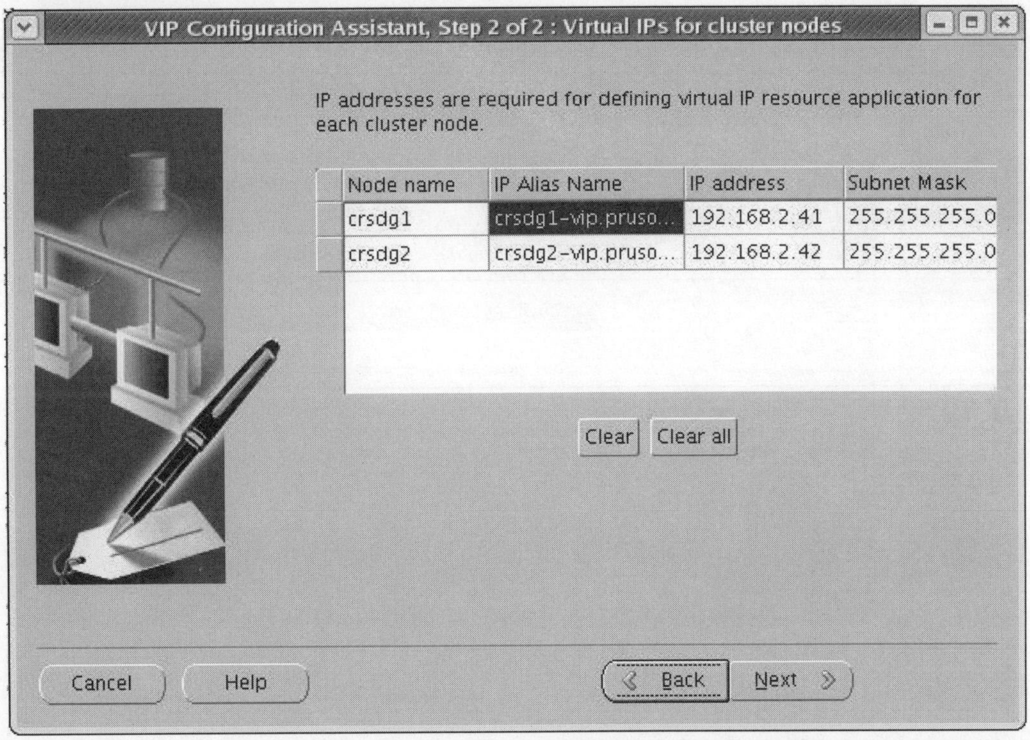

- Summary

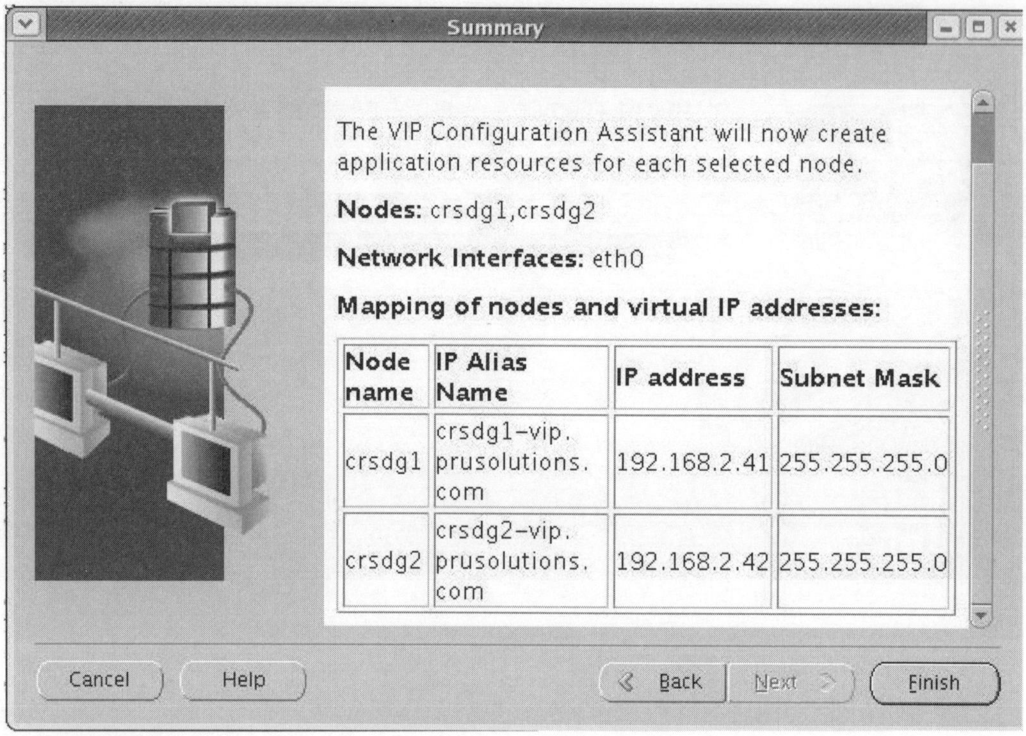

- Install Complete

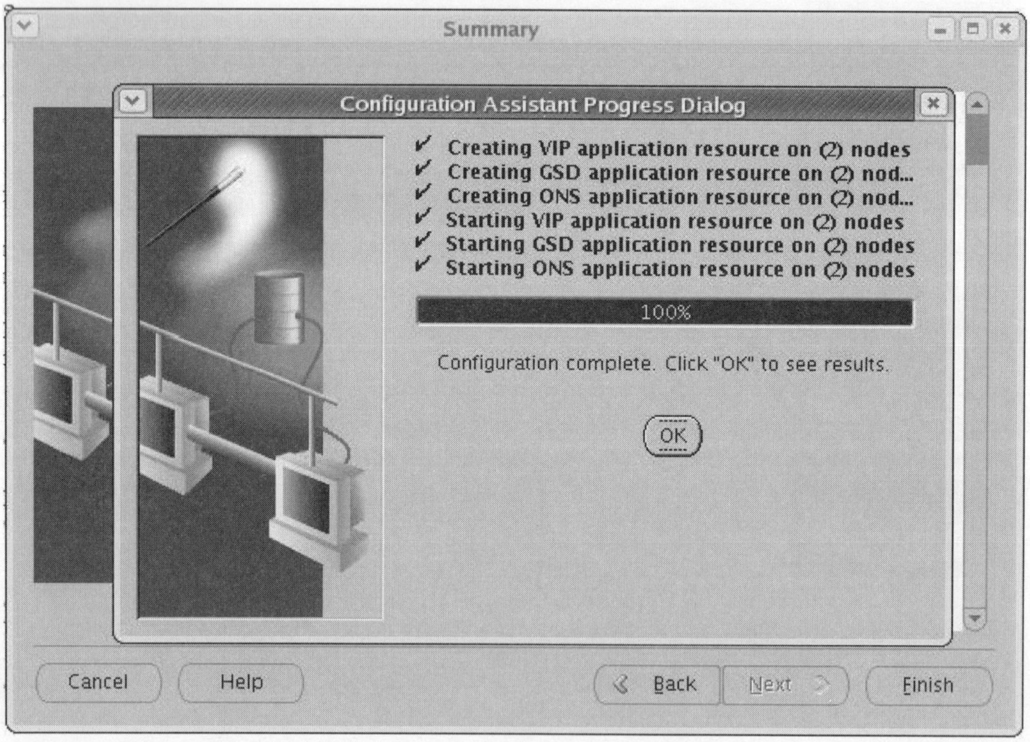

- Configuration Results

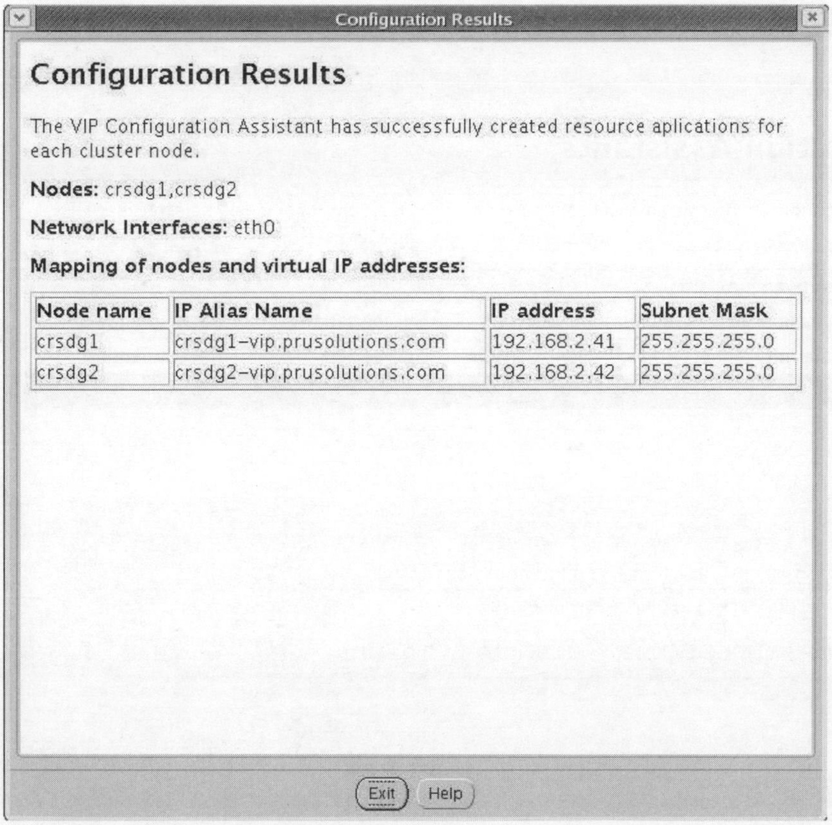

- Execute Configuration Scripts

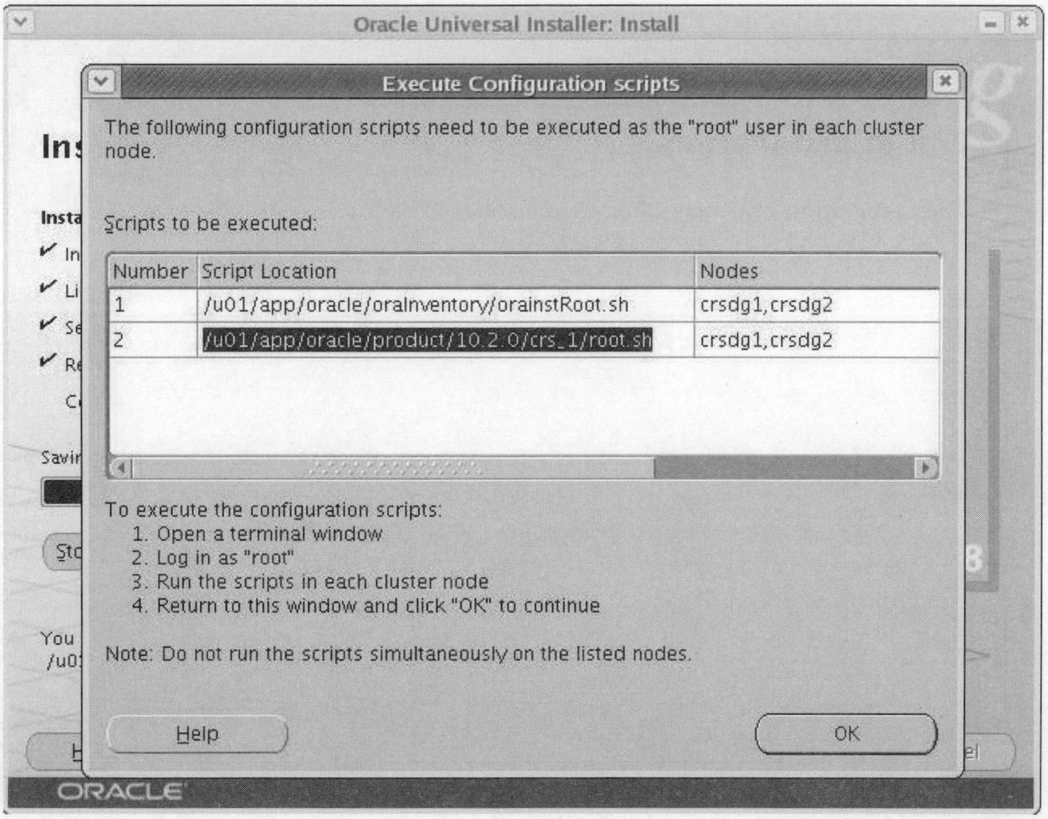

- Configuration Assistants Succeeded

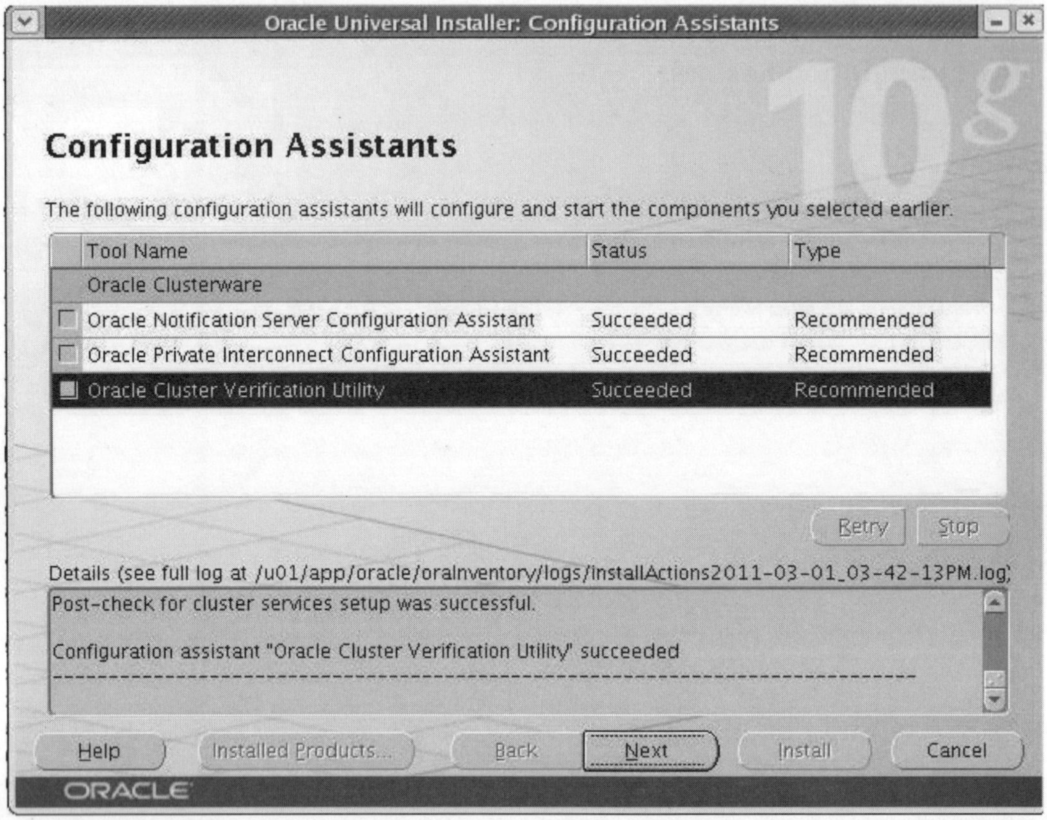

- End of Installation

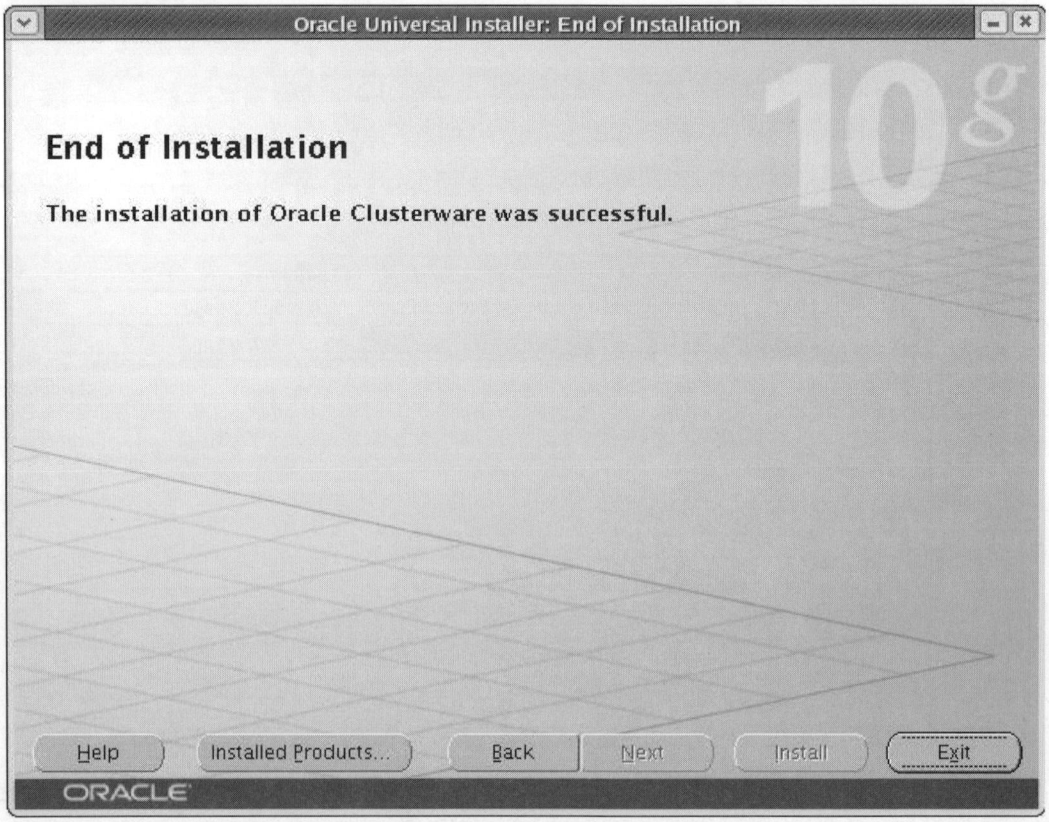

9.8 Install and configure ASM

[oracle@crsdg1 cluvfy]$ /u01/software/clusterware/cluvfy/runcluvfy.sh stage -pre dbinst -n crsdg1,crsdg2 -verbose

Ignore Linux package version warnings
[oracle@crsdg1 ~]$. /home/oracle/asm_profile
[oracle@crsdg1 ~]$ echo $ORACLE_HOME
/u01/app/oracle/product/10.2.0/asm_1

- Install ASM Software

  [oracle@crsdg1 database]$. /runInstaller

- Welcome Screen: Click Next
- Select Installation Type: Enterprise Edition (1.24GB)
- Specify Home Details

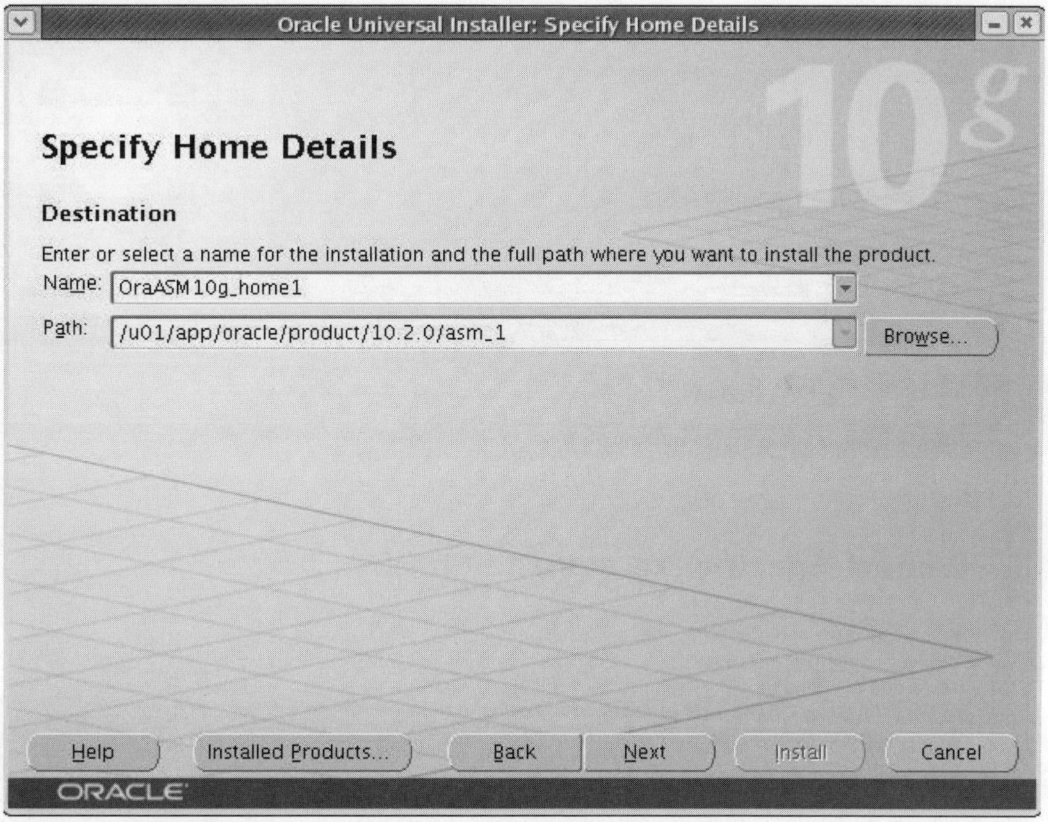

- Specify Hardware Cluster Installation Mode

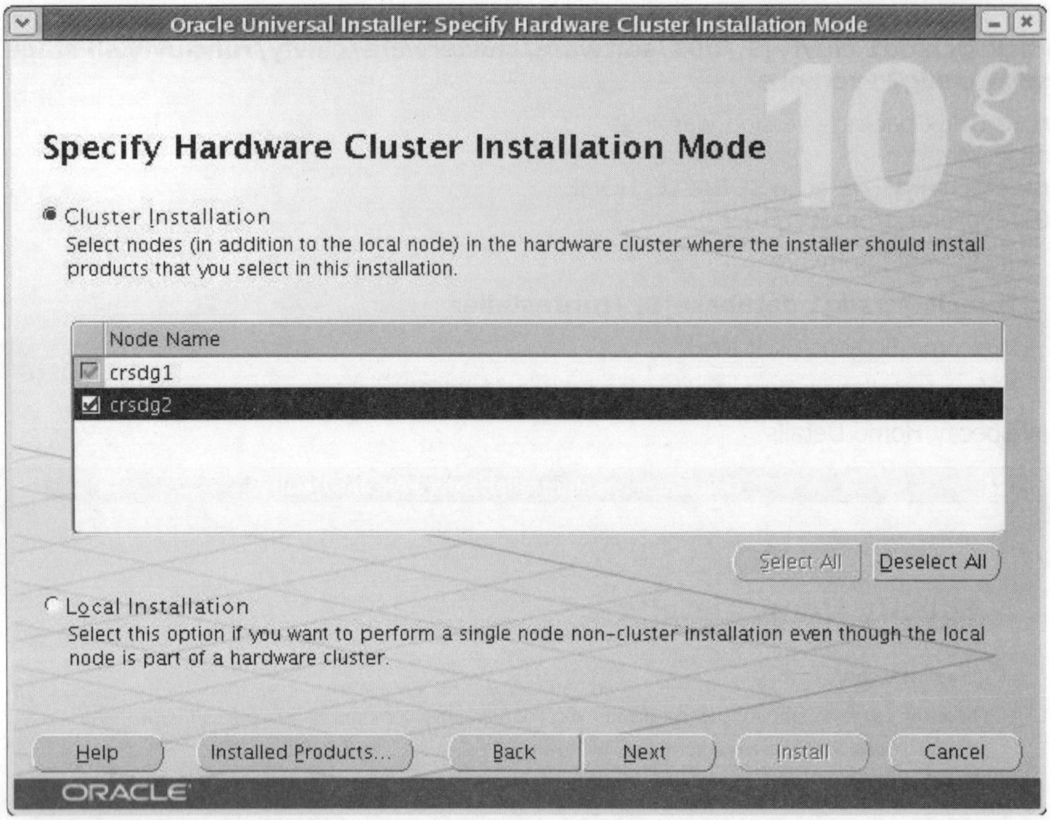

- Product-Specific Prerequisite Checks

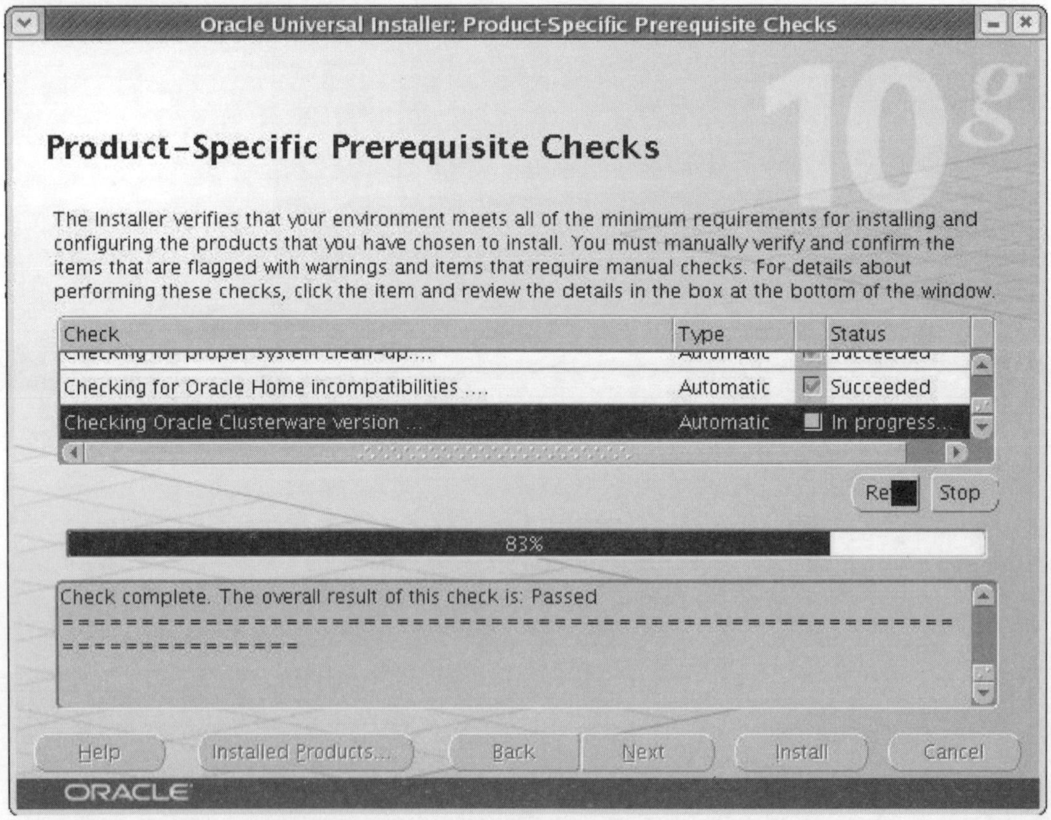

- Select Configuration Option

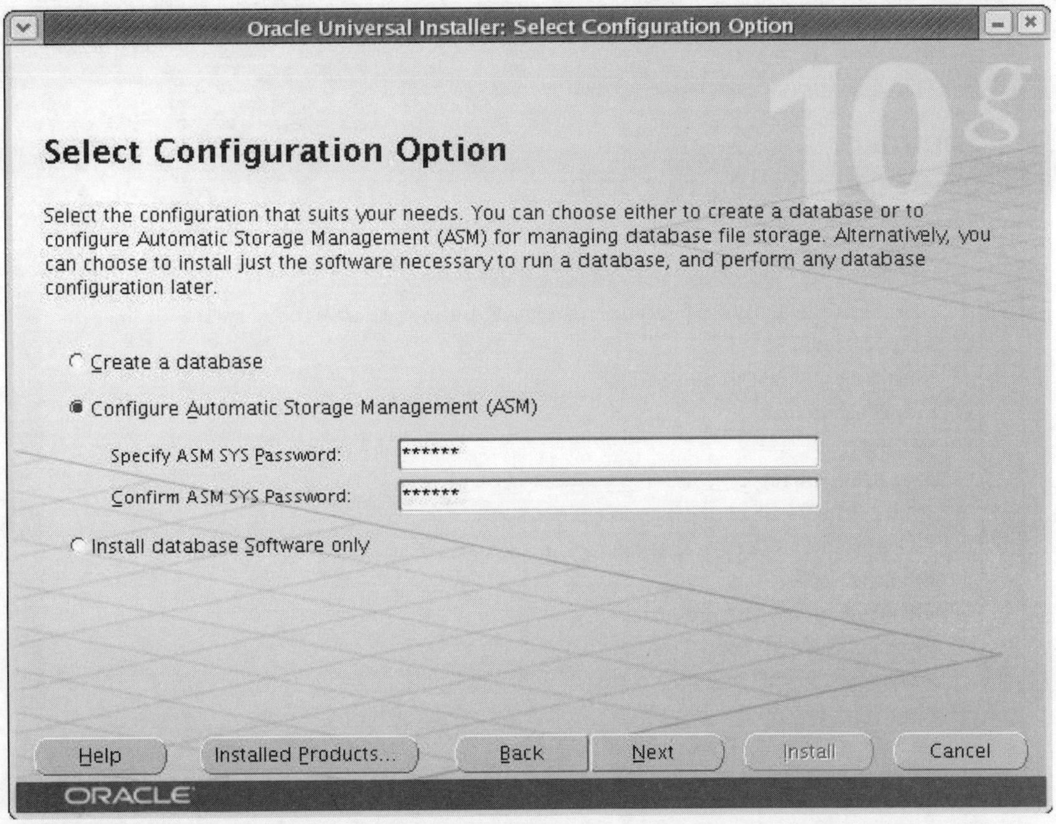

- Configure Automatic Storage Management

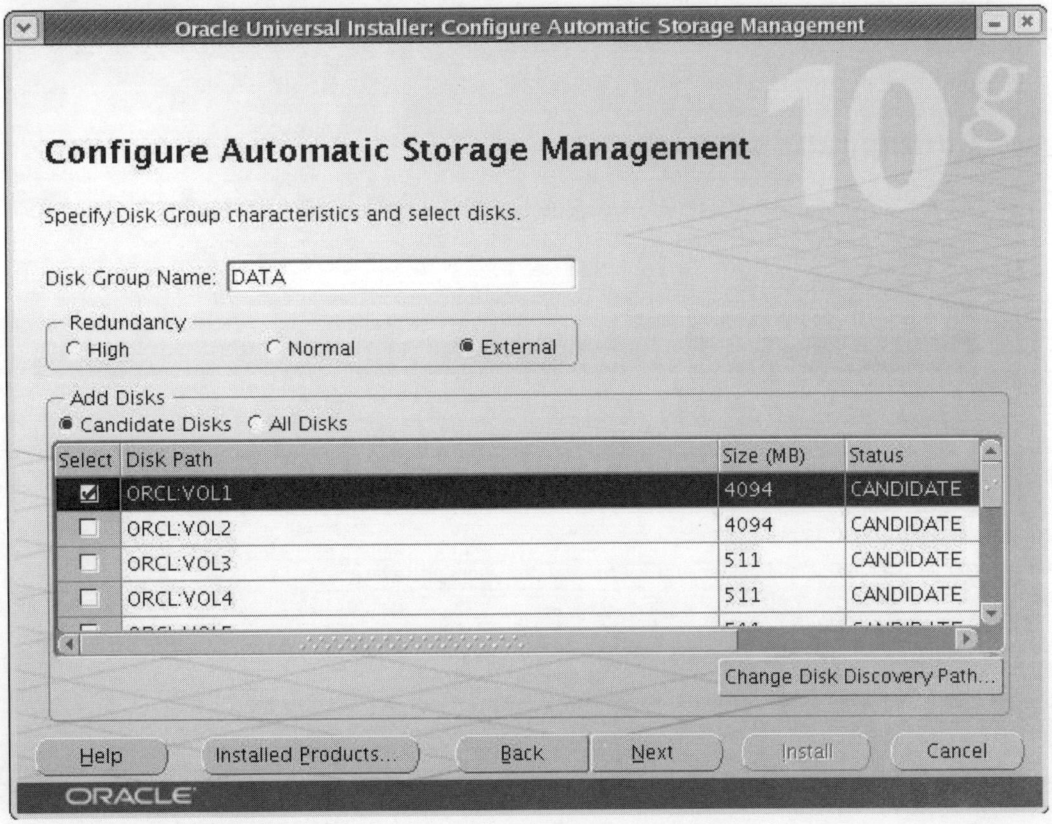

- Summary

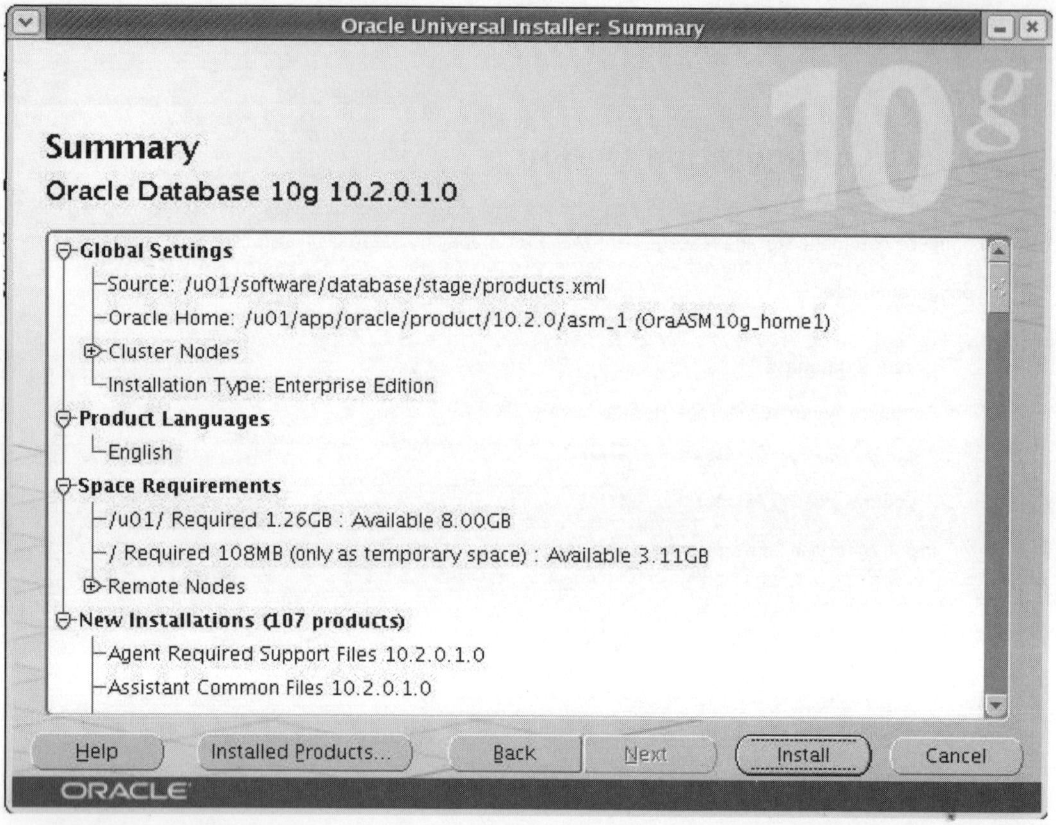

- Configuration Assistants

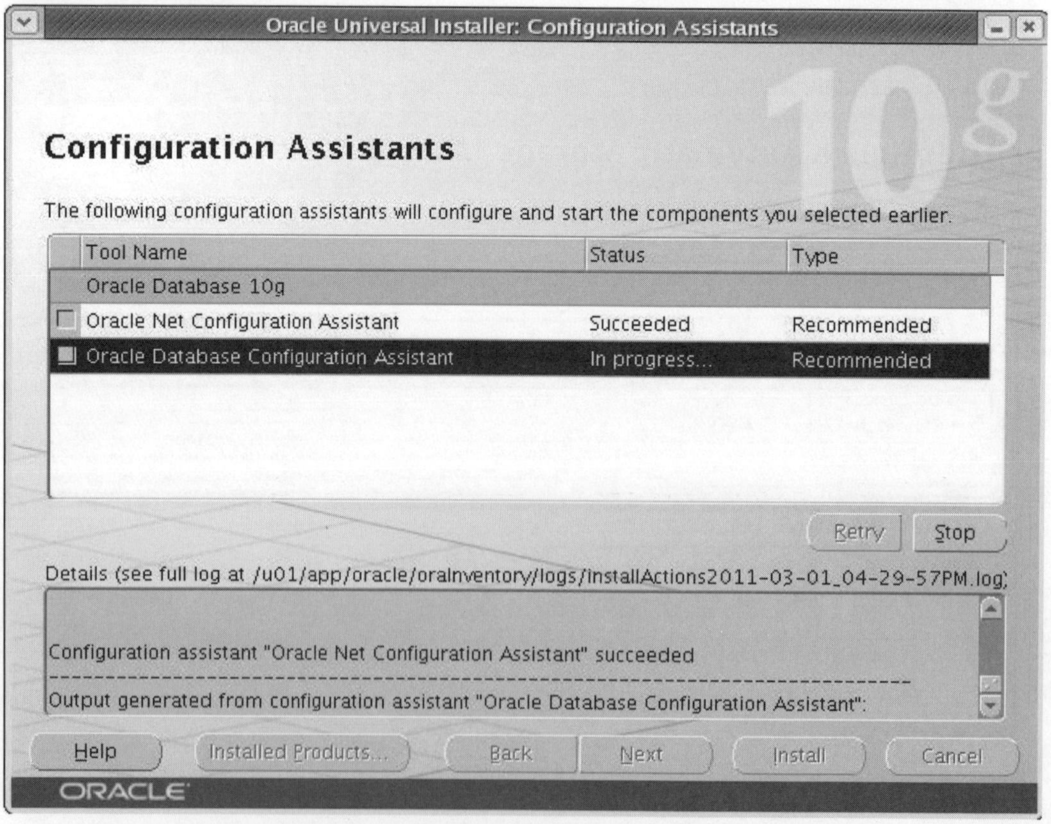

- Execute Configuration Scripts

[root@crsdg1 oracle]# /u01/app/oracle/product/10.2.0/asm_1/root.sh
Running Oracle10 root.sh script...

The following environment variables are set as:
    ORACLE_OWNER= oracle
    ORACLE_HOME= /u01/app/oracle/product/10.2.0/asm_1

Enter the full pathname of the local bin directory: [/usr/local/bin]:
    Copying dbhome to /usr/local/bin ...
    Copying oraenv to /usr/local/bin ...
    Copying coraenv to /usr/local/bin ...

Creating /etc/oratab file...
Entries will be added to the /etc/oratab file as needed by
Database Configuration Assistant when a database is created
Finished running generic part of root.sh script.
Now product-specific root actions will be performed.

[root@crsdg2 oracle]# /u01/app/oracle/product/10.2.0/asm_1/root.sh
Running Oracle10 root.sh script...

The following environment variables are set as:
    ORACLE_OWNER= oracle
    ORACLE_HOME= /u01/app/oracle/product/10.2.0/asm_1

Enter the full pathname of the local bin directory: [/usr/local/bin]:
    Copying dbhome to /usr/local/bin ...
    Copying oraenv to /usr/local/bin ...
    Copying coraenv to /usr/local/bin ...

Creating /etc/oratab file...
Entries will be added to the /etc/oratab file as needed by
Database Configuration Assistant when a database is created
Finished running generic part of root.sh script.
Now product-specific root actions will be performed.

- End of Installation Screen

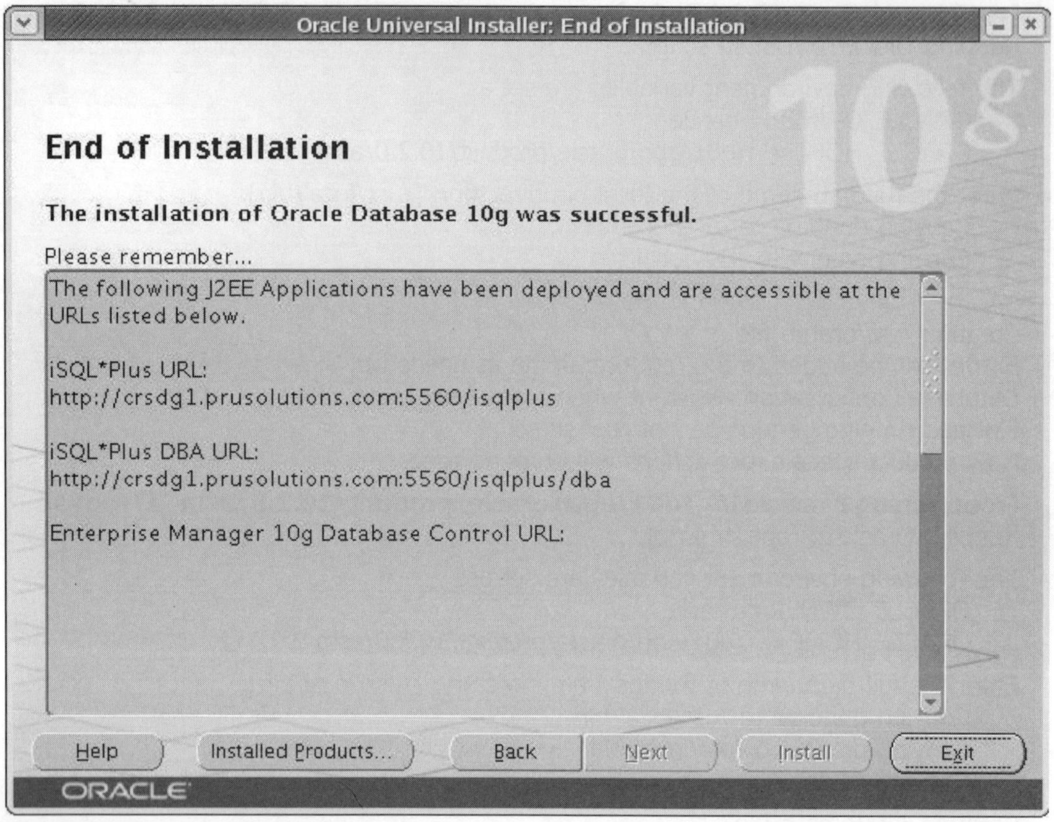

9.9 Install Database Software

[oracle@crsdg1 ~]$. /home/oracle/.bash_profile

[oracle@crsdg1 ~]$ echo $ORACLE_HOME
/u01/app/oracle/product/10.2.0/db_1

[oracle@crsdg1 ~]$ /u01/software/clusterware/cluvfy/runcluvfy.sh stage -pre dbinst -n crsdg1,crsdg2 -verbose

Ignore Linux packages version warning

- Welcome Screen: Click Next
- Select Installation Type: Enterprise Edition (1.24GB)

- Specify Home Details

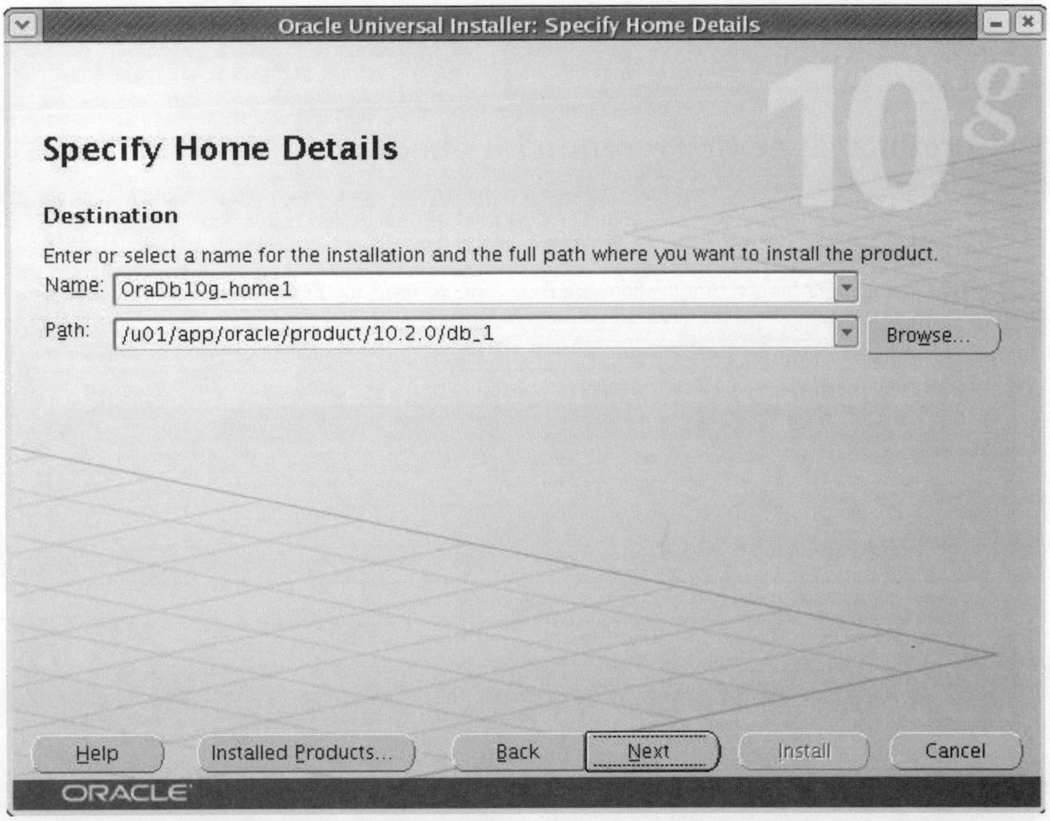

- Specify Hardware Cluster Installation Mode

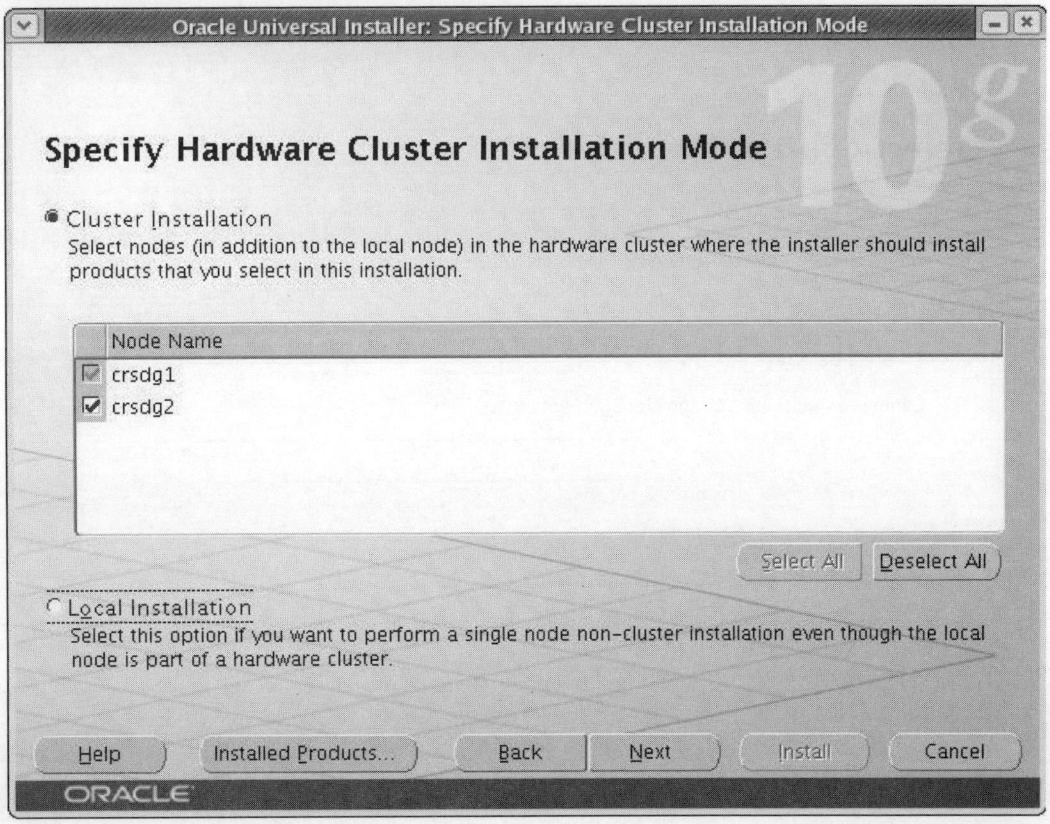

- Product–Specific Prerequisite Checks

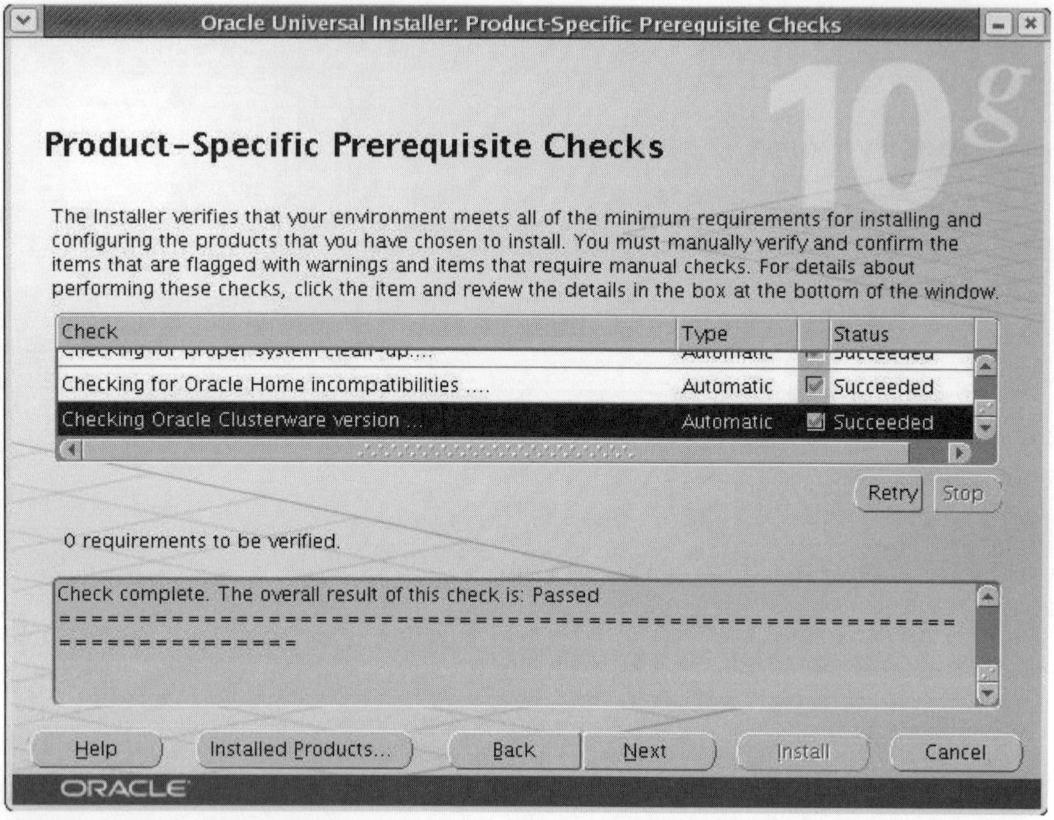

- Select Configuration Option

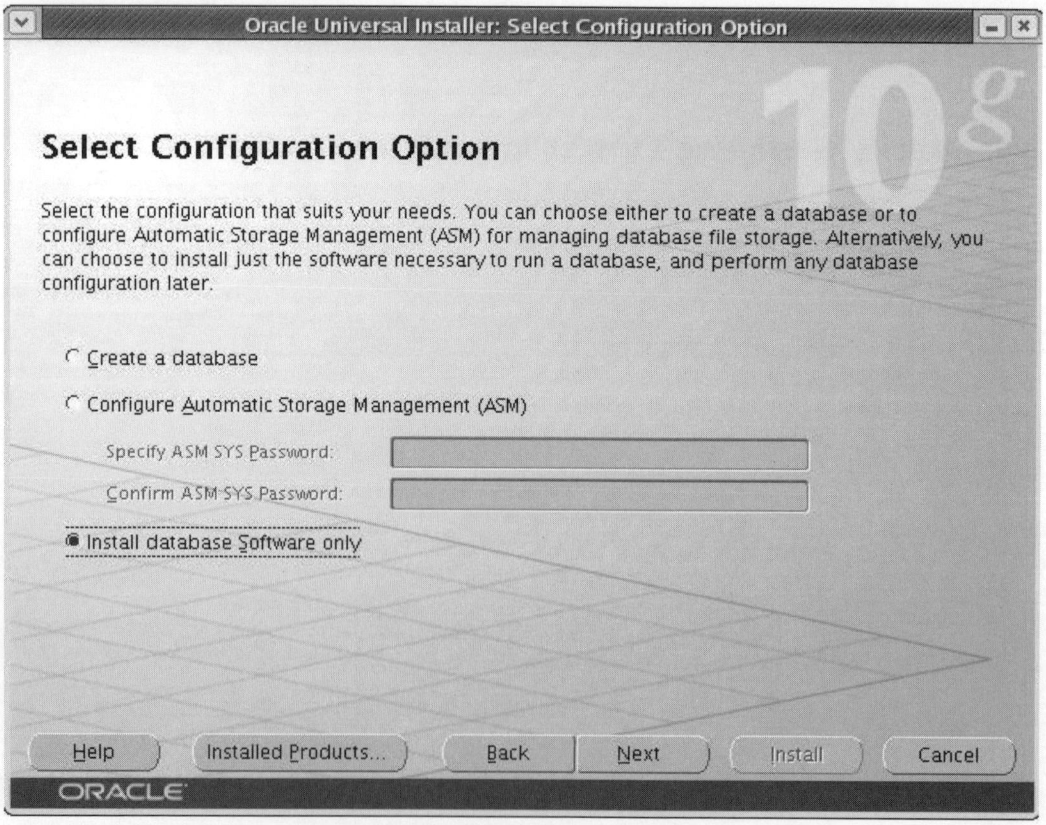

- Summary

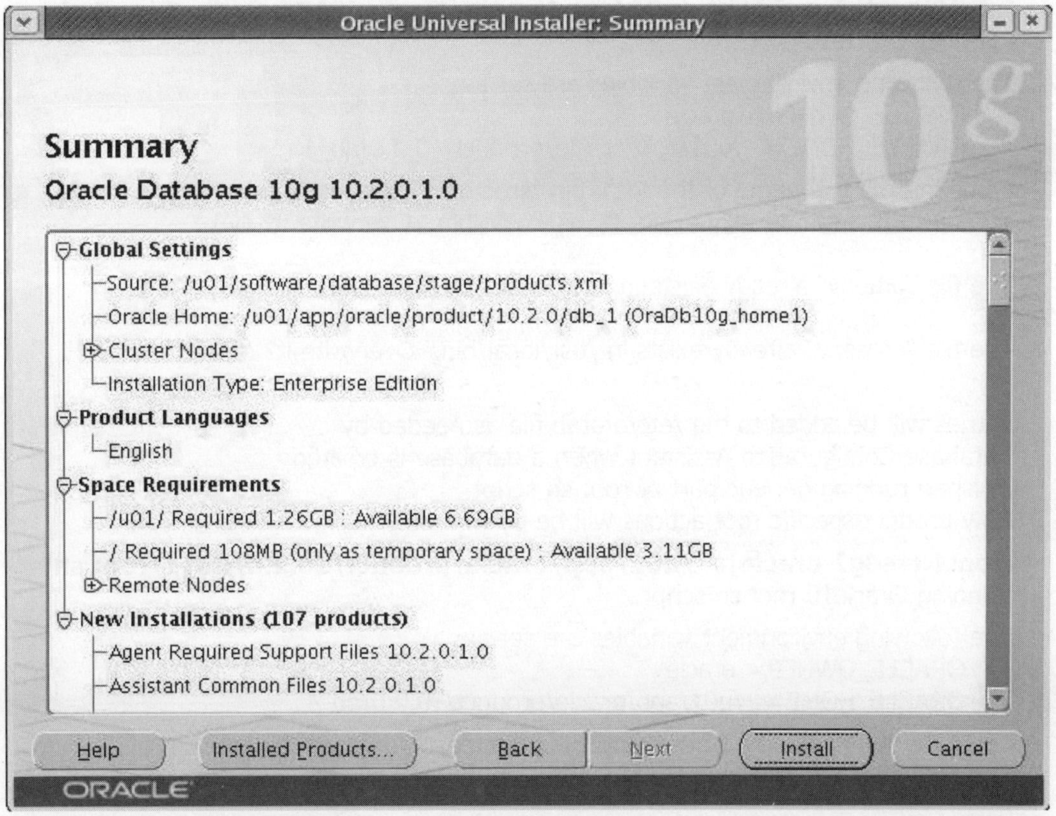

- Execute Configuration Scripts

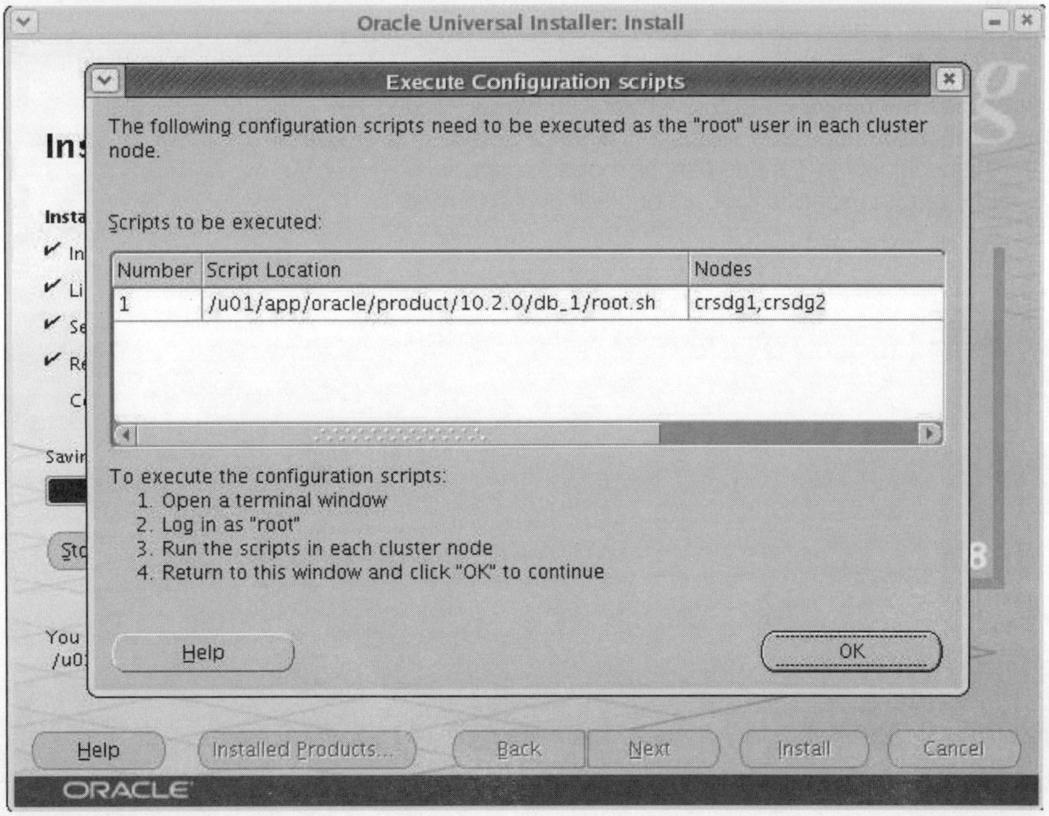

- Open a new terminal and sudo su and execute configuration script

[root@crsdg1 oracle]# /u01/app/oracle/product/10.2.0/db_1/root.sh
Running Oracle10 root.sh script...

The following environment variables are set as:
    ORACLE_OWNER= oracle
    ORACLE_HOME= /u01/app/oracle/product/10.2.0/db_1

Enter the full pathname of the local bin directory: [/usr/local/bin]:
The file "dbhome" already exists in /usr/local/bin. Overwrite it? (y/n)
[n]:
The file "oraenv" already exists in /usr/local/bin. Overwrite it? (y/n)
[n]:
The file "coraenv" already exists in /usr/local/bin. Overwrite it? (y/n)
[n]:

Entries will be added to the /etc/oratab file as needed by
Database Configuration Assistant when a database is created
Finished running generic part of root.sh script.
Now product-specific root actions will be performed.

[root@crsdg2 oracle]# /u01/app/oracle/product/10.2.0/db_1/root.sh
Running Oracle10 root.sh script...

The following environment variables are set as:
    ORACLE_OWNER= oracle
    ORACLE_HOME= /u01/app/oracle/product/10.2.0/db_1

Enter the full pathname of the local bin directory: [/usr/local/bin]:
The file "dbhome" already exists in /usr/local/bin. Overwrite it? (y/n)
[n]:
The file "oraenv" already exists in /usr/local/bin. Overwrite it? (y/n)
[n]:
The file "coraenv" already exists in /usr/local/bin. Overwrite it? (y/n)
[n]:

Entries will be added to the /etc/oratab file as needed by
Database Configuration Assistant when a database is created
Finished running generic part of root.sh script.
Now product-specific root actions will be performed.

- End of Installation

9.10 Use dbca to add on Data Guard Cluster Nodes

The name and number of disk group as in crs1 and crs2 more Diskgroup in crsdg1 and crsdg2 be the same.

- Below id the screen shot of disk groups on crs1 and crs2

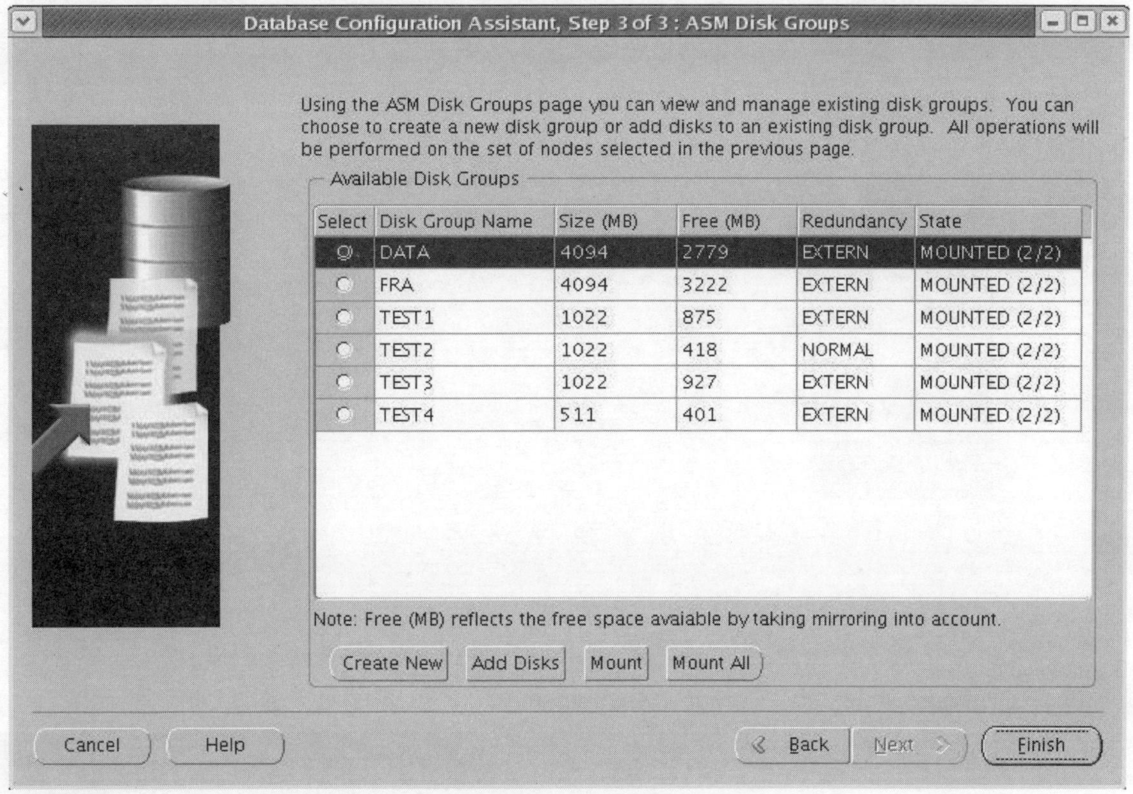

- Using dbca on crsdg1 create extra disk groups as in crs1

[oracle@crsdg1 ~]$. /home/oracle/.bash_profile

[oracle@crsdg1 ~]$ echo $ORACLE_HOME
/u01/app/oracle/product/10.2.0/db_1

[oracle@crsdg1 ~]$ dbca

- Welcome Screen: Select Oracle Real Application Cluster Database, Click Next

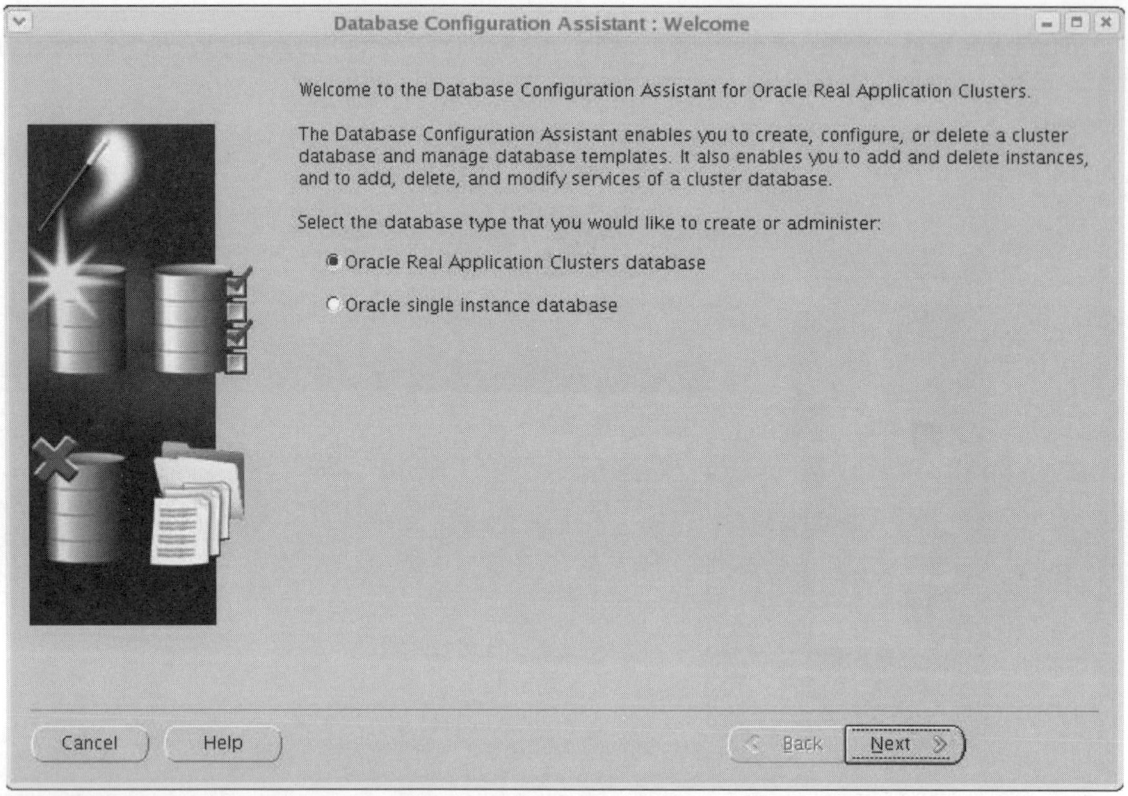

- Configure Automatic Storage Management

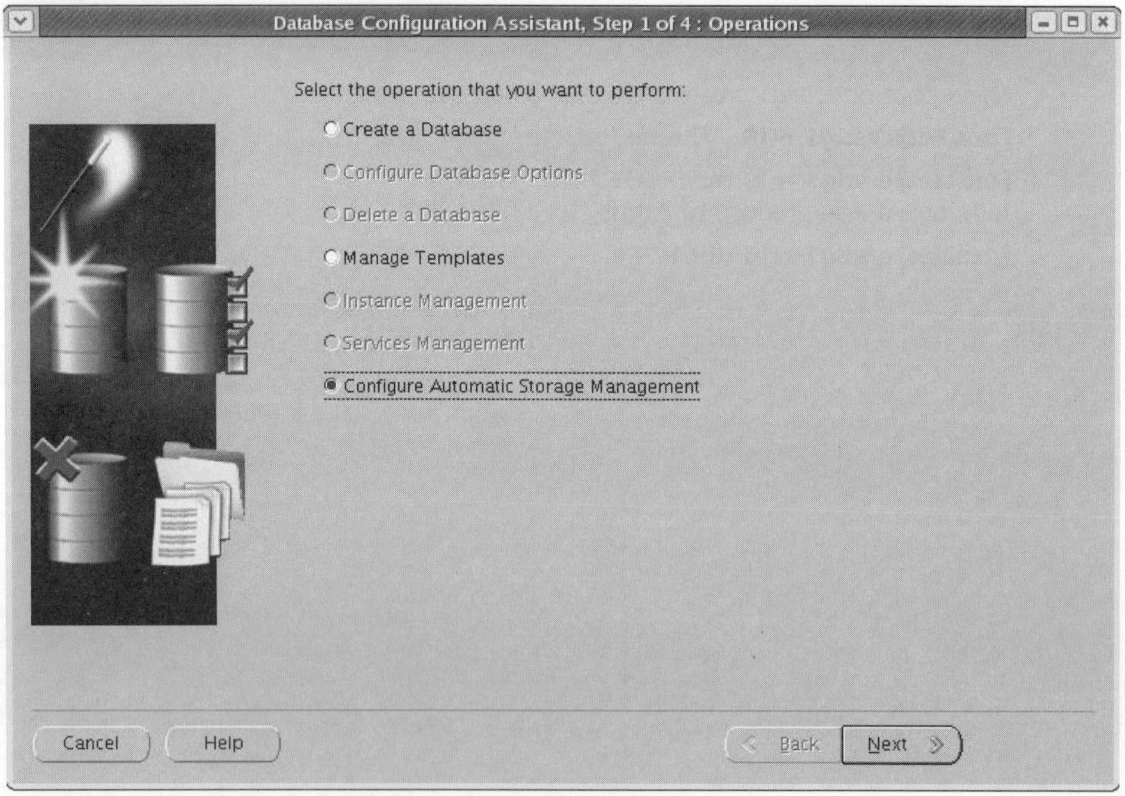

- Node Selection: Select both crsdb1 and crsdg2

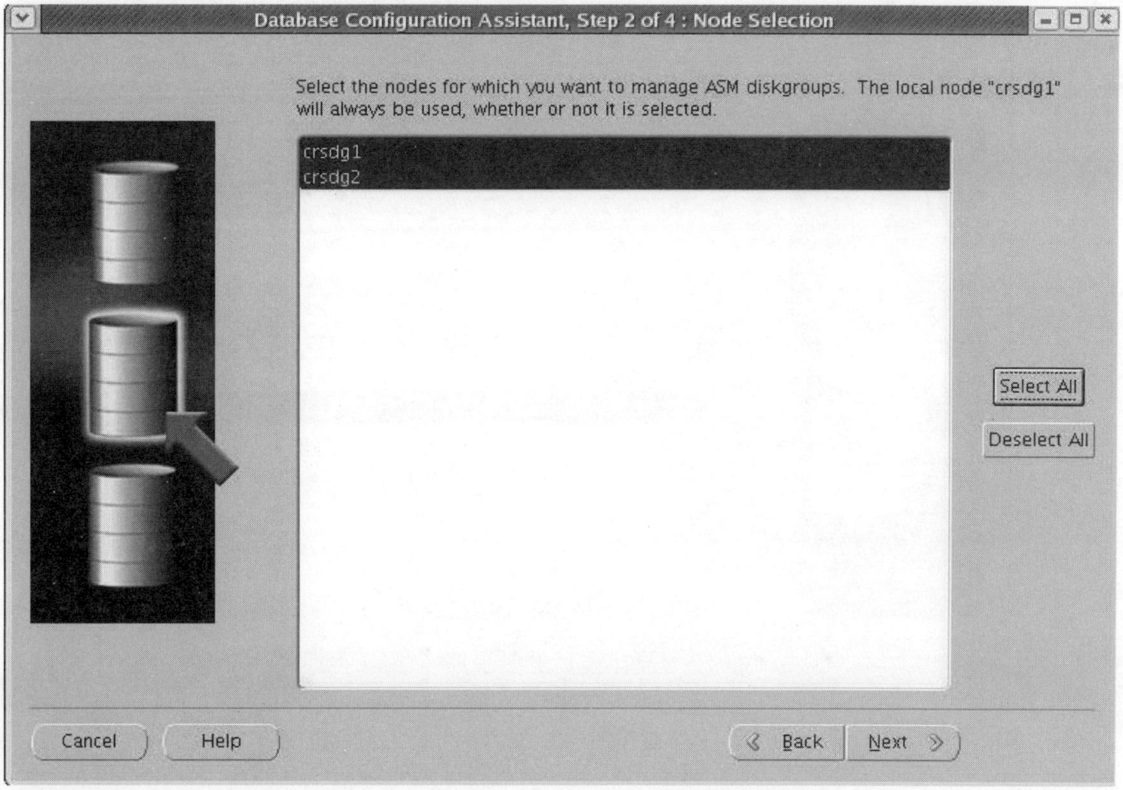

- Create Disk Group: ASM disk group FRA created on Data Guard Cluster ASM

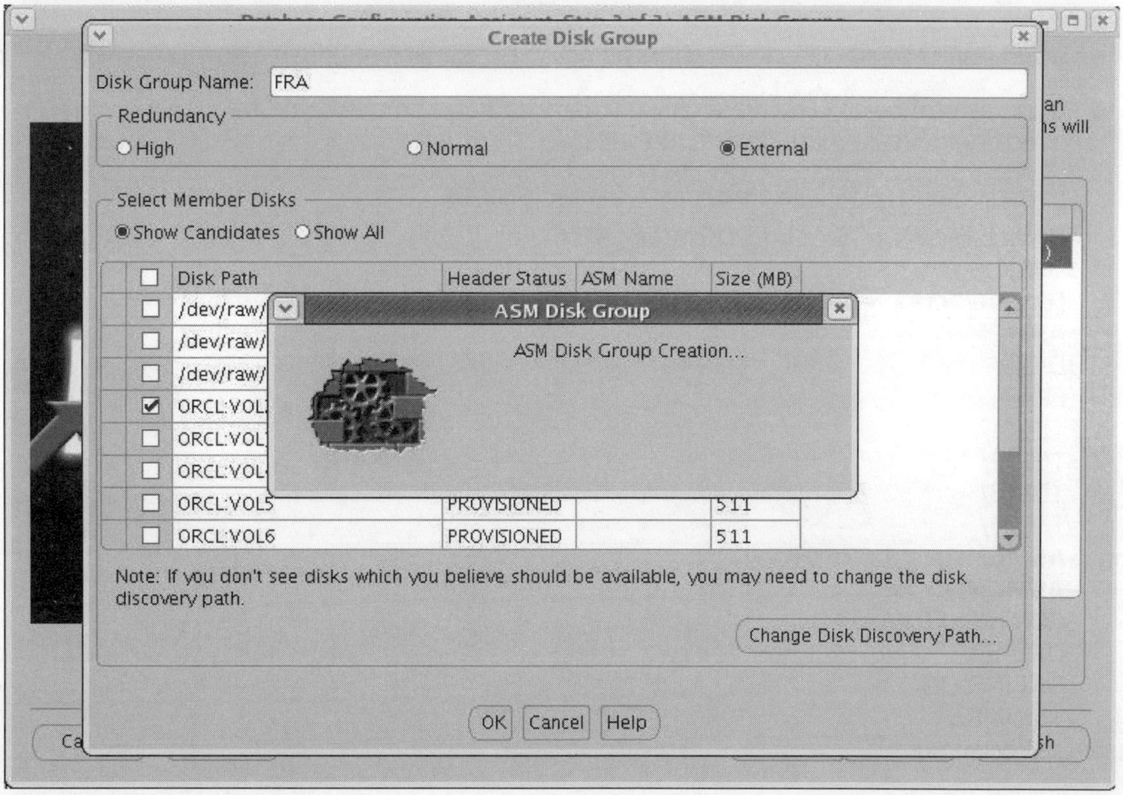

- In same way all other ASM Disk Groups are created on crsdg1 and crsdg2

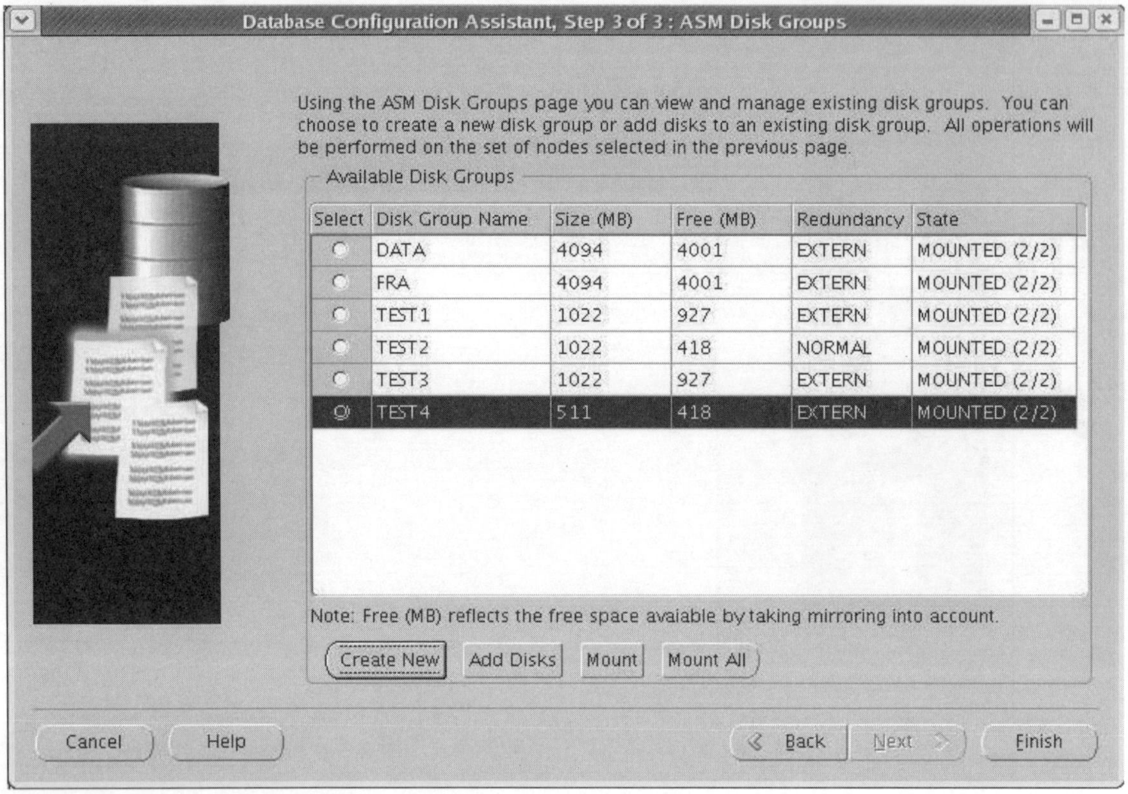

9.11 Using ASMCMD add directories

Using ASMCMD add directories same as on crs1, crs2 as mentioned below on asmdisk on crsdg1 or crsdg2

- Using asmcmd, you can create only one directory at a time and you have change directory to that directory to create more inner directories.

```
[oracle@crs1 ~]$ . /home/oracle/asm_profile
[oracle@crs1 ~]$ echo $ORACLE_SID
+ASM1
[oracle@crs1 ~]$ asmcmd
ASMCMD> ls
DATA/
FRA/
TEST1/
TEST2/
TEST3/
TEST4/
ASMCMD> cd CRSDB
ASMCMD> ls
CONTROLFILE/
DATAFILE/
ONLINELOG/
TEMPFILE/
spfilecrsdb.ora
```

- Below is the example to create sub directories in +DATA/CRSDB

CONTROLFILE
DATAFILE
ONLINELG
TEMPFILE

[oracle@crsdg1 ~]$. /home/oracle/asm_profile

[oracle@crsdg1 ~]$ asmcmd

ASMCMD> ls

DATA/
ASMCMD> cd +DATA

ASMCMD> mkdir CRSDGDB

ASMCMD> cd CRSDGDB

ASMCMD> mkdir CONTROLFILE

ASMCMD> mkdir DATAFILE

ASMCMD> mkdir ONLINELOG

ASMCMD> mkdir TEMPFILE

ASMCMD> cd +FRA

- In the same way, create all directories and sub directories in **CRSDGDB** directory on crsdg1 as in crs1

+FRA/CRSDGDB/ ARCHIVELOG
+FRA/CRSDGDB/ CONTROLFILE
+FRA/CRSDGDB/ FLASHBACK
+FRA/CRSDGDB/ ONLINELOG
+TEST1/ CRSDGDB/ DATAFILE
+TEST2/ CRSDGDB/ DATAFILE
+TEST3/ CRSDGDB/ DATAFILE
+TEST4/crsdgdb/controlfile

- Make sure you can view all directories and sub directories in crsdg2 as in crs1

9.12 Shutdown and Backup cluster nodes

Shutdown and Backup cluster nodes CRSDG1 and CRSDG2 for future exercises

Copy c:/vm/rac/crsdg1 to c:/vm/backup/crsdg1
Copy c:/vm/rac/crsdg2 to c:/vm/backup/crsdg2
Copy c:/vm/rac/shareddg to c:/vm/backup/shareddg

9.13 Start crs1, crs2, crsdg1 and crsdg2 machines

- Make sure crsdb database is up and running on both crs1, crs2

[oracle@crs1 ~]$ crs_stat –t

Name	Type	Target	State	Host
ora....SM1.asm	application	ONLINE	ONLINE	crs1
ora....S1.lsnr	application	ONLINE	ONLINE	crs1
ora.crs1.gsd	application	ONLINE	ONLINE	crs1
ora.crs1.ons	application	ONLINE	ONLINE	crs1
ora.crs1.vip	application	ONLINE	ONLINE	crs1

```
ora....SM2.asm   application   ONLINE   ONLINE   crs2
ora....S2.lsnr   application   ONLINE   ONLINE   crs2
ora.crs2.gsd     application   ONLINE   ONLINE   crs2
ora.crs2.ons     application   ONLINE   ONLINE   crs2
ora.crs2.vip     application   ONLINE   ONLINE   crs2
ora....db1.srv   application   ONLINE   ONLINE   crs1
ora....db2.srv   application   ONLINE   ONLINE   crs2
ora....EST1.cs   application   ONLINE   ONLINE   crs1
ora....db1.srv   application   ONLINE   ONLINE   crs1
ora....EST2.cs   application   ONLINE   ONLINE   crs1
ora....db1.srv   application   ONLINE   ONLINE   crs1
ora....EST3.cs   application   ONLINE   ONLINE   crs1
ora....b1.inst   application   ONLINE   ONLINE   crs1
ora....b2.inst   application   ONLINE   ONLINE   crs2
ora.crsdb.db     application   ONLINE   ONLINE   crs2
```

- Make sure nodeapps and asm are running on crsdg1 and crsdg2

[oracle@crsdg1 ~]$ crs_stat –t

```
Name             Type          Target   State    Host
-------------------------------------------------------
ora....SM1.asm   application   ONLINE   ONLINE   crsdg1
ora....G1.lsnr   application   ONLINE   ONLINE   crsdg1
ora.crsdg1.gsd   application   ONLINE   ONLINE   crsdg1
ora.crsdg1.ons   application   ONLINE   ONLINE   crsdg1
ora.crsdg1.vip   application   ONLINE   ONLINE   crsdg1
ora....SM2.asm   application   ONLINE   ONLINE   crsdg2
ora....G2.lsnr   application   ONLINE   ONLINE   crsdg2
ora.crsdg2.gsd   application   ONLINE   ONLINE   crsdg2
ora.crsdg2.ons   application   ONLINE   ONLINE   crsdg2
ora.crsdg2.vip   application   ONLINE   ONLINE   crsdg2
```

9.14 Manually Create Physical Standby

- Configure oracle database parameter db_broker_config_file

For RAC/ASM first change the location of db_broker_config_file to shared disk from $ORACLE_HOME/dbs

SQL> ALTER SYSTEM SET DG_BROKER_CONFIG_FILE1 =
'+DATA/crsdb/datafile/dr1crsdb.dat' SCOPE=BOTH;

System altered.

SQL> ALTER SYSTEM SET DG_BROKER_CONFIG_FILE2 =
'+TEST1/crsdb/datafile/dr2crsdb.dat' SCOPE=BOTH;

System altered.

- Make database crsdb in force logging

SQL> ALTER DATABASE FORCE LOGGING;

- Make staging directory for backup same path on all instances both on primary and secondary

$ mkdir –p /u01/app/oracle/stage

- RAC Database crsdb parameters changes

Either you can use alter system or manually edit pfile after creating it from spfile. As RAC instance were started using spfile the default value for sid is sid='*', so no need to mention sid='*' in alter system command.

Always before modifying, any parameters make a backup of pfile

- Create pfile from spfile

  Never create pfile having instance name like initcrsd1.ora as it contains location of spfile, which will be overwritten

  [oracle@crs1 dbs]$ cat initcrsdb1.ora
  SPFILE='+DATA/crsdb/spfilecrsdb.ora'

  SQL> CREATE PFILE='/u01/app/oracle/product/10.2.0/db_1/dbs/initcrsdb.ora.bck1';
  FROM SPFILE;

  File created.

- Set database db_unique_name= crsdb

  SQL> ALTER SYSTEM SET db_unique_name='crsdb' SCOPE=SPFILE;

  System altered.

- Setting dg_config=(crsdb,crsdgdb)

  SQL> ALTER SYSTEM SET log_archive_config='dg_config=(crsdb,crsdgdb) '
  SCOPE=SPFILE;

  System altered.

- Setting location for log_archive_dest_1 for primary database

  SQL> ALTER SYSTEM SET log_archive_dest_1='location=use_db_recovery_file_dest
  valid_for=(online_logfiles,all_roles) db_unique_name=crsdb' SCOPE=SPFILE;

  System altered.

- Setting location for log_archive_dest_2 for Secondary database

  SQL> ALTER SYSTEM SET log_archive_dest_2='service=crsdgdb lgwr async
  valid_for=(online_logfiles,primary_role) db_unique_name=crsdgdb' SCOPE=SPFILE;

  System altered.

- Setting location for log_archive_dest_3 for Standy Role

  SQL> ALTER SYSTEM SET log_archive_dest_3='LOCATION=use_db_recovery_file_dest
  VALID_FOR=(STANDBY_LOGFILES,STANDBY_ROLE) DB_UNIQUE_NAME=crsdb'
  SCOPE=SPFILE;

  System altered.

- Enabling the log_archive_dest_state

  SQL> ALTER SYSTEM SET log_archive_dest_state_1 = enable SCOPE= SPFILE;

  System altered.

  SQL> ALTER SYSTEM SET log_archive_dest_state_2 = defer SCOPE=SPFILE;

  System altered.

  SQL> ALTER SYSTEM SET log_archive_dest_state_3 = enable SCOPE=SPFILE;

  System altered.

- Setting remote_loging_passwordfile=exclusive

  SQL> ALTER SYSTEM SET remote_loging_passwordfile=exclusive SCOPE=SPFILE;

  System altered.

- Setting fal_server as Secondary database for Primary database

  SQL> ALTER SYSTEM SET fal_server='crsdgdb' SCOPE=SPFILE;

  System altered.

- Setting fal_client for Primary database

  SQL> ALTER SYSTEM SET fal_client = 'crsdb' SCOPE= SPFILE;

  System altered.

- Setting log_file_name_convert ='crsdgdb','crsdb'

  This means after switch over secondary (crsdgdb) when redo will be transported from new primary (crsdgdb) to new secondary (crsdb) the log file name will be converted from crsdgdb to crsdb. Same changes will apply to db_file_name_convert.

  SQL> ALTER SYSTEM SET log_file_name_convert='crsdgdb','crsdb' SCOPE= SPFILE;

  System altered.

  SQL> ALTER SYSTEM SET db_file_name_convert = 'crsdgdb','crsdb' SCOPE=SPFILE;

  System altered.

- **If the Diskgroup is different on primary and secondary, add Diskgroup name also.**

  SQL> ALTER SYSTEM SET log_file_name_convert = '+**RECOVERY**/crsdgdb','+DATA/crsdb' SCOPE = SPFILE;

  SQL> ALTER SYSTEM SET db_file_name_convert = '+**RECOVERY**/crsdgdb','+DATA/crsdb' SCOPE = SPFILE;

- Setting standby_file_management to auto

  SQL> ALTER SYSTEM SET standby_file_management = auto;

  System altered.

- Setting standby_archive_dest location

  SQL> ALTER SYSTEM SET standby_archive_dest ='location=use_db_recovery_file_dest' SCOPE=SPFILE;

  System altered.

- Again create pfile backup2 from spfile

  SQL> CREATE PFILE='/u01/app/oracle/product/10.2.0/db_1/dbs/initcrsdb.ora.bck2' FROM SPFILE;

  Shutdown database and restart to make sure there are no errors in parameters. If there, is any problem in startup database then Shutdown the database immediately change the parameter, which has problem in latest pfile backup, and again restart the database

  [oracle@crs1 dbs]$ srvctl stop database -d crsdb

  SQL> STARTUP nomount;

  ORACLE instance started.

  ```
  Total System Global Area  285212672 bytes
  Fixed Size                  1218992 bytes
  Variable Size             100664912 bytes
  Database Buffers          180355072 bytes
  Redo Buffers                2973696 bytes
  ```

  SQL> SHUTDOWN immediate;

  ORA-01507: database not mounted
  ORACLE instance shut down.

- Restart database and service using srvctl command

  [oracle@crs1 ~]$ srvctl start database -d crsdb

  [oracle@crs1 ~]$ srvctl start service -s TEST1 -d crsdb

  [oracle@crs1 ~]$ srvctl start service -s TEST2 -d crsdb

  [oracle@crs1 ~]$ srvctl start service -s TEST2 -d crsdb

- **The other option is to modify above parameters in Primary Database pfile directly instead of alter system commands**

  *.db_unique_name= 'crsdb'

  *.log_archive_config='dg_config=(crsdb,crsdgdb)'

  *.log_archive_dest_1='location=USE_DB_RECOVERY_FILE_DEST valid_for=(online_logfiles,all_roles) db_unique_name=crsdb'

  *.log_archive_dest_2='service=crsdgdb lgwr async valid_for=(online_logfiles,primary_role) db_unique_name=crsdgdb'

  *.log_archive_dest_3='LOCATION=use_db_recovery_file_dest ALID_FOR=(STANDBY_LOGFILES,STANDBY_ROLE) DB_UNIQUE_NAME=crsdb'

  *. log_archive_dest_state_1 = enable

  *. log_archive_dest_state_2 = defer

  *. log_archive_dest_state_2 = enable

  *. remote_login_passwordfile=exclusive

  *.fal_server='crsdgdb'

  *.fal_client='crsdb'

  *.db_file_name_convert='crsdgdb','crsdb'

  *.log_file_name_convert='crsdgdb','crsdb'

  *.standby_file_management='AUTO'

  *. standby_archive_dest ='location=use_db_recovery_file_dest'

- After database is restarted, again create a pfile from spfile and make a copy

  SQL> CREATE PFILE='/u01/app/oracle/product/10.2.0/db_1/dbs/initcrsdb.ora.bck' FROM SPFILE;

- Make a copy of latest pfile backup for secondary database instances

  [oracle@crs1 dbs]$ cp initcrsdb.ora.bck initcrsdgdb.ora.bck

- Modify parameters below in copied Secondary Database pfile,changes marked in bold

[oracle@crs1 dbs]$ cat initcrsdgdb.ora.bck | grep -i crs

crsdgdb2.__db_cache_size=134217728

crsdgdb1.__db_cache_size=176160768

crsdgdb2.__java_pool_size=4194304

crsdgdb1.__java_pool_size=4194304

crsdgdb2.__large_pool_size=4194304

crsdgdb1.__large_pool_size=4194304

crsdgdb2.__shared_pool_size=138412032

crsdgdb1.__shared_pool_size=96468992

crsdgdb2.__streams_pool_size=0

crsdgdb1.__streams_pool_size=0

*.audit_file_dest='/u01/app/oracle/admin/**crsdgdb**/adump'

*.background_dump_dest='/u01/app/oracle/admin/**crsdgdb**/bdump'

*.control_files='+DATA/**crsdgdb**/controlfile/current.260.743634235','+FRA/**crsdgdb**/controlfile/current.256.743634235','+TEST4/**crsdgdb**/controlfile/controlfile3.ctl'

*.core_dump_dest='/u01/app/oracle/admin/**crsdgdb**/cdump'

```
*.db_file_name_convert='crsdb','crsdgdb'
*.db_name='crsdb'
*.db_unique_name='crsdgdb'
*.dg_broker_config_file1='+DATA/crsdgdb/datafile/dr1crsdgdb.dat'
*.dg_broker_config_file2=' +TEST1/crsdgdb/datafile/dr2crsdgdb.dat'
*.dispatchers='(PROTOCOL=TCP) (SERVICE=crsdgdbXDB)'
*.fal_client='crsdgdb'
*.fal_server='crsdb'
crsdgdb2.instance_number=2
crsdgdb1.instance_number=1
*.log_archive_config='dg_config=(crsdb,crsdgdb) '
*.log_archive_dest_1='location=use_db_recovery_file_dest  valid_for=(online_logfiles,all_roles)
db_unique_name=crsdgdb'
*.log_archive_dest_2='service=crsdb lgwr async  valid_for=(online_logfiles,primary_role)
db_unique_name=crsdb'
*.log_archive_dest_3='LOCATION=use_db_recovery_file_dest
VALID_FOR=(STANDBY_LOGFILES,STANDBY_ROLE) DB_UNIQUE_NAME=crsdgdb'
*.log_file_name_convert='crsdb','crsdgdb'
*.remote_listener='LISTENERS_CRSDGDB'
crsdgdb2.thread=2
crsdgdb1.thread=1
crsdgdb2.undo_tablespace='UNDOTBS2'
crsdgdb1.undo_tablespace='UNDOTBS1'
*.user_dump_dest='/u01/app/oracle/admin/crsdgdb/udump'
```

- You can also see the difference between crsdb and crsdgdb pfile.

  [oracle@crs1 dbs]$ diff initcrsdb.ora.bck initcrsdgdb.ora.bck

- Add following lines for Secondary database crsdgdb1 and crsdgdb2 in tnsnames.ora of both crs1 and crs2

```
CRSDGDB =
  (DESCRIPTION =
    (ADDRESS = (PROTOCOL = TCP)(HOST = crsdg1-vip.prusolutions.com)(PORT = 1521))
    (ADDRESS = (PROTOCOL = TCP)(HOST = crsdg2-vip.prusolutions.com)(PORT = 1521))
    (LOAD_BALANCE = yes)
    (CONNECT_DATA =
      (SERVER = DEDICATED)
      (SERVICE_NAME = CRSDGDB)
      )
  )

CRSDGDB2 =
  (DESCRIPTION =
    (ADDRESS = (PROTOCOL = TCP)(HOST = crsdg2-vip.prusolutions.com)(PORT = 1521))
    (CONNECT_DATA =
      (SERVER = DEDICATED)
      (SERVICE_NAME = CRSDGDB)
      (INSTANCE_NAME = CRSDGDB2)
      )
  )
```

```
CRSDGDB1 =
  (DESCRIPTION =
    (ADDRESS = (PROTOCOL = TCP)(HOST = crsdg1-vip.prusolutions.com)(PORT = 1521))
    (CONNECT_DATA =
      (SERVER = DEDICATED)
      (SERVICE_NAME = CRSDGDB)
      (INSTANCE_NAME = CRSDGDB1)
      )
    )
```

- TNSPING crsdgdb, crsdbdg1 and crsdgdb2 from both crs1 and crs2 to check connectivity

  [oracle@crs1 admin]$ tnsping crsdgdb

- Copy parameter file on crs1 into /u01/app/oracle/stage directory

  /u01/app/oracle/product/10.2.0/db_1/dbs/initcrsdgdb.ora.bck

- Copy network files on both crs1 and crs2 into their /u01/app/oracle/stage directory

  /u01/app/oracle/product/10.2.0/db_1/network/admin/tnsnames.ora /u01/app/oracle/product/10.2.0/**asm_1**/network/admin/listener.ora
  /u01/app/oracle/product/10.2.0/**asm_1**/network/admin/sqlnet.ora

- On primary take rman backup to staging directory /u01/app/oracle/stage

  [oracle@crs1 stage]$ rman target /

  RMAN> backup device type disk format '/u01/app/oracle/stage/%U' database plus archivelog;

  RMAN> backup device type disk format '/u01/app/oracle/stage/%U' current controlfile for standby;

- Ftp all the files in /u01/app/oracle/stage from crs1 to crsdg1 and from crs2 to crsdg2

  Copy network files in /u01/app/oracle/stage on crsdg1 and crsdg2 to

  $ cp tnsnames.ora /u01/app/oracle/product/10.2.0/db_1/network/admin/tnsnames.ora

  $ cp listener.ora /u01/app/oracle/product/10.2.0/**asm_1**/network/admin/listener.ora

  $ cp sqlnet.ora /u01/app/oracle/product/10.2.0/**asm_1**/network/admin/sqlnet.ora

- Modify networks files are mentioned below

  - On crsdg1 before changes listener.ora

```
SID_LIST_LISTENER_CRS1 =
  (SID_LIST =
  (SID_DESC =
    (SID_NAME = PLSExtProc)
    (ORACLE_HOME = /u01/app/oracle/product/10.2.0/asm_1)
    (PROGRAM = extproc)
    )
  )

LISTENER_CRS1 =
  (DESCRIPTION_LIST =
  (DESCRIPTION =
    (ADDRESS = (PROTOCOL = IPC)(KEY = EXTPROC1))
    (ADDRESS = (PROTOCOL = TCP)(HOST = crs1-vip.prusolutions.com)(PORT = 1521)(IP = FIRST))
    (ADDRESS = (PROTOCOL = TCP)(HOST = 192.168.2.131)(PORT = 1521)(IP = FIRST))
    )
  )
```

- On crsdg1 after changes listener.ora

```
SID_LIST_LISTENER_CRSDG1 =
  (SID_LIST =
  (SID_DESC =
    (SID_NAME = PLSExtProc)
    (ORACLE_HOME = /u01/app/oracle/product/10.2.0/asm_1)
    (PROGRAM = extproc)
    )
  )

LISTENER_CRSDG1 =
  (DESCRIPTION_LIST =
  (DESCRIPTION =
    (ADDRESS = (PROTOCOL = IPC)(KEY = EXTPROC1))
    (ADDRESS = (PROTOCOL = TCP)(HOST = crsdg1-vip.prusolutions.com)(PORT = 1521)(IP =
    FIRST))
    (ADDRESS = (PROTOCOL = TCP)(HOST = 192.168.2.141)(PORT = 1521)(IP = FIRST))
  )
```

- On crsdg2 before changes listener.ora

```
SID_LIST_LISTENER_CRS2 =
  (SID_LIST =
  (SID_DESC =
    (SID_NAME = PLSExtProc)
    (ORACLE_HOME = /u01/app/oracle/product/10.2.0/asm_1)
    (PROGRAM = extproc)
    )
  )

LISTENER_CRS2 =
  (DESCRIPTION_LIST =
  (DESCRIPTION =
    (ADDRESS = (PROTOCOL = IPC)(KEY = EXTPROC1))
    (ADDRESS = (PROTOCOL = TCP)(HOST = crs2-vip.prusolutions.com)(PORT = 1521)(IP = FIRST))
    (ADDRESS = (PROTOCOL = TCP)(HOST = 192.168.2.132)(PORT = 1521)(IP = FIRST))
    )
  )
```

- On crsdg2 after changes listener.ora

```
SID_LIST_LISTENER_CRSDG2 =
  (SID_LIST =
  (SID_DESC =
    (SID_NAME = PLSExtProc)
    (ORACLE_HOME = /u01/app/oracle/product/10.2.0/asm_1)
    (PROGRAM = extproc)
    )
  )

LISTENER_CRSDG2 =
  (DESCRIPTION_LIST =
  (DESCRIPTION =
    (ADDRESS = (PROTOCOL = IPC)(KEY = EXTPROC1))
    (ADDRESS = (PROTOCOL = TCP)(HOST = crsdg2-vip.prusolutions.com)(PORT = 1521)(IP =
    FIRST))
    (ADDRESS = (PROTOCOL = TCP)(HOST = 192.168.2.142)(PORT = 1521)(IP = FIRST))
    )
  )
```

- Modify following lines in tnsnames.ora on crsdg1 and crsdg2
  - **Before changes**

```
LISTENERS_CRSDB =
  (ADDRESS_LIST =
    (ADDRESS = (PROTOCOL = TCP)(HOST = crs1-vip.prusolutions.com)(PORT = 1521))
    (ADDRESS = (PROTOCOL = TCP)(HOST = crs2-vip.prusolutions.com)(PORT = 1521))
  )
```

  - **After Changes**

```
LISTENERS_CRSDGDB =
  (ADDRESS_LIST =
    (ADDRESS = (PROTOCOL = TCP)(HOST = crsdg1-vip.prusolutions.com)(PORT = 1521))
    (ADDRESS = (PROTOCOL = TCP)(HOST = crsdg2-vip.prusolutions.com)(PORT = 1521))
  )
```

- Test connection from crsdg1 and crsdg2 to crsdb database

```
[oracle@crsdg1 stage]$ sqlplus /nolog
SQL> connect sys@crsdb as sysdba
     Enter password:
     Connected.
SQL> SELECT db_unique_name FROM v$database;

     DB_UNIQUE_NAME
     ____________________
     crsdb
```

- Create pfile and spfile as mentioned below for both crsdg1 and crsdg2 have path for spfile for crsdgdb database
  - On crsdg1 filename initcrsdgdb1.ora

```
[oracle@crsdg1 dbs]$ cat /u01/app/oracle/product/10.2.0/db_1/dbs/initcrsdgdb1.ora
SPFILE='+DATA/crsdgdb/spfilecrsdgdb.ora'
```

  - On crsdg2 filename initcrsdgdb2.ora

```
[oracle@crsdg2 dbs]$ cat /u01/app/oracle/product/10.2.0/db_1/dbs/initcrsdgdb2.ora
SPFILE='+DATA/crsdgdb/spfilecrsdgdb.ora'
```

  - On crsdg1, create spfile from pfile copied from crs1

```
SQL> CREATE SPFILE='+DATA/crsdgdb/spfilecrsdgdb.ora' FROM
     PFILE='/u01/app/oracle/stage/initcrsdgdb.ora.bck';
```

- Create oracle password file both on crsdg1 and crsdg2

  To enable transmission of redo make sure database uses password file and sys user is identical on every system

```
[oracle@crsdg1 dbs]$ orapwd password=oracle file=orapwcrsdgdb1 entries=5
[oracle@crsdg2 dbs]$ orapwd password=oracle entries=5 file=orapwcrsdgdb2
```

- Startup database crsdgdb in nomount state

```
[oracle@crsdg1 stage]$ sqlplus / as sysdba
SQL> STARTUP nomount;
SQL> SHOW PARAMETER db_unique_name
```

NAME	TYPE	VALUE
db_unique_name	string	crsdgdb

- Start RMAN and connect to primary and secondary instances

[oracle@crsdg1 stage]$ rman target sys/oracle@crsdb1 auxiliary /

```
Recovery Manager: Release 10.2.0.1.0 - Production on Sun Mar 6 08:00:30 2011
Copyright (c) 1982, 2005, Oracle.  All rights reserved.
connected to target database: CRSDB (DBID=572850618)
connected to auxiliary database: CRSDB (not mounted)
```

RMAN> duplicate target database for standby;

```
Starting Duplicate Db at 06-MAR-11
using target database control file instead of recovery catalog
allocated channel: ORA_AUX_DISK_1
channel ORA_AUX_DISK_1: sid=152 instance=crsdgdb1 devtype=DISK
contents of Memory Script:
{
   restore clone standby controlfile;
   sql clone 'alter database mount standby database';
}
executing Memory Script
Starting restore at 06-MAR-11
using channel ORA_AUX_DISK_1
channel ORA_AUX_DISK_1: starting datafile backupset restore
channel ORA_AUX_DISK_1: restoring control file
channel ORA_AUX_DISK_1: reading from backup piece /u01/app/oracle/stage/0em6ffpf_1_1
channel ORA_AUX_DISK_1: restored backup piece 1
piece handle=/u01/app/oracle/stage/0em6ffpf_1_1 tag=TAG20110305T153055
channel ORA_AUX_DISK_1: restore complete, elapsed time: 00:00:25
output filename=+DATA/crsdgdb/controlfile/current.257.745056097
output filename=+FRA/crsdgdb/controlfile/backup.256.745056105
output filename=+TEST4/crsdgdb/controlfile/controlfile3.ctl
Finished restore at 06-MAR-11
sql statement: alter database mount standby database
released channel: ORA_AUX_DISK_1
contents of Memory Script:
{
   set newname for tempfile  1 to
 "+DATA/crsdgdb/tempfile/temp.263.743634265";
   switch clone tempfile all;
   set newname for datafile  1 to
 "+DATA/crsdgdb/datafile/system.256.743634151";
   set newname for datafile  2 to
 "+DATA/crsdgdb/datafile/undotbs1.258.743634153";
   set newname for datafile  3 to
 "+DATA/crsdgdb/datafile/sysaux.257.743634153";
   set newname for datafile  4 to
 "+DATA/crsdgdb/datafile/users.259.743634153";
   set newname for datafile  5 to
 "+DATA/crsdgdb/datafile/example.264.743634277";
   set newname for datafile  6 to
```

```
  "+DATA/crsdgdb/datafile/undotbs2.265.743634431";
  set newname for datafile  7 to
  "+TEST1/crsdgdb/datafile/test1.256.744125767";
  restore
  check readonly
  clone database
  ;
}
executing Memory Script
executing command: SET NEWNAME
renamed temporary file 1 to +DATA/crsdgdb/tempfile/temp.263.743634265 in control file
executing command: SET NEWNAME
executing command: SET NEWNAME
executing command: SET NEWNAME
executing command: SET NEWNAME
executing command: SET NEWNAME
executing command: SET NEWNAME
executing command: SET NEWNAME
Starting restore at 06-MAR-11
allocated channel: ORA_AUX_DISK_1
channel ORA_AUX_DISK_1: sid=152 instance=crsdgdb1 devtype=DISK
channel ORA_AUX_DISK_1: starting datafile backupset restore
channel ORA_AUX_DISK_1: specifying datafile(s) to restore from backup set
restoring datafile 00001 to +DATA/crsdgdb/datafile/system.256.743634151
restoring datafile 00002 to +DATA/crsdgdb/datafile/undotbs1.258.743634153
restoring datafile 00003 to +DATA/crsdgdb/datafile/sysaux.257.743634153
restoring datafile 00004 to +DATA/crsdgdb/datafile/users.259.743634153
restoring datafile 00005 to +DATA/crsdgdb/datafile/example.264.743634277
restoring datafile 00006 to +DATA/crsdgdb/datafile/undotbs2.265.743634431
restoring datafile 00007 to +TEST1/crsdgdb/datafile/test1.256.744125767
channel ORA_AUX_DISK_1: reading from backup piece /u01/app/oracle/stage/0bm6ffge_1_1
channel ORA_AUX_DISK_1: restored backup piece 1
piece handle=/u01/app/oracle/stage/0bm6ffge_1_1 tag=TAG20110305T152605
channel ORA_AUX_DISK_1: restore complete, elapsed time: 00:03:48
Finished restore at 06-MAR-11
contents of Memory Script:
{
  switch clone datafile all;
}
executing Memory Script
datafile 1 switched to datafile copy
input datafile copy recid=9 stamp=745056393 filename=+DATA/crsdgdb/datafile/
system.258.745056165
datafile 2 switched to datafile copy
input datafile copy recid=10 stamp=745056395 filename=+DATA/crsdgdb/datafile/
undotbs1.262.745056167
datafile 3 switched to datafile copy
input datafile copy recid=11 stamp=745056396 filename=+DATA/crsdgdb/datafile/
sysaux.259.745056165
datafile 4 switched to datafile copy
```

```
input datafile copy recid=12 stamp=745056397 filename=+DATA/crsdgdb/datafile/
users.264.745056169
datafile 5 switched to datafile copy
input datafile copy recid=13 stamp=745056397 filename=+DATA/crsdgdb/datafile/
example.260.745056167
datafile 6 switched to datafile copy
input datafile copy recid=14 stamp=745056399 filename=+DATA/crsdgdb/datafile/
undotbs2.263.745056169
datafile 7 switched to datafile copy
input datafile copy recid=15 stamp=745056399 filename=+DATA/crsdgdb/datafile/
test1.261.745056167
Finished Duplicate Db at 06-MAR-11
RMAN>
```

RAC STANDBY DATABASE CRSDBDB IS CREATED

- Add standby redo log files on both primary and secondary by the formula below.

```
SQL> SELECT thread#, group#, bytes
     FROM v$log
     ORDER BY 1, 2;
```

- Total # of standby files should be:

  (Maximum # of logfiles +1) * Maximum number of threads

  There are two online logfiles for each thread. Thus, the number of standby redo logs be
  (2+1)* 2 = 6 standby redo logs each on primary and secondary

- Add 3 Standby redo logfile on each thread on both Primary and Secondary Database.

  Execute sql below both on crs1 and crsdg1

```
SQL> ALTER SYSTEM SET standby_file_management = manual;
SQL> ALTER DATABASE ADD STANDBY LOGFILE THREAD 1 GROUP 5 SIZE 50M,
     GROUP 6 SIZE 50M, GROUP 7 SIZE 50M;
SQL> ALTER DATABASE ADD STANDBY LOGFILE THREAD 2 GROUP 8 SIZE 50M,
     GROUP 9 SIZE 50M, GROUP 10 SIZE 50M;
SQL> ALTER SYSTEM SET standby_file_management = auto;
```

  Two Standby log members are created for each group and each member is of 50m size. One member is created in the directory specifiled by init parameter db_create_file_dest and other by db_recovery_file_dest

- Use following select statements to get details of redo logs and standby logs

```
SQL> SELECT * FROM v$log;
SQL> SELECT * FROM v$standby_log;
SQL> SELECT * FROM v$logfile;
```

- You can add more standby log members by using following command

```
SQL> ALTER DATABASE ADD STANDBY LOGFILE MEMBER
     '+DATA/crsdb/onlinelog/stdredo04.log' REUSE TO GROUP 4;
```

- Immediately set Secondary database crsdgdb flashback on

```
SQL> ALTER DATABASE FLASHBACK ON;
```

- Start managed recovery and real-time apply on standby database.

```
SQL> ALTER DATABASE RECOVER MANAGED STANDBY DATABASE USING CURRENT
     LOGFILE DISCONNECT;
```

- Verify Data Guard Configuration

  Standby is now mounted and functional. Check alert log file to see if the standby database is receiving archive logs properly. Can also query V$ARCHIVED_LOG view to verify that redo logs are received. Execute following sql on crsdg1, crsdg2

```
SQL> SELECT db_unique_name,
            database_role,
            protection_mode,
            protection_level,
            open_mode
     FROM   v$database;

SQL> SELECT THREAD#,
            SEQUENCE#,
            FIRST_TIME,
            NEXT_TIME
     FROM   V$ARCHIVED_LOG
     ORDER BY SEQUENCE#;
```

  Archive current logfile on Primary and again execute above command on both Primary and secondary to check the sequence in v$archived_log are being applied on secondary;

```
SQL> ALTER SYSTEM ARCHIVE LOG CURRENT;

SQL> SELECT THREAD#,
            SEQUENCE#,
            FIRST_TIME,
            NEXT_TIME
     FROM   V$ARCHIVED_LOG
     ORDER BY SEQUENCE#;
```

- Register database crsdgdb to Cluster OCR

  - Register the standby database and the database instances with OCR using the SRVCTL utility.

    [oracle@crsdg1 dbs]$ srvctl add database -d crsdgdb -o /u01/app/oracle/product/10.2.0/db_1

    [oracle@crsdg1 dbs]$ srvctl add instance -d crsdgdb -i crsdgdb1 -n crsdg1

    [oracle@crsdg1 dbs]$ srvctl add instance -d crsdgdb -i crsdgdb2 -n crsdg2

  - If ASM instances are NOT part of OCR then also add those using commands below

    [oracle@crsdg1 ~]$ srvctl add asm -n crsdg1 -i +ASM1 -o /u01/app/oracle/product/10.2.0/asm_1 -p /u01/app/oracle/product/10.2.0/asm_1/dbs/init+ASM1.ora

    [oracle@crsdg1 ~]$ srvctl add asm -n crsdg2 -i +ASM2 -o /u01/app/oracle/product/10.2.0/asm_1 -p /u01/app/oracle/product/10.2.0/asm_1/dbs/init+ASM2.ora

  - Establish dependencies between ASM instance and Database instance

    [oracle@crsdg1 ~]$ srvctl modify instance -d crsdgdb -i crsdgdb1 -s +ASM1

    [oracle@crsdg1 ~]$ srvctl modify instance -d crsdgdb -i crsdgdb2 -s +ASM2

    [oracle@crsdg1 ~]$ srvctl enable asm -n crsdg1 -i +ASM1

    [oracle@crsdg1 ~]$ srvctl enable asm -n crsdg2 -i +ASM2

9.15 Install agent on RAC using agent deploy

- Start oem server, listener, oemdb database oem agent and oms server to start Oracle Enterprise Manager Grid Control
- On Data Guard nodes check jdk is installed or not (jdk was installed in Chapter 1).

  [oracle@crsdg1 ~]$ which java
  /usr/bin/java
- Logon to oms machine where Oracle's OEM Grid software is installed and secure copy agentDownload.linux to target machine parent directory where agent has to be deployed

  <OMS_HOME>/oms10g/sysman/agent_download/10.2.0.1.0/linux

  [oracle@oms linux]$ scp agentDownload.linux crsdg1:/u01/app/oracle/product/10.2.0/

  The authenticity of host 'crsdg1 (192.168.2.141)' can't be established.
  RSA key fingerprint is f4:ac:d2:7e:05:e8:4e:47:a9:6f:80:99:46:f9:f7:58.
  Are you sure you want to continue connecting (yes/no)? yes
  Warning: Permanently added 'crsdg1,192.168.2.141' (RSA) to the list of known hosts.
  oracle@crsdg1's password:
  agentDownload.linux 100% 22KB 22.3KB/s 00:00
- On node crsdg1, execute agent_profile

  [oracle@crsdg1 10.2.0]$. /home/oracle/agent_profile

  [oracle@crsdg1 10.2.0]$ echo $ORACLE_HOME
  /u01/app/oracle/product/10.2.0/agent10g
- Change directory to parent directory of <AGENT_HOME>

  [oracle@crsdg1 ~]$ cd /u01/app/oracle/product/10.2.0

  [oracle@crsdg1 10.2.0]$ ls –ltr
- Change agentDownload.linux file permission

  [oracle@crsdg1 10.2.0]$ chmod 755 agentDownload.linux
- Install Oracle Agent

  [oracle@crsdg1 10.2.0]$./agentDownload.linux -b /u01/app/oracle/product/10.2.0 -m oms.prusolutions.com -r 4889 -c "crsdg1, crsdg2" -n crs
- Execute Configuration Scripts using root user on both crsdg1 and crsdg2

  [root@crsdg1 oracle]# /u01/app/oracle/product/10.2.0/agent10g/root.sh

  [root@crsdg2 oracle]# /u01/app/oracle/product/10.2.0/agent10g/root.sh
- Return back to crsdg1 agent install window to check status of agent install
- Once agent is installed, secure agent and upload agent to Oracle's OEM Grid.

  Here $ORACLE_HOME is <AGENT_HOME> password for secure oms was set in chapter 3 "**oracle123**"

  [oracle@crsdg1 10.2.0]$. /home/oracle/agent_profile

  [oracle@crsdg1 10.2.0]$ echo $ORACLE_HOME
  /u01/app/oracle/product/10.2.0/agent10g

  [oracle@crsdg2 ~]$. /home/oracle/agent_profile

  [oracle@crsdg2 ~]$ echo $ORACLE_HOME
  /u01/app/oracle/product/10.2.0/agent10g
- Perform following steps on both crsdg1 and crsdg2

  $ORACLE_HOME/bin/emctl stop agent

  $ORACLE_HOME/bin/emctl secure agent

```
$ORACLE_HOME/bin/emctl clearstate agent
$ORACLE_HOME/bin/emctl start agent
$ORACLE_HOME/bin/emctl upload
```

- Configure and View crsdgdb Database in OEM Grid Control
  - On Targets Tab, Hosts Page Click crsdg1 and crsdg2 to configure Database ASM

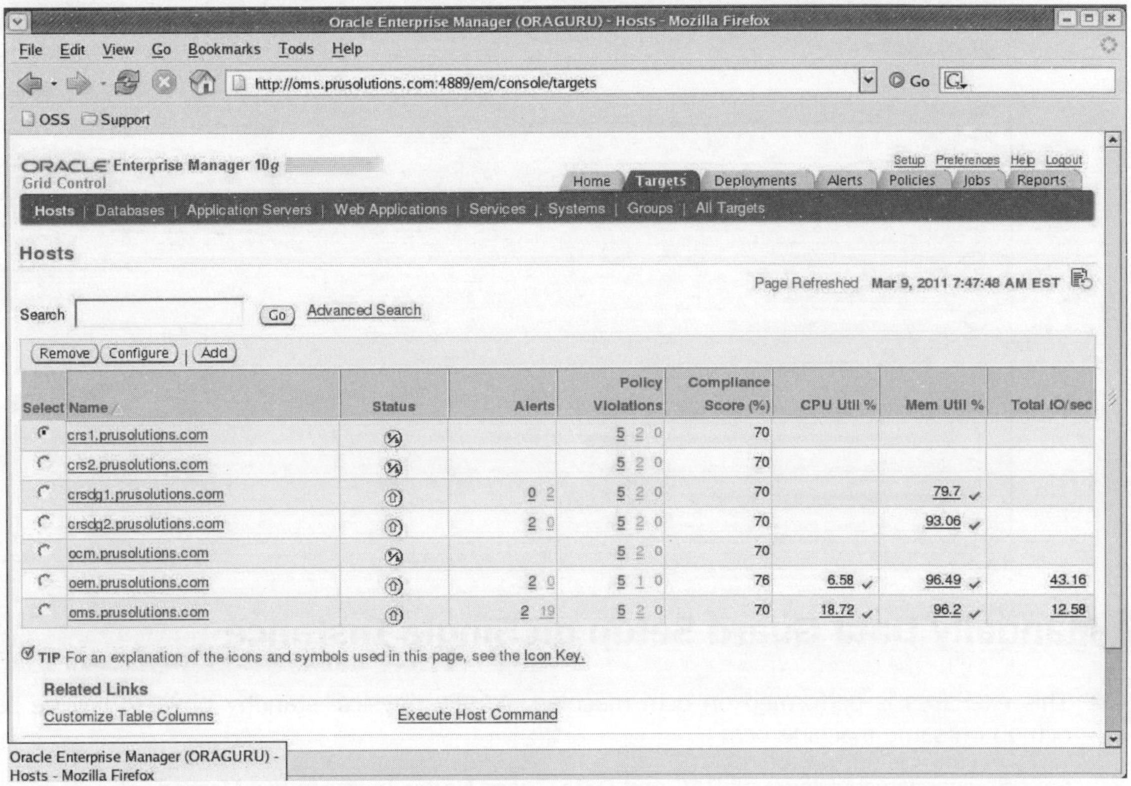

- Configure ASM for crsdg1 and crsdg2

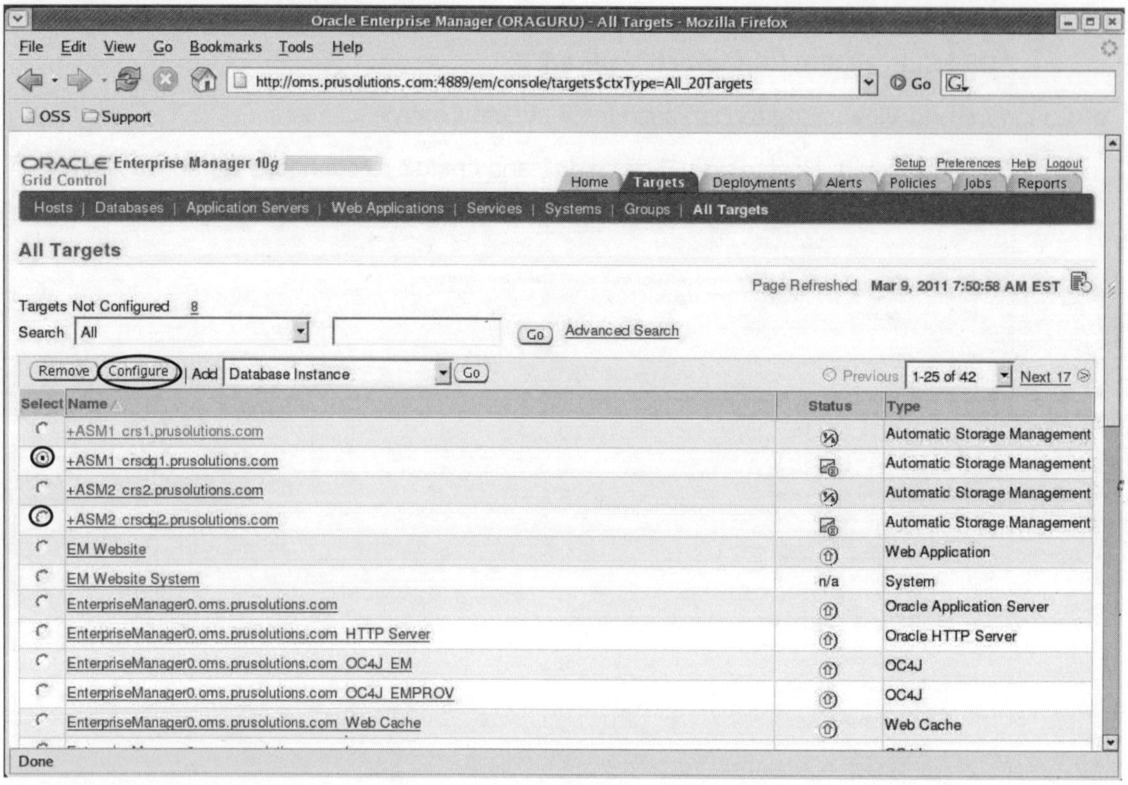

9.16 Manually Data Guard Setup on Single Instance

- This exercises is performed on ocm machine. A new physical standby phyocm will be setup for primary ocmdb on same machine ocm

  For this exercise shutdown all RAC and Data Guard Nodes increase the Memory of ocm machine to 3 GB and start ocm machine

- Make database in Force Logging Mode

  SQL> ALTER DATABASE FORCE LOGGING;

- Make following Directories for Dataguard Setup

```
[oracle@ocm ~]$ mkdir -p $ORACLE_HOME
[oracle@ocm ~]$ mkdir -p $ORACLE_BASE/admin
[oracle@ocm ~]$ mkdir -p $ORACLE_BASE/oradata/disk1/phyocm
[oracle@ocm ~]$ mkdir -p $ORACLE_BASE/oradata/disk2/phyocm
[oracle@ocm ~]$ mkdir -p $ORACLE_BASE/oradata/disk3/phyocm
[oracle@ocm ~]$ mkdir -p $ORACLE_BASE/oradata/disk4/phyocm
[oracle@ocm ~]$ mkdir -p $ORACLE_BASE/oradata/disk5/phyocm
[oracle@ocm ~]$ mkdir -p $ORACLE_BASE/admin/phyocm/control
[oracle@ocm ~]$ mkdir -p $ORACLE_BASE/admin/phyocm/cdump
[oracle@ocm ~]$ mkdir -p $ORACLE_BASE/admin/phyocm/bdump
[oracle@ocm ~]$ mkdir -p $ORACLE_BASE/admin/phyocm/udump
[oracle@ocm ~]$ mkdir -p $ORACLE_BASE/admin/phyocm/adump
```

[oracle@ocm ~]$ mkdir -p $ORACLE_BASE/admin/phyocm/scripts

[oracle@ocm ~]$ mkdir -p $ORACLE_BASE/flash_recovery_area

- Dataguard parameter changes for ocmdb database

  - Create pfile from spfile

    Never create pfile backup having instance name like initocmdb.ora as it contains location of spfile, which will be overwritten

    SQL> CREATE PFILE='/u01/app/oracle/product/10.2.0/db_1/dbs/initocmdb.ora.bck1' FROM SPFILE;

    File created.

  - Set database db_unique_name= ocmdb

    SQL> ALTER SYSTEM SET db_unique_name='ocmdb' SCOPE=SPFILE;

    System altered.

  - Setting dg_config= (ocmdb, phyocm)

    SQL> ALTER SYSTEM SET log_archive_config='dg_config=(ocmdb,phyocm) ' SCOPE=SPFILE;

    System altered.

  - Setting location for log_archive_dest_1 for primary database

    SQL> ALTER SYSTEM SET log_archive_dest_1='location=use_db_recovery_file_dest valid_for=(online_logfiles,all_roles) db_unique_name=ocmdb' SCOPE=SPFILE;

    System altered.

  - Setting location for log_archive_dest_2 for Secondary database

    SQL> ALTER SYSTEM SET log_archive_dest_2='service=phyocm lgwr async valid_for=(online_logfiles,primary_role) db_unique_name=phyocm' SCOPE=SPFILE;

    System altered.

  - Setting location for log_archive_dest_3 for Standby Role

    SQL> ALTER SYSTEM SET log_archive_dest_3='LOCATION=use_db_recovery_file_dest VALID_FOR=(STANDBY_LOGFILES,STANDBY_ROLE) DB_UNIQUE_NAME=ocmdb' SCOPE=SPFILE;

    System altered.

  - Enabling the log_archive_dest_state

    SQL> ALTER SYSTEM SET log_archive_dest_state_1 = enable SCOPE= SPFILE;

    System altered.

    SQL> ALTER SYSTEM SET log_archive_dest_state_2 = defer SCOPE=SPFILE;

    System altered.

    SQL> ALTER SYSTEM SET log_archive_dest_state_3 = enable SCOPE=SPFILE;

    System altered.

  - Setting remote_loging_passwordfile=exclusive

    SQL> ALTER SYSTEM SET remote_login_passwordfile=exclusive SCOPE=SPFILE;

    System altered.

  - Setting fal_server as Secondary database for Primary database

    SQL> ALTER SYSTEM SET fal_server = 'phyocm' SCOPE=SPFILE;

    System altered.

- Setting fal_client for Primary database

  SQL> ALTER SYSTEM SET fal_client = 'ocmdb' SCOPE= SPFILE;

  System altered.

- Setting log_file_name_convert ='phyocm','ocmdb'

  This means after switch over secondary (phyocm) when redo will be transported from new primary (phyocm) to new secondary (ocmdb) the log file name will be converted from phyocm to ocmdb. Same changes will apply to db_file_name_convert.

  SQL> ALTER SYSTEM SET log_file_name_convert = 'phyocm','ocmdb' SCOPE=SPFILE;

  System altered.

  SQL> ALTER SYSTEM SET db_file_name_convert = 'phyocm','ocmdb' SCOPE=SPFILE;

  System altered.

- Setting standby_file_management to auto

  SQL> ALTER SYSTEM SET standby_file_management = auto;

  System altered.

- Setting standby_archive_dest location

  SQL> ALTER SYSTEM SET standby_archive_dest ='location=use_db_recovery_file_dest' SCOPE=SPFILE;

  System altered.

- Again, create pfile backup2 from spfile;

  SQL> CREATE PFILE='/u01/app/oracle/product/10.2.0/db_1/dbs/initocmdb.ora.bck2' FROM SPFILE;

- Shutdown database and restart to make sure there are no errors in parameters. If there, is any problem in startup database then shut down the database immediately change the parameter, which has problem in latest pfile backup, and again restart the database.

  SQL> SHUTDOWN immediate;

  SQL> STARTUP;

OR

- Modify init.ora Parameters for Primary in initocmdb.ora

  *.db_unique_name= ocmdb

  *.log_archive_config='dg_config=(ocmdb,phyocm)'

  *.log_archive_dest_1='location=USE_DB_RECOVERY_FILE_DEST valid_for=(online_logfiles,all_roles) db_unique_name=ocmdb'

  *.log_archive_dest_2='service=phyocm lgwr async valid_for=(online_logfiles,primary_role) db_unique_name=phyocm'

  *.log_archive_dest_3='LOCATION=use_db_recovery_file_dest VALID_FOR=(STANDBY_LOGFILES,STANDBY_ROLE) DB_UNIQUE_NAME=ocmdb'

  *. log_archive_dest_state_1 = enable

  *. log_archive_dest_state_2 = defer

  *. log_archive_dest_state_2 = enable

  *. remote_login_passwordfile=exclusive

  *.fal_client='ocmdb'

  *.fal_server='phyocm'

  *.db_file_name_convert='phyocm','ocmdb'

*.log_file_name_convert='phyocm','ocmdb'

*.standby_file_management='AUTO'

- Copy initocmdb.ora.bck2 to initphyocm.ora and modify parameters below

  [oracle@ocm dbs]$ cp initocmdb.ora.bck2 initphyocm.ora

- Modification of]init.ora Parameters for Secondary database phyocm

  *.db_file_name_convert = 'ocmdb','phyocm'

  *.db_unique_name = 'phyocm'

  *.log_archive_config = 'dg_config(ocmdb,phyocm)'

  *.log_archive_dest_1 = 'location=use_db_recovery_file_dest valid_for=(online_logfiles,all_roles) db_unique_name=phyocm'

  *.log_archive_dest_2 = 'service=ocmdb lgwr async valid_for=(online_logfiles,primary_role) db_unique_name=ocmdb'

  *.log_archive_dest_3='LOCATION=use_db_recovery_file_dest VALID_FOR=(STANDBY_LOGFILES,STANDBY_ROLE) DB_UNIQUE_NAME=phyocm'

  *.remote_login_passwordfile=exclusive

  *.log_archive_dest_state_1 = enable

  *.log_archive_dest_state_2 = enable

  *.fal_server = 'ocmdb'

  *.fal_client = 'phyocm'

  *.db_file_name_convert = 'ocmdb','phyocm'

  *.log_file_name_convert = 'ocmdb','phyocm'

  *.standby_file_management = auto

  *. standby_archive_dest ='location=use_db_recovery_file_dest'

  *.local_listener='LISTENER_PHYOCM'

Modify other parameters for Secondary like ..dump_dest for Dataguard

  *.audit_file_dest='/u01/app/oracle/admin/phyocm/adump'

  *.background_dump_dest='/u01/app/oracle/admin/phyocm/bdump'

  *.core_dump_dest='/u01/app/oracle/admin/phyocm/cdump'

  *.user_dump_dest='/u01/app/oracle/admin/phyocm/udump'

- Add following lines to listener.ora files for Dataguard listener on non-default port

```
LISTENER_PHYOCM =
    (DESCRIPTION_LIST =
    (DESCRIPTION =
        (ADDRESS = (PROTOCOL = TCP)(HOST = ocm.prusolutions.com)(PORT = 2012))
        )
    )

SID_LIST_LISTENER_PHYOCM =
    (SID_LIST =
    (SID_DESC =
        (GLOBAL_DBNAME = phyocm)
        (ORACLE_HOME = /u01/app/oracle/product/10.2.0/db_1)
        (SID_NAME = phyocm)
        )
    )
```

- Add following lines to tnsnames.ora for PHYOCM database

```
LISTENER_PHYOCM =
    (DESCRIPTION_LIST =
    (DESCRIPTION =
        (ADDRESS = (PROTOCOL = TCP)(HOST = ocm.prusolutions.com)(PORT = 2012))
        )
    )

PHYOCM =
    (DESCRIPTION =
    (ADDRESS_LIST =
        (ADDRESS = (PROTOCOL = TCP)(HOST = ocm.prusolutions.com)(PORT = 1521))
        )
        (CONNECT_DATA =
        (SERVICE_NAME = phyocm)
        )
    )
PHYOCM_TEST =
    (DESCRIPTION =
    (ADDRESS_LIST =
        (ADDRESS = (PROTOCOL = TCP)(HOST = ocm.prusolutions.com)(PORT = 2012))
        )
        (CONNECT_DATA =
        (SERVICE_NAME = phyocm)
        )
    )
```

- Also, modify SID_LIST_LISTENER in listener.ora .Add SID_DESC mentioned below in BOLD for phyocm database

```
SID_LIST_LISTENER =
    (SID_LIST =
   (SID_DESC =
        (GLOBAL_DBNAME = phyocm)
        (ORACLE_HOME = /u01/app/oracle/product/10.2.0/db_1)
        (SID_NAME = phyocm)
        )
        (SID_DESC =
            (GLOBAL_DBNAME = ocmdb)
            (ORACLE_HOME = /u01/app/oracle/product/10.2.0/db_1)
            (SID_NAME = ocmdb)
        )
        (SID_DESC =
            (SID_NAME = plsextproc)
            (ORACLE_HOME = /u01/app/oracle/product/10.2.0/db_1)
            (PROGRAM = extproc)
            )
        )
```

- Reload listener changes and tnsping secondary database.

[oracle@ocm admin]$ lsnrctl reload listener

[oracle@ocm admin]$ tnsping PHYOCM

[oracle@ocm admin]$ tnsping PHYOCM_TEST

- Create password file for phyocm database having same sys password as on ocmdb database.

[oracle@ocm dbs]$ orapwd password=oracle file=orapwphyocm entries=5

- Make staging directory and take backup of ocmdb database

[oracle@ocm ~]$ mkdir -p /u01/app/oracle/stage

[oracle@ocm stage]$ rman target

RMAN> backup device type disk format '/u01/app/oracle/stage/%U' database plus archivelog;

RMAN> backup device type disk format '/u01/app/oracle/stage/%U' current controlfile for standby;

- Create spfile from pfile for dataguard database phyocm

SQL> CREATE SPFILE='/u01/app/oracle/product/10.2.0/db_1/dbs/spfilephyocm.ora' FROM PFILE='/u01/app/oracle/product/10.2.0/db_1/dbs/initphyocm.ora';

- Set ORACLE_SID=phyocm and start phyocm database in nomout state

[oracle@ocm stage]$ export ORACLE_SID=phyocm

[oracle@ocm stage]$ echo $ORACLE_SID

[oracle@ocm stage]$ sqlplus / as sysdba

SQL> STARTUP nomount;

[oracle@ocm stage]$ rman target sys/oracle@ocmdb auxiliary /

RMAN> duplicate target database for standby;

Finished Duplicate Db a ..

Here standby database created

- Create standby redo log files on both primary and secondary by the formula below.

[oracle@ocm ~]$ echo $ORACLE_SID
phyocm

SQL> SELECT thread#, group#
FROM v$log
ORDER BY 1, 2;

Total # of standby files is:

(Maximum # of logfiles +1)* Maximum number of threads

(3 +1)*1 = 4 standby redo logs each on primary and secondary

SQL> ALTER SYSTEM SET standby_file_management = manual;

SQL> ALTER DATABASE ADD STANDBY LOGFILE THREAD 1 GROUP 4 SIZE 50M, GROUP 5 SIZE 50M, GROUP 6 SIZE 50M, GROUP 7 SIZE 50M;

SQL> ALTER SYSTEM SET standby_file_management = auto;

Open a New terminal, connect to ocmdb database, and create standby redo logfiles

SQL> ALTER SYSTEM SET standby_file_management = manual;

SQL> ALTER DATABASE ADD STANDBY LOGFILE THREAD 1 GROUP 4 SIZE 50M, GROUP 5 SIZE 50M, GROUP 6 SIZE 50M, GROUP 7 SIZE 50M;

SQL> ALTER SYSTEM SET standby_file_management =auto;

SQL> SELECT group#, MEMBER FROM v$logfile;

SQL> SELECT * FROM v$log;

SQL> SELECT * FROM v$standby_log;

- If required you can create additional members for standby redo logfiles on ocmdb and phyocm

  ALTER DATABASE ADD STANDBY LOGFILE MEMBER '/u01/app/oracle/oradata/disk1/ocmdb/stdredo04.log' REUSE TO GROUP 4;

  ALTER DATABASE ADD STANDBY LOGFILE MEMBER '/u01/app/oracle/oradata/disk1/ocmdb/stdredo05.log' REUSE TO GROUP 5;

  ALTER DATABASE ADD STANDBY LOGFILE MEMBER '/u01/app/oracle/oradata/disk1/ocmdb/stdredo06.log' REUSE TO GROUP 6;

  ALTER DATABASE ADD STANDBY LOGFILE MEMBER '/u01/app/oracle/oradata/disk1/ocmdb/stdredo07.log' REUSE TO GROUP 7;

  ALTER DATABASE ADD STANDBY LOGFILE MEMBER '/u01/app/oracle/oradata/disk1/phyocm/stdredo04.log' REUSE TO GROUP 4;

  ALTER DATABASE ADD STANDBY LOGFILE MEMBER '/u01/app/oracle/oradata/disk1/phyocm/stdredo05.log' REUSE TO GROUP 5;

  ALTER DATABASE ADD STANDBY LOGFILE MEMBER '/u01/app/oracle/oradata/disk1/phyocm/stdredo06.log' REUSE TO GROUP 6;

  ALTER DATABASE ADD STANDBY LOGFILE MEMBER '/u01/app/oracle/oradata/disk1/phyocm/stdredo07.log' REUSE TO GROUP 7;

- Flashback on phyocm database.

  Turn Flashback ON before start of managed recovery and real-time apply on standby database

  SQL> ALTER DATABASE FLASHBACK ON;

- Enable log_archive_dest_state_2 both on primary and secondary database;

  SQL> ALTER SYSTEM SET log_archive_dest_state_2=enable;

- Start managed recovery and real-time apply on standby database

  If you forget to turn on flashback on and started managed recovery and real-time apply on standby database then to turn it on as mentioned in next section.

  SQL> SELECT db_unique_name FROM v$database;

  DB_UNIQUE_NAME

  ---

  phyocm

  SQL> ALTER DATABASE RECOVER MANAGED STANDBY DATABASE USING CURRENT LOGFILE DISCONNECT;

  Database altered.

- Verify Data guard Configuration

  - Standby is now mounted and functional. Check alert log file to see if the standby database is receiving archive logs properly. Can also query V$ARCHIVED_LOG view to verify that redo logs are received.

    SQL> SELECT SEQUENCE#, FIRST_TIME, NEXT_TIME
    FROM V$ARCHIVED_LOG
    ORDER BY SEQUENCE#;

  - Archive the current log on the primary database using following statement.

    SQL> ALTER SYSTEM ARCHIVE LOG CURRENT;

  - Again, check on standby database if the archivelog is received

    SQL> SELECT SEQUENCE#, FIRST_TIME, NEXT_TIME
    FROM V$ARCHIVED_LOG
    ORDER BY SEQUENCE#;

If archivelog(s) are received, means standby has been created successfully.

- To check if the archive logs are successfully applied on standby, use the below query

SQL> SELECT MAX (al.sequence#) "Last Seq Received",
MAX (lh.sequence#) "Last Seq Applied"
FROM v$archived_log al, v$log_history lh;

9.17 Turn Flashback on after start of managed recovery

- To make Database flashback on Standby, use following command.

  - Issue the following query to find out if the standby database is performing Redo Apply or. real-time apply. If the MRP0 or MRP process exists, then the standby database is applying redo.

    SQL> SELECT PROCESS, STATUS FROM V$MANAGED_STANDBY;

    - If log apply services are running, cancel them as shown in the following command

    SQL> ALTER DATABASE RECOVER MANAGED STANDBY DATABASE CANCEL;

    SQL> ALTER DATABASE FLASHBACK ON;

    - Restart Redo Apply or real-time apply. To start Redo Apply, issue the following statement:

    SQL> ALTER DATABASE RECOVER MANAGED STANDBY DATABASE DISCONNECT FROM SESSION;

    OR

    SQL> ALTER DATABASE RECOVER MANAGED STANDBY DATABASE THROUGH ALL SWITCHOVER DISCONNECT NODELAY;

    OR

    SQL> ALTER DATABASE RECOVER MANAGED STANDBY DATABASE FINISH FORCE;

    - To test the archived logs are being applied of not on standby.

    SQL> SELECT SEQUENCE#, FIRST_TIME, NEXT_TIME FROM V$ARCHIVED_LOG ORDERBY SEQUENCE#;

    SQL> SELECT RECOVERY_MODE FROM V$ARCHIVE_DEST_STATUS;

    SQL> ALTER SYSTEM ARCHIVE LOG CURRENT;

    SQL> ALTER SYSTEM ARCHIVE LOG CURRENT;

    SQL> SELECT SEQUENCE#, FIRST_TIME, NEXT_TIME FROM V$ARCHIVED_LOG ORDER BY SEQUENCE#;

  - You will notice the sequence# is advanced in both primary and standby.
  - If DGMGRL was already configured there will warning which can be fixed by enabling and disabling configuration

    Warning: ORA-16826: apply service state is inconsistent with the DelayMins property

    DGMGRL> Disable Configuration

    DGMGRL> Enable Configuration

9.18 Managing Data Guard using DGMGRL

- Make dg_broker_start= TRUE on both primary (ocmdb) and secondary (phyocm) databases.

  SQL> SHOW PARAMETER dg

  SQL> ALTER SYSTEM SET dg_broker_start=TRUE SCOPE=BOTH;

- Configure listener.ora for DGMGRL

  These '<db_unique_name>_DGMGRL' entries in the listener.ora files on each system are required for Broker operations invoked using DGMGRL that require connecting remotely to a database to function normally. Without them, the Broker cannot connect to the target database when it is down, as is the case in a switchover or failover or any other operation that requires a restart of a database.

  As non-default port, local listener is used for ocmdb and phyocm. Add SID_DESC for DGMGRL for both Primary and Secondary on non-default port listener SID_LIST as mentioned in **BOLD**

```
SID_LIST_LISTENER_OCM =
    (SID_LIST =
    (SID_DESC =
        (GLOBAL_DBNAME = ocmdb)
        (ORACLE_HOME = /u01/app/oracle/product/10.2.0/db_1)
        (SID_NAME = ocmdb)
        )
    (SID_DESC =
        (GLOBAL_DBNAME = ocmdb_DGMGRL)
        (ORACLE_HOME = /u01/app/oracle/product/10.2.0/db_1)
        (SID_NAME = ocmdb)
        )
    )

SID_LIST_LISTENER_PHYOCM =
    (SID_LIST =
    (SID_DESC =
        (GLOBAL_DBNAME = phyocm)
        (ORACLE_HOME = /u01/app/oracle/product/10.2.0/db_1)
        (SID_NAME = phyocm)
        )
    (SID_DESC =
        (GLOBAL_DBNAME = phyocm_DGMGRL)
        (ORACLE_HOME = /u01/app/oracle/product/10.2.0/db_1)
        (SID_NAME = phyocm)
        )
    )
```

- Run "netmgr" and verify that the Oracle Net pre-requisites for using the DGMGRL command line interface have been satisfied.

- LISTENER_OCM

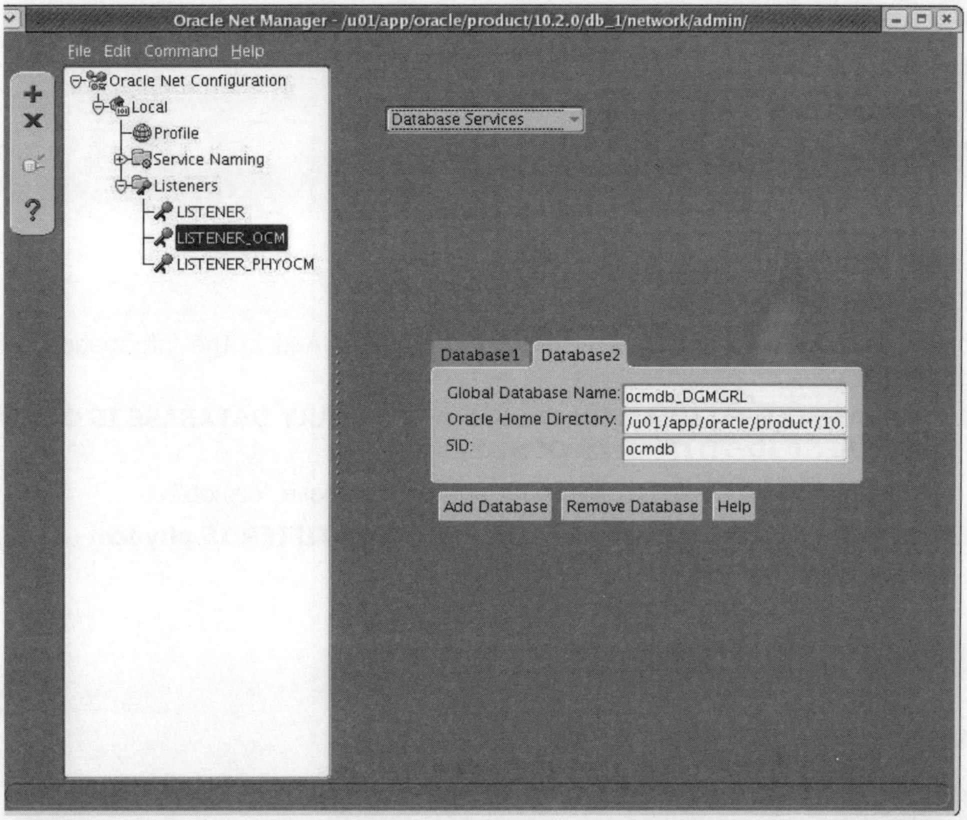

- LISTENER_PHYOCM

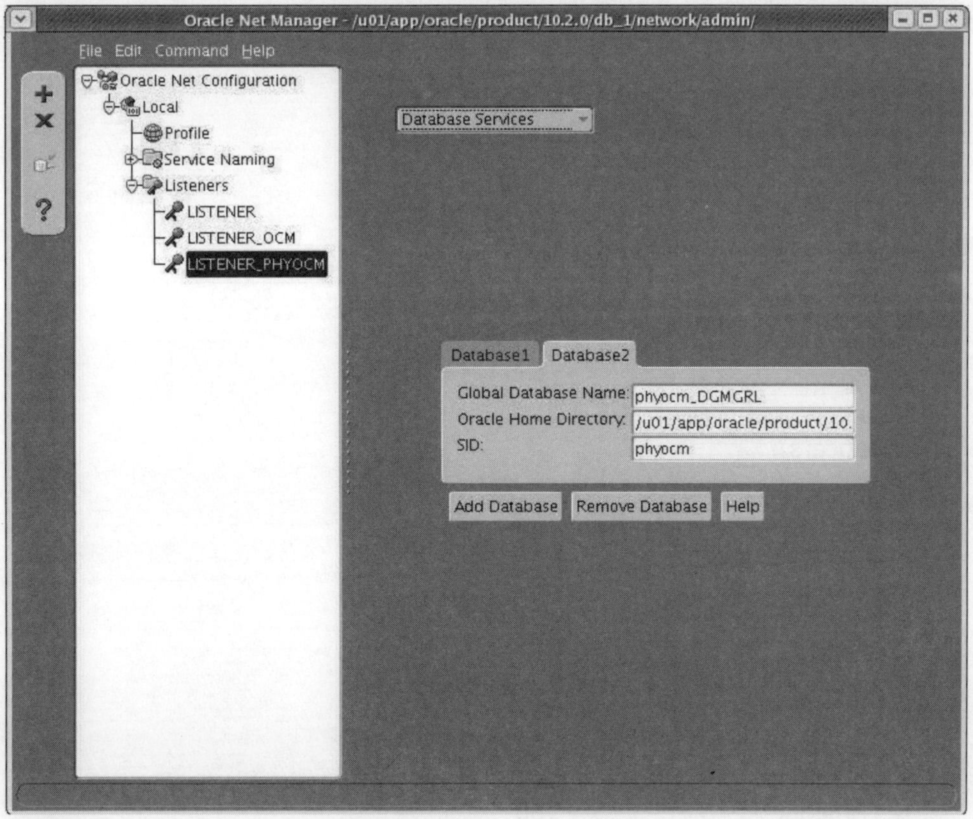

- Commands to get dgmgrl help

```
DGMGRL>help edit
DGMGRL>help remove
DGMGRL> help enable
DGMGRL> help start
```

- DGMGRL Create Configuration

```
[oracle@ocm ~]$ dgmgrl
DGMGRL> connect sys@ocmdb
```

Create configuration with "ocmdb" as the Primary database. Add in the information about the physical standby database

```
DGMGRL> CREATE CONFIGURATION OCMDB AS PRIMARY DATABASE IS OCMDB
        CONNECT IDENTIFIER IS OCMDB;
        Configuration "ocmdb" created with primary database "ocmdb"
DGMGRL> ADD DATABASE phyocm AS CONNECT IDENTIFIER IS phyocm
        MAINTAINED AS PHYSICAL;
        Database "phyocm" added
DGMGRL> enable configuration;
        Enabled.
DGMGRL> show configuration;
        Configuration
        Name:            ocmdb
        Enabled:         YES
        Protection Mode:    MaxPerformance
        Fast-Start Failover: DISABLED
        Databases:
        ocmdb  - Primary database
        phyocm - Physical standby database

        Current status for "ocmdb":
        SUCCESS
DGMGRL> show database verbose ocmdb;
        Database
        Name:          ocmdb
        Role:         PRIMARY
        Enabled:       YES
        Intended State:  ONLINE
        Instance(s):
        ocmdb

        Properties:
        InitialConnectIdentifier        = 'ocmdb'
        LogXptMode                      = 'ASYNC'
        Dependency                      = ''
        DelayMins                       = '0'
        Binding                         = 'OPTIONAL'
        MaxFailure                      = '0'
        MaxConnections                  = '1'
        ReopenSecs                      = '300'
        NetTimeout                      = '180'
```

```
LogShipping                     = 'ON'
PreferredApplyInstance          = ''
ApplyInstanceTimeout            = '0'
ApplyParallel                   = 'AUTO'
StandbyFileManagement           = 'AUTO'
ArchiveLagTarget                = '0'
LogArchiveMaxProcesses          = '2'
LogArchiveMinSucceedDest        = '1'
DbFileNameConvert               = ''
LogFileNameConvert              = 'phyocm, ocmdb'
FastStartFailoverTarget         = ''
StatusReport                    = '(monitor)'
InconsistentProperties          = '(monitor)'
InconsistentLogXptProps         = '(monitor)'
SendQEntries                    = '(monitor)'
LogXptStatus                    = '(monitor)'
RecvQEntries                    = '(monitor)'
HostName                        = 'ocm.prusolutions.com'
SidName                         = 'ocmdb'
LocalListenerAddress    = '(ADDRESS=(PROTOCOL=TCP)(HOST= ocm.prusolutions.com)
        (PORT=2010))'
StandbyArchiveLocation          = 'location=use_db_recovery_file_dest'
AlternateLocation               = ''
LogArchiveTrace                 = '0'
LogArchiveFormat                = '%t_%s_%r.dbf'
LatestLog                       = '(monitor)'
TopWaitEvents                   = '(monitor)'

Current status for "ocmdb":
SUCCESS
```

- Managing Databases using DGMGRL

  You can view and change database properties using dgmgrl

  DGMGRL> show database ocmdb logxptmode;
  LogXptMode = 'ASYNC'

  DGMGRL> show database ocmdb nettimeout;
  NetTimeout = '180'

  DGMGRL> show database phyocm logxptmode;
  LogXptMode = 'ASYNC'

  DGMGRL> show database phyocm nettimeout;
  NetTimeout = '180'

- Using sqlplus connect to primary database and change value of log_archive_max_processes parameter

  SQL> SHOW PARAMETER log_archive_max_processes;

  The current value is two, increase it to five and again check database configuration from dgmgrl

  SQL> ALTER SYSTEM SET LOG_ARCHIVE_MAX_PROCESSES=5 SCOPE=MEMORY;

- Use show configuration command to get Dataguard status

  DGMGRL> show configuration;

  ```
  Configuration
  Name:            ocmdb
  Enabled:         YES
  ```

```
Protection Mode:     MaxPerformance
Fast-Start Failover: DISABLED
Databases:
        ocmdb - Primary database
        phyocm - Physical standby database

Current status for "ocmdb":
Warning: ORA-16608: one or more databases have warnings
```

- Use show database verbose ocmdb to get ocmdb database details

```
DGMGRL> show database verbose ocmdb ;
Database
Name:            ocmdb
Role:            PRIMARY
Enabled:         YES
Intended State:  ONLINE
Instance(s):
ocmdb
Properties:
InitialConnectIdentifier        = 'ocmdb'
LogXptMode                      = 'ASYNC'
Dependency                      = ''
DelayMins                       = '0'
Binding                         = 'OPTIONAL'
MaxFailure                      = '0'
MaxConnections                  = '1'
ReopenSecs                      = '300'
NetTimeout                      = '180'
LogShipping                     = 'ON'
PreferredApplyInstance          = ''
ApplyInstanceTimeout            = '0'
ApplyParallel                   = 'AUTO'
StandbyFileManagement           = 'AUTO'
ArchiveLagTarget                = '0'
LogArchiveMaxProcesses          = '2'
LogArchiveMinSucceedDest        = '1'
DbFileNameConvert               = ''
LogFileNameConvert              = 'phyocm, ocmdb'
FastStartFailoverTarget         = ''
StatusReport                    = '(monitor)'
InconsistentProperties          = '(monitor)'
InconsistentLogXptProps         = '(monitor)'
SendQEntries                    = '(monitor)'
LogXptStatus                    = '(monitor)'
RecvQEntries                    = '(monitor)'
HostName                        = 'ocm.prusolutions.com'
SidName                         = 'ocmdb'
LocalListenerAddress            = '(ADDRESS=(PROTOCOL=TCP)(HOST=ocm.prusolutions.com)
                                  (PORT=2010))'
StandbyArchiveLocation          = 'location=use_db_recovery_file_dest'
AlternateLocation               = ''
LogArchiveTrace                 = '0'
LogArchiveFormat                = '%t_%s_%r.dbf'
LatestLog                       = '(monitor)'
TopWaitEvents                   = '(monitor)'
```

Current status for "ocmdb":
Warning: ORA-16792: configuration property value is inconsistent with database setting

- Get database inconsistent properties and fix the problem

DGMGRL> show database ocmdb inconsistent properties;

```
INCONSISTENT PROPERTIES
 INSTANCE_NAME   PROPERTY_NAME          MEMORY_VALUE   SPFILE_VALUE  BROKER_VALUE
        ocmdb    LogArchiveMaxProcesses            5              2             2
```

SQL> ALTER SYSTEM SET LOG_ARCHIVE_MAX_PROCESSES=2 SCOPE=MEMORY;

DGMGRL> show database ocmdb inconsistent properties;

```
INCONSISTENT PROPERTIES
INSTANCE_NAME  PROPERTY_NAME   MEMORY_VALUE   SPFILE_VALUE   BROKER_VALUE
```

DGMGRL> show configuration;

```
Configuration
Name:             ocmdb
Enabled:          YES
Protection Mode:     MaxPerformance
Fast-Start Failover: DISABLED
Databases:
       ocmdb  - Primary database
       phyocm - Physical standby database

Current status for "ocmdb":
SUCCESS
```

Open new terminals connect to ocmdb and phyocm using sqlplus and execute following sql

```
SQL> SELECT db_unique_name,
            database_role,
            protection_mode,
            protection_level
       FROM v$database;
```

- Edit Database property using DG Broker

DGMGRL> edit database ocmdb set property LogArchiveMaxProcesses=10;
Property "logarchivemaxprocesses" updated

DGMGRL> edit database ocmdb set property LogArchiveMaxProcesses=10;
Property "logarchivemaxprocesses" updated

- Change configuration set Protection Mode to MaxAvailability from MaxPerformance

When you try to change set Protection Mode to MaxAvailability, it will give error, as Standby database phyocm property logxptmode is 'ASYNC'

DGMGRL> edit configuration set protection mode as maxavailability;
Error: ORA-16627: operation disallowed since no standby databases would remain to support protection mode
Failed.

Check database property logxptmode

DGMGRL> show database ocmdb logxptmode;
LogXptMode = 'ASYNC'

DGMGRL> show database phyocm logxptmode;
LogXptMode = 'ASYNC'

Change LogXptMode to SYNC of Physical Standby database **PHYOCM ONLY** and then change the protection mode

```
DGMGRL> edit database phyocm set property logxptmode='SYNC';
        Property "logxptmode" updated
DGMGRL> show database phyocm logxptmode;
        LogXptMode = 'SYNC'
DGMGRL> edit configuration set protection mode as maxavailability;
        Operation requires shutdown of instance "ocmdb" on database "ocmdb"
        Shutting down instance "ocmdb"...
        Database closed.
        Database dismounted.
        ORACLE instance shut down.
        Operation requires startup of instance "ocmdb" on database "ocmdb"
        Starting instance "ocmdb"...
        ORACLE instance started.
        Database mounted.
```

Now change the property LogXptMode of ocmdb database to 'SYNC'

```
DGMGRL> edit database ocmdb set property logxptmode='SYNC';
        Property "logxptmode" updated
DGMGRL> show database ocmdb logxptmode;
        LogXptMode = 'SYNC'
DGMGRL> show configuration;
        Configuration
        Name:          ocmdb
        Enabled:       YES
        Protection Mode:    MaxAvailability
        Fast-Start Failover: DISABLED
        Databases:
              ocmdb  - Primary database
              phyocm - Physical standby database
        Current status for "ocmdb":
        SUCCESS
```

If due to some reason, the Dataguard Protection modes is not change to MaxAvailability using DGMGRL then do it from SQLPLUS

ALTER DATABASE SET STANDBY DATABASE TO MAXIMIZE AVAILABILITY;

Open new terminals connect to ocmdb and phyocm using sqlplus and execute following sql

```
SQL> SELECT db_unique_name,
            database_role,
            protection_mode,
            protection_level
     FROM   v$database;
```

- Switch Over to Standby database phyocm

```
DGMGRL> switchover to phyocm;
        Performing switchover NOW, please wait...
        Operation requires shutdown of instance "ocmdb" on database "ocmdb"
        Shutting down instance "ocmdb"...
        ORA-01109: database not open
```

```
Database dismounted.
ORACLE instance shut down.
Operation requires shutdown of instance "phyocm" on database "phyocm"
Shutting down instance "phyocm"...
ORA-01109: database not open

Database dismounted.
ORACLE instance shut down.
Operation requires startup of instance "ocmdb" on database "ocmdb"
Starting instance "ocmdb"...
ORACLE instance started.
Database mounted.
Operation requires startup of instance "phyocm" on database "phyocm"
Starting instance "phyocm"...
ORACLE instance started.
Database mounted.
Switchover succeeded, new primary is "phyocm"
```

If instances are down start them in mount mode, the primary database will automatically open

SQL> STARTUP MOUNT;
DGMGRL> show configuration;

```
Configuration
Name:                ocmdb
Enabled:             YES
Protection Mode:     MaxAvailability
Fast-Start Failover: DISABLED
Databases:
    ocmdb  - Physical standby database
    phyocm - Primary database

Current status for "ocmdb":
SUCCESS
```

Open new terminals connect to ocmdb and phyocm using sqlplus and execute following sql

```
SQL> SELECT db_unique_name,
            database_role,
            protection_mode,
            protection_level
     FROM   v$database;
```

- Switchover back to ocmdb

DGMGRL> switchover to ocmdb;
DGMGRL> show configuration;

```
SQL> SELECT db_unique_name,
            database_role,
            protection_mode,
            protection_level
     FROM   v$database;
```

- Failover to phyocm
  - From sqlplus shutdown, abort primary database

```
[oracle@ocm ~]$ echo $ORACLE_SID
ocmdb
SQL> SHUTDOWN abort;
```

  - Using dgmgrl connect to new phyocm

```
[oracle@ocm ~]$ dgmgrl sys/oracle@phyocm
DGMGRL> failover to phyocm;
DGMGRL> show configuration;
        Configuration
        Name:          ocmdb
        Enabled:       YES
        Protection Mode:   MaxPerformance
        Fast-Start Failover: DISABLED
        Databases:
           ocmdb  - Physical standby database (disabled)
           phyocm - Primary database
        Current status for "ocmdb":
        SUCCESS
```

  - The Protection Mode automatically goes back to MaxPerformance, but the logxptmode properties remains 'SYNC'

```
DGMGRL> show database ocmdb logxptmode;
        LogXptMode = 'SYNC'
DGMGRL> show database phyocm logxptmode;
        LogXptMode = 'SYNC'
```

  - Open a new terminal and set ORACLE_SID for phyocm

```
[oracle@ocm scripts]$ export ORACLE_SID=phyocm
SQL> SELECT db_unique_name,
            database_role,
            protection_mode,
            protection_level
     FROM   v$database;
```

  - Connect to ocmdb and startup database in mount state

```
SQL> STARTUP mount;
```

  - Now reinstate database ocmdb as physical standby

```
DGMGRL> reinstate database ocmdb;
        Reinstating database "ocmdb", please wait...
        Operation requires shutdown of instance "ocmdb" on database "ocmdb"
        Shutting down instance "ocmdb"...
        ORA-01109: database not open
        Database dismounted.
        ORACLE instance shut down.
        Operation requires startup of instance "ocmdb" on database "ocmdb"
        Starting instance "ocmdb"...
        ORACLE instance started.
        Database mounted.
        Continuing to reinstate database "ocmdb" ...
        Reinstatement of database "ocmdb" succeeded
```

If reinstate fails for first time again start ocmdb database in mount state and reinstate, it will succeed in second or third attempt.

- Switchover back to ocmdb to make ocmdb as Primary Database

DGMGRL> switchover to ocmdb;

```
Performing switchover NOW, please wait...
Operation requires shutdown of instance "phyocm" on database "phyocm"
Shutting down instance "phyocm"...
ORA-01109: database not open

Database dismounted.
ORACLE instance shut down.
Operation requires shutdown of instance "ocmdb" on database "ocmdb"
Shutting down instance "ocmdb"...
ORA-01109: database not open

Database dismounted.
ORACLE instance shut down.
Operation requires startup of instance "phyocm" on database "phyocm"
Starting instance "phyocm"...
ORACLE instance started.
Database mounted.
Operation requires startup of instance "ocmdb" on database "ocmdb"
Starting instance "ocmdb"...
ORACLE instance started.
Database mounted.
Switchover succeeded, new primary is "ocmdb"
```

DGMGRL> show configuration;

```
Configuration
Name:              ocmdb
Enabled:           YES
Protection Mode:     MaxPerformance
Fast-Start Failover: DISABLED
Databases:
    ocmdb  - Primary database
    phyocm - Physical standby database

Current status for "ocmdb":
SUCCESS
```

- Fast Start Failover
  - Connect to physical standby using dgmgrl

    [oracle@ocm ~]$ dgmgrl sys/oracle@phyocm

  - Currently the Protection Mode is MaxPerformance, For fast start failover the Protection Mode should be MaxAvailability.

    Anytime to change configuration to "MaxAvailability" make sure the primary database property is logxptmode is "ASYNC" and standby database "logxptmode" is "SYNC then only it can be changed to "MaxAvailability" otherwise it will fail. If maxavailability does not work with DGMGRL then you do it from SQLPLUS

    ALTER DATABASE SET STANDBY DATABASE TO MAXIMIZE AVAILABILITY;

    DGMGRL> show database phyocm logxptmode;

    LogXptMode = 'SYNC'

```
DGMGRL> show database ocmdb logxptmode;
        LogXptMode = 'SYNC'
DGMGRL> edit database ocmdb set property logxptmode='ASYNC';
        Property "logxptmode" updated
DGMGRL> show database ocmdb logxptmode;
        LogXptMode = 'ASYNC'
DGMGRL> edit configuration set protection mode as maxavailability;
        Operation requires shutdown of instance "ocmdb" on database "ocmdb"
        Shutting down instance "ocmdb"...
        Database closed.
        Database dismounted.
        ORACLE instance shut down.
        Operation requires startup of instance "ocmdb" on database "ocmdb"
        Starting instance "ocmdb"...
        ORACLE instance started.
        Database mounted.
        Now make primary database "logxptmode" is "SYNC
DGMGRL> edit database ocmdb set property logxptmode='SYNC';
        Property "logxptmode" updated
```

- Make sure both primary and secondary databases have FLASHBACK ON

```
SQL> SELECT db_unique_name,
            database_role,
            open_mode,
            flashback_on
     FROM   v$database;
```

- Edit database property faststartfailovertarget and enable fast_start failover

```
DGMGRL> edit database phyocm set property faststartfailovertarget=ocmdb;
        Property "faststartfailovertarget" updated
DGMGRL> edit database ocmdb set property faststartfailovertarget=phyocm;
        Property "faststartfailovertarget" updated
DGMGRL> enable fast_start failover;
        Enabled.
DGMGRL> show configuration;
        Configuration
        Name:             ocmdb
        Enabled:          YES
        Protection Mode:     MaxAvailability
        Fast-Start Failover: ENABLED
        Databases:
            ocmdb  - Primary database
            phyocm - Physical standby database
            - Fast-Start Failover target
        Current status for "ocmdb":
        Warning: ORA-16608: one or more databases have warnings
DGMGRL> show database verbose ocmdb;
        You will see warning in the end mentioned below
        Current status for "ocmdb":
        Warning: ORA-16819: Fast-Start Failover observer not started
```

- Connect to ocmdb using sqlplus and execute following commands

SQL> SELECT fs_failover_status, fs_failover_current_target, fs_failover_threshold
FROM v$database;

SQL> SELECT fs_failover_observer_present, fs_failover_observer_host
FROM v$database;

Now go to FSFO Observer window and start it >it is best recommended to use the '-logfile' qualifier on the DGMGRL command to direct any of its output message to a file that can be examined in case of a problem. Additionally it is also suggested to specify unique data file name that Observer uses. This can be done by adding the 'FILE=' command to the 'start observer' command.

This will also allow you to start multiple Observers for multiple Primary/Standby pairs on the same Observer system using the same Oracle Home. In this example, since everything is on the same system, the log in was made using the current ORACLE_SID, which was setup to be the standby database phyocm. In a real setup neither of your databases should be on the Observer system so you would have to use the '@tnsname' qualifier on the 'sys/password' login

[oracle@ocm ~]$ export ORACLE_SID=phyocm

[oracle@ocm ~]$ echo $ORACLE_SID
phyocm

[oracle@ocm ~]$ dgmgrl -logfile $ORACLE_HOME/rdbms/log/dgmgrlOCMDB.LOG sys/oracle

DGMGRL for Linux: Version 10.2.0.1.0 - Production

Copyright (c) 2000, 2005, Oracle. All rights reserved.

Welcome to DGMGRL, type "help" for information.
Connected.

DGMGRL> start observer file='/u01/app/oracle/*afo*ocmdb.dat';

> Make sure to correct observer file correctly having "afo<db_name>.dat" in start

Connect to ocmdb using sqlplus and execute following commands

SQL> SELECT fs_failover_status, fs_failover_current_target, fs_failover_threshold
FROM v$database;

FS_FAILOVER_STATUS	**FS_FAILOVER_CURRENT_TARGET**	**FS_FAILOVER_THRESHOLD**
SYNCHRONIZED	phyocm	30

SQL> SELECT fs_failover_observer_present, fs_failover_observer_host
FROM v$database;

FS_FAIL	**FS_FAILOVER_OBSERVER_HOST**
YES	ocm.prusolutions.com

- Open a new session using dgmgrl and connect to standby database phyocm

[oracle@ocm ~]$ dgmgrl sys/oracle@phyocm

DGMGRL> show configuration;

```
Configuration
Name:                 ocmdb
Enabled:              YES
Protection Mode:      MaxAvailability
Fast-Start Failover: ENABLED
Databases:
   ocmdb  - Primary database
   phyocm - Physical standby database
```

```
    - Fast-Start Failover target
Current status for "ocmdb":
SUCCESS
```

- Connect to ocmdb database and shutdown abort;

```
SQL>  SHUTDOWN abort;
      ORACLE instance shut down.
```

OR

$ps –ef | grep –i pmon

Kill pmon process to primary database ocmdb to failover

```
DGMGRL> show configuration;
      Configuration
      Name:              ocmdb
      Enabled:           YES
      Protection Mode:      MaxAvailability
      Fast-Start Failover: ENABLED
      Databases:
          ocmdb  - Physical standby database (disabled)
          - Fast-Start Failover target
          phyocm - Primary database
      Current status for "ocmdb":
      Warning: ORA-16608: one or more databases have warnings

DGMGRL> show database ocmdb;
      Database
      Name:          ocmdb
      Role:        PHYSICAL STANDBY
      Enabled:       NO
      Intended State:  ONLINE
      Instance(s):
      ocmdb
      Current status for "ocmdb":
      Error: ORA-16661: the standby database needs to be reinstated
```

- Connect to ocmdb instance and startup

```
[oracle@ocm ~]$ export ORACLE_SID=ocmdb
[oracle@ocm ~]$ sqlplus / as sysdba
SQL>  STARTUP;
      ORACLE instance started.
      Total System Global Area  536870912 bytes
      Fixed Size                  1220460 bytes
      Variable Size             209715348 bytes
      Database Buffers            314572800 bytes
      Redo Buffers               11362304 bytes
      Database mounted.
      ORA-16649: database will open after Data Guard broker has evaluated Fast-Start Failover
      status
```

- It will take few minutes to get database synchronized. Execute following sql on both primary and secondary.

```
SQL>  SELECT db_unique_name, open_mode, database_role FROM v$database;
SQL>  SELECT fs_failover_status, fs_failover_current_target, fs_failover_threshold
      FROM v$database;
```

```
DGMGRL> show configuration;
        Configuration
        Name:            ocmdb
        Enabled:         YES
        Protection Mode:     MaxAvailability
        Fast-Start Failover: ENABLED
        Databases:
            ocmdb  - Physical standby database
            - Fast-Start Failover target
            phyocm - Primary database
        Current status for "ocmdb":
        SUCCESS
DGMGRL> STOP OBSERVER;
        Done.
DGMGRL> disable fast_start failover;
        Disabled.
DGMGRL> show configuration;
        Configuration
        Name:            ocmdb
        Enabled:         YES
        Protection Mode:     MaxAvailability
        Fast-Start Failover: DISABLED
        Databases:
            ocmdb  - Physical standby database
            phyocm - Primary database
        Current status for "ocmdb":
        SUCCESS
```

- Switchover back to ocmdb

```
DGMGRL>  switchover to ocmdb;
         Performing switchover NOW, please wait...
         Operation requires shutdown of instance "phyocm" on database "phyocm"
         Shutting down instance "phyocm"...
         ORA-01109: database not open
         Database dismounted.
         ORACLE instance shut down.
         Operation requires shutdown of instance "ocmdb" on database "ocmdb"
         Shutting down instance "ocmdb"...
         ORA-01109: database not open
         Database dismounted.
         ORACLE instance shut down.
         Operation requires startup of instance "phyocm" on database "phyocm"
         Starting instance "phyocm"...
         ORACLE instance started.
         Database mounted.
         Operation requires startup of instance "ocmdb" on database "ocmdb"
         Starting instance "ocmdb"...
         ORACLE instance started.
         Database mounted.
         Switchover succeeded, new primary is "ocmdb"
```

9.19 Manually managing Dataguard using SQL commands.

- All Activities mentioned below should be performed on Primary Database

```
SQL> SELECT  db_unique_name,
             database_role,
             open_mode,
             flashback_on
     FROM    v$database;
```

DB_UNIQUE_NAME	DATABASE_ROLE	OPEN_MODE	FLASHBACK_ON
ocmdb	PRIMARY	READ WRITE	YES

```
SQL> SELECT * FROM v$dataguard_stats;
     no rows selected
SQL> SELECT switchover_status FROM v$database;
```

SWITCHOVER_STATUS
SESSIONS ACTIVE

```
SQL> SELECT SID, PROCESS, PROGRAM
     FROM V$SESSION
     WHERE TYPE = 'USER' AND SID <> (SELECT DISTINCT SID FROM V$MYSTAT);
```

SID	PROCESS	PROGRAM
266	17161	oracle@ocm.prusolutions.com (TNS V1-V3)
233	4075	emagent@ocm.prusolutions.com (TNS V1-V3)
236	18174	dgmgrl@ocm.prusolutions.com (TNS V1-V3)
232	4075	emagent@ocm.prusolutions.com (TNS V1-V3)

- Stop Agent and If there is any DGMGRL configuration, please disable them and disconnect from DGMGRL

```
[oracle@ocm ~]$ . /home/oracle/agent_profile
[oracle@ocm ~]$ emctl stop agent
Oracle Enterprise Manager 10g Release 10.2.0.1.0.
Copyright (c) 1996, 2005 Oracle Corporation.  All rights reserved.
Stopping agent ... stopped.
DGMGRL> disable configuration;
        Disabled.
DGMGRL> exit
SQL> SELECT SID, PROCESS, PROGRAM
     FROM V$SESSION
     WHERE TYPE = 'USER' AND SID <> (SELECT DISTINCT SID FROM V$MYSTAT);
     no rows selected
SQL> ALTER SYSTEM SET job_queue_processes=0;
     System altered.
SQL> SELECT SID, PROCESS, PROGRAM FROM V$SESSION;
SQL> SELECT  db_unique_name,
             database_role,
             protection_mode,
             protection_level
     FROM    v$database;
```

DB_UNIQUE_NAME	DATABASE_ROLE	PROTECTION_MODE	PROTECTION_LEVEL
ocmdb	PRIMARY	MAXIMUM AVAILABILITY	MAXIMUM AVAILABILITY

```
SQL> ALTER DATABASE SET STANDBY DATABASE TO MAXIMIZE PERFORMANCE;
     Database altered.
SQL> SELECT  db_unique_name,
             database_role,
             protection_mode,
             protection_level
     FROM    v$database;
```

DB_UNIQUE_NAME	DATABASE_ROLE	PROTECTION_MODE	PROTECTION_LEVEL
ocmdb	PRIMARY	MAXIMUM PERFORMANCE	MAXIMUM PERFORMANCE

- Make log_archive_dest_2 in 'ASYNC' mode

```
SQL> ALTER SYSTEM SET log_archive_dest_2='service=phyocm lgwr async
     valid_for=(online_logfiles,primary_role) db_unique_name=phyocm' SCOPE=BOTH;
     System altered.
SQL> SHOW PARAMETER log_archive_dest_2
```

NAME	TYPE	VALUE
log_archive_dest_2	string	service=phyocm lgwr async va lid_for=(online_logfiles,prima ry_role) db_unique_name=phyocm

```
SQL> SELECT switchover_status FROM v$database;
```

SWITCHOVER_STATUS
TO STANDBY

```
SQL> ALTER DATABASE COMMIT TO SWITCHOVER TO PHYSICAL STANDBY;
     Database altered.
SQL> SHUTDOWN IMMEDIATE;
     ORA-01507: database not mounted
     ORACLE instance shut down.
SQL> STARTUP MOUNT;
     ORACLE instance started.
     Total System Global Area  536870912 bytes
     Fixed Size                  1220460 bytes
     Variable Size             213909652 bytes
     Database Buffers          310378496 bytes
     Redo Buffers               11362304 bytes
     Database mounted.
SQL> SELECT  db_unique_name,
             database_role,
             protection_mode,
             protection_level
     FROM    v$database;
```

DB_UNIQUE_NAME	DATABASE_ROLE	PROTECTION_MODE	PROTECTION_LEVEL
ocmdb	PHYSICAL STANDBY	MAXIMUM PERFORMANCE	MAXIMUM PERFORMANCE

- All Activities mentioned below should be performed on Secondary Database

[oracle@ocm ~]$ export ORACLE_SID=phyocm

[oracle@ocm ~]$ sqlplus / as sysdba

```
SQL> SELECT db_unique_name,
            database_role,
            protection_mode,
            protection_level
     FROM   v$database;
```

DB_UNIQUE_NAME	DATABASE_ROLE	PROTECTION_MODE	PROTECTION_LEVEL
phyocm	PHYSICAL STANDBY	MAXIMUM PERFORMANCE	MAXIMUM PERFORMANCE

```
SQL> ALTER SYSTEM SET log_archive_dest_2='service=ocmdb lgwr async   ;
     valid_for=(online_logfiles,primary_role) db_unique_name=ocmdb' SCOPE=BOTH;
     System altered.
SQL> SHOW PARAMETER log_archive_dest_2
```

NAME	TYPE	VALUE
log_archive_dest_2	string	service=ocmdb lgwr async val id_for=(online_logfiles,primar y_role) db_unique_name=ocmdb

```
SQL> SELECT SWITCHOVER_STATUS FROM V$DATABASE;
```

SWITCHOVER_STATUS
TO PRIMARY

```
SQL> ALTER DATABASE RECOVER MANAGED STANDBY DATABASE CANCEL;
     Database altered.
SQL> ALTER DATABASE COMMIT TO SWITCHOVER TO PRIMARY;
     Database altered
```

- Open another terminal and check alert log file

[oracle@ocm bdump]$ tail -f alert_phyocm.log

- Open another terminal and check alert log file

[oracle@ocm bdump]$ tail -f alert_ocmdb.log

```
SQL> ALTER DATABASE OPEN;
     Database altered.
SQL> SHUTDOWN IMMEDIATE;
     Database closed.
     Database dismounted.
     ORACLE instance shut down.
SQL> STARTUP;
     ORACLE instance started.
```

```
Total System Global Area 536870912 bytes
Fixed Size                  1220460 bytes
Variable Size             176160916 bytes
Database Buffers          348127232 bytes
Redo Buffers               11362304 bytes
Database mounted.
Database opened.
```

- Execute following sql statements on both Primary and Secondary

```
SQL> SELECT  db_unique_name,
             database_role,
             protection_mode,
             protection_level
     FROM    v$database;
SQL> SELECT SWITCHOVER_STATUS FROM V$DATABASE;
```

- For next, exercise Switch, back to ocmdb through either sqlplus or dgmgrl
- If you are using dgmgrl then have to remove and add configuration again

```
[oracle@ocm bdump]$ dgmgrl sys/oracle@phyocm
DGMGRL for Linux: Version 10.2.0.1.0 - Production
Copyright (c) 2000, 2005, Oracle. All rights reserved.
Welcome to DGMGRL, type "help" for information.
Connected.
DGMGRL>  enable configuration;
         Enabled.
DGMGRL>  show configuration;
         Configuration
         Name:            ocmdb
         Enabled:         YES
         Protection Mode:     MaxPerformance
         Fast-Start Failover: DISABLED
         Databases:
             ocmdb  - Primary database
             phyocm - Physical standby database
         Current status for "ocmdb":
         Warning: ORA-16607: one or more databases have failed
DGMGRL>  show database ocmdb;
         Database
         Name:          ocmdb
         Role:          PRIMARY
         Enabled:       YES
         Intended State:  ONLINE
         Instance(s):
         ocmdb
         Current status for "ocmdb":
         Error: ORA-16816: incorrect database role
DGMGRL>  remove configuration preserve destinations;
         Removed configuration
```

```
DGMGRL> CREATE CONFIGURATION OCMDB AS PRIMARY DATABASE IS PHYOCM
        CONNECT IDENTIFIER IS PHYOCM;
        Configuration "ocmdb" created with primary database "phyocm"
DGMGRL> ADD DATABASE ocmdb AS CONNECT IDENTIFIER IS ocmdb MAINTAINED
        AS PHYSICAL;
        Database "ocmdb" added
DGMGRL> enable configuration;
        Enabled.
DGMGRL> show configuration;
        Configuration
        Name:           ocmdb
        Enabled:        YES
        Protection Mode:     MaxPerformance
        Fast-Start Failover: DISABLED
        Databases:
            phyocm - Primary database
            ocmdb  - Physical standby database
        Current status for "ocmdb":
        SUCCESS
```

- Switch over to ocmdb for next exercise

```
DGMGRL> switchover to ocmdb;
        Performing switchover NOW, please wait...
        Operation requires shutdown of instance "phyocm" on database "phyocm"
        Shutting down instance "phyocm"...
        ORA-01109: database not open

        Database dismounted.
        ORACLE instance shut down.
        Operation requires shutdown of instance "ocmdb" on database "ocmdb"
        Shutting down instance "ocmdb"...
        ORA-01109: database not open

        Database dismounted.
        ORACLE instance shut down.
        Operation requires startup of instance "phyocm" on database "phyocm"
        Starting instance "phyocm"...
        ORACLE instance started.
        Database mounted.
        Operation requires startup of instance "ocmdb" on database "ocmdb"
        Starting instance "ocmdb"...
        ORACLE instance started.
        Database mounted.
        Switchover succeeded, new primary is "ocmdb"
```

9.20 Converting Physical Standby to Logical Standby

- Check Protection Mode is MaxPerformance or change it to MaxPerformance
- Check LogXptMode is 'ASYNC' or change LogXptMode to 'ASYNC'
- Disable configuration and exit from dgmgrl

```
DGMGRL> disable configuration;
        Disabled.
DGMGRL> exit
```

- Change directory of log_archive_dest_3 to physical location instead of using db parameter use_db_recovery_file_dest

> Flash recovery area is not supported as a standby archive log destination for logical standby.

Change parameter log_archive_dest_3 on both primary and secondary

```
[oracle@ocm ~]$ mkdir /u01/app/oracle/flash_recovery_area/OCMDB/STANDBYLOG
SQL> ALTER SYSTEM SET log_archive_dest_3='LOCATION=
     /u01/app/oracle/flash_recovery_area/OCMDB/STANDBYLOG
     VALID_FOR=(STANDBY_LOGFILES,STANDBY_ROLE) DB_UNIQUE_NAME=ocmdb' SCOPE=BOTH;
[oracle@ocm ~]$ mkdir /u01/app/oracle/flash_recovery_area/PHYOCM/STANDBYLOG
SQL> ALTER SYSTEM SET log_archive_dest_3='LOCATION=
     /u01/app/oracle/flash_recovery_area/PHYOCM/STANDBYLOG
     VALID_FOR=(STANDBY_LOGFILES,STANDBY_ROLE) DB_UNIQUE_NAME=phyocm'  SCOPE=BOTH;
```

- Find tables without unique logical identifier in the primary database.

```
SQL> SELECT OWNER, TABLE_NAME
     FROM DBA_LOGSTDBY_NOT_UNIQUE
     WHERE (OWNER, TABLE_NAME) NOT IN
     (SELECT DISTINCT OWNER, TABLE_NAME FROM DBA_LOGSTDBY_UNSUPPORTED)
     AND BAD_COLUMN = 'Y';
SQL> ALTER TABLE <table_name> ADD PRIMARY KEY <column_name> RELY DISABLE;
```

- Make sure Database supplemental logging is enabled.

```
SQL> SELECT SUPPLEMENTAL_LOG_DATA_PK, SUPPLEMENTAL_LOG_DATA_UI
     FROM V$DATABASE;
```

- Cancel log applying on standby (phyocm)

```
[oracle@ocm ~]$ echo $ORACLE_SID
phyocm
SQL> ALTER DATABASE RECOVER MANAGED STANDBY DATABASE CANCEL;
     Database altered.
```

- Make dg_broker_start =FALSE on both primary and secondary

```
SQL> ALTER SYSTEM SET dg_broker_start=FALSE SCOPE=BOTH;
     System altered.
SQL> show parameter dg
```

- Following commands will be executed only on Primary Database ocmdb

```
SQL> SELECT     db_unique_name,
                database_role,
                protection_mode,
                protection_level
     FROM       v$database;
SQL> EXECUTE DBMS_LOGSTDBY.BUILD;
     PL/SQL procedure successfully completed.
```

- Archive all online redologfile

```
SQL> ALTER SYSTEM ARCHIVE LOG CURRENT;
     System altered.
SQL> ALTER SYSTEM ARCHIVE LOG CURRENT;
     System altered.
SQL> ALTER SYSTEM ARCHIVE LOG CURRENT;
     System altered.
```

- Following commands will be executed only on Secondary Database phyocm

```
SQL> SELECT    db_unique_name,
               database_role,
               protection_mode,
               protection_level
     FROM      v$database;
SQL> ALTER DATABASE RECOVER MANAGED STANDBY DATABASE CANCEL;
     Database altered.
```

- Open another terminal and check alert log file

```
[oracle@ocm bdump]$ tail -f alert_phyocm.log
SQL> ALTER DATABASE RECOVER TO LOGICAL STANDBY phyocm;
SQL> SHUTDOWN IMMEDIATE;
SQL> STARTUP MOUNT;
SQL> ALTER DATABASE OPEN RESETLOGS;
SQL> SELECT    db_unique_name,
               database_role,
               protection_mode,
               protection_level
     FROM      v$database;
SQL> ALTER DATABASE START LOGICAL STANDBY APPLY IMMEDIATE;
SQL> ALTER SYSTEM SET dg_broker_start=TRUE SCOPE=BOTH;
```

9.21 Install Oracle Agent using Mass Agent Deploy Application

- **Shutdown ocm, oms, oem crs1, crs2, crsdg1 and crsdbg2**
- Backup current copy of]oem and oms machines and use oms and oem from last backup in section 4.3
  - Take backup of current machines

    Copy c:/vm/rac/ocm to c:/vm/backup_current/ocm
    Copy c:/vm/rac/oem to c:/vm/backup_current/oem
    Copy c:/vm/rac/oms to c:/vm/backup_current/oms
  - Restore machines from backup

    Copy c:/vm/backup/ocm to c:/vm/rac/ocm
    Copy c:/vm/backup/oem to c:/vm/rac/oem
    Copy c:/vm/backup/oms to c:/vm/rac/oms
- Backup current copy of crs1 and crs2 machines and use crs1 and crs2 from last backup in section 9.13
  - Take backup of current machines

    Copy c:/vm/rac/crs1 to c:/vm/backup_current/crs1

Copy c:/vm/rac/crs2 to c:/vm/backup_current/crs2
Copy c:/vm/rac/shared to c:/vm/backup_current/shared

- Restore machines from backup

  Copy c:/vm/backup/crs1 to c:/vm/rac/crs1
  Copy c:/vm/backup/crs2 to c:/vm/rac/crs2
  Copy c:/vm/backup/shared to c:/vm/rac/shared

- Backup current copy of crsdg1 and crsdg2 machines and use crsdg1 and crsdg2 from last backup in section 10.12
  - Take backup of current machines

    Copy c:/vm/rac/crsdg1 to c:/vm/backup_current/crsdg1
    Copy c:/vm/rac/crsdg2 to c:/vm/backup_current/crsdg2
    Copy c:/vm/rac/shareddg to c:/vm/backup_current/shareddg

  - Restore machines from backup

    Copy c:/vm/backup/crsdg1 to c:/vm/rac/crsdg1
    Copy c:/vm/backup/crsdg2 to c:/vm/rac/crsdg2
    Copy c:/vm/backup/shareddg to c:/vm/rac/shareddg

- Modify the memory of the all above machine in vmware to 900 MB and start all of them.
- Set <AGENT_HOME> on all machines.

  . /home/oracle/agent_profile

- Ping all the machines from oms server from where ssh will be setup.

  [oracle@oms ~]$ ping ocm.prusolutions.com

  [oracle@oms ~]$ ping oem.prusolutions.com

  [oracle@oms ~]$ ping crs1.prusolutions.com

  [oracle@oms ~]$ ping crs2.prusolutions.com

  [oracle@oms ~]$ ping crsdg1.prusolutions.com

  [oracle@oms ~]$ ping crsdg2.prusolutions.com

- Execute following script for ssh setup
  - Sample Script

    <OMS ORACLE HOME>/sysman/prov/resources/scripts/sshUserSetup.sh –hosts " host1 host2 " -user oracle

  - Actual Script Executed

    [oracle@oms ~]$ /u01/app/oracle/OracleHomes/oms10g/sysman/prov/resources/scripts/sshUserSetup.sh -hosts "ocm.prusolutions.com oem.prusolutions.com crs1.prusolutions.com crs2.prusolutions.com crsdg1.prusolutions.com crsdg2.prusolutions.com" -user oracle

  - Input yes when prompted.

    Do you want to continue and let the script make the above mentioned changes (yes/no)?
    yes

  - Provide Oracle Password for all machines when prompted

    oracle@ocm.prusolutions.com's password: **<password>**

  - Following will be result for each machine ssh setup

    If you any other output beside the output of DATE command or if you are prompted for password, it means ssh setup has not been successful, set ssh again.

Mon Apr 4 18:35:41 EDT 2011

SSH verification complete.

- **Shutdown ocm, crsdg1 and crsdbg2 as we install first agent only on crs1 and crs2**
- Make sure Oracle Cluster is up on crs1, crs2

  [oracle@crs1 database]$ crs_stat –t
- Make sure as oracle user you can sudo su – on both crs1, crs2

  [oracle@crs1 ~]$ sudo su -
- Install agent from OEM grid Control
  - On Home Page in Agent Installation Section Click Install Agent

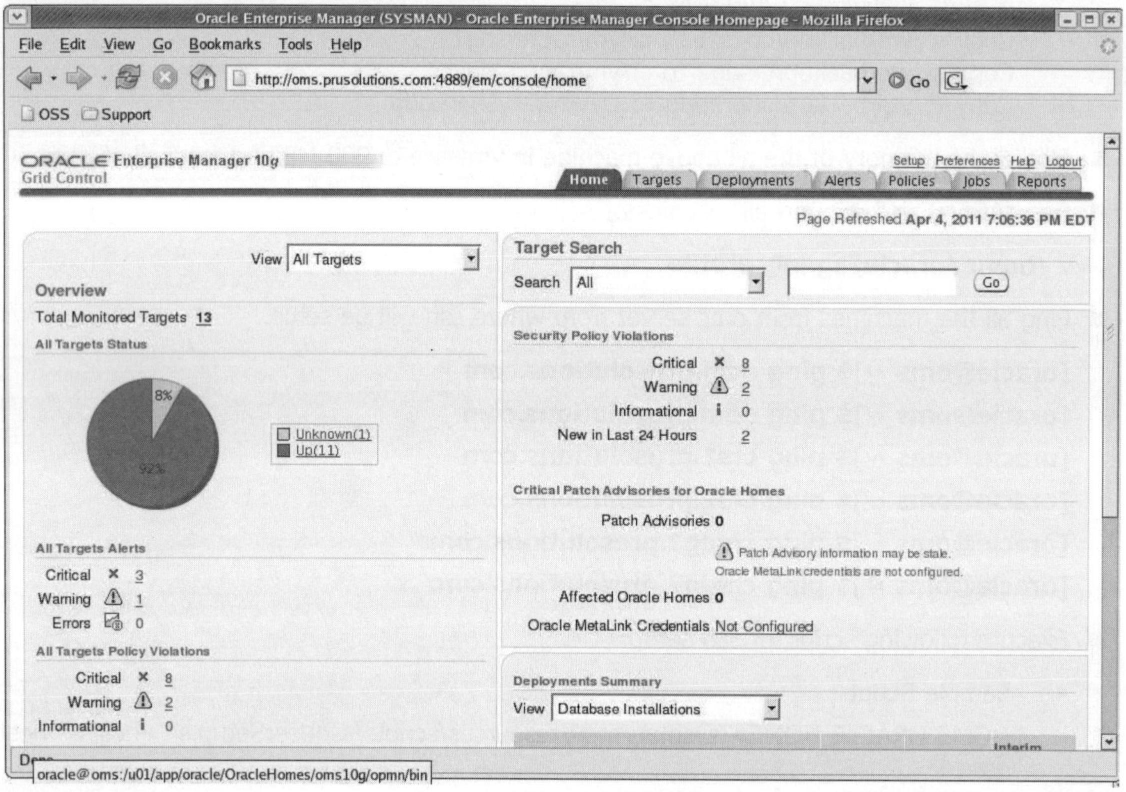

- Agent Installation Section: Click Install Agent

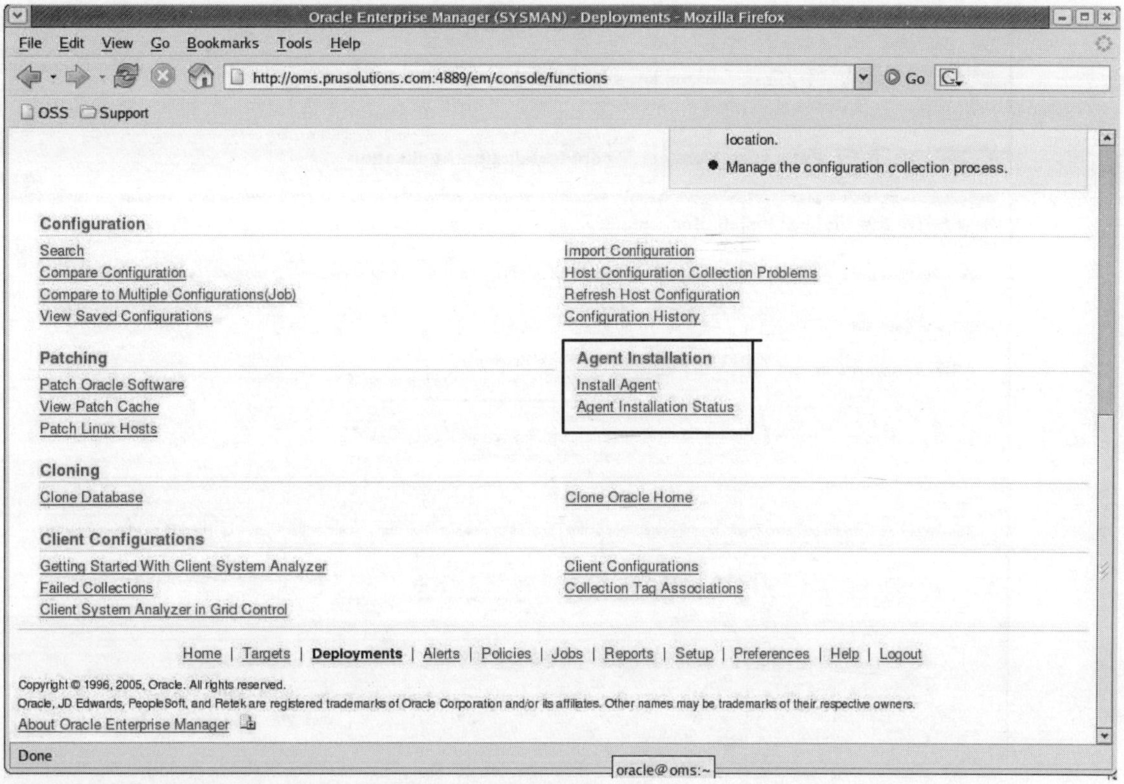

- Agent Installation Application : Click Fresh Install

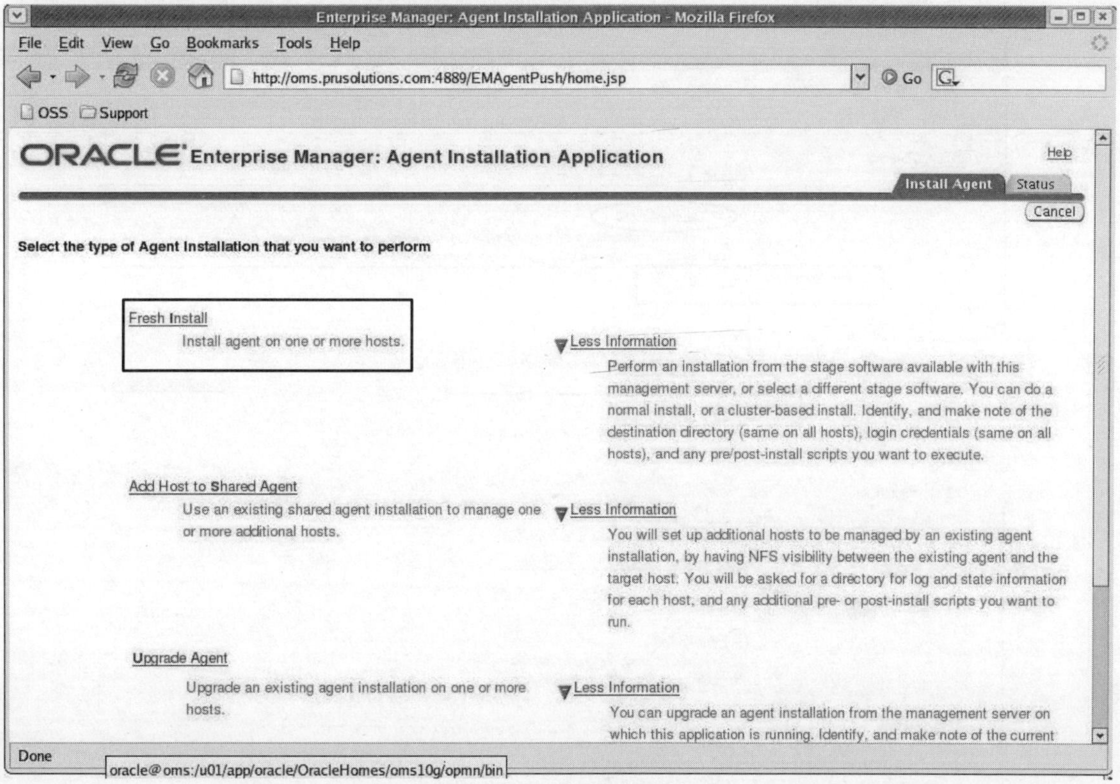

- Source Software : Select Default from Management Server Location

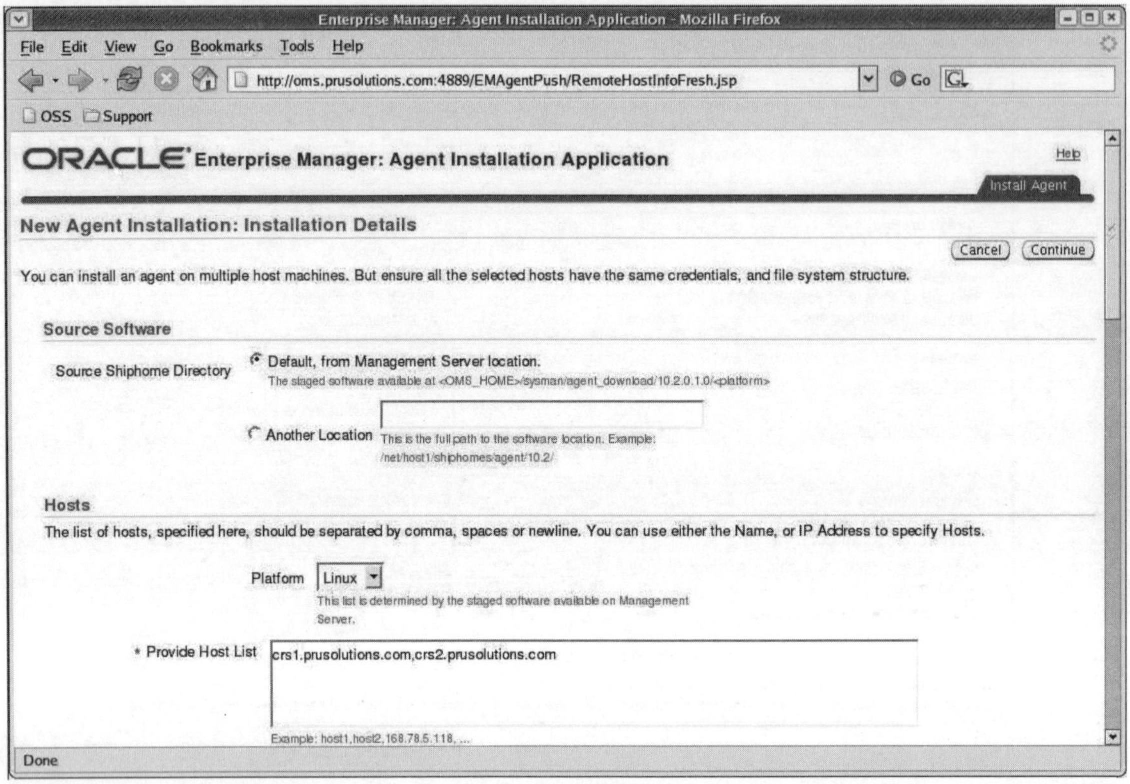

- Cluster Install , Cluster Node List: crs1,crs2, Cluster Name: crs, OS Credential: oracle/oracle **Deselect Run root.sh**

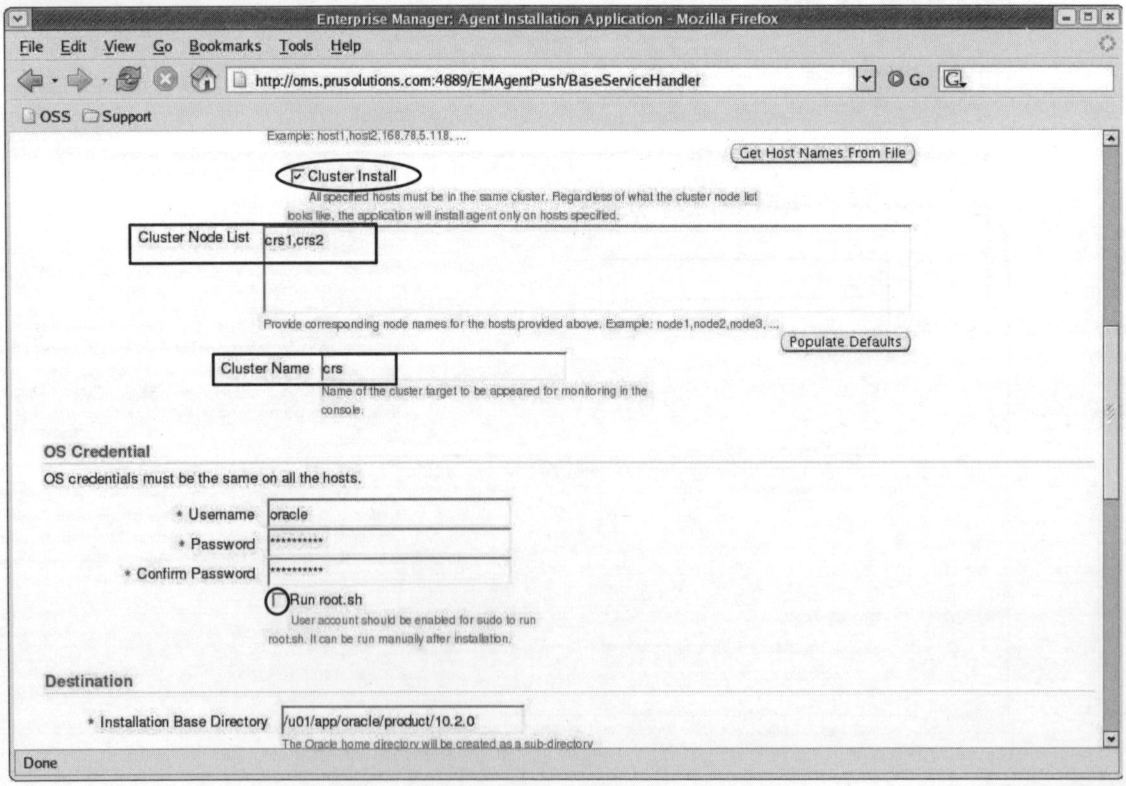

- Management Server Security: Enter password for oms security: **oracle123**

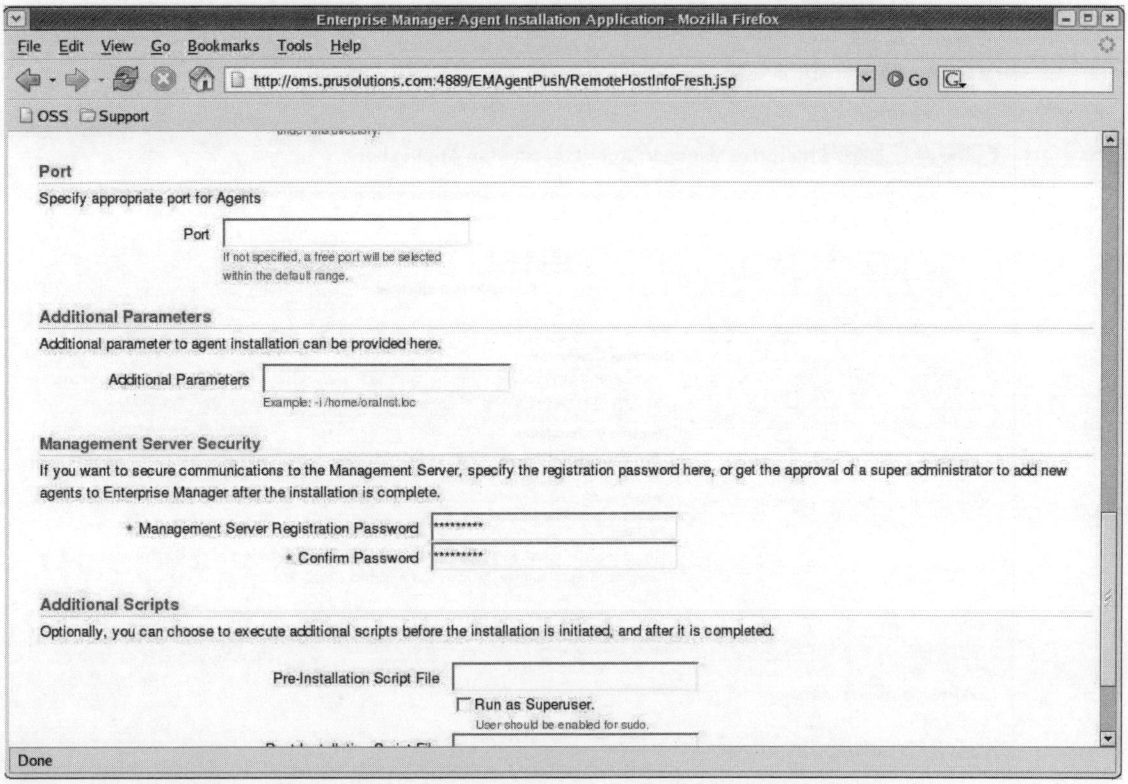

- Enterprise Manager: Agent Installation Application: Checking Connection

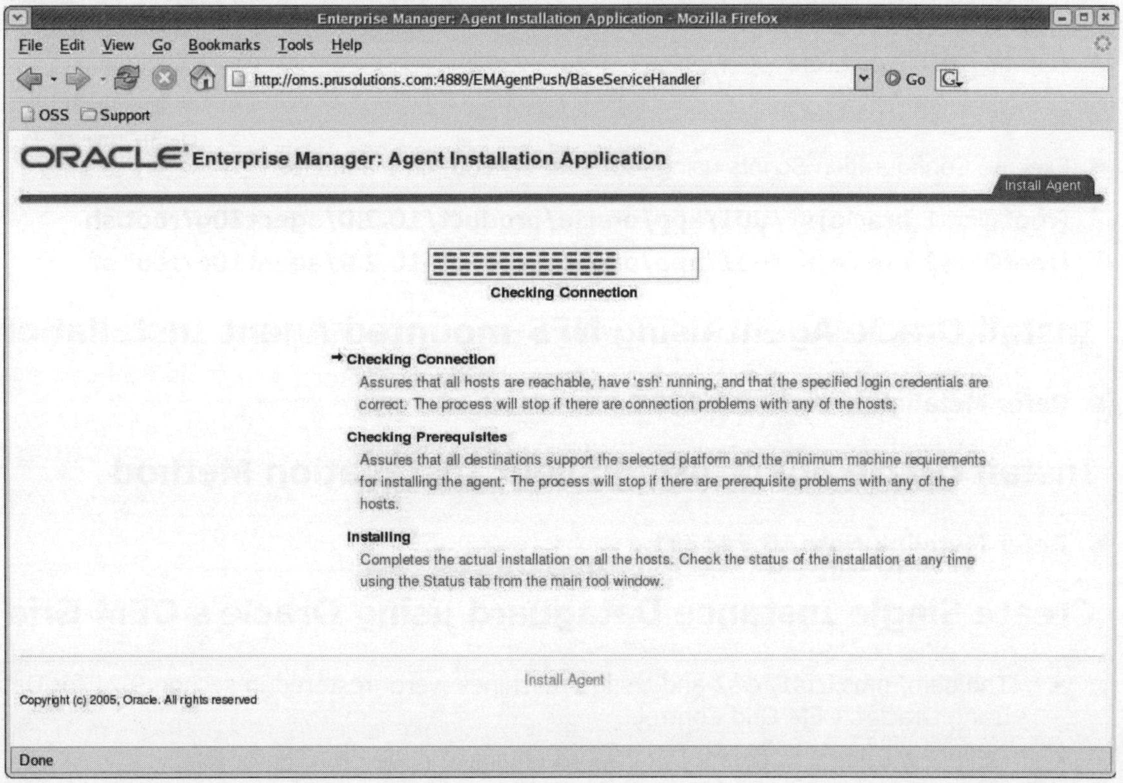

- Enterprise Manager: Agent Installation Application: Checking Prerequisite

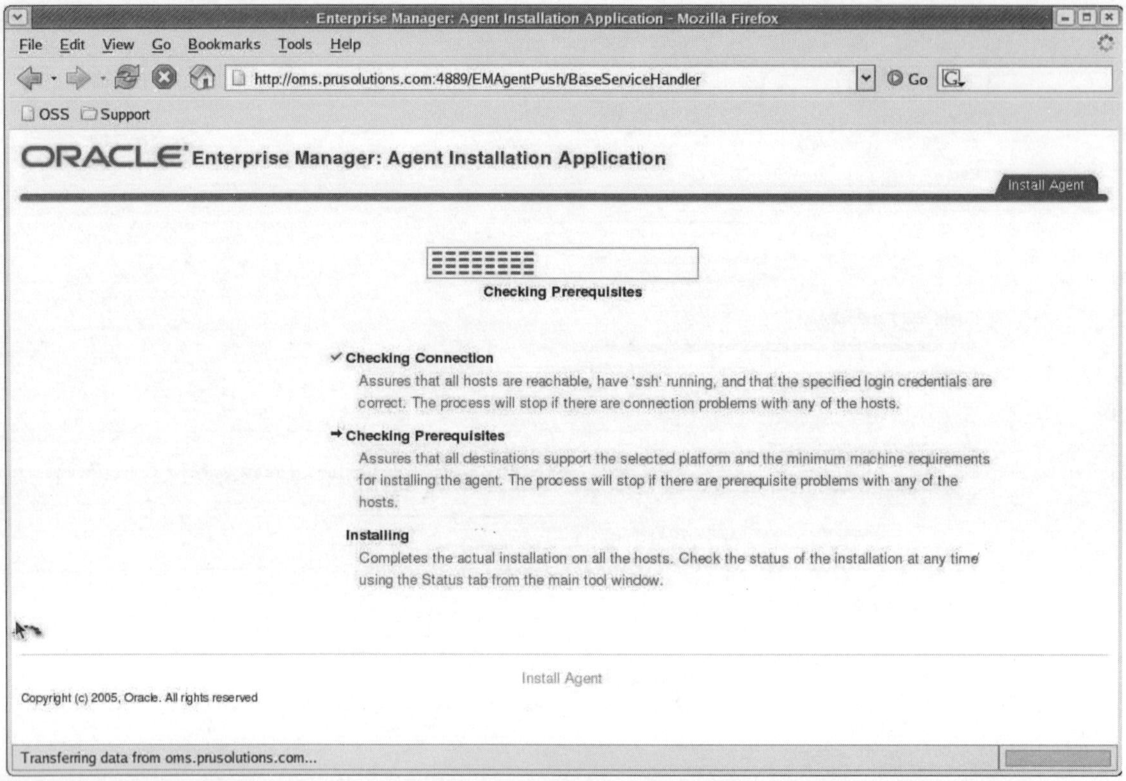

- **If you get TIME ZONE error apply OEM Patch Mentioned below and repeat all the Steps mentioned above again**
  - gc_10205_part1of2
  - gc_10205_part2of2
- Execute Configuration Scripts using root user on both crs1 and crs2

[root@crs1 oracle]# /u01/app/oracle/product/10.2.0/agent10g/root.sh

[root@crs2 oracle]# /u01/app/oracle/product/10.2.0/agent10g/root.sh

9.22 Install Oracle Agent using NFS-mounted Agent Installation Method

- **Refer Metalink Note ID 735133.1**

9.23 Install Oracle Agent using Silent Installation Method

- **Refer Metalink Note ID 744391.1**

9.24 Create Single Instance Dataguard using Oracle's OEM Grid Control

- The oem, oms, crs1, crs2 and crsdg1 machines were restored in section 9.21 for Data Guard practice using Oracle's OEM Grid Control.
- OEM Grid Control to create Data Guard on single node on ASM for RAC
- For this, you have to install ASM and Database Software on single node crsdg1
- Below are the screen shots to Setup Dataguard using OEM Grid Control

- On Cluster Database crsdb, Page Maintenance Tab. In Data Guard Section Click Setup and Manage

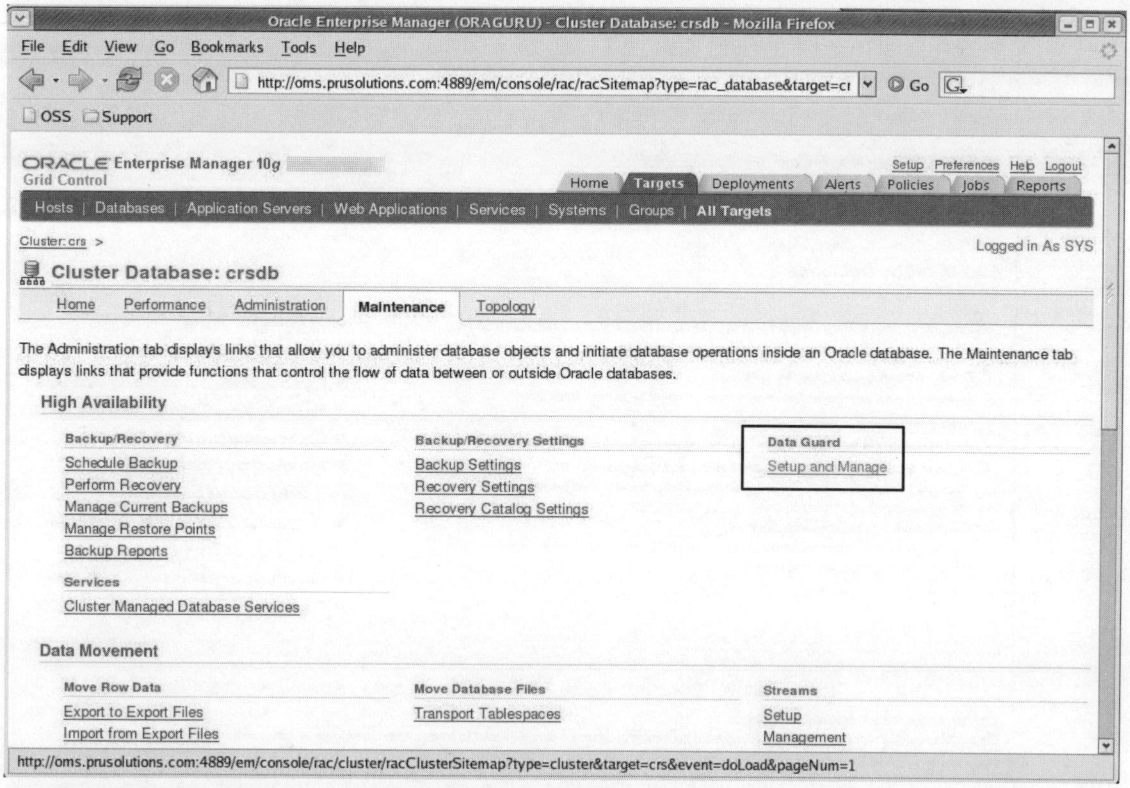

- On Data Guard Page: Double Click Use Data Guard Broker

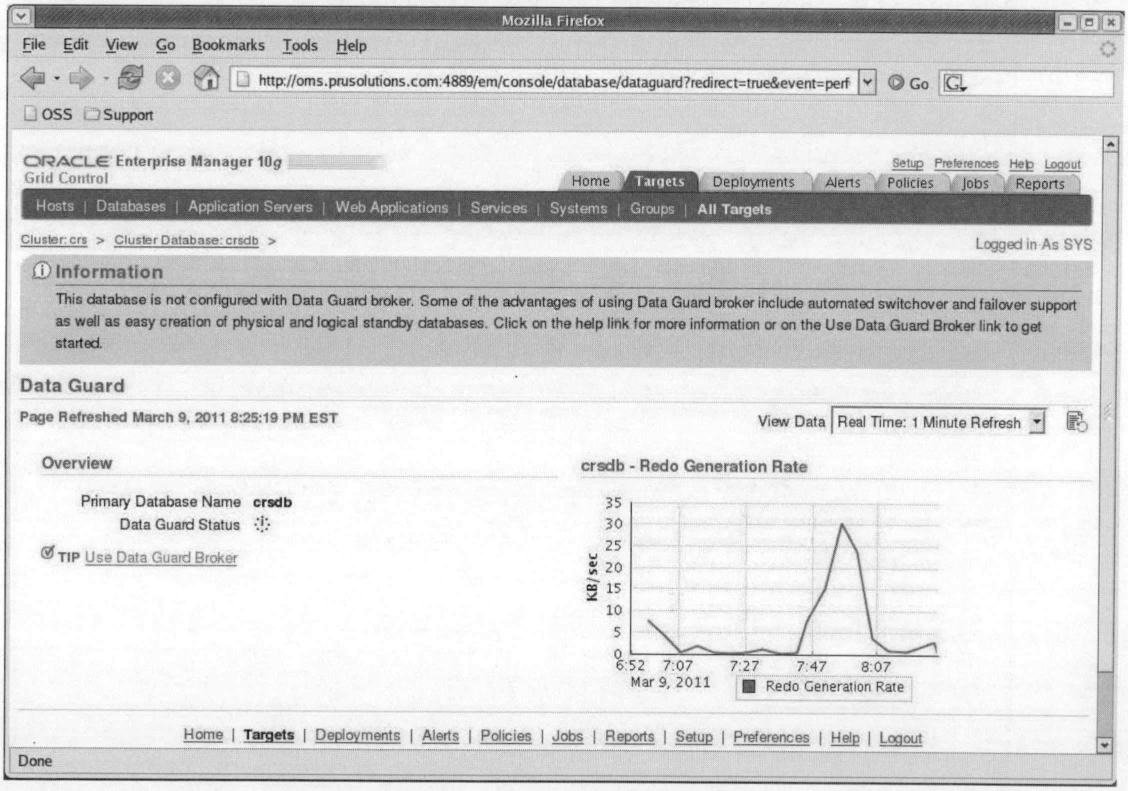

- On Add Standby Database page : Choose a new physical database

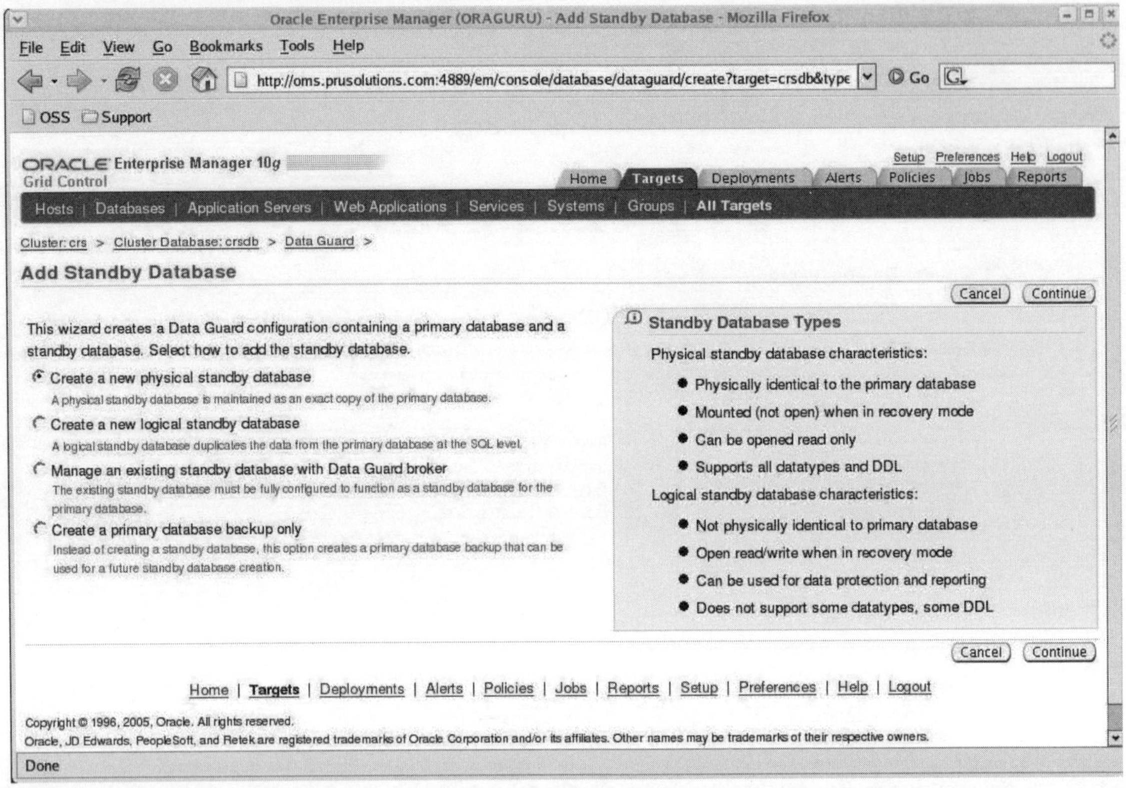

- On Warning page : Make sure, if non-standard port is used then the LOCAL_LISTENER is set both on Primary and Secondary databases. Click Yes and continue.

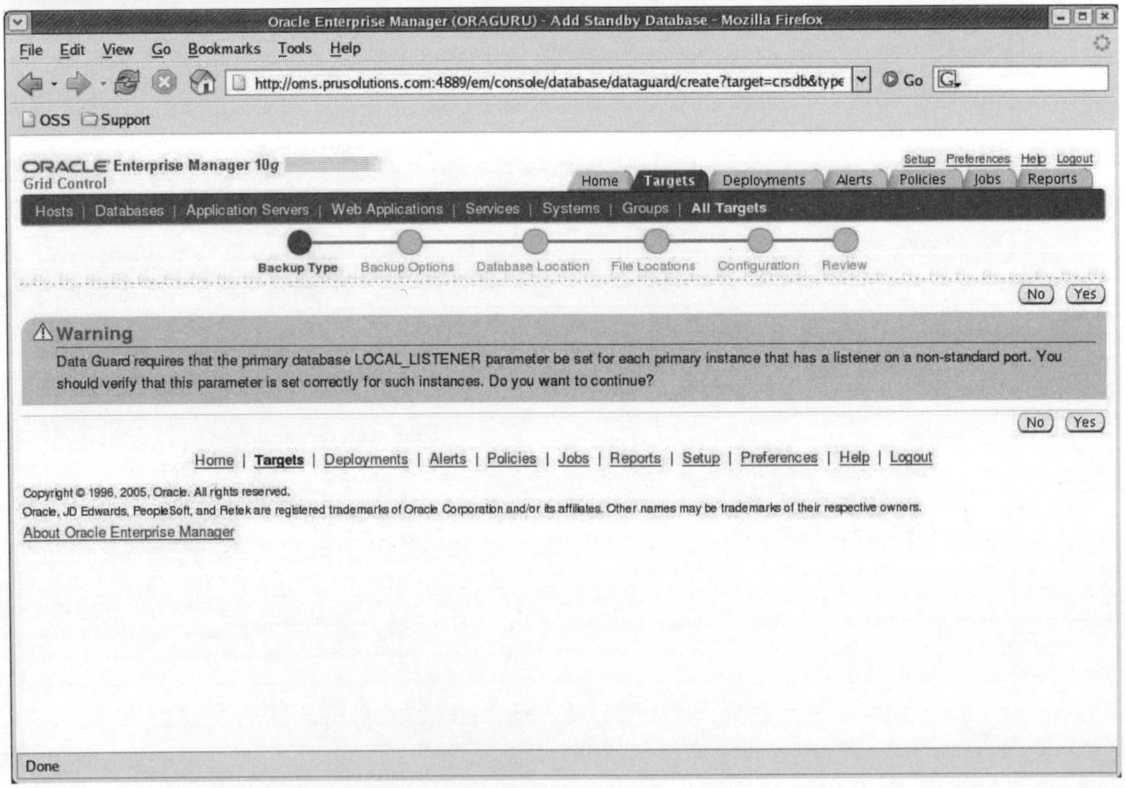

- On Add Standby Database Backup Type : Select Perform a live backup of the primary database

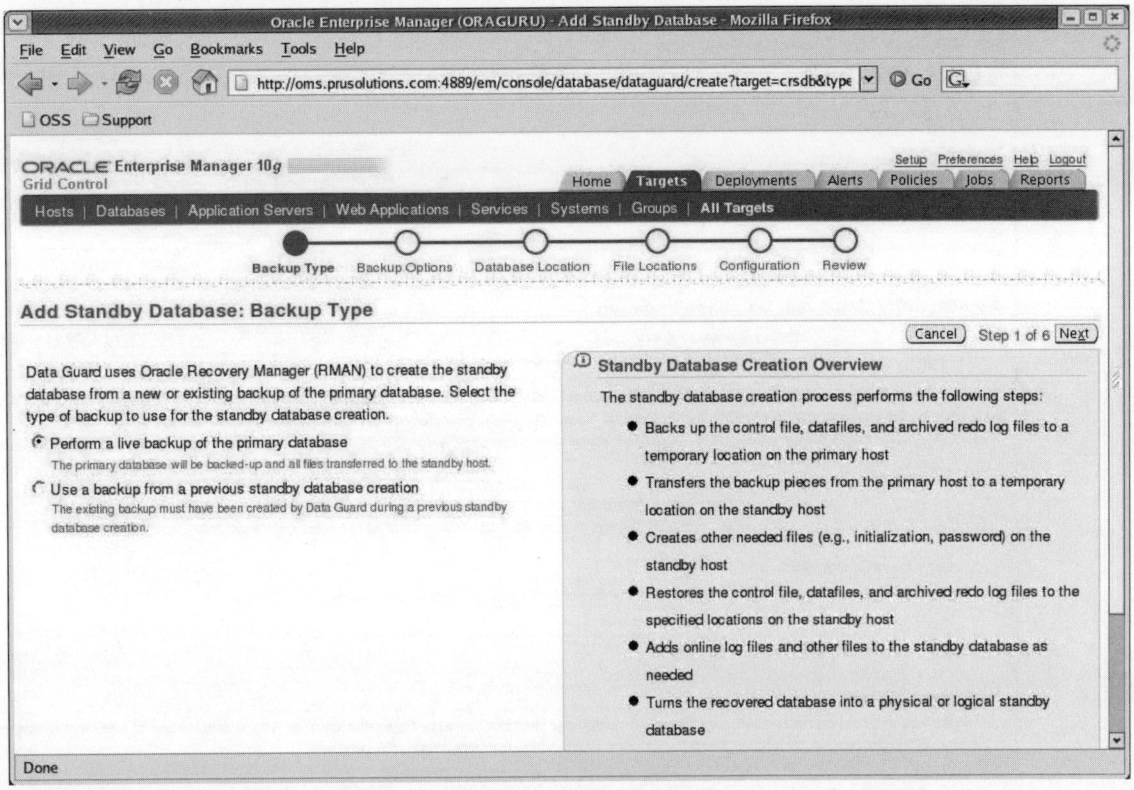

- Backup file Directory : /u01/app/oracle/stage, Select Delete directory, Provide Primary Host and Database Credentials.

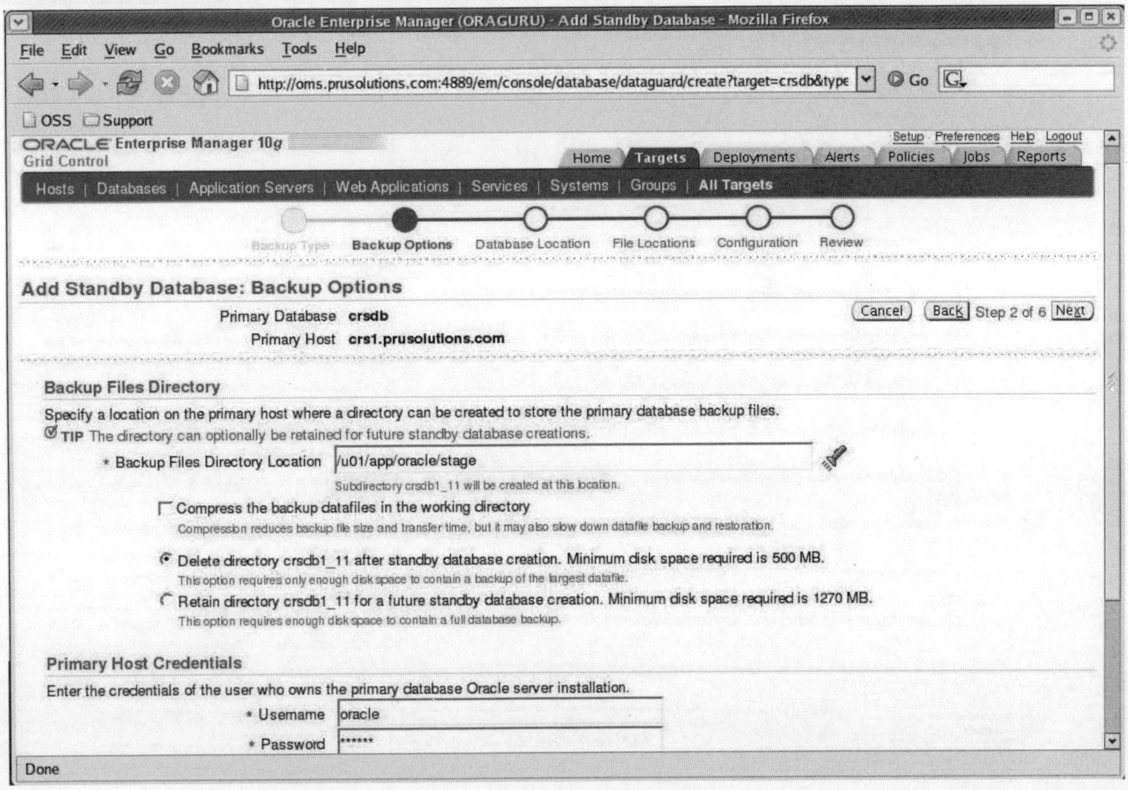

- Standby Database: Instance Name: crsdgdb1 , Provide Standby Host and Database Credentials.

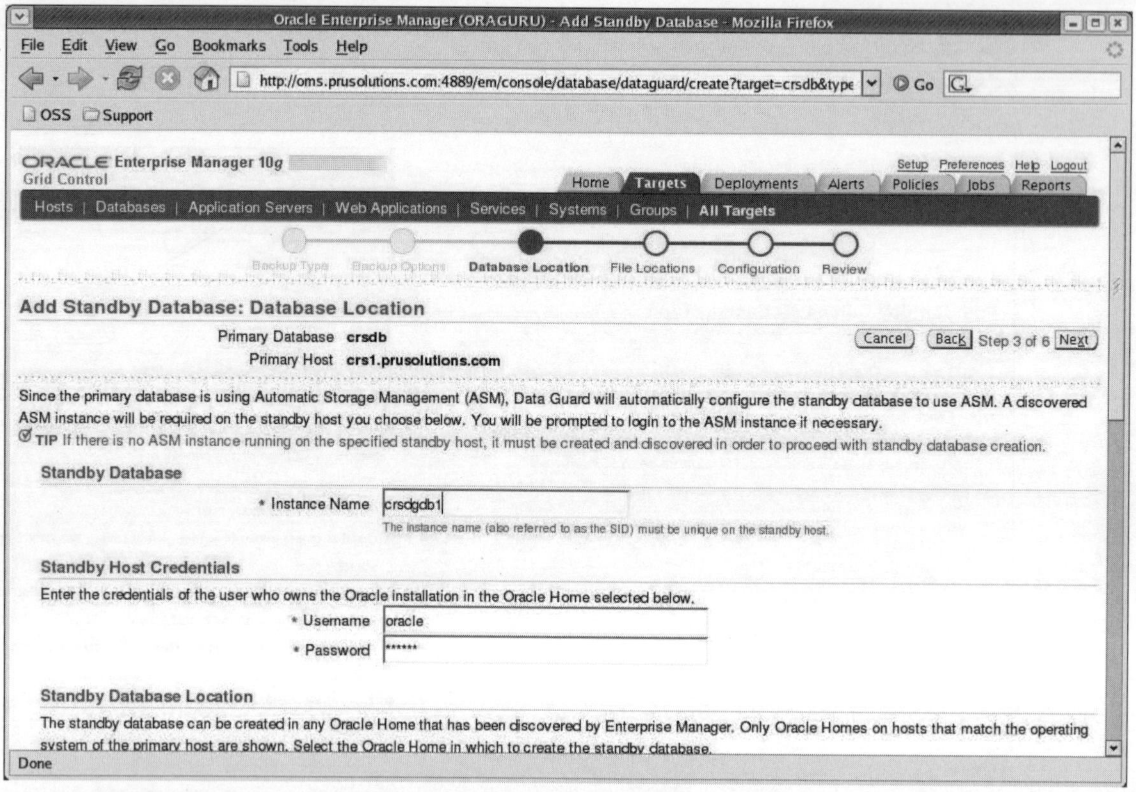

- Select Standby Database Location: Select crsdg1 which is not used by any Data Guard Configuration.

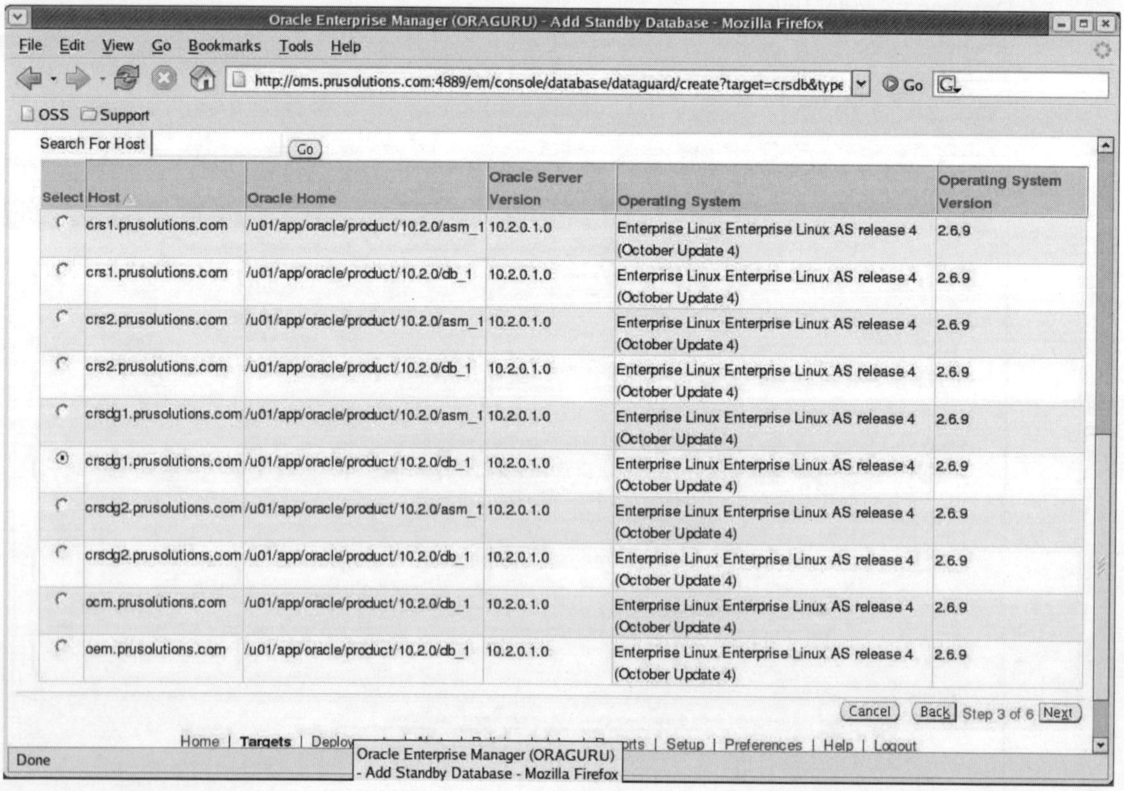

- Standby Host Backup File Access: Transfer files from primary host backup files directory to a standby host directory. Provide Directory path:/u01/app/oracle/stage, File Transfer FTP.

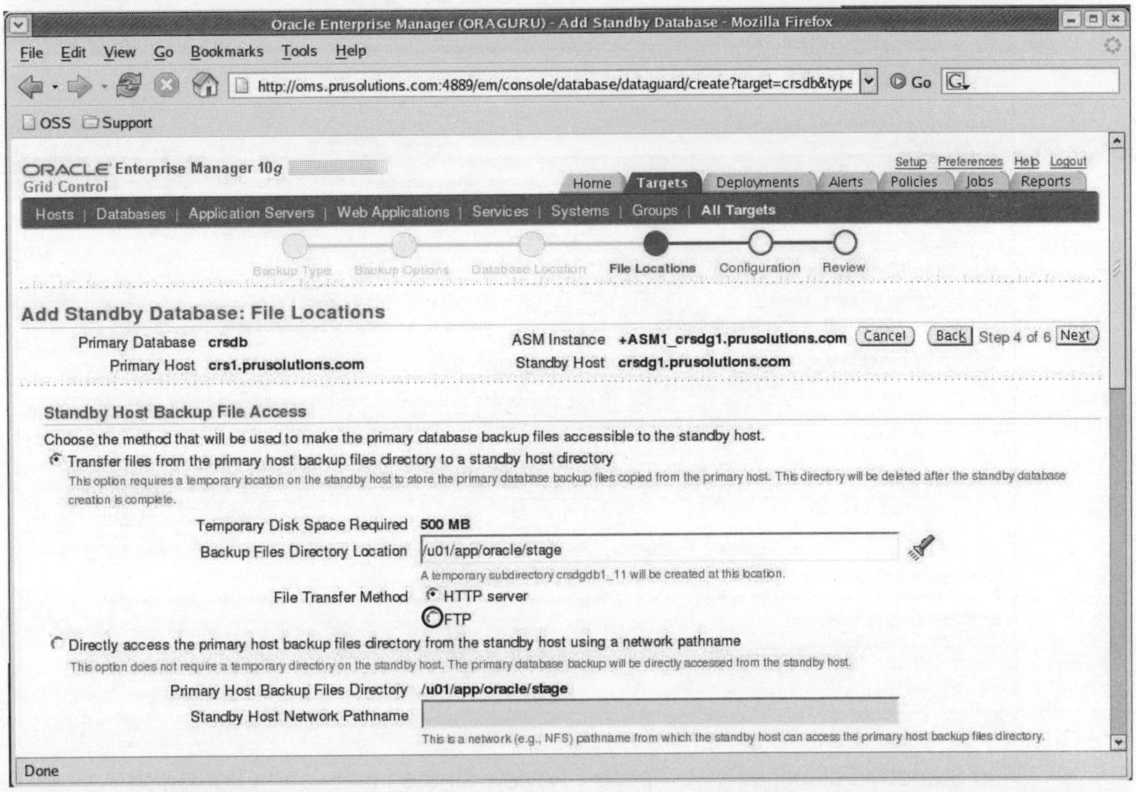

- Provide Database Area : DATA, Flash Recovery Area FRA and Network configuration file location

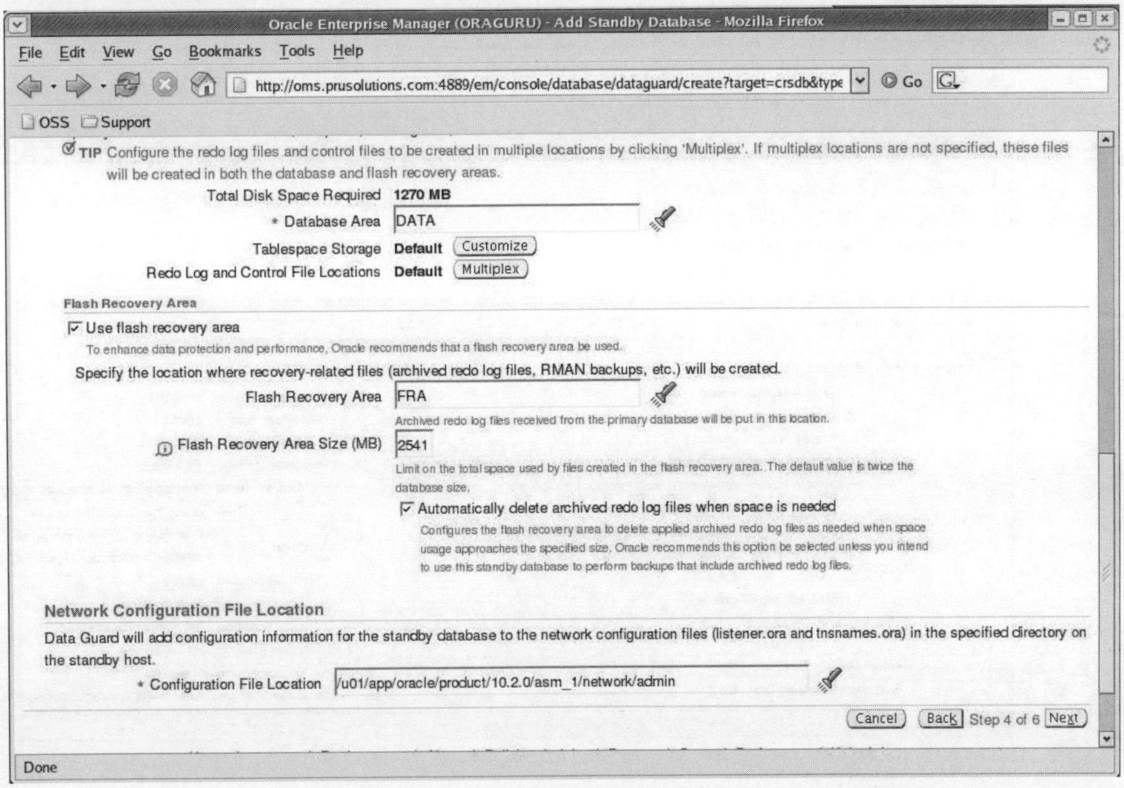

- Provide Database Unique Name: crsdgdb , Target Name crsdgdb and Click Next

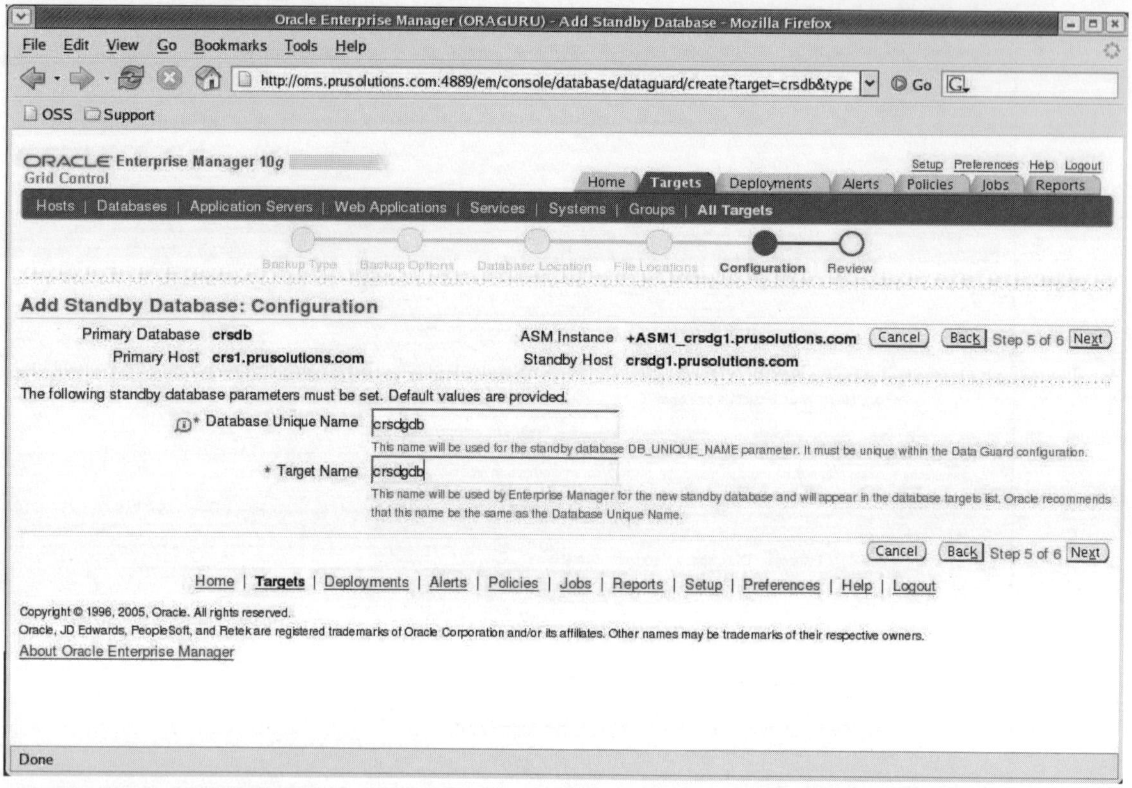

- Add Standby Database Review page : Review all the inputs and Click Finish

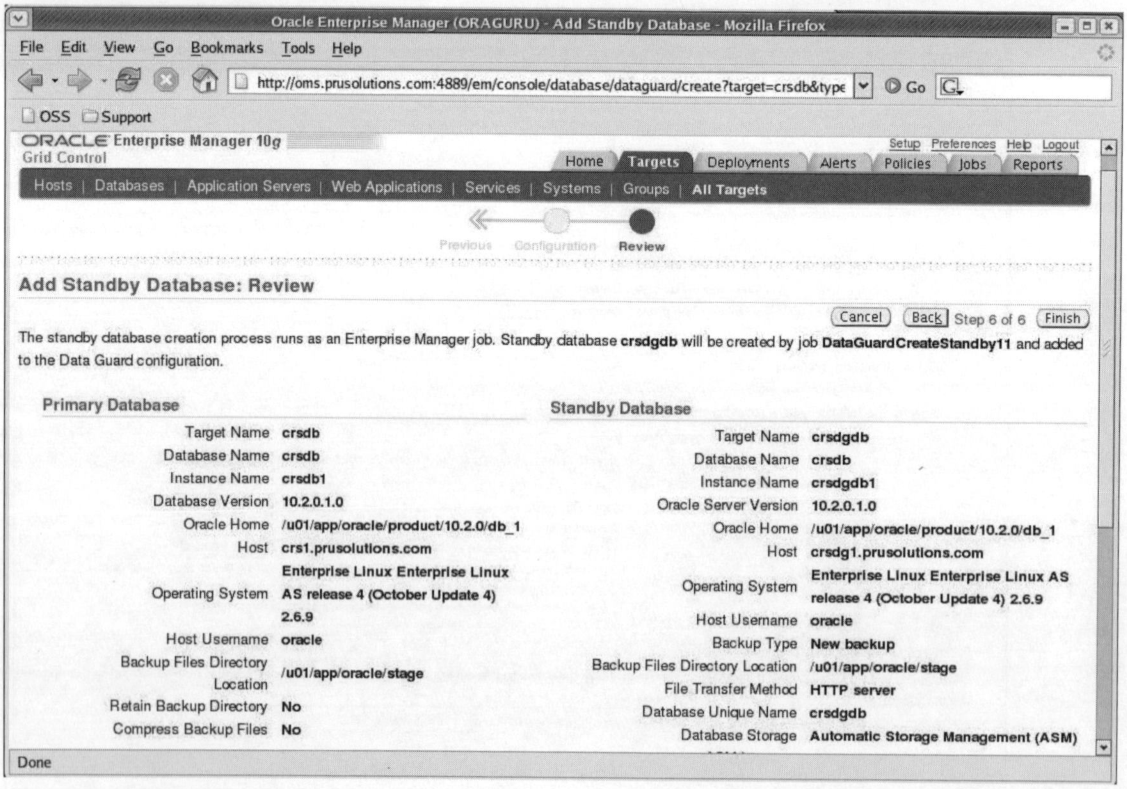

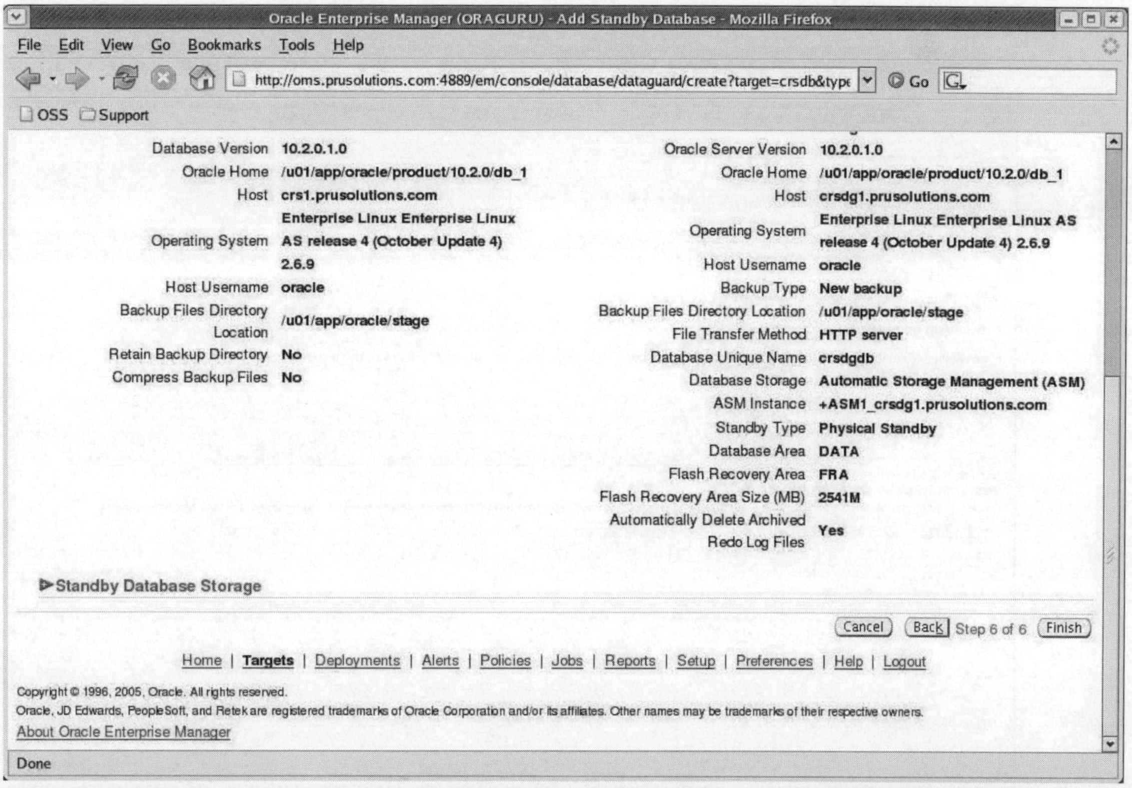

- Enterprise Manage Job will be created after processing parameters for Add Standby Database

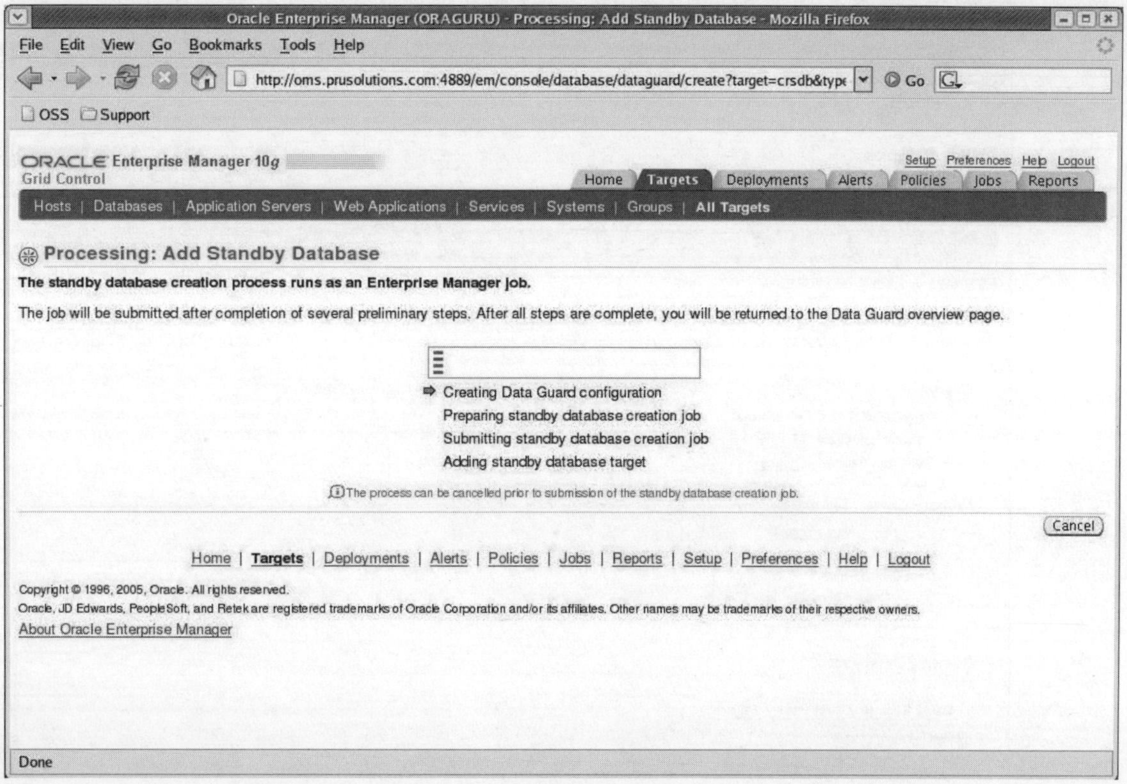

- Processing Completed

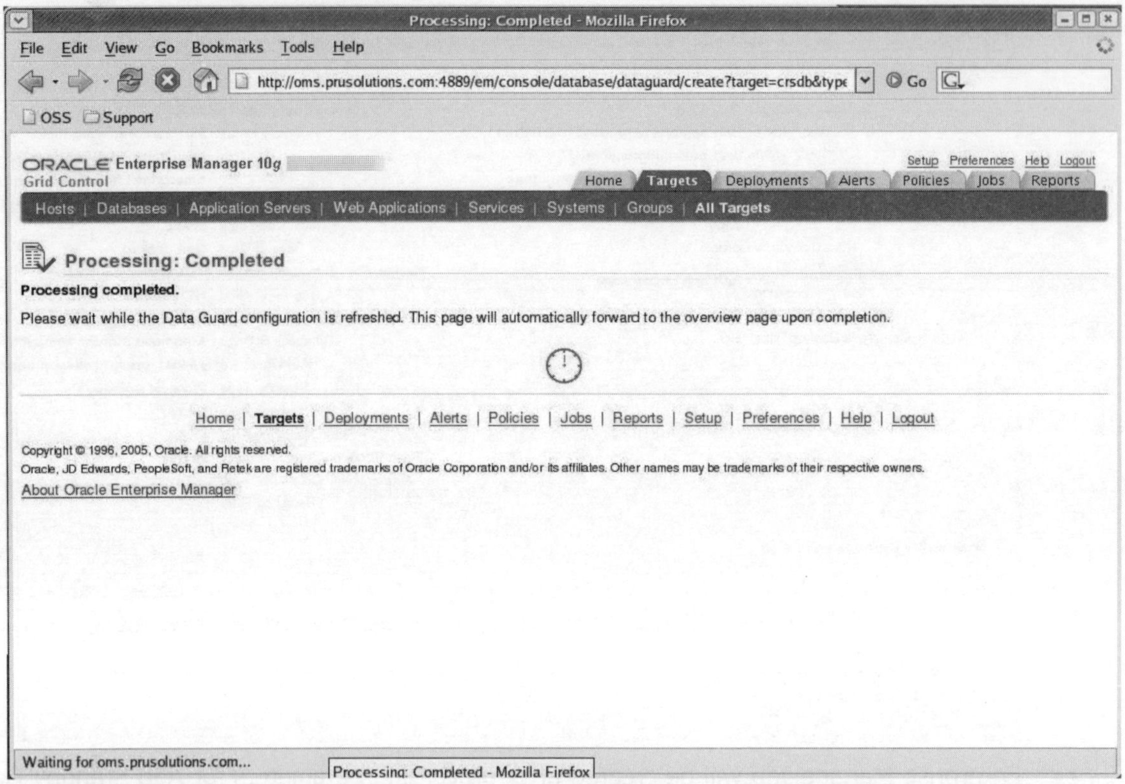

- Data Guard Overview Page have details of Broker and Job Processing Status

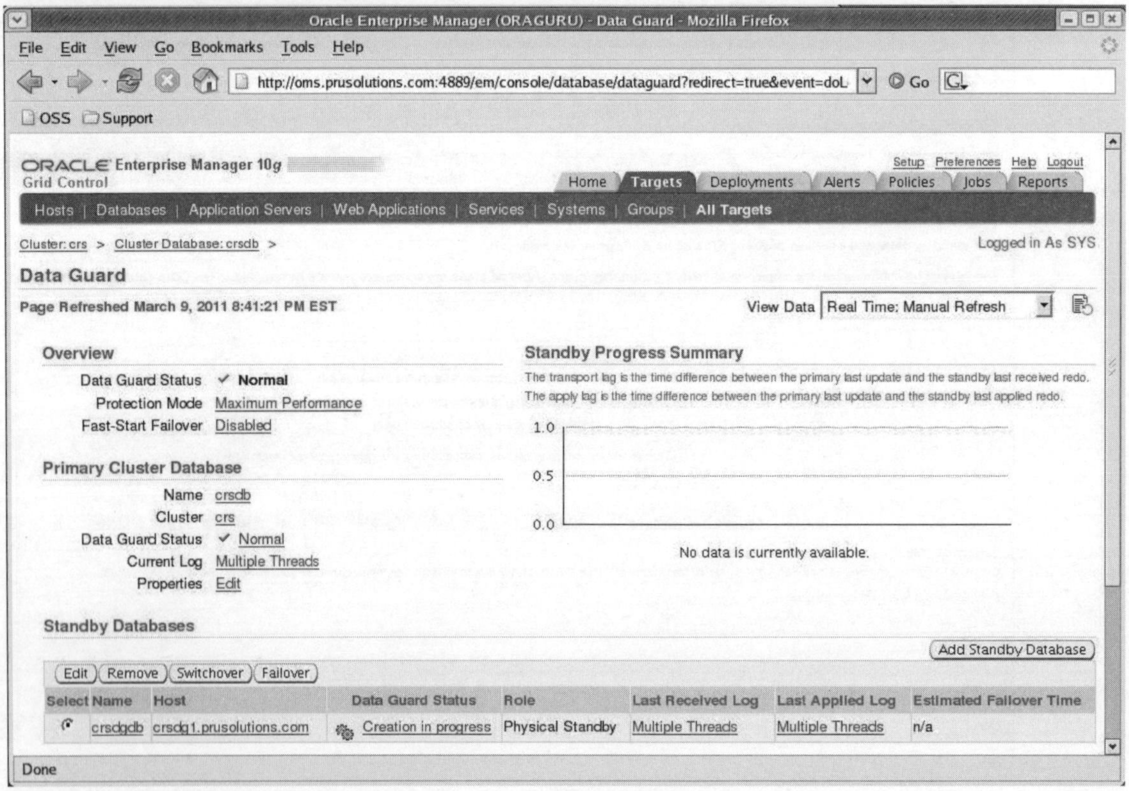

- Status of Job: Running and after job is finished Standby Database is created, Verify Configuration to add Standby redo log file

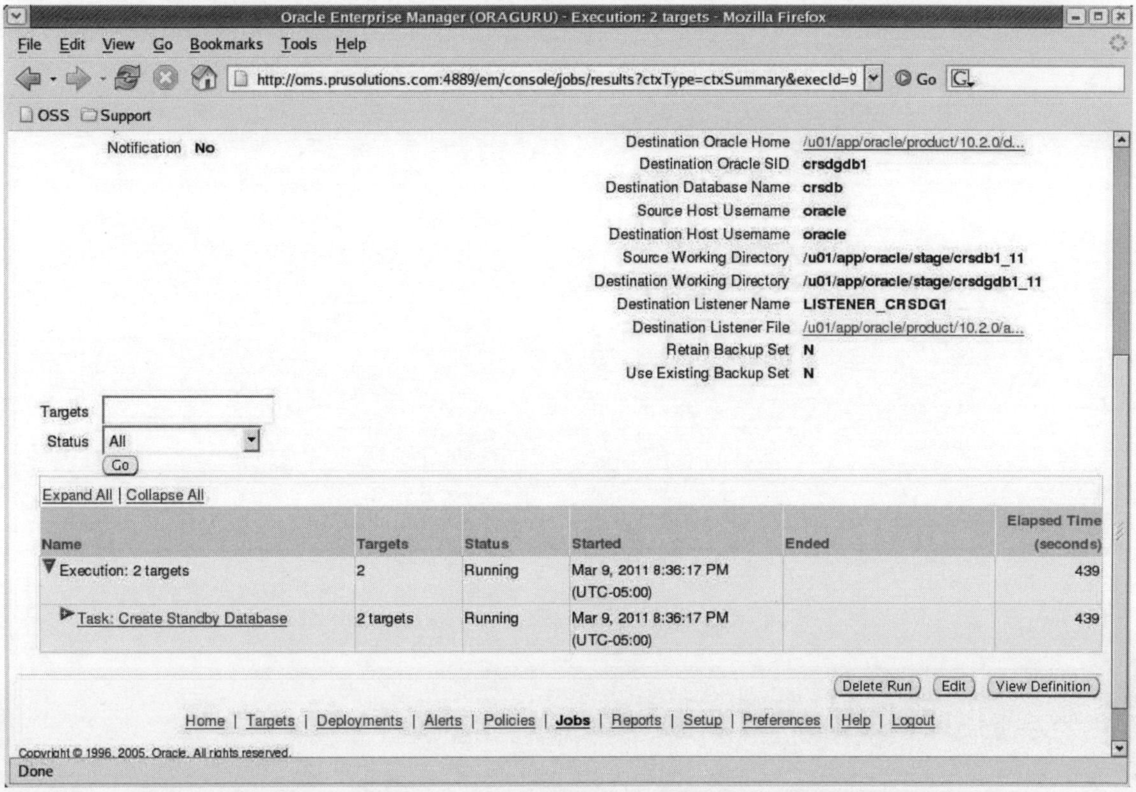

- On Data Guard home Page Click Verify Configuration and add Standby Redo log files both on Primary and on Secondary. Do Switchover, Failover of crsdb using Oracle' OEM Grid Control.
- Practice conversion of Physical Standby to Logical Standby using Oracle's OEM Grid Control.

Appendix

1. Configure Linux Machines on VMware

- Read about installation of Linux on VMware from VMware website.

2. Server Configuration

- Navigate through Oracle Documentation to get to Database creation script

  Oracle Database Documentation Library > Books > ADM > Administrator's Guide > HTML

  On contents page Ctrl f and search for *"CREATE DATABASE"* you will reach database creation statement.

- Navigate through Oracle Documentation to get to Temporary Tablespace details

  Oracle Database Documentation Library > Books > ADM > Administrator's Guide > HTML

  On contents page Ctrl f and search for *"Temporary Tablespaces"* you will reach Temporary Tablespaces.

- Navigate through Oracle Documentation to get to Undo tablespace without search tab

  Oracle Database Documentation Library > Books > ADM > Administrator's Guide > HTML

  On contents page Ctrl f and search for *"Undo Tablespaces"* you will reach Managing Undo Tablespaces.

- Navigate through Oracle Documentation to get to listener.ora file without search tab

  Oracle Database Documentation Library > Books > NET > Net Services Reference > HTML

  On contents page Ctrl f and search for *"listener.ora"* you will reach sample listener.ora file.

- Navigate through Oracle Documentation to get to Transparent Application Failover without search tab

  Oracle Database Documentation Library > Books > NET >* Net Services Administrator's Guide *> HTML

  On contents page Ctrl f and search for "Configuring Transparent Application Failover" you will reach sample Configuring Transparent Application Failover.

- Navigate through Oracle Documentation to get to Dynamically Register Services without search tab

  Oracle Database Documentation Library > Books > NET >* Net Services Administrator's Guide *> HTML

  On contents page Ctrl f and search for "Listener Architecture" you will reach Dynamically Register Services.

- Navigate through Oracle Documentation to get to tnsnames.ora file without search tab

  Oracle Database Documentation Library > Books > NET > Net Services Reference > HTML

  On contents page Ctrl f and search for *"Perform Functional Upgrade"* you will reach sample tnsnames.ora file.

- Navigate through Oracle Documentation to get to sqlnet.ora file without search tab

  Oracle Database Documentation Library > Books > NET > Net Services Reference > HTML

  On contents page Ctrl f and search for *"sqlnet.ora"* you will reach sample sqlnet.ora file.

3. Enterprise Manager Grid Control

- Navigate through Oracle Documentation to get to Overview of Enterprise Manager without search tab

    Oracle Database Documentation Library > Books > ENT > Enterprise Manager Concepts > HTML

    On contents page Ctrl f and search for *"Overview of Enterprise Manager"* you will reach Overview of Enterprise Manager.

4. Managing Database Availability

- Navigate through Oracle Documentation to get to RMAN Commands without search tab

    Oracle Database Documentation Library > Books > BAC > Backup and Recovery Reference > HTML

    On contents page Ctrl f and search for *"Commands"* you will reach RMAN Commands

5. Data Management

- Navigate through Oracle Documentation to get to SQL*Loader Commands without search tab

    Oracle Database Documentation Library > Books > UTI > **Utilities**> ***HTML***

    On contents page Ctrl f and search for "SQL*Loader Case Studies" you will reach SQL*Loader Case Studies which will give location of sqlldr files in $ORACLE_HOME/rdbms/demo.

    On contents page Ctrl f and search for "Assembling" you will reach "Assembling Logical Records from Physical Records" which will give examples for assembling logical records from Physical records.

- Navigate through Oracle Documentation to get to Partitioning in Data Warehouses without search tab

    Oracle Database Documentation Library > Books > DAT > Data Warehousing Guide> HTML

    On contents page Ctrl f and search for "Partitioning in Data Warehouses"you will reach Partitioning in Data Warehouses, which will give details for all partition types.

- Navigate through Oracle Documentation to get to Managing Partitioned Tables and Indexes without search tab to learn partition exchange methods

    Oracle Database Documentation Library > Books > ADM > Administrator's Guide > HTML

    On contents page Ctrl f and search for "Managing Partitioned" you will reach Managing Partitioned Tables and Indexes, which will give details for Managing Partitioned Tables and Indexes.

- Navigate through Oracle Documentation to get to PL/SQL LOB Demonstration Files

    Oracle Database Documentation Library > Books > ADM > Application Developer's Guide - Large Objects > HTML

    On contents page Ctrl f and search for *"PL/SQL LOB Demonstration Files"* you will reach PL/SQL LOB Demonstration Files

- Navigate through Oracle Documentation to get to Parallel Execution in Data Warehouses without search tab

    Oracle Database Documentation Library > Books > DAT > Data Warehousing Guide> HTML

    On contents page Ctrl f and search for "Using Parallel Execution" you will reach Using Parallel Execution, which will give details for Parallel Execution.

6. Data Warehouse Management

- Navigate through Oracle Documentation to get to External Tables without search tab

  Oracle Database Documentation Library > Books > ADM > Administrator's Guide > HTML

  On contents page Ctrl f and search for "External Tables" *you* will reach External Tables, which will give details of External Tables.

- Navigate through Oracle Documentation to get to ORACLE_DATAPUMP without search tab

  Oracle Database Documentation Library > Books > UTI > **Utilities**> ***HTML***

  On contents page Ctrl f and search for "14 The ORACLE_DATAPUMP Access Driver" you will reach The ORACLE_DATAPUMP Access Driver which will give location of ORACLE_DATAPUMP.

- Navigate through Oracle Documentation to get to Change Data Capture without search tab

  Oracle Database Documentation Library > Books > DAT > Data Warehousing Guide> HTML

  On contents page Ctrl f and search for "Change Data Capture" you will reach Change Data Capture, which will give details for all Change Data Capture types.

7. Performance Management

- Navigate through Oracle Documentation to get to DBMS_ADVISOR Package without search tab

  Oracle Database Documentation Library > Books >PL/> PL/SQL Packages and Types Reference > HTLM

  On contents page Ctrl f and search for "DBMS_ADVISOR" you will reach DBMS_ADVISOR section

- Navigate through Oracle Documentation to get to Automatic Shared Memory Management

  Oracle Database Documentation Library > Books > ADM > Administrator's Guide > HTML

  On contents page Ctrl f and search for "Automatic Shared Memory Management" you will reach Automatic Shared Memory Management.

8. Real Application Clusters

- Navigate through Oracle Documentation to get to Real Application Clusters Installation Guide for Linux without search tab

  Oracle Database Documentation Library > Books > DAT >

  On contents page Ctrl f and search for "Real Application Clusters Installation Guide for Linux" you will reach Real Application Clusters Installation Guide for Linux. Click **HTML** to go Contents page.

9. Data Guard

- Navigate through Oracle Documentation to get to Data Guard without search tab

  Oracle Database Documentation Library > Books > HIG >

  On contents page Ctrl f and search for "High Availability Best Practices" you will reach High Availability Best Practices. Click **HTML** to go Contents page.

References

NIEMIEC, RICHARD. ORACLE DATABASE 10g Performance Tuning Tips & Techniques. United States of America: The McGraw-Hill Companies Inc., 2007.

The book is good to refer while preparing for OCM: Oracle Database 10g Administrator Certified Master Exam.

Monitor, analyze, and optimize Oracle Database 10g using the tested methods and insider advice contained in this definitive volume. Written by Oracle Certified Master Richard Niemiec, Oracle Database 10g Performance Tuning Tips & Techniques is packed with detailed case studies, best practices, and code samples illustrating Oracle's new tuning features. Find out how to select optimal indexing options, effectively manage drives and disk arrays, troubleshoot queries, and reliably predict future performance. You'll also get detailed coverage of PL/SQL performance enhancements, initialization file tweaks, and the latest database surveying and reporting utilities.